BEING AND BECOMING UTE

Being and Becoming Ute

The Story of an American Indian People

SONDRA G. JONES

THE UNIVERSITY OF UTAH PRESS | Salt Lake City

The Defiance House Man colophon is a registered trademark
of The University of Utah Press. It is based on a four-foot-tall
Ancient Puebloan pictograph (late PIII) near Glen Canyon, Utah.

LIBRARY OF CONGRESS CATALOGING-IN-PUBLICATION DATA
Names: Jones, Sondra, 1949- author.
Title: Being and becoming Ute : the story of an American Indian people /
  Sondra G. Jones.
Description: Salt Lake City : The University of Utah Press, [2018] | Includes
  bibliographical references and index. |
Identifiers: LCCN 2018037972 (print) | LCCN 2018041046 (ebook) | ISBN
  9781607816584 | ISBN 9781607816577 (pbk. : alk. paper) | ISBN
  9781607816669 (cloth : alk. paper)
Subjects: LCSH: Ute Indians—History. | Ute Indians—Ethnic
  identity—History. | Ute Indians—Cultural assimilation—History. | Ute
  Indians—Economic conditions—History.
Classification: LCC E99.U8 (ebook) | LCC E99.U8 J66 2018 (print) | DDC
  979.004/974576—dc23
LC record available at https://lccn.loc.gov/2018037972

COVER PHOTO: Andrew Frank, respected Northern Ute leader at the turn of the twentieth century, by L.C.
Thorne. Used by permission, Uintah County Library Regional History Center, all rights reserved.

Errata and further information on this and other titles available at UofUpress.com.
Printed and bound in the United States of America.

Contents

Illustrations

MAPS

Abbreviations

ARCIA. *Annual Report of the Commissioner of Indian Affairs*

BIA. Bureau of Indian Affairs

BOR. U.S. Bureau of Reclamation

BYC. Brigham Young Collection, located in the Historical Archives of The Church of Jesus Christ of Latter-day Saints, Salt Lake City, Utah

BYMH. Brigham Young, "Manuscript History," located in the Historical Archives of The Church of Jesus Christ of Latter-day Saints, Salt Lake City, Utah

BYU-HBLL. Brigham Young University, Harold B. Lee Library

BYU-SC. Brigham Young University, Harold B. Lee Library, Special Collections & "Americana"

CHC. *Comprehensive History of the Church*, by B. H. Roberts (1930), 6 vols.

CHL. Church History Library, The Church of Jesus Christ of Latter-day Saints, Salt Lake City, Utah

DOI. U.S. Department of the Interior

DUP. Daughters of Utah Pioneers

GAS. George A. Smith Collection

JD. *Journal of Discourses*, Located in the Historical Archives of The Church of Jesus Christ of Latter-day Saints, Salt Lake City, Utah

JH. *Journal History*, located in the Historical Archives of The Church of Jesus Christ of Latter-day Saints, and on microfilm

MANM. Mexican Archives of New Mexico (microfilm), located in New Mexico State Historical Archives, Santa Fe, New Mexico

OCSC. Omer C. Stewart Collection, Norlin Library, University of Colorado, Boulder

OIA. Office of Indian Affairs, Letters Received. Microfilm. RG 75, M-234

OIA-UT. Office of Indian Affairs, Letters Received, 1824–1881, Utah Superintendency, 1849–1880. National Archives Record Group. RG 75, M-234, rolls 897–898

RSI. *Report of the Secretary of the Interior*

TANM. Territorial Archives of New Mexico (microfilm), Located in New Mexico State Historical Archives, Santa Fe, New Mexico

USHS. Utah State Historical Society Archives, Salt Lake City, Utah

USIA. Utah Superintendency of Indian Affairs, Letters to the Office of Indian Affairs

UTMC. Utah Territorial Military Correspondence (microfilm). Located in the Utah Historical Society Archives

WR. War of the Rebellion, U.S. Department of War, A Compilation of the Official Records of the Union and Confederate Armies (1897)

Preface and Acknowledgments

As a child, I used to gaze across Utah Valley and wonder if there had ever been any Indians where I grew up. Little did I know.

I would not learn the answer to this question until, as an undergraduate, my interest in Native America was reawakened after I participated in a sixteen-week archaeological field school, made anthropology my minor, and married an aspiring cultural anthropologist. Because we did most things together, I initially envisioned this book as a short historical framework for his ethnographic study of the Utes. However, my project soon took on a life of its own. My early research began with the many well-researched secondary sources on Ute history and ethnography. However, these were primarily topical studies: a few biographies, studies of specific Indian "wars," analyses of intercultural relations, individual state and tribal histories, and numerous anthropological studies of religion, culture, or folklore. However, until recently, no one has attempted to pull all of this together into a comprehensive and inclusive story, and few have attempted to tackle the equally fascinating part during the twentieth century.

These early secondary sources soon sent us to archives to locate original material, beginning with the Smithsonian where we acquired copies of John Wesley Powell's handwritten notes on language, kinship, and folklore, as well as Anne Smith's extensive folklore collection (both since edited and published by other historians). I found more material in state and historical society archives in New Mexico, Colorado, and Utah, as well as in special collections in city and university libraries, and in church archives (Mormon and Catholic).

Government documents and early correspondence were a major resource, including Indian agency letters and agency reports (from the 1850s through the early 1900s), as well as the annual reports of the commissioners and superintendents of Indian Affairs and copies of original treaties and agreements.

Military records and militia correspondence (1850–1860s) helped me see the Provo and Walker Wars, while correspondence between Civil War governors and commanders stationed in Utah and Colorado provided insight into attitudes toward Indians and Indian fighting in the 1860s when militia commanders perpetrated massacres of Ute neighbors. The findings and opinions in twentieth- and twenty-first century court cases were valuable, as were testimonies collected in several congressional hearings, and the archived Ernest Wilkinson papers regarding the Confederated Utes' Land Claims Case.

Memoirs, diaries, journals, and letters of mountain men and mid-nineteenth-century travelers, explorers, pioneers, and Mormon leaders provided firsthand reports during the early and mid-1800s, as did reports published in nineteenth-century newspapers. The Mormon Church's Journal History included a scrapbook of collages of contemporary accounts of Indian relations in early Utah. During the late-twentieth and twenty-first centuries—because the three tribes have become political and financial powers within their states—journalists reported extensively on Ute tribal affairs, as did the tribes themselves on expansive tribal web pages and in online tribal newspapers. Active internet sparring between political factions, on and off the reservations, continues today.

Personal contact was also important. From 1979–1981 my husband and I spent our summers on the Northern Ute Reservation as part of his graduate field research, working with the Northern Ute tribal historian and museum director, Fred Conetah. With Conetah's help and tribal permission, we camped on the Sundance grounds one summer and observed and participated in their two Sundances. Over the next years we were involved in more Sundances (my husband danced in four), witnessed or participated in healing ceremonies and sweats, and visited all three reservations. We (and more recently I) conducted formal and informal interviews and conversations with medicine men, spiritual advisors, and tribal representatives, along with general members and mixed-bloods from the Northern and Southern Ute reservations. We also camped in, explored, and drove through traditional Ute lands and along traditional Ute trails in Utah, Colorado, and northern New Mexico.

In addition to the Utes themselves, many others have helped me in my quest for knowledge and understanding of the Ute people, including the many unnamed archive librarians who helped me locate original source material and unpublished studies. However, certain individuals need special thanks. Included among these are John R. Maestas, one-time director of BYU's Indian Education Department, and historian and editor Howard Christy, both of whom provided moral and financial assistance during the research's very early stages. Hal Christy also traveled with us to visit tribal councils in the 1980s, provided militia correspondence microfilm, and became a great sparring partner for arguing Utah's Ute history. Fred Conetah was a thoughtful host while we did research in his archive, shared insights on Ute history, and provided taped oral interviews. Darrel and Colleen Gardiner encouraged my husband to participate in the Sundance and provided his outfit, and later provided insight into the Ute and mixed-blood controversy. Both Eddie Box and "Bishop" Arrochis, recognized Ute medicine men, spent time talking to us in the early 1980s, and Clifford Duncan, a Northern Ute elder, offered positive comments on an early, much shorter draft of this history. Some years later I interviewed additional tribal employees, including Larry Cesspooch, then a tribal liaison and today a recognized cultural spokesperson and storyteller, who provided me with additional insights into Northern Ute enterprises and modern Ute thinking.

Omer C. Stewart, an ethnohistorian and recognized expert on Ute affairs, was especially helpful. He not only shared his insights and personal experiences with us, but he also gave us several large files of unpublished source data from his Ute case notes and two unpublished preliminary articles on the Western and Eastern Utes. (These I have since deposited in the Stewart collections in the archives of the Marriott Library, University of Utah, and the Norlin Library, University of Colorado.) More recently, historian Paul Reeve provided much-needed support, encouragement, suggestion, and mentoring in finalizing the penultimate version of this book, as have new readers in offering ongoing encouragement and suggestions on its published form. Not the least of these are historians Greg Thompson, director of the Marriott Library Special Collections, and John Alley at the University of Utah Press.

And through it all has been my husband, Bob Jones, whose early research reignited my interest in American Indians and especially in writing about Ute history. His insights as a trained anthropologist, his experiences as a Sun-dancer, and his life as an urban Indian have been invaluable.

Chapter 1

Introduction

In the late 1970s a small group of Northern Utes decided to eschew modern life and culture and return to the "old ways." With this in mind they retreated to tribal land near the Uintah Mountains where they set up tipis and attempted to live traditionally.

They did not, however, eschew cars, pickups, or horses, nor did they cease hunting with rifles or fishing with commercial gear. Some of their buckskin clothing had been assembled and decorated using commercial leatherworking tools and beading equipment, and their tipis were made of canvas. Their nostalgic traditionalism incorporated layers of cultural and technological adaptations that had been acquired through centuries of adjustment to changing cultural, ecological, and technological environments. Like many other Native Americans who especially felt a loss of cultural identity following the 1950s era of Termination, Relocation, and the rise of urban living, this small group of Utes sought to restore their sense of identity through native symbols, spirituality, and a return to nature. But this kind of traditionalism cherry-picks aspects of a recent, stereotyped, and perhaps romanticized way of life—an idealized existence frozen at a specific moment in time rather than the earlier hardscrabble lifestyle that more accurately reflected the world of their ancestors before the arrival of Euro-Americans and European commodities.

TRADITIONALISM AND IDENTITY

The problem in attempting to define "tradition" is that no cultural group exists in complete stasis. Rather, cultures exist in a complex and ever-changing continuum of time, space, and collective perceptions. And while both scholars and native people struggle to reconstruct pristine *traditional* cultures, they can only paint a portrait of a people at a particular time, in a particular place, and in particular circumstances.[1] It would probably be more accurate to view cultural history as an ongoing *journey* during which events and circumstances have molded a people into who they are today, and placed them on a trajectory toward who they may become tomorrow. The historian can only pick a point along the path and then follow it to another predetermined spot. Thus, this work is not a static portrait of the Ute people, but a description of a passage from their first sixteenth-century encounters with Euro-Americans to their corporate tribal modernity of the twenty-first century.

During the early decades of the twenty-first century, scholars have revised many long-standing stereotypes about "traditional" Indians. Where Native Americans were once stereotyped as noble, bloodthirsty, victimized, or savage, historians now describe the complexities of native cultures and politics among a tremendous variety of native peoples—over 560 different tribes—while giving them a new and more human face. Nobility and malevolence are necessarily a part of these images since human nature is inherently complex. So historians now seek to cast aside the stark black-and-white hats that once populated the nationalistic narratives of progress and pacification, as well as the later revisionist histories that simply reversed the roles from noble savage to noble victim. They have also recognized that a more complete history must move beyond the old political and military frameworks to include the sociocultural readjustments that were triggered by internal politics as well as intertribal and international conflicts. As relationships shift over time and in different places, people adapt and adjust their perceptions, attitudes, behaviors, and responses.

The Utes illustrate this metamorphosis well. Over time they were impacted by shifting territory, technology, and cross-cultural relationships. As this happened, they changed, too. They adopted new ideas and technology, abandoned older beliefs, and adapted the new within existing worldviews. For example, Western Utes were hunters and gatherers, with a subsistence culture that resembled other Great Basin Indians. On the other hand, their Eastern Ute relatives were migrating into regions bordered by people culturally very different. Here they interacted with the sedentary Pueblo Indians and later Spanish settlers, from whom they acquired new commodities such as textiles and cultivated food. By the mid-1700s they had adopted horses and guns and expanded their hunting territory deeper into the Great Plains, where they adopted a horse and bison economy typically associated with Plains Indians. And yet the cultural resemblance of these southern Utes to other Plains and Pueblo Indians remained little more than a recently acquired veneer. As late as the 1930s, Eastern Utes still recognized they and their western cousins had been and were "a single people." Regardless of external differences in their material culture, they all spoke the same language and *thought* like Utes. As one historian put it, "A man may put on a new hat, but it doesn't necessarily change the way he thinks."[2]

By the second half of the nineteenth century, pulp fiction and Wild West shows had popularized the stereotypical image of a buckskin-clad, horse-riding, tipi-dwelling Indian based on the Siouxan culture of its native performers, a stereotype that would be perpetuated by Hollywood; but this image was a fragmentary and disjointed reflection of Native America.[3] The Ute people were—and are—more than the Plains Indian veneer adopted by some. And many Utes never did fit this image.[4]

The question of *who* or *what* a Ute is also taps into a larger question, one that continues to plague Indian America today: Who are native American Indians—really—and what is it that identifies a person as not only a "real" Indian, but also qualifies them to be a bona fide member of a specific Indian community? Unlike a tongue-in-cheek attempt in the 1930s to acquire federal recognition for the large community of Indian actors in Hollywood as "DeMille Indians,"[5] many Native Americans today are fighting real and very substantive battles for recognition as "authentic" American Indians. They desperately wish to restore a sense of their own ethnic identity as well as to gain access to the significant resources reserved for tribes and their members.

The political, cultural, and economic history of the Ute Indians is the story of but one native group, but it illustrates the kinds of forces that have shaped the history of native America.

TRANSFORMING NATIVE IDENTITY

Until the 1890s, ethnic native identities and tribal membership remained fluid and changeable. As scholars have pointed out, the acquisition of European goods, technologies, and alliances caused an upheaval in native societies, including modifications in material cultures, sociocultural and political relations, homelands, and traditional identities.[6] Throughout North America, European and Indian trade partners developed continually shifting symbiotic relationships for commercial trade and as defensive alliances. Complex identity-changing associations and contests varied dramatically depending on place, period, and other circumstances. Confederacies coalesced, imperial contests reshaped alliances, mounted hunting bands waged territorial battles across the Great Plains, and a complex array of shifting alliances and misalliances entangled Utes, Comanches, Apaches, Pueblos, and Hispanic settlers.

The repercussions of European encounters spread through native America, decimating populations through disease, war, and slaving; transforming their technologies and economies; and increasing conflict over trade and resources. A deadly ripple effect not only struck those who dealt directly with Europeans but also reached second- and thirdhand groups via complex networks of trade, social intercourse, and warfare.[7] Those without European goods became prey to, or were displaced by, those made powerful (and aggressive) through European commodities—including weapons. Technology changed the ground rules and shifted the balance of power in the ongoing competition for scarce resources. This increasingly violent competition helped solidify group identities as *we* fought against *them*—the *other*—and everyone resisted relocation and struggled first against domination by other Indians and then against Euro-American colonialists.[8]

As a result of these competitions and cultural transformations, tribal identities coalesced; but because of the continual intermixing of people, such ethnic groups did not correlate exactly with blood relationships: they were never genetically pure. Membership in a native community was not determined, as it often is today, by a certain quantity (or "quantum") of ethnic-specific *blood*. That amorphous concept originated as a European legality related to inheritance laws (as in "blood relatives"), and it was later racialized in the Americas to codify the distinctions between indigenous populations, African slaves, and Americans of European descent.[9] The distinction between "red" American Indians and "white" Euro-Americans became racialized during bloody colonial competitions over land, resources, native sovereignties, and the right of Indians to *be* Indian. During these conflicts the earlier distinctions between specific European ethnic identities (such as German versus English settlers) dissipated as "white" colonists banded together against "red" natives. Thus skin color joined with perceived blood heritage as a physiological indicator of racial or ethnic identity.[10]

During this same time the intellectual children of the Enlightenment and Scientific Revolution were seeking to categorize their world, and physical appearance and ethnicity played to these impulses. By the nineteenth century, scholars were specifically using the theory of race to categorize people. Darwinian theories of biological evolution soon informed new theories of social evolution that justified social and racial hierarchies as well as political and social oppression. As such, race and blood became a significant political phenomenon. The belief that one drop of (contaminated) blood damaged the white race was becoming increasingly popular. For example, novelist James Fenimore Cooper's iconic character, Hawk-Eye, proudly—and continually—referred to himself as having "no cross" in his blood, meaning he had the skills of an Indian but not the taint of Indian blood. By the twentieth century federal officials were measuring how "Indian" Native Americans were by the amount of Indian blood (genetic inheritance) they could prove.[11]

However, from their earliest encounters with rogue fishing fleets off the coast of Newfoundland in the sixteenth century, North America's native people faced mounting turmoil and social dislocation that transformed traditional identities. Disease, war, and slaving caused mass demographic upheavals as populations were decimated and conflict forced relocation. Refugees migrated, amalgamated, reconstructed, and confederated for mutual defense and social stability in multitribal, multilingual societies. Ritual, vengeance, or opportunistic warfare traditionally allowed others—typically captives or refugees—to be integrated into the social and biological fabric of native communities as slaves, servants, wives, or adopted replacement children. After European colonization, hundreds of white captives were also incorporated into these societies, as were European traders who formed alliance marriages to cement or gain access to trading privileges. Some indentured servants and runaway African slaves "went native" and voluntarily joined Indian communities, while Indian slave-holders sired mixed-blood children with their black slaves just as their white counterparts did on Southern plantations. All of these factors contributed to the increasingly complex racial and cultural mix among Native Americans.[12] The integration of nonnative people into the social community and genetic pool of Native Americans, not to mention the amalgamation of refugee natives into new communities, means that any reference to a racially pure tribe is little more than wishful—and perhaps nationalistic—nostalgia.

Until the seventeenth century American Indian identity was not a construct of race, for that very idea was a relatively recent fabrication of Europe's rising scientific anxiety to comprehend the world by classifying it into its component parts.[13] Indian identity had traditionally been understood through a person's linkage to family, clan, or residence. Thus a mixed-blood Métis could be either white French or red Indian, depending on whether they were raised in their mother's native community (*métis bâtards*), or in their father's French Canadian settlement (*métis legitimes*). In the American southeast, sedentary Indians were typically identified by the village in which they lived. Nomadic tribes were often identified by where they winter-camped, their food or food-gathering areas, or some other unique feature. If these identifiers changed, so did the name by which they were known. Thus, when the Timpanogos Utes amalgamated with other Western Utes on the Uintah Reservation, they all became Uintah Utes; the Tabeguaches became the Uncompahgre Utes after they relocated near the Uncompahgre River; and the Yamparika were identified by both their preferred food (yampa root) and the yampa-rich lands along the Yampa River. By the late 1800s the Yampa Utes joined other bands at the White River agency where they became collectively known as the White River Utes.[14]

Thus throughout native America, identities were defined and redefined when groups migrated, fled, or were forced out of traditional territories, shifted their methods of subsistence, or realigned kin (family), cliques (friends), and clans. Despite attempts by modern tribes to solidify their claims of unalterable ethnicity and, in some cases, an ancient nationhood, the very concepts of *ethnicity*, *tribe*, and *nation* are modern political and economic constructs formulated by non-Indian officials for the purpose of negotiating for and laying claim to Indian land and resources. Native ethnicity (or tribal identity) is not grounded in culture or biology—although these are significant factors—but is primarily a social and political identity. And ethnic identity is constantly evolving over time—a type of ethnic evolution scholars refer to as *ethnogenesis*.[15]

A significant fact in the ethnogenesis of major tribal groups was the competition for resources, especially after they encountered and traded with exploring and colonizing non-Indians. This competition continued as federal Indian policies successfully demanded further solidification and codification of Indian identities for the purpose of negotiation, administration, and relocation. Indian policies demanded a formal racial definition and headcount to determine who was (or was not) an Indian and thus eligible for government aid or reserved Indian land. In the twentieth century federal policies toward these codified and enumerated tribal entities led to reorganization and creation of corporate tribal entities. And within these corporate entities, the competition over tribal and federal resources continued to define Indian and tribal identity. Thus a stroke of a pen now defines a person as *Indian* or strips them of their Indian or tribal identity regardless of genetic makeup, kinship, communal relations, shared sociality, history, upbringing, or sense of being Indian.

The history of the Ute Indians, then, is that of a native people surviving in a harsh environment, competing and strategizing for scarce resources, and ultimately resisting the colonial domination of expansionist Euro-Americans. Exposed to changing economies and technologies, they exploited, adapted, and

6

sometimes resisted cultural exchanges. This history explores the complex paths that led the Ute people from their roots as relatively undifferentiated Numic-speaking hunter-gatherers who migrated from the Great Basin to the Rocky Mountains, Colorado Plateau, and Great Plains, to assertively self-identified and reservation-defined tribal (and corporate) entities by the beginning of the twenty-first century. The story includes how the Utes resisted change or domination through a variety of strategies: defensive as well as offensive violence, alliance and negotiation, a defiant resurgence of traditional politics and religion, and the celebratory assertion of tribal and Indian identity.

The tale encompasses external cultural and religious changes as well as the metamorphosis of the Utes' social and political identity. While this includes the transitional periods when most Utes became buckskin-clad, tipi-dwelling, nomadic hunter-warrior equestrians, the story involves much more than this romanticized era. Though it would be this transitional phase that the nostalgic traditionalists of the 1970s wanted to believe epitomized the traditions of their ancestors, they were not remembering a precontact period, or even a precolonial time. Ironically, this nostalgic era was a relatively brief period of prosperity that resulted from their ancestors incorporating nontraditional, non-Indian technology and ideas. It was a snapshot of a people who were continuing to evolve and adapt to changing physical and social environments.

Thus, the story of the Ute people is not a static portrait frozen in time, nor is it a tragedy in which vanishing Native Americans sink into oppressed oblivion; instead, while it contains elements of tragedy, it is ultimately a dynamic and continually transforming story that demonstrates the resilience of an American Indian people.

Chapter 2

Out of the Desert
The Núu-ci

Most biographies begin generations before a subject's birth. After all, who a person becomes is, in part, determined by who they were and where they came from. The same is true for cultural biographies. However, a biography must begin somewhere. So to understand the Ute people we must first explore their cultural ancestry and then begin their story at an arbitrary point in time. After a brief nod to theories of ancestral origins, we will begin by looking at the cultural and social context of the Ute people just before the transformative effects of Europeans and their life-altering commodities. By looking at what *was*, we can better appreciate who the Ute people *became*, both within the context of extensive transformations as well as the persistent continuities that remained.

IN THE BEGINNING

The Utes are a Shoshonean people who fall within the Uto-Aztecan language family, a linguistic group that includes over thirty different languages spoken from Montana to Central America and encompasses such disparate groups as the Ute, Hopi, and Aztec Indians. The ancestors of today's Utes were members of a culturally similar Great Basin people whom scholars call the *Numa*, which means "The People." Linguistically, Shoshonean has been divided into three major families. Western Shoshonean includes the Northern Paiutes, Bannocks, and Mono Indians; Central Shoshonean consists of the Shoshones, Goshutes, and Comanches; and Southern Shoshonean are comprised of the Chemehuevi, Kawaisu, Southern Paiutes, and Utes. In 1873 the explorer John Wesley Powell called these people *Numas*, reflecting what they called themselves, including the *Numu* (Shoshone), *Neme* (Northern Paiute), or *Nimici* (Southern Paiute). Utes still refer to themselves as the *Núu-ci* (or Nooche), meaning "The People," and call Indians who are "not one of us" *núu nuakati*.[1]

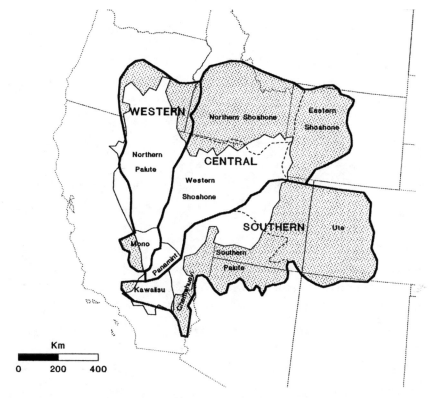

2.1. Distribution of Numic-speaking peoples (from Madsen and Rhodes, *Across the West*, 25).

What the *Núu-ci* did not call themselves was Ute, and scholars still do not agree on the origin of that name. The term *Yuta* (or Eutaw, Utah, Ute) first appeared in early Spanish documents and continued to be used by trappers, traders, explorers, settlers, and federal officials to identify the *Núu-ci*.

In the Before Time

The origins of the Ute people remain controversial. At one time scholars believed that the Great Basin had been populated for thousands of years by a culturally homogenous people they dubbed the Desert Culture. When nineteenth-century travelers encountered the Great Basin people and saw that their staple food source was roots, the travelers rather derogatorily dubbed them "Digger Indians." In later years, many scholars assumed that because the so-called "Diggers" had a survivalist toolkit similar to the remains found in ancient archaeological sites, they must be direct descendants of these earlier people. More likely the harsh environment, along with the existence of a successful technology for living in it, simply produced similar weapons, basketry, grinding stones, nets, and the like.[2] In any case, not all areas of the Great Basin were equally harsh. Many parts—especially along its western and eastern fringes and wherever water supplies collected near mountain ranges—were rich in plant, animal, and aquatic life, which native people took advantage of. Many of the early pejorative names for the Great Basin people—such as "Digger Indians"—were actually descriptions of a people who had been displaced from the more productive regions by travelers and traders on early western trails. For practical reasons, these trails had appropriated the most fertile corridors along rivers, streams, lakes, and springs. Subsequent settlers in the same areas continued to force native people to relocate and adopt a significantly more hardscrabble lifestyle.[3]

Scholars continue to argue whether the expansion of Shoshonean language groups implies a replacement of native peoples or the merging of new people with old. What is known is that the earliest people appeared on the more fertile fringes of the Great Basin and along the Wasatch Front as early as twelve thousand years ago, including along the shores of Lake Bonneville, a large lake that once filled much of the Great Basin.[4] Over the next several thousand years the lake subsided, but Basin natives continued to live near the remaining lakes, marshes, and natural springs, in small family-based bands. As their hunting and gathering techniques improved, the marshland population increased, and by 2000 BCE small bands of hunters and gatherers had pushed beyond the wetlands and were camping in the upland and mountain regions where their nomadic mobility provided increased resources. More small and large game entered their diet, as well as mountain berries, nuts, and roots. Over the next two thousand years the climate grew cooler and moister. Water levels rose, and the marshland and springs flooded. Lakeshore populations dropped significantly, and some sites were abandoned. Small family bands may have relocated into the mountains or moved to the desert steppe lands. Many appear to have simply not survived the climatic and ecological shift in their environment.

Between AD 900 and 1150 a northern finger of pueblo (village) culture stretched into the Great Basin and the Wasatch Front. The short-lived Fremont culture brought clusters of durable stone dwellings, along with horticulture, improved basketry, and simple pottery. This group was similar to but not the same as the Anasazi pueblos of the Colorado Plateau to the south, but both people disappeared or retreated southward about the same time the Numic and Athabascan (Apache and Navajo) people migrated into the region.[5] The climate had changed again, likely prompting these migrations, although they may also have had conflicts with the new Numic and Athabascan people who replaced them.[6]

The Numic People

Numic-speaking peoples were living in the southwest corner of the Great Basin near Death Valley and Owens Valley by at least as early as AD 800. Over the centuries, individual bands made up of family and friends (kin-clique bands) began fanning out north and east across the Great Basin. Time, separation, and competition for scarce resources solidified group identities, and the Pai-utes, Goshutes, Shoshones, Bannocks, and Utes developed increasingly dis-crete languages and identities. As some Ute bands migrated beyond the Great Basin into the Wasatch and then Rocky Mountains, the geographic barriers and differing ecologies amplified cultural differences between Utes who lived east or west of the Green and Colorado Rivers. Despite these external differ-ences, Utes continued to perceive themselves as one people due to their shared language and worldview.

Utes and Shoshones migrated into and claimed the more fertile regions north and east of the Great Basin; as they developed big-game-hunting skills, they ranged into the mountains and beyond. As they grew more prosperous, they also became more powerful. By the mid-1500s when the Spanish first encountered them in what is today northern New Mexico, bands of Utes could be found throughout the valleys and mountains of central Utah, among the slopes and heights of the Rocky Mountains in Colorado, and on the often-contested western fringe of the Great Basin.[7]

This is the scholarly view of Ute origins. Ute storytellers have given differ-ent accounts, typically variations of this one recorded in the 1920s:

> In the beginning there were no people in the world. Siná-wavi, the creator (Wolf), cut some straight bushes into several bundles of sticks without telling his brother Yukwu-pi-ci (Coyote) what he was doing or why. After cutting the sticks about the same size, Siná-wavi put them into a bag with its mouth facing the east. Yukwu-pi-ci, a curious crea-ture, untied the bag to peek in. Suddenly people came out, running and shouting. By the time Yukwu-pi-ci was able to retie the bag, only a few people were left in it. Siná-wavi distributed the people who were left, calling them by name and saying that people who spoke different lan-guages would fight with each other because Siná-wavi's plan had gone awry. The Núu-ci were a very small group but they were very brave and

would be able to defeat the rest. This is how the Ute ended up living in the land where White men discovered them.[8]

At one time this tale or a variant of it was sufficient to explain Ute origins. It defined Ute identity contra others, delineated language and interethnic enmities, explained the Ute position in the physical world, and shed light on their increasing conflict with others. Implicit was the knowledge that their ancestors had been in their homelands from the beginning and had won the right to remain there. They were rooted in and hence sovereign over their lands. As one Ute elder explained in 1979, "No one knows the history of the Ute; how can anyone hope to write it?"[9]

However, historians, archaeologists, and anthropologists seek science-based answers. To this end, they have sifted the sand and refuse from caves; poked, probed, measured, and compared the skeletal remains of ancient and modern natives; studied historical documents; and dissected and analyzed the patterns of languages. From this research scholars created—and debated—their own stories of Ute origins.

THE CULTURAL LIFEWAYS OF THE NUMIC PEOPLE[10]

The native people of the Great Basin, nearby mountains, and Colorado Plateau utilized a variety of methods to survive. In arid regions small family groups exploited available resources and traveled more frequently in regular nomadic circuits, clustering with other families only during the winter, for specific communal hunts or harvests, or for brief social gatherings. In the more fertile wetland areas and in the mountains where resources were more abundant, family-bands clustered near stable resources, supplementing their diet with seasonal hunting and foraging circuits.[11]

Who is My Brother? Early Numic Society

Among Numic people, the most basic social unit was a small individualistic group composed of relatives and friends.[12] These bands typically consisted of at least a nuclear family but might also include grandparents, grandchildren, siblings, nieces, nephews, as well as spouses, in-laws, and occasionally friends. Related but independent bands often camped near each other during the winter or united for communal game drives, piñon nut harvesting, or social activities. In more fertile regions, including central Utah and western Colorado, more permanent clusters developed. After the Utes acquired the horse, these family-band clusters evolved into loosely organized larger bands; however, a Ute's essential identity remained rooted inextricably in who they were related to and where their family-band preferred to hunt and forage.

Group leadership was primarily vested in the wisdom and authority of age and experience. While an ethos of individualism permeated Ute culture, a system of loose, directive authority was an ingrained part of Ute leadership. Language reflected and perpetuated the importance of kinship and respect for age, and it was laced with a complex array of words that defined gradients of age and reciprocal relationships. For a Ute, the world was one in which authority was rooted in experience or success, labor was based on gender, and the social community was grounded in family relationships.

Although men provided the skills and leadership for social affairs, hunting and fishing, and nomadic migration, women were the nexus of a complex web of marriage-based kinship networks.[13] A man usually joined his wife's family and band.[14] Marital relations were fluid, easily entered into, and theoretically easily broken up, in what some anthropologists have called "brittle monogamy." However, many unions were long-lasting, and jealousy-induced violence was not uncommon in cases of stolen, runaway, or philandering wives or husbands. Certainly social expectations demanded at least the show of fighting for one's spouse. In the mid-1800s Wákara and Kanosh furiously, and fruitlessly, pursued their respective runaway wives. We also have descriptions of men punishing philandering wives or of women brawling with their husbands' paramour(s).[15] Among the Southern Paiutes, nineteenth-century slave trading resulted in such a significant gender imbalance that men frequently fought in bloody scrums over potential brides.[16]

Polygamy was acceptable, and not uncommon. Men often married sisters, and widows might marry their brother-in-law.[17] It was, after all, more practical for a widower to marry his sister-in-law and remain within the same family and camp-group.[18] These arrangements were highly pragmatic since it was easier to care for children in a wife's household, while her family retained the valuable skills of a son-in-law. In later years men also integrated female captives as wives. For example, the widowed Ouray married his wife's foster-sister, Chipeta, a Kiowa captive who had been raised by the Tabeguache family as a Ute.[19]

Extended households, polygamous marriages, or marriage to a series of different spouses was not unusual and complicated family relationships. Children could have full siblings, half-siblings, stepsiblings, and cousins, all within the same household or in related camps if parents remarried. Kinship was based on age and gender. For example, brothers and male cousins (to the third degree) were all either younger brother or older brother, while sisters and female cousins were either younger or older sister. When good friends were integrated into a family-band, they became brothers and sons as well.[20]

This arrangement of extended relations provided an additional survival strategy in a region with widely dispersed and seasonal resources. If the piñon nuts failed to ripen one fall, the family-band could merge with cousins who knew where yampa roots were abundant. However, these relationships were often misunderstood by nineteenth-century settlers and officials who confused family structure, size, and relationships because they applied their own rigid European systems for reckoning kinship. Utes must have appeared to have very large families.

Family-bands were directed by experienced leaders who led camp movements, winter encampments, and communal rabbit drives. However, antelope drives, the Bear Dance, or other social dances were led by chiefs with shamanistic or medicine powers (*puwá*). During the mid-nineteenth century, some especially successful and prosperous war leaders were believed to have strong medicine power and attracted many followers. But when they ceased to be successful, followers fell away, because the chief's *puwá* had clearly left him or rebounded on him for ill.[21]

The Way to a Man's Heart: Food

Early Utes were nomadic hunters and gatherers who exploited the seasonal abundance of different foods, moving through varied geographic and climate areas from the arid steppes of the eastern Great Basin to the forested Wasatch and Rocky Mountains. Here they exploited varying ecological zones where they could find hundreds of different species and subspecies of mammals, fish, reptiles, and edible insects, as well as a variety of herbs, berries, shrubs, and trees.[22]

Western Utes ranged through the valleys and slopes of the Wasatch Mountains and subsisted primarily on wild vegetal foods including roots, berries, nuts, seeds, and greens, which they augmented with the meat from fish, small mammals and occasional big game, as well as insects, grubs, and reptiles. Utes further east similarly exploited the wild plant foods but also had greater access to big game, including bison. However, because early Utes lacked sophisticated weaponry, hunting big game was difficult and chancy, typically requiring major communal efforts. Some scholars have suggested that because of this, the eastern bands may have incorporated larger band organizations for hunting big game even before they acquired the horse.[23]

14

One critical food source were piñon nuts, and folk legends describe how the Creator brought important piñon nuts to the People.[24] Family-bands would camp near abundant sources when the nuts ripened in the fall, and clusters of family camps frequently wintered together near favored piñon groves. Utes also enjoyed wild berries, but gathering them was dangerous because bears enjoyed the same food. Numerous folktales recount the exploits, adventures, and trauma of encountering bears on such berry-gathering quests.

Protein-rich insects were another important food, especially for the Western Utes and their Great Basin cousins, a practice that startled Euro-American settlers. Every half dozen years or so, regions of the Great Basin were overrun by hordes of cicadas, Rocky Mountain locusts (*Melanoplus spretus*), and Mormon crickets (*Anabrus simplex*), actually a shield-backed katydid. When swarms of these insects appeared, women knocked them to the ground with sticks, corralled them in low brush pens or pits, or drove them into streams, ditches, or trenches where they were trapped and later roasted. Goshutes and Shoshones also collected crickets from windrows washed up near the Great Salt Lake. While these insects could be eaten raw, they were usually baked or parched in trays over hot coals. Ground cricket "meat"—or black flour—could be mixed with mashed berries and dried as a "desert fruitcake." Roasted ground crickets were described as "quite palatable and nourishing," "very rich," and "great delicacies."

Goshutes took an early settler, Howard Egan, on a cricket drive and demonstrated how to force the crickets into grass-covered trenches, fire the grass, and bake the insects. Lorenzo Dow Young (brother of Brigham Young) also provided a vivid description of cricket infestations in the early 1850s and of Indians gathering them. Mormon crickets still swarm in parts of the Great Basin, and the crawling hordes have been described by tourists and farmers alike. Matted ants and crushed grubs were also added to stews.[25] Early settlers described eating seed meal and insect-laden stews with their Paiute neighbors:

> [The stew] was darkish grey color with like chunks of bacon in it, we tasted the flour…[which] tasted much like buck wheat flour or bean meal, what we fancied to be pieces of bacon, I have been told were bunches of matted ants, one of the brethren tasted this food and said these clusters tasted very oily but knew not the cause.[26]

Most desert-dwelling Numas also dug lizards out of their holes, ate snakes when killed, harvested tortoises, but avoided amphibians as bad luck.

Fish and marsh birds were another important source of food for the Utes and were available in abundance. For example, hundreds of Western Utes gathered in Utah Valley for an annual spring fish festival during the spring spawning runs. During this time fish were harvested in great numbers, especially from the Timpanogos River (Provo River), dried, and stored for winter use.[27] Fish swarmed upstream in such abundance that rivers were "full from bank to bank as thick as they could swim for hours and sometimes days together, and fish would be taken from morning until night for weeks together." Peter Gottfedson described arriving where a Ute had been fishing:

> There was about forty fish lying on the bank of the creek and thousands more in the little creek.... I ran down the stream three or four rods and started to throw out fish. By the time the others had un-saddled and unpacked they came and stopped me. I think I had about 300 fish and I was down on my knees throwing them out with both hands. They threw back those that were still alive but we took 210 to camp.... The fish in this locality go up the small streams to spawn in such numbers that they can hardly move.[28]

Timpanogos Utes also used nets or artificial shallows and constructed bulrush rafts from which they speared, line-fished, or shot fish with barbed fish arrows, or ice fished in the winter.[29]

In addition to fishing, Utes hunted waterfowl and game birds and collected their eggs in the spring, but they avoided predatory or scavenger birds except for their feathers.[30] When a person consumed an animal, they absorbed the characteristics of that animal along with its meat, and it became part of them.[31] Utes also hunted, trapped, ambushed, or stalked small game, which was an important source of meat as well as for decoration and charms. Women used porcupine quills to decorate clothing before beads became available, while men used weasel and ermine fur for caps, decoration, or to trim their braids.[32]

One of the most important meat staples—especially for Western Utes and Paiutes—was the ubiquitous rabbit. Rabbit and antelope populations fluctuated in boom-bust population cycles of between six to eight years, and Egan described a year when "black-tailed rabbits [clustered] in bands so thick they could not all get in the shade of the sagebrush." During such years Utes and Paiutes harvested abundant meat during communal drives.[33] Nets resembling coarse fishnets were stretched across the mouth of a gully, between hills, or in other suitable locations. Then women, children, and elders beat the brush and drove the rabbits toward the nets where hunters waited to shoot them with arrows or club them to death. The rabbits were skinned in long strips, the strips dried, and the fur woven into rabbit-skin blankets, which were often the only covering used among many groups. Remnants of rabbit nets have been found in Utah and Nevada, dating back a thousand years.[34]

Utes also hunted big game—the Eastern Utes to a greater extent than their cousins in central Utah. The most important big game included bighorn sheep as well as deer, antelope, and elk (in the winter). Mouache Utes who frequented the "plains of the Yutas" east of the Rockies also hunted bison. Coronado saw bison-hunting Indians—Utes included—whom he called *Querechos*, while later Spanish officials referred to the then-equestrian hunters as *Vaqueros* (cowboys).[35] Conflict with other mounted Plains Indians eventually drove the Mouache off the Yuta Plains and back into their mountains except during seasonal hunting trips.

Since simple weapons made stalking game risky, communal hunts were more effective. Small bands of hunters used ambuscades and pits and stampeded game into traps or over dropoffs where other hunters waited to dispatch animals not killed outright. Evidence of such traps or butchering sites have been found in western Colorado dating from as early as 7000 to 4000 BCE, and a more recent bison kill site was found north of Salt Lake City in Shoshone territory. On the plains hunters stalked only weak, disabled, or young bison, especially near water holes.[36] Elsewhere, nonequestrian Great Basin Numas drove antelope into winged brush corrals where they could be methodically slaughtered or trapped in a constricting circle of beaters and hunters, although this technique was disclaimed by later Utes.[37]

Early hunters avoided moose and bear. The moose, or "water deer," was considered unlucky because it was associated with water where evil sprites or "water babies" (*páa-ʔáapa-ci*) could be encountered and a hapless individual seduced, killed, or possessed.[38] Bears, on the other hand, were respected for religious as well as practical reasons, and they were feared, avoided, and placated. Utes only hunted bears in the spring when still drowsy from hibernation, or if they were forced to kill them in self-defense. Bears also carried sacred significance as near-relatives and (according to some lore) primal ancestors. When speaking of or to bears, Utes used kinship terms such as grandmother or aunt.

One of the Ute's oldest communal ceremonies was dedicated to the bear, a spring fertility ceremony called the "woman's forward-stepping dance," also called the Mating Dance or Bear Dance. This weeklong ceremony incorporated

18

2.1. Bear Dance at Ignacio, 1890 (Denver Public Library, Western History Collection, H. S. Poley, P-712)

aspects of a bear ceremonialism common in much of northern Native America, which linked the awakening of the bear (its turning over, signified by thunder) with the end of the starving time of winter and the awakening fecundity of spring. Dancers, believing bears slowly woke and danced in the mountains, sympathetically mimicked them on the dance grounds. As a means of accumulating medicine power, the ceremony also served as a forum for occasional individual healing rituals, as well as a communal social event that helped reestablish and reinforce the ties of dispersed bands and provided a venue for courtship, sexual dalliance, and marriage.[39]

Some animals were only killed in self-defense or hunted for their skins, which were used as blankets, clothing decoration, and saddle blankets. However, after Utes became integrated into the commercial hide trade with non-Indians, they sometimes hunted deer, beaver, weasels, or ermine solely for their skins or furs.[40]

Ute Dress and Shelters

The Numic people spent a major portion of their time acquiring the necessities for survival, and there was limited time and few resources to produce extraneous fine arts and crafts. So they applied skill and artistry primarily to necessary handicrafts: hunting equipment; woven baskets, bowls, trays, and jars (at which Ute women excelled); and woven rabbit skin blankets, tanned robes,

2.2. Pah-ri-ats, a western Ute in summer hunting attire, c. 1873 (Used by permission, Utah State Historical Society, J. K. Hillers Photo #14556)

and where prosperity permitted, woven plant-fiber or buckskin clothing. After the southeastern bands integrated into the Spanish frontier border trade and then the central Rockies fur trade, they became very skilled at tanning hides and preparing beaver pelts for commercial trade as well as for personal use.[41]

While buck- and doeskins became common apparel among Eastern Utes, elsewhere, especially among Western Ute bands, nudity was common, especially during the hot summer months, while rabbit-skin blankets were often their only covering in the winter. In 1776 Escalante described Timpanogos Utes wearing some buckskin clothing, but he found the natives wearing no more than buckskin loincloths south of Utah Valley. In 1830 the trapper Warren Ferris wrote that "wild natives [Sanpitch Utes] ventured into our camp...stark naked."[42] Colorado Utes hunted big game in the mountains and bison on the Great Plains and used their hides for clothing or blankets, while the Timpanogos Utes exploited bighorn sheep as well as rabbits, musk-rats, beaver, and deer, the skins of which were used to make tunics, vests,

2.3. Rabbit-skin blankets were frequently worn by the Numic people during the cold winters. (Church of Jesus Christ of Latter-day Saints, Church History Library, P4544)

leggings, moccasins, and robes. When animal skins were especially scarce and the weather demanded it, scanty clothing could be woven from plant fibers, including knee-length skirts for women, poncho-like shirts, twined plant-fiber leggings, and twined-fiber moccasins.[43] Many Utes, Paiutes, Goshutes, and Shoshones relied mainly or solely on rabbit-skin blankets to keep them warm, their hands tucked inside.[44]

Utes used their pragmatic ingenuity to create shelters from existing resources. Some early shelters were simply rough lean-tos thrown together to mediate the effects of the weather or small-domed huts covered with brush, bark, or grass and tules, although Weeminuches and Western Utes sometimes constructed larger-domed ones.[45] After Utes acquired horses and European weapons and were influenced by interactions with Plains Indians, they began to construct skin tipis. Still, only successful hunters could afford this luxury, for it took six to ten elk or bison hides to make one. Primarily, these tipis

2.4. Brush tipis and wickiups were still being used into the twentieth century. (Photo c. 1880, Denver Public Library, Stobie Collection, X-30353)

were used by the more interculturally influenced equestrian Utes of central and southern Colorado, although northern Colorado and Utah bands eventually adopted them during the nineteenth century. Bernardo Miera's 1776 map of the Domnguez-Escalante expedition illustrated these cultural differences when he drew tipis to indicate southern and central Ute locations, and small, domed huts for the northern and western bands.[46] After hunting was curtailed during the early reservation years, skin tipis were replaced with poorly insulated canvas-covered tipis and military-style tents.[47]

Many Utes today construct brush houses—enclosed ramadas or square shade houses—that they refurbish and use annually at modern communal events like the Sundance, Bear Dance, or powwows, sometimes building them near homes. These shade houses merged and adapted the traditional brush dwellings with the Spanish ramada. Framed with solid poles, they were roofed and, by the mid-twentieth century, walled with fresh branches each season. Cross ventilation, and breezes through moist green leaves, kept such summer shelters comfortably cool and humid.[48]

Medicine and Power

Traditional Ute religion has been described as "shamanism based on individual powers."[49] Later Ute contact with non-Indian Christians and non-Numic Indians led to the integration of new religious conceptions and pan-Indian rituals and ceremonies. While these later religious movements were new, Utes imbued them with traditional spiritual meanings and adapted their practice so that they fit easily within older religious perceptions. In essence, late nineteenth-century syncretic religious adaptations like the Sundance or the peyote religion became overt expressions of traditional Ute beliefs in a new, hybridized form.[50]

Early Utes believed in an earthly cosmos that was filled with an animating and fertile supernatural force (*puwá* or *puwá-vu*), and their language incorporated elements that clearly separated the sacred from the mundane. Shamans (*puwarat*), also known as medicine men or Indian doctors, could acquire supernatural power, as could witches or bad-medicine shamans (*awu puwarat*). The supernatural domain also included otherworldly harbingers or things imbued with increased powers such as coyotes or piñon nuts. *Puwá* could also be accumulated in objects, during ceremonies, and by elderly people who had lived long, or perhaps too long, accruing power by virtue of simply living.[51]

Medicine power was neither good nor bad, it was simply there. It became good or bad depending on how it was controlled and who used it. *Puwá* was expressed in terms of human life, health, and prosperity: good powers healed or revitalized, while bad powers (*awu puwá*) caused illness or death. The many medicinal hot springs that dotted Ute country were imbued with medicine power and were deeply valued. For example, in the nineteenth century southern Utes battled Navajos over the possession of the medicinal Pagosa Hot Springs; some post-reservation Utes continued to visit the hot springs and hot-vapor caves at Glenwood Springs; the 1873 participants in a Ghost Dance camped at the hot springs near Fountain Green; and in 1850–1851 the measles-plagued Timpanogos Utes sought relief (though many found death) in the hot springs north of Utah Lake.

A multitude of mischievous or benevolent sprites filled the Ute world. Some, like moose, the evil *páa-ʔáapa-ci* "water babies," or dangerous *pituku-pi* dwarves were to be avoided; others such as horned toads or collared lizards could be propitiated for good luck.

The most potent reservoir of power was the sun, though powerful animals such as elk, bear, bison, and eagle were also significant reservoirs of *puwá*. The physical and spiritual fluids of life—water, sap, and blood—held power, and *puwá* was sometimes referred to simply as "water." In the Sundance, for example, the east-facing entrance to the dance corral was called a "water path," a path of power leading from the rising sun and always kept clear of observers, while vision-questing men sought personal water paths. Utes could tap these reservoirs of supernatural power and use it, ideally, for the good of themselves and others. Prosperity and success indicated a person possessed medicine power, while failure signaled its loss or that it had rebounded for evil.

Puwá could seek out a person, usually in dreams where spirit tutors gave specific instructions, or individuals could seek out *puwá* for themselves. For example, in 1914 Northern Ute healers explained how they had been visited by supernatural entities or "spiritual tutors," who gave them their powers and told them what to do; Teddy Pageets described multiple visits from a "little green man," first seen when he was very young, and who taught him his medicine songs in dreams. Mrs. (White Bear) Washington, a shaman and herbal doctor, was visited by a spirit "represented by an eagle," who "taught her what to do."[52] These were *puwarat*,[53] men (or women) with power or medicine. The purpose of a shaman's power was to heal; above all else, he was a healer—a doctor. *Puwá* was literally "medicine," but like all medicine it could be used for good or ill. A powerful Indian doctor had good medicine with which he could heal the sick; a successful chief had strong medicine to bring prosperity to his band; and medicine talks could heal emotional or political rifts between individuals, families, bands, or tribes.

Although women could gain power and heal, and sometimes did, most *puwarat* were men. Medicine women tended to be more accomplished with their use of herbal specifics and nursing skills, valued for their knowledge of herbal medicines. Shamans were, in theory, altruistic and self-sacrificing. Payment for their services was not required, although gifts were generally expected, usually given, and often generous. Power was a gift, usually from specific supernatural animal familiars, the spirit tutors. During recurring dream visions, a novice was instructed over a long period in the ways of his power, learned his personal medicine songs, and understood what to put in his medicine bundle.

A medicine man was expected to be relatively circumspect and follow the ideals of social behavior; he could not refuse a call upon his powers, yet the exercise of them sapped him and left him open to personal danger. Shamans risked having their powers turn bad if they were overworked, misused, abused, or degenerated as a person aged. Bad power caused illnesses, disease, and sometimes death. A man with bad power could cause illness by directing his powers against someone; his *awu puwá* could kill his patients instead of healing them; or he might use his powers to steal life from young people to extend his own. Old shamans (and very old men and women) were feared because the potential for their power to sour grew greater each day.

Once power had "tasted blood" it could never be controlled for good again, and bad power could only be destroyed through the death of the *awu puwarat*. Although many medicine men died of old age, more than one found an early grave when grieving relatives suspected witchcraft in a patient's death. For example, Chief Ignacio's father was reputed to have been a medicine man who was killed when a patient died, and his shaman brother was killed by the brother of another patient who died. Tamouchi, a Capote war chief, shot a shaman who failed to heal his wife, and Buckskin Charley dispatched a shaman in his band. Shavano, a prominent Uncompahgre leader and medicine man, was shot and killed in front of the Ouray agency amidst a score of his warriors, who promptly executed the killer and dumped his body into a nearby river. Within days another Uncompahgre shaman was accused by a grieving father of causing the deaths of his two sons. In this case the medicine man preemptively shot his accuser.[54]

For the most part, however, the Ute people honored and respected (if cautiously) those with *puwá*. Their religion was a flexible system of beliefs whose major purpose was the health and welfare of the individual and community. It was holistic, intimately linking religion, physiology, and psychology. Because illness could be caused by thinking bad thoughts, violating taboos, having an *awu puwarat* direct bad powers against a person, or by being tricked by a mischievous sprite or ghost, dream analysis was often an integral part of curing, for it was critical for a doctor to know the disturbing thoughts or "visions" that might have induced physical malfunction. Faith healing, or drawing on the powers of a patient's mind, was an important factor in Ute religion.[55]

Curing ceremonies were all-night affairs, timed so the patient could rise up with the vigorous sun in the morning. The shaman offered prayers to his power, smoked so his words would be carried heavenward, and sang from his personal repertoire of medicine songs to summon *puwá*. Others present were usually invited to join in singing to amalgamate their efforts in calling out the medicine power. Such singing during curing ceremonies was a common practice among most Native Americans; for example, the Shoshonean term for curing literally means "singing," while Navajo curing ceremonies are called "sings" and their medicine men, "singers."[56]

While the Utes had an extensive knowledge of medicinal plants, one of the most visible means of curing was the dramatic and often violent shamanistic exorcism of the illness-causing evil. A medicine man summoned *puwá* and then used himself as a healing tool, pressing his head against the diseased body and "sucking out" or extracting the intrusive power and then spitting it into his hand where it could be destroyed—often by swallowing it so the power within him could "devour" the evil. Similarly, a shaman could draw the evil out by lying under the patient and then pulling the disease into their own body where it could be destroyed. Others used pain to drive out the evil, burning a patient's body in patterns with live coals, or scarifying it with supernaturally potent obsidian knives.[57] A powerful medicine man could also use the light down-feather from an eagle, which symbolized the soul and the breath of life, to call back the spirit of a patient who was close to death.

By the end of the nineteenth century, Utes began incorporating older beliefs into new pan-Indian religions, including the Sundance and peyote meetings. For example, Peyote road chiefs used a traditional syndication of healing powers: an all-night curing ritual combined with traditional sources of *puwá* in the smoke, music, and medicinal specifics. Many of the first Ute peyote chiefs were also traditional medicine men, and some early meetings incorporated traditional sucking treatments into the ritual. And holy men continued to doctor patients with a sacred eagle-wing fan at the end of these new ceremonies as well as in private curing rituals.[58]

As disease and death took its toll in the wake of Euro-American colonization and confinement on reservations, there was also a high turnover in medicine men. Even in the mid-twentieth century, some Ute Mountain Ute shamans were killed when their patients died. Still, many Utes continued to seek out native doctors, disliking and distrusting non-Indian ones and preferring to take "Indian" ailments to Indian doctors. By the end of the twentieth century, although Indian Health Service clinics were busy, many Utes continued to harbor a basic distrust of non-Indian medicine.[59]

Paramount to the inherent individualism of the Utes was the belief that there were many paths to god (divine power or *puwá*), and the purpose of religious ceremonies was to direct one's thinking to do good and prepare the mind and body to receive dream visions or the whispering inspiration that came with power. So when Christianity was introduced, few Utes found it inconsistent to be both Christian and Indian. Many Western Utes became Mormons at first, and when relocated to the Uintah Reservation leaned toward Presbyterianism and then Episcopalianism,[60] while southern Utes were proselyted by Catholic and Protestant missionaries. Reverend James Russell, who ran the Presbyterian mission at Towaoc, noted how Ute Mountain Utes found no incompatibility between attending mass, the Sundance, and peyote meetings. One Episcopalian priest at Whiterocks, a Sioux, sought his own communion with god in "sweats," Sundances, and Christian services. As Ouray once pragmatically noted, "If one religion is good, two religions are much better."[61]

The traditional way of life for most Utes would be dramatically altered with the approach of nonnative Euro-Americans, but even before contact the influence of trade, technology, and increased intertribal conflict had already begun to impact the *Núu-ci* way.

Chapter 3

First Encounters

Commerce and Colonialism, to 1846

As have other nomadic or migrating groups, the Utes inevitably met, interacted with, and exchanged culture with new people. As their Numic ancestors spread across the Great Basin and into the Rocky Mountains and Colorado Plateau, they encountered resident natives as well as other migratory people. By at least the fourteenth century this included a group of south-migrating Athabascans, later known as Apaches and Navajos.[1] Utes responded in various ways, from intermarriage, integration, symbiotic commerce, and adoption of new subsistence technologies to conflict, exploitation, decimation, conquest, and the replacement and removal of older residents. New environments demanded adapting subsistence methods, and interacting with new people facilitated the spread of ideas and technologies.[2] Consequently, an ongoing aspect of Ute existence was their practical adaptability to changing circumstances.

As Utes migrated into the Rocky Mountains and Colorado Plateau, they interacted with nomadic bison hunters on the plains, sedentary Pueblo agriculturalists, and, by the mid-1500s, Spanish and Mexican explorers and colonizers. Competition over natural resources and trade led to military and economic alliances that formed and reformed, and the balance of power between native groups continually shifted as they integrated new European technologies. By the late 1600s a new horse culture was spreading, slave raiding was increasing, and competitive violence was rising.[3] All of this would transform Ute culture, even as significant continuities remained.

This impacted the Ute worldview, often shifting how they thought of and defined themselves. Increased competition for resources hardened the cultural carapaces that delineated native groups, creating boundaries between even such close linguistic cousins as Utes, Paiutes, Shoshones, and Comanches. Meanwhile, social and material culture was changing as new commodities and ideas were adopted—and adapted—within a framework of more traditional perceptions.

CONTACT, CULTURE CHANGE, AND CULTURAL CONTINUITIES

Migrating Utes became part of a shifting mosaic of peoples who fluctuated between dominance and retreat as they won or lost access to resources and trade. Because of environmental changes like the Little Ice Age or intermittent droughts, as well as domestic strife, intercultural relations, and the intrusion of migrating people, traditional native territories were seldom static. This was true for the Utes just as it was for most Native Americans, and especially for eastern bands where they became part of an ever-changing kaleidoscope of "others" from whom they borrowed and exchanged new ideas and goods.

By the fifteenth century the Shoshones generally ranged north of the Utes, though a few bands were beginning to migrate south and east. Although these Shoshone bands—known to the Utes as Comanches—were at first Ute allies, by the 1750s the two groups had become bitter enemies. The easternmost Utes also encountered Plains Apaches, who were migrating south and transitioning from a northern Athabascan culture. By the 1500s, some of these Apaches were moving beyond the Great Plains and into the Southwest and Mexico, most having vacated the Plains by the later 1700s as newly armed and mounted Pawnee, Arapahoe, Cheyenne, Kiowa, and Sioux expanded deeper into the central and northern Plains. As they dominated the plains, the Comanche and Kiowa Apache shifted further into the southern Plains. By the 1500s southern Ute bands were colliding with and alternately fighting, trading, and even merging with the Athabascan Navajo west and northwest of the upper Rio Grande, even as they traded with and raided the agricultural Pueblo Indians. Ute oral traditions remember a time when Ute traders commonly visited the northeastern Pueblos, and Pueblo trade caravans ventured into Ute country.[4] The southern Ute bands were first to interact with foreign cultures. These were the Mouaches (*Mogwá-ci*), Capotes (*Kapúuta*), and Sabuaganas, and they were most heavily impacted by the subsequent intercultural exchanges. Bands roaming more distant areas lagged behind these bands in acquiring and incorporating this borderland culture; among these were the still-unmounted "walking Mouaches," or *mogwá-taví?waa-ci*, later known as Tabeguaches. However, the easterly Mouaches had migrated early to the borderland and by 1540 had begun adopting the diet, dress, and shelters of bison-hunting Plains Indians, forming larger bands, and growing more aggressively territorial. Early

Spanish records describe large bands (up to one thousand people) of "valiant and courageous" Plains Utes who traveled in protective close-order formations and were prepared for battle with long and short bows, arrows, war clubs, spears, and hide shields.[5]

Cultural change accelerated after the arrival of Hispano-Americans. This occurred as early as Vásquez de Coronado's 1540–1542 expedition to the Upper Rio Grande and his foray onto the Great Plains. Coronado's travels resulted in direct contact and rumors among the Indians about the foreigners and their domestic animals. As a consequence, Indians were fearful and hostile, as well as anxious for new goods, when they encountered subsequent European expeditions. Most encounters remained transitory until 1598, when Spanish colonizers arrived under the leadership of Don Juan de Oñate. This shifted native relationships drastically, as large numbers of new European goods entered Indian trade networks and intertribal power relations shifted.[6]

Horses and European weapons transformed native cultures and revolutionized hunting and warfare. These were, as one historian put it, "the cotton gins and steamboats of the high plains."[7] Nomadic Indians could now accumulate and transport more tangible wealth, while new hunting and warring tactics led to protectively larger bands and transformed social and political relations. Violent competition flared over resources and trade. At the same time virulent epidemics of European diseases were ravaging native people. Populations plummeted, even as the demand for labor to produce trade goods commodified captives and led to an increase in slave raiding and trading. This in turn spurred even greater levels of warfare. Meanwhile, the borderlands became increasingly multicultural and multiethnic, as all groups incorporated and assimilated a greater number of "strangers"—including traders, intertribal spouses, captives, and their mixed-heritage children. Such hybridizing also created new and complex intercultural and intertribal kinship networks and alliances.[8]

Location was key. The Mouache Utes were integrated into the Spanish-Pueblo border trade as well as a native trade network that stretched from today's Mexico to the Yellowstone River and from the Colorado to the Mississippi.[9] Borderland Utes traded with and raided pueblo villages in a "symbiotic, nutritional interdependency," as did Apaches and other nomadic tribes. The Pueblo Indians needed meat and hides to supplement their agriculture-based diet, since (with the exception of turkeys and dogs) they lacked domestic animals and had (by the fifteenth century) overhunted local game. At the same time nomadic Indians coveted Pueblo textiles along with carbohydrate-rich

29

3.1. Hunter's camp with elk or bison-skin tipi; skin from a newly killed deer and "jerky" are drying on poles. (L. Tom Perry Special Collections, Brigham Young University, Provo, Utah, Adams Bros. P-259, Neg. #6317)

foods like maize, squash, and beans to supplement their winter diets. Nomadic bands developed long-standing trade relationships with some Pueblo villages while targeting other villages for raids. Utes also had fluctuating trade-and-raid relations with certain Navajo bands.[10]

Early Spanish explorers described Plains hunters as *Querechos* or "bison followers" (a term adopted from the Jemez), or *Vaqueros* "cattle herdsmen."[11] While these people are often identified as Plains Apaches, early chroniclers knew the mountain-based Utes (Yutas) were seasonal bison hunters. Juan Amando Niel wrote in 1702 that the *Vaqueros* mentioned by Gerónimo de Zarate Salmarón in 1621 were Yutas, and the region northeast of Taos was the "plains of the Yutas." This beautiful, fertile region was filled with game, and the Mouaches were understandably defensive, especially after newly mounted enemies increasingly competed for the land. Ute presence is indicated by aggressive trading and raiding activities with the Pueblos, already evident by 1540 when Coronado described the ruins of Tewa pueblos and adjoining lands laid

3.1. Approximate location of Ute, Comanche, and "Payuchi" bands, as recognized by contemporary Spanish chroniclers, c. 1750.

waste and depopulated by the attacks of "brave men from the north." These appear to have been the Utes. After the Capotes acquired the horse, they joined the Mouaches on the Plains and by the early 1700s were another important presence in the borderlands.[12]

Southern Ute bands became skilled big game hunters and hide processors. Each fall, when Pueblo harvests were in and the season's hunting concluded, Utes came to annual trade fairs in Taos and Pecos where they bartered beautifully tanned hides, chamois skins (mountain sheep), meat, and salt. This trade intensified after the Spanish arrived and eventually included horses. Although Spanish law forbade Indians owning horses in the seventeenth century, Utes acquired them nonetheless. As early as 1626 they were stealing them, recovering strays, and buying old, worn out horses they called "big dogs" because, like dogs, they used them as beasts of burden to pull travois. By 1640 the knowledge of equestrianism had spread, and records describe bands of mounted Indians, including the Utes. The most likely vector in this spread were Indian slaves or servants who watched or worked with horses and inevitably took that knowledge (if not an occasional horse) with them when they were emancipated, ransomed, or escaped.[13]

Economic conditions improved dramatically for the Utes after they acquired the horse, and their material and social culture morphed accordingly.

Conflict increased as well, for Indians raided each other for horses or the captives that could be traded for the horses. A hunter-warrior complex quickly developed on the Plains. This was the beginning of a two-hundred-year legacy of the mounted Plains warrior, noted by nineteenth-century military officers as the finest light cavalry in the world, but also a culture that would be stereotyped in later Wild West shows and the celluloid of Hollywood.[14]

Though the Utes never adopted a full-blown war ethic like that found among other Plains cultures, they did grow increasingly warlike. As early as 1621 the Yutas were described as being "of good physique, valiant and full of spirit...equal in manliness to the *Apacha* with whom they war. They...never turn their backs to the enemy, but conquer or die." And in 1686 they were "greatly feared."[15] This aggressive stance was heightened with new hunting and raiding patterns and the need to defend against increasingly hostile neighbors. Equestrianism also brought ecological stress and impacted band movement as larger horse herds competed for and overgrazed available grass. Equestrian bands coalesced into larger and more permanent groups for hunting or raiding as well as for protection.[16] Social stratification began to develop as individuals accumulated greater wealth. More efficient hunting provided more hides and meat, allowing equestrian Utes to barter for more luxury items including metal tools, trinkets, textiles, clothing, and decorative items like tin, yarn, or beads. Diets altered and the language expanded to include jargonized trade words for products such as corn, beans, and squash, as well as cabbages, peaches, oranges, apples, coffee, beef, and mutton. Not only were new commodities being exchanged, but so were new ideas.[17]

Horses became *the* symbol of wealth and prestige. A man with many horses could travel, hunt, trade, or raid more easily and was free to be generous with his goods, which in turn elevated his status and influence. Horses were also an important medium of exchange, including as fee payments for shamans, bride-price gifts, or ceremonial gift exchanges. Female captives also increased a man's ability to prosper, since more women could prepare more hides for commercial trade. War captives—especially women and children—were also valuable trade commodities and were bartered to transient traders, at trade fairs, or through the native trade network that spanned the Great Plains.[18]

Weapons were important for maintaining a balance of power between groups. Over time a disparity began to develop between Plains Indians who, by the mid-1700s, were obtaining weapons from French traders on the upper Missouri and Platte Rivers and, by the 1800s, from Americans. Although some Ute bands continued to make seasonal hunting and raiding forays onto the

TABLE 3.1. UTE AND PAIUTE BAPTISMS IN NEW MEXICO, 1700–1880[1]

	1700s	1710s	1720s	1730s	1740s	1750s	1760s	1770s	1780s	1790s	1800s	1810s	1820s	1830s	1840s	1850s	1860s	1870s
Total Yutas	0	5	0	1	5	8	9	9	23	15	163	124	56	90	207	62	41	2
"Ute" (general)				1	5	8	9	9	23	15	162	112	49	71	157	43	26	1
Eastern Ute bands											1	3		1	2	1		
Pahvant														1	2			
Paiute												2	1	7	44	18	15	1
Timpanogos												7	6	10	2			

1. Data from Brugge, *Navajos in the Catholic Church Records*, frontispiece, 30.

Note: For most of the 1700s, Utes were not differentiated by bands, and the term Yuta or Ute might refer to Utes or related Paiute or Pahvant. As Utes warred with Comanche after 1752, the number of Ute captives baptized rises. After trade increased in the interior after 1780, there is a sharp surge in the number of captives, and Pahvant, Paiute, and Timpanogos Utes appear (suggesting interactions with both Spanish traders and Comanche raiders). There is a sharp rise in numbers during 1800–1820 then a decline for a decade. The notorious slave trader Wákara claimed his father had traded in captives. When Wákara and his kin entered the trade, c. 1835–1856, the number of western captives spikes.

plains, they were being hemmed into their mountains by more arms- and horse-rich Plains Indians who had better access to American trade to the east as well as raiding opportunities in Texas. Groups like the Comanche, Cheyenne, and Arapaho grew in power while the Utes remained relatively horse- and gun-poor.[19]

By the late 1700s and early 1800s, Utes who lived even more distant from the resource-rich Plains or the borderland trade—yet equally desperate to obtain horses—began to exchange captives or even their own children or orphaned kinsmen for horses. Mounted Eastern Utes ridiculed their western cousins along the Wasatch Front as "poor" because they had few horses and were so destitute they sometimes used them as food. With most of the Plains and borderland Indians mounted by the early 1700s, horses became the ultimate tool for survival and power—for subsistence, prestige, and defense/offense against aggressive tribes.[20]

The borderland market economy also encouraged the flourishing commercial slave trade. As the demand for manufactured goods rose, the need for the labor to produce trade commodities increased on both sides, and this propelled slave raiding. Captives were used to supplement low population groups and as laborers, and women were incorporated as both domestics and consorts in Indian and non-Indian societies alike. Polygyny increased among Indian groups, even as Hispanic settlers sired children with their Indian women captives. Wealthy Spanish officials used slaves to produce textiles for commercial trade, and as the Navajos incorporated sheep into their economy, the Navajos raided for herdsmen, field hands, and weavers. Similarly, Comanches needed women to process and tan hides and boys to tend their growing herds of horses.[21]

Spanish officials reported in the early 1700s that both Comanches and Utes raided for large numbers of women and children, only some of whom were ever sold or ransomed back. Utes traded large quantities of expertly tanned buckskins and became noted for their exquisite beadwork, but these were labor-intensive commodities; so, even as Utes negotiated peace with the Spanish, they continued to take captives from their Indian enemies. For example, the well-known nineteenth-century Ute chief Ouray had an Apache father and a Kiowa wife who were both tribally integrated captives. Although the Utes never institutionalized slavery the way the Spanish, Navajo, or Comanche did, captives continued to replace populations and labor. When there is a demand for labor to produce valuable commodities—or labor populations decrease due to disease or war—societies justify slave or exploited labor. Native Americans were no different.[22]

Equestrianism impacted Ute social and political organization as well. As family groups clustered and bands grew larger and more permanent, civic leadership morphed to meet increasingly complex needs, and the status and importance of raiding chiefs and their lieutenants increased. This transforming leadership appeared earliest and most clearly among the Mouaches and Capotes who coalesced into larger bands, but the pattern was repeated as other bands also acquired equestrian mobility. Respected elders had once directed activities in small family bands, basing their leadership on a traditional collective cultural conscience and haranguing members about their duties, responsibilities, and morals.[23] In larger bands, this traditional leadership was revised to meet new needs. Here the main camp leader remained an authoritative, respected elder, who coordinated major movements, negotiated, and was a good "talker," but who was increasingly assisted by a council of influential elders and younger subchiefs who were typically leaders of hunting or raiding bands. Meanwhile, specialty chiefs and shamans remained influential. Utes began to differentiate the varied chiefly roles with titles such as "band chief," "the man," "leader of the camp," or "war leader." Women rarely, if ever, sat in council or held leadership positions.[24]

Individuality, personal opinion, and dissension remained, and Utes, if dissatisfied, would simply associate with other leaders. Chiefs, though, won and held their positions by dint of their physical prowess, personality, assertion of authority, and *puwá*—the fertile sacred powers demonstrated in the prosperity they brought to their followers.[25] Social expectations and tradition reinforced a leader's position so long as he was successful. Still, bands remained predominantly associations of family and close friends who traveled in familiar country they were attached to by strong ties of emotion and identity. Separating from kin and country was traumatic and disruptive to the social identity within a family and territorial home. So while Utes were free to disassociate from a leader they didn't like, it was typically preferable to adjust to that leader than endure a self-imposed exile.

Nevertheless, general band membership remained fluid and individualistic, and marriages outside bands reinforced that. During the early agency years, 1863–1880, Utes often registered with more than one agency to receive extra rations or benefits. Because of their widespread kin, Ute travels often brought them near more than one agency, making such an arrangement eminently practical. Even band affiliations of prominent Ute figures shifted. Sapowaneri, Ouray's lieutenant and successor among the Uncompahgre, signed the Treaty of 1868 as a Mouache and the 1880 agreement as a White River. Ignacio

35

identified himself as a Mouache in 1868, although he gained prominence as a Weeminuche chief. Piah was identified as a White River and Denver Ute, but in 1880 he took his kinsmen to join the Mouaches and Capotes so he could stay in Colorado. Similarly, Colorow associated with whichever group (or agency) suited his interests, signing the 1863 Tabeguache Treaty but calling himself a Yampa on the 1868 Treaty; he was also associated with the Denver Agency and after 1872 was variously identified as an Uncompahgre or a White River. In fact, some sources suggest he was actually an adopted Comanche captive raised by Mouache parents. Many other prominent Utes were similarly fluid in their choice of band association.[26]

Larger social groupings demand increasingly centralized authority, and those who associated with prospering bands grew more dependent on directives from leaders or prominent families—but the *family* (kinsmen) endured as the nucleus of social regulation. Chiefs remained little more than committee chairmen who only directed collective economic and social activities. In matters of justice, the family remained the court of first and last appeal, and decisions were meted out according to traditional patterns. For example, in the case of theft, an authoritative older relative arranged just punishment and restitution. For murder—including death by witchcraft—grieving kinsmen took vengeance on the perpetrator or their family. Murder, theft, or personal violence were not crimes against society, but violations of individual or family honor and as such needed to be redressed by those directly affected. Thus, band chiefs were respected for their advice but were neither police nor judge, and their authority stopped at the door of a man's lodge.[27]

The continuities as well as changes to Ute patterns of social organization and leadership illustrate how the Utes adapted to and revised social patterns within older perceptions of how things ought to work. Despite new economies, new material goods, and transforming social and subsistence patterns, traditional beliefs continued to undergird Ute values and behavior.

COMPETITION, ALLIANCES, AND THE BALANCE OF POWER

Spanish explorers and colonizers were motivated by several often-competing desires, among them imperial rivalries, the reclamation of heathen souls, the promulgation of the Catholic Church, and the personal accumulation of wealth and power. Not only did Spanish officials engage in agriculture, husbandry, mining, slave trading, manufacture, and commerce, rumor and myth also impelled them to continue searching for new sources of legendary treasure. The golden kingdom of Quivira was somewhere on the High Plains, and Teguayo and the Lake of Copala of Aztlan—the legendary home of the Aztecs—lay deep within Yuta country. These myths fueled Spanish imagination and pushed explorations through the 1700s.[28] Meanwhile, Native Americans were equally motivated by the desire to accumulate wealth through trading and raiding opportunities.

Spanish colonizers also believed they were surrounded by hostile enemies and constantly vulnerable to Indian attacks; therefore, they used a variety of "foreign-relations" policies to solidify their rule. Over time officials varyingly invoked punitive expeditions to chastise or exterminate hostile Indians, or they negotiated peace agreements that emphasized gift-giving and trade regulation for the purpose of creating mutually beneficial relations. The colony was, after all, dependent on its ability to farm securely and trade safely. Thus, the Utes, along with other borderland Indians, were alternately benefited or harmed by the shifting winds of official policies that blew according to the wisdom or whim of the serving governor.[29]

Spanish colonization initially disrupted and shifted the borderland trade economy, at first because taxes and tribute drained away trade goods the Pueblos normally used for borderland trade. As trade decreased, Apache and Ute raiding increased. This led to punitive military expeditions. Some Spanish officials also saw these wars as "providential," since they provided an excuse to acquire profitable captives in "just" wars that were used locally or sold south into the silver mines of Parral. New Spain was hungry for cheap labor and starved for it on its northern frontiers. Spanish landowners and Catholic missions used the bound labor of Pueblo Indians and the slave labor of nomadic heathens—non-Christians—captured during just wars or "ransomed" (*rescato*, rescued) at trade fairs. These captives then worked off the cost of their fictive ransom as domestics and field hands. As the demand for these commodity-producing laborers increased, the slave trade flourished.[30] Although Spain had passed laws against enslaving Indians, the latter could be enslaved for a set period of time if captured in battles as legitimate "foes of Christ" and Spain. But the idea of a just war was slippery and conveniently defined. Declaring war against wild tribes ostensibly justified taking prisoners who could then be set to work. Some religious leaders also condoned enslavement as a convenient means to gain converts to Christianity.[31]

Simply put, Indian wars were good strategy and good for business—for outsiders. And, in a vicious twist, Spanish and later American officials in New Mexico found that intertribal warfare accomplished several strategic goals: not only were the settlements supplied with labor and converts, wars weakened tribes and redirected their antagonism toward one another. José de Gálvez wrote in 1767 that "the vanquishment of the heathen consists in obliging them to destroy one another." Even early American officials encouraged tribes to raid other tribes since war captives helped fund the war *and* galvanized rival tribes to destroy each other.[32]

The Yuta and Apache Indians were targeted early by Spanish officials who sent expeditions against them as early as 1606, and especially from 1637 to 1641. Governor Luis de Rosas, a notoriously greedy slaver, propagated Indian wars primarily as an excuse to harvest slaves. During one four-year war he enslaved at least eighty "Utacas" in his textile works in Santa Fe where they were forced to manufacture serapes and mantas. Naturally, conflict escalated as Utes and other native people retaliated, provoking a cycle of even more resistance, death, and reprisals.[33]

But not all governors believed in a big-stick policy. By the 1670s Governor Antonio de Otermín attempted to negotiate peace with the Utes, but in 1680 the Pueblo Indians revolted and drove the Spanish out of the Upper Rio Grande.[34] Ute complicity in that uprising remains conjectural; however, Popé, the leader of the revolt, visited both Utes and Navajos where he learned "many of their tricks" and "juggleries" with which to overawe and gain the confidence of his Pueblo revolutionaries. The Utes undoubtedly knew of the impending revolt but took no active part in it. They even allowed visiting Spaniards to leave their camps safely during the disorder.[35]

Whatever their role, the Utes benefited by the Spanish defeat. In addition to a windfall of horses, in the absence of Spanish protection the Utes raided the Navajos, Hopis, and Pueblos more frequently. Twelve years later, the returning Spanish found Pueblo and Hopi Indians forted up on mesa tops and lowland villages abandoned. The new governor negotiated with the Utes, offering peaceful trade, while reminding the Pueblos of how much they needed the Spanish for protection against Ute raids.[36]

During the 1600s the Mouache Utes also competed with migrating Jicarilla Apaches for territory north and east of Taos, and they formed an alliance with south-migrating Comanche, a group of Shoshone splinter bands. The Comanche, or *kumá-ci* in Ute, meant enemy, stranger, foreign person, non-Ute, or left-handed kinsman, and it was typically applied to Shoshones or related Comanches. It was a backhanded acknowledgement of their Shoshonean kinship, because the left hand was considered the bad-luck or witching hand. Allies at first, Eastern Ute bands introduced these Comanches to Pueblo trade in the early 1600s, and by the early 1700s mounted Comanche bands had become a formidable force. During the first half of the 1700s, mounted Ute and Comanche allies warred against the Jicarillas, hunted bison on the plains from the Arkansas River to the panhandle of Texas, and resumed raiding Pueblo settlements.[37]

But raids again provoked armed responses from the Spanish military and their Indian allies. In 1716 acting Governor Martinez launched a punitive campaign against the Mouaches and Comanches during which they killed many Utes and took numerous captives. But this didn't stop the cycle of raiding and retaliation—instead it grew more vicious and expansive. What had begun as raids for goods, livestock, and captives escalated into a killing war that continued for over thirty years.[38]

Meanwhile, imperial rivalries ramped up the conflict, especially after Spanish officials learned that French traders were making alliances with the Plains Pawnee and selling them weapons—a significant technological advantage that promised to shift the balance of power on the Plains. The competition for Indian allies increased intertribal violence as native groups scrambled for parity.[39] By 1724 Mouaches and Comanches were raiding as far south as Jemez and west into the Chama Valley. By the 1730s the Capote Utes had joined the fray, raiding east of the Divide and striking Navajos to the southwest. Between 1747 and 1768, the "giant barbarians"—Utes—forced the Jicarilla Apaches out of Ute-claimed territory and pressured the Navajos out of the upper San Juan River drainage. Meanwhile, they continued to raid Navajo camps as far south as modern-day Cuba and Grants (New Mexico), initiating a defensive alliance between the Navajos and the Spanish.[40] Once Navajos and Jicarillas had been expelled, Ute attacks focused on the Chama River Valley.

Colonizers had established the villages of Río Ojo Caliente, Abiquiú Creek, and Chihuahueños near Chaguagua Creek during the early decades of the 1700s. But this was Capote and Chaguagua (Sabuagana) hunting grounds,[41] frequently visited by other Indian raiders, and a major trading and raiding route. The isolated settlements were highly vulnerable to attack and quickly became opportunistic prey of raiding Utes and other Indians. Beginning in 1744 Utes and Comanches conducted a series of raids on these villages; in response to a 1746 Comanche attack on Abiquiú, Spanish troops and allies destroyed a peaceful Ute camp. This triggered more reprisal raids by enraged Capote and Chaguagua Utes. By 1749 the Chama River Valley had been abandoned.[42]

But officials needed settlements on this northern frontier, to act as buffers to protect the central towns and later to protect miners. Colonists were forcibly resettled in 1750 and reinforced in 1754 with *genízaro* grantees. Genízaros were detribalized, Hispanicized Indians—emancipated captives or acculturated Pueblo exiles. These genízaros were familiar fixtures in frontier settlements and militias, as well as guides and interpreters. Because of their mixed heritage, they sometimes provided links to complex native kinship networks as well.[43] By the mid-1750s, some governors recognized that violence only exacerbated hostilities, which disrupted colonization and hurt the economy. Both sides actually preferred peace and friendship to protect their people and to encourage a mutually beneficial trade. So Governor Vélez Capuchín successfully negotiated peace through conciliation and gifts, and by 1754 mestizo and genízaro settlers had safely returned (albeit reluctantly) to the Chama Valley.[44]

By this time the Ute-Comanche alliance was souring, further motivating the Utes to negotiate peace with the Spanish. Because the Comanche had pushed deeper onto the Plains, they had developed new networks of Indian alliances that gave them access to French arms and ammunition, positioned them on the grassy southern Plains, and placed them within reach of horse-rich Texas ranches. Many of their new allies were also traditional enemies of the Utes. As Plains tribes grew stronger, the Mouaches and Capotes could only hunt bison seasonally. With their access to the Plains trade network disrupted, trade became limited to the local borderlands economy. By the mid-1700s the Utes, with few to no European weapons and significantly fewer horses, had become the technological inferiors of their Comanche cousins. Making things worse, in the 1740s borderland commerce was damaged by a serious drought that reduced agricultural production. Tensions escalated. When the Utes negotiated peace with the Spanish in 1752, the still-warring Comanches turned on their former allies. Utes and Comanches would be bitter enemies for decades to come.[45]

As Comanche raids on borderland settlements increased, the Utes allied with both Spanish and Apache troops against them. On one occasion in the 1760s, violence flared around the Taos Valley. In response Utes and Spanish troops stormed a Comanche camp and hundreds of warriors fled, apparently trying to lead the enemy away. As Spanish troops chased down and ultimately killed over four hundred Comanche men, the Utes remained to plunder the abandoned camp, driving off over one thousand horses and mules and taking several hundred women and children captive. Eventually, the Comanches did negotiate peace with Governor Cachupín. Southern Ute bands, still at odds with the Comanche, responded by forming a lasting buffer alliance with their old enemies, the Jicarilla, as well as tightening their mutually beneficial trade links with the Spanish.[46]

As allies, Utes increasingly acted as valuable auxiliaries on Spanish expeditions against Comanches and Navajos.[47] Teodoro de Croix reported that "to withstand [the Navajos], no better means has been found than that of availing ourselves of the arms of the Ute. It is sufficient that the latter declare war to make the Navaho desist from war on us." Conflict between the Spanish and Navajo increased after an 1804 campaign against the Navajos when Spanish troops, with their Mouache and Jicarilla allies, massacred a large band of Navajos in Canyon de Chelly. This triggered a decades-long bloody war between Navajo and Spanish settlers that would not end until the 1860s. The united efforts of Spanish troops and the "brave Ute and treacherous Jicarilla" also brought peace with the Comanche on the northern frontier.[48]

Although the Mouaches restricted their raiding against borderland settlements, the Capotes did not. Instead, they allied with the Navajo against the Hopi, and Spanish officials feared the two would turn on Spanish settlements. This alliance, along with a vigorous border trade in contraband weapons, prompted a 1778 *bando*—a proclamation—prohibiting any trade between the Utes and Spanish settlers or Christian Indians.[49] Eventually, the Capotes realized trading was more profitable (and safer) than raiding and allied with the Spanish as well.

Then in 1783 the new American republic was recognized, and Spanish land claims faced a new threat from the expansionist young republic. Officials soon discovered that Utes and genízaro traders made good frontier spies, as well as excellent trade partners.[50]

OPENING UTE COUNTRY

During the early 1800s, Spanish and then Mexican officials continued conciliatory gift giving—or paying tribute—to the Utes to maintain peaceful relations. It also suited the Utes to remain on peaceful terms because, after 1765, commodity-rich Spanish traders and explorers began trekking deeper into Ute country. So even as Spanish and genízaros from frontier borderlands fought the Navajos, some were also members of annual trade expeditions who were welcomed by Utes in western Colorado and central Utah. Two major routes wound out of Abiquiú: either northwesterly into Colorado, central Utah, and eventually south to southern California, or the Armijo route westward through northern Arizona to the southern leg of the California trail. These routes would become known collectively as the Old Spanish Trail.[51]

These routes were originally blazed by explorers commissioned by Spanish officials seeking a northern route to California. Tomás Vélez Cachupín ordered the first exploration in 1765. This expedition, led by Juan María de Rivera, had three main goals: to discover the source of silver traded by a Ute in Abiquiú; to find a route across the Colorado River (known as the Río del Tizón); and to gather more information about the fabled *Teguayo* and Lake of Copala, the mythical Aztlan of the Aztecs, which was rumored to exist within Yuta country. Teguayo was purported to be near a great salt lake and was associated with other fabled sites. A lost colony of Spaniards was also rumored to exist there, along with a numerous, wealthy, and civilized people.[52]

Rivera travelled as far as the La Sal Mountains and the Colorado River near today's Moab, Utah. Ironically, he found only lead in the Sierra de la Plata (Silver Mountains) where Americans would later find rich deposits of silver in the mid-1800s. He also discounted the river crossing his Ute guides showed him, although it *was* the crossing, and would be used by subsequent traders for decades to come.[53] On Rivera's trek he described the Payuchis and Weeminuche, as well as the Tabeguache and Sabuagana Yutas, who provided hospitality and guides.

The Sabuagana warned him to beware of angry Comanches from whom they had just stolen horses. They also told Rivera the region across the river had never been visited by Spaniards but was filled with a dangerous group of fair-skinned, fair-haired, bearded men led by a "Castillian" who spoke Spanish. They described a tribe within a day's travel who were so destitute they sometimes ate their own children, and they confirmed that there was a large lake at the base of some mountains where numerous Indians lived.[54] But they also warned Rivera of the perils across the river, a place they held in superstitious awe and were fearful to enter. Among the dangers were cannibalistic troll-like creatures—not the *páa-ʔáapa-ci* water babies of Ute lore, but *pituku-pi*, evil dwarves that would attack and devour men. It was a tradition that would be remembered by more traditionalist Uncompahgre Utes even as late as the 1980s.[55]

In 1776 officials dispatched another expedition through Ute country. Spain had begun colonizing in Alta California after 1768 in response to fears that Russian interests were moving south along the Pacific Coast. Contrary ocean currents made supplying Alta California hazardous, and Southern Apache and Yuma hostilities had closed the southern overland route.[56] So in 1776 Fray

3.2. Route of two Spanish explorations through Ute country: Rivera in 1765, and Domínguez and Escalante in 1776.

Francisco Atanasio Domínguez and his young companion, Fray Silvestre Vélez de Escalante, embarked on a new exploratory expedition in hopes of locating a northern route to California as well as suitable locations to establish missions among the Utes. Among those who accompanied the trek were genízaro traders and guides, Andrés Muñis, possibly an acculturated Ute, and his brother Antonio, both of whom had been with Rivera and spoke Ute.[57]

At first the Franciscans retraced Rivera's route but then turned north along trails used by northern and western Utes. They saw only a few Tabeguache Utes, although they encountered a sizable group of Sabuaganas on the north fork of the Gunnison River near the Colorado River who claimed they knew nothing about the route westward. However, the friars engaged a visiting Timpanogos or "Laguna" Indian as a guide to Lake Timpanogos. These Utes were also known as Fish Eaters or "water-edge people," because they relied heavily on abundant quantities of fish found in their valley's large freshwater lake and rivers.[58]

The Timpanogos guide, now christened Silvestre, agreed to lead them; however, the Sabuaganas now repeatedly warned them—in harrowing detail—of the hazards awaiting them. The trail led through enemy territory of the *Yamparica Comanche*, a people with whom they were at war.[59] Even the guide Silvestre grew hesitant, but the friars were insistent. Their genízaro guides were now thoroughly frightened and joined the chorus to convince the missionaries to turn back. Failing this, they pulled out contraband weapons they had hidden in their packs for surreptitious trade (to the friars' consternation), which they now decided were better used to protect themselves.[60]

Notwithstanding, the company continued on and made it to Lake Timpanogos (Utah Lake) without incident.[61] They saw "wisps" of smoke and hoof prints in the Uintah Basin and were told that both Comanches and Lake Utes hunted there. In Utah Valley the Lake Utes—once they discovered the mounted party were not Comanches—greeted them warmly. They appeared to listen intently to the friars' sermons, embraced them when they departed, and appeared eager for their return the following year to set up their planned missions.[62]

This eagerness may have been as much for military reasons as for religious fervor, considering the precarious condition in which these Western Utes then existed. Unarmed and unmounted—but rich in natural resources—they were vulnerable prey to the aggressive mounted and armed Shoshones and Comanches who neighbored them to the north and east, and who raided them intermittently. It is likely the Timpanogos welcomed the possibility of a Spanish settlement with its military strength and political alliance as a check on these depredations. Seventy-five years later the Southern Paiutes would similarly welcome Mormon settlements for much the same reason—as protection against mounted Western Utes who preyed upon them.

Escalante described the Timpanogos Utes as docile, good featured, some bearded, and speaking the Yuta language with a noticeable accent. They lived in willow-brush huts and subsisted on fish, rabbits, birds, seeds, and herbs. They were poorly dressed, their best apparel a few buckskin shirts, jackets, leggings, and moccasins, with supplementary rabbit-skin blankets for cold weather. The

44

Timpanogos told the missionaries that bison existed in the large valley just to the north, but it was Shoshone territory so they did not hunt there.

Traveling south from the hospitable valley, the company encountered few Indians, though they met one old man with a beard "so long and matted he resembled one of the Hermits of Europe."[63] Near the Sevier River they met more bearded Indians whom Escalante described as looking like "Capuchin priests or monks," save for the polished bone ornaments they wore in their noses. These *Barbones* or *Tirangapui*, possibly Pahvants, were friendly and appeared to listen to their message of Christian salvation. Escalante described tears flowing upon their departure, reinforcing their plans to return and establish missions and pueblos among the "poor lambs of Christ, wandering about for want of the light."[64]

Then their Timpanogos guide abandoned them.

Short of supplies and with winter coming on, the company suspended their attempt to reach California and started searching for a way back to Santa Fe. They began to encounter small bands of "timid" Indians, probably Southern Paiutes, who fled or exhibited great fright. Pressing on, they survived several attempts by seemingly helpful Paiute guides who tried to lead them astray. After navigating a difficult trek through slickrock wilderness, they finally located a passable ford and crossed the Colorado on November 7, 1776, leaving their names and date etched in nearby sandstone. Later, Americans would call this the Crossing of the Fathers. Of course, local Paiutes were already crossing here, and after mounted Utes started using it to access Navajo country, native people began calling it the Ute Crossing, an important link on an equally new Ute Trail. After 1829, Mexican traders began using this same crossing on the Armijo route between New Mexico and California, and beginning in 1858 it was used by Mormons trekking into northern Arizona. This difficult crossing was replaced in 1870 by Lee's Ferry further downstream, and today it is more than five hundred feet below the waters of Lake Powell.[65]

In 1779, after his successful return, Escalante wrote a letter to the governor debunking many of the legends that had lured explorers into the interior. Quivira was nothing more than Wichita villages; Teguayo was only pueblo ruins; and the lost Spanish civilization of armored and bearded men were just the poor bearded Indians south of the Timpanogos Utes.[66]

Though Domínguez and Escalante did not locate their overland route to California, they did explore and map a region previously unknown to Europeans, opening it for further exploitation by borderland profiteers. Neither was

Domínguez able to establish missions; instead, diverted by internal religious politics, he left to defend himself in Mexico City. Rather than build missions, Spanish traders began trafficking deeper into Ute country where they traded with Tabeguache, Sabuaganas, and Western Utes in central Utah.

More distant Utes were being integrated into the expanding borderland economy, especially the lucrative trade in human merchandise. The previously isolated Western Utes initially turned to this commodity because it was, at first, their only merchandise valuable enough to lure traders the long distances to their territory. As Western Utes acquired horses, some bands began to raid not only for horses and plunder, but also for women and children to sell to Spanish traders. Paiutes and Goshutes, technologically weaker than Utes, became easy targets for Ute raids or forced trade. By 1804 the Timpanogos were grazing herds of horses and mules in the grasslands by their lake, but by 1813 they were demanding Spanish traders buy slaves. The San Pete and Sevier valleys became the apex of a major Spanish trade trail where buyers rendezvoused with Western Utes at least as early as the 1830s, and probably earlier. By this time Western Utes were also exploiting the web of Spanish trade trails as they exacted tolls, gifts, and barter from traders and explorers; ventured southeast along the trails to trade and raid in Navajo and Spanish borderlands; and by 1835, headed southwest to raid California horse herds.[67]

A lucrative illicit trade grew, with most Spanish traders ignoring the regulatory licenses that were required but only intermittently enforced. Officials tried to regulate trade and the behavior of traders, halt the flow of contraband weapons and slaves, and protect the peace of the frontier by passing increasingly restrictive trade laws beginning in 1778 and again in 1812 and 1824.[68] But frontier Indian trading was lucrative, long-standing, welcomed by the Utes, and worth the risk of getting caught.[69]

By at least 1813 such seasonal extralegal expeditions were becoming more frequent and seasonally regular, and Ute traders rendezvoused with Spanish traders at established locations. Several incidents illustrate this predictable if unofficial trading, as well as the Utes' hunger for horses and the violent intertribal competition over them.

Sabuaganas told Rivera in 1765 that they raided Comanches for horses (who raided Utes in return), and Domínguez and Escalante were warned against marauding, horse-stealing Yamparica Comanches in 1776. In 1804 Manuel Mestas, an old genízaro trader and Ute interpreter, landed in court after he attempted to retrieve horses and mules he thought had been stolen by the Timpanogos Utes raiding in northwestern Colorado. Actually, the stock had been stolen by Comanches, then stolen again by Timpanogos raiders, who brought them home to graze with their Utah Valley herds. Mestas and a band of armed men found his stock there, forcibly recovered them, and headed back to Abiquiú. But en route, Kiowa raiders attacked and drove off his stock—again.[70] Clearly, the demand for horses had upped stakes and raised the level of violence, sending Ute raiders out of traditional homelands to steal horses and mules, while luring Plains Indians into their mountains on the same business.

Meanwhile, Lewis and Clark's 1806 report of a "fur bonanza" in the western mountains sparked additional interest in Indian trade. American, British, and Spanish companies began sending out companies to trap and trade in the mountains, and after 1825 American trappers remained there year-round. Trade with the Indians was welcome but peripheral, as these mountain men and others rendezvoused annually with their fur company to exchange pelts for supplies.[71]

Although Western Utes participated in the hide and fur trade to some extent, they were not enthusiastic about large-scale commercial trapping; there were only a few trade forts within their territory; and all of the rendezvous were in Shoshone country (Utes stopped attending after only two). Instead, Western Utes preferred to trade primarily in captives. We know only snatches of this trading since it was illegal and not reported. However, two traders did land in court in 1813, accused of illegal trading for slaves with the Ute Indians.

In court Mauricio Arze and Lagos García claimed that they and their small company had trekked into Utah Valley hoping only to cash in on the new beaver trade. Instead, they said, the Timpanogos refused to trade in furs and demanded they purchase their slaves as Spanish traders had done "on other occasions." When they purportedly refused, the Utes retaliated by killing some of their horses. Arze and García gathered their remaining stock and led the company south the next morning. Near the Sevier River, trade overtures were again rebuffed, and they were threatened by a small band of bearded Indians. Then, near the Green River crossing, they met more Utes who were camped and waiting for seasonal Spanish slave traders. These were led by Chief Guasache (Wasatch) and were possibly Sheberetch Utes. Once again, the traders were threatened if they didn't purchase the Utes' supply of captives, so the Spaniards acquiesced and bartered for a dozen—grudgingly, they claimed. If they had indeed been seeking pelts rather than slaves, then it was an unprofitable and disappointing four-month journey. They had acquired few pelts and were caught with the contraband slaves, which then became prima facie evidence of their illegal trade. Or perhaps their testimony had been no more than an elaborate cover story spun to explain their surreptitious slave-trading expedition. In any case, it is clear that by 1813 Western Utes had grown powerful, aggressive, and practiced slave traders, and that they were expecting seasonal Spanish traders.[72]

48

Clearly, things were changing. Within three decades of Domínguez and Escalante's visit to the "docile" and easygoing Lake Utes, their need for horses had made them more aggressive. As mounted warriors, they too could enter into the horse and raid/trade economy. And by the 1830s, traditional survival skills were no longer enough; wealth, power, defense, and basic survival now depended on the strength and cunning of warriors who could barter or raid for valuable commodities. Those lacking these tools remained naked, destitute, and "miserable human beings," as Warren Ferris described nonequestrian Utes and Paiutes in 1832.[73] They also became the prey of their technologically superior neighbors.[74]

But Spanish colonizers and traders were only the first of many new relationships. French-Canadian traders had been affecting intertribal relations since the mid-1700s. Trade was also spreading west from French Louisiana and later from the American Ohio Valley. These trade goods reached the various Plains Indians first, substantially shifting the native balance of power. The demand for power-enhancing weapons, metal tools, and horses was enormous and desperate. But in this competition, the Utes became the technological inferiors of their Plains Indian enemies. Conflict followed a tumultuous arms race as the have-nots fought to have these culture-changing tools.

Still, up to this point the Utes had remained relatively aloof and on the periphery of Euro-American influence, safe within their mountain fastness. This would soon change.

Chapter 4

Americans among the Utes
Trade, Trapping, and Trails

In 1805, after Meriwether Lewis and William Clark brought word of a beaver bonanza in the western mountains, hundreds of hunters and trappers swarmed into western Indian country. Although the trapping business would be symbiotically linked with good relations among local Indians, the arrival of hundreds of non-Indians and their valuable goods heightened intertribal conflict and set the stage for the radical revision and ultimate dispossession of Indian societies. In addition to bringing large amounts of culture-changing trade goods, these trappers and traders expanded animal and Indian trails into rough commercial thoroughfares that were used by subsequent waves of American emigrants. They also established supply bases, rendezvous sites, and trading forts that became the nuclei of future Euro-American settlements. As Thomas Jefferson later reminisced, these rough traders and trappers were "the overture to...American settlement of the West."[1]

Euro-Americans were also imbued with contemporary racial prejudices against darker-skinned people and assumed a racist hierarchy that placed "whites" above "less civilized" people like Africans, Mexicans, and Indians. Journals and memoirs are rife with denigrating and condescending descriptions of Mexican and Indian "savages" with whom traders exchanged gifts, patronized, or fought. Such attitudes laid the groundwork for the ultimate conquest and dispossession of native people and "unprogressive" Mexicans to make way for the presumably civilized and superior white race that could better cultivate, improve, and develop the land.[2]

Mountaineers and explorers filled their letters and journals with descriptions of western land that read like an avid land speculator's survey, replete with detailed notes on agrarian or mineral potential. Jedediah Smith contrasted the Paiute's barren "Country of Starvation" with the fertile and "promising" Western Ute country. Rufus B. Sage described the "romantic," "beautiful," and "fertile" lands of what is today northern New Mexico and Utah, as well as the promising mineral wealth and abundance of game. Osborne Russell described the bountiful grasses of Utah Valley, and the "beautiful and fertile" valley of the Great Salt Lake that was "intersected by streams and rivers that with little labour and expense [could be] made to irrigate the whole Valley." Daniel Potts waxed eloquent about "beautiful transparent streams," "picturesque...moun-tains," the "beautiful country," and plentiful grass. Trapper George Yount wrote about Spanish-held California and the "tragedy" of "Anglo Saxon enterprise [that had] permitted these treasures, and this land of prodigious wealth and resources, this Elysium in point of climate and comfort to remain unimproved during so many long centuries."

British explorer George Ruxton was enthusiastic about the fertile soils, plentiful game, and grazing lands he found in Ute country, especially in the San Luis Valley, South Park, and along the Front Range, while John C. Frémont bla-tantly surveyed the West in anticipation of the manifestly destined expansion of the United States. His report to Congress included glowing descriptions of Western Ute country with its "great pastoral promise" and abundant streams. Utah Valley, he wrote, included "a plain, where the soil is generally good, and in greater part fertile; watered by a delta of prettily timbered streams. This would be an excellent locality for stock farms; it is generally covered with good bunch grass, and would abundantly produce the ordinary grains."[3] These reports became a catalyst to subsequent westward expansion.[4]

These fur-trade entrepreneurs also brought with them an attitude of rapa-cious, unconstrained exploitation of the environment—first for furs, then the land, water, minerals, and timber. And the lure of trade goods drew many Utes and Shoshones into this mindset as well, for not only non-Indians but also native hunters fell into the trap of overhunting for the commercial hide and pelt markets.[5]

TRADING, RAIDING, AND EXPLOITING THE OLD SPANISH TRAIL

By the 1840s the subsistence patterns of most Utes had been altered, their nomadic circuits expanded, and their hunting and gathering supplemented with a commercial capitalism that included trading large quantities of tanned hides or—among the Western Utes—slaves. Some Utes were also actively exploiting the trails. In addition to stealing horses and selling them to travel-ers or outfitters (as well as redistributing them through the tribe), they solic-ited gifts, demanded use fees, scavenged abandoned goods, and stole stock

4.1. Old Spanish Trail with annotation (Courtesy of the Old Spanish Trail Association, online).

from travelers. The Southern Paiutes became especially adept at replacing lost resources with traveler goods. For practical reasons, trader and emigrant routes wound through the most fertile parts of the region, and the water, forage, and food-plants on which Utes and Paiutes depended disappeared beneath the hooves or into the stomachs of Spanish, Mexican, and American livestock. Occasionally, unthinking travelers even loosed their livestock into Paiute corn fields or raided Ute and Paiute food caches. So gifts, handouts, tolls, scavenging, and theft were seen by native groups as fair compensation for land and game lost to non-Indians.[6]

These frontier byways had been initiated by Spanish explorers and exploited by Spanish traders, many of whom had originally been lured deeper into the interior by a lucrative slave trade.[7] By the mid-1830s, Mexican and American explorers had opened routes between Santa Fe and southern California. Ever larger mule-team caravans and herds of horses, mules, and sheep pushed through or near Ute and Paiute country, and by the 1840s emigrants were impinging on Shoshone, Goshute, and Western Ute country to the north. Meanwhile, following Mexican independence in 1821, American entrepreneurs and fur traders began plying the Santa Fe Trail between Missouri and today's New Mexico, as well as establishing routes on the upper Missouri and along the Platte River to the Rocky Mountains. While large numbers of trappers and traders increased the amount of trade goods available, the increased traffic on the trade trails damaged local ecologies and further disrupted native societies.

But expanded trail use also provided a variety of new opportunities. Utes and Paiutes met Spanish Trail caravans or rendezvoused with trappers and traded for (or stole) goods, including food, guns, ammunition, horses, and other stock. At first local Indians exchanged friendship gifts. Paiutes offered rabbits, fish, pumpkins, or corn, while Utes brought meat, hides, pelts, and slaves. But as the numbers of travelers increased, the ritual gift exchange transformed into begging or more assertive demands for tolls and tribute.[8]

Finding themselves on major commercial crossroads, the Utes were quick to exploit their new opportunities, and these trade routes became as much Ute trails as they were Spanish or American. Some Western Utes were especially noted for their trading and raiding activities on the Spanish Trail, growing prosperous with their high-quality horses, most either stolen from California rancheros or extorted from Mexican traders on their way back from California. By the late 1840s, some trappers were trading with the Utes *for* horses, rather than the other way around.[9]

The Euro-Americans who flooded into Ute country inevitably influenced Ute perspectives and attitudes as well. Mountaineers were generally a rough lot, lured to the mountains by the promise of quick money, adventure, or an escape from the sins of their past. Many have also been called "expectant capitalists" whose goal was to make their fortunes quickly and retire to invest in capitalist ventures back home.[10] These enterprising mountaineers influenced the Utes directly and indirectly when power dynamics fluctuated as bands variously gained more or less access to manufactured goods and trade opportunities. As early as the mid-1820s, Jedediah Smith reported that the Utes had more guns than the Shoshone, while travelers in the 1840s described Utes and Arapahos competing over fertile mountain parks like "Bayou Salado" (South Park). Numerous contemporary descriptions highlighted how well-armed and well-mounted the Utes were.[11]

As native ecology changed, local demographics likewise shifted. One historian called the exploration, exploitation, and settlement of Indian country "a series of environmental traumas."[12] And it was. Travelers used or stole the often scarce resources and exploited Indian women and children. The quantity of manufactured trade goods, horses and mules, and other livestock altered material cultures and changed traditional economies as the opportunity for raids, trade, tribute, and charity drew Indians into an opportunistic free-enterprise economy. Now more prosperous and mobile, bands of Western Ute raiders were able to prey on others, especially the Southern Paiute.

These Paiutes lived in marginal, environmentally fragile lands and in much smaller numbers than the Utes. Both their ecosystems and their society were disrupted when the new trade routes entered and transected their country, including the Virgin River basin, where traditional hunting and gathering sites were located. Socially disrupted and physically dislocated and scattered, these small family bands never coalesced into larger groups the way Utes did, and they were unable to obtain sufficient numbers of power-enhancing horses or weapons. As a result, they remained vulnerable, loosely organized family bands, unable to resist their enemies.[13]

For several decades selling women and children became an important component of Ute economy. Southern Utes traded Plains Indian war captives and may have raided their San Juan Paiute neighbors, while more isolated northern Ute bands exchanged their own children or orphaned relatives for Mexican horses and other goods. Even influential figures exchanged their children; for example, Chief Ignacio bartered a son for a horse, and an 1865 report by Indian agent Lafayette Head indicated that half of the Ute servants in the San Luis Valley had been purchased from other Utes. Many of the Indian children baptized in New Mexico were also Utes. However, some of these Hispanicized servants later returned to their people, and in so doing became important cultural mediators. Two of the best known were Chief Ouray and his sister Susan, both raised among the Spanish. Such acculturated children brought new perspectives and skills. Equally important, acculturated genízaros who remained in borderland settlements occasionally maintained kinship ties with Indian relatives, facilitating peaceful relations and trade.[14]

The Western Ute slave trade was far more predatory, for some bands coercively traded with or raided the Southern Paiutes on a regular basis. Some better-positioned Paiutes also participated as middlemen by trading for children with less prosperous and "more distant Trybes," for the purpose of trading them to the Utes and later Mormon settlers. By the early 1840s, several prominent Ute bands had become notorious for this traffic—especially those associated with Wákara and his kinsmen, whose influential father had been similarly engaged for decades.[15] Because the Utes had targeted the Paiutes and Goshutes for years, the ethnic boundaries between these culturally and linguistically related people was solidified, leading to a long-lasting antipathy between them

53

and creating a distinct power hierarchy that placed Utes at the top.[16] Western Utes grew wealthy, even as the human and natural resources of the Southern Paiutes were decimated.

Spanish slave trading expeditions encouraged this commerce. By 1800 trade expeditions were regularly heading out from Abiquiú—and later Taos— first conducting their traditional trade among Capotes, Mouaches, and Tabeguaches, and then continuing on to the Sanpete and Utah Valleys where they traded for Indian children and women. For the first decades of the Spanish Trail's existence, these central Wasatch valleys were the destination of traders who sought slaves, as well as hides and the occasional peltry. Even after 1830 when the traffic between Santa Fe and southern California introduced more intercolonial commerce, most traders still included valuable captives as part of their cargo. It was a lucrative trade, for Indian boys brought nearly $100 each while girls fetched $100–$400 in the Mexican settlements.[17]

Mexican slave traders also targeted the vulnerable Southern Paiutes. By the mid-1820s, American mountain men were also willing to snatch Paiutes or buy captives from Utes to sell in Mexican settlements along with their furs.[18] As a result, Paiutes equated mounted riders with slave raiders, and at the sight of them women hid their children or fled with them into the brush.[19] The Southern Paiutes were especially vulnerable to slave predation because of their location on the trade and emigrant trail to California. Displaced from better resources around the springs and streams along the trail, they remained physically, martially, and politically weak, their small and vulnerable family-bands dependent on scattered garden patches and widespread foraging. Begging, scavenging, theft, and the sale of their children became increasingly common survival options for many trailside Paiutes.[20]

On the other hand, Western Utes had been fortunate in claiming and holding the more fertile regions of the Wasatch Mountains, especially in the San Pete Valley and near the lush wetlands of "Utaw" Lake.[21] But relatively prosperous as they were, they remained the "poor relations" of the even more prosperous eastern bands that ranged through the Rocky Mountains and hunted on the Plains. These bands not only had access to more abundant big game and bison, but they benefited from a longer involvement in the borderland trade. However, the Western Utes continued to subsist primarily on plant sources, supplemented by fish, birds, insects, and small and occasionally large game. Clothing remained sparse, and they continued to use brush huts as well as tipis. But once they began to acquire horses and weapons, their status improved. Where Warren Ferris described the Sanpitch Utes as naked, destitute, and "miserable human beings," by 1840 some had joined the Timpanogos as predatory mounted warriors.

By the 1830s travelers and American settlers equated equestrianism with Ute and pedestrianism with Paiute, sometimes referring to the latter as Piede Indians, from the French *pied* meaning "foot." For example, the "Piede" Utes around Koosharem and Circleville, who ate horses instead of riding them, were often assumed to be Paiute because of their diet, although they considered themselves Ute (as did their neighbors), a detail confirmed during the 1950s Indian Claims Commission hearings. The distinction was slippery and recent, however, and some Paiutes also told ethnographers that although these people were Utes, they were not "real" Utes, but only half-Ute. They only thought they were Ute because they had relocated further north and the men were "dressed like a Ute" and "wore [their] hair in two braids."[22]

By the 1820s Spanish and Mexican trade into Ute country was shifting native economies, and the equestrian and more mobile Western Utes were prospering at the expense of weaker neighbors. When large numbers of mountain men began to stream into the Rocky Mountains, they added to these accelerating changes. Shrewd and ambitious Utes incorporated free-enterprise capitalism into their traditional economy and some—like Wákara, Arapeen, Sanpitch, and Ammon—not only benefitted from trade on the trails, but they also became involved in the emigrant outfitting businesses through large-scale stock rustling. They grew more prosperous, as did their noncombatant kinsmen who benefitted second- and thirdhand from the redistribution of their plunder. Under the informal tutelage of Hispanic traders and American hunters, the Utes were quick to adapt to new situations and exploit new resources to replace or augment the old.

TRAPPERS, TRADERS, EXPLORERS, AND FORTS

Trappers and traders entered Ute country from three directions: Spanish New Mexico, the British-dominated Northwest, and the American Mississippi and Missouri River settlements. Independent trappers and fur company employees flooded into the mountains seeking individual wealth, even as imperial rivals sought to claim territory through their exploration. From 1807 to 1811 American, British, Spanish, French Canadian, as well as Shawnee, Delaware, and other Indian entrepreneurs raced to stake claims for fur trading or trapping enterprises.[23] Meanwhile, American exploration and mapping expeditions were launched, including the 1806 Zebulon M. Pike company, which explored up the Arkansas and deep into Mouache Ute country, and the Stephen H. Long expedition that followed in the early 1820s.[24]

By 1811 American trappers were encroaching on Eastern Ute territory, and the Utes were ambivalent about their presence. While some were cautiously willing to trade or assist the trappers by giving or selling them meat and other supplies, they also worried that these newcomers would drive away their "Indian cattle" (bison wintering in their mountain valleys) and tried to forbid their hunting.[25] But attempts to regulate trappers were unenforceable. Euro-Americans began living year round with the Indians or at newly established trading forts where they exploited native women as well as natural resources. Some integrated into local Indian populations by marrying women who subsequently bore them mixed-race children. In the 1840s, one British traveler described the multiethnic nature of trader posts in a typically biased manner: "Four Taos women, and as many squaws of every nation, comprised the 'female society' on the Upper Arkansa [sic]...giving good promise of peopling the river with a sturdy race of half-breeds, if all the little dusky buffalo-fed urchins...arrived scathless at maturity."[26]

While such racially charged language was common among early European adventurers, the traders and Indians throughout frontier America and Canada generally welcomed such interethnic relations because, in these early years, it was mutually beneficial to all parties involved. Women were important intercultural liaisons. The fur trade business could not have succeeded without them, for Indian wives were invaluable participants in the trade. Marriage alliances gave traders a kinship status that facilitated interaction with their wife's band, justified trapping within her band's territory, and integrated his wife's kinsmen into an expanding and profitable trade network. Many women even sought these marriages, since a trader's wife gained status and wealth through better access to women's trade goods including cloth, thread, ribbons, awls, beads, and needles. Their mixed-heritage children often gained status as well. It wasn't until large numbers of settlers arrived and the economy shifted that their status changed. Clergymen, missionaries, and settlers, with their typically moralistic and racist ideologies, denounced trappers' "Indian custom" marriages as illicit, their wives concubines, and their children bastards. While some trappers ignored convention, the status of "squaw-man" or "half-breed" eventually became a liability for most traders in the expanding white settlements.[27]

While some trappers and traders made Indian women their common-law wives, others exploited native women both sexually and economically. In some cases they were enslaved by post traders and shared for a price, or they were passed around, sold, or gambled away. In other cases women prostituted themselves for reasons similar elsewhere: for profit, survival, or addiction (in many cases, alcohol). But women were important to their people, were not always given up lightly, and their marital and sexual exploitation resented. Indian men also desired wives and family alliances and were protective of their mothers, sisters, wives, and daughters. In fact, the blatant sexual exploitation of Ute and Shoshone women was a contributing factor in attacks during the 1840s on raucous forts like "Winty" (Uintah) and Uncompahgre. Other factors included commercial jealousy (white men trapping Indian pelts) and a war between the Utes and the Mexicans that broke out in 1844.[28]

The first tentative attempts to trap within Ute country occurred during the 1811–1812 season but failed when the small party of American trappers were killed by Indians, probably Utes or Arapahos. But another expedition returned in 1815. After Mexican Independence in 1821, traffic on the Santa Fe Trail developed quickly, and fur trappers were among the first to use it. Taos and Santa Fe soon became headquarters for a growing number of fur companies and a body of ethnically diverse trappers. At the same time British trappers began exploring south, even as American trappers drifted in from the east.[29] But the new Santa Fe Trail transected Comanche grasslands and the old Yuta Plains, and the traffic damaged forage for Indian horses and bison. This split or drove herds away, and Utes and Comanches responded by preying on and plundering the traders' pack and later emigrant wagon trains."[30] This did not, however, deter trade or travel on the trail.

Expeditions into Ute country began in earnest in 1821. That year at least three major American expeditions set out for the mountains from Santa Fe or Taos, trapping on the upper Rio Grande, the upper Arkansas, and in the San Luis Valley—all in Ute country. The following year four more American fur brigades arrived. Not only were the number of expeditions increasing, but they were also growing larger; for example, the 1824 fur brigades were triple the size of the year before.[31] Nor were these the reclusive mountain men of Hollywood film; rather, expeditions included at least twenty to thirty men who formed smaller companies of specialists, including trappers, wranglers, camp-keepers, and hide-preparers. Later expeditions numbered eighty to one hundred men. Thus, during the 1830s and 1840s, the Ute and Shoshone mountains were filled with a constantly fluctuating population of hundreds of trapper-hunters.[32] Such an invasion—friendly or otherwise—could not help but affect the Utes and their resources.

By 1825 competing British, American, and Mexican fur companies were clashing over the right to trap in "Snake" (Shoshone) and Ute country. British and Americans contended along the Weber River and in Cache Valley, both in Shoshone country, while Taos-based French Canadians were trapping near the Uintah Basin and Utah Valley.[33] These expeditions introduced large amounts of Indian trade goods including weapons, ammunition, paint, food, tobacco, textiles, blankets, sewing equipment, ribbons, beads, and "frufraws." One typical pack train included fourteen mules loaded just with trade goods for the Indians. All of the western Indians expected gifts in exchange for their friendship or alliance, and contemporary accounts are replete with examples of Utes demanding—or at best, expecting—gifts to work in or cross through Ute country.[34] Traditional gift exchange rituals were rapidly transforming into demands for tolls and tribute as the number of foreigners increased.

In the 1830s, Western Utes attacked William Hamilton's trapping party after they refused to pay for being in Ute country. In 1844 Frémont described Wákara's band "journeying slowly towards the Spanish trail to levy their usual tribute upon the great California caravans," and noted how the Utes "conduct their depredations with form and under the color of trade and toll for passing through their country." Four years later Kit Carson encountered Wákara and his band, again on their way to levy "their yearly tribute" from the Spanish trade caravans, a toll "which the tribe exact as the price of a safe-conduct through their country." In the 1840s Utes on the western slopes of the Rockies were also harassing emigrant trains and demanding use fees for free passage. As late as the 1850s, trapper Dick Wootton claimed he fully expected to pay for "formal permission to go through their country," but Tabeguache Utes on the Uncompahgre River first tried to raid his sheep herd before extorting several hundred pounds of flour along with ammunition and other goods for the right to pass unmolested.[35]

Because weapons were such a significant trade item, the competition over commercial trade, as well as the arms trade itself, also escalated intertribal warfare. By the 1830s Plains Indians were growing hostile toward trapper-traders for supplying the weapons Utes used against them. Wootton, for example, claimed he once raced to the safety of a party of Utes in order to escape hostile Jicarilla Apaches, as did Étienne Provost following an 1824 Shoshone attack on the Jordan River. Kit Carson tested an unknown war party north of Taos by speaking to them in Ute to ascertain if they were friend (Ute) or foe (not Ute). During the 1840s, Frémont and George Ruxton were both caught in the middle of Ute-Arapaho hostilities in the mountains near North and South Parks and were attacked by Arapahos for being the presumed suppliers of Ute weapons.[36]

These conflicts of interest were an ongoing problem for traders, explorers, and later American settlers, as they juggled relations with and between warring tribes. Jedediah Smith attempted to not only negotiate a treaty with Western Utes in Utah Valley for fair use of their resources, but he also urged them to agree to a truce with the Shoshones so Americans could work safely and avert hostile crossfire. Trappers tried to avoid entanglements whenever possible since they jeopardized relations. In 1828 Tom "Peg-Leg" Smith tried to excuse himself from joining his Ute kinsmen in a foray against the Shoshones by pleading a blind horse (overruled), and in the 1840s Arapahos asked Frémont and his men to join an attack on the Utes (tactfully refused). A few years later Wákara demanded the Mormon militia ride with his warriors against Shoshones who had raided his freshly rustled herd of California horses pastured in Utah Valley (declined).[37]

Conflict escalated when the presence of trade goods attracted enemies bent on plunder as well as trade. Certain regions became notorious as intertribal "battlegrounds," including the Bear River and the Little Wind River region. The southern Rocky Mountains, traditionally Ute territory, attracted Arapaho, Jicarilla, and Navajo bands, while Plains Indians, Utes, and Jicarillas competed for trade around Bent's Fort on the Arkansas. Arapahos and Utes fought bitterly over South Park, and for decades Shoshones and Western Utes exchanged bloody raids as they competed for trade, plunder, and natural resources.[38]

BLAZING TRAILS, SHIFTING ECONOMIES, AND STEALING HORSES

In 1825 frontiersman William Ashley introduced the idea of rendezvousing with his American trappers to pay them for their furs and sell them fresh supplies. His first rendezvous was a simple sober business meeting with no Indians invited; subsequent rendezvous, however, became wild revelries with plenty of games, gambling, and carousing.[39] Lured by the trade and alcohol, Indians also joined these large encampments and incorporated them into their regular cycle of communal gatherings. But because all the rendezvous were held in Shoshone country, Utes were hesitant to attend, although they were specifically invited to the first few. They were present at the 1827 Bear Lake rendezvous when Blackfeet attacked, and they were applauded for their skill and bravery when they joined the Shoshones and mountain men to repel them. Nevertheless, Utes remained vulnerable in enemy territory and ignored future rendezvous.[40]

Regardless of rendezvous attendance, Ute culture was inexorably affected by the influx of trade goods, weapons, and horses, both directly and indirectly. With more horses and guns available, they could hunt more effectively and increase their profits from raiding and long-distance trade. As early as 1825, Ashley remarked on the unexpected wealth of the Utes in the Uintah Basin. He had

> expected to find them a poor lifeless set of beings, destitute of the means or desposition to defend themselves; alarmed at the sight of a white man but to the contrary, they met me with great familiarity and Ease of manner were clothed in mountain sheep skin & Buffalloe robes superior to any band of Indians in my knowledge west of Council Bluffs—have a great number of good horses & about the one half, well armed with English fuseeze [fusils] others with bows & arrows Tomahawks & a number of them were ornamented with perl & sea shells which they informed me the[y] purchased from Indians who lived on the borders of a great lake [the Pacific Ocean].[41]

Ashley was also surprised when the Utes "expressed great friendship for the Americans," spoke some English, and showed "full acquaintance with white men [with] no fear or hostility." But his attempt to buy pack horses was frustrated because "such is the use that the[y] make of their horses and the value the[y] set on them that I with difficulty purchased two."[42]

Trapper trails also opened new routes for trade and commerce. Following the 1826 rendezvous, Jedediah Smith and other trappers trekked south through Ute and Paiute country, crossing the southern Great Basin to arrive in California. In blazing this route, Smith opened up the southern leg of the Spanish Trail and completed the commercial route that would link the Upper Rio Grande and California. However, Smith found Spanish officials less than friendly to the Americans, so he returned to Bear Lake by way of a central (and waterless) Great Basin route.[43] During this trip Smith and his brigade trapped through the "Utaw Mountains" (Uintah and/or Wasatch Mountains) and in "Utaw" Valley where he paused to negotiate a treaty with Timpanogos Utes and their principal chief, probably the prominent leader Conmarrowap (or Quimanuapa), who later led another east-central Utah band of "Py-Euts" (perhaps Sheberetch).[44]

Supply bases, forts, and trading posts established by trappers served as a nexus for intercultural relations. These catered to and supplied trappers, provided defense against potential Indian attacks, and became wilderness centers of commerce for an ethnically diverse population of travelers, traders, and a variety of Indians. Fort Uintah (Fort Winty) was also graphically described as the site of drunken debaucheries with exploitative trafficking of Indian women to "spice up" the legitimate trade.[45]

Most early forts were established on the fringes of Ute country. Bent's Fort, built in 1832 on the Arkansas River, tapped into the trade in bison robes and mountain furs and supplied travelers on the Santa Fe Trail. Over the next few years a string of small adobe trade forts also appeared on the South Platte at the base of the Rockies: Forts Saint Vrain, Lupton, Vasquez, and Jackson. Another appeared further up the Arkansas on Hardscrabble Creek, and Fort Pueblo was built in 1842.[46] Other forts were constructed deeper inside Ute territory. In 1826 an early but short-lived trade fort was built near Utah Lake, while trapper Antoine Robidoux established both Fort Uintah in the Uintah Basin and Fort Uncompahgre in western Colorado. Both posts were abandoned in 1844, although Fort Uintah was revived by another veteran trapper, Charboneau "Jim" Reed, whose descendants through his Shoshone wife would figure prominently among later Uintah Utes and Uintah mixed-bloods.[47] Utes and Shoshones both visited Fort Bridger, just north of the Uintah Mountains,[48] as they did Fort Davy Crockett ("Fort Misery") in Brown's Hole.[49]

As long as the fur trade remained vigorous, Utes visited these forts regularly and conducted incidental trade. But by 1840 fashions had changed, the fur market stagnated, and the price of beaver pelts plummeted.[50] The last rendezvous was held in 1840, Fort Davy Crockett was abandoned in 1841, and Forts Uintah and Uncompahgre were abandoned in 1844.

Another factor in the abandonment of forts was the outbreak of Ute hostilities in 1844, following the ambush of a southern Ute delegation at the Governor's Palace in Santa Fe. Ute leaders had come to Santa Fe seeking compensation for an unprovoked attack on a peaceful camp. The negotiations, however, erupted into violence when the governor became enraged and killed a chief. Soldiers then poured into the building, and a number of Ute leaders were killed before others broke free and escaped with the remaining survivors. Furious at the ambush, the Utes rampaged from Santa Fe through the Chama Valley and then northward. Hostilities spread, and Utes attacked Mexicans on the trails and at Fort Uncompahgre where they killed all the Mexican employees. The lone American was spared and sent to Fort Uintah with the message that Robidoux's furs would not be molested. The Mexicans at Fort Uintah precipitately abandoned the post and fled home, leaving it to the Utes.[51] Hostilities would last for another several years.

4.1. Jim Bridger was a fur trapper, mountain man, and trader who became an outfitter, guide, and regional "consultant" for later emigrants. (Used by permission, Utah State Historical Society, Photo #11757)

During the fur trade's two-decade heyday, however, trappers, traders, adventurers, and explorers became a familiar sight throughout Ute country. Some mountain men remained to influence subsequent events; others left vivid descriptions of Western Utes and Paiutes—their mode of living and quality of their country.[52] These letters, reports, and memoirs provide a glimpse into Ute life in transition. During the 1820s the Western Utes were mounted but remained more impoverished than their eastern cousins because of a lack of bison. According to trapper Daniel Potts, the Timpanogos Utes still used bulrushes to construct homes "resembling muskrat houses … in which the Indians remained during the stay of the ice."[53] In the 1830s the Timpanogos Utes were described as "neither ugly nor prepossessing. They are brave, but extremely suspicious; are candid, never treacherous, and are not inhospitable, though they rarely feast a stranger who visits them . . . but in general ask for something to eat themselves . . . Unlike the Crows or Snakes, they *never* steal; . . . [but] they are the most accomplished beggars." Potts also noted that they were rarely "corpulent" but tended to be in excellent physical condition. They were well dressed but lacked buffalo hides for all but a few skin tipis; instead they constructed "cabins of cedar branches" during the winter.

Ute dietary protein still came primarily from small animals like the ubiquitous rabbit. They were expert horsemen, made frequent visits to Taos and California, and many spoke passable Spanish.[54] But by 1840 Western Utes had grown more prosperous, owned "fine horses and lodges," and were "very partial to the rifles of the white man." Trapper Osborne Russell wrote that a contented Ute was a man with eight or ten good horses and a rifle with which to hunt. These Utes still remembered when large herds of bison roamed the Great Salt Lake Valley, though by 1830 these had disappeared.[55]

Trappers—such as Tom Smith and Jim Beckwourth—also drew Utes into profitable escapades that some Utes then adopted as their own. Smith had lost a foot during a skirmish with Indians in North Park (Colorado), and he had been carried by fellow trappers to the Uintah Basin where Utes successfully doctored him during the winter using shamanic singing and a generous application of medicinal herbs and roots.[56] That spring, Smith's trapper companions fashioned him a wooden stump and began calling him Peg-Leg. In later years, Smith would boastfully claim the Utes also gave him several wives and rechristened him Waketoco or "tough man." Later historians suggested this meant "man with one foot," but the Ute language does not support this. It is more likely that Smith was simply giving a polite translation of the Ute word *wa?á-qa-ti*, which means male, macho, stud, or "horny." Reportedly, Smith's Indian kinsmen *were* impressed with his fortitude.[57]

Following the 1828 rendezvous, Smith trapped on the Virgin and Santa Clara Rivers then purportedly followed Jedediah Smith's trail to California. He sold his furs but then stole 300 to 400 horses and mules that he drove back to Taos via the Spanish Trail where he sold them.[58] A few years later Smith repeated this exploit—this time bringing along Western Ute accomplices who enjoyed the foray so much they returned repeatedly to steal more horses with or without their trapper associates.

By the 1830s an increasing number of traders were traversing the Spanish Trail through Ute lands as well as through Navajo and Hopi country on the southern Armijo route. Californians wanted New Mexican textiles and sheep, while New Mexicans desired high-quality California mules and horses. For

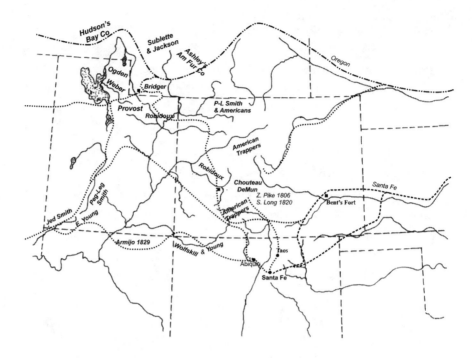

64

4.2. Mexican, British, and American traders, fur trappers, and explorers began penetrating into Ute country by 1800, describing the region and opening routes that would later be used by emigrants.

the same personal and commercial reasons, Western Ute raiders also used the trail.[59]

Around this time the United States began launching new explorations. Proponents of Manifest Destiny assumed their new country was destined to expand to at least the Pacific Coast. Captain Benjamin Bonneville led explorations into the Great Basin in 1832, and trapper Joseph Walker located a route to California through the Great Salt Lake Valley and along the Humboldt River, opening a major emigrant trail through Goshute and Northern Paiute country. A southern route connected Great Salt Lake Valley with the Spanish Trail and cut directly through Ute, Pahvant, and Southern Paiute country. By the late 1840s, the Santa Fe and Spanish Trails had become a central route to the coast. And in 1843–1844, 1845–46, and 1848, the flamboyant John C. Frémont explored—and then popularized—the Far West, including much of Ute country.[60] Frémont's publications, along with a growing number of published travel adventures written by mountain men and early travelers, excited the imagination of Americans and inspired thousands of emigrants to head west. This massive influx of settlers would have a devastating effect on the Utes.

EXPLOITING THE TRAILS

As the economy of the west moved from fur to emigration, some trappers transformed their strategically placed supply forts into emigrant outfitting posts or
established new ones. Several one-time trappers and Utes helped supply these
posts with stolen livestock. For example, Peg-Leg Smith ran a post near Bear
Lake, frequently dealing in horses carrying California brands.[61] Meanwhile, Jim
Bridger and Louis Vasquez established a fort in Bridger Valley (Wyoming) that
became a center of commerce for emigrants and Indians alike.[62]

In fact, many of these outfitting posts became major outlets for stolen
stock.[63] In 1835–1836 a band of Timpanogos and Sanpitch Utes under the leadership of Wákara joined Smith and Beckwourth in raiding for horses in California.[64] The mixed company took a supply of furs and captives to California,
and as Smith and Beckwourth were conducting trade in town, Wákara and
his men rounded up some six hundred head of horses and headed back up
the Spanish Trail. Smith and Beckwourth left shortly thereafter—accessories
after the fact if not direct collaborators, but certainly willing to turn a profit at
Bent's Fort with their share.[65]

Four years later, Wákara and a group of 150 Utes and possibly a few Shoshones and Paiutes joined Smith, Beckwourth, and four other Americans in a
major California raid. Beckwourth scouted ranches while Smith and Wákara's
Utes perpetrated one of the largest horse raids in southern California, striking
almost every major ranch and purportedly stealing thousands of horses. They
made it over Cajón Pass, and then Wákara and his men waited in ambush.
When their Mexican pursuers stopped to rest, Wákara's men stole their horses
as well.[66]

These large-scale horse raids became more common after 1840. George
Ruxton wrote that "the more irresponsible traders soon found it easier to procure the animals by raid than by trade [and] horse stealing became a regular
feature of the traffic" on the trade and emigrant trails. Ruxton met Wákara
and his men on their way to steal horses in California, and he also claimed
Joe Walker's 1833 trail-blazing trek over the Sierras ended up as "more of a
horse-stealing expedition than anything else." Ruxton reported that Wákara
sold 400 or 500 California horses at Bent's Fort to California-bound American
troops during the Mexican War (1846). The chief even ambushed other Indian
raiders returning on the Spanish Trail and stole horses the raiders had just
stolen. Stock rustling became endemic as demand on emigrant trails increased.
By 1850 horse raiders had become notorious figures in southern California as

Utes, Paiutes, Mojaves, and a diverse collection of non-Indian horse and later cattle thieves devastated California's southeastern ranches in the 1840s and early 1850s.[67]

By the late 1840s, the Utes had adeptly adjusted to the shifting market-driven economy of the several trails that wound through their homelands, demanding tolls and use fees, and rustling and selling horses. Wákara epitomized this shift. Called variously Walker, Walkara, or Wákara, his name was actually 'Oáqari (or "Rucca"), meaning yellow or brass-colored (a yellowish metal). However, according to one tradition, he received a new name in a dream-vision: Iron Twister, or Pan-a-karry Quin-ker (*Panáqari Kwín'wáyke*), words that carry the meaning of shining metal, money, golden and twisted, or one who twists gold. It was an apt name for the wily entrepreneur who grew prosperous exploiting western trails.[68]

By the 1860s the Utes began to shift their attention to a rising demand for cattle. The western cattle industry had begun to grow in this decade, especially after the Civil War when cattle ranching spread rapidly throughout Colorado and Utah. Western Ute raiders began to prey on Mormon-owned cattle in central Utah, not only to replace lost food resources but also to supply the growing market for beef at American military forts. Clearly, Ute entrepreneurs had been using the trapper and trade trails for their own purposes for decades, first to extract trade, gifts, and tolls; then to enrich themselves with California horses; and by the 1860s, to drive stolen cattle to new American markets at military posts in Fort Bridger or Santa Fe.[69]

The influx of foreign traders, trappers, and explorers shifted sociocultural relations and intertribal power dynamics while transforming and diversifying native economies. Equestrianism, weapons, and the lure of trade goods increased intertribal warfare as native groups—including Utes—aggressively competed for resources and trade. Competition solidified tribal identities, even as small family groups clustered in larger offensive and defensive bands. Authoritative and prominent men were increasingly propelled to the fore as spokesmen, "talkers," and intercultural negotiators.

As local ecologies were damaged by large herds of domestic stock, populations were forced to relocate and exploit new kinds of subsistence. Trading, raiding, begging, demanding tolls, scavenging, and selling other Indians became part of an increasingly diverse subsistence economy. Meanwhile, the Utes, still independent and free roaming, grew increasingly prosperous even as they grew increasingly dependent on Euro-American goods.[70]

Still, up to the 1830s Utes had escaped most of the ill effects of Hispanic and American colonization while reaping the economic and material benefits that trading supplied. But this best-of-both-worlds lifestyle ended when traders, explorers, and mapmakers were followed by farmers, ranchers, and miners. For the Utes, whose culture was based on nomadism and mobile trading and raiding, permanent settlements could mean only one thing: the abandonment of their traditional lifestyle and for most, relocation.

Chapter 5

Colonization
Utah Territory

Through the 1840s the Utes experienced an influx of non-Indians with their trade goods and domestic animals. This improved prosperity but increased stress on the environment. Utes and non-Indians alike overhunted big game for meat, commercial hides, and sport. During the 1820s and 1830s, travelers commented on the abundance of game in the Ute mountains, but by the late 1840s, Western Utes complained that "they av no game," and mountaineers remarked on the depletion of beaver and withdrawal of bison. Meanwhile, large herds of domestic stock were driven along trade routes, destroying trail-side ecologies and disrupting native subsistence.[1] Colonization would be even more devastating.

Utes were experiencing significant changes—but these had primarily augmented traditional cultural patterns while core social values remained. Bands were larger but still clusters of kinsmen and associates, and leadership remained loose and nonauthoritarian. Although raiding, trading, slaving, toll-taking, and scavenging along trade routes became new and important supplements to subsistence, older patterns were not completely abandoned; the understanding of what constituted hunting and gathering was simply expanded to include raiding and trading. And most importantly, foreigners only trekked *through* traditional homelands. Ute country remained Ute country. Bands were free to travel, share resources, demand fair-use fees from outsiders, and make transitory hunting or raiding excursions into enemy territory. But their homeland continued to be the regions they had inhabited for at least 600 to 700 years. This would change.

In the 1840s, Mexican and American settlers pushed into Mouache and Capote country, Mormons flooded onto the Wasatch Front, and then prospectors swarmed into the Rocky Mountains. Military subjugation and political negotiations led to increased land loss. The free-ranging Utes were criticized

5.1. Major Ute bands as recognized by contemporary chroniclers, 1850.

for their nomadism and profligate use of the land and were prodded toward an agrarian assimilation. As land and natural resources dwindled and their territory was restricted, Utes became, of necessity, increasingly dependent on gifts, handouts, predation, and supplies obtained at government-administered agencies.

By the 1850s American political expectations and economic expediency froze the once-dynamic band identities as officials struggled to categorize and pigeonhole who Utes were, where they could be found, and who represented whom. American officials also solidified tribal leadership when federal king-makers demanded—even created—political representatives (and allies) who would amicably negotiate in the name of an illusory "confederated" tribe of Ute Indians. But negotiators often spoke past each other, perpetuating mistrust. Neither side fully understood what the other side was agreeing to or promising, nor did they grasp the concept of ratification by other parties not present at the negotiations. The result was that both sides inevitably failed to live up to agreements made at treaty councils. Regardless, American negotiators legally bound the Utes to agreements made by a few leaders, and militias or the American military enforced them. The Utes had to adjust to and cope with dispossession, restrictions, and demands for Euro-American assimilation—and with it, the loss of their traditional ethnic identity.

It began in Utah Territory. New Mexico, Kansas, and Colorado Territories were not far behind.

Colonization in what would shortly become southern Idaho and Utah Territories did not occur gradually nor in tentative increments. Instead, the Western Utes and their Numic cousins—Shoshones, Goshutes, and Paiutes—experienced the onslaught of rapid, organized colonization on a grand scale. The impact was enormous as key campsites were lost to settlements, fields, and fenced pastures. Natural resources were depleted or usurped, and colonizers expected Utes to accommodate their arrival by abandoning traditional nomadism as well as profitable trading, raiding, and toll-taking.

Mormon American colonizers arrived during the summer of 1847 and settled first in a borderland shared by Utes, Goshutes, and Shoshones. Because it was a middle ground, these colonizers were able to sink deep roots there before native residents realized its ultimately devastating effect on their lives. Although the incoming Mormons had a unique perspective on what their relationship with Indians was supposed to be, they carried with them typical nineteenth-century American attitudes: Indians were racially inferior but should be assimilated, acculturated, and Christianized as a means of integrating them peacefully—if not equally—into American society. Or they should just be moved out of the way and interred on reservations. Or exterminated. But the intercultural relations between Mormons and Indians were more complex than elsewhere in America. And native people resisted change. Not surprisingly, while most Utes were willing to incorporate subsistence-enhancing goods or technology, few were willing to peacefully abandon their lifestyle, religion, or homelands. As both Mormon and federal authorities explored their relationship with the Numic people, their Indian policies fluctuated as theories were tested, incorporated, or discarded.

The new immigrants were members of The Church of Jesus Christ of Latter-day Saints (Mormons); they had been forcibly expelled from Illinois the year before and were deliberately seeking refuge in western isolation. The new colony took root in the valley of the Great Salt Lake, a middle ground that had buffered Ute and Shoshone enmity for years. Three native groups intermittently used and sometimes confronted each other in the area, though most recognized it as primarily Shoshone territory. With the main populations of Utes, Shoshones, and Goshutes concentrated elsewhere, few were concerned

5.1. Mormon pioneers in Echo Canyon, early 1860s (Courtesy, The Church of Jesus Christ of Latter-day Saints Church History Library, P-731-1)

if the newcomers settled in there, for it would provide a handy new trade market.[2]

On the other hand, the populous Yuta Valley lay just to the south, and beyond that, territory dominated by the warrior-raider Wákara, and his kinsmen Arapeen, Sanpitch, and Ammon.[3] Wákara had grown wealthy and influential exploiting the trade and emigrant trails, and the new arrivals promised a potentially lucrative source of new trade and plunder closer to home. However, he was ambivalent toward them. For the next six years he vacillated between hand-clasped friendship and open hostility.

The Mormon approach to Indian relations would differ from what Eastern Utes had experienced. These Americans were numerous and openly colonialist, and their goal was an inland empire that included all of Western Ute territory along with large portions of Shoshone, Goshute, and Paiute country. Because of repeated religious and political violence against Mormon settlements in Ohio, Missouri, and Illinois, Joseph Smith—the founder of the movement—knew he needed to remove his people from hostile non-Mormon populations. In the years before his death, Smith had begun gathering information for a move further west. A number of colorful reports describing the far West had already been published.

When threats to Smith's life rose sharply in the 1840s, he planned an escape and expressed a desire to reconnoiter the Rocky Mountains, a location that he had prophesied would be a new refuge for his Saints.[4] He was murdered a short time later, but his successor, Brigham Young, completed Smith's dream. With the aid of journals, books, and maps—and sparked by John C. Frémont's popular description of the valleys fronting the Wasatch Range—Young followed the general route of the Oregon Trail before turning south into the valley of the Great Salt Lake.[5]

Convinced the exodus was divinely inspired, Brigham Young believed God had given Mormons the western lands and that they had a sacred right to occupy them. In 1854 he preached,

> I did not devise the great scheme of the Lord's opening the way to send this people to these mountains. Joseph contemplated the move for years before it took place, but he could not get here...I had [nothing] to do with our being moved here, that was the providence of the Almighty.[6]

Divine providence notwithstanding, Brigham Young—like the biblical Joshua—was prepared to do battle for the lands they had been given: "When we first entered Utah, we were prepared to meet all the Indians in these mountains, and kill every soul of them if we had been obliged so to do."[7] Such an attitude did not bode well for the Utes or their Numic cousins.

But Jim Bridger had warned Young to avoid the fertile Yuta Valley and its fish-filled lake. While the land was good, the Utes had become more protective of their resources, as well as more aggressive and opportunistic. Unlike earlier descriptions of friendly Utes, Bridger (possibly influenced by his close association with the Shoshones) warned that the Timpanogos Utes were a "bad people; if they catch a man alone they are sure to rob and abuse him, if they don't kill him."[8] Young apparently listened. A few days before arriving in the valley, he told his counselors that "it would be better to bear toward the region of the Salt Lake," a more "neutral ground," and that it would be wiser "not to crowd upon the Utes" until they all had a better chance to get acquainted. "The Utes," he explained, "may feel a little tenacious about their choice lands on the Utah Lake."[9] This was certainly an understatement.

So the first Mormon colonizers settled in Great Salt Lake Valley, an ultimately better location after all. Not only was it a more neutral middle ground, it was (as reports promised) also fertile when irrigated. The fledgling settlement soon found itself athwart a recently opened route to California, and when gold

5.2. Brigham Young, Mormon prophet, territorial governor, Indian superintendent, and early colonizer of Utah, Idaho, Arizona, and Nevada. Earliest known photo, 1853. (L. Tom Perry Special Collections, Brigham Young University, Provo, Utah)

was discovered two years later, it became a major outfitting center for a flood of emigrants heading to the California gold fields.

However, Great Salt Lake City was only the beginning, for Brigham Young envisioned a truly vast empire. Within the year, he established a string of small settlements north into Shoshone country and planned more to the south. To expand south, however, Young had to broach Utah Valley and establish a settlement there. Within a week of arriving, Mormon scouts were making their first reconnaissance of the valley.

Meanwhile, both Shoshones and Utes were reconnoitering the new Salt Lake colony in turn. Non-Indians had long been an important source of trade goods, especially guns, livestock, and luxury commodities, as well as a market for slaves, peltry, and horses. Even after conflict erupted between Mormons and Western Utes, Wákara would explain that he never wanted to expel the Mormons, because if they left he would have no more herds to plunder or partners with whom to trade.[10]

So the Indians generally welcomed the new settlers. However, jealousy over trading rights quickly erupted between Shoshones and Utes. Borderland or not, the new settlement lay within territory claimed primarily by Wanship's Shoshone band. The recognized boundary between Ute and Shoshone territory was Traverse Mountain, which separates Utah and Salt Lake valleys. So when a small band of Utes showed up within a day, wanting to barter with the new settlers, the Shoshones objected to potential equal trading rights.[11] Making matters worse, that night three Ute teenagers stole Shoshone horses and fled south toward Utah Valley and Little Chief's camp. The furious Shoshones pursued them the length of the valley, killed two of the young thieves, and recovered the horses.[12] Clearly, the Mormons needed to waste no time formulating a policy for dealing with their diverse Indian neighbors.

DEVELOPING INDIAN POLICIES

Federal Indian policy in the nineteenth century typically consisted of assimilation at the core, as well as assertive discipline, even military might to enforce federal directives. The Indian policy Brigham Young devised would follow similar lines, though with a unique theological justification.

The Latter-day Saint religion was founded on the Book of Mormon, a set of ancient American records written on golden plates that Joseph Smith claimed he discovered and translated with divine help. This record chronicled ancient events in the New World and primarily detailed the cultural demise of a once-flourishing group of Israelite refugees, the Nephites and the Lamanites. These tribal-clan identities became generic descriptions of righteous and industrious believers (Nephites) versus wicked and indolent nonbelievers (Lamanites). The Lamanites "dwindled in unbelief," and became "a dark, and loathsome, and a filthy people, full of idleness and all manner of abominations."[13] Over time, they were

> led by their evil nature ... [becoming] wild, and ferocious, and a bloodthirsty people full of idolatry and filthiness; feeding upon beasts of prey; dwelling in tents, and wandering about in the wilderness with a short skin girdle about their loins and their heads shaven; and their skill was in the bow, and in the cimeter, and the ax ... and they were continually seeking to destroy [the Nephites].[14]

This description placed the Lamanites in stark contrast to the "white and delightsome" Nephites.[15] Mormons believed American Indians were the direct descendants of these wicked Lamanites.

However, their scriptures also said "the remnants of Jacob [the Indians], who have been cursed and smitten because of their transgression, [need to] be converted from their wild and savage condition to the fullness of the everlasting gospel," after which they would "flourish in the wilderness" and "blossom as the rose."[16] Thus, Mormon doctrine both condemned the Indian's fallen state but demanded they be culturally and spiritually redeemed. This theme would permeate Mormon-Indian relations and Mormon official policies toward Native Americans.

Nevertheless—and despite rhetoric from their leaders to the contrary—rank-and-file Mormons generally held negative views about American Indians. Like most nineteenth-century Americans, they were grounded in a deep-seated racial prejudice that defined whites as God's supreme creation in a natural, scientifically provable hierarchy of races. They believed American Indians (along with all dark-skinned people) were intellectually and morally inferior to whites and biologically doomed to remain so. Early pseudoscience claimed to affirm this, and by the 1870s evolutionary theories, incorporated into so-called Social Darwinism, reinforced this entrenched racism.[17] Indians were despised for their perceived lack of civilization and humanity as well as their religion that seemed to lack moral law, consisting of "a tissue of childish fancies...a conglomerate of senseless fables." In the Rockies and Wasatch Mountains, both Mormon settlers and passing immigrants were shocked by the "barbarous" and "savage" practices of the "turbulent" Utes. Instances of Ute cruelty to women, children, and slaves were recorded in diaries and letters to exemplify this savagery and to justify the prevailing American prejudices against them.[18]

Nevertheless, Mormons were directed to preach Christianity to the Lamanites. Joseph Smith had declared that a testimony of Jesus Christ should

> come to the knowledge of the Lamanites.... And for this very purpose are these plates [Book of Mormon] preserved, which contain these records...that they may believe the gospel and rely upon the merits of Jesus Christ, and be glorified though faith...[and] repentance.[19]

And in 1855 another Mormon leader preached that "the Lord has caused us to come here for this very purpose, that we might accomplish the redemption of

5.3. Mormons actively proselyted American Indians; here Shivwits Band Paiutes are baptized in 1875 (Charles Savage photo, courtesy, The Church of Jesus Christ of Latter-day Saints Church History Library)

these suffering degraded Israelites." He warned that "if we are thus indebted as a people [for the Book of Mormon]—woe be unto us... if we neglect to pay the debt by our exertions to save them."[20]

Federal Indian policy included acculturation and assimilation as a major part of its agenda.[21] So did Mormon Indian policies. Literacy and technical education in the domestic and agricultural arts were prime requisites for the cultural and spiritual redemption of Indians. So long as Indians struggled to survive and

> have to hunt in the mountains and kanyons for food, and to eat snails, snakes, and crickets, in order to keep themselves alive,... you cannot make them think of God.... If you want them to learn knowledge, and to acquire it in the best way, and with the least expense to yourselves, feed and clothe them, and then instruct them.[22]

While redeeming the Indians was an ecclesiastical duty, it was also a practical necessity. Brigham Young intended to settle a proposed state of "Deseret," a word meaning honeybee and symbolizing an industrious population.[23] This empire would have encompassed today's Utah, Nevada, and parts of Idaho, Colorado, Arizona, and southern California. Mormons perceived it as their divinely given right as the Lord's new stewards to colonize as much of the land as fast as possible. That they were displacing the Indian occupants was of concern—but only because the Indians failed to convert to being born-again agriculturalists. Young envisioned the two peoples living side by side in peace and at first even suggested they intermarry, if it was politically expedient, to create kinship alliances.[24] Unsurprisingly, the notion of interracial marriage soon broke down, since Indian men resented the loss of their women. It seemed even less tenable after some chiefs asked for white wives in return. Wákara, for example, courted two women, but one went into hiding and the other hurriedly married her brother-in-law as a plural wife.[25]

To coexist and assimilate, native people would have had to completely reorder their lives, which was difficult to do in a single generation. Nomads could not live off a land settled by sedentary agriculturalists and ranchers, since settlements were invariably established in the most fertile portions of the country, often on established camp or foraging sites.[26] Traditional seedbeds were replaced by farms and pastures, and livestock grazed on (and trampled) the plants on which the Indians traditionally lived. And even when Indians did attempt to farm, they were displaced as colonies expanded and often unthinkingly usurped most of the land and all the available water.[27] Meanwhile, grazing livestock as well as timber-gathering and mining in the canyons caused ecological damage and spring floods, driving wild game deeper into the mountains. Adding insult to injury, in Utah Mormon authorities also banished the lucrative Mexican trade from the territory.

As settlements spread, native subsistence had to come, one way or another, from the colonizers. But settlers would not tolerate raids on their livestock, government aid was not always forthcoming, and gifts and handouts lasted only as long as settler supplies held out. And, despite Brigham Young's rhetoric that Indians should not be killed for the stealing that ensued, most Mormons found it difficult to overcome traditional frontier prejudices that stereotyped Indians as savages to be cleared away along with the weeds and predators that infested the land. Ongoing colonization also negated missionary efforts when waves of settlers expropriated land and water until none was left for Indians.

Like most Americans, Mormons agreed that even though Indians might be brought up and educated among whites, as racial inferiors they would never be able to rise to the same level as whites. Southern-born Garland Hurt, a non-Mormon Indian superintendent for Utah, exemplified this attitude when he wrote that the Indians of Utah Territory shared "in common with all the inferior tribes of our species... [the] mental inferiority... [of the] colored races," a racial aspect that was a "fixed and demonstrable fact." Indeed, "the idea of their future elevation to an equality with the Caucasian race [was] utterly preposterous, and [could] only exist in the misguided wanderings of a perverted imagination," for they were akin to "some species of the gregarious animals, whom they approximate."[28] While not quite as bigoted, Young still echoed these sentiments when he wrote to his Washington lobbyist friend in 1850 suggesting the need for Indian removal and linking them to other wild predators needing to be dealt with in the new territory. And although he acknowledged they were "human beings," he thought they were "most awfully degraded."[29]

Given the typical prejudices of the day, it is not surprising that the "industrious," agriculturalist Mormons not only misunderstood but feared and resented the pilfering of "indolent," predatory Utes who threatened their livelihoods and the establishment of civilization. On the other hand, the Utes understandably resented the usurpation of their lands and grew desperate as settlements proliferated, Euro-American populations soared, and resources disappeared. Disease, starvation, and war took a devastating toll on kinsmen and friends.

As competition escalated over rapidly dwindling resources, conflict was inevitable. Consequently, an important aspect of Brigham Young's evolving Indian policy was the development of a strong defense in case conciliation, negotiation, and benevolence failed—which it too often did. Young first instituted a policy that mandated centralized towns similar to the British manorial-village type that was common in New England. These were protected by strong fortifications and armaments. Each settlement also maintained a militia, sometimes known as the Nauvoo Legion. Thus prepared for hostilities if need be, Young cautiously opened a mailed fist to treat with the Indians whose land he intended to appropriate for his new empire.[30]

And appropriate the land they did. Although few Indians recognized the concept of property ownership, some Shoshones did offer to sell land-use rights to the new settlers. However, the Saints had little with which to pay, and they were reluctant to set a buy-out precedence lest the Utes ask for compensation, too. Heber C. Kimball, Young's counselor, explained that "the land belongs to our Father in Heaven, and we calculate to plow and plant it; and no man shall have the power to sell his inheritance for . . . it belongs to the Lord."[31] And initially no land was bought and sold, for settlement leaders allocated all land, often by drawing lots. However, it was not long before property was being bought and sold freely among white settlers.

But the Utes and Shoshones were aware they were due payment and that the federal government was compensating other tribes. Yet Mormon settlers continued to usurp Indian land without payment and with no consideration for earlier native land-use. This was disastrous to the Indians, though they attempted to reap some payment. As one federal official complained, settlers were "forced to pay a constant tribute to these worthless creatures, because they claim that the land, the wood, the water, and the grass are theirs, and we have not paid for these things."[32]

The Mormons were also aggressive, well-organized colonizers—not unlike the Spanish with their missions, pueblos, and presidios. The church was the colonial authority that determined who colonized, where they colonized, and how the land was allotted. Sites were picked and men conscripted based on their skills and the needs of each colony. Once established, settlements were organized and centrally directed through a church hierarchy. Local bishops (ministers) allotted the land in clustered, often fortified villages with agri-cultural fields outside. A rapidly expanding population cultivated the land, diverted water, grazed growing herds, built homes, and started industries. Mechanical shops appeared, timber was harvested, and mills multiplied on canyon streams.[33]

This worked well for the Mormons, but it was a disaster for the Indians. As waves of Mormon settlers poured in, Indians were quickly outnumbered and outgunned. After Utah became a territory in 1850, Brigham Young proposed that the federal government buy out and "transplant" the Indians through treaty, and negotiations were held. However, no land was successfully sold to Mormon settlers, no federal treaties were ratified by Congress, and the region was never officially opened for settlement.[34] And yet Mormon colonies multi-plied and continued to have unofficial "trade and intercourse" with the Indians (including active proselyting)—all of which were theoretically regulated by the government in Indian Country. Some small, federally funded and locally operated Indian farms were established, but they were sold in the 1860s to feed the by-then destitute Indians.[35]

Attitudes fluctuated as non-Indians flooded into and through Ute coun-try. Wákara and the influential elder, Sowiette, were among those who first approached the colonists to trade. According to Mormon tradition, Sow-iette embraced the new arrivals and commiserated with them as exiles in the mountains.[36] Wákara was less certain. On one hand the Mormons were often generous with their gifts, promised a nearby market for trade, and were a ready source for incidental rustling; on the other hand, their settlements posed a threat to Ute subsistence and independent lifestyles. Jim Bridger and Louis Vasquez added to the discontent. They cultivated Wákara's antipathy after California-bound emigrants began bypassing their outfitting post in favor of stopping in Great Salt Lake City. The old trappers warned Wákara of impending land loss and sold arms to his band.[37] Mormon lore claims that Wákara agitated for war as early as 1847 and was only subdued when Sow-iette asserted his authority and flogged Wákara with a riding crop in front of a council of elders.[38] Wákara and Sowiette would remain at odds for years. Meanwhile, an uneasy détente existed between Wákara and the Mormon leaders as they exchanged assurances and gifts while jockeying for the best advantages for themselves and their followers.

Other Utes were less ambivalent. For example, Cone and his small Tim-pany band (Timpanogos) swore to live by raiding Mormon stock. Mormon livestock was displacing wild game and eating the wild seed grasses Indians traditionally used for food.[39] Therefore, they reasoned, the livestock was fair game, and capturing enemy property was not the same as theft. The issue was how to define the Mormons: friend or foe? In any case, the capture of occasional livestock was little more than a fair-use fee for the land, not unlike the tolls and tribute they had been requiring for decades. As Brigham Young noted in his journal, "The Indians supposed the land to be all theirs, and are in the habit of taking a share of the grain [or stock] for the use of the land."[40]

Mormons did not agree with the Utes' reasoning.

So despite wanting peaceful relations, Brigham Young deplored the general thievery and needed to formulate a strategy to combat it. However, he also condemned the brutality with which some of his people wished to punish the offenders. It was wrong, he argued in 1847,

> to indulge in feelings of hostility and bloodshed toward the Indi-ans...who might kill a cow, an ox or even a horse; to them the deer, the buffalo, the cherry and plum tree, or strawberry bed were free. It was their mode of living to kill and eat....I realize there were men among us who would steal, who knew better, whose traditions and earliest

teachings were all against it. Yet such would find fellowship with those who would shoot an Indian for stealing.[41]

But as thefts continued, Young and his counselors grew less patient.

When stock was again stolen in March 1848, a heavily armed posse was sent after Cone's raiders into Utah Valley. However, Cone's leader Little Chief stepped in and punished them himself, extracting a promise to behave and promising he would protect and support the Salt Lake colony.[42] But Cone's predation continued, and in February 1849 another detachment was sent after them and ordered to "put a final end to these depredations." The militia engaged the four raiders near Mt. Timpanogos on a stream subsequently renamed Battle Creek; during the fight they killed the men and took their women and children prisoners. Four days later, a Mormon council approved a preplanned colony in Utah Valley.[43]

But the show of force stunned rather than cowed the Timpanogos Utes. The battle had been witnessed, and descriptions of it inflamed Valley Utes. Relatives of the raiders swore future enmity, including Patsowett, Chief Opecarry (Stick-on-Head), and the noted warrior Pariats (Big Elk). Even Little Chief cursed the Mormons and warned that small, unprotected parties would no longer be safe in the valley. These men would form a growing, influential cadre for whom peaceful coexistence with the Mormons became impossible.[44] Over the next years Mormons discovered what modern military advisors have since relearned: killing insurgents multiplies enemies as kinsmen join the ranks of the aggrieved.[45]

The Mormon hierarchy was also displeased and censured the expedition's commander, John Scott, because the generalized policy of "shed no blood" had marked Mormon-Indian relations up to this point.[46] Regardless, Mormon leaders were determined to plant a colony in Utah Valley. A few weeks later—without negotiating with or notifying the Timpanogos Utes—a company of over 150 settlers set out for Utah Valley.[47]

Unsurprisingly, the Utes were not happy to see the colonizers. Utah Valley was no middle ground; it was a center of Western Ute population. Broad expanses of seed grasses, tuberous plants, and game-rich marshes fed their people. Nearby canyons provided berry bushes and wild game and opened trails eastward into the Uintah Basin or north toward bison country. Especially important were the freshwater lake, marshes, and rivers that provided a wealth of waterfowl and fish. It was also the site of an annual spring festival that brought Utes from two hundred miles around to take advantage of the spring spawning run. Thousands of fish, including an abundance of freshwater trout and suckers, swarmed upriver to spawn in such numbers that "often the river would be full from bank to bank as thick as they could swim for hours and sometimes days together, and fish would be taken from morning until night for weeks together."[48]

These Lake Utes were indeed a little tenacious about their valley. Angry men blocked the incomers, but the colonizers negotiated with elders and swore with uplifted hands that they would never drive the Utes from their valley. With these assurances, they were reluctantly allowed to continue to a site near the mouth of the Provo River. Within weeks they had ensconced themselves within a palisade from which stared the muzzle of a small cannon. With good reason, the settlement was called Fort Utah.[49] A year later, plagued by mosquitoes and sloughs of spring floodwater, the settlement relocated two miles east and was eventually renamed Provo after the prominent French Canadian trapper, Étienne Provost.[50]

Shortly thereafter, Wákara arrived for the fish festival following another successful horse raid in California. He was furious to see the non-Indian settlement and lobbied for war. Other belligerents joined him, including Patsowett, Opecarry, and the hostile Pariats, a six-foot-tall heavily muscled warrior known to mountain men as the "terror of the mountains" for his animosity toward Americans. But Wákara had too few supporters and was restrained by Sowiette.[51] Shortly thereafter, Wákara shifted positions and one-upped the Timpanogos bands when, in June, he met with Young, proffered his friendship, and invited Mormons to settle in "his" Sanpete Valley.[52]

Wákara had long been estranged from the Utah Valley bands, a pique that purportedly stemmed from the alleged murder of his father by a Timpanogos faction. According to oral tradition, tribal factions had argued over whether to send war parties after raiding Shoshones. One group with blood ties to the Shoshones argued against, while the war hawks, led by Wákara's father, sued for action. The pro-Shoshone faction assassinated Wákara's father, so Wákara and his kin-brother Arapeen avenged his death and then retreated to the Sanpete and Sevier valleys.[53] Here he established a base of operation in a location convenient to the Old Spanish Trail. Nevertheless, he and Arapeen continued to visit Utah Valley.[54]

Now Wákara was exploiting the new situation, hoping to raise his influence with the white settlers while cultivating potential trade advantages. Shortly after the Battle Creek incident, he told Brigham Young that "it was good to kill the Timpany Utes," that they "ought to kill some more," and that he wanted the

Mormons to "settle a Co. in his valley." A few months later Wákara met with Young and claimed "he don't care about the Land but wants the Mormons to go & settle it." In return, Young proposed to teach the Utes agriculture, husbandry, and letters—or more precisely to acculturate them into the Mormon-American way of life. Of this, Wákara seemed to approve.[55] Four months later Utes guided over two hundred colonists into the Sanpete Valley.[56]

At first the new Manti settlement was a successful example of Indian-Mormon friendship and cooperation, marked by amicable reciprocity. Utes helped the Mormons move supplies and equipment, and the Mormons responded with gifts, medicine, and priesthood blessings for the sick, perceived by Utes as shamanic power. A devastating measles epidemic struck during the winter of 1849–1850. Because Utes had never been exposed to the disease and had no immunities, it was especially virulent and horrific. In Utah Valley Mormons buried at least thirty-six Utes in one mass grave, and many more remained unburied, especially near the medicinal hot springs north of Utah Lake.[57]

In Manti, settlers generously shared their food supplies with the Utes, nursed the sick, and offered priesthood blessings. Although many died, including Wákara's mother and Arapeen's daughter, others recovered under Mormon ministrations. By early spring, Wákara and Arapeen had both been baptized Mormon and ordained into the Melchizedek priesthood (as was Sowiette, later).[58]

How converted these raiders were, is problematic. The Utes were mystics in whose lives the supernatural played an important part. Mormon memoirs claim Wákara had received a vision as a young man in which he died and went to "heaven" where a white-robed Lord gave him a new name—"Iron Twister" (*Panáqari Kwín'wáyke*)—and told him he would meet a race of white people who would be his friends and whom he must treat kindly. While the story smacks of Christian theology and a Mormon perspective, if even partly true, it helps explain his ambivalence toward the Mormons.[59] However, Wákara's conversion was as much rooted in pragmatism as mysticism. As a mystic he was willing to tap into any source of *puwá* medicine, but as an opportunist the cagey chief undoubtedly viewed his baptism as a means of sealing his political and economic alliance with the Mormons as well.

However, with this alliance came demands. The Mormons mistakenly assumed that Wákara held authority over all Utes and expected him to help discipline them. And to some extent he did. That winter he hunted down and executed several Utes who stole Manti livestock, and when some Timpanogos

Utes clashed with Mormons in Utah Valley, he warned his men to steer clear of the trouble.[60]

Relations were far less friendly in Utah Valley. In August of 1849, three Mormons (Richard Ivie, Jerome Zabrisky, and John R. Stoddard) killed a Timpanogos elder, "Old Bishop," during a scuffle over an allegedly stolen shirt. They clumsily tried to hide the evidence by disemboweling the corpse, filling it with stones, and throwing it into the Provo River. Then, within the safety of the fort, they boasted of their actions. Of course, the Utes soon discovered the mutilated body and demanded the perpetrators be handed over for justice—or at least be given some livestock as a blood payment. When the settlers refused, Ute leaders ordered them out of the valley. When they didn't leave, Utes began to harass them.[61] By mid-October Fort Utah leaders were complaining to Brigham Young that the Utes were "saucy, annoying and provoking," were killing livestock, and were threatening to kill them. No mention of the precipitating murder was made. A frustrated Young rebuked the settlers for failing in their duties toward the Indians.[62]

But the situation escalated. Both sides purchased guns and ammunition from California-bound emigrants. Utes stepped up their theft of livestock, began taking potshots at the fort and isolated workers, and harassed a federal survey party near Utah Lake. Meanwhile, the fort's "minute men" began to drill daily, and Indians were no longer allowed into the fort for any reason. In stark contrast to the Manti settlers, Fort Utah Mormons refused to help the starving, measles-ravaged Utes that winter. When Pariats came begging for medicine, he was literally and very roughly kicked out.[63]

The frustrated colonists repeatedly sought permission to chastise the Indians, but Young remained adamant: if they killed Indians for stealing they would have to answer for it. But by January 1850, with the fort virtually under siege, Isaac Higbee traveled to Great Salt Lake City and demanded punitive action be taken. Parley P. Pratt, only recently returned from exploring routes south of Utah Valley, agreed. As colonizers they had but three choices: abandon the colony (breaking lines of communication south); leave the settlers to their destruction (unthinkable); or defend the settlers and destroy the Indians. Apparently, the idea of diplomatic peace negotiations did not come up.[64]

Badgered on all sides, Young finally conceded:

> They must either quit the ground or we must—we are to maintain that ground [Utah Valley] or vacate this [Salt Lake Valley]—we were [told] three years ago—if we don't kill those lake Utes they will kill us—every

man told us the same—they all bore testimony the Lake Utes lived by plunder and robbing—if we yield in this instance—we have to yield this land.[65]

And Young had no intention of yielding the land.

Captain Howard Stansbury, whose federal survey party had been harassed by Utes, seconded the decision to send a punitive expedition, as did John W. Gunnison, another government explorer at the meeting. Stansbury argued that "the contemplated expedition against these savage marauders was a measure not only of good policy, but one of absolute necessity and self-preservation." He also offered military aid and the services of a doctor.[66]

Four years later, Father James Bean of Fort Utah told Young about the Old Bishop murder that had triggered hostilities. Young would annotate his journal, claiming he had been opposed to the war and had only been persuaded by Higbee's report.[67] The inundation of hawkish military advice undoubtedly influenced his decision as well. Regardless, like the Battle Creek incident, the 1850 Provo War proved a strategic blunder. While it brought temporary peace, it sowed the dragon's teeth of future conflict, as embittered Ute refugees once again spread a hatred and thirst for vengeance that would fuel subsequent conflicts.[68]

Orders were issued to the Salt Lake City militia to cooperate with the Fort Utah militia "in quelling and staying the operations of all hostile Indians," and to act "as the circumstances may require, *exterminating* such, as do not separate themselves from their hostile clans, and sue for peace."[69] Young also wrote, "I say go kill them...Let the women and children live if they behave themselves...We have no peace until the men [are] killed off."[70] Two weeks later he reiterated this policy: "If the Indians sue for peace, grant it to them, according to your discretion and judgment [but]...if they continue hostile pursue them until you use them up—*Let it be peace with them or extermination.*"[71]

Concerned over the rising tensions, a number of Utes (including a south-valley chief named Black Hawk) came to the fort to offer aid and reassure the Mormons that they were peaceful. Even Chief Opecarry unsuccessfully attempted to negotiate peace, but the war leader, Pariats, was now determined to drive the Mormons out.[72]

On February 7, 1850, a large force of militiamen travelled to Utah Valley where they joined the local militia under the command of Peter Conover. Early the next morning, the combined force attacked Opecarry and Pariats' fortified camp, with orders to "take no hostile prisoners," to "do the work up clean,"[73] and not to "leave the valley until every Indian was out of it."[74] The militia laid siege to the camp with guns, cavalry, and a death-dealing cannon. But despite frigid temperatures and more than two feet of snow, the entrenched Utes determinedly held off the Mormon forces for two days and nights, lighting up the night with their muzzle flashes. On February 10, Major general Daniel H. Wells arrived with reinforcements—but during the night the surviving Utes had fled. The wounded and sick (many starving, freezing, or dying of measles) retreated eastward toward a "difficult gorge" (Rock Canyon), while others fled south.[75]

Wells pursued the fleeing Utes and engaged them in a rousing battle on Goshen Marsh. Horses slid about on the ice and warriors shot at the militia from prone positions. In the end, a number of Utes were killed and the rest taken prisoner. But the warriors refused to swear eternal peace, and the next morning they were dealt with in "a most summary manner." All the men were shot while "trying to escape," and their women and children taken captive to Fort Utah.[76] The next day Stansbury's military surgeon and members of the militia collected the heads of the dead Utes, hacking them off with pocket-knives so the skulls could be used for scientific research.[77] However, they were not properly prepared and most rotted and were unusable. Disturbingly, Ute prisoners at Fort Utah—the wives and children of the slain—were taunted with these gruesome trophies.[78]

After roving militiamen killed a few more Utes, they finally returned to finish up at Rock Canyon. Sharpshooters overlooking the camp opened fire, killing a few Utes, though most escaped up the canyon on snowshoes—including Opecarry and Patsowett. In the end, two dozen Utes lay dead in the camp, many of them women and children, most dead of exposure, hunger, fatigue, or disease. Among them was Pariats, who had succumbed to battle wounds and disease, and his wife, who tried to escape up the icy cliffs but fell to her death (giving the precipice its name: Squaw Peak).[79]

The militia returned to Great Salt Lake City, taking with them captive women and children who were distributed into foster families, where they remained through the winter before returning to relatives in the spring. Captured livestock was given to the Cumumbahs.[80]

Later that spring Brigham Young tried to calm the troubled waters when he initiated formal peace talks with Black Hawk (either he of later renown, or more likely his father or father's kinsman).[81] Young hoped to reassure Utes who remained in the valley that despite the recent bloodshed, Mormons were "their friends and not their enemies." The Mormons did "not want their horses, women, or children" and would return prisoners and as much of the confiscated Ute property as possible. Fort Utah residents, Lot Huntington and James Bean, went to Black Hawk's camp southwest of present-day Payson, where they endured the humiliation of being struck "severely" with a riding crop before Black Hawk would consent to speak to them. Following negotiations, Lot and Bean invited the Utes to come into the fort where a feast was prepared and peace declared.[82]

But Pandora's Box was already open. The spirit of war had been released, and Young's utopian plan for peaceful coexistence with and redemption of the Lamanites was foundering. Without the support of rank-and-file Mormons, and in the face of mounting Indian resentment of usurpation of their homelands, the idealistic rhetoric about peaceful relations was useless. Young later complained that because Fort Utah colonizers had behaved badly, he had been forced "to confiscate all [the Utes'] property—and then put them in the heat of battle and kill them."[83]

Though Indian resistance had temporarily ceased, it did not ensure peace. Embittered Ute refugees fought in subsequent uprisings, like the younger Black Hawk who witnessed the 1850 war and had kinsmen among those who fought and were killed and mutilated. Other refugees joined Shoshone and Goshute bands and incited them.[84]

Despite the supposed peace, sporadic vengeance killings continued. Isaac Higbee wrote that Patsowett and his brother had been killing cattle and threatening to kill "every white man he can." Higbee's men had found and killed the brother, and he now urged Wells to "search for [Patsowett], and if he can be found in [Salt Lake] valley, kill him before he can do any more mischief." A short time later Patsowett was arrested as he left Young's office and was summarily tried and executed.[85] Clearly, a new policy was in force—the extermination of hostile Indians. With the help of Utes still friendly to them, Mormon officials continued to round up suspected hostiles and execute "justice."[86]

Because family relationships were important, Ute aggression typically developed along personal lines, as was the case with Patsowett and Pariats. However, most Western Utes remained relatively peaceful, and many Mormons continued as helpful friends of the Indians. Raiding was predominantly engaged in by a minority of men—usually young, unmarried adventurers or kinsmen of the dominant raiders like Wákara and Ammon, who often settled down once they had a family.[87] That these raiders were belligerently aggressive had given the Timpanogos Utes their bad reputation.

Wákara's alliance with the Mormons, however, was soon tested. During the spring of 1860, shortly after his baptism, Wákara met with Brigham Young during the spring fish festival near Utah Lake. When Shoshones raided the festivities-rich Ute camp and drove off a sizeable number of good horses (many belonging to Wákara), he demanded that Young, his new ally, order his militia to join him in retaliatory pursuit.[88] Of course Young could hardly acquiesce. Mormon settlements depended as much on Shoshone peace to the north as Ute peace to the south—and peace between the two tribes, if possible.

Wákara was furious. He had caught and punished Utes who had stolen Mormon stock and expected the same courtesy in return. He and Arapeen led their men in pursuit of the raiders and were successfully revenged in Echo Canyon. Back in Sanpete they staged a victory celebration outside the gates of Manti where Shoshone women were humiliated, scalps displayed, and victory dances held for over two weeks. Once their initial fright waned, curious settlers visited the camp to watch the "savage pageantry."[89] Then Wákara returned to Utah Valley and, according to Mormon lore, tried again to foment an attack on the Mormons but was rebuffed by Sowiette who announced that he and his followers would defend the white people. This incident, often retold, solidified a Mormon belief that Sowiette was their friend, and Wákara could not be trusted.[90]

Meanwhile, tensions continued to escalate. Ute provocateurs stirred up Shoshones in the Ogden area, resulting in a cycle of thefts and retaliatory killings—although the militia there was warned to "be careful not to get into further difficulty with [the Indians] if possible".[91] On the other hand, when displaced and hungry Goshutes stole livestock, local militias were ordered to chase and destroy the depredating Indians. Still acting on the orders to "let no hostile Indians escape," Goshutes were shot in battle and prisoners summarily executed. Porter Rockwell argued it was "unwise to turn the thieves…loose to commit more depredations and perhaps shed the blood of some useful citizen and they were sacrificed to the natural instincts of self-defense."[92] One militia commander even requested arsenic to poison Goshute water supplies. The action would not have been without colonial or frontier precedence, because poisoning or deliberately infecting Indians with virulent diseases was not unheard of. One Colorado newspaper argued that it was "cheaper pecuniarily [to poison Utes] than to kill them with powder and lead, and, withal, fully as effective." The Utah commander's request was denied.[93]

Not everyone agreed with this brutality. Both Jacob Hamblin and Dudley Leavitt placed their own bodies in front of Goshute prisoners to stop executions, calling it murder.[94] By 1851 church officials realized the extermination policy was not working. General Wells rescinded orders to pursue Goshutes (probably after talking to Brigham Young) and argued, "We may expect to expend more time and money in running after Indians than all the loss sustained by them."[95] A few weeks later Young reiterated this when he responded to renewed trouble near Ogden, saying it did not become the Mormons to "make a wanton attack upon the nation and take their property in retaliation" for the deeds of a few. Instead he urged settlers to "heal the breach," return Shoshone property, and compensate them for any Indian deaths. "It is cheaper by far, yes hundreds and thousands of dollars cheaper to pay such losses, than raise an expedition...to fight Indians."[96] Shortly thereafter, Young began urging the government to establish Indian farms and pressed again the peaceful redemption and education of Indians. Three years later, Young was claiming he had

> uniformly pursued a friendly course toward them, feeling convinced that independent of exercising humanity towards so degraded and ignorant a race of people, it was manifestly more economical and less expensive, to feed and clothe, than fight them.[97]

It was a pragmatic conclusion argued by other federal Indian agents as well.[98]

The sixteen-month policy of extermination had been costly, and relations sorely chafed. Even peacemaker Sowiette exclaimed in 1852 that "American— Good! Mormon—no good! American—friend, Mormon—kill—steal." U.S. Indian Agent Henry Day reported that the Utes and Shoshone had "little confidence in anything the Mormon people say to them," and that they stood "in much fear of them."[99]

When Brigham Young first learned that Utah was to be organized as a territory, he had begun to explore additional means for resolving his Indian problem. The day after he received the news, Young dispatched a letter to his Washington representative, John Bernhisel, to suggest "the extinguishment of the Indian title to the land and the removal to, and location of the Indians at, some favorable point" away from his colonies—such as the Sierra Nevadas or Wind River Mountains. This would help "the prosperity of civilization" and be for the "good of the Indians."[100]

But there was no removal, and coexistence quickly became a necessity. In just five years the non-Indian population had mushroomed. In Utah Valley alone, four of the nine settlements (Provo, American Fork, Lehi, and Payson) already totaled 7,600 people—four times the number of Valley Utes—with 7,800 head of cattle, 950 horses, 3,600 sheep, and various factories and mills.[101] Despite Mormon promises to not drive the Utes out of their valley home, Utes were inexorably being displaced by rapid colonial expansion. Land and resources had been lost, populations reduced by disease and conflict, and trade and raid resources severely curtailed. Gifts and tribute from travelers were replaced by gifts and handouts from settlers. Both federal and Mormon policies demanded assimilation, acculturation, Christian redemption, and a sedentary lifestyle to accommodate the rapid influx of agricultural Americans. But these new-comers also viewed the nomadic Utes as racially inferior and incompetent stewards of their valuable but undeveloped land, and therefore felt justified in appropriating all of it. Few recognized prior rights for nomadic Indians whose land rights seemed no more valid than those of the wild animals to which they were frequently compared.

As Western Utes and Mormons struggled to develop the new terms—and a final solution—for their forced coexistence, bloody conflict and cultural changes were inevitable.

Chapter 6

Conciliation and Defeat
Western Utes, 1851–1855

Gifts and negotiations had brought an uneasy truce between Utes and Shoshones. However, Western Utes and their native neighbors watched in dismay as ongoing Mormon colonization efforts followed a course of rapid, systematic, and continuous expansion into the choicest parts of their homelands. By the fall of 1851, Utah Indian Superintendent J. H. Holeman reported that the Indians in Utah Territory had become

> very much excited by the encroachments of the Mormons, as they are making settlements, throughout the Territory on all the most valuable lands.... The Indians have been driven from their lands and their hunting ground destroyed, without any compensation...they are in many instances reduced to a state of suffering, bordering on starvation.[1]

By 1852 even the once-friendly Sowiette told U.S. Indian Agent Henry Day that the Indians had "little confidence in anything the Mormon people say to them" and stood "in much fear of them." In 1853, Sowiette and his band fled Utah Valley and sought refuge in the Uintah Basin.[2] By the 1860s the initially friendly and welcoming Southern Paiutes found themselves displaced by a flood of new settlers and had become increasingly destitute and hostile.[3] Worse, Indian children were dying. By 1872 Kanosh lamented that Pahvant children were "all gone, all sick, no shoot, die sick"; Ute leader Sowooksobet ("Indian Joe") grieved that he had no children because they had "all died and gone into the ground." Settlers also noted that because of disease the bands had "dwindled down to a mere handful of warriors." The Southern Paiute population had dropped 90 percent by 1861, and by 1870 the Western Ute population had plunged from eight thousand to eight hundred.[4]

Meanwhile, travelers and settlements on the Spanish Trail were interfering with the Utes' most profitable enterprises—the slave trade and horse-stealing operations. Mormons stopped the Mexican trade in Utah Territory, even as a new military presence in California and settlements at Las Vegas and San Bernardino strangled escape routes and restricted resources on the trail.

Mormon converts streamed into Utah Territory, and they needed land. To accommodate the influx and assert dominion, Mormon leaders laid claim to an immense swath of territory through a network of strategically placed colonies. In addition to appropriating Utah's central valleys (Western Ute country), colonies appeared as far north as the Shoshone and Bannock's Salmon River Valley, west into the Goshute's Tule (Tooele) valley and the even more distant Northern Paiute territory in Carson Valley, and south into the Paiute country of southwestern Utah and southern Nevada. Settlements were even attempted in peripheral Hopi country.

In the meantime, the Ute and Shoshone's old trading partners, the entrenched American mountaineers and Mexican traders, began cultivating Indian antipathies toward the new settlers. Trade on the emigrant trails was lucrative, and Jim Bridger and Louis Vasquez hoped Indian troubles would dislodge their Mormon competitors. Bridger's blunt prediction that the Mormons would displace the Indians was uncomfortably accurate.[5] Neither the Utes nor the Shoshones were fools—many were aware that this was exactly what was happening.

Exacerbating intercultural relations, racial bigotry remained rampant despite diplomatic overtures of friendship and the brotherly rhetoric of Mormonism. This latent racism too often found expression when responding to ongoing pilfering and petty theft—both perfectly acceptable games by Ute standards. This led to friction, minor conflicts, and rising tension.[6]

But Brigham Young needed an atmosphere of peace for his colonization efforts to succeed, for his far-flung outposts were isolated and vulnerable. Nor could he afford to take sides with any one tribe, since he needed all as peaceful allies. Therefore, he worked to negotiate peaceful relations between his settlers and their Indian neighbors, as well as resolve long-standing intertribal conflicts. The predatory slave trade that targeted Paiutes had to be curbed, and the Ute-Shoshone feud needed to be resolved. To ameliorate Ute-Shoshone relations, Mormon leaders and a string of federal Indian agents worked as diplomatic peacekeepers. In September 1851 Young urged Ute leaders to attend a major peace council at Laramie, but Western Utes refused, fearful of Mormon

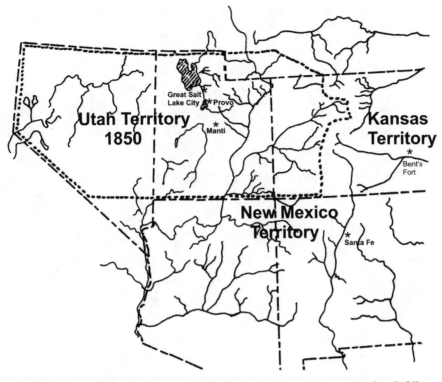

6.1. Utah Territory, Kansas Territory, and New Mexico Territory, 1850; most Ute bands fell within the jurisdiction of Utah Territory, except for the Mouache and Capote, who ranged into New Mexico.

intentions. The Mormons had recently waged a "war of extermination" against Utes and Goshutes, and Sowiette and Wákara feared the invitation was a ruse to have them all killed.[7]

Nevertheless, Ute and Shoshone leaders joined agent Henry Day at Fort Bridger shortly after the Laramie talks. Laying aside their traditional animosity toward one another, they unitedly denounced Euro-American colonizers, particularly Mormons, and aired their grievances over the usurpation of land and resources. Both Shoshone chief Washakie and Ute chief Sowiette asked Day if the U.S. government could protect them against Mormon colonization. Another informal peace parlay six months later also failed to yield results. However, within a year Western Ute and Shoshone leaders did negotiate a lasting peace after meeting with Indian agents and Mormon leaders in Great Salt Lake City.[8]

ENDING THE MEXICAN-INDIAN SLAVE TRADE

Commerce with Mexican traders on the Old Spanish Trail was a significant source of contention between Utes and settlers. While the slave trade had become an economic mainstay for many Western Utes, it created major problems for the Mormons.

The issue was not slavery, per se; slavery was, after all, legal in the United States. However, that was *black* slavery. Slavery had been a controversial political issue throughout the 1830s, 1840s, and 1850s and had negatively impacted Mormons in Missouri and Illinois. Consequently, members had been cautioned against open abolitionist rhetoric. Nevertheless, most Mormons disapproved of chattel slavery, although, like most Americans, they remained decidedly racist. Most Mormons (including Brigham Young) also bought into the belief that black Africans had been appropriately cursed with dark skin and perpetual servitude because of their supposed descent from the biblical Ham (a folkloric tradition now discredited by the LDS Church).[9]

Indians, however, were another story. Mormons believed that Lamanites—whom they alleged were the ancestors of American Indians—had been cursed with dark skin because of the wickedness of their ancestors, but not with perpetual servitude. Rather, they were believed to be descendants of Abraham and Jacob and were therefore among God's covenant people who could be redeemed.[10] Because of this, Mormons were disturbed to see Indians enslaved and outraged when they witnessed the often-abusive treatment of women and children by Ute captors. But even more important, stopping the slave trade was a diplomatic necessity. Mormon colonizers needed peaceful relations with their immediate Indian neighbors and were, by political expediency, allied with each tribe. They could not allow Utes to prey upon their Paiute or Goshute allies—but neither could they afford to antagonize the Utes with an armed resistance.[11]

An opportunity to interdict the trade came during the fall of 1851 when veteran slave trader Pedro León Luján arrived in Sanpete at the head of his annual trade caravan.[12] Don Pedro León had been leading slave-trading caravans into central Utah since at least 1827. However, by 1851 he knew he must follow new protocols in the recently created Utah and New Mexico Territories. Thus, he tracked down a touring Brigham Young to obtain permission to trade with the Indians. But Young refused. As ex officio superintendent of Indian affairs, Young invoked the recently extended Trade and Intercourse Act to deny the Mexicans permission to trade with Indians in Utah Territory.

Disgruntled, Luján agreed to leave the territory and sent most of his large party back to New Mexico while he and seven companions lingered long enough to buy supplies in Great Salt Lake City. But Ute traders—with their human merchandise already in hand—had other ideas. They raided the Mexican camps, appropriated horses and mules, and offered or left captives in exchange. In short order the traders were in possession of nearly a dozen captives, eleven children and one woman, *prima facie* evidence of having "traded" illegally with the Indians. Local nonslaving Sanpitch Utes snitched, and Luján and his companions were arrested, tried, and found guilty of illegal trading (not slaving) with the Indians without a license.

The decision was not surprising, given the tenor of the Mormon-dominated court and that most White Americans at that time were as prejudiced against Mexicans as they were Indians. The court confiscated the Mexicans' trade goods to pay court fines, including their horses, mules, and captives, which were distributed among friends of court officials (for a price). Then the Mexicans were expelled from the territory. Although Brigham Young gave them food and supplies for their return trip, they were forced to walk home, through the mountains, in midwinter.[13] Shortly thereafter, Utah's territorial legislature debated the issue of slavery and passed a law making the traffic in Indian slaves illegal, establishing regulations governing the purchase of Indian children as indentured servants and/or adopted children. (In the same session, the legislature also laid out regulations governing the treatment of black slaves.)[14]

The law against the Mexican trade was a crippling blow to Western Utes who, by 1852, derived a substantial portion of their livelihood from the slave trade. The following fall, Arapeen attempted to trade children to Provo residents for guns. But Governor Young had recently enacted strict regulations against trading any arms or ammunition with the Indians. When the settlers refused to trade, the volatile chief flew into a rage and denounced Mormons and Mormon law. If the Mormons had stopped the Mexicans from buying slaves, he stormed, then the Mormons should buy them instead. Grabbing a child by her feet, he dashed her head against the ground and flung the limp body at the horrified Mormons. "You have no hearts or you would have bought it and saved its life," he declared.[15]

As early as 1851, Brigham Young had already begun urging Mormons to purchase or trade for Indian children. Reports of Ute cruelty toward their captives was one incentive, but Brigham Young had an even nobler plan for redeeming the Lamanites:

> Buy up the Lamanite children as fast as [you can], and educate them and teach them the gospel, so that many generations would not pass ere they should become a white and delightsome people,... the Lord could not have devised a better plan than to have put us where we were in order to accomplish that thing. I knew the Indians would dwindle away, but let a remnant of the seed of Joseph be saved.[16]

Many of these children were Southern Paiutes, traded from either Ute slavers or destitute parents, as were Goshute and Shoshone children. Mormons also raised children orphaned during military actions against their families. Ultimately, more than 350 Indian children would be fostered/indentured by Mormons during these decades, with mixed results.[17]

The expulsion of Mexican traders weighed heavily on Wákara and those under his influence. In 1852 the trading chief wintered among the Moqui (Hopi) Indians until February, but when he returned, so did the Mexican traders.[18] This time they traveled under the purported leadership of a Dr. C. A. W. Bowman, a belligerent former mountain man then living in Abiquiú. With him was his Abiquiú neighbor, Pedro León Luján, traveling as a "peon" though undoubtedly acting as guide and advisor. Bowman deliberately sought out and confronted Brigham Young in Provo, "accost[ing]" him "in a very abrupt manner," and acting "in an insulting and threatening manner." Boasting that "he had four hundred Mexicans on the Sevier awaiting his order," Bowman told Young that his traders "feared nothing for law, and would not be restrained from any pursuit which they chose to follow."[19]

There was no army of Mexican traders. Nevertheless, Young was alarmed at the possibility of Mexicans instigating an Indian uprising. He ordered an immediate military alert, issued a general mobilization order, and commanded a forty-man detachment to travel through the settlements to locate and apprehend every "strolling Mexican party" as well as to ascertain Ute movements. Ultimately, nothing came of Bowman's threats. A few Mexican traders were arrested, held briefly, and then released and allowed to leave the territory peacefully. However, angry Utes did kill Bowman after he supposedly tried to cheat them (although rumors persisted that Mormons had killed him and blamed the Utes).[20]

The territory remained on high alert as both Brigham Young and the Utes anticipated trouble. Young gave orders to arrest Wákara "if he was not disposed to live peaceably."[21] Meanwhile, major Ute chiefs began to decamp. Wákara and his band abandoned Parowan and headed to Sanpete, even as his furious

6.1. Wákara and his brother Arapeen, Western Ute war chiefs, 1853 painting. (Drawing by Solomon Nunes Carvalho, c. 1853, used by permission, Utah State Historical Society, #14421)

lieutenant-brother, Arapeen, rode from Manti in a huff. That night Sanpete warriors demonstrated angrily outside another settlement just north of Manti, keeping the Mormon colonists in arms through the night, before they and other Utes "headed to the mountains." At the same time the Spanish Fork chief Bateez (possibly Wákara's son) abandoned Spanish Fork and took his band up Provo Canyon to "see how the battle went."[22]

But neither Wákara nor Young wanted a war. Wákara and Arapeen sent word that they wanted peace, and Young immediately responded with gifts and a letter telling Wákara to "behave."[23] However, when 150 Yampa Utes appeared near Wákara's camp—hoping to receive gifts from their new superintendent of Indian affairs, Brigham Young—rumors circulated that they had come to reinforce Wákara›s "war" band.[24]

The two leaders were at an impasse. Wákara wanted a presettlement status quo while Young intended to continue expanding his cultural and political empire. But these goals were mutually exclusive, and Young distrusted Wákara. In April Young told a congregation that

> It is truly characteristic of the cunning Indian, when he finds he cannot get advantage over his enemy to curl down at peace and say "I love you."...I am resolved however, not to trust his love...and I shall live a long while before I can believe that any Indian is my friend, when it would be to his advantage to be my enemy.

Wákara would keep the peace, Young asserted, but only because the Utes "dare not be any other way....They will be kind and peaceable because they are afraid to die, and that is enough for me."[25]

If the Utes continued to resist territorial law and persist in illegal trading and raiding, Young was determined to oppose them by force: "If [Wákara] become[s] hostile and wishes to commit depredations," Young threatened, "he shall be wiped out of existence and every man that will follow him."[26] Thus tensions continued to rise, and the Utes grew increasingly belligerent. By mid-May 1853, the territory had become a powder keg waiting for the spark that would ignite an inevitable war.[27]

THE "WALKER" WAR

The simmering hostilities exploded on June 17, 1853, when several Utes attempted to trade trout for flour at James Ivie's farm in Utah Valley. An altercation erupted over the fairness of the trade, which ended in a brawl that left two Utes dead, one injured, and a single bystander left to carry the tale to their kinsmen in Wákara's camp.[28] Although authorities in nearby Springville immediately offered the Utes a blood payment of cattle, Wákara refused, demanding Ivie himself be given up for punishment, the same way Utes had turned over Ute offenders for Mormon justice. When officials declined, Wákara abandoned negotiations and declared war.[29] Breaking camp, he joined Arapeen in Peteetneet (Payson) Canyon where other chiefs joined them in a council of war.

The alarmed Springville colonists mustered out their militia but continued to try diplomacy. The next day Captain Stephen C. Perry and seven men headed up Peteetneet Canyon, unaware that they were riding toward a war camp.[30] As they approached the camp, Ute warriors raised the war whoop and the air rang with their horrid yells which would have appalled the stoutest heart, in a moment a rush was made in [our] direction…we seemed placed in eminent danger, to retreat seemed madness, to proceed death stared us in the face.[31]

Notable Western Ute chiefs were at the war council, including Wákara, Arapeen, Tabby, and Sanpitch. The Mormon ambassadors were allowed to speak, but the chiefs again refused a blood payment. The kinsmen of the dead men were especially hostile, particularly Arapeen and Wyonah, but the other leaders agreed to allow Brigham Young to mediate.[32]

Believing immediate danger had been averted, the peace party rode down to the Payson fort. However, they were trailed by Arapeen and a hostile party. For the first few miles, a Ute friend named Oneship nervously rode with Perry and warned him that some Utes were still planning to seek revenge by killing Mormons and stealing cattle.[33] At the fort, Arapeen spurred forward to join Perry. Still hoping for conciliation, and despite Oneship's warnings, Perry invited him and his men into the fort to eat. But as the Utes rode out of the fort later that evening, the last man (likely Arapeen) turned and shot and killed a guard just then assuming his post. With war cries and threats, the war party swept back up the canyon, firing on farms and stealing two dozen head of cattle along the way. The war camp withdrew over the ridge into Salt Creek Canyon and Sanpete Valley beyond.[34]

The territory erupted into war.

Utah Territory had an impressive military force it could call on. Unlike most western settlements, Mormon colonies were part of a highly organized territorial militia that, though theoretically secular, was under the direct control of the LDS Church through its ranking ecclesiastical leaders. Each settlement had a militia, and the territory was divided into military districts according to counties. District militia commanders could assume emergency leadership authority over both militia and civilian populations and could call out, at a moment's notice, a regularized town posse or a volunteer army of civilians.[35]

Following the attack in Payson, this systemized militia sprang into action. Within the hour commanders in Springville and Provo were notified. Colonel Stephen Markham led the Springville militia to Palmyra (Spanish Fork), recruited more volunteers, reconnoitered Peteetneet Canyon, and then rode on to Payson. Meanwhile, Colonel Peter Conover mustered fifty men from Provo and by midnight had also reached Payson. After sending a hurried dispatch to military headquarters in Great Salt Lake City, Conover and Markham led their hundred-man contingent on a rapid journey southward. They were realistically fearful for settlers in the isolated and sparsely inhabited Sanpete Valley, Wákara's home ground. They may have also wanted to be in the forefront of the anticipated battles. By July 20 they had reached Manti.[36]

As feared, Ute raiders began to plunder Mormon settlements. Springville, Spanish Fork, and Nephi were all attacked July 19, as were settlements in Sanpete and dispatch riders in between.[37] When Conover's message reached militia headquarters in Great Salt Lake City, the response was immediate—but not what Conover and Markham had anticipated. Instead of exterminating hostiles, Brigham Young ordered, militia commanders should make all efforts to *conciliate* any hostile Utes even as they defended consolidated, forted-up settlements. "No retaliation [should] be made and no offense offered.... No threats or intimidations are to be made or exercised toward the Indians no more than nothing unusual had occurred."[38]

General Daniel H. Wells ordered two more companies south, and colonels Markham and Conover were ordered to pursue the hostile Indians, recover stolen stock, and capture the leaders of the rebellion, in particular, Wákara, but "in no case act upon the offensive."[39] Rather, they should "avoid... the shedding of blood, but endeavor to obtain the desired object and prevent by mildness and judiciary management a recurrence of the present Indian hostilities."[40]

But Conover and Markham were already onsite and planning *offensive* maneuvers similar to those conducted during the Provo and Goshute conflicts.[41] Conover had even sent out patrols to search out "hostile" Utes.[42]

George Albert Smith of Provo was furious with Conover for abandoning his regular military command at a time of crisis. A ranking ecclesiastical authority and close associate of Brigham Young, Smith reported Conover to authorities.[43] As a result, General Wells appointed Smith to the command of a newly created Southern Military Department, which included all militia districts south of the Salt Lake Valley.[44]

Nevertheless, Conover's offensive strategies were well under way. One of his patrols was headed by Jabez Nowlen, a Provo neighbor who had been wounded in the face during the Provo War and who held no love for Utes. Near Pleasant Creek (Mt. Pleasant) Nowlen's patrol accosted a hostile Ute camp and killed six men.[45] With Ute blood spilled, the war escalated.

Shortly afterwards, Conover and Markham were compelled to return home and comply with the conciliation and defense orders. When Conover resisted, he was temporarily relieved of command.[46] Now Colonel Smith made a whirlwind tour of southern Utah Territory to enforce the new general orders. Forts were to be completed immediately, settlers were to return to forts from outlying farms, and all surplus livestock (a magnet for Ute raids) driven to Salt Lake Valley.[47] Some distant settlers, who felt they were in no danger, including residents of Cedar City, angrily resisted sending their cattle north and armed themselves. They were arrested, jailed briefly, and released. (They subsequently left Utah and were excommunicated.)[48]

Meanwhile, Young continued to work for a negotiated peace.[49] He sent word to Wákara, calling him a fool for fighting his best friend, offering him beef cattle and flour, and inviting him to meet when he became "good natured again."[50]

But the overtures came too late. Although Wákara also counseled against further blood vengeance, others were determined to continue hostilities. On June 28, raiders made a stunningly successful daylight attack on Allred's settlement, driving off two hundred head of cattle and horses. After the disgruntled settlers finally obeyed orders and evacuated to Manti, Utes returned to burn the settlement to the ground. Though no blood was shed, it was a devastating psychological blow.[51]

Notably, most Utes did not participate in the uprising. The raiders were primarily members of Wákara's band and those most affected by the loss of the Mexican slave trade. Thus, the conflict that would become known as the Walker War was, in essence, a bloody feud between Mormon settlers and some of Wákara's band—particularly Arapeen and Wyonah, who were closely related to the men killed at the Ivie farm, and whose deaths had triggered the conflict. But as in most feuds, tit-for-tat retaliation inevitably escalated the conflict.

As early as July 28, the friendly Pahvant chief Kanosh assured Colonel Smith of Pahvant support, offered to help fight Wákara, and warned of impending trouble.[52] Eleven days later, the pacifist Sowiette and members of his band approached Springville to guarantee their peace, but the alarmed settlers drove off his kinsmen and arrested and threatened to shoot him. The shaken chief was eventually released, but he promptly relocated his band in the Uintah Basin where he thence remained prudently distant from the Utah Valley settlements. Other Ute chiefs met with Colonel Smith and indicated they too desired peace, including White Eyes (Yampa) and Antero (Uintah). Wákara, who was actually not actively involved in the conflict, soon traveled south on the Spanish Trail, stopping to trade with Mexicans on the Green River, and then wintering "as usual" in New Mexico Territory.[53]

But local hostilities continued, primarily hit-and-run raids on cattle and horses. Soon a spiraling cycle of bloody retaliation developed, and atrocities were committed on both sides.[54] Rogue Pahvants killed a guard at Fillmore, then at Manti settlers confronted and shot down a group of visiting Utes, and Arapeen boasted he would never make peace.[55] The Palmyra (Spanish Fork) militia attacked a camp of Utes at dawn, killing six and wounding many more.[56] Six days later Mormon teamsters were attacked, the freight vandalized, and their mutilated bodies left as a mute testimony of growing Ute rage.[57]

Angry Nephi authorities brought in friendly Utes from a nearby camp and summarily "shot [them] down without even considering whether they were the guilty ones or not…like so many dogs, picked up with pitchforks [put] on a sleigh and hauled away."[58] An hour later guards shot and killed another Ute man and took his young son prisoner.[59] Three days later Utes killed and mutilated two Mormons near Manti, and ten days after that Utes attacked harvesters digging potatoes near Summit Creek (Mona).[60]

Civil and military leaders in Great Salt Lake City were desperate to stop the mayhem. Brigham Young preached against this retaliatory warfare, condemning Mormons who punished whatever Indians were at hand for the misconduct and crimes of others. While this might be the custom of Indian warfare, he argued, it was the Mormons' duty to teach better conduct—which they could hardly do if they were as guilty, if not more so, than the Indians themselves. Young pled with military commanders for a cessation of hostilities and renewed his offers to negotiate peace.[61]

In the midst of the turmoil, Captain John W. Gunnison arrived in Utah with a government survey party, looking for a route for the Central Pacific Railroad. Despite warnings, Gunnison remained unconcerned because he had made friends among both the Pahvants and Utes during an 1849–1850 expedition. Unfortunately, non-Mormon immigrants had recently scuffled with and killed a Pahvant elder, whose son had sworn revenge against Americans.[62] Traditional justice demanded vengeance be wreaked on offending tribes, not specific individuals, and by this time most Utah Indians saw a clear distinction between the two non-Indian tribes in Utah: Americans (*mericats*) and Mormons (*mormonees*). Because Gunnison's survey party members were clearly *mericats*, the rogue Pahvant war party killed Gunnison and all of his party except four men who managed to escape .[63]

The slaughter of the government party shocked Indians and non-Indians alike and marked an end to the bloodshed—although stock raids continued. By November, nineteen Mormons and at least twice that number of Utes had been killed, and even more displaced Utes would die of starvation and disease in the months to come. The warmer valleys where Utes had once wintered were now unsafe, so they shivered and starved through the cold winter in the canyons and the Uintah Basin.

Meanwhile, the Gunnison Massacre aroused national ire. Kanosh cooperated fully, expressing his regrets over the rash actions of a few members of his band, berating the perpetrators, and returning what government property he could. But officials still arrested and tried eight Pahvants, including Kanosh. However, the Mormon jury in Nephi infuriated federal officers with a verdict of manslaughter against only three of the defendants, all elderly men, picked by the Pahvants to stand proxy for the tribe. They were sentenced to three years' imprisonment in the Utah penitentiary, from which they "escaped" a short time later.[64] Apparently, Mormons had a marked prejudice in favor of the Pahvants, with whom they had to live as neighbors, as opposed to Americans whom most Mormons preferred to live without.

Nonetheless, the Walker War was not yet resolved. Stock raids kept the territory on guard and halted further colonization southward. In December, Governor Young offered total amnesty to all Utes who had participated in the recent hostilities if they agreed to the same terms as Mormons.[65] He also offered to reopen informal trading relations and tried to induce his people to trade food, clothing, and other goods to the Utes. But winter was the starving time, and raiding continued, including a masterly roundup of a hundred head of cattle from Springville and Palmyra to feed Arapeen's band. The uneaten cattle were returned in the spring as part of peace negotiations.[66]

After Wákara returned to southern Utah in mid-February 1854, he initiated his own peace talks. A wagonload of gifts were sent, and Superintendent Young was notified. He, in turn, sent E. A. Bedell, a non-Mormon Indian subagent, to treat with the Indians regarding the purchase of land in Sanpete.[67] But Wákara backed away from the deal, preferring to coexist peacefully with his cattle-rich Mormon neighbors. So tensions continued as Wákara defended the Utes' right to pilfer cattle and his right to exact tribute from travelers. Church president Young responded by threatening the chief with excommunication.[68]

Wákara responded, proposing his own peace terms: full economic freedom, no interference with Mexican traders, and a large number of presents to cement the peace.[69] Young refused these status quo demands, but in May he and other dignitaries traveled south of Nephi to negotiate with the chief.

Ute leaders poured out their grievances. One emaciated and scarred elder complained that "Americats have no truth. Americats kill Indians plenty.

Americats see Indian woman—he shoot her like deer. Americats…have no mercy." Sanpitch tearfully described how white men had murdered his wife and son while they were hunting rabbits.[70] The following morning Young distributed gifts of cattle, blankets, and clothing, after which Wákara spoke:

> When Walkara is absent, then Americats come and kill his wife and children…. Walkara is accused of killing Capt. Gunnison. Walkara did not. Walkara was three hundred miles away when the Mericat chief was slain. Mericats soldiers hunt Walkara, to kill him…Walkara hear it; Walkara come home…Walkara heart very sore…Walkara no want to fight more. Walkara talk last night to Payede, to Kahutah, Sanpete, Parvain—all Indian say, "No fight Mormon or Mericats more."[71]

Both sides formally pledged peace on May 11.

But the war had been lost for the Western Utes before it ever began. By 1853 Euro-Americans vastly outnumbered the native population, and settlements had spread into most valleys previously occupied by Western Utes. Every settlement was fortified in a strict defensive posture, herds guarded. Even more overwhelming was their vastly superior number of weapons. Even with the arms supplied by disgruntled Mexican slavers, American traders, or other Indians, Ute raiders were no match for the number of armed settlers who defended their targets.[72]

By May 1854 Wákara, notable as a successful and power-filled raid chief, had been curtailed. Raids were too costly; hostilities between Shoshones and Utes had been resolved; slave raiding and trading had been prohibited; Mexican traders had been effectively expelled from the territory; and access to the southern California horse herds had been restricted.[73] Wákara's *puwá* had been broken. Eight months later on January 29, 1855, he died from a cold that "settled into his lung" (probably pneumonia). With him he reportedly took a wealth of trade goods and trinkets. Fifteen of his best horses were killed along with two Paiute consorts, and at least one—possibly two—Paiute children, who were entombed alive with him.[74]

Wákara was a highly visible symbol of how Western Ute life had changed in only a few decades. With rapid American colonization, the major bases of Western Ute economy disintegrated. Western Utes retrenched, many trying to return to traditional hunting and foraging, splitting into smaller kin-cluster bands and exploiting what resources remained. Meanwhile, Mormons and federal officials continued to demand representative chiefs with whom to negotiate, and these talkers did their best to work these sources for gifts or subsidies. With the best parts of their land unavailable, most native people in Utah Territory were forced to beg, steal, or starve. No matter how generous the handouts (and they were often limited), they were never sufficient.

Since ranching was not yet an option for most Utes, farming was the only viable recourse for peaceful coexistence—assuming that conflicts over water rights actually allowed Indians to farm. But farming was difficult, and few Ute men were willing or able to adapt because working with plants and the soil marked a woman's sphere. In 1855 few Utes acknowledged the need for such a dramatic shift in cultural identity, and they continued to fight it for years to come. For the Western Utes the next decades would be filled with increasing hardship, exposure, hunger, degradation, and death.

Chapter 7

Colonization
Kansas/Colorado Territory

Colonization among eastern and southern Ute bands (in today's Colorado and New Mexico) was less dramatic than in Utah Territory but was ultimately just as traumatic. And unlike the Mormons, few settlers made any pretense of loving Indians or even being willing to coexist with them. Neither Mormon, American, nor Mexican colonizer could conceive of Utes needing the vast acreage through which they roamed, and if not directly usurping land, settlers justified negotiating Utes out of their homelands for this rationale. They reasoned that Utes simply could not make as good use of it as industrious farmers, ranchers, or miners could. Spanish settlements on the northern frontier had typically been established with land grants given to lower caste *genízaros*, Mexican Indians, or mestizos, and these areas acted as borderland buffers against invading Plains or mountain Indians. These settlements pressed against the borders and sometimes pushed into Ute and Jicarilla territory, as did several herding operations north of Abiquiú. But attempts to colonize Ute country were not successful until after 1849, when the region became part of the United States. Ten years later the discovery of gold in the Rocky Mountains precipitated a major rush of Euro-American fortune hunters into this Ute fastness. Thus, Ute affairs in Colorado and New Mexico now fell under the purview of American officials and their military might, both working to control intercultural and intertribal relations with the Utes and initiate attempts to bring them into conformity with U.S. Indian policies of containment, acculturation, and assimilation.

EXPANDING NORTHWARD: THE SAN LUIS VALLEY

Colonial inroads into Eastern Ute country had begun as early as 1806 when Zebulon Pike built a log structure at the junction of Fountain Creek and the

Arkansas River, a prime winter camp for the Utes. Fur trappers and traders would use the same site off and on until 1842, when traders constructed a cluster of small wood and adobe buildings that became known as Fort Pueblo. It housed a diverse population of relatively sedentary families of traders married to women of Taos and Mora, and a constantly fluctuating population of trappers with their Indian wives.[1]

In 1833 the first permanent settlement on the Santa Fe Trail was established on the Arkansas River. Bent's Fort commanded commerce on the plains—including bison robes, hides, and furs—as well as the occasional herd of horses stolen in California. Shortly thereafter, a series of small, independent posts also appeared, some along the Front Range and others well within Ute territory. While the former posts were peripheral to Ute trade, three other forts were not: Forts Uncompahgre (1828), Uintah (1832), and Davy Crockett (1836) were established on the western slopes of the Rocky Mountains and in the Uintah Basin and would become important trade centers for the next decade.[2]

At first these trading forts attracted only incidental residents. But Mexican officials grew concerned that these posts were harbingers of American colonization—which they were, for in time some became hubs for settlement as traders turned to ranching and farming. To address these concerns, officials pushed for formal Mexican colonization of the San Luis Valley, hoping to solidify Mexico's claim to their northern frontier and thwart the expansionist United States. It would also address another problem: land shortages. Competition over land had increased after 1772, resulting from a series of political and economic reforms and a rising demand for commercial wool textiles. Population and livestock herds expanded rapidly as new settlers moved in and the number and size of sheep herds increased. Desperate for more grazing land, settlers and sheepherders were willing to brave the dangers of moving deeper into Indian country. Thus, in the early 1830s, officials confirmed the Conejos and Sangre de Cristo grants in the San Luis Valley and the Tierra Amarilla grant forty-five miles north of Abiquiú.[3]

But all three grants lay well within Mouache and Capote homelands and included winter-camp valleys and summer hunting grounds. The Mouaches were jealous of their rights in South Park, and the San Luis Valley, and firmly repelled early attempts to colonize there, forcing trespassers out of the Conejos grant in 1833 and again in 1840. But in Tierra Amarilla country, sheepherders refused to leave despite intermittent raids on their herds.[4]

Tensions worsened after 1840 when Mexican officials began to fear a possible alliance between Capote Utes and Navajos. Because of these fears—or perhaps in spite of them—officials failed to distribute the customary conciliatory peacekeeping gifts to Utes. Friction increased. Blood-trouble began in September 1843 when a band of Mexican mercenaries was unsuccessful in its search for Navajos to plunder and attacked a peaceful Ute rancheria just north of Abiquiú instead. They killed ten Utes, took captives, and stole horses and mules.[5]

Alarmed, citizens of Abiquiú attempted to placate the incensed Utes. Diplomacy had worked before, so both parties agreed to negotiate a settlement. Over one hundred Capotes led by Chief Panasiyave headed to Santa Fe in September 1844, all well-armed and decked out as if for war. They intended to sue for blood payments as compensation for the unprovoked attack and learn why they had not received their customary tribute. The conciliatory peace policy of the previous decades had included an unwritten agreement in which Utes punished Utes who stole from or killed settlers, and Mexican officials reciprocated by compensating Utes for thefts or murders committed by the settlers. However, Governor Mariano Martínez de Lejanza was new and unseasoned, and he distrusted the Utes. Expecting treachery, he positioned armed soldiers behind draperies in the audience room of the Governor's Palace. When arguments escalated, the nervous governor struck and killed the chief and signaled his soldiers to attack. Servants, guards, and citizens joined in as angry Utes poured into the Governor's Palace. Nearly a dozen warriors died before they retreated.[6] A new "Ute War" had begun.

As the Capote swept up the Chama Valley, they killed Mexicans and stopped specifically in Tierra Azul to kill the man who had escorted them to Santa Fe, and his family. At Abiquiú, those who attempted to sue for peace were killed on the spot. Punitive raids continued, and within two years other Utes had joined the hostilities. The Mouaches raided as far south as Las Vegas (New Mexico) while Utes in the north killed Mexicans employed at Fort Uncompahgre and attacked Fort Uintah.[7] Yet even as Mexican trappers and their employees were being attacked, trade traffic on the Old Spanish Trail remained active and unmolested. Some long-time Mexican traders and members of militias who willingly fought and killed Comanches, Navajos, or Jicarillas refused to fight against their Ute trade partners. For example, Pedro León Luján, the veteran slave trader with the Western Utes in Utah, was an Abiquiú citizen, an officer in the militia, and a veteran Indian fighter—but he never fought Utes.[8]

AMERICAN JURISDICTION, MILITARY PRESENCE, AND FIRST TREATIES

When American troops under Stephen W. Kearny entered New Mexico in 1846, the northern frontier of Nuevo Mexico was under siege: Mouache, Jicarilla, Comanche, and Kiowa were raiding east of the Sangre de Cristos, and the Capote and Navajo were raiding to the west. After crushing a bloody but short-lived uprising of Mexican and Pueblo allies near Taos (the "Taos Revolt"), Kearny firmly established U.S. control in the region. When the Mexican-American War ended in 1848, the Indian "problem" of Mexico's northern frontier became the Indian problem of the United States' new Southwest. Among Kearny's promises to the New Mexicans was his guarantee to protect them from Indian attacks. Because the Utes now fell under U.S. jurisdiction, this shift in imperial politics had immediate and drastic results. Their previous relationship with the relatively accommodating Spanish/Mexican settlers did not prepare them for this new situation, nor for the impending influx of Americans. In addition to a powerful and more aggressive military, Americans also brought a whole new set of racist attitudes and restrictive federal policies toward Indians. Within five years the Mouache and Capote Utes, along with their Jicarilla Apache allies, would be decisively defeated and maneuvered into ceding away their lands and legal rights.[9]

Establishing peaceful relations with Indians in the new territory was a high priority for the United States, and one of Kearny's first acts was to negotiate a temporary truce with the Mouache. Led by Kaniache, sixty Mouaches journeyed to Santa Fe with William Gilpin (a member of Kearny's forces and later first territorial governor of Colorado) where they conferred with Colonel Alexander Doniphan. With the memory still fresh of the 1844 treachery at the Governor's Palace as well as a recent attack by U.S. troops, the Capote refused to attend.[10]

Minor, intermittent raids or demands for tribute continued as they demonstrated ownership of the San Luis Valley and the upper Arkansas, but otherwise Utes remained generally peaceful at first, especially compared to Comanche and Plains Indian violence on the Santa Fe Trail.[11] But before the year was out, the Utes had become hungry and their men began to steal more stock. The military response was quick: punitive expeditions that killed Ute men and destroyed lodges, equipment, and provisions. In return, Mouache Utes killed two veteran mountaineers in 1848 who were retrieving equipment and goods cached by John C. Frémont several years earlier. The following year a Jicarilla war party, augmented by Mouache allies, attacked travelers on the Santa Fe Trail, killing a Mr. J. M. White and capturing his wife and daughter.[12] Three hundred troops were dispatched into "Utah" country to stop these depredations, recover stolen property, and demonstrate United States military power. In December principal Capote chief Quixiachiagiate and twenty-seven "subordinate chiefs" met with James S. Calhoun, an idealistic and sensitive man who served as New Mexico's first Indian agent and then as short-lived governor and superintendent of Indian Affairs in New Mexico. In Abiquiú the Capote leaders signed a formal treaty that gave the United States carte blanche authority over not just the Capote but *all* Utes, then and in the future.[13] Though it was primarily Capotes at the negotiations, among the signatories was the notorious Mouache leader Chico Velasquez, who had sworn eternal enmity toward Americans and Mexicans. After signing the treaty, however, he would become a noted ally of the Americans.[14]

The rest of the Mouaches, however, rejected Velasquez's authority to act in their name and refused to be party to the Capote treaty. In any case, it isn't likely the Capote leaders recognized the full ramification of what they had signed. In a pattern that would be repeated across the West, American negotiators did not understand—or refused to acknowledge—the limited scope of a chief's authority and the individualism of those who followed him. Neither did most Indian leaders fully comprehend that they were selling their land (not leasing or granting use-rights), agreeing to restrict their behavior, and binding other bands who had not attended the parlays.

The 1849 Treaty with the Utes reflected the restrictive and assimilative goals of American Indian policy, and future treaties and agreements followed similar patterns. In exchange for "such donations, presents, and implements, and . . . such other liberal and humane measures, as said Government may deem meet and proper," the Capote leaders unknowingly bound the entire "Utah tribe of Indians" to "acknowledge and declare they are lawfully and exclusively under the jurisdiction of the Government of said States: and to its power and authority they now unconditionally submit." They promised perpetual peace and amity, to return all stolen property and captives or make restitution, and to submit to all laws then in force—or any that might be passed—regulating trade and intercourse with Indians. They agreed to guarantee safe passage through Indian lands for all Americans and to allow military posts to be built to protect the interests of Americans and Utes.

Then, in particular, the Utes "relying confidently upon the justice and liberality of the United States," agreed to allow the government to set or adjust their territorial boundaries" (i.e., create reservations) as it deemed fit at some convenient time in the future. They also agreed to "build up pueblos, or to settle" so that they could "cultivate the soil, and pursue such other industrial pursuits as will best promote their happiness and prosperity," to "abstain for all time to come, from all depredations; to cease the roving and rambling habits...; to confine themselves strictly to the limit which may be assigned them; and to support themselves by their own industry."[15]

The 1849 Treaty was negotiated with just a handful of prominent leaders from only one or two Ute bands, and few Utes were ever aware of this early, legally binding agreement. Over the next three decades American officials would continue to negotiate similar treaties with a supposed "confederated" Ute tribe, though such a united nation never existed. But all that government negotiators needed was a representative number of signatures, preferably including leaders from prominent bands.

But the treaty did not ensure peace. In mid-May of 1850, a large war party of Jicarilla, with "straggling" Ute and Comanche accomplices and (rumor claimed) several Mexican collaborators, attacked a mail train on the Santa Fe Trail near Wagon Mound, New Mexico, killing eleven. The Eastern press published sensational eyewitness accounts, horrifying the nation and putting pressure on officials to solve the "Indian Problem" in New Mexico.[16] Ute leaders who had not signed the 1849 Treaty were urged to negotiate peace and demonstrate their good intentions, and in June 1850 chiefs from the northern Ute bands traveled to Abiquiú and signed an addendum to the 1849 Treaty. However, they insisted that as a *tribe* they had committed "no acts of hostility, or depredations." Nonetheless, a significant number of independent Ute adventurers continued to roam with the Jicarilla and share in their depredations.[17]

One motivation for the ongoing attacks was simple survival. The Mouache and Capote lands were being flooded with non-Utes after 1848. Thousands of settlers and ranchers, and then prospectors, miners, and entrepreneurs, poured into territory traditionally claimed by Eastern Utes, including today's mountainous western Colorado and northern New Mexico. Meanwhile, their Plains enemies, armed by American traders and negotiators, and with plunder stolen on the Santa Fe Trail, also invaded their mountains to prey on the more poorly armed Utes. Many Utes lacked the guns and ammunition they needed to hunt, even as game declined under the pressure of stock grazing and overhunting. When hunting failed and gifts, tribute, or trade were not forthcoming, hunter-warriors turned to raiding.[18] Christopher "Kit" Carson warned that the Utes were starving for lack of game, and another traveler described Ute women as so hungry that they were eating bark from trees. Settlements and livestock were attractive lures for raiders trying to provide for themselves and their families. So sporadic "banditry" continued. But raiding led to punitive reprisals, and the Army of the West was ready to enforce peace with the sword.[19]

To counter Indian depredations, Calhoun forbade the sale of articles of war, but Utes demanded—sometimes belligerently—the guns and ammunition they needed to hunt. Occasionally, illegal trade in New Mexico and legal trade with Mormon and American traders near Great Salt Lake City and Fort Bridger left some Utes with a "superabundance of Powder and Lead." For instance a large, well-armed band of Utes (Capotes, Tabeguaches, or possibly visiting Western Utes) camped north of Abiquiú in 1850, claiming they had "procure[d] their munitions of War from the *Mormons*, and a trading post near the Great Salt Lake."[20]

The Utes at this time were also locked in a spiraling cycle of hostilities with settlers, while competition for disappearing resources fanned intertribal enmities. Plains Indians resented Ute hunting and raiding forays on the plains and retaliated with raids of their own.[21] And all continued to raid settlements to replace declining game and to create herds of their own.

Thus, Indian agents were duly appointed and plans begun for agencies and future reservations. General Cyrus Choice arrived in Abiquiú in January 1850 to act as agent for the Capote, where he served until his death nine months later and the agency closed. It reopened in 1854, was moved north to Tierra Amarilla in 1872, and eventually ended up at Amargo (near Dulce) in 1881. Meanwhile, a second agency was established in 1851 at Taos where John Greiner acted as agent until it was temporarily closed two years later. It was reopened in December 1853 with Kit Carson as agent. However, it was only minimally successful because of a lack of funds, a situation typical for the times. Nevertheless, both the Capote and Mouache frequented this agency, and the Jicarilla were soon added, as were the Tabeguache after they drifted south for a time.

These bands also obtained subsidies from temporary agencies located at Cimarron and at Lucien Maxwell's ranch, a palatial home set on a million-acre grant east of Taos and strategically located on the Santa Fe Trail.[22] It became a favorite center for the Mouache and Capote, not only for the supplies and gifts there, but as a place to socialize and trade. One traveler described sleeping

7.1. Utes at the Abiquiú agency, 1880. (Courtesy Palace of the Governors Photo Archives [NMHM/ DCA], #087555)

on the hardwood floor amidst the "mighty men of the Ute nation," watching the crackling fire and the silent interplay between "half a dozen chiefs," Kit Carson, and Lucien Maxwell as they conversed in sign language throughout the night. The Utes respected Maxwell and Carson and considered both men to be friends, benefactors, and possibly allies.[23]

The efforts of agents and New Mexican officials helped maintain peaceful relations with the southern Ute bands that at first gained them paternalistic praise as "good Indians." Both Calhoun and Greiner reported that the "Eutaws are the easiest managed of any Indians in the Territory," were "peaceable and kindly disposed towards our Citizens," "behaved well," were "patient," and could "be relied on." Calhoun added, "No Indians could have behaved better for the last two years, than the Utahs,...inviting all Americans, except those who are endeavouring to take forcible possession of their lands to come out and trade with them."[24] Decades of friendly relations on the borderlands had taught these Utes that trade and gift alliances were generally more productive than war, and the mutually beneficial trade relationship had held for decades. But colonization and military encampments were another matter. In 1850 a new push was made to colonize the San Luis Valley, recommendations were made for an overland trail to California through Ute country, and the army proposed new military posts within or near Ute territory.

Ending subsidies also precipitated conflicts. Governor William Lane had been subsidizing supplies for the Utes while he made plans to relocate them near agencies and teach them to be agriculturally self-sufficient. But when the commissioner of Indian Affairs George Manypenny abruptly terminated Lane's program, rations dwindled and the Utes grew discontented. In 1853 Lane's successor, David Meriwether, inherited a growing problem: the lack of supplies was leading to increased thefts and violence. Meriwether warned that "unless these Indians be whipt or fed, the territory will soon be in a sad condition."[25]

But more supplies were not forthcoming, and the army was already planning to "whip" the Indians. A number of strategically located military posts were under construction as part of General Edwin Sumner's overall defensive strategy for the Southwest. Such posts were an essential element for keeping the peace between Indians and settlers as well as controlling intertribal hostilities.[26] Although the army spent a minority of its time fighting Indians, when it did fight the effects could be devastating. Within just a few years it was poised to crush Ute resistance should it arise.[27]

As non-Indian populations swelled in the early 1850s, the Utes had to compete for the right to access their own natural resources. As in Utah, colonizing and fort-building took many traditional food-gathering sites, especially in the San Luis Valley, South Park, and along the Front Range. It also forced Utes into increased contact with non-Indians, which in turn amplified cultural exchanges and heigthened the growing need for strong negotiator-leaders. As dependence on handouts, subsidies, and annuities increased, Utes came to expect them not only as reciprocal gift-giving between friends, but as fair payment for ceded land and lost resources.

Relations continued to sour as colonization in the San Luis Valley pushed forward. Utes had driven settlers out in 1833, 1842, and 1843, but colonists were persistent and Utes continued to harass them. One traveler in 1846 described the colonists as poverty-stricken, living in "wretched hovels on sufferance from the barbarous Yutas... [allowing] themselves to be bullied and ill-treated." He supposed "the politic savages" were only suffering the colonists to stay to supply them with "corn or cattle without the necessity of undertaking a raid on Taos or Santa Fe."[28] Of course the Mouache were not "suffering" the settlers to remain in the valley to plunder them; more likely they hoped their constant threats would eventually force the colonists to leave. By 1849 a settlement on the Costilla River was established that did survive, and it was augmented by more settlements two years later.[29]

But the Utes remained strongly opposed to colonization. The San Luis Valley was "their Winter hunting ground that it contains the bones of their Fathers, and they cannot & will not give it up quietly," and they threatened to "resist to the death" all attempts to settle there. Calhoun appealed for military intervention to stop the expansion—which was not forthcoming—and large numbers of "insolent and provocative" Utes began to threaten several ranches in the "Costillo" Valley. Rumors also circulated that the Utes were stockpiling weapons.[30]

But colonists were determined to lay claim to the rich San Luis Valley—for they held legal land grants and intended to develop them. Under the direction of Charles Beaubien (former proprietor of Bent's Fort and owner of the Sangre de Cristo grant), three small villages were planted and irrigation canals dug: San Luis (1851), San Pedro (1852), and San Acacia (1853). In 1854 Lafayette Head, who had come to New Mexico as a soldier during the Mexican-American War and later married into a prominent Mexican family, led another colony that settled at Conejos.[31] Additionally, a central summer route to the California gold fields was being recommended along Robidoux's old trapper trails. This route wound up the Huerfano River, through the Sangre de Cristo Pass, across the San Luis Valley, over Cochetopa Pass, and then on to the Spanish Trail.[32]

The army was also establishing military posts. Fort Union was built in 1851 on the Santa Fe Trail near Las Vegas (New Mexico),[33] and Fort Massachusetts was completed in 1852 in the San Luis Valley at the base of Blanca Peak. At first Utes believed the fort was erected to fulfill federal obligations to protect them from Plains Indian incursions since the treaty specified "protection to all the people and interests of the contracting parties." In 1858 the post was moved six miles south—but not to benefit the Utes. The new Fort Garland was strategically located where it could help regulate intertribal relations but more explicitly to protect San Luis Valley colonists.[34] Rather than safeguarding the Utes, both Forts Massachusetts and Garland would serve as staging points for punitive expeditions against them.

By 1854 diminished game, reduced subsidies, and increased colonization had pushed the generally peaceful Capotes and Mouaches into another all-out war.[35] Tierra Blanco, a hawkish Mouache chief, began leading Mouaches and allied Jicarilla Apaches on stock raids near Taos, along the upper Red River, and in the San Luis Valley. Alarmed noncombatant Capote and Jicarilla bands withdrew into the La Plata Mountains, hoping to disassociate from the aggressive Mouaches.[36]

When some Jicarilla and (probably) Mouache allies stole cattle from a Fort Union beef contractor, the army retaliated. A punitive expedition "cut up" the war party and killed Lobo Blanco, a prominent and hostile Jicarilla chief. In response, Jicarilla warriors lured troops from Cantonment Burgwin (south of Taos) into a murderous ambush.[37] General John Garland, now in command of the Military Department of New Mexico, angrily dispatched troops on a major retaliatory campaign against the Jicarilla with orders to "give them neither rest or quarter until they are humbled to dust."[38]

Augmented by Pueblo, Mexican, and American auxiliaries (including Kit Carson as scout), the troops doggedly tracked the Jicarilla and their Mouache allies until they finally turned to defend themselves. The battle was brief; the Indians scattered and troops seized or destroyed their equipment, food, and horses, while many fleeing women and children died during a major blizzard following the battle.[39] Still the troops kept them on the run and starving until they were "most thoroughly humbled." Though small-scale raiding by hungry Indians continued through the summer, by fall the defeated Jicarillas and Mouaches negotiated separate peace treaties.[40]

In October 1854 Chico Velasquez, Tierra Blanco, and Tamouche parlayed with David Meriwether at Abiquiú. Among the gifts distributed were a number of decorated blanket coats or *capotes*; by the time the Utes returned to the mountains, smallpox had broken out among them. Every man who received a blanket died in agony or grew desperately ill and was scarred for life. The Utes blamed the American superintendent, believing he had deliberately introduced the disease among them.[41]

The furious Mouaches turned on the Americans, again. Chico Velasquez had succumbed to the pox, and with his death the more aggressive Tierra

Blanco assumed leadership. Confrontations increased in the San Luis Valley and along the Arkansas. Then on Christmas Day in 1854, Blanco—horribly disfigured by smallpox scars—led Mouache raiders in a series of attacks against isolated posts along the Arkansas and its tributaries, then they forced their way into Fort Pueblo. There the Utes killed all fourteen men, took a few captives, and drove off two hundred horses. As they swept back into the Sangre de Cristo range, they killed more non-Indians and non-Utes along their way and stole another one thousand sheep. Over the next months the Mouaches continued their campaign to expel settlers on the upper Arkansas, and by the summer of 1855 the area was clear of all but two Americans and a few employees.[42]

The U.S. military retaliated with five companies of regulars and volunteers led by Colonel Thomas T. Fauntleroy (Fort Union commander) and Lieutenant Colonel Ceran St. Vrain, former trapper, trader, and now head of the New Mexico Volunteers. An angry General Garland railed against "the peace establishment" that advised war be pursued only against the hostile faction of Indians and urged Fauntleroy to wage war against "the whole of [the] nation."[43] Kit Carson agreed the Utes needed to be chastised and recommended the expedition be augmented by a local, less-forgiving citizen militia. The Utes, he argued, acted as if they were "master of the country," and the region would remain "in its impoverished state as long as them [*sic*] mountain Indians are permitted to run at large. . . . The only remedy is [to] compel them to live in settlements, cultivate the soil, and learn to gain their maintenance independent of the general government."[44]

Over four hundred men headed north on a search-and-destroy mission in early February 1855. By mid-March and over the next several months, they engaged Blanco's Mouaches in a series of running battles through rugged mountain passes and on the Purgatoire River, as well as attacking winter camps. Dozens of Utes were killed, their supplies and equipment destroyed, and the plundered livestock recovered.[45] Militarily defeated, unable to hunt on the run, and further debilitated by Plains Indian raids, Mouache resistance was effectually halted. Kit Carson later reported that the lack of game for Indians now made subsisting by hunting nearly impossible, so the "government [had] but one alternative, either to subsist and clothe them or exterminate them." In August 1855, one thousand Capotes met with Governor Meriwether, again in Abiquiú, and signed a new treaty; by September the Mouaches had come in as well.[46]

Once again Ute leaders agreed to relinquish all land rights to the United States, adopt an agricultural lifestyle, and concede all legal and political

117

jurisdiction. They also agreed to the right of the United States to survey their reservation land and make individual land allotments if the government deemed it desirable; to exchange other land for mineral land that might be discovered on the reservation; to preserve the right-of-way for travel across the reservation; and to establish military posts if necessary. The government also reserved the right to regulate or create laws governing Indians on the reservation and demanded the right of extradition of any Indian who might make depredations on or off the reservation. In return for these concessions, the United States promised to deliver to each of the two bands goods and services equal to $66,000, spread out over a twenty-seven-year period—or about $2,500 a year per band. Among the Ute signatories were Mouache chiefs Kaniache and Tierra Blanco.[47] However, the Senate refused to ratify the treaties because some of the territory reserved for the Capote and Mouache's exclusive use included parts of the already occupied San Luis Valley.[48]

For the time being, Utes were at peace again, but their way of life had changed. While still free to "rove and ramble" freely throughout most of southcentral Colorado, traditional Ute subsistence patterns had been ruptured. Despite promises for peace (by the Utes) and support (by the government), southern bands were forced to seek alternative subsistence. Even as they became more dependent on sporadic government annuities, they still had to raid, steal, or beg to make up the difference. Over the next years agents, agencies, and the military provided intermittent annuities, employed Utes, and sanctioned profitable warfare (and plundering) as military auxiliaries or allies. Meanwhile, Ute leaders grew more powerful as their role as tribal negotiators and peacekeepers solidified.

Still, in spite of signing agreements to become sedentary agriculturalists (to them a feminine occupation), most Utes remained firmly committed to the freedom of their masculine—if reduced—nomadism. As long as the government did not need to enforce their restriction, Utes remained free.

Then in the summer of 1858, gold was discovered in Colorado.

THE GOLDEN DREAM

Gold had been discovered in Ute country as early as 1806 when James Purcell, a member of Zebulon Pike's expedition, picked up a few small pieces in South Park. However, nothing came of this initial discovery. Forty-four years later, Lewis Ralston, an educated and experienced Cherokee prospector on his way to the California gold fields, found a small amount of gold dust in rivers east of

7.2. "Pike's Peak or Bust": The Colorado Gold Rush 1859 (Denver Public Library, Western History Collection, O. William, X-21803)

the Rockies. Then, during an 1857 military campaign against the Cheyenne, Fall Leaf, a Delaware scout, picked up a few small nuggets. The following year both Ralston and Fall Leaf guided separate parties of mixed-blood Cherokees and American prospectors back to the Front Range, which was then the far western edge of Kansas Territory. Placer deposits on Cherry and Ralston Creeks yielded minimal returns, but they were enough to whet the appetite of hopeful prospectors, suggest rich lodes deeper in the mountains, and fuel exaggerated rumors of vast deposits of gold already found. And as in California, the gold rush became a product of clever journalistic promotion by land speculators and suppliers who stood to profit from the sale of land, supplies, equipment, and newspapers.[49]

Samples of gold dust were displayed in stores, and newspapers proclaimed that there was "Gold in Kansas!!!"; that the area was "The New Eldorado!!" and a "second California"; and that "gold is found everywhere you stick your shovel." Towns along the Missouri River competed to outfit the prospectors who streamed westward in the spring, and land speculators developed more than a half dozen roistering new settlements along the front face of the Rockies by the fall of 1858. Facing each other across Cherry Creek, the rival cities of Auraria (gold) and Denver (named for the Kansas governor) became the most prominent.[50]

Over one hundred thousand prospectors trekked toward the purported gold fields, many with slogans such as "Pike's Peak or Bust" painted on wagon covers. Some fifty thousand completed the journey only to find the rumored wealth in gold to be only that: rumors. Half returned home disgusted and embittered at the "Pike's Peak Humbug." Others threatened to lynch the promoters of the "Pike's Peak hoax," including newsmen such as W. N. Byers, founder of the *Rocky Mountain News* and active Denver land speculator.[51]

But tens of thousands remained, reasoning that the gold dust found in the creeks must have a rich source in the mountains. When significant amounts of gold *were* discovered in the mountains west of Denver in 1859, the towns emptied and prospectors poured into the mountains from South Pass to the headwaters of the Rio Grande.[52] Prospectors overran the southern and eastern boundaries of Ute homelands as well as the passes they used to access the Plains. Numerous mining camps sprang up near Pike's Peak and old Fort Pueblo, and prospectors ventured deeper into the haunts of the Mouaches, then those of the Capotes and Tabeguaches. They squatted in Middle Park, a favorite Tabeguache hunting ground and location of several sacred medicinal springs.[53] They even camped as far west as the Durango-Dolores region. Conflict was inevitable.

Making matters worse, stepped-up military actions against the Navajos in New Mexico in 1858–1859 pushed Chief Cayetano's aggressive band of Navajos north to camp along the Animas River. The Navajo intrusion forced Capotes eastward, even as the Tabeguaches were shifting southward from pressure in central Utah. By 1860 Tabeguaches were in the San Luis Valley, once considered Mouache country but now occupied by nearly six thousand Euro-American and Hispanic settlers. They also ranged northeast onto the plains to hunt buffalo along the Arkansas River and camped near Cañon City.[54] The competition for resources was growing critical.

During this time national events and shifting federal policies fused to redefine American territorial boundaries and jurisdictional claims. The Civil War in particular had a resounding impact. The economic benefits of the mineral wealth in the Ute's "Shining Mountains" made the creation of a new territory not only feasible but economically advantageous to the war-torn Union; however, the United States could ill afford to spare troops for Indian wars unless Indians significantly interfered with government operations. Western Kansas brought gold and silver into Union coffers and was strategically located to counter Confederate troops from Texas, who threatened New Mexico. On February 28, 1861, Colorado Territory was formed from eastern Utah, western Kansas and Nebraska, and a portion of New Mexico Territories.[55] Requisite to the smooth operation of government, mining, farming, and ranching interests, officials needed a solution to the problem of the Utes who claimed the mineral and agriculturally rich lands in the western half of the new territory.

The first half of the 1800s had been but a prelude to the rapid dispossession of Eastern Ute bands. Until gold was discovered, these Utes had roamed freely, binding their identity to their equestrian skills and big-game hunting, raiding, and trading prowess. But increased encounters with new people, ideas, and commodities resulted in significant social, political, and cultural changes. While horses and guns had improved hunting, they had also led to overhunting and the depletion of game. Many Utes grew increasingly dependent on gifts and federal subsidies or justified hunting domestic food on the hoof as a rightful payment for lost resources. But such raids or attempts to dislodge encroaching settlements invited retribution by the newly arrived and powerful American Army of the West.

The inevitable military response, along with threats of starvation, brought Capotes and Mouaches to the negotiators' table. But cultural differences meant all parties talked past each other, and misunderstandings were perpetuated. Band leaders, increasingly identified as power-wielding chiefs, unwittingly signed legal documents that ceded away the rights of *all* Utes to their home-lands and all-natural resources therein, while placing them under the direct military and legal jurisdiction of the United States.

It was only a matter of time before the federal government enforced those treaties.

Chapter 8

Containment
Colorado, 1855–1873

After the discovery of gold in the Rockies, succeeding waves of miners, ranchers, and colonizers wanted unencumbered access to the gold- and silver-riddled Rocky Mountains and the ranching paradise of its fertile high valleys and western slopes. Politics and emerging social theories also continued to impact Ute affairs. The Civil War had serious repercussions as the military focus shifted to the East and Indian-hating militias were left unfettered in the West. The Union also needed safe access to the wealth being extracted in California and Colorado.

Both intertribal and intercultural competition for resources increased. Farmers and ranchers encroached on Ute homelands, even as raiding by Plains enemies escalated. The Utes grew more insecure, for not only was there less game, they had fewer hides to trade. They were also growing militarily weaker than their enemies, because the Plains Indians were acquiring weapons and horses from raids on the emigrant trails, while the Utes were not. Not surprisingly trails, settlements, and mining camps in the mountains became tempting targets for plunder and subsistence, while newly established agencies increased dependency with their promise of goods and subsidies. Most Utes saw these payments as a continuation of the fair-use fees they had long collected and which they felt were their due.

Meanwhile, encounters multiplied as non-Indians flooded into Ute country and Ute material culture continued to change, especially among those in multiethnic borderlands. By the 1850s Southern Utes had adopted much of the bison culture of the Plains and supplemented this with Navajo, Hispanic, and American goods. The changes were most apparent in their dress, food, dwellings, and hunting/raiding accoutrements as well as in practical and decorative goods that included cookware, weapons, clothing, blankets, jewelry, and trinkets.

The sociopolitical atmosphere was shifting as well. After the disastrous 1854 conflicts, leaders of the Mouache, Capote, and Tabeguache recognized the power of the American military and turned to diplomatic negotiations to protect their people and accommodate their changing circumstances. Increasingly, authoritative chiefs manipulated these parlays as best they could, trying to negotiate the most advantageous deals possible to compensate for lost resources, but this was difficult during a climate of land greed and active hostility toward Indians. Nevertheless, Utes were successful in cultivating military alliances and negotiating treaties that at least promised generous compensation for ceded land. But government presents came at a cost, in the form of land loss and the growing insistence that Utes abandon the hunting, gathering, and trading nomadism that defined them in favor of a sedentary agricultural ideal envisioned by assimilationists and evolutionary social Darwinists.

Treaty negotiations impacted band and tribal identities as well. American officials needed to create administrative categories into which they could pigeonhole the loosely organized Utes so that they could treat with them. This resulted in identity-altering name changes that were based not on nomadic circuits or behavior, but on agencies and roll taking. These agency-assigned band identities began to solidify after 1868 and formed the basis of today's tribal identities. At first bands remained fluid as Utes worked the agency system by identifying with multiple sources of Indian supplies while maintaining a rambling hunter-trader circuit. But after 1868, and especially after 1873, the clustered kin-clique bands began to merge into the geographically based administrative agency identities incidentally imposed on them by federal officials.

The seven major but loosely associated groups of Eastern Utes were amalgamated into three agency-administered "bands." At first these identities were simply reference categories—the Utes who appeared, collected subsidies, and were enrolled at a particular agency, for example, Los Piños, Cimarron, or Denver. But because this identification fell within traditional naming customs (by location, subsistence, chief, or cultural quirk), such identifiers were eventually accepted by the Utes themselves. And as the years passed, these clustered bands solidified as single groups, often with recognized territorial boundaries, and in opposition to others—including other Utes.

SURVIVAL THROUGH DIPLOMACY AND ALLIANCES

Traditional patterns of subsistence were shifting, and the pragmatic Utes incorporated new economic strategies to supplement their income. For a number of years Southern Ute bands added *sanctioned* raiding and warfare, especially the Mouaches, who acted as military auxiliaries to the American army. During the Navajo Wars and Civil War, Ute warriors assisted the army as guides, spies, fighters, and adjunct raiders. American officials and army officers tapped into the long-standing enmity between Utes and Navajos, and Utes profited from the plunder they took. They also helped repel an attempted Confederate invasion during the Civil War. Though initially cautious (only a few dozen warriors were recruited at first), Albert Pfeiffer later rode with as many as 500–600 Ute auxiliaries in one expedition against the Navajo. By the end of the Navajo Wars, officials estimated as many as 4,000–8,000 Utes had participated as military auxiliaries, primarily from the Mouache, Capote, and Tabeguache bands, but may have included men from Northern and western bands as well.

During the Civil War, Utes guarded herds, acted as spies and guides, fought with Union troops, and attacked, harassed, and interdicted supply trains.[1] After the Civil War they continued to fight for the Americans, this time against their old enemies on the Plains who were creating havoc on the Santa Fe Trail. They fought with Colonel Kit Carson against Comanches and Kiowas at the Battle of Adobe Walls in 1864, and against the Kiowas in 1865. Armed with government-issued weapons and ammunition, and with assurances that their families would be provided for at forts, Ute war parties made sorties against the Plains Indians at the behest of Colonel Carson and Brigadier General Calhoun.[2] But by 1870 these opportunities disappeared: the Civil War was over (bringing a flood of displaced Southerners to the West), and the Plains Indians had been defeated and relocated on distant reservations.

Another side effect of the Civil War was that the Union and Confederacy recalled most of their soldiers. With professional troops gone, attacks on trails and settlements increased. Responding to these depredations were the more brutal local or imported citizen militias. Some of the tragic results included a scorched-earth sweep of Navajo country, and their roundup and Long Walk to Fort Sumner, 1864–1865; the perpetration of the 1863 Bear River Massacre in Idaho by Patrick Connor and his California Volunteers; and the Sand Creek Massacre of peaceful Cheyenne and Arapaho by John Chivington's Colorado militia. The Utes escaped this bloody triangle of terror in part as a result of strong-fisted leadership and their recourse to diplomacy and alliances of friendship.

Ute diplomacy began even before the Civil War, when the Colorado gold rush demanded a resolution to the question of American access to the mineral-rich Rocky Mountains. In 1860 officials recommended an agency be established for the Tabeguache at Fort Garland in the San Luis Valley.[3] The Tabeguache had originally fallen under the jurisdiction of the Utah Indian agency in Great Salt Lake City, but after 1857 when they drifted south, it was more practical to place them within the Abiquiú agency. Between 1860 and 1861, jurisdiction shifted to a newly created subagency in Denver, and again to a new agency at Conejos in the San Luis Valley. The new agent, Lafayette Head, had arrived in New Mexico with the Missouri Volunteers in 1848, married into a prominent Mexican family, founded settlements in the San Luis Valley, and had become the "boss" of the upper Rio Grande. Though he was now an Indian agent as well, "his" agency remained little more than a paper promise from a financially preoccupied Washington.[4]

In the meantime, the Capote and Weeminuche bands ignored Conejos and continued to receive supplies at Abiquiú and a subagency at Tierra Amarilla. The Mouache visited the Taos agency until it was closed in 1862, and their affairs were shifted to Maxwell's Ranch on the Cimarron.[5] An additional agency was authorized at Hot Sulphur Springs, ninety miles northwest of Denver, for the northern bands living in the Uintah Basin and along the Yampa, White, and Grand (Colorado) Rivers. A few Utes made private pacts with individual ranchers as well. After the 1854 uprising, Felipe Baca, a wealthy rancher and friend of Colorow, made compacts of friendship with the Utes and Arapaho who agreed to not molest him or his herds in return for food and supplies.[6]

But waters remained roiled. Even as Mouache and Capote auxiliaries were helping the Union war effort to the south, Utes in the north were raiding on the Overland Mail Route in the north. This route generally followed the Oregon/California Trail and was a critical communications lifeline between California and the East. Stations along the trail were stocked with large herds of horses, which made them enticing targets. During the summer of 1863, Utes stole horses from Fort Halleck and the Pass Creek station, food and clothing from the Medicine Bow station, all the horses from the Cooper Creek station, and hundreds of horses from a herd near Fort Laramie.[7] Troops pursued and engaged 250 Utes in a running battle through the mountains until the Utes scattered. Sobered after twenty were killed and another forty wounded, chiefs from the northern bands traveled to Fort Bridger where they joined the Shoshone, who were still reeling from the January massacre at Bear River. They sat in council with General Patrick Connor and Utah Governor James Doty and agreed to cease depredations along the telegraph and stage lines.[8] Peace councils were also held that summer in Spanish Fork (Utah) and Conejos.

But even as northern Ute leaders negotiated peace at Fort Bridger, Fort Halleck was raided again. The Colorado Cavalry pursued Tabeguaches with orders to "punish the hostiles," but the Utes eluded the cavalry and returned to Conejos. There they complained loudly that the horses in question were "legitimate" booty taken from the Sioux with whom they were at war. The Sioux had raided the Overland Stage Company, not them; the Tabeguaches had simply captured stock from their enemies. Moreover, they argued, the soldiers had no right to interfere with their dispute with the Sioux.[9]

Despite alliances and peace parlays, the Utes were understandably unhappy with American expansion, and some began to agitate for war. That fall, northern Utes from Colorado even joined western bands in an angry council of war near Spanish Fork.[10] For their part, Coloradoans were anxious to clear all Indians out of the agricultural land east of Denver and mineral-laced mountains to the west. Creating reservations was their first attempt. The Treaty of 1849 was considered legally binding on *all* Utes since it identified its Capote signatories as "representing the Utah tribe of Indians." Officials pointed out that the Utes had already agreed to government supervision, farming, and to create reservation boundaries at a convenient time in the future—which was now. Governor John Evans, an inveterate Indian hater determined to divest Colorado of all its Indians, proposed that the Utes be relocated to the arid Four Corners near the headwaters of the San Juan where they could take up farming. A delegation went to Denver to confer with Governor Evans. However, the Tabeguache and northern Ute bands refused to relinquish their mountains, and besides, the Weeminuche and Capote already claimed the proposed area.[11]

Undeterred, officials invited a delegation of Tabeguache chiefs to travel to Washington during the summer of 1863, where they were treated to a display of the gathered military might of a nation arrayed for war. Back home the Tabeguache leaders wisely ignored a Utah war council and the rhetoric of more volatile men and assembled at Conejos to negotiate a treaty.[12]

But only a few came. The Yampa and White River bands had gone to Spanish Fork; the Weeminuche sent a terse message that they would neither consent to any reservation boundaries nor agree to farm. The Capotes ignored the negotiations entirely, and only three Mouache leaders attended. Most Mouaches were camped near Fort Union guarding military herds and refused to sign the proposed treaty. Only the Tabeguaches and a few Grand River chiefs participated and signed the 1863 treaty. But the U.S. government conveniently viewed absence not as rejection but as default, and the Tabeguaches and Grand River chiefs in attendance were allowed to represent a fictive "confederated" Ute tribe. The treaty also established the legal precedent for future negotiations.[13]

The Ute leaders at Conejos met with agent Lafayette Head (Conejos), agent Simeon Whitely (Hot Sulphur Springs), New Mexico superintendent Michael Steck (southern Utes), Colorado governor John Evans, and treaty commission secretary and special agent John Nicolay (Lincoln's private secretary). In the conspicuous presence of five hundred American soldiers, the Ute leaders signed the treaty. Among the signatories was a subordinate Tabeguache chief and interpreter named "U-ray" (Ouray), and Grand River chiefs Colorow and Nevava (or Novavetuquaret), who claimed leadership over all of the northern Ute bands.[14]

In the treaty the Utes again acknowledged the supremacy of the United States and the "right of the United States to regulate all trade and intercourse with them." This wording would answer the bitter question Ouray later posed: "If we are a conquered nation, who has conquered us?"[15] The treaty also specified a boundary around and reserved for the Tabeguache, most of their traditional hunting grounds. Government negotiators used the legal fiction that the ceded territory was also claimed by the Tabeguache (for which they would be compensated). However, most of the land the Tabeguaches ceded was territory claimed by other Ute bands and not theirs to give away. It was a practical cession, though, because it included the San Luis Valley and nearby mountains, which were already appropriated by thousands of non-Indian farmers and miners.

The Tabeguache and Grand River signatories believed they had simply agreed to define a boundary around *their* traditional hunting grounds, confirming and preserving their right to their homelands. Perhaps they assumed separate treaties would be drawn up with the absent bands later. However, the treaty specified that the Ute negotiators had "exclusive right" to the entire mountain region of western Colorado. By boycotting the Conejos council, the other bands effectively abdicated their rights and allowed the Tabeguache and Grand River leaders to inadvertently cede away their territory. The Tabeguache chiefs were also unaware that the government negotiators never viewed the reservation as anything but a temporary reserve. Officials knew that new mines would be found and more settlers would arrive, and they were already looking forward to restricting the Utes to a much smaller reservation. The treaty also included provisions that if rich mines were later discovered, Americans could enter the reservation and begin mining operations. This alone would provide sufficient excuse to negotiate new treaties later.[16]

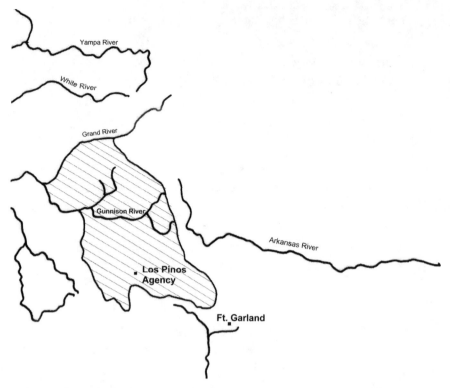

Yampa River

White River

128

Grand River

Gunnison River

Arkansas River

Los Pinos
Agency

Ft. Garland

8.1. Treaty of 1863, the "Tabeguache Treaty" (Los Piños agency added for orientation).

The Tabeguache Treaty of 1863 granted rights to the Tabeguache and affiliated Grand River bands and pledged to place the Utes on the "white man's road" to civilization, promising them an administrative agency, livestock, blacksmith, annuities, and services equivalent to up to $20,000 per year for ten years (after that, it was assumed they would be self-reliant). They would also be provided with the materials needed to cultivate the soil and raise stock—whether they wanted to farm or not.[17]

The terms of the treaty were not unlike other treaties. Notions of redeeming, civilizing, and assimilating Indians were underlying theories behind most Indian policies throughout the Colonial and National periods. Most Euro-Americans accepted the premise that civilization was dependent upon an agrarian base. Thomas Jefferson promoted the idea that the success of democracy was dependent on a nation built on yeomen farmers earning an independent living from honest toil, stating that "those who labour in the earth are the chosen people of God... whose breasts he has made his peculiar deposit for substantial and genuine virtue."[18] The theories of developing independent and virtuous people through farming infused nearly all attempts to civilize the American "savage" from the seventeenth-century Indian plantations in New England to the land allotment acts of the 1880s.[19] Kit Carson, southern Ute agent from 1854 to 1859, argued that "a man who owns his own house and fields won't go to war unless someone threatens him. Give the Indian his own land and he'll stop fighting."[20] Similarly, Utah superintendent Garland Hurt echoed biblical injunctions when he insisted that Indians must earn their bread by the "sweat of their own faces."[21]

What these idealists did not grasp was that Indians already had land, and that was precisely what they were fighting for. The real issue was not land *ownership* but land *use*.

The goal of agriculturalism was also influenced by pioneer anthropologist Louis Henry Morgan and his assimilated Seneca informant, Ely S. Parker. Parker became Ulysses S. Grant's adjutant during the Civil War, his military secretary after it, and later Commissioner of Indian Affairs. He and Morgan were the architects of Grant's Peace Policy that advocated negotiating treaties then placing Indians on reserved lands and helping them assimilate within American society. But this required abandoning nomadism and the wholesale adoption of an agricultural lifestyle. Subsequent theories of Darwinian social evolution reinforced these ideas.

In 1877 Morgan argued that all societies must move through specific evolutionary stages: from savagery, to barbarism, to civilization. Most American Indians were seen as "savage," a phase marked by hunting, gathering, and the use of simple weapons like bows and arrows. They needed to evolve to barbarism, a stage marked by basic animal domestication and agricultural lifeways, before they could move on to civilization, a state marked by writing and intellectual and technological innovations.[22] These goals were also pragmatic: sedentary Indians could be contained on restricted allocations of land, throwing the rest of their vast territories open to American settlement. Agriculture, assimilation, and restrictive reservations would be inherent in every treaty or agreement signed by the Utes.

LAND CESSIONS, DISPLACEMENT, AND CONTAINMENT

Although the 1863 Treaty was ratified by Congress, because the country was distracted by war, treaty obligations were largely ignored—except the government now laid legal claim to and took the lands Ute chiefs had ceded. Since the treaty preserved all mineral rights for the United States, any earlier protection of the reserved lands were effectively negated, for "any citizen of the United States [could] mine, without interference or molestation, in any part of the country hereby reserved to said Indians where gold or other metals or minerals may be found."[23]

Kingmakers and Principal Chiefs: The Rise of Ouray

Initially, little changed as a result of the unfulfilled and unenforced Treaty of 1863, or "Kit Carson's Treaty for San Luis Valley." The Utes continued to visit their old agencies, there was no attempt at farming, and they continued to occupy and hunt in their traditional lands. However, they did begin to rely more on subsidies and gifts from settlers and agents. When a disastrous early snowstorm in 1863 prevented the Tabeguaches from making their annual fall expedition to hunt on the plains, starving Utes congregated near Colorado Springs and begged for food. The old Conejos agency finally sent supplies, and local settlers grudgingly relinquished some of their own provisions so the Utes could return to their winter camps.[24]

Among the leaders to sign the 1863 Treaty was a minor leader named Ouray. He had acted as interpreter, translating from Ute to Spanish, even as other interpreters translated the Spanish into English. More importantly, he had been instrumental in convincing many of the chiefs to attend the council. As a result, American officials began to view Ouray as an excellent ally. As Ouray's influence as a committed peace negotiator increased over the next decade, the kingmakers in Washington anointed him head chief of all the Colorado Utes and authorized him to speak on their behalf. Ironically, although Ouray considered himself Tabeguache, he was only half Ute by both blood and culture.

Ouray's precise parentage remains unclear and continues to be argued by scholars, but most contemporary accounts suggest he was the son of a Jicarilla Apache, Guera Murah, and a Tabeguache mother. He was born during the summer of 1833, the year an unusually spectacular Leonid meteor shower lit up the skies. His parents often camped near Abiquiú or in the Taos and San Luis Valleys, territory frequented by the Capote, Mouache, and Jicarilla. At some point Ouray, his sister Susan, and his brother Quenche became unfree servants of wealthy Taos families, either jobbed out or sold. There Ouray spent his youth where he was christened Catholic, tutored by Franciscans, herded sheep, and learned Spanish, some English, and Plains sign language. By the time Ouray rejoined the Utes in about 1850, Spanish was his first language. He not only spoke it fluently but later admitted he continued to think in it as well.[25]

8.1. Ouray, 1868; Ouray quickly rose to prominence in Colorado (Scan #20101020, History Colorado)

In 1846 the teenaged Ouray witnessed the military might of the United States when General Stephen Kearny and his army marched into New Mexico during the Mexican-American War, and again when Kearny brutally quelled the Taos Revolt. A few years later eighteen-year-old Ouray abandoned (or escaped) the Mexican settlements to join the Tabeguaches where he solidified his place by marrying into a prominent family. When his wife died several years later, he married her adopted younger sister, a Ute-acculturated Kiowa captive named Chipeta.[26]

Though a man of few close friends, Ouray won respect as a skilled hunter, fierce warrior, and hot-tempered man who enjoyed a good fight. Despite family ties to the Tabeguaches, by the 1860s he had allied himself to the powerful northern Ute chief Nevava.[27] Stories claim he killed at Nevava's behest in order to enforce discipline, thus gaining a reputation as a dangerous man who never hesitated to kill when necessary. Few were willing to cross him.[28]

In spite of this reputation, Ouray uniformly struggled for a negotiated peace between the Utes and Americans. He was acquainted with three cultures, had the ability to think in non-Ute ways, and possessed the linguistic skills to negotiate directly with his American and Ute adversaries. He was an arrogant, often self-serving loner, but under his iron-fisted leadership the Utes in Colorado escaped the disaster of an Indian uprising against the United States until the relatively late date of 1879, and so avoided the devastating retaliation that inevitably followed such uprisings. Utes and non-Indian historians continue to debate whether this was because Ouray was a visionary, a realist, or a traitor.

From an early period, Ouray demonstrated his diplomacy and willingness to make peace under any circumstance. In addition to a long-time friendship with Kit Carson, he had also seen firsthand the futility of opposing the military might of the United States.[29] He refused to join proposed hostilities against Euro-Americans, sometimes thwarted plans to attack settlements, and took rebellious Utes prisoner, either remanding them into American custody or harming them outright. His actions left a string of seething enemies but illustrate Ouray's determination to police "his" people and demonstrate his loyalty to Washington. Sidney Jocknick, a cowboy at the Los Piños and Uncompahgre agencies, praised Ouray, calling him a "shining light" and attributing the agency workers' safety solely to his influence. Ouray's actions also guaranteed that federal largesse would continue and that open warfare would not break out.[30]

Secretary of the Interior Carl Schurz claimed Ouray had "pondered much" about the condition of the Indian and the question of their future:

> [Ouray] spoke like a man of a high order of intelligence and of larger views who had risen above the prejudices and aversions of his race....He comprehended perfectly the utter hopelessness of the struggle of the Indians against the progress of civilization. He saw clearly that nothing was left to them but to accommodate themselves to civilized ways or

perish. He admitted that it was very hard to make his people understand this; that so long as they did not fully appreciate it, they should…be kept out of harm's way; that it was the duty of influential chiefs to cooperate with the Government to make the transition as little dangerous and painful as possible.[31]

In a more colloquial tone, one colorful journalist wrote,

> These Southern Utes ain't going to make trouble….Ouray'll keep 'em quiet….He told Chief Ignacio and the rest of 'em straight out, "my beloved brethren, it's no use your kicking; the white man has a gun for every tree….He'll hold 'em down right enough, whatever old thing the Governor wants out of 'em.[32]

Ouray exemplified the changing roles of increasingly authoritative chiefs while still working within the traditional framework of leadership. To protect his people from external threats and assure their subsistence, he made the best economic and political deals he thought possible through diplomatic dealmaking. Although these deals included repeated concessions, he fought for favorable terms and used his oratorical skills to convince others of their inevitability. But non-Tabeguaches resented his assumption of power and his influence with the Americans; however, with the formidable federal government behind him, and by using his skills, knowledge, and oratorical ability, Ouray developed significant—if grudging—influence among most of the Colorado bands.

Without a doubt Ouray was a tool the U.S. government used to manage Eastern Utes. Officials lumped together the disparate and fluid Ute bands within the (wishful) rubric of a confederated Ute tribe, and then they appointed the eloquent and iron-handed Ouray as its principal chief. The United States needed to negotiate with the Utes through an established set of leaders, but for the most part ignored the complexities of Ute leadership or band affiliations. There was little the Utes could do about American officials who preferred to work with compliant rather than obdurate leaders.

Warfare, Manipulation, and Negotiations

Despite continually reneging on treaties, Washington was still less close-fisted with Utes in Colorado than Utes in Utah. Although the compensations promised in 1863 never materialized, subsequent treaty obligations were more or less fulfilled. Agencies were built and manned, and cattle, annuities, and monies were distributed on a semiregular basis.[33] Of course this was pragmatically political: gold- and silver-rich Colorado was a desirable and cooperative territory, while Utah was perceived as cantankerous and obstructionist. The power struggle between Mormons and federal officials generated bitter animosities, made worse when Mormons leaders advised their people to stay aloof from the Civil War. Thus, Utah remained a financial drain on national coffers while offering little in return during this national crisis. Worse, officials believed Mormons and Indians were allies against the federal government's authority. Rumors circulated that Mormons were trying to tamper with Colorado's Utes as well. As early as the 1857 Utah War, for example, Kit Carson delivered extra supplies to Colorado Utes to keep them from joining the Mormons.[34]

Colorado, in contrast, poured a glittering stream of wealth into the national treasury. In return for peaceful access to their lands, the Utes received a relatively stable supply of goods. "Buy their good will," wrote Special Agent John Nicolay in 1863. "The expense of such a system will in a given number of years be found to be less by far than the expense of active military campaigns against them, which its neglect may render necessary."[35] American officials, too, recognized that it was cheaper to "feed the Indian than to fight him." Even so, as more mineral deposits were discovered and Coloradoans pressed for more land, state officials searched for an excuse to divest themselves of the Utes entirely.

Particularly anxious to rid his territory of all Indians, Governor Evans sought to provoke their removal. There was little he could do about Utes who had signed the 1863 treaty. However, negotiations with the Cheyenne and Arapaho failed. Spring raids in 1864 triggered punitive expeditions by local militias, mostly made up of the dregs of Denver saloons who were eager to harass Indians. The militias conducted indiscriminate Indian-killing forays, provoking equally bloody retaliation. The terrifying summer of 1864 culminated in November with a dawn attack on a peaceful Cheyenne village camped along Sand Creek.[36] The national outcry against Colorado for this dubious "victory" was loud and immediate. But the war had achieved its purpose, and the plains tribes were forced to relocate outside Colorado's borders.

Meanwhile, an only slightly subdued Colorado citizenry wanted to rid itself of its Utes, as well. The Treaty of 1863 was unsatisfactory because it failed to restrict Utes or safely open more mineral lands. In 1865 new deposits of gold, silver, and coal were discovered in southwestern Colorado. Miners poured in and the inevitable clashes occurred. The Tabeguaches pulled back to the

134

Uncompahgre and Grand Rivers but continued to make occasional nipping forays against miners, while the Mouaches and Capotes made increasing demands for supplies from the government and loitered near agency settlements where illicit alcohol was too easily obtained. Overworked agents mediated disputes and struggled unsuccessfully to induce their charges to remain near agencies and away from non-Indian settlements.[37]

The presence of miners within reservation boundaries was an ongoing invitation for trouble, so officials sought to renegotiate the 1863 treaty in hopes of removing Utes from the Front Range completely. Ouray relayed the invitations, but Nevava refused to attend; he believed the mountains belonged to the Utes, and they could hold them by holding the passes. Thus, Ouray effectively usurped Nevava's position by approving the council and appointing himself chief spokesperson.

A preliminary council, convened in 1866 in the San Luis Valley, accomplished nothing. However, officials also met with Yampa River and Uintah Utes to negotiate a temporary treaty of "amity & friendship" in order to guarantee unmolested road building through their country. Nevava reasserted his position by signing this agreement—but it was never ratified.[38] The Utes were not interested in making further cessions, despite the increasing pressure.

The peace councils, treaties, and attempts to establish reservations in 1863 had been but an initial attempt to settle Indian affairs that had been neglected during the Civil War. Once the war was over, the country turned its attention back to the pressing needs of western expansion. In 1865 Congress authorized a committee to investigate the condition of Indian tribes in the West, but most observers already knew Indian populations were declining because of disease, starvation, wars, loss of hunting grounds, and diminishing game. And who should administer Indian services? Fraud and ineptitude were found among agency employees and military officers alike.[39] Many believed that without reforms, and unless "civilized," Indians would inevitably become extinct.

The Doolittle Report, published in 1867, concluded that the only way to end the Indian wars and establish peace was for the Indians to give up their nomadic lifestyle, accept limited reservations protected from non-Indian encroachment, and learn to "walk the white man's road and become fully acculturated into the white-man's world." Five years later the commissioner of Indian Affairs argued that the government needed to buy off

the hostility of the savages...exasperated as they are...by the invasion of their hunting grounds and the threatened extinction of game.... [When] the last hostile tribe becomes reduced to the condition of suppliants for charity... [this would be] the only hope of salvation for the aborigines... They must yield or perish.... [Placing the Indian] in a condition of complete dependence and submission... is the true permanent Indian policy of the Government.

The Doolittle Commission did recognize that the United States had taken Indian lands, and it argued that a national morality required the government to

provide some substitute for the means of subsistence which it has destroyed... not by systematic gratuities... but by direct[ing] these people to new pursuits which shall be consistent with the progress of civilization... helping them over the first rough places on 'the white man's road.'[40]

As a result of the Doolittle Report, Congress authorized a Peace Commission, and delegations of treaty makers were sent west. Their task was to end Indian resistance to American expansion through the creation of restricted reservations and implementation of assimilative agricultural programs. The administration of Indian affairs was also reformed and agencies placed in the care of Christian denominations in hopes of escaping the sordid fraud that had plagued other agencies.

Treaties and Restrictions: 1868–1873

For decades political battles would rage in Washington over how to and who should administer western Indian affairs—the Department of the Interior or the Department of War. Adherents of the Peace Policy were at loggerheads with those who advocated a "Force Policy." General of the army William T. Sherman believed in "Americanization at the point of a bayonet," arguing (and practicing) the policy of exterminating hostile Indians, meaning any Indian found outside the boundaries of a reservation.[41] This definition initiated major military actions at the Washita River and the Little Bighorn, both featuring General George Armstrong Custer.

When Utes were urged to attend new treaty negotiations in 1868, it was one of many Peace Policy councils held with western Indians from 1867–1868. Not surprisingly, Ute feelings about a new treaty were mixed. Southern bands remained adamantly opposed to it, but some prominent northern chiefs favored the new offers. Unable to sway the southern bands, Ouray suggested

8.2. Treaty of 1868.

that another delegation of leaders travel to Washington for the final negotiations. Ten chiefs along with attendant officials and agents (including Kit
Carson) traveled to Washington, and on March 2, 1868, they signed the new
treaty. Among the signatories was the "principal" Ute chief, "U-re" (Ouray);
a reluctant Kaniache of the Mouaches; Piah (Nevava's nephew), and a young
White River leader who gained later infamy, Nicaagat or Captain Jack.[42]

The treaty provided for a fifteen-million-acre reservation (the western
third of Colorado) for the "absolute and undisturbed use and occupation" of
the "Confederated Utes." Excluded were the San Luis Valley, the Yampa River
Valley, and (despite Ouray's objections) Middle and North Parks, areas already
overrun by non-Indians. Two new agencies would be established: one on the
White River to replace the agency at Hot Sulphur Springs, and another on

8.2. Colorow (with late-model Maynard rifle), Nicaagat (top, far left), Piah (top, fourth from left) and others pose in Colorado Springs, 1875 (Photo incorrectly identifies Colorow as Ouray.) (Denver Public Library, Western History Collection, X-30557)

the Los Piños. The White River agency would serve northern Ute bands who ranged around the Yampa, White, and Grand Rivers. Subsequently, because their affairs were administered from the White River agency, these people were lumped together under the sobriquet of White River Utes. The southern agency on the Los Piños was supposed to serve the Tabeguaches, Mouaches, Capotes, and Weeminuches.[43] A third unofficial agency functioned in Denver until 1876, by which time the bison that had lured Ute hunters through Denver and onto the plains had been nearly exterminated.

Ute hunting bands that traveled through Denver capitalized on local markets for their bison hides. These Utes were often criticized as hang-about Indians, for in Denver they "learned only the white man's vices and none of his virtues." With a surfeit of supplies, it was claimed, they grew idle, shiftless, insolent, domineering, and greedy, and were typically drunk, demoralized, and often in the "calaboose." One close observer wrote that their downfall from a proud and independent people had been the extermination of the bison that led them to beggary and theft. Kit Carson expressed similar concerns about the Mouaches and Capotes who "hung about" the settlements.[44]

Though "civilizing" Utes was integral to the treaty, Ouray declared that he only signed with the understanding that all references to mills, farming, machinery, schools, and relocation to a reservation be struck out. The Utes refused to be confined by invisible boundaries set on a paper contract.[45] Instead, they continued to view reservations as land *reserved* to them, the boundaries defining where non-Indians could not go rather than where Utes must stay. However, the government had no intention of redlining those references, and once the signatures had been obtained, Colorado and New Mexico officials pressed to confine all Utes to the newly established reservation as quickly as possible. But they resisted relocation. Four months later, two thousand Utes and all of the leading chiefs gathered in Denver to protest—but no one would hear their complaints.[46]

Instead, officials later located the principal Ute chiefs and obtained their signatures on the ratified and amended treaty. Every band was represented, including the Tabeguache (Ouray), Grand River (Piah), Uintah (Antero), Yampa (Colorow and Nicaagat), Mouache (Kaniache and Sapowaneri), Capote (Sobata), and Weeminuche. Notably absent was the influential Weeminuche chief, Ignacio.[47]

During the spring of 1869, the resigned Tabeguaches headed for the site of their new Los Piños agency, but when they reached one of their traditional summer hunting grounds near Cochetopa Creek—at least sixty miles northeast of the recognized Los Piños River and short of the reservation boundaries—they refused to move any farther. A tributary of the Cochetopa was promptly named "Los Piños" and the agency was erected on the site.[48] New Indian agents arrived and workers began constructing houses for the agents and non-Indian employees, corrals, a schoolhouse, warehouse, mills, and a carpenter-blacksmith shop. A home was also built for Ouray.[49]

However, both the Lost Piños and White River agencies generated heated controversy. Lucrative Indian contracts had become an important boost to

8.3. Encampment at Los Piños, 1874. (L. Tom Perry Special Collections, Brigham Young University, Provo, Utah, BYU 1608 p66-b2-f2-134)

local economies. Governor Hunt was accused of graft and "finessing" away Ute contracts for the agency in Denver. Lafayette Head complained bitterly of Colorado's "sleight of hand" in moving the agency closer to Saguache and out of Conejos where he had profited handsomely from Indian contracts (and gained a reputation for selling Indian supplies and substituting spoiled goods). Instead, the Los Piños agency became a windfall for entrepreneur Otto Mears. And in New Mexico the governor called the "political kidnapping of the aborigines" an "audacious trick." Southern Utes were furious, too. Capotes and Weeminuches insisted (correctly) that the treaty referred to their Los Piños, a well-known river that flowed through Capote homelands and on which they often camped.[50]

Both agencies were also poorly located. The White River agency was situated in an unpleasantly cold canyon, so the Yampas lobbied to have it moved north to the Yampa Valley. The Los Piños agency was set high in the mountains, which was fine for summer hunting but impractical during winter, when the Tabeguaches moved to warmer campsites on the Uncompahgre.

And southern Utes utterly refused to go to an agency on the Cochupatu River, referring to the nearby "Pass of the Buffalo"; instead, they stubbornly continued to frequent the old agencies at Abiquiú and Maxwell's Ranch. Meanwhile, the Weeminuche refused to go to either agency, in part because Ignacio had killed Kaniache's brother, an important Mouache chief, and a feud was raging between the bands.[51]

And despite the treaty, prospectors continued to trespass on reservation lands. The army responded by threatening to enforce boundaries, but angry Coloradoans protested the prospect of white blood being spilt by white soldiers on behalf of Red Indians. Military protection was quietly withdrawn, and Indian agents were ordered to keep their charges on the reservation by withholding rations or dispensing them on a travel-limiting schedule.[52]

Political Ascendancy of the Tabeguache

By 1870 the southern bands were openly resentful of the Americans and their treaties; they wanted the miners gone and their homelands returned. Ignacio complained that "whites did not keep their word. They give us land and a home where we always lived. They find gold and silver and take our land from us.... They promise much but do little.... They eat the bread and give us the crust."[53]

The bad feelings were aggravated when officials ordered that supplies no longer be dispensed from Cimarrón or Abiquiú, and they informed southern Ute leaders they must get their supplies at the Los Piños agency. When the Weeminuches, Capotes, Mouaches, and associated Jicarilla Apaches refused to travel to the mountainous Los Piños agency, they were left with no government supplies. This especially rankled the Mouaches because they had been faithful military allies during two wars. New Mexico superintendent Nathaniel Pope and his agents at Abiquiú and Cimarrón warned the commissioner of Indian Affairs that the government must either

> clothe these Indians or fight them, and thus choose between the expenditure of a few thousand dollars for clothing, or of hundreds of thousands of dollars to fight them; ... for however expensive it may be to feed and clothe Indians, it is a great deal cheaper than to fight them.[54]

By this time the Capotes had grown dependent on supplies from Abiquiú and from raiding the expanding Tierra Amarilla herds. Some chiefs, like the Weeminuche Ignacio or Sobata and Chavez of the Capotes, worked to maintain relations by helping to retrieve stolen horses. Other Capotes blatantly preyed on the herds where, one agent noted, "they have got the art of stealing down to a science."[55]

Further east the Mouaches were dealt a major blow when the Maxwell Grant was sold to the Maxwell Land Grant and Railway Company. The Mouaches had always considered the million-acre grant to be Mouache and Jicarilla land on which they *allowed* Lucien Maxwell to live because of their friendship. It was a great wrong, they believed, to sell the land and withhold the proceeds from them, the rightful owners. Unsuccessful attempts were subsequently made on Maxwell's life. Mouaches began to douse their anger with illicit whiskey and watched as their enemies received plentiful supplies to placate and bribe them into peace. Some suggested darkly that "the surest way for them [Mouaches] to obtain goods was to imitate other tribes...[and] kill a large quantity of stock and about a dozen citizens, and then they would have heaps of goods very soon."[56]

Political turmoil was also increasing among northern bands. After Nevava died in 1868, northern Ute leaders jockeyed for power, among them Douglas, Johnson, Colorow, and Nicaagat. In the end, Nevava's kin-brother Douglas was accepted as the principal speaker for the amalgamated White River Utes. However, ultimate political chieftainship now lay with Ouray, who was recognized by Washington as spokesperson for *all* Utes. And by now Ouray himself had begun to view other Ute leaders as little more than subordinate chiefs. Resentment smoldered against Ouray's usurpation of power.[57]

The Tabeguache also seemed to get preferential treatment; however, this was primarily because the Los Piños agency was closer to supply lines, treaty obligations were easier to fulfill, and the Tabeguaches were generally less troublesome. In contrast, the White River agency was isolated and poorly managed while resident Utes were more independent and less compliant.[58]

The Los Piños agency was ostensibly well run and well supplied, receiving over one thousand sheep and six hundred cattle. Otto Mears—the savvy, opportunistic, and shady businessman from Saguache who held the government contracts—provided a relatively steady supply of cattle and other promised goods, and he built and maintained roads to the agency.[59] Mears, who spoke Spanish and Ute, was personally acquainted with many Utes who traded in Saguache and Conejos. Because of this overt friendship, he developed mutually profitable business relations with the agency, the Indians, and Saguache merchants.[60]

But graft, fraud, and occasional mix-ups sometimes left the agency short of rations, and the stock was of poor quality. Ouray refused most of the first shipment because the cattle were the "poorest, scrubbiest and ordinariest Texas cattle that ever passed through the territory"—despite treaty stipulations that they be supplied with only "gentle American cow[s]" and not "Mexican or Texas breed" cattle. There were few breeding bulls, and the majority of the sheep were castrated wethers that were clearly not "suitable for... increase and propagation."[61] Still, everyone profited to some extent: the Tabeguaches received relatively stable supplies, suppliers made profits, and Coloradoans could continue mining in relative peace.

But unrest was brewing. During the mid-1860s Black Hawk had attempted to recruit Colorado Utes for his Utah war, and after 1870 both northern and western Ute bands participated in the recently introduced and visibly anti-white millennial Ghost Dance. Yampas left their agency during the summer of 1872, in part because of an epidemic of respiratory diseases from which dozens died, and attended an 1872 Ghost Dance in Sanpete Valley.[62]

Poor management and a high agent turnover at both agencies also exacerbated conditions. In 1871, for example, the Unitarian Church appointed an ascetic, well-educated, but tight-fisted agent named Jabez "Neversink" Trask to administer the Los Piños agency.[63] Trask and the Tabeguaches took an instant dislike to each other. In his "indiscreet haste to civilize and Christianize the Utes all in a day," Trask alienated everyone. Utes considered him eccentric while citizens of Saguache thought him crazy. Ouray complained that Trask "shut himself up in his house, refused to issue rations to their squaws and children when they were starving, and treated them like dogs." A new agent was appointed. The Utes lobbied for Albert Pfeiffer, a well-liked New Mexican subagent and former military officer with whom they had served in the Navajo War; instead they got "General" Charles Adams, a former militia commander and relative of Governor McCook, though a good administrator.[64]

A series of inept agents also served at the White River agency, which quickly fell into disrepair. By 1871 the mill had burned, buildings were dilapidated, lumber for fencing was scarce, plows were nonexistent, and Indian livestock (1,600 horses and several hundred head of sheep and cows) overran available agricultural land. The cattle delivered in 1871 were a mixture of domestic stock and scrubby Texas longhorns. Because of the excessive cold, alkaline soil, and scarcity of game, Ute leaders again petitioned to have the agency moved, but officials again refused.[65]

Other Utes simply refused to go to their respective agencies, preferring to camp near Denver. These Denver or Plains Utes—led by northern chiefs like Colorow and Piah or southern chiefs like Kaniache and Curecanti—declared

143

144

8.4. Kaniache, Mouache chief and enemy of Ouray, c. 1873 (Denver Public Library, Western History Collection, A. Zeese & Co., X-30715)

that if government goods were not forthcoming, they would simply "roam where they pleased, hunt where they happened to find game, beg in the towns, and steal from ranchmen."[66]

UNPROFITABLE SERVANTS: AGREEMENTS AND DEALMAKING, 1873

As prospectors continued to encroach on reserved land, the Tabeguaches grew increasingly annoyed. They and their agents refused permission to those who asked to enter and warned trespassers to leave; still, prospectors continued to trek into the San Juan Mountains. When the Little Giant Lode was discovered in 1871 (near today's Silverton), a new wave of prospectors flooded in. The Utes complained of "frequent intrusions" and the utter failure of the government to protect their claims, and the Capotes threatened to drive the miners out by force.[67]

At the same time, Coloradoans demanded the vast Ute reserve be reduced and the country legally opened to prospectors. In January 1872 Edward McCook—a one-time Tabeguache agency employee and now governor of Colorado Territory—argued that the Ute "savages" had too much land. Their reservation included great mineral wealth and some of the most productive farmland in the territory. The Utes, he insisted, should either cede the land or be expelled from the territory entirely. The territorial legislature promptly solicited President Ulysses Grant to renegotiate the Ute treaty, again contending the Indians were "unprofitable servants"—some five thousand Utes roamed freely on almost 15 million acres, which they neither worked nor allowed others to work. That was 3,000–4,000 acres of free land for every "aboriginal vagrant," while American citizens were entitled to only 160 acres—and they had to either pay or work for it.[68]

In April, Washington authorized a renegotiation of the 1868 treaty, claiming the Ute reservation was "much larger than is necessary for the number of Indians located within its limits" and because "valuable gold and silver mines have been . . . discovered in the southern part of it, the discoveries being followed by the inevitable prospecting parties and miners."[69] In July, Charles Adams and Otto Mears accompanied a delegation of Utes to meet with Governor McCook and Denver agent James B. Thompson to arrange for the renegotiation.[70] However, it was not a treaty the officials sought this time, but an agreement. An 1870 Supreme Court decision found that "no Indian nation or tribe within the territory of the United States shall be acknowledged or recognized as an independent nation, tribe, or power with whom the United States may contract by treaty." Thus, the court denied tribal sovereignty of Indian nations and distinguished between making treaties with independent foreign nations and making agreements with dependent Indian tribes. Congress subsequently passed an act prohibiting future treaties with Indian tribes, and after March 1872 tribes were to be considered dependents of the United States and subject to all of its laws and executive orders.[71]

In late August of 1872, nearly fifteen hundred Utes with their respective agents and interpreters assembled at the Los Piños agency to negotiate a new agreement. Mouache, Capote, White River, and even a few Jicarilla Apache

8.5. Ute delegation in Washington to sign Brunot Agreement, 1874. L to R, back row: Washington, Johnson, Nicaagat, John and (?); middle row: U. M. Curtis (interpreter), J. B. Thompson (Denver), Charles Adams (Los Piños), Otto Mears; first row, Guerro, Chipeta, Ouray, Piah. (Denver Public Library, Western History Collection, X-19251)

leaders attended. American officials included agent W. F. M. Arny and inter-preter Uriah Curtis, Felix Brunot (chair of the Board of Indian Commissioners), and Governor McCook with his two brothers-in-law, agents James B. Thompson and Charles Adams. On their heels was a crowd of curious Coloradoans.[72]

But Ouray denounced the renegotiations as unjust, and he refused, on behalf of all Utes, to consider the idea. He also argued that should the Utes one day wish to farm or ranch—which was, after all, the goal of the assimilationist Indian policy—they would need the valleys. In any case, relations with non-Indians were better when there was a mountain range between them. Nevertheless, Ouray eventually—but grudgingly—agreed to compromise and allow the prospectors to mine their "heaps of gold and silver," but he was adamant against settlers in the valleys, as they frightened away game.[73]

Officials were not satisfied and sent new proposals to Ouray. They suggested the Utes voluntarily move to Indian Territory (today's Oklahoma), sell the southern portions of the reservation and keep to the north, or just give up the area already being illegally occupied by the miners. Ouray responded with a bitter tirade. While the Utes kept their end of agreements, the United States did not. They could not police their own people who trespassed on Indian land with impunity, failed to deliver rations or allowed them be stolen, provided poor-quality supplies, and delivered steers that could not breed.[74]

It was an impasse. Colorado officials were determined to negotiate a new agreement, but the Utes had given them no excuse to abrogate the existing treaty. McCook argued that it was impractical to remove the swarm of miners, and a "collision" between Utes and Americans was inevitable. Since the miners would never leave, he asserted, the Utes *must* yield. In November, officials sent another delegation of Utes to Washington, but they returned to Colorado without an agreement.[75]

Colorado officials and press stepped up the pressure on Washington to force the Utes to cede the San Juan region. The press raged against Indian claims and asserted a moral right to displace them. "The fairest portion of Colorado and some of the richest mining country is closed," cried one newspaper, and "an Indian has no more right to stand in the way of civilization and progress than a wolf or a bear." Another complained the government had no right to use U.S. bayonets to hold back civilization, "interposing in behalf of a few straight-haired vagabonds against the property rights of a brave, energetic, intelligent class of white men." To another, it was an atrocity that a "small band of dirty nomads [could] idly roam over 20,000,000 acres of hunting ground."[76]

Federal and state officials continued to woo Ouray, seeing in him the linchpin to successful negotiations. After the pragmatic Mears suggested they offer a "nice gift" to Ouray to encourage cooperation, officials proposed to formally appoint him principal chief of the so-called Confederated Ute tribe and pay him one thousand dollars a year for as long as he retained his influence and the tribe remained at peace. It was not a bribe, they explained, but a salary to compensate him for time spent at political duties rather than hunting. Ouray later added it also compensated him for his loss of dignity as the manipulated "straw boss" of his people, and it provided some insurance for his wife if he was assassinated by his increasingly numerous enemies.[77]

But Ouray continued to refuse demands to cede the San Juan district, echoing Ute sentiments when he said "the mountains with the mines we will sell, but those where the mines are not in we will not sell;... the whites can go and take the gold and come out again. We do not want them to build houses there."[78]

The next ploy was to offer to locate Ouray's long-lost son. Years earlier Ouray's only child, six-year-old Paron ("Apple"), had been stolen by a Sioux (or Kiowa) raiding party. During a secret meeting with Brunot, Ouray finally agreed that if they located his son, he would "do what I can for the Government in regard to our lands."[79] Eventually, Brunot found the son—he had been traded to the Arapaho and raised by Chief Friday. But he had also become, heart and soul, Arapaho. Despite a striking resemblance between Ouray and "Ute Friday," the young man denied that Ouray was his father, and the dismayed Ouray refused to acknowledge him as his son.[80]

But with the earlier promise that his son would be delivered, the principal chieftainship assured, and the proffered salary all but in hand, Ouray assembled the major Ute chiefs at Los Piños in the fall of 1873. He used his influence to convince the leaders to sign the new agreement. There was little else they could do, Ouray reasoned, because despite their protests, miners would continue to come. The other leaders reluctantly agreed to cede the mining country—but not the agricultural lands—and officials allowed them to continue to believe that they were ceding mineral rights only. What the agreement actually said was that except for hunting rights, the "Ute Nation" relinquished "*all* right, title, and claim and interest in" all of the ceded portions of the reservation. Within days of signing, and even before ratification, stockmen began driving cattle into the San Juan region.[81]

The agreement was ratified on April 29, 1874, and returned for final signatures. But many had developed second thoughts. Chief Ignacio—who refused to recognize any agreement made by Ouray—signed his own private agreement for farming and mining rights on a small tract near today's Hesperus. Five of the seven northern Ute chiefs refused to sign the ratified agreement, and southern Ute leaders ignored it entirely (even though they were the most heavily affected).[82] But rejection through abstention was still not recognized, and Washington simply accepted the agreement through default.

The Agreement of 1873, or Brunot Agreement, split the confederated reservation. Most of the four-million-acre San Juan country was ceded in return for a revised tribal payment equal to $25,000 per year in perpetuity, and the Utes retained their hunting rights as long as they remained at peace. But the Tabeguache lost a strip of Uncompahgre Park that contained rich soil and sacred hot mineral springs, and despite attempts to assert their rights, non-Indian squatters quickly moved in. The Mouaches, Capotes, and Weeminuches were assigned a narrow fifteen-mile-wide, 110-mile-long reservation on the

Map labels: Ft. Steel, Laramie, Ft. Sanders, Ft. Russell, Ogden, Ft. Bridger, Salt Lake City, Whiterocks Agency, Ft. Collins, Greeley, Uintah, Green R., Provo, White River Agency, Central City, Boulder, Denver, White R., Nephi, Fairview, Green R., Georgetown, Ute Reservation, Gunnison, Fillmore, Sevier R., Richfield, Canon City, Ft. Cameron, Uncompahgre Agency, Saguache, Pueblo, Colorado R., Lake City, Del Norte, Kanab, Paria R., San Juan R., Animas, Pagosa, Ft. Garland, San Juan R.

149

8.3. 1873 Agreement, the "Brunot Agreement" (ARCIA 1879).

southern border of Colorado, and by 1878 they were pressured into abandoning northern New Mexico and restricting themselves to this limited reservation.[83]

Many Utes resented Ouray for pushing through the Brunot Agreement. Animosity escalated and Ouray escaped more than half a dozen assassination attempts—including by his brother-in-law, Sapowaneri—and killed some of his attackers. He now began to use a system of informants, maintained an arsenal of at least five rifles, and eventually insisted his Mexican servant Mariano sleep armed at his bedroom door.[84]

The Civil War and the development of evolutionary social theories had dropped a heavy hand on Native Americans, and they were forced into two camps: those willing to negotiate and those who futilely resisted. Most Utes negotiated. While chiefly authority was still associated with those who most successfully directed band movements, the definition of how bands survived was changing. By the 1860s a successful leader required intercultural communication and negotiation skills as well as hunting and warfare abilities. A knowledge of the Other became more important than knowledge of natural resources or skill with weapons. Negotiated reserves and the paternalistic hand of the federal government increasingly focused native identities on the administrative agencies where supplies were available or expected, and where long-term camping intensified and solidified intraband relations.

In Colorado, the desire to exploit Ute homelands led to a wholesale invasion of Eastern Ute territory. The demand for these mineral-rich and fertile farmlands necessitated a policy of containment and land cession. A cadre of increasingly strong and culturally adept Ute leaders negotiated with American officials for the best terms possible. But by 1873 even the conciliatory Ouray had grown resentful with few illusions about federal promises.

In 1873 most Coloradoans viewed Utes as unprofitable servants on an immense expanse of valuable land that was far in excess of what they needed and could better be developed by a "superior" white race. Ironically, within a hundred years Coloradoans were clamoring to protect Colorado's wilderness from development in favor of a burgeoning and economically lucrative recreational tourism industry. By the 1970s the incomparable Ute wilderness had become a mecca for outdoor enthusiasts who wanted to curtail development and preserve their hiking, biking, trail-riding, skiing, and hunting paradise.

Chapter 9

Conflict and Removal
Utah, 1855–1879

The Mormon incursion into Western Ute territory began with the utopian dream of making the barren desert blossom as the rose—in which in their minds they succeeded—while redeeming its Native American occupants—in which they failed. Thus, despite the Western Utes' hopeful vision of profitable new trade markets or the idealistic redemptive vision of Mormon leaders, Ute–Mormon relations eventually devolved into the familiar pattern of Western conquest: usurpation, conflict, destitution, and removal.[1]

Mormon industry created an agricultural oasis along the Wasatch Front that included farms, fruit orchards, and rose gardens. But these came at the expense of the native environment and native inhabitants. New domestic plants and animals reordered native ecology and restricted grasslands; game decreased; poor land management resulted in destructive erosion, especially in canyons stripped of timber and overgrazed by cattle and sheep; dammed-up rivers destroyed fish populations by diverting water for irrigation and introducing destructive species; and most devastating of all, the introduction of unfamiliar microbes decimated vulnerable Indian populations. Hundreds died from smallpox, measles, tuberculosis, pneumonia, and other diseases.[2] At least half of all Indian children died in infancy, fewer than a quarter grew to be adults, and almost the entire adult population suffered from various sexually transmitted diseases and tuberculosis. In 1860, Sanpete County reported that "the aborigines in this part of the Territory seem to be wasting away very fast, and the band, which under Walker, their former chief, was the terror of the surrounding tribes and of Lower California and New Mexico, has dwindled down to a mere handful of warriors." Even many of the Indian children Mormons fostered succumbed to diseases.[3]

Thus, as with other native people throughout the Americas, the ecological and microbial conquest was far more devastating than any military conquest.

By 1890 disease, war, and displacement-induced starvation had reduced the Western Ute population by 70 to 90 percent.[4] And with their relocation, reduced populations, and amalgamation of autonomous bands into an administratively identified single tribe, the Western Utes not only lost their land and resources but their individual band identities as well. After 1873 they were no longer Moanunt, Sanpitch, Timpanogos, Piede, Sheberetch, or Uintah. Instead, the southern bands in Colorado continued to refer to Western Utes with the generic description, *pagwá-núu-ci* ("water-edge Utes"),[5] while federal officials knew them as "Uintah Utes," or simply "Uintahs." Within a few years, most Western Utes lived with that new amalgamated identity.

The destruction of Indian people in Utah was not deliberate, although some Mormons—like Puritans before them—believed the disease-induced decimation was the providential hand of God either clearing the land for their occupancy or punishing their enemies.[6] Instead, as non-Indian populations and settlements proliferated, Mormon leaders made significant efforts to create political alliances and build bridges to span the cultural and economic divide; many Mormons genuinely wanted to teach their nomadic Indian neighbors their own way of life. But the reality was that predatory nomads simply could not coexist with sedentary agriculturalists. Mormon leaders, like other idealistic reformers, earnestly hoped to create sturdy yeomen farmers no longer dependent on the vagaries of nature, theft, or unearned gifts. Thus, for pragmatic, political, and religious reasons, Mormons attempted to reorder Indian values and proselyte them into not just their religion, but also into a cultural worldview of individualism and a Puritan ethic of hard work, property ownership, and land development. But their efforts soon foundered, not only from the incompatibility of cultures and worldviews, but also from the prejudice, impatience, politics, frustration, fears, and sometimes blatant greed of Mormons and Indians alike.

Efforts to reorder Ute values so that Utes could integrate into an agrarian society generally failed. Most Ute men balked at the perceived emasculating work of farming and ridiculed those who did. Gender roles were important in the Ute worldview, inherent even in their language that marked specific masculine and feminine spheres. The inanimate world of plants and domestic tools such as digging sticks, pots, scrapers, and seed baskets were feminine, while the animate world of hunted game, plunder from raids, and the supernatural realm were masculine. But even if Ute men had wanted to farm, a flood of incoming emigrants took the best farmland and preempted their water rights.[7]

As resources dwindled and farming failed, Utah's Indian population grew more destitute, and intermittent conflict increased. Mormon and federal officials regarded relocation as the best solution. Some Utes, like Sowiette's band, sought refuge in the Uintah Basin early rather than risk confrontations with either settlers or hawkish Utes. But the cold, arid valley was not their first choice. Although a small mixed band of Ute-Shoshones had clustered near old Fort "Winty" since the 1830s, most western and northern Ute bands considered the basin a hunting ground and few chose to live there year round.[8] By the mid-1860s, they would have little choice.

ACCULTURATION AND INTEGRATION

Western Utes and Mormons did try to coexist for the first two decades after Mormons arrived. Missionaries were sent to preach doctrine and teach farming, and settlers were encouraged to hire Indians so they could learn new skills on the job and earn the gifts they were given, as workfare. Hundreds of Paiute and Goshute Indian children were purchased from Ute slavers or more frequently from struggling Indian relatives, then indentured and adopted into Mormon homes with the goal of acculturating them into Mormon-American society. Mormons also experimented with racial amalgamation in an early and short-lived attempt to cement tribal alliances through intermarriage. A few adopted girls married Mormon men as polygamous wives when the girls grew older.[9]

Agricultural Missions and Indian Farms

As part of their acculturation efforts, Mormon leaders and federal officials would establish several reserved Indian farms that would function between 1850–1862. Even earlier, colonizers in Utah, Sanpete, and Little Salt Lake valleys had been instructed to teach local Indians agriculture, and the southern settlements had initially been set up as religious and agricultural missions.[10] But despite Brigham Young's admonitions that Indians should be a primary concern, self-interest eventually prevailed, and these missionary settlements soon expanded into economic enterprises at the expense of neighboring Indians. Jacob Hamblin, the "buckskin apostle" who ministered most of his life to various Indian groups, was forced to relocate his family after he invoked his neighbors' ire by criticizing them for appropriating all available water and leaving Paiute fields to wither.[11]

The first Indian farm was set up in 1851 with federal assistance and local labor near a traditional campsite in the fertile bottomlands of the Spanish Fork River. Two years later, farms were established for Utes on Twelve Mile Creek south of Manti and for Pahvants at Corn Creek south of Fillmore. Another small farm was later established in Thistle Valley near today's Indianola. Even Sowiette (unsuccessfully) requested a farm in the Uintah Basin. Goshute and Shoshone survivors of the Bear River Massacre also attempted farms. Church leaders commissioned missionaries to help run them (for which they were paid by the government), and under their experienced hands, the farms at first flourished.[12]

However, it soon became obvious that the agricultural experiments would not succeed except through the direct labor of Mormon missionaries, local Mormon farmers, or government employees. Most Utes considered the farms a supplement to their nomadic hunting and foraging circuit. While some Utes were willing to help with work seasonally, they were frequently absent. But the farms were also fated for failure due to mismanagement, politics, greed for valuable Ute land, and a growing desire to relocate and isolate "the bothersome Utes." Crops were sold to pay debts instead of providing food, and on one occasion troops from Camp Floyd scavenged and destroyed what few crops had been raised on the Spanish Fork farm.[13]

Political conflict also interfered. In 1857 non-Mormon territorial officials accused Mormons of fomenting insurrection, and President James Buchanan inadvisably dispatched troops to quell a supposed Mormon rebellion. As Colonel Albert Sidney Johnston and his Utah Expedition neared Utah Territory, local Mormons worried that the non-Mormon agent at the Spanish Fork farm would incite the Utes to rise up against them. So a large contingent of Spanish Fork militia marched on the farm and its agent, Garland Hurt, fled to Johnston with exaggerated tales of Mormon misdeeds. The farm was left in disarray.[14] By spring the brouhaha had been resolved, American troops set up Camp Floyd in Goshute country east of Lehi, and a new non-Mormon governor and Indian superintendent were installed.[15]

But mismanagement continued, the farms deteriorated, and the new governor, Alfred Cumming, tried to distance himself from them. Indian men could never learn to farm, he declared, not under any circumstances. It was cheaper and more efficient to simply concentrate them on reservations and feed them. Indian superintendents past and present defended the farms, arguing that the only way to feed a man was to teach him to grow his own food, but Cumming's position prevailed.[16]

By the early 1860s the Indian farms had been abandoned and the land sold. Utes, settlers, and soldiers stripped the abandoned farms of equipment, tools, lumber, and what scanty food stores or stock remained. A few informal efforts at farming continued, but the experiment was ultimately abandoned. Despite the infusion of cash from government employment, most Mormons considered "supporting" the Indians and their farms a "burdensome tax."[17] Although Brigham Young preached otherwise, few Mormons viewed these efforts as compensating the Utes for the resources they had taken.

Mormonees and Mericats

One unexpected repercussion of Mormon attempts to work with local Indians was that federal officials viewed the friendship as an unholy alliance. Government benefits were often withheld from Indians in Utah Territory, and non-Mormon agents and military leaders seldom lost an opportunity to disengage the relationship between Indians and Mormons, even encouraging antipathy. In the process, Western Utes became unwitting pawns in a political war waged between Washington and Utah Territory.

Federal Indian agents were dispatched to Utah Territory in 1848, just as they had been to Colorado and New Mexico. At first, agents Jacob Holeman, Garland Hurt, and Henry R. Day worked under the jurisdiction of Utah's ex officio superintendent of Indian affairs, Brigham Young. But in short order relations grew strained.[18] Federal agents considered Young arrogant, high-handed, and self-serving. He was not only superintendent of Indian affairs, but territorial governor and, significantly, the president of the Mormon Church. As such, Young was firmly entrenched as the de facto theocratic dictator in the territory. Holeman complained that no one dared oppose Young, and no Mormon officer would "disobey his will."[19] Garland Hurt grumbled that he could not procure an interpreter because they were all missionaries and refused to work for him without Young's permission.[20] Officials also questioned Young's motives as superintendent of Indian affairs since, as leader of his decidedly expansionist Mormon colonizers, this was a sizable conflict of interest.

By 1851 Brigham Young had initiated his "cheaper to feed than fight" policy, and he openly acknowledged that they were indebted to the Indians for destroying their livelihood. "We are drinking their water, using their fuel and timber, and raising our food from their ground," therefore, "it is our duty to feed these poor ignorant Indians."[21] Pragmatically, he instructed his followers to "buy [the Ute's] good will . . . by a generous liberality. . . . The expense of such a system will . . . be found to be less by far than the expense of active military campaigns against them."[22] He asked his settlers to feed and clothe the Indians and turn a blind eye to the occasional stolen stock, while he stepped up agricultural and domestic-arts missionary efforts.

Yet federal agents criticized even this policy. Hurt complained that this built up expectations that could not be realized, and "instead of bettering their condition, tended rather to lull them into supineness [*sic*] and leave them in a worse condition than they were when we found them." Nevertheless, he also confessed that the policy was probably the most encouraging one for such "wild nomadic creatures...even admitting that they [were] suspectible [*sic*] of civilization."[23]

Although Mormons attempted to support the increasingly impoverished Indians, their resources were limited. Young knew that Indian affairs more appropriately belonged within the jurisdiction and financial responsibility of the federal government. Thus, as superintendent of Indian Affairs he had drawn on the financial resources of that office to "lavish" gifts on Ute and Shoshone leaders. But this also angered federal agents, because Young seldom clarified from whom the gifts came. Holeman protested that Young misused his office and federal funds to promote his personal and church agendas.[24]

These complaints only emphasized the separation between the two enemy tribes—the *Mormonees* and *Mericats*—a distinction that existed in the minds of Mormons, Indians, and government officials alike. A close-knit group, Mormons drew clear boundaries around themselves and non-Mormon "gentiles." As one traveler put it, "I was an American, in contradistinction to Mormon."[25] But federal Indian agents felt this was "prejudicial to the interests of [Americans]."[26] An 1877 court found that Mormon proselyting had "very much increased the disloyalty of the Indians...[and] their hostility" toward non-Mormons, and that Indians classified "all whites as either Mormonees or 'Merikats,' the former being called friends and the latter enemies."[27] Mormons taught that they "were a superior people to the Americans, and that the Americans were the natural enemies of Indians, while the Mormons were their friends and allies."[28]

Mormons did in fact preach this. Brigham Young told Wákara that Wákara was a "fool for fighting your best friends...everyone else would kill you."[29] And the Indians needed no help in seeing the difference between how transient *Mericats* treated them compared to the *Mormonees* who lived as their neighbors. One traveler wrote that Indians in Utah were sometimes "wantonly and cruelly shot down, like so many wild beasts, by the American emigrants to California," or they were shot at "just to see them jump."[30]

As Mormon–federal relations continued to deteriorate, some Mormons sought to cultivate their Indian-ally relationships even further, suggesting that Indians should be the "battle ax of the Lord."[31] Southern settlers were told to "obtain [the Paiute's] love and confidence, for they must learn that they have either got to help us, or the United States will kill us both."[32] By 1857 non-Mormons were accusing Mormons of instigating the Indians to hostilities "against our [American] citizens, and…exciting amongst the Indian tribes a feeling of insubordination and discontent."[33] It is not surprising that Jacob Holeman asked for stricter enforcement of the Trade and Intercourse Act that barred any but authorized government agents or appointees from treating, bargaining, or proselyting among the Indians.

Rumors circulated that every Indian depredation against non-Mormons on the Oregon and California trails were perpetrated with the support or encouragement of Mormons—or by costumed Mormons themselves.[34] Meanwhile, officials refused Young's demands for more federal funds to feed the increasingly destitute Indians. After all, they argued, it was the Mormons who were the authors of the trouble through their usurpation of Indian lands and resources.[35] As early as 1856, Garland Hurt was predicting an Indian war of desperation unless the Utes were protected from further encroachment by creating an off-limits reservation. But Washington officials were reluctant to do anything that might help the Mormons. Even after Young was replaced in 1858 as superintendent of Indian Affairs in Utah, Indian relations changed little. He remained the most influential mediator with Utah Indians, and Mormon settlements continued to expand.

The Uintah Reservation

By the early 1860s, Western Utes struggled for a means of survival. Hurt complained that "the fertile valleys along the base of the mountains, from which [the Indians] ever derived their subsistence are now usurped by the Whites, and they are left to starve or steal, or to infringe upon the Territories of other bands."[36] Though most Utes refused to take sides during the Utah War of 1857, some offered to ally with U.S. troops in driving the Mormons out. The brief conflict also provided new opportunities for Utes to raid Mormon horses and cattle. As intermittent stock raids increased, Young opened his larders more freely, hoping to regain Indian friendship.[37]

Nonetheless, violent incidents continued to fan smoldering resentments. In the fall of 1858, two drunken Utes raped a Mormon woman and her young daughter near the Spanish Fork farm. Dragoons from Camp Floyd were dispatched but trampled Indian crops before arresting one of Arapeen's sons (Pintuts, a noted friend of the Mormons), and then killed him when he tried to escape. Arapeen responded with a series of reprisal attacks and threatened to incite the Navajos to the south. Four temporary military outposts were set up, but Arapeen sued for peace and the Utes drifted back to their old farms where they were virtually imprisoned, allowed off only with permission from the superintendent.[38]

But the farms were already dying. Harvests at the Spanish Fork farm had to be sold to pay debts, or they were appropriated by Utes who had not worked on the farm.[39] The farm closed in 1860, and Mormon "sooners" began to survey and move onto the abandoned land. A series of very hard winters made things even worse. Agent Benjamin Davies reported that Utes who remained in traditional campsites near the abandoned farm were in a "state of nakedness and starvation, destitute of shelter, and dying of want," and were "sleeping in snow and sleet, with no covering but a cape of rabbit's fur and moccasins lined with cedar bark."[40]

Mormons and non-Mormons alike offered food and clothing—partly out of compassion, but also to preserve peace. When food could not be found, the Utes fell back on their traditional methods of survival: splintering into smaller food-gathering parties and, when the competition became too fierce, into raiding parties to steal what they could not beg.[41]

Officials began looking for a more isolated site to establish an Indian reservation for the five western bands along with the Yampa, White, and Grand River Utes. Governor Cumming lobbied for a reservation devoid of white settlements but near an adequately supplied agency where its Indian residents could be supported and trained in agricultural skills.[42] The "Winter Valley"—"Winty" or Uintah Basin—seemed promising, since reports indicated significant agricultural potential. As early as 1851 Brigham Young had suggested the region for Indian settlement.[43] But when it was again recommended in 1861, he hurriedly dispatched a survey party to assess its potential for Mormon expansion before giving his approval. When the Mormons found no "fertile vales, extensive meadows, and wide pasture ranges," Young's reluctance disappeared.[44]

That year, Abraham Lincoln set aside the Uintah Basin for "the Indians of Utah," officially creating the reservation by executive order (though not ratified by Congress until May 4, 1864). However, no provisions were made to survey the region, establish boundaries, or appropriate funds for an agency there.[45] The attempt to create a Utah reservation came at a bad time: the nation was fighting a civil war and Congress had few funds to spare. Although officials attempted to open an agency as early as 1862, there were no provisions, no buildings, and few Indians.[46] Not only was the area ecologically inadequate to support a large population of nomadic foragers and hunters, it had marginal agricultural potential and was isolated from even its nearest supply points hundreds of rugged miles away. Later American homesteaders also struggled to survive there. Farming didn't become sustainable or profitable until a military post brought in money and federal contracts in the mid-1880s and extensive irrigation projects brought water from the mountains.[47]

Nevertheless, in 1864 Utah got a new superintendent of Indian Affairs, Orsemus H. Irish, and he was determined to resolve Indian problems in Utah and permanently settle the tribes on reservations.[48]

Before Irish could act, the bloody Black Hawk War erupted.

CONFLICT AND RELOCATION: THE BLACK HAWK WAR

In 1865 Ute–Mormon relations disintegrated, and reciprocal atrocities ruptured the veneer of brotherly love. For several years the charismatic chief Autanquer, or Black Hawk,[49] led a highly successful insurrection and wholesale cattle rustling operation that predominantly targeted Sanpete and Sevier settlements. The war was an expression of Ute anger against Mormon expansion and an attempt to stop it. While initially successful, in the long run it became disastrous. Though most Utes were noncombatants, they were forced to flee the Mormon-occupied valleys and seek refuge in (or were relocated to) the desolate Uintah Basin. The war-induced dislocation resulted in starvation and disease, Ute populations plummeted, kin-bands survived in tatters, and band leadership was disrupted.

The Utah conflict should also be positioned within the broader context of Indian unrest in the West. After the outbreak of the Civil War in 1861, western Indians heard about or felt the heavy hand of irregular armies and local militias that replaced the professional troops who had gone east to fight. In Utah, Colonel Patrick Connor's California Volunteers set up camp just east of Great Salt Lake City at Fort Douglas, and they began patrolling the vital communication and commercial trails linking California to the Union. Starving Western Shoshones and Northern Paiutes who plundered these routes in Nevada were killed, and in January 1863 Northwestern Shoshones who had been nipping at the Oregon–California Trail were slaughtered during the Bear River Massacre.[50] In November 1864 Colonel John Chivington, who had been corresponding with Connor and may have been emulating his tactics, led his own Colorado irregulars against a camp of peaceful Cheyenne and Arapaho in the Sand Creek Massacre.[51] And in New Mexico Territory, Kit Carson led scorched-earth expeditions against the Navajos that culminated in the infamous Long Walk to a New Mexico concentration camp where hundreds more Indians died.[52]

Indian hostility grew throughout the West, including an increase in Ute and Shoshone hit-and-run raids. In April 1863, Connor's troops pursued a band of Shoshone raiders into Utah Valley and up Spanish Fork Canyon, where local Utes repulsed them. Additional troops were dispatched, but other Utes intercepted and besieged them in Pleasant Grove. Angry officers claimed that nearly 150 Mormons watched from "their house tops, barns, sheds, and haystacks, without offering the slightest assistance" as the raiders pinned the troops down, plundered their supplies, and tried to steal their horses and mules. The report even alleged that Mormons helped the Utes round up the scattered army stock.[53]

In reprisal, Colonel George S. Evans attacked a Ute camp in Spanish Fork Canyon. Local Mormons, including a former Indian farm employee and later Black Hawk confederate named Isaac Potter, tried to warn the Utes, but they were too late. The Volunteers killed at least thirty before the rest escaped up the canyon. Potter and other Mormons retrieved and buried the bodies.[54] Following this incident, some Western Utes joined White Rivers in raiding the overland mail route in Wyoming and were rumored to be inciting the northern Ute bands to go to war.[55]

Nevertheless, in July six hundred to seven hundred Western Utes met with Superintendent J. D. Doty and Colonel Connor and exchanged promises of peace. Among those present were prominent leaders including Antero, Tabby, Ankatowats, Black Hawk, and the Pahvant chief, Kanosh. Connor believed the Utes were "heartily tired of war" and would be "the last to break the peace."[56]

But the Mormonees and Mericats continued to cultivate the Utes for their own purposes, opening their storehouses to conciliate Indians while warning them of the perfidy of the other. Mormon efforts to "feed not fight" local Indians continued to be seen as a collusive alliance, a perception that was reinforced when Connor's men found a supply of Mormon grain in the Shoshone camp after the Bear River battle. Connor complained that "the Indians are congregating in large force in the vicinity of the Mormon settlements . . . with a view of depredating on the overland mail and emigrant routes, and are incited and encouraged in their hellish work by Brigham Young, by whose direction they are also supplied with food, and by his people with ammunition."[57] He also reported exaggerated rumors of triumphant war parties boasting of their exploits and exhibiting "reeking scalps" in Mormon towns. He was, he raged, "surrounded by enemies, white and red."[58]

During the fall of 1863, Black Hawk called a war council at the old Spanish Fork farm, where Western Utes were joined by northern Ute bands from Colorado. Although Uriah Curtis, the Hot Sulphur Springs agency interpreter, tried to convince "his" Utes to return to treaty negotiations at Conejos, they refused. However, Doty was successful in dissuading the Utes from waging all-out war in Utah by promising them food and supplies at the new Uintah agency. Unfortunately, these supplies were not forthcoming, and small-scale raids for food and horses persisted.[59]

By this time Western Utes had been devastated by the accumulated effects of lost resources, disease, and a series of very severe winters. Curtis, long acquainted with the Utes, was surprised when he saw "the wasted numbers of these [Western] bands," and he noted that "Chiefs, who a few years before, had led hundreds of warriors, now [did] not have as many as dozens."[60] Second-generation Ute reactionaries were now gravitating to Black Hawk, angry with the Mormon settlers who were the immediate cause of their difficulties. Black Hawk would later explain that while starvation forced the war, it was anger, frustration, and unkept promises that maintained it.[61]

Apparently oblivious to the rising tensions, several Mormons picked this inauspicious moment to propose developing cattle ranching in central Utah to the Indians. These lucrative new enterprises were on the rise throughout the West as a demand for beef rose rapidly; in consequence, 1864 had seen a "tremendous burst of expansion" of settlement and cattle ranching from Bear Lake to southern Nevada. Brigham Young later denounced Mormon "greed for land and stock" and selfish land promoters for causing the Black Hawk War.[62]

Among these promoters were Orson Hyde, a Mormon apostle, and Elijah Barney Ward, a one-time mountain man, Shoshone kinsman, and Mormon convert. Hyde and Ward lobbied successfully for the expansion of Mormon settlements south from Sanpete, along the Sevier River, across 150 miles of prime grazing lands, and, coincidentally, through the last of the good hunting and foraging territory. During the early winter and summer of 1864, a dozen new colonies—including Salina, Richfield, Marysvale, Circleville, Panguitch, and Long Valley—were threaded along the tenuous route. Although Hyde proposed purchasing the valleys for two dozen head of cattle, Sanpitch, Sowoksoobet, and Black Hawk all laughed at the meager offer. But the offer was merely a polite overture to legitimize what was in fact taking place, for the

161

settlements were already under construction and the land "alive with stock." In the first raid of the war, the Utes netted over eighty head of cattle, and Orson Hyde would fume that the "scamps" had stolen four times his offer for the land.[63]

Before the war was over, the Mormons would pay a much higher price.

The disastrous winter of 1864–1865 brought tensions to a head. O. H. Irish had freighted his own supplies to Utah rather than purchasing them at inflated local prices. But heavy early snows delayed the shipment and kept Utes in Sanpete Valley from heading into the hills for the fall hunt. Many were trapped near Manti with neither an adequate supply of venison nor their government supplies.[64] Although the supplies eventually arrived in Spanish Fork, deep snow prevented transporting them to Manti. Instead, Irish sent money to his Sanpete subagents to purchase supplies locally.[65]

But subagents L. B. Kinney, John Lowry, Jerome Kempton, and George Bean instead lined their own pockets. (Bean later confessed to being a "little tricky" in his affairs, and "investing" government money that was not his.) This was not a new problem: it had been going on for years as both non-Mormon and Mormon agents and contractors feathered their own nests for years at the expense of agencies and Indians. On the Spanish Fork farm, F. W. Hatch had hired friends and family, sold Indian supplies, and made the Utes pay for their own goods. In Manti, Kinney was even worse. But this fraud was particularly dire during the exceptionally hard winter of 1864–1865.[66]

The Utes in Sanpete grew desperate; some starved and others succumbed to virulent winter diseases that ravaged their hunger-weakened bodies. They stole more than a dozen head of Mormon cattle for food and appeared too frequently on doorsteps begging for more. Black Hawk voiced their bitterness when he declared he would never again hold a hungry child he could not feed.[67] When an epidemic of smallpox and measles ravaged a camp near Gunnison, the Utes blamed local Mormons and accused them of using witchcraft (*awu puwá*) to inflict the ghastly illness and death on them.[68]

By February 1865, agent Lowry heard rumors that the Utes intended to raid settlement herds when the passes through Salina Canyon (the old Spanish Trail route) were free of snow, but he dismissed it as "big talk." But when Utes slaughtered his prize breeding bull, he promoted a peace parlay to end depredations. Ute leaders assembled in Manti on Sunday, April 9, 1865. Sowoksoobet and Toquana (son and representative of the aging Sowiette) clearly wanted peace, while others were clearly hostile, including a sullen Black Hawk and "Jake Arapeen" (Yenewood), a son of Arapeen.[69] Only a week earlier Black

Hawk had been involved in an altercation at the old Spanish Fork farm during which his face had been kicked "to a pulp."[70] Black Hawk was reputed to be a born fighter with an "impulsive and unforgiving spirit."

Jake Arapeen listed Mormon injustices and angrily accused Lowry and Kempton of stealing Ute supplies, which they had. The purportedly drunk Lowry responded, and despite efforts by Sowoksoobet and Toquana to calm the situation, the confrontation became physical. The Utes withdrew, with Jake and Black Hawk shouting dire threats. Within hours all valley Utes were prudently heading for the hills.[71] The Black Hawk War had begun.[72]

It was, ironically, the same day Robert E. Lee surrendered at Appomattox, effectively ending the Civil War.

To some extent Utah's Indian uprising was probably part of the widespread hostilities that exploded in the wake of the Sand Creek and Bear River Massacres. But the Utes had their own grievances, along with the avarice of white collaborators who urged them to steal the cattle they both profited from, and the tacit permission they received from the American military (i.e., Connors) to help themselves to Mormon property without fear of government reprisals. While it began as a war bred of anger, it was driven by desperation. But it also became an opportunity to profit from the antipathy between Mormonees and Mericats, as well as from the growing demand for beef and horses in expanding markets.[73] The war grew brutal as the Mormon dream of a utopian interracial brotherhood disintegrated in an escalating cycle of bloody attacks, vicious reprisals, and reciprocal atrocities.

While it is tempting to suggest the Black Hawk War was an example of a pan-Indian uprising, it never became a united native rebellion. Black Hawk did attempt to recruit fighters from all Ute bands, as well as among the Paiutes, Shoshones, and Navajos, and officials believed his band was augmented by warriors from several Indian groups. But it remained primarily a Ute uprising reinforced by occasional non-Ute adventurers or opportunists. Only a handful of Southern Utes and very few Shoshones became involved, and no more than a few hundred Ute fighters, usually fewer, rode with Black Hawk or his Sheberetch lieutenant at any time. Most of the raiders were Sheberetch (or Elk Mountain) Utes and some Timpanogos and Sanpitch Utes, while most Utes remained noncombatants, even in Utah. Southern Ute raiders knew the mobile Black Hawk, and rumor suggested he and his followers even joined in sheep raids at Tierra Amarilla on a few occasions.[74]

It is unlikely that any Tabeguaches ever joined Black Hawk since they had a long-standing superstitious dread of the region "across the river" and, according to some modern Utes, would not have willingly crossed into central Utah.[75] Attempts by Black Hawk's brother, Quibets, to recruit Navajos were also unsuccessful. However, the Ute insurgency did encourage Navajo holdouts to conduct their own raids against southern Mormon settlements and isolated ranches. And Black Hawk managed to enlist some collusive noncombatant help from Pahvants, Piedes, and Paiutes, the latter making a few small opportunistic raids. However, for the most part the Southern Paiutes preferred to ally with the Mormons, especially against their perennial enemies, the Navajos.[76]

Using the vastness of the rugged Emery County and San Rafael wilderness as refuge, and the unexplored mountains and easily defensible canyons as a base of operations, Black Hawk and his confederates swept down on central Utah settlements, routing large herds of livestock and terrifying settlers. They drove off hundreds of cattle and horses at a time, destroying animals that could not keep up and mutilating the abandoned carcasses as a warning to pursuers. The raiders did not seek out and kill settlers; however, those who got in their way were killed—sometimes brutally. At first Black Hawk's tactics were successful, and he left in his wake a population terrorized and economically crippled.[77] In addition to some seventy-five people killed, the war cost $1,500,000 in lost property and forced the abandonment of twenty-seven settlements. But the costs in the end were much higher for the Utes. The conflict precipitated and unexpectedly implemented Irish's plan to remove the Utes to their unprepared reservation. By the end of the war in 1872, the already decimated Western Ute population had dropped by half again.[78]

The war also triggered a moral disintegration among hard-hit Mormons in Sanpete and Sevier settlements, as a war-induced hysteria peeled away the veneer of religious piety, unleashed previously suppressed prejudices and hatred for Indians, and helped justify reciprocal atrocities against them. Sermons vilified the raiders as descendants of the wicked first murderer, Cain. Apostle Orson Hyde, the ranking ecclesiastical authority in Sanpete, argued that only a few Utes were actually the children of Israel as the Mormon religion taught. Rather, most were descendants of the Gadianton Robbers—an evil secret cabal in the Book of Mormon who had murdered to get gain and, like the Utes, retreated into mountain sanctuaries. By so preaching, leaders justified a war of extermination against the Utes. Despite church doctrine about the sanctity of Lamanite/Indian life, Hyde absolved the militia, promising that it was no sin to kill any member of a raiding Ute band—men, women, elderly, or children—because they were all Gadianton Robbers.[79] Within a year General

Warren Snow announced the deaths of suspected raiders by writing that he had made three new "good" Indians in the encounter.[80]

Many settlers believed that even Indians who professed friendship were merely spies for Black Hawk, and the war with the Indians was a war between a *people*, not just against a few renegade raiders. Hyde wrote Brigham Young that he intended to pursue the "murderous villains," shooting all he could not capture. Although Young immediately responded that there should be no wanton killing, especially of innocent people, evidence suggests that Hyde may have given secret and unauthorized orders to slaughter Indians of all ages. One militia member confided in his diary that he and others were ordered to attack a small camp near Manti that was suspected of harboring visiting raiders, and to kill *all* the Utes they found in camp, including elders, women, and small children.[81]

Even as Young continued to urge conciliation and defense, sending messages urging Black Hawk and his followers to negotiate peace, the war ground on with the hallmarks of modern guerilla warfare and insurgencies. Noncombatants were suspected sympathizers, either harboring raiders or acting as informants. Militias searched villages for raiders who, if found, were summarily executed. And noncombatant Utes at this time did profit from the redistribution of war spoils. But collaboration of any sort became the criteria by which Mormons determined friend from foe. Even Young wrote that "many of them...are treacherous, and, while professing friendship...are conniving with murderers to aid them in their schemes of plunder and murder." Although he urged commanders "not to injure innocent Indians," the term innocent was difficult to define. Young justified harsh measures, claiming "we cannot submit to the murder of our brethren" by raiders or their "accessories." He also argued that "if these indians [sic] who profess to be friendly will not help...treat them as Enemies."[82]

One early victim of this policy was Quibets, Black Hawk's brother. Although Quibets was nominally sympathetic to the Mormons, Spanish Fork officials arrested him and tried to force him to lead them to his brother. He escaped and joined the uprising.[83] Other Utes were also compelled to flee, threatened not only by nervous Mormons who saw an enemy in every Indian, but also by fellow Utes who suspected them as colluders. Ute insurgents, for instance, punished Mormon collaborators like Kanosh who tried to stay neutral. One of Kanosh's wives was persuaded to run away with a raider and take all his cash, most of his large wardrobe, and his extensive horse herd.[84]

Some Mormons retaliated with indiscriminate attacks against Utes and Paiutes, and a few overzealous settlers waged their own unauthorized wars of extermination, determined to shoot "until the last Indian was destroyed that could be found."[85] Militia commanders began taking hostages and demanded Black Hawk surrender. Sanpitch was especially targeted, not only because he was an influential leader, but because Mormons believed he was supplying Black Hawk with ammunition, supplies, and tactical information about "the most feasible points for stealing cattle." But taking hostages only hardened the battle lines. Native sympathizers helped hostages escape, but the fugitives, including Sanpitch, were hunted down and killed.[86]

The mistakes and brutality of nervous and poorly trained militias also fueled the conflict. These green troops sometimes responded badly under stress, as in the infamous "Squaw Fight" when captured women were shot down when they rushed guards in an attempt to escape. And in many cases the actual events remain controversial, because firsthand accounts vary. For example, descriptions of a fight near Koosharem taken from separate diary accounts by militia members relate how the tired militia was surprised to discover a hunters camp behind a hill they were resting near, and the subsequent fighting was disorganized, though ultimately disastrous for the Utes. However, oral histories passed down by Southern Paiutes and Pahvants claimed the militia attacked a sleeping camp and killed them in their blankets, or that they tried to tell the soldiers they were peaceful and carried a "treaty" paper but were shot down anyway. Both stories echo too closely the Sand Creek Massacre.[87]

Inept militias were sometimes ambushed, routed, or inadequately equipped to chase Indians long distances. And the quality of the militia further deteriorated when, in the absence of federal military help, Mormons began to hire mercenaries from northern settlements, typically footloose young rowdies, lured by the promise of money and adventure.[88]

Atrocities occurred on both sides. Settlers in Circleville arrested nearby Piedes, among whom were two Ute war messengers. That night and the next morning the settlers systematically slaughtered all but a few small children (for which Brigham Young later pronounced a curse on the settlement). Panguitch men also arrested and shot two Paiutes.[89] St. George militia pursued, arrested, and "executed" Kaibab Paiutes they believed had collaborated with Navajo raiders in attacking a Pipe Springs ranch.[90] After Ute raiders hit Scipio and killed James Ivie, Ivie's son Richard took revenge by shooting the first Indian he saw—an elderly Pahvant shaman. Although a Scipio official quickly issued an extermination order to cover the murder, Richard Ivie was tried for murder at Brigham Young's insistence. Ivie's Circleville peers acquitted him, but he was subsequently excommunicated. Young later preached there would be "eternal condemnation" for unexpiated murder, including for Indians. (One hundred years later Ivie's descendants would have his excommunication reversed, arguing the murder was a justifiable act in the heat of war.) Perhaps it is not coincidental that the hot-tempered James and Richard Ivie were both involved in triggering two early conflicts, the Provo and Walker wars.[91]

Throughout the conflagration the conflict remained personal, a war fought between one-time neighbors and friends. Black Hawk and his raiders primarily targeted Sanpete and Sevier settlements.[92] These Utes had camped near settlements, worked for Mormon farmers, and received handouts at their kitchen doors. Thus, Utes sometimes directed attacks on certain settlers, hurled taunts or insults, by name, at particular men during battles, or treated bodies differentially. During the first year of the war, some corpses were brutally mutilated while others were treated with respect.[93]

Cattle and horses were the main target, and much of the raiding was carried out as part of a wholesale rustling operation. Utes stole more than two thousand head of cattle in 1865, most driven south along the Spanish Trail to be sold in New Mexico markets, or north for emigrant outfitters on the Oregon–California trails and to military commissaries at Fort Bridger. White collaborators also aided the raiders, including former Mormons Isaac Potter and Richard James. These men were accused of riding with the enemy, and even leading some attacks. Potter was seen during a fight in Thistle Valley, and James's horse was found dead after a battle in Diamond Fork Canyon. Potter had been identified as one of several outlaw white men who promoted the Black Hawk Indian War by urging Utes to "go down to Sanpete, and gather up a large lot of the Horses and Cattle there and drive them down East" where they would meet them "and trade the Horses and Cattle to Emigrants, and get them money, Tobaco [sic], Whiskey, and Horses, that would be their own." With this money, Ute raiders armed themselves with surplus weapons available in the wake of the Civil War.[94] Brigham Young lamented that "were there no white men to purchase stolen stock, and supply the Indians with whiskey and ammunition there would be fewer Indian thieves, and scarcely any Indian difficulties."[95]

The stealing of stock and selling it to emigrants had been an ongoing dilemma, but it had not happened on this scale.[96] Exacerbating the problem were non-Indian cattle thieves, so-called White Hawks, who had also been lured into the territory. Even as the Utes rustled cattle wholesale in central Utah, White Hawk rustlers were running their own territory-wide operation.[97]

The blatant marketing of rustled cattle was possible, in part, due to antipathy between the military and the Mormons. The rabidly anti-Mormon General Connor allegedly told Black Hawk it was "all right for him…to help Kill the Mormons" and "steal Mormon animals" because "it will not be in [Connor's] province to chastise them for it." Army quartermasters turned a blind eye to Mormon brands on the beef they bought.[98]

Meanwhile, Brigham Young did his best to suppress inflammatory news about the Indian uprising for fear of bringing in more federal troops.[99] With no help from local troops, Young turned the management of the war over to local militias or hired mercenaries who were typically ill trained, inept, and at times brutal. Not until 1872 did federal troops get involved, and only after militias were deemed illegal.

At first Young attempted to manage the war through his old policy of defense and conciliation, ordering settlers to abandon small settlements, build defensive fortifications, and guard cattle heavily or sell them to buy weapons.[100] In time defenses were tightened, settlers better armed themselves, roving militias were stationed, herds were guarded or sent north for safekeeping, and a system of telegraph lines was built. As a result, stealing stock grew more difficult for the "Indian Rover" and his "Indian desperadoes." Raids became more wide-ranging and audacious, and Ute casualties mounted.[101]

Meanwhile, the hopeful superintendent Irish believed he could solve the problem of Indian raids by simply moving Utes away from white settlements. Following the first big raid in April 1865, he called for a treaty conference of all Western Ute leaders. With the Civil War over and more funds available—and with the increase in Indian hostilities to justify it—the Ute "problem" could be put off no longer. Ute leaders again met with Irish on June 6, 1865, at the old Spanish Fork Indian farm.[102]

Most of the major Western Ute chiefs attended—although Black Hawk and his insurgents were conspicuously absent. However, Ankatowats was there, as was Black Hawk's brother, Quibets. Federal and military officials were also invited, and, much to their ire, so was Brigham Young. Irish knew the Utes trusted Young, and it was Young's advice that ultimately convinced them to sign the treaty. However, Young's name would only appear on the treaty as a witness.

Thanks in part to Irish's gifts and Young's influence, the council was a success. As Irish explained, "the fact exists, however much some might prefer

9.1. Provo erected a mud wall for protection during the Black Hawk War, c. 1865 (L. Tom Perry Special Collections, Harold B. Lee Library, Brigham Young University, Provo, UAP 2, Folder 2)

it should be otherwise, that [Young] has pursued so kind and conciliatory a policy with the Indians that it has given him great influence over them." Others disagreed, and most officers refused to attend because Young had been invited. They angrily declared that "they would rather the Indians, than the Mormons, would have the land."[103]

Although Young was respected by Ute chiefs, he was foremost a colonizer and head of a rapidly growing population of Mormons. Pragmatically—and bluntly—he told the Utes,

> I am looking for your welfare. Do you see that the Mormons here are increasing? We have been and calculate to be friends all the time. If you do not sell your land to the government, they will take it, whether you are willing to sell it or not. This is the way they have done in California and Oregon. They are willing to give you something for it and we want you to have it. If you go to Uintah, they will build you houses, make you a farm, give you cows, oxen, clothing, blankets and many other things you will want.... The land does not belong to you, nor to me, nor to the Government! It belongs to the Lord. But our Father at Washington is

disposed to make you liberal presents to let the Mormons live here. We have not been able to pay you enough, although we have helped you a good deal. We have always fed you, and we have given you presents, just as much as we could, but now the great father is willing to give you more; and it won't make one particle of difference whether you say they may have the land or not, because we shall increase, and we shall occupy this valley and the next, and the next, and so on until we occupy the whole of them and we are willing you should live with us. If you will go over there and have your houses built and get your property and money, we are perfectly willing you should visit with us.... We feel to do you good and know that this treaty is just as liberal and does everything for you and your people that can be done. If it were not so, I would not ask you to sign it. But as for the land, it is the Lord's and we shall occupy it, and spread abroad until we occupy the whole of it.[104]

And the treaty *was* fair, at least compared to others drawn up at the time. However, Ute leaders did not fully understand that the treaty required full removal and relocation. Most believed it simply guaranteed the government would build and manage farms for them in the Uintah Basin, pay them annuities, and still let them hunt and gather as they always had. No one corrected this misunderstanding. Sixteen chiefs affixed their marks to the treaty, including Sowiette, Kanosh, Tabby, Sowoksoobet, Ankatowats, and—very reluctantly—Sanpitch.[105]

But the treaty was never ratified by Congress. Instead of the houses and support they expected, the Utes who dutifully removed to the Uintah Basin under Chiefs Tabby, an aging Sowiette, and Toquana found an ill-prepared agency, poor farmlands, and little money or food. Worse, the roads leading to the agency were often impassable in winter. As a result, the harsh winters would wreak havoc among Western Utes on their barren reservation.[106]

As the promises continued to be unmet, Western Utes viewed the situation as a breach of oath and act of poor faith on the part of the government and Mormons, specifically Young. In June 1866, Agent F. H. Head wrote that "the Indians...were still enraged at not having been fed during the winter, and the winter being an unusually severe one, many had nearly perished of starvation and a great part of their animals had perished.... The starvation and nakedness of the Indians [is] entirely attributable to Congress." Not mentioned by Head was the ongoing theft of Indian provisions.[107] Thus, previously noncombatant

Utes now began to prepare for combat. Even pacifist Tabby planned to lead his Uintahs in an all-out war as soon as the trails became passable.[108]

Around this time, other winter-starved Utes were making sporadic raids on Spanish Fork, Heber, and Fairview settlements, but they refused to venture into Mormon settlements to talk peace, claiming Mormons had threatened to cut their throats.[109] But Brigham Young was determined to reassert Mormon friendship, negotiate an end to hostilities, and forestall the threatened Uintah uprising. As soon as the passes allowed, he sent wagons full of supplies and a herd of seventy head of cattle to the Uintah agency. His emissaries found the Utes in an uproar that devolved into an armed standoff. Colonel William Wall faced down a gauntlet of angry men to join Tabby and Head for a peace parlay. Young's conciliatory letter was read, and need overcame scruples. Tabby accepted the proffered peace and Mormon offerings, along with Head's government supplies. That spring of 1866, agent Thomas Carter arrived with new employees. Indian and non-Indian workers cleared land, built fences, dug irrigation ditches, and planted twenty-five acres—the first real efforts toward agriculture—and the reservation returned to an uneasy peace.[110]

But that year Black Hawk was still successfully raiding, and he continued to attract followers. His brilliant raiding triumphs demonstrated his accumulation of *puwá* "medicine" power, and Black Hawk carried an aura of spiritual as well as military influence. But his spectacular luck changed after a daring raid on Scipio in June 1866. Although his men drove off over two hundred head of stock, Black Hawk was seriously wounded during their escape. When the wound failed to heal and he grew weak, and as subsequent raids failed disastrously, his followers melted away. Clearly, his *puwá* had soured, and the Mormon god was now in ascendancy.[111] The final blow hit in 1867 when Mormons arrested Black Hawk's good friend and accomplice, Isaac Potter, and he was killed while trying to escape. Ten days later Black Hawk sent word that he wanted to negotiate peace.[112]

In August Black Hawk agreed to stop his own warriors from depredating, but he could not control the Sheberetch.[113] To seal his pledge, Black Hawk asked Head to cut his hair, an action with double meaning. He had kept it long as a symbol of defiance against white ways and as a proclamation of his own Indianness. The act of cutting hair was also a traditional symbol of mourning.[114]

Black Hawk kept his promises, but the Sheberetch continued to raid under the direction of Augavorum and Tamarits (renamed Shenavegan, meaning "saved by almighty power").[115] They would not negotiate peace until August

1868, when they met with Superintendent Head in Strawberry Valley, even as Mormon leaders met with other chiefs in Ephraim, Nephi, Heber City, Coalville, and the abandoned Salina,[116] although final treaties were not signed until 1872.

But the Uintah agency remained ill prepared for an influx of more Indians. Head complained that "the Indians must be fed by the government, or by the settlers.... If not done, like their superiors in civilization, they will steal before they will starve. This leads to pursuit, recrimination, and war."[117] But the government appropriated too few funds, supplies did not always arrive, and early crops were destroyed by plagues of grasshoppers. Even Black Hawk rose from his sick bed and threatened agency employees, declaring he would "rather have his throat cut than starve to death." Minor subsistence raids continued.[118]

By 1869 Black Hawk was dying. He had grown skeletal from the ravages of his still-festering wound, syphilis, and tuberculosis. In response to ongoing threats against him and his band, and with a desire to make peace with the triumphant Mormon god, he sought Brigham Young's aid. Young ordered Mormons to not molest Black Hawk or his people and advised Black Hawk to make things right with God by seeking forgiveness from the settlements he had raided. Between July and December, the emaciated, enfeebled, but dignified chief traveled from Santaquin to St. George, at times in company with Quibets and Tamarits, and under heavy Mormon guard. He explained his actions and asked forgiveness. Most voted to accept his repentance, but some—like the Ivies—continued to consider him a black murdering devil and vehemently opposed him. Six months later, Black Hawk was dead.[119]

But his war was not. Petty, sporadic raiding continued, as did rancor between Utes, Mormons, and Mericats. Some Utes attempted to return to Sanpete and Sevier valleys, but despite Young's promise that "we are perfectly willing you should visit with us," or his attempts to censure his people's unchristian attitudes, the Utes were not welcome.[120] When Tamarits continued to raid, relations worsened, and visiting Utes fled back to the hills. Several had already been killed by Sanpete settlers, including Jake Arapeen, who was brutally murdered by a gang of young men. By the same token, Mormons—once considered Ute allies—had become *personae non gratae* on the Uintah Reservation, and even former friends who ventured there were angrily driven away.[121]

By 1867 Western Ute social and political identities were shifting rapidly. Tabby, Sowiette, and Sowiette's son, Toquana, had jockeyed for leadership over Ute émigrés in the Uintah Basin. In 1865 these three chiefs, already possessing influence in the Uintah area, had been eager to sign treaty agreements while other leaders balked. For the latter, this hesitancy came, in part, for fear of

9.2. Tabby (c. 1892) was the Uintah Band Chief who became most influential after the western Utes were forced onto the Uintah Reservation. (Denver Public Library, Western History Collection, X-30635)

losing not only their traditional land and land-based identity, but also their claim to leadership. They and their people would be subsumed in a geopolitical shift, taking them to the Uintah Basin where the three influential Ute leaders already held sway.[122]

Western Ute refugees were finding asylum in the basin, and Tabby was becoming the most prominent "talker" for not only his small Uintah band, but for all the Timpanogos, Santaquin-Goshen, Moanunts, Sanpitch, Piede, and Sheberetch remnants who joined them. Not only did other band chiefs lose influence, all bands had been fragmented and nearly decimated. The boundaries separating these shattered kin-bands, clustered on the Uintah Basin, inevitably blurred, even as the loss of their homelands shredded their land-based identities. As their common travails began to unite them, they focused on the Uintah agency for survival. New social boundaries emerged to define a new reservation and agency-dependent identity. Interband marriages created new family alliances and enhanced this conflated identity. Within a few years, except in occasional memory of a bygone era, the disparate Western Ute bands had become the amalgamated Uintah Utes.

REVITALIZATION MOVEMENTS AND FINAL REMOVAL

The Uintah Utes found that the war with the Mormons and the scant aid from a reluctant federal government had left them destitute on a barren reservation—and with nowhere else to go. Attempts to farm fared poorly, and members still roamed on and off the reservation hunting, foraging, begging, and occasionally stealing supplies. Sometimes they travelled off the reservation to collect supplies at agencies in Wyoming, White River, and Denver, even as northern Ute bands sometimes collected annuities at Uintah.[123]

Then in 1870 a hopeful new religious philosophy swept out of western Nevada—the Ghost Dance. This revitalization movement was a syncretic merging of native and Christian elements, promising that with right living, faith, prayers, and marathon dancing, Euro-Americans would disappear and Indians would return to an Indian paradise where game was abundant and their many recently deceased relatives would rejoin them.[124]

This movement appealed to many Indians because it promised a way out of their increasingly desperate conditions: a cataclysmic end to the white man's oppression and debilitating vices, and a return to an idealized pre-white world. In 1870 Uintah, Yampa, and Tabeguache Utes joined Bannocks, Shoshones, and Goshutes at a dance in Bridger Valley. The following year a dance was held on the Bear River without Utes.[125] But in 1872 thousands of Utes and other Indians attended a dance near sacred hot springs in Sanpete Valley. It would be the last major Ghost Dance in which the Utes would participate, and when an 1890 Ghost Dance revival spread across the West, few Utes had anything to do with it.

In the early 1870s Uintah Utes had grown to resent all Euro-Americans, but especially Mormon Americans. Congress never ratified the treaty Brigham Young had advised them to sign, which seemed to prove Mormon treachery. Worse, many Utes had died during the war, most from starvation and disease caused by their abrupt relocation and lack of federal support. Completing the rupture, relocation to a distant reservation had effectively placed Utes outside Mormon influence. There were no more gifts or new acts of friendship. Most

Uintahs were now convinced that their destitution was the fault of the Mormons who had fenced their lands to raise wheat and cattle without sharing the bounty of the land that was rightfully theirs. They also believed that "Brigham's Bishops" were now helping dishonest agents pilfer what Washington did send them, forcing them to raid and fight.[126]

Mormons, however, were convinced that it was the neglect and dishonesty of the gentile agency employees that was causing the problems, and that federal officials were still encouraging Indians to supply themselves with Mormon cattle so that officials could appropriate government supplies for their own use.[127] The situation was undoubtedly nuanced, but there was enough fraud from both Mormons and non-Mormons to fuel rumors.

The seething unrest culminated during the 1872 Ghost Dance summer when Western and some Eastern Utes gathered near Fountain Green, twenty-five miles north of Manti. In April, Chief Douglas led a large band of White River Utes through the Uintah Valley on their way to Sanpete. They stopped to ridicule Uintah men who were attempting to farm, "calling them squaws." They told the farmers to join them and leave the farming to white employees, because "Washington did not intend that they should work."[128]

More than two thousand Indians converged on Sanpete Valley that summer, including White Rivers, Uintahs, Capotes, Sheberetches, Weeminuches, and Navajos.[129] Negative feelings ran high against the Mormon settlers. The Uintahs were angry that the terms of their treaty had never been met and argued that since they had not been paid for the land, it had not been sold; therefore, they had as much right to the valley as the Mormons. Begging grew into demands by "despotic savages"; unscrupulous dealers arrived with liquor; and the Sheberetches accused the Mormons of sorcery and blamed them for a recent epidemic that had all but exterminated their band. The Sheberetch withdrew to their old Grass Valley rendezvous and began to raid the settlements again, killing several settlers.[130]

Mormons responded by killing Indians in return, sending falsified reports of depredations to government officials, and requesting federal military intervention in hopes that the inevitable clash would destroy the Indians once and for all. One bishop declared they would no longer listen to the pacifist counsel from Salt Lake City or Brigham Young since they did not "care a dam [*sic*] for the People of Sandpitch." He would no longer "play the squaw" but would seek peace "if he had to kill every Indian to get it."[131]

The old conflict between federal officials and Mormons only complicated matters, because each thought the convocation of Indians was a plot hatched by the other. Federal officials believed Brigham Young was assembling an Indian army to help carve out his mountain kingdom, while Mormons presumed the Indians had been sent by government agents to destroy them. The new Uintah agent, John J. Critchlow, arrived with Colonel Henry Morrow to help defuse the situation. Most Indians left, although a few small bands remained to hunt, forage, beg, and occasionally steal through the summer. By fall nearly all had left for the fall hunt.[132]

SETTLING UTAH AND SETTLING IN AT UINTAH

One of the tragic ironies of the Black Hawk War was that a battle begun to curtail Mormon expansion ultimately facilitated even more sprawl and the Western Utes' final removal. The end of hostilities in 1872 ushered in a new era of expansion in Utah. Settlers followed routes that were blazed by military expeditions chasing raiders or searching for Black Hawk's strongholds. These expeditions had also been looking for new routes and possible Colorado River crossings.[133] Even in the midst of the war, Brigham Young was making plans to settle southeast Utah in an attempt to block expanding southern Colorado cattle outfits.[134] Thus, even as the ink dried on the 1872 peace agreements, colonists prepared to move into the Utes' summer strongholds in Grass Valley, Rabbit Valley, Castle Valley, and the Paiute's Potato Valley (Escalante).[135]

Meanwhile, affairs were improving at the Uintah agency. In 1868 it was relocated from Rock Creek to a location on the Uintah River, near the old Reed trading post, and central to several trails. Though the agency had at first been ineptly managed by a series of revolving-door agents, in 1871 the stable and efficient John J. Critchlow took control. He was appalled at the agency's neglect and disrepair and wrote angrily to the superintendent of Indian Affairs:

> [I] found the employees—some of them utterly depraved and worthless—the Indians completely discouraged...roaming about discontented and hungry, having access to every place except the commissary, in which there was little, except flour, worth keeping from them....[And the] amount of tillable land and its vast products never existed on this agency, except on paper and in the fertile imagination of those who penned those reports.[136]

During the summer of 1872, Critchlow and his non-Indian staff planted and tended seventy-five acres. When the wandering Utes returned in late fall they found, for the first time, that a good harvest had been made.

Tabby led nearly two hundred Utes in farming the next summer, and with the help of agency employees harvested twelve hundred bushels that fall. In 1874 Critchlow brought his wife to the reservation, where she attempted to open a school. It failed, as did subsequent efforts to convince Ute parents to send their children to the White Man's school. But the movement to provide formalized education had begun.[137]

Though most Uintah Utes settled into their reservation, a few did not. Sowoksoobet and his small band returned to Thistle Valley, Koosharem reset-tled a small band in Grass Valley, and the Pahvants remained near Fillmore. The remnants of the once-powerful Sheberetch refused to go to Uintah, and most of the few survivors of a virulent epidemic were absorbed into the Weeminuche band, with only a few joining Uintah kinsmen.[138]

The "Uintah Valley, in the Territory of Utah," had been set apart for "the permanent settlement and exclusive occupation of such of the *different tribes of Indians of said territory* as may be induced to inhabit the same."[139] How-ever, most non-Utes refused to relocate on the same reservation as their tradi-tional enemies. This included the Paiutes, Goshutes, Northwestern Shoshones (including the so-called Weber Utes), and Cumumbahs (Shoshone-Ute mixed-bloods). Southern Paiutes told John Wesley Powell that not only were they repelled by the notion of joining so many people,

> [The Utes] had been their enemies from time immemorial; had stolen their women and children; had killed their grandfathers, their fathers, their brothers and sons and, worse than all were profoundly skilled in sorcery and that under no consideration would the Pai-Utes live with them.[140]

Powell—explorer, ethnographer, and researcher—had visited the Uintah Reservation as well as the Southern Paiutes in 1873. With the support of Presi-dent Ulysses S. Grant, Powell influenced the development and creation of new conservation and Indian policies that were subsequently implemented in the West. Like Lewis Henry Morgan, he advocated locating all Indian populations on protective reservations. Not so coincidentally, at the time of his visit to Utah and thereafter, federal pressure mounted on Critchlow to concentrate all Utah Indians on the Uintah Reservation.[141] However, Critchlow and his reservation now represented the gentile faction in Utah, and Mormons well knew it. The Presbyterian Critchlow, like other non-Mormon agents, dealt with Mormons only when forced to and preferred non-Mormon merchants and agents whenever possible. Critchlow even investigated the possibility of building a road to Bridger or Green River to bypass Salt Lake City altogether.[142]

Despite the Indian wars, Mormon Church policy still called for the redemption of the Lamanites. Relocating the majority of Utes had helped relieve Mormon settlements, but it had alienated them from Mormon influence. Now, ironically, Brigham Young used his authority to keep Indians off the reservation. Critchlow believed that

> leaders of the Mormon Church have . . . tried to keep the Indians of this Territory under their control. . . . Not only has it been exerted upon those Indians outside [the reservation], to keep them away, but on those who are located here, to induce them to leave. . . . They have baptized all they could get to submit to their rites. Kenosh and Captain Joe [Sowoksoobet] are members of the Mormon Church, as are also many, if not all, of their bands.[143]

Church leaders did in fact urge Mormon Utes to gain title to their own land and not go to the reservation. Local bishops in central Utah helped Indians buy homesteads, legitimized under the 1887 Indian Homestead Act, though it required Indians to renounce tribal membership. The church deeded land to others, including Kanosh and his 125-member Pahvant band who remained near Corn Creek. Likewise, Sowoksoobet's all-Mormon band in Thistle Valley and Koosharem's band in Grass Valley acquired deeded land with help from local bishops. With legal title to their land, only the military could chase them from their homes. And with the help of Mormon neighbors, they were generally successful. At one point Sowoksoobet's small band had as much land under cultivation in Thistle Valley as in all of the Uintah Reservation.[144]

Mormons were again accused of tampering with the Indians to keep "obnoxious" gentile settlers from entering Mormon-dominated lands.[145] On a fact-finding mission, Critchlow visited the holdout settlements and found that Mormons were attempting to keep or lure Indians off the reservation. However, he also found that Mormon-influenced Indians were faring better than their reservation counterparts. He concluded they should not be forced onto the reservation or its overburdened rolls (and supplies).[146]

On the reservation, Critchlow continued his efforts to enlarge the farms and develop the agency, and under his administration the Uintahs remained relatively peaceful. But by 1878 non-Indians were beginning to settle on Ashley Creek, just eighteen miles east of the reservation, and rumors spread that the reservation was about to be thrown open. Though these rumors were soon laid to rest, the reservation did receive an unexpected influx of new residents a year later. In 1879 White River Utes attacked federal troops, killed agency employees, and kidnapped the women. Refusing to be caught up in the affair, the Uintahs rushed to protect their agent instead.[147] In the aftermath, both the White River and Uncompahgre bands were expelled from Colorado and forcibly relocated either to the Uintah Reservation or to a new, even more barren reservation adjoining it.

It would be the beginning of a new era for these three bands.

Chapter 10

Conflict and Removal
Colorado, 1873–1881

As the Euro-American population in Colorado multiplied, they turned increasingly envious eyes on the territory to the west that had been guaranteed to the Utes. The mountains were rich with precious minerals, and the western slopes promised farmland and pastures for the growing cattle and sheep industries. Non-Indian squatters continued to encroach on reserved land, Utes registered complaints, and tensions rose. Although the Utes at the White River agency were generally "disposed to be friendly with white settlers," the Utes at the Los Piños agency were becoming a progressively "troublesome class of Indians." They showered their agent with complaints about exhausted supplies and clamored for the immediate removal of a small settlement of squatters in their Uncompahgre Valley. Although the squatters knew their presence was illegal, they refused to leave, even after troops were called and a time limit set for them to decamp. Nevertheless, and despite being "thoroughly dissatisfied," the Utes never "molested the squatters," and their agent reported they had "proved themselves to be far superior to those unscrupulous persons who have endeavored to dispossess the Indian of his land, and . . . willfully set at naught the rights of others."[1]

However disgruntled, most Utes remained at peace—to the frustration of a rabidly anti-Indian governor and his journalistic cohorts. With no "incidents" to exploit, they could not lobby for Ute expulsion as had been done with Plains Indians.[2] But during the late 1870s, the northern Ute bands suffered a series of unfortunate incidents, including lost and undelivered supplies and the arrival of an agent whose loose tongue and forceful agrarian demands led to a brief but bloody—and sensationalized—uprising. It was the fulcrum needed to lever most Utes out of Colorado.

LAND HUNGER AND ESCALATING TENSIONS

After the 1873 Brunot Agreement when large portions of Ute territory in the San Juan Mountains were ceded away for mining and ranching, many non-Tabeguache Utes grew increasingly bitter against Ouray. Northern bands accused him of selling Utes down the river for his $1000 annual salary. When the government failed to fulfill some of its obligations or pay agreed-upon sums, some accused Ouray of conspiring with agents to misappropriate the monies. Attempts were made on his life.[3]

Meanwhile, the Los Piños agency underwent major changes. Because it had been delegated to the Unitarian Church, in 1875 the experienced and well-liked Charles "One-Talk" Adams (a Catholic) was dismissed and replaced by the Unitarian Reverend Henry F. Bond. Bond's first act was to move the poorly located Los Piños agency, which was not only high in the mountains, but also outside reservation boundaries. The new site was in the Uncompahgre Valley where the Tabeguache traditionally wintered. For the next five years the old agency would serve as a summer subagency.[4] Though official correspondence continued to refer to the agency as the Los Piños, the band soon began referring to themselves as the Uncompahgre, a traditionally appropriate land-based identity.

However, the difficult move was not without incident, for more than two hundred head of cattle were lost, most appropriated by non-Indian ranchers invoking the "maverick law." Bond was blamed, the cost garnished from his wages, and the cattle replaced; however, the loss—coupled with Ouray's accusations that Bond was stealing and selling Indian supplies—led to Bond's resignation, and a succession of short-tenured agents ensued.[5]

At this time southern Ute bands continued to travel throughout their traditional territory in southern Colorado and New Mexico. But New Mexico officials wanted the Utes removed, as the 1873 agreement had promised. In 1875 money was appropriated for their relocation; the Cimarrón agency was closed in 1876; and finally, in July 1878, Congress ordered the southern Ute bands to relocate and remain on their approved reservation: a fifteen-mile-wide, 110-mile-long strip on the southern Colorado border. Agents Francis Weaver and Benjamin Thomas constructed an agency on the traditional Los Piños River where it was intended to administer to the Mouaches, Capotes, and Weeminuches. It would become the nucleus of a small town, subsequently named for the prominent Weeminuche chief, Ignacio.[6]

10.1. Location of Ute agencies in Colorado and Utah, 1879 (towns added for orientation).

Regardless of reservation boundaries, most Utes continued to hunt and travel freely throughout their traditional territories, as legitimately provided for by their reserved hunting rights. Some grew increasingly belligerent as non-Indians continued to penetrate, mine, and settle their land, and wild game grew scarcer. And yet, although squatters rarely heeded occasional orders to leave reservation land, there were surprisingly few skirmishes.

Several factors contributed to this grudging peace. Foremost, the Utes were a pragmatic people who did not go to war simply for the glory of combat. Rather than being "blood-thirsty," they were generally diplomatic, "quiet in demeanor," "perfectly peaceable...[and] lacking...those fierce and predatory instincts which characterize so many of the western tribes."[7] War was a practical activity: to obtain food, clothing, wealth, horses and armaments, or general booty. Killing was usually incidental to a raid, for Utes seldom killed maliciously, except when justice demanded a death for a death. Rarely did Utes attempt a consolidated all-out "war of retribution" against encroachers or in defense of their land.[8]

Conflicts were also buffered by the vast open territory. In 1876, nearly one third of Colorado was reserved Ute land. Most intruders were miners, not land-intensive farmers or ranchers; and most of the encroachment was concentrated in specific areas, requiring less territory. The Utes still had access to adequate hunting in the mountains and on the plains, and they received a relatively consistent supply of goods and annuities at agencies. Thus, even by the 1870s most Colorado Utes remained generally independent. However, traditional territories, sacred places, and medicinal hot springs were being invaded, and their free movement curtailed. There were also a few openly antagonistic factions. But their backs were not yet against the wall, and influential leaders like Ouray and Ignacio helped defuse potential upsurges in hostilities. Unfortunately, because they were peaceful, Utes began to be stigmatized by Colorado officials and journalists as "arrant cowards, as well as arrant knaves," mocking any threats as "vaporings."[9] Officials were still searching for an excuse to divest themselves of the land-rich Utes.

The push for total expulsion began in earnest in 1876, when Colorado became a state. Its first governor, Frederick W. Pitkin, and his party were elected on a popular platform: "Get the Utes out of Colorado." Pitkin had long advocated Ute removal. A New Englander, he had come to Colorado Territory for his health and remained to make a fortune mining silver in the San Juan region. As a leading voice for mining interests, he had led the charge to expel Utes from this region—successfully accomplished in the 1873 agreement.[10]

However, Coloradoans also coveted the western slopes of the Rockies, now considered a new Eden because it contained the finest agricultural and grazing land in the state. With cattle and sheep ranching on the increase it had, in Pitkin's opinion, been unfairly closed to American settlement:

> It…is nearly three times as large as the State of Massachusetts. It is watered by large streams and rivers, and contains many rich valleys and a large number of fertile plains. The climate is milder…Grasses grow there in great luxuriance, and nearly every kind of grain and vegetables can be raised without difficulty.…No portion of the State is better adapted for agricultural and grazing purposes than many portions of [the Ute] reservation."[11]

A campaign was launched against the improvident Utes. Although they were admittedly "not particularly quarrelsome or dangerous," newspapers complained the Utes were "exceedingly disagreeable neighbors." Journalist William Vickers excoriated the supposedly wastrel Utes: "Even if they would be content to live on their princely reservation, it would not be so bad, but they have a disgusting habit of ranging all over the state, stealing horses, killing off game, and carelessly firing forests."[12] But without provocation, there was little Colorado could do to rid themselves of the "troublesome" Utes.

Then in 1876 Custer was defeated by the Sioux at the Battle of the Little Bighorn. As Utes had once done in New Mexico, some acted as scouts for federal troops during the Sioux campaign.[13] But an unfortunate byproduct of the Sioux uprising was that popular American sentiment turned against *all* Indians. Federal officials banned the sale of arms to all Indians, or even the possession by them—friend or foe—and in many cases Indian hunters were shot and killed simply for carrying rifles. The interdiction of weapons was a serious blow to Indian survival, independent of government rations and regulation.

The Uncompahgre Utes grew increasingly dependent on government annuities, especially after the ban on arms sales. Still Ouray urged "his" Uncompahgre to remain peaceful. He had ample reason to enjoin that peace: he now owned a fenced five-hundred-acre tract of land at the new agency, on which he raised fifty acres of hay, grain, and vegetables. There he lived in a new four-bedroom adobe house, slept in a bed, and ate at a table with plates and utensils. He owned rugs, curtains, good furniture, china, and silverware, and he kept cigars and wine for guests and regularly wore a broadcloth suit and tie, assuming native dress only when he hunted or posed for photographs. He sat in a chair when he held council with his subchiefs, while they sat on the floor around him. And, unless hunting, he rode in a carriage pulled by a team of horses driven by his Mexican servant, Mariano, who also acted as his private secretary and personal bodyguard.[14]

Ouray's ready adoption of this lifestyle in the face of a general rejection of farming and house living by other Utes may be accounted for by his youthful association with and perhaps envy of the Mexicans he had grown up with in Taos. His relative wealth also gave him prestige among his own people; not only could he acquire the symbols of wealth by both Ute and American standards, but he also had the wherewithal to dispense favors among his followers. Despite his increasing frustration and disgust with what Americans were doing to his people, he continued to work for peace until the day of his death.

10.1. Nathan Meeker, idealistic agent to the White River Utes. (Denver Public Library, RMN-041-1413)

We can only speculate why. Ouray may have been influenced by military scenes from his youth in New Mexico, or as U.S. Secretary of the Interior Carl Schurz believed, "he saw clearly that nothing was left to them but to accommodate themselves to civilized ways or perish." Brunot argued in 1873 that regardless of whether the Utes sold their land to the United States, the miners would mine there anyway. Attempts to drive miners out would result in a war that would destroy the Utes and force them out. The only way for the Utes to gain anything in the war of diplomacy, according to Brunot, was to sell the land for as much as they could get and preserve as much of it for themselves as they could.[15] In 1873 Ouray told Washington reporters that "the agreement an Indian makes to a United States treaty is like the agreement a buffalo makes with his hunters when pierced with arrows. All he can do is lie down and give in."[16]

FORCING UTES DOWN THE WHITE MAN'S ROAD

Every negotiated land cession had been accompanied by stipulations that the Utes learn "civilized" ways of living. With nomadism impossible on restricted reservations, Utes were forced to depend on government supplies and learning new agricultural skills. Since Washington did not want to support the Utes

forever, teaching them to farm was imperative. Although there had been little follow-through with the first treaties, by 1875 the first serious attempts at
tethering and "domesticating" Eastern Utes had begun.

At the White River agency, the White River, Yampa, and Grand River
bands remained contemptuous of any attempts to make them farmers. When
H. E. Danforth arrived at their agency and urged them to help farm, they
adamantly refused. They had no intention of relinquishing hunting, traveling,
and racing fine horses for a sedentary, socially demeaning, and drudgery-filled
life. Only five years earlier they had derided their Uintah cousins, calling them
squaws and fools for working in the fields, since this was the responsibility of
agency employees.[17]

The isolation of the agency was another problem. Supplies had to be
freighted over 175 miles of rough roads from the rail station in Rawlins,
Wyoming, and delivery was erratic. Red tape, inefficiency, misunderstandings,
and misappropriated goods sometimes led to no goods at all. After the Sioux
uprising, miscommunication led to the agency receiving no annuities for two
years straight. Because they were also denied guns and ammunition, the Utes
could not hunt. Danforth resigned in disgust.[18]

Danforth's replacement was the idealistic journalist Nathan C. Meeker.[19]
Meeker had been a poet before the Civil War, a war correspondent during it,
and an agricultural correspondent for newspaper editor Horace Greeley after.
With backing from Greeley and other investors, Meeker founded a socialistic
agricultural commune near the Cache la Poudre River that he called Union
Colony (today's Greeley). The colony was a success but made no money. Meeker
lost the investments, and Greeley's heirs threatened to sue him. Desperate for
money, Meeker jumped at the chance to go to the White River agency, where
he envisioned creating a new agricultural utopia.

Meeker believed the salvation of Indians lay in their pursuing an industrious life as agriculturalists. In 1856 he wrote a novel about a seaman cast ashore
on a South Sea island who taught ignorant natives the practical wonders of the
industrial world but none of its vices. Perhaps the aging Meeker, economically
shipwrecked and cast away in the isolated mountains of western Colorado,
wished to do the same.[20] However, Meeker had no idea how to work with
Indians. He was pushy, impatient, and often angry, and the northern Ute bands
had trouble dealing with the new volatile agent.

Meeker's first act was to move the agency fifteen miles downriver to a location in Powell's Valley where there was ample farmland, water for irrigation,
good timber nearby, and coal for fuel. Naturally, Meeker's discovery was not

10.2. Douglass and Johnson (Quinkent and Canavish), leaders at the White River Agency during the Meeker "Massacre" (Scan #10045265, History Colorado)

original. Protected from heavy snows, the valley had long been used by Utes for winter pasture for their thousands of horses. It was also the site of a favorite racing course.

The move fractured the bands. One faction followed the aging Quinkent (Douglas), moved to Powell's Valley, and the following spring reluctantly built an irrigation ditch, assisted constructing fences, and helped white employees plow and plant crops. The other faction followed Nicaagat ("Captain Jack") and defiantly refused to farm, insulting those who did. Nicaagat told Meeker that "the site of the old agency had been settled by treaty, and that [Nicaagat] knew of no law or treaty that made mention of the new site." Meeker arrogantly responded that the Utes "had better all move down below, and that if we did not we should be obligated to; that for that they had soldiers."[21]

During the spring of 1879, Meeker began constructing the new agency and plowed the first forty acres of land. He also hired seven non-Indian employees to act as tutors to the "apprenticed" Ute laborers. But most Utes left to follow traditional hunting and gathering circuits. Only after a great deal of talk, entreaty, and browbeating did Quinkent's followers grudgingly assist in the work—before eventually deserting the agency as well. The inveterate letter-writing Meeker complained that "their needs are so few that they do not wish to adopt civilized habits [and] the great majority look upon the white man's ways with indifference and contempt."[22]

Meeker now launched an offensive against Ute "slothfulness." He first declared war on their large herds of horses. These were anathema to all his plans for quick acculturation: horses competed with cattle for graze; they carried Utes away from the agency; they seduced farm laborers into gambling away their time and money in horse racing; and they took children away from their studies. Meeker was determined to replace the vast herds with a few draft horses for farm work. Once the Utes were forced to remain near the agency and dependent upon government rations, he would issue his coup de grâce—denial of rations to all who would not cooperate with him—even to the point of starvation.[23]

However, the Utes still had their horses and preferred to travel on and off their reserved land, even as the number of non-Indian settlers near the reservation grew. Governor Pitkin and the journalist Vickers's blatant hate crusade intensified hostilities. Inadvertently, the inept Meeker abetted this campaign.

Meeker's fanciful pen busied itself with descriptions, opinions, expectations, and complaints about the White River agency and the barbarous Utes. He wrote numerous letters to government representatives and newspapers. In 1879 the *Greeley Tribune* published Meeker's editorial that reservation lands did not actually *belong* to Indians but were being held in trust for them by the federal government. In an imaginary conversation he argued, "If you [Utes] don't use it and won't work, white men away off will come in and by and by you will have nothing."[24]

Expanding on the theme of the unprofitable servant, Vickers proclaimed, "The Utes Must Go!"

> The Utes are actual, practical Communists and the government should be ashamed to foster and encourage them in their idleness and wanton waste of property. Living off the bounty of a paternal but idiotic Indian Bureau, they actually become too lazy to draw their rations in the regular way but insist on taking what they want wherever they find it. Removed to Indian Territory, the Utes could be fed and clothed for about one half what it now costs the government.[25]

The phrase "The Utes Must Go!" became a popular theme for applause-seeking Colorado orators during the summer of 1879. Then Vickers stepped up his campaign by fabricating incidents upon which the public could focus and politicians could build to rid the state of unwanted Indians. That year a number of naturally occurring forest fires burned vast acreage in the mountains. Vickers and Pitkin telegraphed the commissioner of Indian affairs, falsely accusing Utes of deliberately setting fires that had "burned millions of dollars of timber and…[of] intimidating settlers and miners," all part of an organized effort "to destroy the timber of Colorado." In their opinion, "these savages should be removed to Indian Territory where they can no longer destroy the finest forests in this state."[26] In response, the commissioner ordered Meeker to keep his Indians on the reservation.

Meeker built on his theme that the reservation did not belong to the Utes and that he was the government steward in the White River provinces. When the northern Utes protested, Meeker insisted he had the right to manage the land in any way he wished, and plow anywhere he liked, since it was government land and he was a government agent. Disturbed by Meeker's betrayal and bungling management of the agency, Nicaagat rode to Denver to personally bring his concerns to the governor. Nicaagat assured Pitkin that the Utes had set no fires nor burned any settlers' cabins, and he asked Pitkin to petition Washington for a new agent. The governor promised Nicaagat he would write to Washington immediately. Then, Pitkin sat back and waited for the growing turmoil to erupt into an incident to use to evict the Utes.

Meeker exacerbated the rising tensions by rationing supplies. To keep "his" Utes from leaving the reservation, he distributed supplies once a week, and only to the heads of each family. Although it was an effective tether—a technique used on other reservations—some Utes simply ignored the rations and left the reservation anyway.[27] Friction between Indians and non-Indians neared a boiling point.

VIOLENCE AT THE WHITE RIVER AGENCY

The trigger for the bloody events was pulled in July 1879, and the subsequent actions (and their interpretation) remain controversial among historians even today.[28]

A group of wide-ranging "Middle Park" Utes, probably led by Piah, left the reservation to camp in Middle Park near today's Fraser, where a stage station and horse pastures were located. When the proprietor was unable to evict the Utes, he went to Hot Sulphur Springs for help. When he returned with the sheriff and a posse, the Utes were racing horses. While the Utes were preoccupied, the posse confiscated all the guns and ammunition in camp. When the Utes returned and saw the white men, a youth named Tabernash waved his rifle in greeting. Mistaking the gesture, a trigger-happy member of the posse shot and killed the teen. Shocked, angry, but weaponless, the Utes decamped and headed back to the reservation, stealing horses and killing a farmer in revenge.[29]

Trouble continued to brew. Warriors were seen in war paint, some harassed a mail carrier, and Utes traded nearly five hundred horses for rifles and ammunition at Peck's trading post near Hayden in the Yampa River Valley. Major Thompson, a former Denver agent living in Hayden, was warned that the younger warriors at White River might cause trouble if Meeker continued to run the agency in the same detested manner.[30]

At this time, the horse embodied Ute ideals and was the ultimate means to generate wealth, power, and freedom. They were a man's most-prized possession, and raising, racing, and showing them off his greatest joy. A man with no horses was nothing, and only they would work on farms. Horse racing and gambling were the Utes' main pursuits, Meeker complained, and the combined bands administered to by the White River agency owned up to four thousand horses, with as many as two thousand pastured in Powell's Valley.[31]

The tipping point came when Meeker began to plow a favorite racecourse and field assigned to the influential leader and respected shaman, Canavish (Johnson). Canavish's field was targeted because he had used grain and pastureland from Meeker meant for farming to groom his prized racehorses instead. Feeling betrayed, Meeker angrily ordered Canavish's field plowed; in response, Canavish and his kinsmen intimidated agency workers. When the old leader confronted Meeker about the destruction of his pasture, the agent responded that Canavish had too many horses and to just shoot them. Infuriated, Canavish grabbed Meeker by the coat, dragged and kicked him from his office, and then—to the delighted amusement of his men—gave the frightened agent a strong shove that sent him stumbling backwards to sprawl, undignified, on the ground.[32]

A shaken and furious Meeker immediately wired Washington:

> I have been assaulted by a leading chief, Johnson. Forced out of my own house and injured badly, but was rescued by employees. It is now revealed that Johnson originated all the trouble.... His son shot at plowman, and opposition to plowing is wide; plowing stops; life of self, family, and employees not safe; want protection immediately; have asked Gov. Pitkin to confer with Gen. Pope.[33]

Meeker went on to describe eloquently his misery in the forsaken and isolated agency, where he felt a victim of Ute persecution and perniciousness. He also warned Governor Pitkin that "none of the white people are safe" while Utes were being forced to farm. He needed the whip of government troops to keep them "in line" and on the reservation.[34] Meeker also complained of his humiliation to the prominent journalist W. N. Byers: "I didn't come here to be kicked and hustled out of my house by savages, and if the government can not protect me, let somebody else try it."[35]

The wheels of government turned to comply with the agent's cry for help. Troops were ordered out to protect Meeker and arrest the leaders of the incident, and the secretary of the Interior Carl Schurz traveled to Denver to confer with Pitkin about his Indian problem. Meanwhile, troops left Fort Steele, Wyoming, on September 21, and on September 25 Meeker was informed that 190 officers and troops were on their way under the command of Major T. T. Thornburgh, a Civil War veteran and West Point graduate newly arrived in the West.[36] On September 26, Nicaagat and a small party of hunters stumbled upon the troops sixty-five miles north of the agency. The party stopped to question the troops and then raced back to the agency to warn the others. That night, a few excitable younger Utes held a spontaneous war dance. Alarmed, Meeker sent a hurried note to Thornburgh the next morning, recommending he stop short of the reservation boundary. He should, Meeker advised, bring only a small escort to the agency to appraise the situation.

For years the Utes had been threatened with American military might. Tabeguache chiefs were warned in 1863 that there were enough American soldiers to surround their mountains and wipe them from the face of the earth.[37] Ouray reinforced this fear while pressuring chiefs to sign the 1868 treaty and 1873 agreement. And Meeker had continually threatened Utes at the White River agency: if they made Washington angry, soldiers would imprison their leaders and drive them to Indian Territory. When soldiers did appear on their border the threats became real, and the northern Ute bands prepared to defend themselves and their home. "The Indians," Meeker wrote to Thornburgh, "seem to consider the advance of troops as a declaration of real war." And to Washington he penned, the "Indians propose to fight if troops advance."[38]

But after consulting his orders and conferring with his officers, Thornburgh decided to ignore Meeker's admonition and continue on at full force so that his men would be within striking distance if there was trouble. He informed Meeker of this but did not notify the Utes.[39] Meeker quickly responded, but his dispatch never arrived. The moment Thornburgh's troops forded the Milk River and crossed onto the reservation, hostilities erupted.[40]

Northern Ute warriors had been watching the troops from the rimrocks above Milk Creek. When the soldiers did not stop but crossed the river, Utes assumed a declaration of war had been made and attacked. Nicaagat later claimed that they had tried to negotiate, the fighting broke out spontaneously, and only fifty warriors were involved (not the hundreds the military reported). He also testified that he didn't know who fired the first shot, Indian or soldier, and that when he tried to stop the shooting, his warriors misinterpreted his "hat waving" as encouragement and fired with more enthusiasm.

As the infantry retreated to the circling wagons a mile behind, warriors raced to cut them off. Thornburgh's scout urged him to open fire, but Thornburgh exclaimed: "My God, I dare not! My orders are positive, and, if I violate and survive, a court martial and an ignominious dismissal may follow." As Utes flanked the troops and opened fire, Thornburgh led a wild charge to open a path allowing most of the soldiers to reach the wagons safely. He and thirteen of his men died in the effort.[41]

The combatants dug in for an extended battle. It was an unusual tactic for the Utes, who seldom engaged in pitched battles, and the Thornburgh incident would become one of the few such battles recorded. Utes typically preferred to hit and run, or fight a running battle until they could scatter and regroup later. There was no glory in being killed in battle, but only in surviving with honor (and booty).

192

Thornburgh's men held out for six days, beset with thirst, hunger, and the stench of dead animals. A few escaped and made their way to Rawlins with news of the conflict, which was telegraphed on to Washington. Another telegram two days later added, "[I] fear Agent Meeker and employees all massacred, as trains and wagons transferring Indian supplies from here have all been destroyed by the Indians."[42] Western newspapers had their sensational Indian war to report.

Outside of Colorado, most newspapers blamed the incident on encroaching miners for inciting hostilities. Rumors also suggested Mormons in Utah had armed northern bands and encouraged them to make war on the government. Other rumors reported that over two hundred Arapahos had joined the northern Utes, or that warriors were headed south to incite the southern bands.[43] Most of these stories were untrue, but many readers believed them.

A flurry of panic beset the Uintah Reservation. The day after learning of the ambush and the fate of the White River agency (as yet unknown to officials), many of the principal Uintahs hurried to their agent, John J. Critchlow. They were fearful the northern Colorado bands might try to force them to join their uprising. Critchlow also reported that white men were hoping "my [Uintah] Indians would get into trouble and be compelled to leave, so that this reserve might be opened for settlement." After reassuring the worried Uintahs, Critchlow informed Washington that all was well on his reservation and the Uintahs would fight to defend him and his family.[44]

But in Denver residents were breaking out armaments and fortifying themselves against Indian attacks. Pitkin alerted citizens that the Indians were "off their reservation, seeking to destroy your settlements by fire, [and] are game to be hunted and destroyed like wild beasts." He created military districts, spread rumors of violent depredations, and was quick to offer the Secretary of War all the troops needed to settle the Indian trouble permanently.[45] Pitkin told reporters that

> Unless removed by the government, [Utes] must necessarily be exterminated. I could raise 25,000 men to protect the settlers in twenty-four hours. The state would be willing to settle the Indian trouble at its own expense. The advantages that would accrue from the throwing open of 12,000,000 acres of land to miners and settlers would more than compensate all the expenses incurred.[46]

193

Meanwhile, Captain Francis S. Dodge, commander of the 9th Cavalry of black troops stationed at Steamboat Springs, force-marched a thirty-nine-man patrol to Milk Creek where he and his *túu-mericats* (black Americans) joined the besieged troops. General Wesley Merritt also headed to Milk Creek from Fort Russell (near Cheyenne) with 200 cavalry and 150 infantry.

At the same time Sapowaneri, an important subchief among the Uncompahgre, arrived at Milk Creek with a written command from Ouray:

> You are hereby requested and commanded to cease hostilities against the whites, injuring no innocent persons or any others farther than to protect your own lives and property from unlawful and unauthorized combinations of horse-thieves and desperadoes, as anything farther will ultimately end in disaster to all parties.[47]

Sapowaneri was accompanied by an American courier with a companion letter to the military commander, informing him of Ouray's letter and reinforcing the request to support efforts to stop hostilities.[48]

Quinkent sent a return message to Ouray, assuring him the troubles would spread no further. The affair concerned only the northern bands at White River, and it was only Nicaagat and his men fighting at Milk Creek. Quinkent explained that now that his men had killed all the employees at the agency and taken the women and children captive, this would be the end of it.[49] But Ouray knew—if Quinkent did not—that it would *not* be the end. The White River debacle was now the affair of every Ute in Colorado.

Once the Milk River siege had been lifted, negotiations began for the release of the women. Ouray threatened to lead other Utes against the northern bands if the captives were not freed; Quinkent's wife Tsashin (Susan)—Ouray's half sister—pleaded on their behalf; and even Chipeta intervened (for which Tsashin and Chipeta would be romantically memorialized in Colorado). After the well-respected former Los Piños agent Charles Adams arrived, the captives were finally released, and the White River band reluctantly agreed to allow the army to move troops onto the reservation.[50]

However, once the captives reached the agency, a full description of the horrors there was published in gruesome detail. Among the dead was Meeker, his head smashed and a barrel stave driven through his mouth—the Utes had often complained he talked too much. Meeker's courier was also found dead twelve miles from the agency with Meeker's last message to Thornburgh undelivered. He had written that there was no sign of trouble at the agency.[51]

And there had been none—initially. But once Utes at the agency learned about the fighting at Milk Creek, they turned on agency personnel. The men were killed and women and children captured and kept in a constantly moving camp. During their captivity, they later testified, they were subjected to abusive threats and taunts and were supposedly "outraged" by Ute men. Meeker's wife took the brunt of the insults, while her liberal college-educated daughter, Josephine, was forcedly to taken to wife. It was an outrage Josephine later crafted into a sensational book that she took on a successful lecture tour.[52]

The troops established a military cantonment on the site of the devastated agency, where it remained for the next four years until officials felt it was safe to be abandoned. As the army departed, their buildings were sold to incoming American settlers who established the new settlement of Meeker.

THE UTES MUST GO!

The attack on Thornburgh's troops and the massacre at the White River agency proved the ultimate calamity for Colorado Utes: Pitkin now had his excuse to expel the Utes. He spoke of Coloradoans "rising up and wiping out the red devils." Vickers evoked the image of the massacre at Little Big Horn in 1876; raised a cry for either Ute expulsion or extermination; and argued it would "be impossible for the Indians and whites to live in peace hereafter." The attack had no provocation, he maintained, and whites were fearful that there was no safe place in the state.[53] Pitkin called successive news conferences, and Coloradoans continued to bear arms and drill militia. The enthusiasm for war was kept alive when Pitkin's associates in the San Juan region falsely claimed that "Chief Ouray...has sent out a courier warning settlers that his young men are on the warpath, and that he cannot control them."[54]

But it took all the media pressure Pitkin could muster to convince a reluctant nation that the trouble had not in fact been instigated by land-hungry, depredating *Americans*. In many quarters, national sentiment was roused against the Colorado "cormorants," who were accused of goading the Utes into war. New York papers attributed the outbreak to "the aggressive miners and the failures of the government to keep faith with the Indians." Meeker, one of the most "upright and competent" agents, had been handicapped by a Congress that failed to pay land cession monies of up to $100,000 to the Utes. Utah papers argued that "If the Indians...were protected as they are entitled to be against the aggressions of marauding miners and the dishonesty of government officials, the outbreak would have no doubt been averted." They pointed out that those journals which at one time cried out for the "extermination of the red devils" now demand a "change in the Indian policy of the Government," and concede the point, always put forth by this paper, that the untutored Indians have been "more sinned against than sinning."[55]

One New York paper quoted a Colorado informant, who said the Utes "were among the most peaceable Indians in the United States and had been defrauded in the most shameless manner by government traders and contractors." Another New York paper concluded a scathingly sarcastic article by saying that "it is manifestly the duty of Congress to see that the Indians are exterminated, with all possible tenderness." A Sacramento paper reported that the more investigators examined the Ute outbreak, the plainer it began to appear that "the Indians were goaded into rebellion by the infamous usage they had suffered at the hands of Congress. Their reservation had been encroached upon and stolen from them by the white prospectors and miners." The San Francisco press supported this, reporting that the hostilities had "unmistakably" been stirred up by the hundreds of prospectors swarming onto the Ute reservation. The *Washington Post* summed it up, "Nearly all our Indian wars— including the present trouble—have resulted from aggressions on the part of the Caucasian on the rights of the red man."[56] Even General Crook, the celebrated Indian fighter, orated against the depredations of non-Indians and the government. "The Indians have no redress against lawless whites, even when Agents are honest and the Interior Department appropriations are sufficient."[57]

At the Los Piños agency on the Uncompahgre, agent Wilson M. Stanley stood behind the Uncompahgre Utes and Ouray. He wrote to the commissioner, hoping the Indian Department would see that the Utes had a fair trial and that the culpability for the incident would be properly affixed:

> I am absolutely disgusted at the conduct of the white people and am not at all surprised that the Indians do occasionally turn upon the traducers and robbers of their rights. The worm will squirm when tread upon and the noble horse defend himself when goaded to desperation, and why not an Indian.[58]

If they took the statements of the Colorado newspapers literally, Stanley added, especially those of the dramatic *Denver Tribune*, one would have to suppose that every Ute was on the warpath, with half the citizens in Colorado murdered and their property burned or stolen. Within a few days, a Chicago newspaper reported, "It is a curious fact that though the Indian scare prevails throughout the State, no trouble is reported since the Thornburgh fight."[59]

Ouray defended the White River Utes, noting that Meeker had made them angry when he forced them to work "for his own glory," and that they had been afraid of a repeat of the Sand Creek Massacre when Meeker sent for the troops to punish them for not working or attending church.[60] Even though overexcited Coloradoans had killed several Utes—some Yampas near Rawlins and Ouray's own uncle and nephew while hunting beaver—Ouray continued to press for a peaceful resolution.[61]

A commission was formed to investigate the incident. Reluctant Ute witnesses appeared—Canavish, Quinkent, Nicaagat, Colorow, and others—but by the time they reached the Los Piños agency, no one could remember anything. They would testify against no one, including themselves. The commission determined that there was insufficient proof of individual culpability at the Thornburgh fight, and the deaths were considered an action of war and therefore excusable. But those who had killed the agency personnel were determined guilty of cold-blooded murder and could be identified and convicted on the testimony of the surviving women. Despite Ouray's strenuous objections to the women testifying—who might simply name those they remembered, not necessarily the guilty—the hearings went on.[62] Quinkent, the government-acknowledged chief of the amalgamated northern bands, was held responsible for the outbreak, notwithstanding his claims denying involvement. (He had, however, taken his share of the spoils, including one of the women.) He and eleven others were to be tried. If the twelve were not surrendered, the entire band would be held responsible, and troops would be ordered to capture them.[63]

A disillusioned Ouray told the commission,

> You want our land; you want our country. You have tried before to get our country away from us, and us from it. You have tried to get it in pieces; you are now trying to get it all. We will not leave our country. We will fight. We will go back into our mountains and we will fight your forty millions.... You are all my enemies.... All of the people of Colorado and New Mexico are our enemies. We will not give these twelve men over to you to be tried by a court of Colorado, where no justice will be shown them. We will give over these men only if they can be tried in Washington, where I know I have at least one friend [Carl Schurz].[64]

The commissioners acquiesced and adjourned. Believing that sufficient evidence could be secured to convict and hang most if not all the accused, General Adams recommended the defendants be taken to Fort Leavenworth until their trial.[65]

But the defendants had disappeared, and no one seemed to know their whereabouts. Ouray suggested they had gone hunting in the rugged wilderness of southeastern Utah where they would be impossible to locate. Frustrated, the commission started for Washington with an armed military escort and only one defendant: Quinkent. Other leaders accompanied them, including Ouray of the Uncompahgre, and southern band chiefs Ignacio, Buckskin Charley, Severo, and Blanco. At train stops in Alamosa and Pueblo, they were verbally abused and physically assaulted, despite their guard. Quinkent was imprisoned at Fort Leavenworth, where he remained until his release a year later, after a Washington court determined he had gone insane.[66]

New hearings on the Ute Question opened in Washington on January 15, 1880. Many of the supposed expert witnesses had never seen an Indian and had only a vague idea of the "problem," but all had definite opinions on its solution. Even before the hearings, Congress had begun debating what was beginning to be called "the Ute Question," and arguing about whether to remove the Indians from Colorado entirely. Congressman James Belford of Colorado worked tirelessly to convince the House to approve the transfer of Colorado Utes to the Uintah Reservation in Utah, arguing once again that they had more land than they could use, and citing precedents of other states removing their Indians.[67]

In December, General Sherman voiced his opinion:

> I pity the poor Indian, but the continent has got to be settled. The supreme command of God has been pronounced, "go forth and multiply and replenish the earth"... and so people have spread to the west and south, and you have Yankees everywhere obeying the divine command. The Indians are entitled to our humanity and consideration. Admit that fact, but at the same time they must do something for their own living and they must get out of the way.... These Indians must submit and deliver up these murderers or take the consequences.[68]

By January, Sherman's opinions had become even harsher. "The only way to deal with the troublesome Indians is to kill them, regardless of whether their treaty rights have been trampled upon or not."[69]

And Colorado officials wanted the valuable Ute land and an atonement for the Meeker Massacre. The Denver press kept public sentiment stirred up against the Utes. While most newspapers outside Colorado took the Utes' side, a growing number began to uphold the right of Colorado to take Ute land:

> It may be that... the past Indian policy of the United States Government is really responsible, and that the Utes have been trained into villainy by villainous whites. But it is... absurd to expect that men who are building up homes for themselves and their children on our far frontiers will let their homes be burned and their families battered in expiration [sic] of the sins of their forefathers, or of some one else's forefather.... We had better get the Utes out of the way of civilized people, and begin a new experiment at making the Utes something very different from what they are, without expecting the people of Colorado to pay the price.[70]

By March 22 the hearings were over and Colorado had won. The White River bands were to be relocated on the Uintah Reservation and their land sold (ceded) to the United States; from that sale, war reparations would be garnished and paid to the families of those killed at the agency. Since the band refused to give up the defendants, the entire band would pay the price. The White River bands were not consulted; having broken their treaty, they had forfeited their right to negotiate. However, the Uintahs were also not consulted about relocating the White Rivers to their land.[71]

Next, officials turned on the Uncompahgre and southern Utes. Though these bands had not broken their treaties—and had even helped broker the end of hostilities and return of the captives—they too occupied valuable agricultural lands. Included in the 1880 debates was the proposal to allot land in severalty instead of creating in-common reservations. Four major arguments favored this: 1) after granting allotments, "surplus" land could be sold to non-Indians; 2) individual land ownership would force Indians to become individualized farmers and help civilize them; 3) as Indians learned to manage their own affairs, their special position as wards of the government could be terminated, and they could assume a position equal to others (many saw this as the final solution to the "Indian Problem"); and 4) individual title would somehow make Indian land less vulnerable to white encroachment. The idealists hoped these homesteads would "improve the condition of the Indian," give them a "fair chance at civilization," and relieve the government of its impossible position of maintaining promises of seclusion it could not keep. Most believed that with private ownership of land (a long-standing American dream), Indians would get homes, mingle with Americans, develop their own business centers, and blend with the white race. But in the coming years, reality would shatter these unrealistic dreams. Instead of protecting Indian land, individual ownership made the land more vulnerable and ultimately resulted in alienating the majority of Indian land everywhere it was implemented.[72]

A foremost advocate of the homesteading principle was George Manypenny, a one-time commissioner of Indian affairs and author of *Our Indian Wards*, a book indicting the use of military might in Indian affairs and calling for a new policy based on Jeffersonian agrarian ideals of creating yeomen farmers out of Indians. Influential eastern reformers, including various "friends of the Indians," the Indian Rights Association, and missionary boards used Manypenny's book and other rhetoric to convince Congress that the time had come to emancipate the Indians as government wards and guide them into a "manly and independent life," having equal citizenship and obligations with other Americans.[73]

Despite some resistance to the land-in-severalty theory, proponents of the legislation (including sympathetic groups who genuinely felt this action was in the Indians' best interests) overwhelmed that opposition. On June 15, 1880, Congress accepted and ratified an agreement "submitted" by the "confederated bands" of Ute Indians in Colorado for the sale of their reservation in return for small portions to be allotted to members of the band severally. A commission was appointed to carry out the act.[74]

On July 8, the commission arrived at the Los Piños agency on the Uncompahgre where they enlisted Ouray to acquire the ratifying signatures of three-fourths of the male membership—a congressional stipulation for the agreement. Ouray's influence was considered critical for this.

After obtaining the Uncompahgre signatures, an ailing Ouray travelled to the Southern Ute agency. But shortly after he arrived, he succumbed to the chronic and painful nephritis that had plagued him for several years. Doctors in Washington had already warned him he had little time left, and by the time he arrived at the Southern Ute agency he was near death. Increasingly disillusioned and depressed, Ouray was already turning his back on non-Indian ways, resuming traditional clothing, and turning to shamanic medicine. Alarmed doctors from the agency and nearby Durango sent word that the influential chief had little time to live. His illness received national attention

10.3. Ouray and Otto Mears, 1880. (Denver Public Library, Western History Collection, X-30561)

and Coloradoans grew alarmed. Without Ouray, they feared few Utes would sign the new agreement within the time limit, in particular the White River bands who were to be expelled by it.[75]

Ouray died on August 24 and, following his instructions, was immediately wrapped in blankets and given a traditional and very secret Indian burial by Chipeta, John McCook (Chipeta's brother), Buckskin Charley, Colorow, and others. Ouray's body lay undisturbed for nearly forty-five years until, after Chipeta's death, Buckskin Charley led men to gather what he claimed were Ouray's bones (rumors persist they were not) for reburial in an Ignacio cemetery.[76]

Newspapers eulogized Ouray as "the greatest Indian of his time…the friend of the white man and the protector of the Indians," and "a remarkable Indian; a man of pure instincts [and] keen perception."[77] But commissioners worried the Agreement of 1880 would languish without this "friend of the white man" to strong-arm Utes into signing it. But shortly after Ouray's death, Chief Kaniache, a long-time enemy of Ouray and outspoken opponent of the agreement, was struck by lightning and killed—clearly an omen. Even more influential, the enterprising entrepreneur and commissioner Otto Mears offered to pay each Ute who signed the agreement two dollars. Embittered Utes declared Mears's two dollars were worth more than all the illusory promises of grants and annuity payments from the government.[78]

Appalled, commission chair George Manypenny refused to endorse the signatures and charged Mears with bribery. But the new U.S. president James Garfield and the new secretary of the Interior Samuel Kirkwood not only exonerated Mears, but they commended him and ordered the federal treasury to reimburse him the $2,800 it had taken to obtain the necessary signatures. Meanwhile, even as Ute commissioners lobbied in Washington against Uncompahgre removal, Kirkwood was offering military aid to enforce it. Mears had told Kirkwood that they could force the move if they would give him "enough troops and [keep] Manypenny and Meacham out of the way."[79]

By October 1880, the necessary signatures had been collected. The White River exiles were to be relocated to "agricultural lands on the Uintah Reservation," while the Uncompahgre would be given individual allotments "upon agricultural lands on Grand [Colorado] River, near the mouth of the Gunnison River." Southern Ute bands were to be allotted agricultural lands along the La Plata River, first in Colorado and then in New Mexico if there was insufficient land in Colorado.[80]

Six months later, the White River Utes were ordered to report to the Uintah Reservation. Although reluctant to leave, they were at last persuaded by the promise of supplies, land allotments, and annuities ($19 per capita). But when allotments were not made and supplies delayed, most returned to northern Colorado. It took renewed efforts to lure, cajole, or force them back to Utah. Even then, some, like Colorow and Nicaagat, continued to invoke treatied hunting rights and led bands back to hunt in their homelands, even as individual families quietly returned to summer-hunt as well. Piah and his Middle Park Utes unobtrusively migrated south to merge with bands not expelled.[81]

Meanwhile, the Ute commission set about locating suitable land for the Uncompahgre.[82] Though Uncompahgre leaders protested that they preferred to stay in the Uncompahgre Valley, the commission, accompanied by an army detachment, reminded them the agreement had already been signed. Negotiations were over.

Now some commissioners questioned what exactly constituted their treatied land. The allotments were supposed to be located along the Colorado, in the vicinity of today's Fruita and Grand Junction. But the commission found multiple reasons the land was unsuitable: there was not enough contiguous land in the quantities needed; it was too far from the river or too sandy for grazing; irrigation projects would also be required that would need skilled labor to build. Even though it was potentially fertile agricultural land, Mears discovered an ambiguous section of the agreement that could be manipulated: "The Uncompahgre Utes agree to remove and settle upon agricultural lands on Grand River near the mouth of the Gunnison River in Colorado, *if a sufficient quantity of agricultural land shall be found there*; if not, then upon such other unoccupied agricultural lands as may be found in that vicinity and in the Territory of Utah."[83]

Mears easily persuaded the commission that "adjacent territory" meant Utah Territory, and the commission made a cursory examination of land in northwest Utah. They quickly determined the area was sufficient to satisfy the Uncompahgres' needs for grazing and agriculture and maintained the Utes should be relocated there. Years later, Mears would claim that he knew the Grand Junction area was fertile, but he felt the Utes should be removed from the "inevitable" confrontation that would occur when Colorado farmers demanded that land, too.[84]

But before the final decision could be made, rancorous arguments broke out among the commissioners. Alfred B. Meacham—outspoken reformer, champion of Indian rights, and strong Ute advocate—was accused of being aggressive, acrimonious, uncompromising, derisive of his opponents, and of "incessantly endeavoring to 'Meachamize'" the other members. The commission was deadlocked, with half wanting the Utes moved into Utah "for the benefit" of Colorado, while the other half, especially Manypenny and Meacham, insisting the terms of the treaty were clear that Uncompahgres should remain in Colorado. A fistfight broke out, a commissioner resigned, and a carefully

10.4. The Uncompahgres were expelled from Colorado at gunpoint in 1881. (Scan #10025742, History Colorado)

chosen replacement ended the deadlock. The Uncompahgres were assigned the vast, barren desert and plateaus just south of the Uintah Reservation with an agency near the junction of the White and Green Rivers. It would be called the Ouray Reservation.[85]

The indignant Uncompahgre delayed their move until officials grew impatient and army troops were instructed to use force if necessary. Colonel McKenzie called a council and inquired of the chiefs whether their people would move to Utah without being forced. When the first Ute speaker began a long oration denouncing whites, McKenzie cut him short:

> It is not necessary for me to stay here any longer, you can settle this matter by discussion among yourselves. All I want to know is whether you will go or not. If you will not go of your own accord, I will make you go.... If you have not moved by nine o'clock tomorrow morning, I will be at your camp and make you move.[86]

One American trooper later described the move:

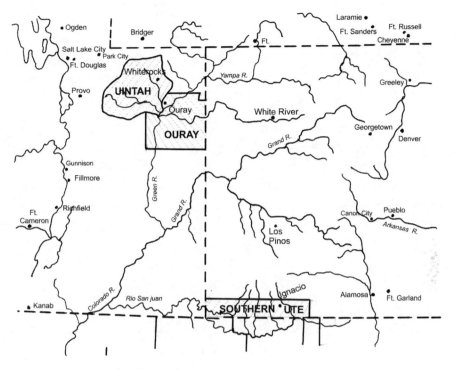

10.2. 1880 Agreement (ARCIA 1879).

The next morning, shortly after sunrise, we saw a thrilling and pitiful sight. The whole Ute nation on horseback and on foot was streaming by. As they passed our camps their gait broke into a run. Sheep were abandoned, blankets and personal possessions strewn along the road, women and children were loudly wailing.

And so we marched behind the Indians, pushing them out, he [Mackenzie] sent word to all the surrounding whites, who hurried after us, taking up the Land.

Our task…was to hold back the civilians. They followed us closely, taking up and "locating" the Indian land thrown open for settlement…we were holding a crowd of these people on the south side of the Gunnison until the Indians had passed Kahnah Creek, thirteen miles distant.…

In three days the rich lands of the Uncompahgre were all occupied, towns being laid out and lots being sold at high prices. With its rich soil and wonderful opportunities for irrigation, the Uncompahgre

Valley—before a desert—soon became the garden spot of Colorado, covered with fruitful fields and orchards.[87]

By the twentieth century, the Uncompahgre's "desert" had indeed become a fruitful garden—however, it took major feats of engineering and a great deal of federal money to divert water for the irrigation needed.[88] It is doubtful either the engineers or the money would have been forthcoming for Indian lands.

The nearly fourteen hundred Uncompahgre men, women, and children marched 350 miles to their incredibly desolate reservation in Utah. They brought with them eight thousand horses and ten thousand sheep and goats. In one last desperately futile gesture, Colorow—who had earlier abandoned the White Rivers to join the Uncompahgres—led a band of painted warriors in a tragicomic charge against the embankment of soldiers before retreating amid the warning thunder of guns and cannon. The Uncompahgres reached their new agency by the end of September, where they found a cluster of hastily constructed buildings.[89]

In Colorado, the Uncompahgre retreat was greeted with enthusiasm. "This is an event that has long devotedly been prayed for by our people," exulted the *Ouray Times*, and "How joyful it sounds and with what satisfaction one can say, 'The Utes have gone.'" Del Norte citizens were urged to "shout the glad tidings...the San Juan is opened."[90]

Behind them the Uncompahgre left extraordinarily rich mineral and farming lands. Moving with Yankee precision and know-how, miners opened the mountains and plundered the rich mineral veins. In the three counties of Ouray, San Juan, and San Miguel alone, nearly $40 million worth of precious minerals were extracted over the next four years. At great expense, railroads and major water projects were gradually built, and farms and ranches soon sprawled across valleys and hills that had once belonged to the Utes.[91]

Thus, land-hungry Euro-Americans were able to expel most of the Utes from Colorado. Using as an excuse the battle at Milk Creek and the subsequent agency murders, Coloradoans applied journalistic hyperbole, manipulative language, legal chicanery, outright bribery, and military force to expel the Utes from Colorado and into Utah. Within hours, much of the Eastern Ute homeland had been claimed by eager land speculators and ranchers.

As Coloradoans rejoiced, the beleaguered Uintahs in Utah were forced to welcome the White Rivers onto their already overcrowded reservation and the Uncompahgres as unwilling neighbors. The bands became administratively known as the Uintah and Ouray Utes, named for the two reservations they now occupied. But they doggedly retained their earlier identities as Uintahs, White Rivers, and Uncompahgres. Washington subsequently reinforced these identities and hardened the boundaries between the three bands when they administered each band as separate entities. Competition for natural resources, government largesse, and political influence increased during the next years. Both competition and bitter recriminations over past events quickly solidified their identities into discrete cultural and competitive political communities.

Chapter 11

The Land Divided

Southern Ute and Ute Mountain
Reservations, 1881–1906

The Uncompahgre and northern Utes were gone, but the dispossession of the Utes was still not complete. Land-hungry farmers, ranchers, and miners continued to covet remaining Ute land. At the same time, well-meaning eastern reformers continued to push formalized plans to save the American Indian from extinction through individual property ownership and farming.

From 1880 to the early decades of the twentieth century, the three Ute "tribes"—the Uintah and Ouray Utes, Southern Utes, and Ute Mountain Utes (with a mix of off-reservation Utes and Paiutes in Utah)—continued to fight for their right to travel and hunt as guaranteed in their treaties and agreements. But competition over resources mounted, especially between Ute hunters and commercial cattle outfits. Unsurprisingly, Utes who remained on reservations were unable to hunt or forage adequately and often starved because of

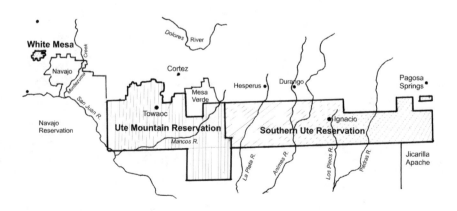

11.1. Southern reservations, including the Southern Utes, Ute Mountain Utes, and White Mesa Utes.

insufficient rations. Not only was the territory too limited for nomadic subsistence, but the land reserved for Indians was typically poor. As H. P. Myton,
a Uintah and Ouray agent, noted about his reservation, it was unsuitable for
white homesteaders because it was land "no one wants" and was "fit only for
Indians."[1]

Despite facing starvation on reservations, Utes who defied reservation
boundaries faced bloody skirmishes with Indian-hating Euro-Americans.
Some Coloradoans renewed attempts to relocate their remaining Utes, even as
new cessions were made for mining lands, and the creation of national forests
and parks reduced or redrew boundaries. The final phase of Ute dispossession
arrived when they were given individual land allotments, and their reservations opened to white homesteaders.

THE SOUTHERN UTE AND UTE MOUNTAIN RESERVATIONS

As they responded to shifting territorial, political, and cultural issues, the once-
nomadic Utes grew less mobile and more firmly linked to their respective
reservations. In this geopolitical adjustment, they began to assume the tribal
identities by which they would be known in the twentieth century.

The Capote and Mouache Utes had long interacted and intermarried with
each other, as well as with racially diverse populations that neighbored them,
including Hispanics, Euro-Americans, and a few African Americans. Additionally, neighboring Hispanic families had been purchasing and incorporating Ute
children into their households as servants since at least the 1700s, sometimes
creating strong cross-cultural bonds. As a consequence, the region was racially
and culturally diverse, and southern Ute bands included a significant number
of interracial mixed-blood members. By the late 1800s, socialization, intermarriage, and political jockeying for administrative power helped subsume
Capote and Mouache band identities within the reservation's administrative
identity as Southern Utes, although a pride in individual traditional heritage
remained. Tribal signs still proclaim that these are the Moache-Capota of the
Southern Ute Indian Tribe.[2]

Conversely, the neighboring Weeminuche retreated to a separate communal reserve around Sleeping Ute Mountain where they grew more isolated,
more stubbornly traditional. In so doing they reinforced and solidified the
boundaries of their discrete identity. In time, they would reservedly accept an
administrative identity linked to the Ute Mountain that dominated their reservation. At the same time, other Weeminuche/Paiutes—even more resistant to

relocation—clung tenaciously to their homelands in southeastern Utah, their identity shifting as their homesteads relocated from Allen Canyon to White Mesa.

While often helpless to redress their losses, the Utes did not accept them passively. Leaders were vocal in their protests; they sometimes tried to initiate changes or were willing to adapt to shifting circumstances; and they began to fight Euro-Americans on the latter's terms: in American courts of law and in the halls of Congress. Confederating to pursue legal claims reinforced a pan-Ute identity, even as politics on reservations substantiated the distinct political identities of northern and southern Ute tribes.

SPIRALING TENSION AND CONFLICT

For years agents in New Mexico had been urging the government to relocate the Capotes, Mouaches, and Weeminuches to a remote location, ostensibly to avoid conflict and "contamination" from non-Indian vices. But this protective isolation remained a fiction.[3] Popular cattle trails crisscrossed the Southern Utes' long, narrow reservation, and cattlemen, Navajos, and rustlers continued to graze sheep and cattle on their land. More worrisome was the threat that Southern Utes would be forced to become farmers on individual land allotments, with the remaining reservation lost to white homesteaders.[4]

While some Capotes and Mouaches under chiefs like Tampuche, Severo, and Buckskin Charley were amenable to farming on allotments, the Weeminuche were adamantly opposed. Led by the commanding six-foot-tall Ignacio, the Weeminuche had always been more isolated and traditional, asserting their right to roam freely on the western portion of the Southern Ute Reservation. Others continued to range throughout southeastern Utah.

By refusing to collect "head money" (annuities), many Weeminuches were not bound to agencies or the increasingly destitute reservation. Exacerbating conditions, a rising non-Indian population was crowding the reservation, who resented the existence of all Indians and of reserved Indian land. The Utes were now locked onto the reservation and were only allowed off with passes (despite treaty guarantees). They were also issued too few supplies to survive, and many ate their stock rather than use them for intended stock-raising enterprises. Without begging permission to hunt or occasionally rustling beef, the reservation-bound Mouaches and Capotes would have starved. It is not surprising that a significant number of Weeminuches preferred to remain untethered on their old homelands in southeastern Utah.[5]

11.1. Buckskin Charlie, 1899 (Scan #20103579, History Colorado)

Those who continued to roam west of the reservation in southeastern Utah freely intermarried and mingled with San Juan Paiutes. These interethnic Indians were often referred to as "Payuchis" or simply Paiutes by non-Indians who saw no difference. It was a unique ethnic mix where the worlds of the San Juan Paiutes, Weeminuche Utes, and Navajos collided, sometimes in conflict, but often—especially in later years—in a fusion of relationships or alliances.[6] Men like Mancos Jim, Mariano, Johnny Benow, Poke (Poco or Polk), Narraguinep, and Posey (a Ute-Paiute brother-in-law of the Ute leader Poke) led these "renegade," "outlaw," or "bronco" Utes in the maze of canyons, gorges, and mountains of southeastern Utah. Together they epitomized the Weeminuche demand for freedom but frequently conflicted with settlers—especially cattle-men—who coveted the same open range.[7]

Following the 1878 agreement, non-Indians flooded into southwestern Colorado and spilled into Utah along the San Juan River. In short order, large commercial cattle companies were vying for the tax-free public range along the slopes of the Blue Mountains and La Sals, home of the Weeminuche and once-powerful Sheberetch.[8] By 1880 tens of thousands of sheep and cattle grazed in southeastern Utah—as many as 11,000 sheep and 32,000 cattle grazed year-round, with another 100,000 driven in from Colorado for winter range. The region became a wild free-for-all no-man's-land for the often lawless and bellig-erent sort attracted to isolated cattle outfits and trading posts, and the increas-ingly defensive and quarrelsome off-reservation Utes and Paiutes. Encroaching Navajo sheepherders added to the tension-filled mix as they spread north, even as a series of new Mormon settlements were established, intent on claiming southeastern Utah against gentile incursions while befriending the Utes, Pai-utes, and Navajos.[9]

As early as 1855 Mormons had attempted a settlement at the main ford of the Colorado on the Old Spanish Trail near the La Sal Mountains (the Elk Mountain mission), but Sheberetch Utes had driven them out. Decimated by smallpox in the mid-1870s, Sheberetch survivors were either absorbed by the Weeminuches or straggled onto the Uintah Reservation. By 1878, settlements began to appear in southeastern Utah, first at the Colorado ford (Moab), and then on the San Juan River (Bluff). A few years later, Bluff Mormons moved north to Piute Springs (Monticello), and then to the foot of the Blue Mountains (Blanding).[10]

In the spring of 1881, conflict erupted and a low-intensity warfare devel-oped. The thousands of sheep and cattle, along with plow-and-fence farming, were destroying Weeminuche range and watering holes, decimating their timber, and causing game to withdraw. Protective Payuchis had attacked a government survey party as early as 1875, and as non-Indians moved in, they continued to beg at doors, steal or mutilate stock, make threats, and destroy property. In response cowboys and settlers abused Indians and threatened retribution, complaining of being "crucified between two thieves" (Navajos and Utes/Paiutes). Colorado newspapers sermonized against the "curse of Indians" and urged citizens to "pursue, [and] kill the red-skinned devils until there is not enough of them left to rob a 'hen roost.'" Rumors spread that bands of whites were secretly planning to "clean out the [Colorado] reservation" and covenanting to wage war against the remaining Indians in the name of "progress."[11]

In May 1881, several Weeminuches were accused of horse theft and badly beaten by a rancher named Thurman near today's Dove Creek. In response, Weeminuches attacked Thurman's ranch where they killed him and two customers, burned the cabin, and stole $1,000 cash, food, arms, tack, and at least one hundred horses.[12] With other Payuchis, they rode into the rugged canyon country west of Bluff, firing on isolated herders and stealing more horses, including some from Bluff. When Bluff residents tracked them to a nearby camp, they found a mixed group of men, women, children, and 150 head of "good quality" horses, some of which bore brands. The men carried "plenty of greenbacks" and had "harness lines…blind bridles and halters." A ranch had obviously been raided.[13]

Despite ongoing petty thefts, the Mormons were on relatively good terms with local Indians, and remained so; in return, Utes and Paiutes primarily targeted gentile ranchers. As one Ute remarked, "We can whip cowboys. Whip soldiers. Mormons no fight. Mormons mostly good friends." Evidence supports this, for of the forty killed by Indians in this region between 1880 and 1920, only one was Mormon.[14] So the Thurman Ranch raiders were amenable to negotiating the return of stolen *Mormon* stock. Shortly after the Mormons left, Mancos Jim—the most prominent bronco Ute leader—joined the raiders and led a combined band north toward the La Sal Mountains, vandalizing property and stock and stealing more horses from non-Mormon ranches.[15]

By this time, a posse of vigilante cowboys and miners from Colorado had headed out to find the "renegade" Utes, anxious to avenge the Thurman ranch killings and to "clean out the redskins." Although the Southern Ute agent, Henry Page, warned against chasing the "fearless and wayward set" of Utes in their "rough and inaccessible" country, Bill Dawson's ragtag posse, along with their hodgepodge of weapons, crossed into Utah. There the vigilantes encountered a military patrol from Fort Lewis (Durango) and were sharply warned to "stay out of Indian fighting business," but the defiant group pressed on.[16]

The posse finally located a large Ute camp on the northwestern slopes of the La Sals. The camp included at least seventy fighting men, along with women, children, and hundreds of sheep, goats, and horses. The posse debated whether to attack or negotiate. Evidence exists that had they negotiated, the Utes would have been amenable, for they had recently seen an ill-omened full lunar eclipse and a bright comet. However, many in the posse seemed overly

214

anxious to kill Indians, so Dawson led his eager posse in a poorly planned and precipitous assault.[17] As Ute women scattered, their men fought a successful rearguard action down Little Castle Valley into Pinhook Draw. There, Ute sharpshooters in the rimrocks ambushed and then picked off a terrified six-man scouting team in a lethal crossfire. Dawson's command disintegrated and fled in disarray. Afterwards, the Utes smashed the victims' heads and laid their remains on display in a gruesome message against further pursuit.[18]

As the surviving posse members retreated toward Colorado, they encountered four companies of African American soldiers from the 9th Cavalry out of Fort Lewis heading into Utah. Their commander, Captain Henry Carroll, was a professional soldier and veteran Indian fighter who was unsympathetic to civilians who interfered in Indian affairs. He chastised the posse for "attacking and disturbing the Indians" and threatened to arrest them.[19]

It had been a disastrous encounter. A dozen men from the posse died, while Mancos Jim claimed he lost at least eighteen "good" and four "average" Ute fighters.[20] Although Poke, Mancos Jim, and a youthful Posey openly boasted they were involved in the incidents, only two reservation Paiutes were reprimanded, neither of them participants. The Ute victory—and their lack of punishment—encouraged another four decades of low-grade conflict in the region and increased the pressure to confine the "insolent renegades" to a reservation.[21]

Trouble flared up again three years later. Three cattle outfits from Colorado set up camp in Montezuma Canyon, Utah; Utes from the reservation with passes to hunt were camped nearby. Within a few days, a brawl erupted over purportedly stolen horses, and in its wake both groups decamped. But Ute warriors followed and harassed the fleeing cowboys, who eventually abandoned their wagons, eluded pursuit, and fled back to Colorado. The Utes plundered and burned their supply wagons and rounded up their horses.[22]

Troops were dispatched from Fort Lewis and ordered to pursue and chastise the "offending" Utes. Captain H. P. Perrine led a forty-nine-man contingent augmented by more than forty eager-for-blood cowboys. They caught up with thirty or forty Ute fighters two weeks later in the rough, unexplored country south of the Blue Mountains. But the Utes had taken up an excellent defensive position in the rimrocks above a narrow cut in the canyon (since known as Piute Pass or Soldiers' Crossing). During a short siege, the Utes were able to hold off the troops, kill a scout and a cowboy, and stalemate the troops. Short of supplies and water, Perrine finally withdrew under a nonlethal hail of warning bullets.[23]

This second ignominious defeat especially rankled cowboys in Utah and Colorado. Most non-Indians viewed reservations as concentration camps on which troublesome Indians should be locked up, with the agricultural and grazing lands left to Euro-Americans. Because of this, some non-Indians felt justified in shooting, on sight, any Indian caught outside reservation boundaries. Ongoing complaints claimed off-reservation bronco Utes were living by stealing cattle and horses. The fight at Piute Pass only intensified the popular opinion that all Indians should be confined. While the charge of horse stealing was undeniable, the Weeminuches and Paiutes were not living off raids nor stealing cattle in large numbers. In fact, cattle rustling by *non*-Indians was a regular occurrence. The Four Corners region facilitated the escape of fugitives who crossed borders at will, and rustlers sometimes wore moccasins to implicate Indians.[24]

In 1885 Coloradoans sent a petition to President Grover Cleveland and Congress demanding the Utes be kept on their reservation by force. The Utes were, they argued, using their government annuities to arm themselves with the best guns and roam at will off the reservation. They accused the "savage fiends" of being "lawless, marauding, savage and bloodthirsty," and of holding white property to be their "hellish sport." Once again Denver newspapers called for the complete expulsion of Utes from Colorado. Cowboys boasted they would no longer shoot Indians "on the wing"; instead, they would use "their own" tactics and shoot them while sitting or sleeping. Several camps of cowboys swore to kill the first Indians they saw off the reservation.[25]

They found their opportunity in June 1885. Thirteen cowboys besieged a Weeminuche family camped on Beaver Creek, north of Dolores. Despite having permits to hunt, and although a mother emerged holding an infant to indicate peace, they were still attacked. A few members of the family escaped, but at least four men, two women, and a child were killed—some while they slept. Utes retaliated by raiding a ranch in Montezuma Valley (Colorado) and killing one man.[26] But where the unprovoked murder of seven (or more) Utes went virtually unnoticed, the death of a single rancher was sensationalized, and headlines proclaimed an "Inhuman Massacre by the Indians." Newspapers again took up the old cry, "The Utes Must Go!," while justifying the attack on the Ute family: "This massacre of Indians may have seemed cruel to many... [but] by adopting their methods the warfare between Indians and whites [was] stopped."[27]

Non-Indians prepared for a siege by hostile Indians, even as the dead Utes lay unburied because none dared venture off their reservation. Furious over the matter, Southern Ute agent Stollsteimer wrote to the commissioner of Indian Affairs:

> We found the bodies of six Indians…attacked and killed while asleep.…The perpetrators of this foul murder have not been discovered…[but] I doubt whether the State authorities would take steps to arrest and punish them. An Indian is hardly considered a human being by a certain class of the Whites with which this part of the country is disgraced.[28]

He threatened action against the cowboys and a feeble investigation was launched, but few non-Indians would talk about the incident. No further violence occurred, and interest waned.[29]

THE UTES MUST GO!—AGAIN

In 1886, Mouache, Capote, and Weeminuche leaders aired their grievances in Washington. Ignacio angrily petitioned the government for a new reservation in southeastern Utah, away from the rapacious cattlemen and miners of southern Colorado. Mouache and Capote leaders bitterly protested that agreement promises had not been kept as expected.[30]

The Utes especially resented the pressure to change their lifestyle and ongoing attempts to force their children into boarding schools. Annuities—which had been given them "not for nothing, but…from the sale of our lands"—were often withheld from parents who refused to send their children to school. Utes—especially Ute women—disliked the separation and restriction of boarding schools and feared their children were being educated away from their Indian traditions (which they were). Boarding schools were also very regimented. Children were rounded up by agents and Indian police, and runaways were sometimes returned at the point of a gun. Once in school, students were forced to cut their hair and wear uniforms, stand in line for flag ceremonies, and sometimes forced to drill like soldiers (making them popular candidates for later war recruitment).[31] Worst of all, children died there. Diseases such as smallpox, measles, pneumonia, and trachoma were rife throughout the reservation, but especially in crowded, often cold and rundown schools with no medical facilities. In 1884 half of the Southern Ute children sent to a boarding school in Albuquerque died. Nevertheless, despite "strenuous opposition," the order to send Southern Ute children to school, by force if necessary, remained in effect until 1893, and was encouraged by agents beyond that.[32]

Meanwhile, Ute leaders continued to be politically active and lobbied for help, but no action was taken on any of their petitions. By this time eastern reformers and Congress were already planning to break up large reservations and dissolve tribal identities toward their goal of Indian individualism, agrarianism, and civilization through individual land ownership.

In 1875 Congress passed the first harbinger of a number of new acts to bring this about. The Indian Homestead Act provided Indians the right to file a claim on land if they agreed to abandon tribal affiliation. Congress passed another Indian Homestead Act in 1884, followed by the Indian Severalty Act of 1885 and the Dawes Severalty (General Allotment) Act of 1887, all of which included provisions for Indians to homestead under the same conditions as non-Indians with the promise of eventual private title to the land.[33]

Some Utes did avail themselves of these homesteading rights. Western Utes had done so at Koosharem and Thistle Valley, as had Pahvants near Corn Creek. To the south, Mancos Jim and other Weeminuche Utes filed on land on Montezuma Creek and in Allen Canyon just south of the Blue Mountains. But while they attempted to work their homesteads, others like Posey, Old Poke, and Johnny Benow continued to lead defiant nomadic bands in the same area.[34]

In the meantime, the government pressed forward with their plans to break up all Indian reservations. Under the new rules of the 1885 Severalty Act and Dawes 1887 General Allotment Act, reservations held in common would cease to exist as they were broken up—or as Theodore Roosevelt later put it, "pulverized"—into plots of individually owned farmland with the remainder of the land thrown open to public sale, homesteading, or grazing. The profits from the land sale would purportedly be returned to the tribe.[35] Well-meaning reformers argued that home, family, and property were the "very anchorages of civilization," that land ownership and farming was a higher level of civilization, and that Christianity was a superior way of life that would "fix" everything. Hard work was ennobling and idleness, evil; individual property ownership was ideal while group identity (tribalism or native communism) was bad. Unless Indians were forced to assimilate, they would become extinct.[36]

One consequence was that Colorado, who hoped to divest itself of the southern Utes as it had its northern and central bands, now found unexpected resistance. The Agreement of 1880 already included provisions for allotting individual held-in-trust homesteads. But agents reported that there was insufficient arable land along the specified La Plata River, and officials again suggested that all Ute claims be shifted to Utah instead. A variety of interests surfaced, ranging from overt fears or simple dislike of Indian neighbors to greed for agricultural or coal lands. The influential Colorado legislature sent numerous memorials to Washington, powerful Colorado senators lobbied, and journalists once again initiated a media blitz maligning Utes and demanding their expulsion. The "savage tribes" deserved extinction so their "rich possessions" could be developed by a "more appreciative race."[37]

Amidst a flurry of public and congressional discussion—twelve unsuccessful removal bills in seven years—Colorado representatives finally succeeded, and a bill for Southern Ute removal passed in 1888. Since Southern Ute leaders adamantly refused to be exiled to Utah's Uintah and Ouray Reservations, a large reservation in southeastern Utah was proposed. But officials who visited the area reported it was not suitable as a home for "Indians who were to be educated for citizenship through the pursuit of agriculture." Still, members of the Southern Ute Commission worked assiduously to persuade the reluctant Utes to sign the agreement anyway. Pressured relentlessly, leaders finally agreed to exchange their Colorado strip for a three-million-acre reservation in southeastern Utah.[38]

But a political stalemate ensued and debate raged for another seven years, as their relocation was blocked by a coordinated outcry from a variety of interests. Meanwhile, with little incentive to improve their farms, Utes could do little more than collect annuities and wait, while speculative non-Indians began to maneuver into the best positions to claim reservation lands. Some even got hired at the agency and brought new farm equipment to store on the reservation.[39]

Mormon settlers in southeast Utah also fought the proposal, objecting to being displaced or surrounded by an Indian reservation. Utah's legislature sent a flurry of resolutions to Congress. But Utah was politically impotent. Instead, the political clout to block the politically powerful Colorado business concerns came from an unexpected alliance. The Pittsburgh Cattle Company neighbored the influential Indian Rights Association in Philadelphia and was one of several major cattle companies with significant interests in southeastern Utah. Europeans and Americans had invested heavily in the burgeoning cattle industry and stood to lose millions if the free range was withdrawn and reserved for Indians. Consequently, this influential lobby exerted considerable pressure on important members of Congress and blocked all attempts to move Southern Utes to southeastern Utah.[40]

But the Utes grew tired of waiting and took matters into their own hands. In 1893 Ignacio and Mariano led a large group of Weeminuches to the Blue Mountains for the fall hunt and then refused to return. Complaints mounted as extensive Ute herds competed for the limited grass and water, and alarmed Utah citizens reacted predictably: they pled for help to save their property and lives from the "anarchy" of the "misguided Utes" and potential "slaughter of women and children." Although Southern Ute agent David Day argued the Utes had always wintered in Utah's San Juan County, cowboys fabricated stories of depredations, and the press shouted that Utah had been invaded by "Bloodthirsty Utes." Officials and the public responded. Utah's governor Caleb West headed for Piute Springs, as did representatives of the Colorado military and Agent Day. Ignacio, Mariano, and Benow met with officials along with a rabble of settlers and cowboys, local Mormons, and armed volunteers. The situation grew explosive as Utes aired their grievances and non-Indians armed themselves. In the midst of heated discussions, Day received orders from Washington to return "his" Utes to their Colorado reservation. The chiefs were incensed, but under threat of both military and vigilante intervention they left, struggling through bitter cold and high snows to return to their reservation.[41] Three months later Congress "disapproved" the 1888 agreement and ordered the Southern Ute Reservation be allotted in severalty.[42]

The stated reason for denying the new reservation was based on "previous settlement," but the real reason was that it was contradictive of the 1885 and 1887 legislations to break up the existing reservations, not create new ones. Moving the Utes to a larger reservation solved nothing, was costly and unnecessary, and violated the intentions of the government's new Indian policy.[43]

Throughout the years of debate, the irascible Weeminuche chief, Ignacio, had persisted in harassing the Office of Indian Affairs (OIA) by pressing Ute claims and demanding the new reservation. Ignacio was the 6'2" son of a Ute medicine man killed by the family of a patient he failed to cure. Ignacio avenged his father's death by killing a dozen members of the patient's family. Many Utes regarded him with awe, while most non-Indians thought him highly intelligent, desirous of peace, but overly demanding. However, most officials considered Ignacio a "thorn in the side," an enemy of progress, and his Weeminuches the most "unprogressive, nomadic, troublesome element in the tribe." Ignacio was "bitterly opposed to everything which points toward civilization," one representative wrote. "Labor is degradation...individual property or thrift a crime against the sacred traditions of his race." He was

11.2. Ignacio, Weeminuche leader (Scan #10038663, History Colorado)

an "unprogressive and civilization-hating old chief" whose "influence over the warlike spirits in his following" was counterproductive and derogatory toward the dignity of the government.[44] By 1892 Ignacio had become so troublesome that officials refused to recognize him as either a spokesman or chief of any southern Ute band, and then fired him as chief of the Indian Police. But Ignacio's influence was strong, and officials were forced to acknowledge his leadership and grudgingly reinstate him as police chief.[45]

Though Ignacio did not gain a Utah reservation, he did garner one concession: the arid western end of the Southern Ute Reservation would remain held in common, a subagency would be established there, and anyone who did

11.3. Issue day at the Navajo Springs subagency, early twentieth century (Denver Public Library, Western History Collection, G. Day, X-30357)

not want to take allotments could go there. However, only the Weeminuches went, for interband feuding eliminated most Mouache or Capotes, and the lack of a reliable water source was daunting. Though irrigation projects were promised, they were not forthcoming. Instead, water had to be hauled in until the 1980s when canals were finally completed as part of the Animas-La Plata water project. Meanwhile, non-Indian incursions continued to be a problem. One of Ignacio's preferred campsites was also a favored route through McElmo Canyon and Navajo Springs, and it continued to be a virtual thoroughfare for Indians and non-Indians alike.[46]

Further to the east, the Southern Utes did have reliable water sources from five major rivers or streams, and attempts were ongoing to develop irrigation. However, non-Indians began early to divert and steal most of the water. Despite guarantees of water rights in their treaties, Utes were subject to Colorado water laws based on prior rights. That is, whoever first took the water and put it to "beneficial use" had the right to it. Agent Day tried to file claims for the Utes in anticipation of an influx of non-Indian homesteaders, but he fought an uphill battle that ultimately ended in court. By 1908 many allotments still had no water, so the government proposed and eventually built the Vallecito Reservoir on the reservation.[47]

A total of 375 allotments were made, family heads receiving homesteads of 160 acres while single men over age eighteen were allotted 80 acres. Some

Coloradoans complained of a "plot" to locate Indians on the best land; a senator investigated, but the allotments were made. Another 500,000 acres on the western portion of the reservation—considered unsuitable for farming—were reserved for grazing and hunting. Meanwhile, under Ignacio's lead, the Weeminuches refused their allotments and took up residence in the barren territory around Mesa Verde and nearby Sleeping Ute Mountain. In 1899 the remainder of the reservation was opened to non-Indians for $1.25 an acre. The Denver and Rio Grande Railroad, anxious for new customers, advertised for homesteaders to claim land in "one of the most fertile portions of Colorado," which promised "unlimited growth" and with a water supply "many times greater than needed" for ranching and agriculture. Hundreds of eager farmers and ranchers filed on thousands of acres during a wild land rush, followed by a steady flow of homestead filings until all remaining land was gone.[48]

The area became a checkerboard maze as Euro-Americans took up plots and Southern Utes leased or ultimately sold their allotments. The Weeminuches, however, remained adamantly opposed to farming, believing that if men were forced to do women's work, it would emasculate the Ute nation. Some threatened to destroy the crops of any Ute who did try to farm. But very few Southern Utes attempted to work their land. Instead, many leased out or contracted their land to Hispanic American sharecroppers who worked for half the crop. (When northern Ute bands attempted to do the same thing, their horrified agent forbade it because the ennobling nature of farming and hard work would be lost if entrepreneurs leased or sharecropped their land.)[49]

Such allotment leases became commonplace nationwide, and the Dawes Severalty Act inadvertently served as the means of ultimate dispossession of Indians from their land rather than assuring tenure and survival. Though most non-Indians championed the act for its humanitarian potential, few, if any, took into account that a people steeped in the tradition of collective ownership with usufruct rights for all tribal members, and with the freedom to roam over the land at will, could not change overnight into individual landowners restricted to a single small plot of ground. Although most proponents of the Dawes Severalty Act were well meaning—if ivory-towered advocates out of touch with real Indians—critics still maintain that many of those responsible for its passage were well aware that allotted land would ultimately end up in non-Indian hands. Evidence exists that some self-interested Indian agents even conspired to help non-Indians gain cheap or free access to Indian land, water, and ditches.[50]

Within ten years, and despite vigorous protests, 70,000 acres of prime grazing and hunting land were also carved from the Weeminuche reserve under the new Antiquities Act, creating Mesa Verde National Park. Although new lands were later appropriated north of Sleeping Ute Mountain, it was a poor substitute for the assets lost to a people already living on a resource-poor land. Rancor persisted for decades.[51]

The split in land use brought a split in the reservation as well as in the "tribal" identities of its residents. The region occupied by the Weeminuches was eventually recognized as the Ute Mountain Reservation, and in 1940 the Weeminuches became known officially as the Ute Mountain Ute Tribe (although they were treated as Southern Utes in United States court cases). They retreated into the fastness of their reservation and tried to turn their backs on non-Indians and non-Indian ways.

Further east, the Mouaches and Capotes remained identified with the Southern Ute agency, but they could not turn their backs on non-Indians. Just as their lands were intermingled with those of Euro-Americans and Hispanics, so were their lives. In time the close social and political proximity of the two bands, as well as their shared struggles, reinforced their identity as Ute Indians and subsumed individual band identities within the overarching political and administrative identity of their reservation. They were becoming not Capote or Mouache, but Southern Utes.

Chapter 12

The Land Divided
Uintah and Ouray Reservations, 1881–1906

While band identities were merging on the Southern Ute Reservation, the opposite was occurring on the Uintah and Ouray Reservations. Instead of accord, rancorous interband competitions quickly developed, crystallizing the boundaries of individual band identities. During the next several years, these three separate identities were unintentionally reinforced when the government treated each band differently—much to the chagrin of acting agents who had to work with them. It would take time to determine leadership and to forge any kind of a working political relationship between the three bickering bands. In the meantime, the northern Utes would remain helpless to stop the further dissolution of their land and livelihoods.

RELOCATION, RECRIMINATIONS, AND CONFLICT

Piah and especially Colorow epitomized the struggle to avoid removal. Over the years Colorow had led the Nevava Utes, a band of 400–500 that generally ignored the Hot Sulphur Springs, White River, and Los Piños agencies. Instead, they hunted in the northern mountains, camped near Red Rocks, and frequented the Denver subagency to collect supplies and sell hides between chasing bison and enemy tribes on the plains. While most Ute bands visited Denver on their way to or from the plains, Colorow and Piah's bands were the most frequent, and there was little love lost between them and Denver agent James B. Thompson. Though Thompson described most Utes as peaceable and of a "quiet demeanor," he did not like Colorow (or "Colorado"), whom he called a "shabby genteel specimen of a big chief" who "wrap[s] himself in the solitude of his own originality and in a very filthy blanket." Thompson complained that Colorow's Nevava band was but a poor offshoot of the "great Nevava" family, afflicted with "many incurable cases of kleptomania and a total want

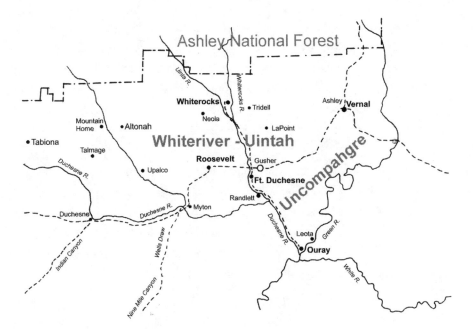

12.1. Uintah and Ouray Reservation, twentieth century, showing general distribution of the three bands: White River, Uintah, and Uncompahgre.

of…gratitude" for the beneficence of the government, sarcastically likening them to Oliver Twist, always asking for more. The feelings were mutual with Colorow's Utes; they called Thompson (behind his back) Old Stiff, Cabbage Head, and a Horse's Ass.[1]

When the Denver agency was closed and the White River Utes ordered to Utah, some free-ranging northern Ute bands shifted their agency identities to suit their own purposes. Thus Piah, for example, signed the 1868 treaty as a Uintah, was referred to as a Nevava Ute in the 1870s, and, after the 1880 agreement, escaped south to the Weeminuches where he became known as Peter Snow. One of his great-grandchildren would later chair the Ute Mountain Utes.[2]

Similarly, after the battle at Milk Creek and massacre at the White River Agency, Colorow and most of his band reappeared among the Uncompahgres. When they too were forced to relocate to Utah, he turned back with a small hunting band and disappeared into the northern hills for their annual fall hunt. Colorow didn't straggle into the Ouray agency until later that winter, and he would continue to exercise hunting rights as promised in the 1873 and 1880 agreements that permitted Utes to hunt on land ceded in Colorado. In any case, agents explained that it was difficult to keep the Utes penned on the reservation when it was "nothing but a desert...[while] on three sides it [was] bounded by mountains where there [was] plenty of water, grass, and game."[3]

Nicaagat also remained defiant, refusing to go to Utah. Instead, he visited the Comanches and then joined Shoshone friends on the Wind River Reservation. While there he was arrested but escaped, shooting and killing a soldier in the process. Angry troops surrounded his tipi and blasted it with a cannon, killing him instantly.[4]

Meanwhile, most of the Tabeguaches/Uncompahgres arrived at the site of their new agency in September 1881—months *before* the reservation was officially established.[5] A military force soon joined them, claiming the best ten acres of bottom- and hay land as a military reserve for the new Fort Thornburgh. However, they soon realized the folly of taking most of the good farmland, and the post was briefly relocated six miles upstream from Ashley; in 1886 it was moved again, this time to its permanent home halfway between the Whiterocks and Ouray agencies. Though General Crook originally envisioned an elaborate post, it only received a $1,500 appropriation. So lumber was scavenged from the old post and used in the construction of the new Fort Duchesne.[6]

The increase of non-Indian settlers on the reservation fringes, and the need to service the new military post, required better roads and rail service. In 1881 the Denver & Rio Grande Railroad cut through the southern edge of the Ouray Reservation, and a second railroad was proposed (but never built). By 1883 three new roads led to the reservations—south from Fort Bridger, east from Park City, and the preferred supply route running north from the railroad near Price. After Fort Duchesne was built in 1886, one responsibility of its troops was to keep the road and telegraph lines from Price in good repair. These new roads not only brought in supplies to the once isolated reservation but also increased non-Indian influences.[7]

The friction between the three Ute bands also increased. On the one hand, agents described the White Rivers as arrogant, intransigent, and insolent. These Utes continued to complain that manual agricultural labor was demeaning, and they argued the government still owed them compensation for the Colorado homelands it had taken. And since Washington had also stolen their traditional means of support, it was obligated to support them with subsidies. This belief was reinforced when money and goods, as well as beef from relocated tribal cattle herds, were distributed to the White Rivers and Uncompahgres. On the other hand, the peaceful Uintah band was forced to support itself through agriculture and day labor for the agency and was given smaller cash payments and beef allotments than their more warlike cousins. Agent John Critchlow complained that the White Rivers

> laugh at the Uintahs for farming, and say they ought to fight and then Washington would furnish them plenty to eat. This seems reasonable to the simple minds of these Indians who have been told that the harder they worked the more they might expect from the government... [but] now see others, parties to a horrible massacre, located on lands which the Uintahs had always supposed their own, and without any effort toward self-support promised abundant subsistence and liberal annuity payments forever, while this tribe, meriting reward and encouragement, are furnished with less than one-fourth of a ration, and... supplied with [almost] nothing.... The Uintahs and White Rivers, if they are to remain together, must be treated with equal liberality... [and] looked upon as members of the same tribe.[8]

The Ute commission added,

> We feed the White River murderers and compel the peaceable Uintahs to largely care for themselves. This course induces the Indians to believe that they must refuse to work, refuse to be orderly and peaceable, and commit some depredations or murder, and then a commission will be appointed to treat with them, and pay them in goods, provisions and money to behave themselves. This looks to an Indian very much like rewarding enemies and punishing friends, and gives him a singular idea of our Christian civilization and our manner of administering justice, which has so much the appearance of rewarding vice and punishing virtue.[9]

From the first, the Uintahs resented having to share their reservation with the White Rivers while already struggling to survive themselves; when they were later compelled to share it further with the Uncompahgres, their resentment grew. For their part, the Uncompahgre resented the White Rivers for precipitating their expulsion from Colorado, while the White Rivers still resented the Uncompahgres who had been led by the Washington-appointed Ouray to the "detriment" of the other bands. The government perpetuated these factions as they continued to deal with each band independently and partially. The boundaries defining band identities tightened, and the three

Ute bands solidified into long-lasting antagonistic factions—and later political entities—that were often at each other's throats. These bitter rivalries continued to shred social and political relations for decades to come, and to some extent persist to this day.[10]

228

Much of the bands' discontent traced directly to their finances and the inequities in their treatment. The White Rivers and Uncompahgre were receiving land payment annuities, of which the peaceful Uintahs had none. No Uintah treaty had ever been ratified, and their ceded land had never been paid for. The White Rivers were also unhappy because reparation money was garnished out of their annuities and given to the survivors of the Meeker Massacre. After a few years they began demanding these blood payments come to an end.[11]

The unrest came to a head in May 1885 and led directly to the construction of Fort Duchesne in 1886. In 1885 the Uncompahgres discovered they had been cheated out of part of their annuity payments, tribal money which was divided and distributed according to the current census rolls.[12] For several years a duplicitous clerk had been padding the rolls and pocketing the extra money (about $3,600, the equivalent of at least 279 nonexistent Utes). The clerk conveniently disappeared just before the May distribution, and the new agent and clerks were left holding the bag. When the Uncompahgres learned of the fraud, they demanded the remainder be disbursed since it was their joint tribal monies; they knew if their agent returned the excess to Washington they would never see it. But federal protocol required all excess money be returned until a revised tribal roll was made for the next disbursement. The Uncompahgres had other ideas. The chiefs—supported by the entire tribe—demanded their money at gunpoint.

Agent Carson counted out the money "pretty quick," wrote out his resignation, and left within hours on the agency's best horse. (However, $3,300 would be withheld from annuities the following year.)[13] The Uncompahgres had been in the right, but this was the last straw in a series of ongoing incidents and complaints. At Whiterocks, the White Rivers had once again roughed up an agent, and a White River had killed a trapper and gone missing. Non-Indian settlers at Ashley and Vernal were also complaining that the Utes were wild, intractable, and uncontrollable. And they sometimes were, in part due to an illegal trade in whiskey that at times produced drunken, frustrated, and often belligerent Utes.[14] Meanwhile, agents were afraid to police Utes who occasionally committed retributive murders within the tribe for personal offenses or shamanistic malpractice. Aggravating the situation were off-reservation hunting trips that antagonized Colorado cattlemen. Although most agency reports described the Utes as "perfectly peaceable," incidents of threatened violence confirmed the need for military intervention. Investigators concluded,

> Unless the Indians were restrained by the presence of a powerful military force, their vicious propensities might lead them to acts of violence. The attitude of the Indians was shown to be defiant and dictatorial toward the Government officials and employees. Being remote from the settlement they had seen but little of civilized life, and did not seem to know or dread the power of the Government.[15]

Rumors had also begun to circulate that Mormons in their new Vernal settlement, currently under legal attack for their practice of plural marriage, had assured Utes that "the Indians and the Mormons combined could successfully resist the Government troops."[16] Responding to all of these concerns, the War Department issued special orders on August 7, 1886, to establish a military fort at a point midway between the agencies at Whiterocks and Ouray. The new post would become a focal point for the two reservations and would eventually host a combined Uintah and Ouray agency to administer all three bands.[17]

However, in 1886 the Utes were understandably alarmed at the news that the military was coming. After all, it was the threatened military invasion of the White River Reservation in 1879 that had precipitated the Thornburgh and Meeker incidents. Uncompahgre and White River warriors prepared to defend their reservation. The situation did not improve when non-Indians spread stories that General Crook was planning to kill some of the Ute chiefs, put others in prison, and drive the rest of the tribe away so the reservation could be given to non-Indians. Provocateurs began to encourage Utes to drive out all whites, plunder agency supplies, and fight the soldiers in the canyons. Uintah chiefs told Special Agent E. E. White that their women and children were terrified, and their men's hearts were "heap sick." White believed that neighboring Mormons were trying to incite the Utes into another Meeker-Thornburgh incident, which would ensure the Utes' swift punishment and removal to Indian Territory and open the reservation to settlement.[18]

Although the situation was explosive, White convinced leading chiefs that another Ute war would lead to their sure destruction and "seal the doom of all your squaws and papooses."[19] But when the Utes discovered that some of the approaching troops were the Black 9th Cavalry, or "Buffalo Soldiers," the crisis was reignited.

According to White, northern bands feared the "Black white men," and that the few African Americans who had chanced among them had disappeared and were never heard from again. Black soldiers held a particularly fearsome reputation among many western Indians, who believed that blacks not only looked like but also fought as fiercely and were as difficult to kill as a wounded buffalo. The agitated Utes wanted White to send the *túu-nigíci* ("black niggers") back.[20]

Determined to allow no troops onto the reservation, a band of three hundred armed White Rivers set up an ambush along the shorter of two routes from Ashley Valley. But warned of the attack, the commander took the longer route and arrived safely at the chosen site for the military post. On August 23, Major Frederick W. Benteen arrived at the makeshift cantonment with two companies of Buffalo Soldiers. Of Little Bighorn infamy, Benteen had been ignominiously assigned to command the 9th Cavalry in what the soldiers called the "American Siberia." After looking the camp over, Benteen moved it to a more strategic site six miles upriver to bench land that overlooked the road linking the Ouray and Whiterocks agencies.[21] Both the ill-housed soldiers and Utes alike suffered through a miserably harsh winter, during which temperatures dropped to a frigid -20°F. Before spring the soldiers were calling the post "Fort Damn-Shame."[22]

Major Benteen, however, did not last so long; within three months of arriving, he was arraigned on charges of mismanagement, continual public drunkenness, and disorderly conduct. Normally known for being even-tempered, Benteen felt humiliated by his new assignment and took to drinking heavily. He disliked commanding black troops, disliked Indians, and disliked Mormons even more. That December, after initiating a fistfight over the presence of Mormons at the post, Benteen was relieved of duty and subsequently court-martialed (though reinstated at rank, in retirement).[23]

A series of commanders followed Benteen until the genial, well-liked Major James F. Randlett settled in at the fort as its commander in 1890. Randlett would remain for years at this post, despite offers at more desirable postings. Unsubstantiated rumors suggested he made under-the-table profits from beef supply contracts. Regardless, Randlett was an effective commander and was well-liked by the Utes.[24]

The fort remained an active bastion to control "hostile" Utes and protect the interests of the region's non-Indians well into the twentieth century, despite several attempts by the War Department to close it. By 1890 most of the military posts originally set up to protect trails or settlements in the West

12.1. Uintah and Ouray Utes at Fort Duchesne, Utah, c. 1895 (Denver Public Library, Western History Collection, T. McKee, Z-218)

were no longer needed. Yet, unusual for the west, Fort Duchesne resisted all attempts to shut it down. Despite recurrent reports that the Utes were peaceful, neighboring non-Indians continued to complain that the Utes were "wild and untamed Indians of the worst type"; they were "whiskey loving...lawless, red devils"; and that without a military presence, the non-Indians and agencies would be left to the mercy of the lawless Utes. One White River agent claimed it was only the presence of the military that kept the Utes from destroying everything at the agency. Oddly, even Major Randlett—a man particularly situated to know the peaceable nature of the Utes—was the only representative of the military who did *not* favor the abandonment of Fort Duchesne. Instead, he sent ominous letters of warning to Washington arguing the necessity of not only keeping a military presence on the reservation but of increasing it.[25]

Yet the Utes caused only minor trouble, mostly due to drunkenness. Rather than fear of Utes, the most likely reason for the extensive lobbying for a military presence was the dependence of local residents on income derived from the post. Many nearby non-Indians as well as large cattle interests relied on military supply contracts and government payrolls. In 1892 a secret agent well acquainted with the area and with Indian and non-Indian residents was hired by the War Department to investigate. He found no one "except those who are deriving some benefits from the traffic with the Post who apprehends any danger from Indians whatever," and he "never saw the Ute Indians more friendly than they are at the present time."

Nevertheless, significant pressure was brought to bear in Washington. Preston Nutter, a Colorado cattle baron whose Strawberry Valley Cattle Company supplied beef to the fort, asked Charles Homer and Alfred and Hermann Schiffer to use their political influence to both garner beef contracts and prevent the abandonment of Fort Duchesne. There are even hints that Major Randlett and the Secretary of War were part of this intrigue. Nutter later wrote that Hermann Schiffer's ability to "get an order of the War Department rescinded showed that he was big medicine." From 1891–1893, the post wavered on the edge of dissolution before receiving a last-minute reprieve. It remained a significant presence on the reservation until 1912, long after most frontier posts had been abandoned.[26]

Meanwhile, reservation land continued to be carved away. First to go was the six-square-mile military reserve.[27] Then S. H. Gilson and Bert Seaboldt used their influence with powerful friends to lobby Congress to remove another seven thousand acres in the middle of the Uintah Reservation to mine a rare form of asphalt found only in the Uintah Basin—Uintaite—later trademarked as Gilsonite. With the aid of a generous supply of liquor, and with the approval of the post commander and agency personnel, the Utes resignedly signed the agreement and unanimously approved the "Whiskey Tent Treaty," agreeing to cede a small tract of land six miles east of Fort Duchesne that was "utterly worthless for any purpose to the tribes."[28]

With the opening of the asphalt operations, a lawless shantytown quickly sprang up in the midst of the reservation that was visited by soldiers, non-Indians, and Utes alike. Because "The Strip" was public domain, Indian agents could not police it, but neither could public law officers because it was in the middle of a large Indian reservation. Only federal officers ever attempted to control its wild collection of rough frontiersmen—and then very gingerly. "Sobertown" became a haven for gamblers, prostitutes, criminals, counterfeiting, and all kinds of corruption. Outlaws frequented The Strip, including Butch Cassidy, the Sundance Kid, and Tabby Weep (celebrated as the fastest gunslinger in Utah, and a Ute). Until the reservation was opened in 1906, the area remained an uncontrolled blister of vice and a significant source of alcohol on the reservation, while liquor merchants near Vernal and peddlers smuggled in the rest. Agent Cornish complained of the "pest hole" and the impossibility of policing it, and Randlett denounced the uncontrolled "dens of gamblers and prostitutes just outside the military reservation" that supplied unrestricted alcohol. The last major incidence of violence there occurred in 1910, when a drunken Tabby Weep shot and killed a non-Indian, who wounded him in return. Liquor merchants on and off the reservation proved disastrous for the increasingly intoxicated Utes, who struggled with poverty, despair, and the growing loss of culture, tradition, and land.[29]

Making matters worse, non-Indians continued to trespass on Ute land. Prospectors and miners strayed onto the sprawling Ouray reservations, while ranchers drove stock across and grazed their herds in the lush Strawberry Valley, which lay on the western edge of the Uintah Reservation. After the General Allotment Act was passed, it became virtually impossible to keep trespassers off the reservations because they anticipated its eventual opening. The Uintah agents and their small contingent of Indian police had attempted to deal with this trespass for years. They had tried to collect grazing fees, fine trespassers or drive them off the land, or even just close the land to any grazing. But the trespass continued. Unable to control it, the agency finally leased grazing rights to the ranchers and left them to police each other.[30] Farmers also usurped Ute water with impunity. Heber Valley residents began to divert water in 1879, and by 1883 the Strawberry Canal Company had fifty stockholders who depended on the illegal water.[31]

The question of Indian hunting rights off the reservations was another source of contention. Each year Colorow led his band to northern Colorado for their fall hunt, where they gathered meat and hides for the winter. This was their right, according to the 1873 and 1880 agreements. But by 1887 the non-Indian population of northwestern Colorado had increased dramatically. The abandoned White River agency had been settled and renamed Meeker, and it now served as the center of ranching activity in the region. Other towns appeared as cattlemen moved in, bringing with them a dislike for Indians who strayed off reservations or grazed large horse herds on their rangeland. Colorado officials were also formulating new game laws because of the surging population as well as non-Indian game exploiters who were decimating deer herds for profit. Ute hunters found hundreds of deer carcasses on their hills, only the hindquarters taken and the remainder left to rot. But, predictably, the rapid decline of deer herds in the 1880s was blamed primarily on Ute hunters.[32]

By 1887, ranchers around Meeker were planning to resist Colorow and his seasonal hunters. Stirred up by a glory-seeking local sheriff who boasted of chasing the "dangerous Indians" out of Colorado, ranchers planned for trouble. When the Utes arrived that fall, Sheriff Jim Kendall and game wardens provoked an incident by accosting women (including Chipeta) picking berries. They made lewd remarks and then accused the Utes of poaching game and stealing horses. An altercation ensued and the posse fired on the Indians, who fired back in self-defense before fleeing. The posse burned the camp along with its winter supply of meat and hides, and then returned home to alert the territory to expect a full-scale retaliation. Alarmed messages were sent to the governor, who dispatched state troops to the aid of the "distressed" settlers.[33]

The messages of alarm also arrived at Ouray, where agent T. A. Byrnes was disbursing annuities. By this time Colorow's hunters were already retreating to the reservation, traveling as fast as their wounded would allow. But as messengers brought descriptions of the conflict, the entire reservation population grew alarmed, and Byrnes acted immediately to try to defuse the situation. He sent Ute messengers to urge the off-reservation Utes to hurry home, guaranteeing safe passage; he also reassured the reservation Utes that there was no need to prepare for war. At the same time, Byrnes sent agency employees to negotiate with the posse and the Colorado troops, even as he sent for his own military assistance from Fort Duchesne and seconded the small detachment then at the agency for immediate action.

Meanwhile, the Colorado troops, anxious to fight Indians, rudely rebuffed Byrnes's negotiator, threatened to pursue the Utes deep into the reservation, and pressed on in their hell-bent pursuit. Unaware that the still-aggressive posse and troops were catching up, Colorow's band paused to rest and eat near the reservation border. Kendall and the troops launched a surprise attack on the unsuspecting camp and engaged the Utes in an all-out battle. As the men desperately held off the Coloradoans, the women and children escaped, after which the men joined the retreat, abandoning all livestock and property. At the border they were met by more than one hundred armed Utes and a cavalry detachment from Fort Duchesne, who escorted the beleaguered band home.

The cost of this brief "war of 1887" was high: fifteen Utes were killed and others wounded, including Colorow; hundreds of horses and several thousand sheep and goats were confiscated by the Colorado ranchers (some stock was later grudgingly returned). Several Coloradoans were also killed, and Sheriff Kendall disappeared shortly thereafter, amid rumors of foul play by angry locals. The following year Colorow died from the effects of his wounds.[34]

Shortly after the incident, Agent Byrnes traveled to the town of Meeker, where he met with Colorado governor Alva Adams, several state representatives, and leading citizens. Byrnes condemned the breach of the Utes' treatied hunting rights and demanded Colorado restore or pay restitution for the Utes' lost property. In time Congress investigated the incident, determined the Colorado ranchers were at fault, and approved reparations of $80,000. However, the compensation came years later, and most Utes remained angry, believing it had never been paid. But Colorado's stance remained hard-line. While the events of the "war" had been unfortunate, the state remained adamant that it would tolerate *no* Utes hunting in Colorado hills, agreement rights notwithstanding. Congressman George Symes even warned Agent Byrnes that any trespassing Utes would be shot on sight.[35]

By this time, the numerous cattlemen on the western slopes were united against two enemies: sheepmen and Utes. Local papers continued to editorialize the annual Indian trek and complained about the lack of enforcement of game laws. At first, Colorado cattlemen were most focused on driving out a large shepherding interest. However, by 1897 the sheepmen were gone, and cattlemen were armed with a new Supreme Court ruling (*Ward v. Race Horse*) that found that once a territory had been granted statehood, its Indians were subject to all local state laws—including game laws—when off their reservations. This effectively annulled any conflicting Indian treaty rights, including hunting rights, unless the state legislated an exception.[36]

In October cowboys spotted Utes in their familiar hunting grounds east of Meeker, and a posse and game warden attempted to arrest several women and elders in camp. An altercation erupted, and the posse killed and wounded several Utes. Once again, the alarmed posse rushed home to sound the all-too-familiar alert that the Utes would be on the rampage—even as the Utes fled for home. On the way they fired a few shots at stray ranch hands and burned a barn and haystack, but the "war of 1897" came to an inglorious close as the hunting party straggled back to the reservation. Once again, Congress launched an investigation, but this time the game warden and posse were exonerated. It was the end of Ute hunting expeditions into the northern Colorado hills.[37] It was not, however, the end of bitter cultural memories. As late as 2008, and despite attempts at reconciliation, White River Utes still feared and disliked Meeker and its "racist" residents, were still crying "breach of treaty," and were still trying to negotiate the return of their "rightful" hunting rights.[38]

Certainly, the Utes had needed these hunting expeditions to supplement subsistence on the reservation, for life had become increasingly intolerable as they faced grave political, economic, and spiritual disorientation. Traditional nomadism had been rendered impossible, and a cosmological orientation and

236

12.2. Whiterocks, Utah, on issue day, 1912 (Used by permission, Uintah County Library Regional History Center, L. C. Thorne Collection, all rights reserved)

identity based on homelands and sacred sites had been wrenched and revised. Trading and raiding were long past; traditional hunting and foraging grounds were off-limits; farmers were stealing water and trespassing on tribal grazing lands; and the threat of allotments portended even further loss of land.

On top of it all, agents were trying to bribe, cajole, or force Ute parents to send their children to school. Year after year, agents reported that Uintah and Ouray Ute parents were as hostile and "violently opposed to sending their children to school" as were their Southern Ute relations. By the early twentieth century, frustrated non-Indian teachers were still complaining that although they "squatted in their filthy wickiups and counseled with the stubborn savages," the teachers were ultimately told that the Ute parents "had no children or that they wouldn't let them go."[39] This was especially true of the Uncompahgre, with one man telling an agent in 1898 that "Me no give 'um children up; fight first." Well into the twentieth century, Uncompahgre parents still disappeared into the mountains to hide their children from agency employees or police sent to round them up and force them into school.[40] This hostility remained, even after the Uncompahgres got their own school at Randlett, a town between Ouray and Fort Duchesne. Agents welcomed the new school, because it was impractical to send Uncompahgre children to the distant and overcrowded school in Whiterocks, and wary parents refused to send their children to Colorado to the new Grand Junction Indian School.[41]

On all four reservations, agents and school superintendents had long struggled to get students into their schools. In the mid-1880s, Uintah agents had tried bribes, paying gratuities to "industrious" parents who sent their children to school. But by the 1890s, like the Southern Ute agents, they were withholding annuities to force parents to send their children. At Whiterocks the earliest attempts to establish schools failed because few children could be recruited, attendance was often irregular, and most children disappeared with parents during fall hunts or spring planting or gathering. School personnel was also limited, buildings were dilapidated and poorly heated, and there were few or nonexistent sanitary facilities or medical help. Later, when enrollment rose to fifty or sixty students and a new school was built, it was still too small for the potential student enrollment. Not surprisingly, disease was an ongoing problem. Seasonal epidemics plagued the Indian population at large, but they were especially virulent among clustered students, and the schools had no means to treat them. Smallpox, measles, trachoma, tuberculosis pneumonia, consumption, and influenza were familiar complaints. When diseases like measles broke out, if the school didn't close (which it was sometimes forced to), parents would often pull children out to be doctored by traditional shamans. For years these medicine men were the bane of the agencies, "found everywhere practicing their fiendish arts" and, according to agency reports, keeping the people mired in the very superstitions agents hoped to eradicate.[42]

Schools thus became a battleground: on one side were agents and educators who wanted to civilize Ute children and wean them from their traditional "savagery," and on the other, "blanket-Indian" parents who vigorously opposed this cultural genocide. And best intentions too often collapsed. For example, after agents struggled to convince parents to send their children to school in 1900, half of the children were stricken with measles a few months later. Before the epidemic was over, seventeen had died, and the Uintah agent had to call out a troop of cavalry to protect the school from being burned by angry parents who suspected witchcraft. A year later, another six Uncompahgre students died at Randlett, and an additional five Whiterocks students perished the following year.[43]

Education was the agency's main tool for civilizing and transforming the Utes. Agents viewed most parents as incorrigible "laze-abouts" and complained continually that Utes had "little disposition to work," and spent all their time

238

12.3. Boarding school at Ignacio, early twentieth century. Students were taught agricultural and domestic skills along with basic reading, writing, and arithmetic (Denver Public Library, Western History Collection, X-30673)

"gambling, horse-racing, and following the hunt."[44] Their children, however, could be molded into productive American citizens who knew how to work. In school they were taught the English language—in fact, they were required to speak it or were punished—as well as reading, writing, and arithmetic. But their most important instruction was learning how to work. Students were provided gender-specific vocational training in domestic arts (girls learned to sew, cook, wash, and clean house) or industrial arts (boys learned carpentry, farming, and stock raising). They were expected to practice these skills by working for the school—cleaning, cooking, washing, planting, harvesting, and hauling water (though parents would object to this exploitation of unpaid labor).[45]

SHIFTING BATTLEGROUNDS AND DISPOSSESSION

The 1890s were a time of significant change, but the Utes were not complacent. Ute leaders now shifted their fights from open battlefields to courts of law and the halls of Congress. Southern Colorado and northern Utah chiefs now united to initiate counterattacks against the government by using lawyers rather than guns and arrows. One of their first actions was a successful defense against non-Indians who tried to claim damages of almost $1 million for depredations in Colorado prior to 1880 (apparently hoping for Meeker-like reparations). About the same time, the Uintah-Ouray and Southern Utes also asked their attorney to represent a "confederated" Ute tribe in an attempt to recover monies for land cessions that had been promised in earlier treaties and agreements but never paid, including large sections of land withdrawn for national forests.[46] These first legal actions were largely unsuccessful (the government claimed the Utes had no right to even hire an attorney), but they demonstrated the new form of warfare Utes needed to wage to protect themselves: legal maneuvering in American courts and direct appeals to Congress.[47]

Meanwhile, non-Indians continued to peck away at the edges of the Uintah and Ouray Reservations. In 1897 Theodore Roosevelt withdrew 1,010,000 acres to be added to the newly created Uintah National Forest.[48] And in Washington, pressure to allot Ute land and open the reservation to non-Indians persisted. But the Uintah and Ouray Utes adamantly opposed allotments or opening the reservation. However, the Uncompahgres had no choice in the matter, because the 1880 agreement already stipulated that "allotment in severalty of said lands shall be made." Politicians now argued that reservation lands had only been held in trust until allotments could be made, and that the remaining mineral-rich lands should have been open to the public long since.[49] One Utah agent expressed his disgust at the "schemes of parties seeking possession of the valuable asphaltum deposits found upon the [Ouray] reservation.... [The] rich asphaltum sharks whose schemes...fruited in unrest and anguish for these wretchedly poor, long-neglected, legal wards of the Government."[50]

In 1894 a specially appointed commission came to the Uintah and Ouray Reservations to convince the Utes—in particular the Uncompahgres—to allow their lands to be allotted. No one consented. Regardless, Congress still ordered the Uncompahgre allotments be made. By April 1, 1898, officials began parceling out these allotments.[51] Despite angry protests and general unrest in the wake of the so-called wars of 1887 and 1897, the allotment was completed within the year.

Since the intent of the allotments was to provide the Uncompahgres with land and opportunity for farming, the commission looked for suitable farmland. But most of the Ouray Reservation was unsuitable for agriculture. Consequently, only eighty-eight allotments were made, and remaining allotments were assigned from lands south of the Duchesne River on the adjoining Uintah Reservation, paid for with these funds from the sale of ceded land in Colorado, held in trust by the government.[52]

Thus, 232 allotments were made on the Uintah Reservation, with the promise of future payment. Each head of household was allotted a 160-acre homestead; single men were given eighty acres.[53] Although the allotments were not approved until 1905, the Ouray Reservation was immediately thrown open as public domain. Unfortunately, the appropriations from Uncompahgre funds to pay for their allotments on the Uintah Reservation were not made for years, and many Uintah and White River Utes still believe the Uncompahgres never paid for the land. Rancor between the bands increased.[54]

Now the pressure mounted to allot the White River and Uintah lands. Officials held more councils to convince the remaining Utes of the need for and advantages of having individually allotted farms, but the Utes remained doggedly opposed, especially the White Rivers. This may have had less to do with farming, since some Uintahs were already improving farms, but rather the specter of the reservation being thrown open to non-Indian homesteaders. Notwithstanding—and despite protests from even the Uintah agent—Congress appointed a commission to make allotments in severalty with a simple majority consent of the tribes. But the Utes continued to balk, even sending a delegation to Washington to reiterate their refusal.[55]

The commission reported that "the Indians were unanimous and determined in their opposition to making cession to the government of any of their lands and to allowing a Uintah or White River Indian to take and hold an allotment in severalty."[56] In response, the Senate resolved to open the reservation without negotiating with the Utes. Certain lawmakers were clearly less interested in bettering and civilizing Indian lives than with gaining access to lands locked away on reservations. Two bills were unsuccessfully introduced in the Senate in an attempt to set aside a new smaller reservation for the Uintah and White River Utes and open up the residue to settlement. This, coupled with numerous requests for leases on Indian lands, precipitated new Senate hearings on the question of Ute lands in Utah. If they could bypass the stubborn tribe, Senate members reasoned, the reservation could just be opened. "There is a sort of feeling among the ignorant Indians that they do not want to lose any of their land," said one commissioner. "You have got to use some arbitrary means to open the land."[57] The fiction of gaining consent from the Utes was crumbling.

Representative George Sutherland from Utah distilled the arguments: The Utes were not the rightful owners of the reservation and need not be consulted, because no treaty had ever been ratified with the Utes in Utah; the Uintah Reservation had been created by the president and Congress, and it could therefore be dissolved by that same authority; the Uintah Reservation had been created for the *Indians* of Utah, and the Uintahs had no more right to it than any other Indians; and the federal government had the power to return a reservation to public domain as it had done with earlier Utah Indian lands (i.e., the Indian farms).[58]

In May 1902 Congress gave the secretary of the Interior the authority to allot the Uintah land and ordered it done, with or without Ute consent.[59] The U.S. Supreme Court had recently ruled in *Lone Wolf v. Hitchcock* that Congress had plenary authority over all Indian relations and thus had the power to arbitrarily pass laws even if they abrogated stipulations in prior treaties or agreements.[60] On March 3, 1903, funds were appropriated to carry out the 1902 order; if consent was not obtained by June 1, 1903, the land would still be allotted.[61] Utes were informed in May that "a recent decision of the Supreme Court of the United States is that Indians have no right to any part of their reservations except what they may require for allotments in severalty or can make proper use of."[62] White River chief Happy Jack responded bitterly: "You are just like a storm from the mountains when the flood is coming down the stream, and we can't get help or stop it."[63]

Officials began to survey the reservation in 1904, despite the protests of overeager non-Indians who claimed the surveys were unnecessary. The allotment commission hurriedly parceled out 103,265 acres in only two months, and in a slipshod manner. Most allotments were arbitrary and scattered between Tabiona and Whiterocks, sixty miles away. The remaining Uncompahgre allotments on the Uintah Reservation were also distributed.[64] Making matters worse for interband relations, the new allotments were only eighty acres per family head and forty acres for single men over age eighteen—half what the first Uncompahgre allottees or Southern Utes had received.[65]

Observers later remarked that "some of the most worthless land on the reservation" was allotted to the Indians and "some of the very best land was opened to entry." Utes complained that their allotments were excessively rocky or located on slopes or gashed with arroyos.[66] Just under 300,000 acres remained unallotted tribal land to be used primarily for communal grazing. By August, one hundred acres had been designated for town sites, and over a million and a half acres had been opened to homesteading and mining claims and reclamation.[67]

The Uintahs and White Rivers also lost the Strawberry Valley. Heber Valley farmers had been diverting its water illegally for years; now Spanish Fork residents hit upon the idea of storing and diverting this water to Utah Valley as well. Power politics, national enthusiasm for reclamation projects, and anticipation of the reservation opening for homesteading all volleyed the question of Basin water, while the Utes' needs—and rights—were essentially ignored.

By 1902 enthusiastic plans were underway to create a reservoir on the Straw-berry River, and the Strawberry Valley Reclamation Service offered to buy the valley from the Utes at the going rate of $1.25 per acre for 56,000 acres. The tribe refused. Leased grazing rights remained an important source of income for the impoverished tribe, plans were in the works to use the valley for tribal stock raising enterprises, and Indian officials voiced concern over diverting water that Utes would need for their allotments. But a growing population of farmers, ranchers, miners, and businesses in Utah Valley needed water. Pow-erful politicians backed the project, and various bills were introduced into the state legislature.

When the Uintah lands were allotted, the Strawberry Valley was promptly reserved to conserve a water supply for Indian *or* general agricultural use—then promptly withdrawn for "irrigation works," as allowed in the 1902 Rec-lamation Act. The secretary of the Interior determined the money received for grazing in the Strawberry Valley could be used to repay the Strawberry reclamation project costs. The Ute agent protested, requesting that the money be paid to the tribe instead, as had been customary. Utah's Senator Sutherland quietly attached an amendment to an Indian Appropriations Act that extin-guished all "title, and interest of the Indians in the said lands." In 1910, Ute title to the land was formally extinguished, and the Reclamation Service paid the tribe its original offer of $1.25 per acre for the ceded land ($71,000).[68]

After allotments had been completed, the remaining reservation land was advertised, and exaggerated tales spread about its natural resources and mineral wealth. In the ensuing land rush, hundreds (including speculators) registered for a drawing to determine the order of entering claims, and troops from Fort Duchesne patrolled the reservation to evict "Sooners" from staking claims early. But the Uintah Basin was just as barren, lacking in a stable water supply, and with questionable soil and climate for farming, as it had been in the 1860s when Mormon explorers first rejected it. The new homesteaders found it nearly impossible to make their dryland farms profitable or generate enough money to repay loans.[69]

In 1906 Congress passed provisions to bring water to the arid farms. Work began on a $600,000 irrigation project that was ostensibly designed to benefit Indian farmers. (There were no Indian farmers, only lands allotted as farms to Indians.) The multimillion-dollar Uintah Indian Irrigation Project provided a system of twenty-two canals, diverting water from most of the Uintah Basin streams and making it available to over 80,000 acres of land, most of which had been allotted to Indians. Included in the program was a plan to clear, fence, and plow Ute allotments, at tribal expense. Once the project was completed, recipients of the aid, whether they wanted it or not, were assessed for water rights and improvements.[70]

Though some Uintahs had requested funds to develop irrigation as early as 1899, most Utes vehemently opposed the expensive 1906 project. Few had any intention of farming and did not wish to finance the building of irrigation canals that would only benefit non-Indians. Regardless of their opposition, the project proceeded. Few Utes worked on it, and after two years and nearly $330,000, less than $7,000 had gone to Indian laborers.[71]

With the breakup of the reservation, the patience of some White River Utes finally snapped. Under the leadership of Red Cap, 365 White Rivers bolted and fled to the Sioux Reservation in South Dakota where, they were convinced, life must be better. Alarmists predicted that "Indian trouble of gigantic proportion is brewing"; journalists described "desperate redskins at bay"; and largely unfounded reports claimed that the traveling band was harassing non-Indians in Wyoming. A military contingent intercepted the band and escorted them to South Dakota. But the Sioux were less than overjoyed to greet the refugees. Their reservation was already overcrowded, and the two tribes were traditional enemies. Nevertheless, the Ute refugees were settled on the reservation where they used Ute tribal money to lease Sioux land and drew annuities at the Sioux agency. But after two years the discouraged and destitute White Rivers—having eaten up all their cattle and supplies—returned to their allotments in the Uintah Basin.[72]

With government protection now all but nonexistent, the stage was set for the Utes' final dispossession, as it was for American Indians throughout the United States. From 1887 to 1933, American Indians lost 87 million acres of reservation land as a result of allotments. For the combined Ute tribes, whose original reservations in Utah and Colorado had totaled almost 23 million acres, the drop to several hundred thousand acres of allotted land was devastating. But the disinheritance had not ended; by 1933 a third of this land had been alienated, too. And land would not be the only loss.

BLOOD QUANTUM AND INDIAN IDENTITY

By 1902 the Utes had lost most of their once-vast homelands, while federal agents did their best to tear away their cultural heritage as well. Individual allotments were scattered across former reservations and were intermixed with non-Indian homesteaders. One response was a retreat into their Indian identity.

The dispersed Utes aligned themselves with kinsmen or other ethnically related Utes who looked like and "thought" as they did. Ethnic boundaries continued to harden, reinforced by religious rituals, inter-reservation visiting, and tribal politics as the Ute people refused to relinquish their identities as Indians and specifically, as Ute Indians. Ethnic boundaries, previously porous, now hardened as the division of resources demanded tribal census rolls and required individuals to prove their right to receive "Indian" privileges, including rations, annuities, and land. Although agencies had always used rolls to track and distribute supplies or annuities to "their" Indians, bands had remained flexible, and interagency visits were common. But the 1887 Dawes Act resulted in hard census rolls on which future Indian—specifically "tribal"—identities would be based, and the once-fluid nature of band identity disappeared.

Most historians agree that the genesis of arguments over Indian identity began with the 1887 Dawes Allotment Act when tribes had to be enumerated, and their members listed on rolls for the purpose of receiving allotments. Reservation land ceased to be a shared commodity, but became a resource to be quantified and then divided up between a specified number of listed members. Resources became a prize in a closed, high-stakes numbers game where bean--counting bookkeepers controlled who got into the game before the doors closed. Greed, graft, fraud, miscalculations, and overworked officials produced less than perfect membership rolls, but the records established a base census from which most tribes continue to lock in membership, and thus a *right* to call themselves Indian. The question of who was a "real" Indian became complex. For example, Reconstruction forced Cherokees to enroll their numerous freed black slaves on tribal rolls; in the Midwest, dishonest attorneys bought fraudulent memberships and allotments for white clients ("$5 Indians"); and white men sometimes romanced Indian women to obtain access to Indian land or resources, then abandoned them or murdered relatives to get their inheritance as well. The variations on fraud were endless as non-Indians tried to claim Indian resources, and many full-blood Indians were lost along the way.[73]

While the Dawes Act had no actual wording about blood quantum until competency reviews were established later, officials, anxious to expedite the allotment procedures, began to invoke the concept of a quantity of "blood" as a means of determining who was Indian and eligible to be entered on the permanent membership rolls of a tribe. It was a racist concept, a biological fiction for a people who had been incorporating others into their societies for generations, and for whom "becoming" Indian had once consisted primarily of playing a cultural role within a society.[74]

244

The racist use of blood quantum had a long tradition in the southern states, used in Virginia, for example, to determine white privilege, persons of "half-American race," "legally inferior persons," or competency of persons of color in courts of law.[75] This racial rule of thumb carried over into the Dawes enrollment process; one-quarter "blood" became the standard measure to define an Indian for federal purposes. However, following tests of tribal sovereignty in 1978 (*Santa Clara Pueblo v. Martinez*), the Supreme Court ruled that only tribes had the right to determine their own membership because it was an internal, sovereign affair. But most tribal rolls, including the Utes', continued to use the notion of blood as a primary component for determining eligibility. Some tribes incorporated higher or lower requirements; others added supplementary restrictions including residency, matrilineal or patrilineal descent, or lineal descent from original members.[76] However, despite the addition of supplementary cultural or traditional membership requirements, the base identity code for authenticating one's Indianness came down to the issue of race. "How much *Indian* are you?" meant "How much Indian *blood* do you have?" or "How much Ute blood do you have?" Blood quantum became a means of authenticating *real* Indians from *ersatz* Indians.

Indian "blood" became a trope of authentic Indianness throughout Indian America at the expense of unenrolled native people. Young Sioux, for example, compared degrees of blood to "see who's more Indian," while blood quantum qualified genuine Native Americans for certain privileges that became increasingly reserved for "real" Indians.[77] Cherokees spoke of feeling a "Cherokeeness" in their blood that made them "act in a certain fashion," and N. Scott Momaday frequently wrote of a Kiowa "blood memory" or "ancestral imagination" that "each of us bears in his genes or blood."[78]

This jealously guarded identity of blood quantum was a legal fiction based on long-discarded scientific theories that suggested blood carried the genetic *and* cultural material to determine allotment eligibility. It was also based on a large body of jurisprudence that spawned the same biological racism of Jim Crow segregation in the South. But it became the basis of tribal membership and initiated increasingly bitter battles between people who should have been both hereditary and cultural kindred and ethnic relatives.

Yet ethnohistorians argue the impossibility of trying to determine true blood quantum or genetic descent, since North American Indian populations are an amalgam of many ancestries (Indigenous American, European, African, Hispanic, Asian, and others), and some "status" Indians have no native biological ancestry at all. Indigenous groups—including the Utes—traditionally incorporated captives and assimilated runaway slaves or indentured servants, while the mixed-blood children of traders or neighboring settlers were raised as members of the native society. Consequently, beginning in the late 1880s, the definition of *Indian* became a political rather than a cultural or biological one—despite being codified in racial terms. And it remains political, because it continues to be primarily about legitimizing access to resources and political power.[79]

Thus, the division of the Ute reservations not only challenged the land-oriented cultural identity of the Utes, but it also revised how they would determine "Uteness" in the future. At the same time, internal boundaries defining individual bands solidified. Interband—and intertribal—relations became a mix of complex issues, including rights to resources, political leadership, identity, and methods of adapting to changing circumstances (traditionalists versus modernists). A shared *Núu-ci* identity—along with shared traditions, language, history, and common travails—bound the people of the three reservations together as *Utes* and allowed them to form a confederation to unitedly fight for their legal rights. However, feuds, recriminations, and competition over the resources that *were* available—as well as intense wrangling of tribal power politics—also split the Utes into warring factions within reservation-defined tribes.

Utes would continue to fight for their physical and ethnic survival during the succeeding decades.

Chapter 13

Religion and the Perseverance of Identity
1890–Present

The period after 1880 was a time of desperation and physical dislocation for most Utes, including the southern bands that had managed to cling to at least a remnant of their traditional homeland. And the population was plummeting. Children, parents, brothers and sisters, aunts and uncles, cousins, grandparents, and friends were dying from starvation and the rampant diseases to which they still had little resistance, and which were made worse by depression, alcoholism, and hunger-weakened bodies. The once widely scattered and loosely related *Núu-ci* bands were now concentrated on reservations where supplies and supplementary hunting were limited. With their world out of kilter, the desperate bands were forced to work together, or at least in sullen conjunction with each other, in order to survive, and under the oversight of government-administered agencies.

The external trappings of their culture were also being stripped away—their traditional leadership being revised by administrative expediency, and their traditional religious expressions scoffed at, feared, and forbidden. Yet it was within these religious rituals, beliefs, and mores that the true essence of being and thinking as a Ute resided. Like the loosely governed and scattered bands, "religion" for the Utes and their Numic neighbors had been an unorganized but loosely connected collection of beliefs and actions used to propitiate or expel evil spirits and to call on the medicinal powers of the cosmos to heal or bring prosperity.

By the 1880s Native Americans everywhere were becoming destitute and desperate, with little but anger to unify them as a people or give them hope for a future. It was into this milieu that a series of new religious movements appeared, providing Native people with a framework within which to incorporate and express traditional beliefs and that could be interpreted within tribal-specific cosmologies. Religion would become an emotional bulwark for the dislocated Utes, a means of revitalizing their flagging spirits and anchoring their identity.

When agency administrators opposed these new pan-Indian religions (as they did all backsliding remnants of Indian "paganism"), they inadvertently enhanced their importance. The new rituals emphasized native values and spiritual expression, and participating in them became a defiant defense of Indian identity. The rituals proclaimed a participant's Indianness and allowed them to seek an internal strength (power) to survive cultural and physical dislocation. And for the three reservation-based Ute tribes, inter-reservation participation strengthened a confederated tribal identity and perpetuated the very essence of being and thinking as *Núu-ci*, even as they and everything else around them seemed to be changing.[1]

Utes were especially apt at merging these new religious rituals into their older cosmological perceptions, in part because they had never had, nor needed, an integrated religious complex. Instead, early individual and communal rituals had been few, relatively simple, and adaptable. Most had been vehicles for family-related bands to socialize or hunt, or for individuals to appease, supplicate, or commune with supernatural powers. In addition to an aspiring shaman's quest for medicine power were communal endeavors during healing ceremonies, various dances, or shaman-directed hunting. These once served as both an individual quest for power, healing, or vision-dreaming, as well as a means of accumulating a generalized cosmic medicine for the good of kin and the larger community. Ceremonies served to direct one's thinking to "do good" and prepare one's mind and body to receive supernatural directions in dream visions or simply the whispering knowledge that came to one with power.[2]

When new rituals like the Sundance and peyote meetings arrived, they were easily incorporated because they drew upon traditional Indian symbols, expressions, and beliefs and could be conceptually molded to fit Ute ideas and to perpetuate their own uniquely Ute spirituality. Because Utes had a vast knowledge and long history of using medicinal herbs and plants, when the Utes were introduced to the Native American Church, many viewed peyote as just another herbal specific as well as a means of spiritual renewal. For example, by the 1990s the Ute Mountain Utes were using peyote meetings as an adjunct to alcohol rehabilitation programs.[3] Similarly, sweat lodges, once used very infrequently if at all, came into increased use in the 1980s, adapted by spiritual advisors to provide a regular forum for spiritual communion, cultural renewal, and physical rehabilitation.[4]

Medicine men ("Indian doctors" or holy men) continued to administer curative blessings, both privately and at communal religious ceremonies, and such healing blessings were integral to the final hours of the Bear Dance and Sundance, when the three- or four-day rituals had accumulated large amounts of *puwá* within the sacred ceremonial enclosures.[5] By the early twenty-first century, however, some traditional beliefs were changing. Spiritual leaders, for example, were no longer referring to themselves as holy men or medicine men, but as spiritual *advisors*, a term now used in most legal and legislative documents.[6]

249

Over time, these religious gatherings grew more social and secular, and were soon joined in the tribal events calendar by purely secular rodeos and powwows. All provided an excuse for inter-reservation visiting and echoed a bygone Ute nomadism of summer and fall social gatherings. The events perpetuated for participants a generalized identity as Indians, specifically Ute Indians. Families refurbished or built shade houses on traditionally located family sites, with occasional trailer or tipi adjuncts. Indian arts and crafts were displayed for sale, along with traditional Indian foods, and crowds gathered to watch or compete in favorite games such as three-card Monte or the even older hidden-object hand games. And it was, above all, a time to celebrate being Indian. Members not only attended and supported participants, but they also displayed traditional clothing and decorative silver, turquois, or beaded accoutrements to proclaim their Indianness.

By the end of the twentieth century, with their world at its nadir, Utes discovered that religious events and social gatherings, while pan-Indian in origin, had become the main vehicle by which they could retain a sense of belonging to a broader and equally abused indigenous world, as well as to perpetuate their own specific sense of being Ute.

GHOST DANCE

The Ghost Dance was the first of the major new religious movements to sweep through western tribes. It was first introduced in western Nevada in 1869 by a Fish Lake (California) Paiute named Wodziwob. He claimed visions of an apocalyptic end of the world and its rebirth without white men. The dance became more widely known the following year but then petered out over the next few years.[7] A new and more lasting version appeared twenty years later, first revived in 1889 by Wovoka (Jack Wilson), the son of Wodziwob's Northern Paiute adherent, Tävibo.[8]

Wodziwob and Wovoka were only the latest in a series of Indian prophets who had emerged in the eighteenth and nineteenth centuries, along with the revitalization or millennial movements they encouraged. Native America saw the rise of such prophets as the Delaware's "Mystic Warrior" (Neolin), the Iroquois' Handsome Lake, and the Shawnee prophet Tenskwatawa. The roots of these religious movements twisted deep into the earliest contacts between Indians and Christian missionaries, during which certain Christian ideas and motifs had become integrated within native interpretations.[9] Similarly, the Ghost Dance religion was a syncretic merging of native and Christian religious philosophies (possibly Shaker and Mormon). Some Mormons even suspected the Lamanites might have received inside mystic information about the Second Coming of Christ with its cataclysmic last days preceding the millennium. For example, when Orson Pratt, an influential Mormon apostle, learned of the Indian prophecies, he began preaching that Mormons should prepare for the Second Coming of Christ.[10]

While the Ghost Dance was not a fulfillment of Mormon millennial hopes, it was a response to the destitution and desperation of Indian tribes. By 1890, when word of Wovoka's visions and gospel spread, primarily through the enthusiastic evangelizing of other American Indians, it gave many Native people renewed hope. However, how the dance was enacted and interpreted varied from tribe to tribe. Wovoka emphasized native unity and peace by calling it the Friendship Dance of the Indian Race, but among the Sioux the dance took on a militaristic shade with echoes of a warrior past. Tragically, the Sioux Ghost Dance's apocalyptic message was misinterpreted as a war dance by inexperienced federal agents and nervous commanders of the 7th Cavalry (Custer's former command) stationed on their reservation, who responded in alarm and then slaughter at Wounded Knee. Although both the 1870 and 1890 movements did express frustration with Euro-Americans, Wovoka's dance had actually preached peace.[11]

The most visible element of the religion was a marathon five-day circle dance in which participants invoked the spirits of their departed ancestors and loved ones. Wovoka also urged Indians to reform themselves by abandoning alcohol, discarding all things warlike, working hard (for the White Man), and practicing peace, honesty, and goodwill. Dancing could bring visions of departed kin, God, and the afterworld. Participants were also told that if they invoked their departed kin through enthusiastic singing, dancing, and (among the Sioux) wearing protective Ghost Dance shirts, they could bring about the cataclysmic end of the world with its accompanying destruction of the White

Man and his debilitating ways. This in turn would usher in a paradisiacal world in which traditional Indian ways would be reestablished. The movement appealed to Native peoples' feelings of frustration and despair, promised a release from the oppressive economic and spiritual deprivation that beset them, and imbued hope in a return to an idealized pre-white paradise.

251

Uintah Utes learned of the 1870 Ghost Dance and were encouraged by other Indians to participate at one in Bridger Basin. Tabby told agency workers that they must "not fail to come as they intend to resurrect their forefathers and all Indians who wish to see them must be there.... They say the white man has nothing to do with this, it is the command of the Indian god and if they do not go they will sicken and die."[12] Tabby, Toquana, Kanosh, and even the dying Black Hawk attended the multitribal gathering that included Bannocks, Shoshones, Goshutes, Uintahs, and Colorado's Tabeguache and Yampa Utes. The following year only Utes, Shoshones, and Bannocks attended a Ghost Dance on the Bear River. A third dance was held in Sanpete Valley in 1872 but was the last dance Utes attended en masse.[13]

Perhaps the inherent fear of ghosts doomed the movement among Utes, or their pragmatism bred disbelief when the looked-for resurrection and Indian millennium did not occur. Although the dance continued among the Fort Hall Shoshones and some Southern Paiutes, Utes quickly abandoned the ritual, and both Navajos and Southern Utes began to ridicule the idea of resurrecting the dead.[14] So the movement passed by in the 1870s with little effect on Western Utes, except to cement their incarceration on their reservation following the 1872 debacle after participating in the ritual in Sanpete Valley and angering settlers by remaining to hunt, beg, and steal. Twenty years later the enthusiasm for the 1890 Ghost Dance made little impression on Utes. Uintah and Ouray Utes sent a delegation to witness the January 1889 Paiute dance, and a number of Utes returned to dance at a second a few weeks later. However, this was likely the extent of their interest. A handful may have continued to dance it in private, unostentatious ceremonies, but within a very few years the ever-pragmatic (and ghost-fearing) Utes at Uintah inverted the Ghost Dance as a "get *rid* of ghosts" dance rather than an invocation *of* the dead. Southern Utes would revise it into a bawdy joking dance.[15]

NUMIC SUNDANCE

The Sundance was another matter entirely and would become the most significant religious gathering on all three reservations.[16] In 1890 a Uintah shaman

13.1. Northern Ute Sundance Lodge, 1979 (Photo: S. Jones)

named General Grant brought to Whiterocks (Utah) a Shoshonean adaptation of the Plains Indian Sun Dance. This dance proclaimed the virtues of Indian ways and turned thoughts toward the old customs of a supposedly less troubled time. The dance incorporated the Utes' traditional reverence of the sun and held echoes of old battle pride. However, because the ceremony demanded a three- to four-day abstention from all food and water, in Ute it is called *tagú-wuní*, the "thirsting dance" or "standing thirsty." Like the earlier Bear Dance, it was held in a sacred brush corral, a medicine lodge constructed new for each dance, and known as the "thirst house" (*tagú-káni*).[17] In English the ritual is simply called the Sundance.[18]

The Sundance carried a spirit of hope—not so much for the destruction of Euro-American hordes as the Ghost Dance had promised, but that they could develop a power within to withstand their current situation with an Indian strength.[19] The Sundance served as a new focus for Indian power, necessitated by the fact that Ute numbers were diminishing at an alarming rate. The Western Ute population in Utah from 1800 to 1840 has been estimated at 8,000; by 1859 it was only 4,500, and by 1877 there were only 800 Western Utes (Uin-tahs)—a 90 percent decline. Even with the influx of Colorado Utes in 1881, agents estimated a combined total of only 4,000 Utes; within ten years they had dwindled to 2,800 and continued to decline until 1930, when they hit a nadir of only 1,750.[20] The Utes looked to the Sundance to save them from both a cultural and physical extinction.

The Uintahs were the first to perform the dance in 1890, but by 1895 White Rivers and Uncompahgres had joined them. Visiting Ute relatives and friends from southern Colorado carried the dance home, and by 1910 the Ute Mountain Utes were sponsoring their own dances and teaching the ritual to Southern Utes.[21]

In the midst of the furor over allotments and the opening of the reservations to non-Indian settlement, Utes turned to the Sundance as an outlet for their frustration and anger as well as to seek spiritual and medicinal recourse. But agency employees were concerned about the new ceremony, and soldiers were sent from Fort Duchesne to police the dance in 1893. Soon the agency forbade its performance altogether, so the dances were defiantly held in secret. Even as late as 1914, when ethnographer Frances Densmore visited and recorded the traditional music of the Northern Utes, she was told the "last" dance had been held that year, still against government orders. But Utes did not abandon the ceremony, and it became a final bastion of Ute identity, a proclamation of Indianness and a symbol of defiance. And like peyote rituals, the religion was accepted as an expression of older Numic beliefs as it merged traditional values and meaning with new symbols. As long-time Sundance chief and holy man Eddie Box Sr. explained, despite a series of transformations, the Sundance preserved "at its core a Ute tradition as old as time."[22]

The dance integrated vestiges of a much older Numic sun reverence, which may be one reason it was so readily adopted. Although the Utes had never worshipped the sun, they had supplicated and utilized its power in curing ceremonies. A number of sun-reverence rituals existed prior to 1880, including the Deer-hoof Rattle Dance, in which dancers painted their bodies in the reds and yellows of a sunset and then danced to supplicate the setting sun and again at dawn to propitiate its rising. Northern Utes also told John Wesley Powell in 1873 about a sun ceremony known as the *ta'-vwi-we-paga* (sun dance), and agency employee Sidney Jocknick described a type of sun reverence among the Uncompahgre in the 1870s that reminded him of Mexican mythology. As late as the 1940s, elders remembered being admonished to rise up early in the morning to offer prayers with the sunrise (*tav-wi-mau'-a-shi*). The new Sundance ritual clearly incorporated aspects of this earlier sun reverence, for it called on that same potent reservoir of power. It also added a formal forum for individuals to vision quest the dream visions of medicine power for their own use, as well as for the good of their family and the community.[23]

13.2. Sundance Dawn, 1979 (Photo: S. Jones)

After its adoption, the Shoshonean Sundance changed little in its outward form and symbolism—although Utes typically provided Christian explanations for symbols to appease agents and anthropologists. The medicine lodge was constructed of twelve sturdy posts and (among Uintah-Ouray Utes) cross-beams, a forked center pole, and was walled up with leafy branches. A door was left open to the east, facing the point of sunrise and establishing a "water path" (water signifying *puwá*) that was always kept clear of spectators. The power of the sun traveled along this path to the center of the lodge, where it was channeled into the medicine lodge through the centrally placed Sundance pole. This pole and the mystic power of the sun became the focus and altar for the dancers. Each morning dancers presented themselves east of the pole and ritually greeted the rising sun.

The dance began after sunset on the first day and only included men. Most Utes believed Sundance power was something women had no business tampering with, and menstruating, pregnant, or nursing women were especially forbidden to approach or enter the lodge. The Southern Utes had allowed women to dance on one occasion, but when one of them died a few months later, the gender restriction was confirmed. (Some women were grudgingly allowed to participate in Shoshone dances but were never allowed in Ute dances.)[24]

During the three- to four-day ceremony,[25] dancers remained inside the medicine lodge, fasting from all food and water, and leaving the Sundance enclosure only to relieve themselves. These Sundance warriors took pride in wearing traditional Indian symbols, including elaborately decorated Sundance skirts, stylized breechcloths or aprons, wide and intricately beaded Sundance belts, medicine pouches, and other Indian jewelry.

The Sundance was very much a community activity. Dancers took positions on the west side of the lodge (the traditional position for respected elders in a tipi) where they blew on eagle-bone whistles tipped with eagle down (symbolizing the breath of life), as they moved rhythmically within their individual paths or sought power-giving dream visions. On the east sat visitors, drum teams, and singers. These drum teams took pride in good singing, which drew out power. Women sat near the drummers and shook willow branches (water plants) to the rhythm of the music as they sang and urged the dancers on.

Dancers sought to prove themselves as men, as well as to seek the dream visions in which they received supernatural instruction and *puwá*. They purified, cleansed, and sanctified their bodies through the ritual fast and blessings received from Ute holy men during the dance. They also renewed and accumulated mystic power for their individual physical and spiritual well-being, as well as for the good of the community. As dancers, singers, and holy men syndicated their efforts, the medicine lodge became a great reservoir of power, and this accumulation was not only available for healing individuals but also to bring good luck and prosperity to the entire Ute community.

Each day dancers further elaborated their costumes, saving their finest accoutrements for the final day, when they also used red ochre paints on their bodies. If a dancer was "going for" vision, they typically did so on the final day. Then they pushed themselves into a semihypnotic state until they fell into an exhausted, unconscious state, during which the symbol-filled visions of power could come.[26] When dancers appeared to be "going for it," the tempo and length of the songs increased in a communal effort to urge and help him on. When a dancer fell, other Sundancers covered him with a sheet where he lay in his personal water path, hidden from the eyes of the curious while he dreamed his visions and experienced his personal epiphanies. Once roused, he was blessed and returned to his place to rest through the remainder of the dance.

In keeping with the focus of traditional Ute religion, healing ceremonies were an integral part of the dance, especially during final hours when the accumulated *puwá* was strongest. Each morning dancers and a few visitors greeted the rising sun, "bathing" in its rays once it broke clear of the horizon. Dancers could also "smudge" or envelop themselves in the incense-like smoke of burning sweet sage, or they might carry a spray of sweet sage. Dancers or others could also seek a blessing at the Sundance pole, a healing ceremony performed by the Sundance chief or other holy man who typically used an eagle-feather fan or sprays of sweet sage. At the conclusion of the ceremony, dancers were given a drink of blessed water, and community-donated gifts were dispersed to families of the dancers. And once all had filed out of the medicine lodge, the structure was completely torn down and everything removed—except for the sacred center pole, which was left standing as a silent sentinel that would "lie down" only when it chose. The following day the Sundance chief hosted a feast for the entire community (a meal the tribe now provides).

The Sundance was—and remains—a source of personal and community religious power. According to one Southern Ute Sundance chief, it is "the most important spiritual ceremony in the Ute tradition."[27] Beyond its spiritual essence, the dance also called upon the ethnic patriotism of the dancers. It was an *Indian* dance, a supplication of Indian power to be used by Indians for the benefit of Indians. Although any man could attend or even participate in the dance—and non-Indians and mixed-bloods occasionally did—through it the community proclaimed the superiority of "real" Indian dancers. Tales circulated of dancers who "couldn't make it," who had to be taken away by parents or who bolted from the lodge; in these stories such dancers were always non-Indians, mixed-bloods, or non-Utes. Throughout the dance, members of the community stood and harangued the dancers, urging them to dance more vigorously and be true to their heritage, sometimes castigating them for their "White ways" that took them away from traditional behavior and values.

In many ways the summer Sundance paralleled the older and more traditional spring Bear Dance. Traditionally, both were performed for three or four
days and were followed by a grand feast; both were directed by individual holy
men, who did so according to their own supernatural instructions; both held
the dance in sacred enclosures or medicine lodges; both ceremonies utilized
medicine music and marathon dancing to call out supernatural powers for the
fertile prosperity of the community; both dances incorporated some doctoring
during final hours; and both ceremonials were communal-gathering affairs
that celebrated being Ute.

PEYOTE RELIGION

Like the Sundance, the peyote religion, or Native American Church, perpetuated older Ute beliefs despite being a pan-Indian religion. Its rituals called
upon a very traditional syndication of healing powers, including an all-night
curing ritual combined with symbols and sources of supernatural *puwá* in
the smoke, music, and medicinal specifics. Traditional Ute healing used two
sources: shamans calling upon supernatural powers and healers who used an
extensive pharmacopeia of medicinal herbs.[28] The basic ritual framework was
standard from tribe to tribe. However, for Ute practitioners the peyote religion
perpetuated Ute cosmological traditions, and medicine men were many of the
first Ute peyote chiefs.[29]

Ethnographers continue to argue whether peyotism was a syncretic
merging of native and Christian elements or a fully aboriginal-based religion
with Christian elements added later as window dressing. (Indians were known
to tell anthropologists "what they wanted to hear"—or to tweak their own
sense of humor at an outsider's expense.)[30] Regardless of the religion's origins,
many Indians found the Native American Church a comfortable way to celebrate a Christian faith within an Indian setting. Under the influence of the
mild hallucinogenic peyote ingested during the ceremony, practitioners might
describe seeing traditional animal powers or the face of Christ. Peyote itself
was sometimes cast in a savior-like role, and prayers could be addressed to
both God and peyote. One morning prayer began, "God, Jesus, Mother Mary,
Peyote, we beg you this morning."[31]

The probable genesis of the modern Native American Church was among
the Lipan Apache around Laredo, Texas (a source of peyote cactus), where
the Lipan Apaches adapted preexisting Mexican ceremonies to Apache-style
music and ritual elements. The adapted ceremony spread first to the Kiowa and

Comanche, and from them to the Arapaho and Cheyenne, where Buckskin Charley, a southern Ute leader, was introduced to it in 1896.[32] However, it was the Uintah and Ouray Utes who first began to regularly practice the ceremonies under the direction of an active peyote missionary, Sam Lone Bear (or "Cactus Pete"), who claimed to be Sioux and to teach the "old Sioux way" (though he may have been a Ute named Ralph Kochampaniskin).[33] Lone Bear settled among the Uncompahgre in 1914 and was influential in spreading the peyote religion among northern Utes and Paiutes.

The Cheyenne and Arapaho were the most active proselytizers of the peyote religion among the southern Colorado Utes. By 1917 meetings were being held under their direction on both southern reservations. Buckskin Charley (or Charles Buck) actively promoted the religion, as did his wife Emma Buck and in-law Isaac Cloud. Although tradition suggests Charles Buck led some of the early meetings, it was Isaac Cloud, brother of Sundance chief Edwin Cloud, who became the recognized leader of the peyote religion on the Southern Ute Reservation.

But interest in the new religion soon flagged among the more acculturated Southern Utes, and it was among the very traditional Ute Mountain Utes that the Native American Church found its strongest hold. The Cheyenne missionary John Peak Heart made annual summer treks to the reservation to teach and conduct strict "moon way" peyote ceremonies. George Mills, the first tribal chair, also became the first Ute Mountain peyote priest, traveling to Oklahoma in 1918 to be trained as a "roadman" and then returning to serve as Peak Heart's apprentice. During the 1920s three more Ute Mountain Utes trained in Oklahoma and returned as peyote chiefs.[34]

Although there were variations in the peyote ceremony from tribe to tribe, and even from roadman to roadman, there were dominant, common characteristics for the religious complex.[35] Participants united their personal quests for *puwá* and the good luck or health inherent in that power. The ritual, typically held in a traditional tipi,[36] began in the evening and lasted through the night until sunrise. Hand drums, eagle-feather fans, eagle-bone whistles, gourd rattles, tobacco, and sweet sage made up most of the ritual paraphernalia. As the participants sat in a circle around a crescent-moon dirt altar and ritual fire, the meeting was directed by a shamanic chief called a roadman, who directed adherents on the peyote path. The peyote plant itself, sanctified on an earthen altar, was Chief Peyote. The roadman led a ritual cycle of four songs to open and close the meeting and to make the midnight or morning water calls, and each participant could sing their own power songs, keeping time to a rattle while holding a staff and eagle-feather fan.

Throughout the meeting, prayers were offered vocally and with proffered smoke, and the hallucinogenic peyote sacrament was passed around. Peyote was bitter in taste, was difficult to chew and swallow, and partakers often became nauseated. However, once ingested, the drug produced euphoria and occasionally dramatic visions that could include both traditional Indian and Christian symbols. Sweet sage was crushed, sniffed, rubbed over the body, and used to beat against the chest for purification. Ceremonies greeted the midnight hour and the dawn and included songs, drinking blessed water, cleaning the altar, and rekindling the fire. In the morning a libation of the blessed water was spilled on the ground and ceremonial blessings given, after which participants adjourned to a moderate breakfast "feast," some participants raising their arms to greet the sun as they first stepped into it.

Except among the Ute Mountain Utes, by the 1980s most Ute practitioners attended peyote meetings irregularly, and many used the rite merely as an adjunctive healing ceremony. By the 1960s, most Uintah-Ouray Utes had taken peyote medicine at one time and used the meetings as prescribed adjuncts to personal curing rituals. Most regular participants, however, belonged to an eclectic group of medicine men or spiritual advisors, who used the meetings to buoy up their personal *puwá*.[37]

Acceptance of the peyote religion varied radically between bands. After the first flurry of interest, it fell into disfavor among Southern Utes, and by 1940 nearly 90 percent had rejected the ritual. Some medicine men emphatically opposed it, including the influential Sundance chief, Edwin Cloud. Not surprisingly, it was vigorously opposed by non-Indians. Superintendent Edward McKean actively tried to suppress it, and the state of Colorado passed a bill in 1917 prohibiting peyote use and making its transportation between reservations illegal. By midcentury, many Southern Utes denounced the ceremonies as too expensive because of the morning feasts; claimed peyotists acted drunk and misbehaved while under the influence; and decried the all-night rituals. As opposition increased, adherents began practicing in secret.[38]

The opposite occurred among Ute Mountain Utes, for whom the peyote religion became firmly entrenched as a rallying point for traditional spiritual expression and cultural preservation. Where 90 percent of Southern Utes rejected peyote, at least 90 percent of Ute Mountain Utes embraced it. Supported from its inception by Jack House, an influential chief and driving force in early tribal councils, it was seen as a means to cure sickness, maintain health, and fight alcoholism and its effects.[39]

"MODERNIZING" UTE RELIGION

Although Ute religious ceremonies continued to promote Uteness and a generic Indianness, after World War II their acculturation accelerated due to increasing interaction with non-Indians, better educational opportunities, and a growing expansion of communication technologies such as radio, television, and later the Internet. Many more Utes absorbed the ever-present mainstream American culture—something that all early assimilation attempts by the Bureau of Indian Affairs (BIA) had been unable to accomplish. As tribes grew larger, more powerful, and more bureaucratic, they took on the responsibility for all community events on reservations, including the Bear Dance and Sundance, formerly the province of shamanic holy men. Increased acculturation also led to a decrease in dependence on traditional beliefs, especially among the younger, educated, and more separated youth. But modernization did not eliminate the elemental function of these religious ceremonies, which was to enhance their Indian—specifically Ute Indian—identity.

One noticeable change in Ute spiritual expression was an increasing emphasis on sweat lodge ceremonies, or sweats, especially after 1980. Ute interest paralleled the growing popularity across the country of sweat lodge ceremonies to incorporate traditional Indian healing ceremonies. This was yet another manifestation of a pan-Indian religious movement, while at the same time a resurrection of an earlier if infrequent Ute practice.

Attitudes toward sweats vary. Some Utes insist sweat ceremonies are a very recent addition (like the Sundance or peyote rituals); however, all pre-reservation bands did use sweat lodges, if only occasionally. In the 1930s, Utes and Southern Paiutes told ethnographers that early medicine men among the Uintahs and White Rivers sometimes used sweat lodges, as did others seeking spiritual and physical purification. On the other hand, as late as 1999 some Uncompahgre claimed their band never used them.[40] Nevertheless, after the resurgence of interest in sweats in the 1980s, both Indian doctors and spiritual advisors began holding ceremonies on a regular basis.

Sweats were used to cleanse and heal mind and body as well as a form of worship or communion with God. As with other native rituals, modern sweat ceremonies were also a means of reinforcing Indian identity and values and

promoting a Ute consciousness. For some, sweats became a vehicle for traditional curative rituals, and doctoring could take place during the ceremonies.
For these Utes, sweats became a form of "going to church" where they could
invoke either traditional powers or the Christian god, or simply meditate to
heal the soul. Ute Mountain Utes began using sweat lodge ceremonies to fight
the debilitating effects of alcohol and drugs. By the twenty-first century, Native
American sweats had become a recognized healing ceremony within a growing
cycle of pan-Indian rights being fought for in prisons.[41] Today sweats are used
nationwide in veterans hospitals and medical centers to fight substance dependency and posttraumatic stress disorder.[42]

Because Ute religion continued to be a vehicle for expressing and
maintaining Indian and Ute identity, it also became a significant focus of controversy. Although the vigorous attempts to suppress Indian religious ceremonials during the first half of the twentieth century eventually gave way to
a grudging acceptance, it did not end the continuous abridgement of Indian
religious freedoms. Neither did it end feuding within tribes over how to or who
could conduct ceremonies. This was especially true after the mid-1950s, when
controversies escalated over the right to claim Indian identity. Additionally,
the manipulation of the religious cycle also threatened to rob ceremonies of
their remaining significance.

The timing of the Bear Dance shifted progressively later in the year to
accommodate farming and school schedules, easing it away from its religious
association with the awakening bear and spring fertility (typically around February), thus transforming it primarily into a social event. The peyote sacrament
was proscribed as a controlled substance, making the rite illegal. And in its
earliest years, Sundances had to be performed in hiding because agents were
fearful of the militaristic overtones: dancers were warriors, the center pole
was ritually killed when harvested, mock battles were once held before the
dance, and escaped war captives were once honored. However, it was eventually allowed—grudgingly—as a "Harvest Dance." Later, as Indian Health Services and area hospitals were promoted and more Utes finally accepted white
medical care, medicine men faded and their roles shifted. In 1980 there were
only three recognized medicine men on the three Ute reservations; by 1999
Utes on the Uintah and Ouray Reservation claimed there were none. Indian
doctors had been replaced by leaders of ceremonies and spiritual advisors (not
holy men). Even though individual blessings could be sought, most of these
leaders worked within the framework of the Sundance, Bear Dance, peyote
meetings, or more popularly, sweat lodge ceremonies.[43]

Sundancing continued to flourish, though numbers varied from year to year and from reservation to reservation, and dancers ranged from fewer than a dozen to well over sixty.[44] By the 1980s tribes sponsored, directed, and sometimes appointed dance chiefs. Tribal councils coordinated schedules, provided funds, and saw to the logistics of the events, including the concluding feast.

Leadership of the dance also reflected tribal politics and changing attitudes toward the legitimized authority of the tribes. The tendency of Southern Utes to channel authority within established familial lines was reflected not only in their politically active families, but in their religious leadership as well. Edwin Cloud was the Southern Ute Sundance chief throughout the 1930s and 1940s, with the mantle falling to Eddie Box for the next four decades until 1994, when he passed the responsibility to Edwin's grandson, Neil Cloud, whom he saw as the rightful chief. Similarly, Terry Knight (whose sister would be tribal chair and was a descendant of Chief Piah) was a recognized Ute Mountain spiritual advisor in the 1980s who conducted sweats and was also a peyote roadman and the tribe's Sundance chief.[45]

The intermeshing of tribal and religious affairs, however, was not always clear-cut. In 1961, for example, the acculturated Southern Ute tribal chair John Baker argued against expenditures for the Sundance and its concluding feast. He questioned the need for the tribe to fund a "private club" (since religious leadership and participation was invested at that time in only a few prominent families), whose activities he did not believe benefited the tribe as a whole.[46]

While the Uintah and Ouray Ute Business Committee had fewer qualms in taking over the logistics and expenses of the Sundance, they did debate the timing. Two dances were being held, one in July and one in August, and members argued over which dance was the legitimate one. They also rotated through a series of unrelated Sundance chiefs. By the end of the twentieth century, some members were criticizing the devolution of Sundance leadership, claiming it had become too easy for a man to declare himself a Sundance chief, simply because he had political clout with the tribal Business Committee. They complained Sundance chiefs no longer needed to be a recognized holy man or even a spiritual advisor (though some considered it helpful), meaning individuals had to rely increasingly on individual vision quests during the dance or advice from personal mentors. Meanwhile, scheduling the Sundance (which was supposed to coincide with the full moon or "Sundance lamp") became more about inter-reservation scheduling conflicts than lunar calendars.[47]

The quest to legitimize the use of peyote was a more difficult and controversial journey. Not until 1965 was the use of peyote by Native Americans protected by federal regulation. However, it still took numerous court cases to safeguard the right of Indians to use the peyote sacrament. A successful challenge to California's anti-peyote laws in the mid-1960s helped overturn Colorado's anti-peyote laws, and in 1967 Colorado courts declared their 1917 law against peyote use to be unconstitutional.[48] Still, it was another eleven years before Congress passed the Indian Religious Freedom Act (1978) to protect the rights of American Indians to "believe, express, and exercise [their] traditional religions."[49]

While this act initiated a process whereby many aspects of religious tradition were protected, it was no cure-all because the law was vague. In theory, American Indians were no longer required to open sacred medicine bundles or amulets for airport security; ceremonials and sacred sites were generally protected; and Indian medicine men were allowed to possess parts of endangered species such as eagles. However, these protections were not always observed, especially for medicine men not enrolled in a recognized tribe. For example, a practicing mixed-blood Uncompahgre "doctor" had a young eagle confiscated from his home because he was not enrolled, therefore not an Indian, and therefore had no right to possess the endangered bird.[50]

Neither was the right of Indians to use peyote as a sacrament consistently recognized. By the 1990s only twenty-eight states protected the right of American Indians to use the drug, although others, including Utah, were willing to turn a blind eye to its use by Indians on Indian lands during Indian religious ceremonies. By 2016 (and after contentious court cases), nine states allowed members of any bona fide religious organization to use peyote. However, other states continued to vigorously prosecute *all* violations of their anti-peyote laws.[51]

The Supreme Court further complicated matters in 1990 when it ruled that the First Amendment did *not* protect the right of Indians to use peyote. In this case, a pair of Oregon respondents had been fired from a private drug rehabilitation organization for using peyote in religious ceremonies, and their application for unemployment compensation was disqualified based on "misconduct" because their firing was drug related.[52] In response, religious freedom advocates successfully lobbied for the Religious Freedom Restoration Act of 1993. The same year Indian leaders met at a national conference to discuss the protection of Indian religious freedom, including their use of eagle feathers and other restricted animal and plant materials. But in 1997 the Supreme Court nullified the Religious Freedom Restoration Act, ruling that Congress had overstepped its authority. They argued it appeared to be a deliberate attempt to circumvent the balance of powers between the legislative and judicial branches, and they charged Congress with trying to interpret the Constitution when it was within the established province of the Supreme Court. Since then, a handful of states have attempted to pass their own Religious Freedom Restoration Acts.[53]

Congress had amended the Indian Religious Freedom Act in 1994 to specifically protect the right of enrolled members of federally recognized Indian tribes to use the peyote sacrament within traditional religious ceremonies. However, a significant number of non-Indians and unaffiliated mixed-bloods continued to press for their rights to religious freedom as practicing members of the Native American Church, regardless of enrollment status. Thus, the issue of peyote use remained heated into the twenty-first century, and states have remained mixed on whether to allow non-Indians to use peyote in religious ceremonies.[54]

Utah is a prime example of this controversy. A years-long battle took place between the Utah attorney general and James "Flaming Eagle" Mooney, a non-Indian, who was conducting peyote ceremonies in his own Oklevueha Native American Church and distributing peyote sacrament to non-Indians. The attorney general argued the church was not a bona fide Indian religion, nor was Mooney from a traditional Indian culture (the Seminole tribe in which he claimed membership had disallowed him and further denied peyotism as a traditional Seminole religion). But Mooney and other non-Indian practitioners argued the laws were not intended to be racially discriminatory, that many of the 300,000 members of the Native American Church were not members of federally recognized tribes, and many had no Indian blood at all. Similar debates were occurring throughout the United States, most remaining unresolved at a federal level. The Utah Supreme Court eventually exonerated Mooney, and in 2004 Utah joined Colorado in making peyote legal in genuine religious ceremonies, regardless of race.[55]

The fight for Indian religious freedom moved into state prisons as well. By the mid-1980s a number of western states began to allow Native American inmates certain religious liberties but not peyote meetings. In Utah a lengthy battle of wills took place over the religious rights of Indian prisoners. The issue of hair length was challenged by Shoshone and Northern Ute inmates who claimed the religious right to wear their hair long. Prison officials disagreed, citing issues of safety, security, and hygiene: weapons could be hidden in hair, long hair was harder to keep clean, prisoners could more easily change their appearance if they tried to escape, and it encouraged homosexuality.[56] But some inmates defiantly refused to cut their hair, with one Lakota Sioux arguing that cutting his hair would be like "slicing away part of his soul," defacing his spirit, and damaging his very identity. Inmates endured repeated isolation

13.3. Darrell Gardiner builds a sweat lodge at the Utah State Prison; maintaining Native American religious rights were a highly controversial issue during the 1980s and 1990s, especially in prisons. (Photo courtesy of Colleen Gardiner)

and maximum confinement when they refused to cut their hair. Then, as part of a 1989 religious freedoms settlement, prison officials agreed (in principle) to allow inmates to wear culturally and religiously based hair styles, but they never actually changed their grooming code and continued to enforce the prohibition on long hair. Two years later, after continued protests, the warden finally agreed to allow Indian inmates to keep their hair long if they had authorized letters from their tribe proving their sincerity in religious beliefs.[57]

However, the fragile agreement was broken within months after a mixed-blood Ute prisoner sued the prison for denying him the right to wear his hair long. Because he was not an enrolled member of any recognized tribe, officials argued he was not an Indian and had no legal right to claim religious freedom protections for Indian beliefs. When the U.S. District Court subsequently ruled that prohibiting long hair did *not* infringe on a prisoner's religious rights, the old grooming code was immediately enforced for everyone.[58] Undaunted, some Native inmates continued their legal appeals until 1993, when the Religious Freedom Restoration Act again forced prison officials to concede the right of Indian inmates to wear long hair for religious purposes.[59]

In the mid-1980s Indian inmates in Utah also demanded the right to hold sweats for religious and therapeutic purposes, but prison officials refused, claiming that security superseded a prisoner's religious rights. Despite examples of other western states allowing Indian inmates to hold sweat lodge ceremonies, based on the 1978 Indian Religious Freedom Act, it was not until 1989, after federal courts ruled that American Indians could hold sweat lodge ceremonies in prisons, that Utah reluctantly allowed the domed lodges to be built and religious leaders to conduct their ceremonies. By 1999 over two hundred inmates were regularly participating in sweat lodge ceremonies at the Utah state prison every four to six weeks.[60]

However, *who* could conduct the ceremonies became another contentious topic that once again raised the touchy issue of Indian identity. Darrel Gardiner, a prominent mixed-blood Uncompahgre spiritual advisor who was often at odds with the tribe, was a Sundance chief at Fort Hall (Shoshone) events, held numerous sweat lodge and curing ceremonies for a national clientele, and worked for the Canadian government as a Native healer in hospitals in western Canada. For ten years Gardiner was prominent among those who travelled to Utah prisons to build sweat lodges and conduct ceremonies.[61] But in 1999 tribal officials objected to his activities. Because he was not enrolled in any recognized tribe, by definition he was not an Indian and therefore not authorized to lead Indian ceremonies in the prisons. By request of the tribe, Gardiner was banned from conducting further sweat lodge ceremonies in Utah prisons.[62] Despite civil rights suits against the state and other officials for abridging inmates' right to worship (it was difficult to find qualified, eligible, and willing leaders), the law was clear: only spiritual advisors authorized by a legally recognized tribe could practice within the prisons.[63]

The Northern Ute tribe's arguments against the mixed-blood practitioner were very much political as well as religious, rooted in a much larger controversy regarding the encroachment of Indian "wannabes" and the growth of New Age religion. Many full-blood Indians believed that non-Indians or unaffiliated individuals with only a smattering of Indian heritage were usurping and prostituting sacred native traditions. For example, in the 1960s, Utes had watched with amused indulgence as a handful of non-Indians and ethnographers sought *puwá* in peyote meetings and the Sundance. After all, these were Indian rituals that summoned Indian power for the specific good of Indian people. Since no Indian would seek out a non-Indian to be either doctored or spiritually advised—which was a root reason for acquiring power—the desire of such men to accumulate Indian power seemed ridiculous.[64] But by the 1990s

Native Americans were no longer amused when non-Indians—from curiosity seekers to nascent New Agers—appropriated, misinterpreted, and misused Indian rituals.

Spiritualists in so-called New Age religions began incorporating traditional Indian rituals in the 1980s, including sweat lodge ceremonies, pipe ceremonies, natural healing, and shamanism. Native Americans labeled these non-Indian spiritualists as "hucksters," "exploiters," "commercial profiteers," and "desecraters of sacred native ceremonies." Some characterized these faddish forays into Indian mysticism as "cultural robbery," the "final phase of genocide," and an assault on the remaining reservoir of Indian identity. Appropriating, misusing, and commercializing religious ceremonies diminished their sacredness and created only "plastic medicine men." These New Age spiritualists, without the years of training or vision questing under the guidance of Indian spiritual advisors, and without a knowledge of traditional Indian languages in which religious meaning was couched, could not fully comprehend let alone properly use the Indian power they claimed to possess. Local press announcements about upcoming Indian rituals began to add caveats explaining they were the "real thing" and not connected to New Age religion, and some tribes threatened to "copyright" their rituals to protect them from misuse.[65]

Some of these New Age spiritualists attempted to legitimize their activities by claiming some Indian heritage or of having learned their ceremonies from bona fide Indian medicine men. Others simply declared that "Indian fundamentalists" were practicing reverse racism by denying them the right to worship because of their skin color or race. One mixed-blood Cheyenne spiritualist argued that "prayer [was] for every race.... If it's godly, it has to be for all people." Some full-blood Indians sided with religious freedom, maintaining that "God just [couldn't] be that exclusive," and one Ute spiritual advisor added that "spirit has no color." Leonard Crow Dog, a prominent Lakota holy man, American Indian Movement activist, and spiritual advisor believed in doctoring anyone who came to him. He affirmed that "in the eyes of the Creator, we are all one. The Spirit really doesn't care what color you are, as long as you are concerned with carrying on the sacred way." Others contended that tribal governments should not determine who could conduct Indian ceremonies, only the participants could.[66]

The heated controversy in Utah over who (or what) constituted an Indian, specifically a Northern Ute, was based on a long-standing controversy resulting from the termination issues of the 1950s. It quickly spilled over into the arena of who could practice Indian religion. But it was a controversy with the weight of legal definition behind it. Congress had set a precedent when it decreed that only individuals with a specific ethnic and/or racial background could practice the peyote religion—that is, only members of a federally recognized tribe. However, while the use of peyote remained technically proscribed by federal law, the Drug Enforcement Agency typically deferred to state laws. Some states prohibited any cultivation, distribution, or use of peyote; others required practitioners to have a certified percentage of Indian heritage or tribal enrollment; while others allowed its use in religious ceremonies, regardless of race.[67] Today, most laws regarding Indian religious rights continue to include the boundary "authorized by a federally recognized tribe." Despite hard-fought legal battles to legalize some religious practices for anyone regardless of race, Indian religion continues to be a racial rather than a spiritual issue.

In modern times, many Utes subscribe to neither Christian nor native religious traditions—except to express their cultural heritage or cursorily attempt to incorporate both. For example, by the year 2000, Christian church attendance was minimal on the Uintah and Ouray Reservation, and traditional ceremonies had evolved into community social events. Some spiritual leaders expressed concern that members were neither Christian nor adherents of Indian religion but were "simply there."[68] On the other hand, the more traditional Ute Mountain Utes continued to fight for the maintenance of traditional beliefs in the face of increasing modernization—and westernization—through the use of peyote and sweat lodge ceremonies as well as the yearly Bear Dance and Sundance.

For many, however, the performance of Indian ceremonies that are perceived as traditional remains a bastion of Indian identity, one that continues to be actively and jealously guarded. Regardless of belief in their intrinsic power, Indian rituals remain a means for Utes, despite their physical acculturation to mainstream America, to maintain and express what they understand to be traditional values and mores. It is a way to preserve the collective consciousness that anchors them within a mythic and historical ethnic identity.

Chapter 14

Travail

1895–1940

Following reservation allotment, the Utes spiraled into a desperate poverty. Most were now corralled on reservations or clustered on allotments, bound to agencies, and dependent on federal annuities and supplies. In the name of assimilation Utes were ordered to farm, and yet they were defrauded of both their land and water rights, disallowed in some cases the right to lease their land (or even allow relatives to use it), and were denied adequate farming equipment or supplies. Those who did attempt to farm were still forced to seek wage work to survive instead of tending their own fields, or they were forced to sell the hay crops needed for their stock. They were set up to fail. And they did. During the decades of the early twenty-first century, the Utes were also inundated with cultural change. Ever a pragmatic and adaptable people, the Utes had long been syncretizing and assimilating cultural innovations—changing externals like dress, diet, and dwellings—even as they tenaciously clung to more deeply embedded beliefs, values, and mores. Thus, while traditional nomadism had been restricted, mobility and close kinship ties continued via inter-reservation visiting and intertribal events. As political patterns shifted, from respected elders and successful hunt-and-raid chiefs to administrative business managers, leaders continued to be the tribe's "talkers" and negotiated with non-Indians on behalf of tribal prosperity. And as the Utes struggled to survive as a people, that very struggle reinforced their ethnic identities as a separate people, as *Indians* and as *Utes*.

Allotment had been intended to pulverize communal reservations and eradicate tribal ties so that Indians would individualize, assimilate Euro-American values, and be absorbed into the dominant culture. Instead, crammed within a limited geographic area, subjected to differential treatment, and forced together to fight against common problems to survive, for Utes the reservation and allotment systems only reinforced the separateness of being Indian and crystallized the definition of tribal identities. Census rolls taken to determine who was or was not Indian (and therefore who was or was not eligible to receive allotted land and tribal benefits) established ethnic boundaries in ways that had never before been defined. The Indian office further confirmed Indian identity by constantly emphasizing the ways they were different from the rest of white America, giving them Indian-only privileges with one hand while denying them most rights enjoyed by non-Indians with the other.[1] Thus, as the Utes entered the twentieth century, they recognized that they were The People—*Núu-ci*—but what exactly identified them as *Núu-ci* was shifting.

DESCENT INTO POVERTY

As tribes lost an increasing amount of American Indian land, a growing number of Indians entered the ranks of the landless poor. Part of the problem Utes faced was that many of their men refused or were unable to farm, yet no one considered training Indian women as farmers or herders, even though farming fell within their gendered sphere of work.[2] Making the situation worse, well-meaning reformers had thrown American Indians into a highly competitive market on marginal lands with hand tools and plows at a time when the very nature of farming in the United States was changing. By the 1910s the agricultural sector was suffering from *over*production due to the fertile Midwest, increased mechanization, the growth of agribusiness, and an enthusiastic wartime push for greater production. Small-scale commercial farming had become increasingly unprofitable in trying to compete with large-scale mechanized farming and in the context of monopolistic, price-gouging railroads and granaries. Yet even as American farmers became the most productive and efficient in the world, creating food surpluses that dropped market prices, in the name of ennobling agriculture and hard work American Indians were typically given small plots of land and were expected to farm by hand. Communal farming was discouraged if not outright forbidden, and the purchase of reapers, harvesters, and even sulky plows was often denied. Hand plows were deemed sufficient for Indian use, and while the secretary of the Interior might allow an agency a few mechanized tools for communal use operated by white employees, it typically refused purchase of labor-saving machinery for Indian farmers. (The Uintah agent was fortunate in acquiring two reapers and a thresher by 1889.)[3]

These policies came from well-intended Indian rights proponents, most of whom had been raised believing in the Jeffersonian agricultural ideal and within a Protestant work ethic that taught physical and spiritual salvation lay in hard work, sobriety, frugality, and individualism, and that the successful amassing of material possessions was a physical demonstration of God's approval. Social evolutionary theories of the time maintained that Indians could only evolve from their savage state into civilization through individual property ownership and physical-labor agriculture.[4]

Yet self-serving agents and superintendents often hampered efforts to transform Utes into farmers and ranchers, as did a variety of Washington-based policies for micromanaging the affairs of so-called "incompetent" Indians (uneducated, illiterate, and unable to speak English). Affairs on the Southern Ute Reservation typified these problems. First, agricultural endeavors were delayed for years while the removal question was debated, inhibiting any attempts to farm, claim water rights, or build schools. Also muddling affairs were the often conflicting interests of agency administrators and employees. For example, Agent Christian Stollsteimer opposed removal because he had almost free use of Ute rangeland near his ranch. However, the unqualified and politically appointed agent Henry Page supported removal because he and several agency employees expected to be in position to file claims on the best land when the Utes were removed. After allotment, other agents benefited from irrigation projects meant to supply water to Ute allotments but reached their own ranches instead. Agency officials often held significant financial interests off the reservation, including irrigation and water companies that stood to profit from delivering water to both Ute allotments and homesteaded farms. Agents also expedited and often profited from the sale of Indian allotments.[5] In theory, Indian land was protected by restricting "incompetent" Indians from selling their land for immediate cash. But agents sometimes declared competency and then facilitated and controlled sales, negated family rights to orphans and claimed guardianship themselves to facilitate sales, or solved heirship issues by selling allotments for cash that was immediately locked up in federally administered Individual Indian Accounts (IIA). Some agents even forced sales and then personally purchased the land at below-market prices. Some Southern Utes were "resettled" on smaller forty-acre allotments clustered in the Pine River and Spring Creek valleys. This seemed a positive move because the land was more fertile, but the allotments were too small to raise the cattle and fodder (i.e., alfalfa) that was the agricultural mainstay of southern Colorado. Thus, the Southern Ute Reservation became a "happy hunting ground for employees" seeking to make personal profits, even as their Ute charges spiraled deeper into poverty.[6]

American Indians across the country also lost large amounts of land and many cattle herds during and just after World War I. Many non-Indians still coveted "unused" Indian land and were anxious for the Indians to either become better farmers or relinquish the land to those who could use it. This was especially true during the war, when the government encouraged American farmers to boost production for the war effort. As part of this, the BIA encouraged and helped Indians produce more, but the commissioner, Cato Sells, was convinced Indians simply lacked the physical capacity to cultivate or make use of all their surplus land. As the country moved into the war, the BIA pushed agencies to lease as much of their extra land as they could to more experienced farmers and ranchers. Thus in places like the Dakotas, Montana, and Wyoming, large-scale and supposedly temporary land leases ultimately alienated hundreds of thousands of acres. Similarly, the best Indian grazing land was lost to large cattle companies, often with the help of unethical BIA employees.[7] Compounding the problem, many Indians were also encouraged to maximize their stockraising profits by selling off their herds while beef prices were high during the war. But the war ended earlier than expected, and by the spring of 1919 the nation's extractive industries (including mining and agriculture) plummeted into a serious postwar depression, and lessees could not pay their debts. Many Indians were left without payment for either land leased or cattle sold. As a result, by 1920, huge swaths of Indian land had fallen into white hands, and many Indians had been stripped of livestock and their livelihood. Not surprisingly, destitute Native Americans, who were very much a part of hard-hit rural America, entered the Great Depression years before the rest of the country.[8]

Not only was "surplus" reservation land lost, allotments were alienated as well. Between 1913 and 1921 alone, nearly one million acres of American Indian land was sold as a result of "emancipating" Indians from federal protection; among these were thousands of acres of Southern and Uintah-Ouray Ute land. By 1936, over 33,000 acres of land allotted on the Southern Ute reservation (46 percent) had been sold to non-Indians, and more than a fourth of Uintah-Ouray allotments were gone. By the end of the 1930s, the combination of opening the reservation and sales of allotted land by destitute Utes had shrunk previously reserved Ute lands by over 90 percent.[9] Only the Ute Mountain Utes, who had successfully refused allotments, remained immune from this continuing land loss. And without a land base, there was little the tribes could do to develop economically.[10]

It is little wonder the Utes were unable to successfully shift from their traditional patterns of subsistence (now untenable) to farming or ranching. According to one historian, with the sudden implementation of allotment

> the Ignacio Utes [Southern Utes] were forthwith expected to behave like industrious farming citizens on their unprepared agricultural tracts, each with grazing land that in most instances was inadequate for running stock. Each family nominally owned funds that were closely guarded from their use in the Treasury or in Individual Indian Accounts. In effect, the Utes were being ordered, like Joseph's people in Egypt, to make bricks without straw.[11]

And Superintendent Walter Runke described the situation on the Southern Ute Reservation in 1914:

> A disgruntled half-starved Ute with a few decrepit head of horses or ponies to help him in his farm work…discouraged because his thin winter diet has sapped the foundation of any ambition. Disgruntled because he feels that the Government is withholding from him what he thinks was faithfully promised to be paid him under their treaty.…Half starved man and beast because the larder was so often nigh-exhausted."[12]

By the early 1900s the Utes on both the northern and southern reservations were abysmally poor. Most subsisted on a mixture of stock raising, farming (mostly done by agency personnel), leasing allotments to Euro-Americans or sharecropping with Hispanic Americans, occasional wage labor, and supplementary hunting and gathering. All, even the independent Weeminuche, were dependent on the rations, annuities, and per capita payments doled out by government agents. Extended families pooled resources and skills to survive, an extension of their traditional collective ethic of sharing.[13] Tribal leaders and individual men and women complained or attempted to obtain redress, but even when they were successful and awarded monetary judgments, the money went into their inaccessible IIAs, which were administered, squandered, garnished, and often lost by federal agents. Making matters worse, the awards were offset by the termination of other government subsidies and a demand that individuals work in exchange for goods or obtain them under a Reimbursable Plan in which tools or matériel were acquired from the tribe through "loans" that individuals had to repay.[14]

Meanwhile, the Office of Indian Affairs (OIA) and their agents persisted in pressuring the Utes to assimilate into the Euro-American mainstream. By the turn of the twentieth century, cotton and wool fabrics, cowboy boots, and hats replaced most buckskin clothing for Utes except on ritual occasions, and beef and mutton replaced wild game. Most Utes still lived in brush shelters, aged skin or canvas tipis, or military-style tents and cooked over open fires. Some small log cabins, frame houses, or shanties were built for acknowledged leaders or shamans—but they were often used for storage. Many owned some livestock, including cattle, sheep, mules, and a diminishing number of horses, though seldom profitably. Like Meeker before them, agents continued to complain about Utes having "too many horses." Agents estimated there were as many as 6,000 to 12,000 horses on the Uintah reservation in the mid-1880s.[15]

Agency administrators also actively—if unsuccessfully—sought to suppress any sign of Indian religion (including social dances and shamanic healing), and they continued to force children into boarding schools and away from the "corrupting" influence of parents.[16] But Utes continued to pool family resources to facilitate survival and retained some mobility through extended inter-reservation visits; participation in Wild West shows (Southern Utes), fairs, and Sundances; and in later years traveling the powwow and rodeo circuits. Of necessity, limited hunting and gathering of traditional foods still supplemented diets. And even though Utes eventually began to accept some "White" medicine, they more frequently turned to traditional shamanic healing until the late twentieth century.[17]

Conditions on the reservations continued to worsen. Sanitation and health care were deplorable because as camps became more permanent, refuse accumulated, breeding germs and disease. A general distrust of white medicine and a preference for traditional medicine men kept Utes away from the minimal health care services that were available. It was a condition paralleled by Native Americans across the country and publicized in 1928 when the Meriam Report was presented to Congress. This report exposed the conditions of American Indians, and it was a scathing denunciation of the failed allotment policy. Indians remained uneducated and untrained, their land had been lost, and the conditions on reservations were appalling. Most Indians were destitute, their living conditions were unsanitary, health was extraordinarily poor, mortality was high, and trachoma, measles, pneumonia, and tuberculosis were rampant. The Indian mortality rate was twice that of the general population, with infant mortality almost triple. Death from tuberculosis was seventeen times the national average in some areas. But health care was practically nonexistent, with the government spending only fifty cents per Indian per year through its health services. Children at boarding schools studied in dirty classrooms and were allotted an average of eleven cents per day for food, while poverty among the general Indian populations had resulted in widespread malnutrition. Most Indians had insufficient incomes and were economically unskilled; half lived on $100–$200 per year at a time the average U.S. income was $1,350. Few understood the value of cash money or land, and the intermittent doling out of "unearned" income from land sales, per capita payments, or leases encouraged idleness and stunted their progress. As a result, most Indians had become apathetic toward economic development, a consequence of despair and an inability to adjust to their new social and economic conditions.[18]

The Utes, too, were locked on limited or unproductive land, in direct competition with American neighbors, but with little history of agrarianism or desire to farm. This was not because they had no history of cultivating food-plants or animal husbandry. The Uintah band was forced to farm or raise stock to survive, and a few families among the White River and Uncompahgre bands owned significant herds of sheep, goats, and even cattle. Among the Southern Ute bands, with a long-standing history of cross-cultural exchange with their Spanish, Pueblo, and Navajo neighbors, some prominent families had owned herds of livestock for decades and now even employed Navajo herders. A few, like chiefs Cabezon and Sewormicha, had reciprocal relationships with Navajo families and unitedly cultivated land along the La Plata, where they planted and irrigated melons, squash, beans, and corn and shared the fruits of the hunt. And the Weeminuche and San Juan Paiutes owned hundreds of sheep, goats, and horses that competed for grazing land with commercial cattle herds.[19] Still, most Utes did not want to farm, not only for gender-related reasons, but because it was foreign and a difficult way of life for anyone in the arid West.[20]

After Congress passed a law in 1908 allowing the secretary of the Interior to lease irrigable allotments with the consent of Indian allottees, many Southern Utes began to let their farms to Hispanic sharecroppers, while others leased their land to Euro-Americans.[21] On the Uintah and Ouray Reservations, out of 80,000 acres within the scope of the ambitious—but costly—Uintah Indian Irrigation Project (UIIP), nearly a third of it was soon leased, and in many cases subsequently sold, to non-Indians. Irrigation canals had been dug as part of the UIIP, and water rights were being assessed to all affected landowners, including Utes, whether farming or not. But by Utah state law, if water was not used for irrigation, after five years it reverted to public domain and could be claimed by non-Indians. Thus, in 1914 a well-meaning agent attempted to

275

preserve the "prior appropriation" water rights of his Uintah and Ouray Utes by advertising for people to utilize Indian lands. As a result, nearly 30,000 acres were leased to non-Indians and much of it ended up being sold.[22] Southern Ute agents pressed for irrigation projects in order to claim water rights under similar western water laws. Regardless of treaties or agreements, the Utes fell under Colorado's "first use" laws. If homesteaders or irrigation companies filed claims first, Utes could only use what was left—if any. Competition over water rights and land would mark Southern Ute relations for decades.[23]

Despite the grandiose irrigation scheme on the Uintah Reservation (or perhaps in part because of it), both Indians and non-Indians found themselves in trouble almost immediately. Most of the Uintah Basin was agriculturally poor and demanded a high input of time and resources. By 1912, even non-Indian homesteaders were in financial distress. And while the Utes had no land payments, they were still being assessed arbitrary land and water improvement fees as if they were farming, even though they had no farm income from which to pay them.[24]

As the Uintah and Ouray Utes hunkered down on their diminished land and watched the gradual disintegration of their traditional ways of life, many turned to alcohol. Drunkenness, disorderly conduct, and alcohol-related violence became a main argument used for maintaining Fort Duchesne—the need to police the Utes.[25] The notorious Strip was a major source of the problem. Whiskey venders in "Sobertown" sold alcohol to Indian patrons as well as to miners and soldiers from Fort Duchesne, and they sent whiskey peddlers into the reservation. Although Major James Randlett attempted to control the sale of liquor to Indians, enforcement was difficult. Local officials passed laws making it illegal to sell liquor to Indians and arrested both liquor venders and drunken Utes. In time, Congress passed a bill prohibiting the sale of alcohol to any Indian, giving more teeth to the laws. Randlett also made the Strip off-limits to soldiers and posted guards on the road. The illegal sale of alcohol and Indian drunkenness dropped significantly.[26]

However, after the reservation was broken up in 1905, the Strip briefly revived, and miners, freighters, travelers, and even a few soldiers and agency employees again smuggled bootleg rotgut whiskey to the Utes. The persistent problem of liquor sales to the Uintah and Ouray Utes and the social disintegration it caused ended only after the military post closed in 1911, law enforcement spread through the fragmented reservation, and the scurrilous businesses on the Strip closed. The problem of alcoholism did not return as a significant issue until after civil rights suits in the 1950s helped repeal the laws that prohibited

276

alcohol sales to Indians (although many tribes, including the Ute Mountain Utes, continue to outlaw the sale of alcohol on their reservations).[27]

A few Hispanic settlements on the fringes of the Southern Ute Reservation produced and sold bootleg moonshine as well. One of these villages, Rosa, was frequented by both non-Indians and Utes who came to drink, socialize, gamble, and race horses, especially after receiving annuities. The Utes were on friendly terms with Rosa's Hispanic residents, protected them from agency protests, refused to testify against them during Prohibition, and offered them favorable leases for grazing sheep on Indian land.[28]

By 1900, Utes were responding more assertively to their new political realities. The northern Utes, with their three bickering bands and competing chiefs, had inherited a decentralized and consequently weak reservation leadership, while the Southern and Ute Mountain Utes maintained stronger, more stable leaders. Although kingmakers in Washington again sought to manipulate leadership—attempting to depose uncooperative chiefs like the Capote's Tabewatch and the Weeminuche's Ignacio—they were generally unsuccessful. Personal popularity and a willingness to voice tribal consensus remained a criteria for Ute leadership. So Ignacio continued to speak for the Utes at Ute Mountain, despite opposition factions led by men like Red Rock and Mariano, while Severo and the generally amenable Buckskin Charley (Charles Buck) remained the most influential leaders of the Southern Utes.[29]

At times these Southern Ute leaders proved significant thorns in the side of bureaucracy, along with later vocal factions who were reinforced with help from non-Ute locals like José Blas Lucero, a prominent Hispanic neighbor, and Barry Sullivan, a successful Euro-American attorney in Durango (both "cordially hated" by agency officials). In 1896 the Southern Utes convened a chiefs consortium and sent a delegation to Washington, D.C., where they were unofficially joined by an angry insurgent faction stirred up by Lucero and Sullivan. The chiefs delegation was able to initiate a lawsuit in the name of the Confederated Bands of Utes to recover money for land ceded during the 1880 removal. In 1910 the Confederated Utes won their lawsuit, and in 1911 the U.S. Court of Claims awarded them $3,408,610—though most of it was deposited and its disbursement controlled by the OIA. In 1930 the Uintah and Ouray Utes were finally awarded a $1.2 million appropriation to reimburse them for reservation land withdrawn and incorporated into the Uintah National Forest.[30]

But with the payment of these debts came the concomitant termination of other benefits. Annuities were suspended while award money was distributed into IIAs, which the "incompetent" Utes were rarely able to access. Although the interest on these awards was usually paid on a per capita basis, tribal members wanted easier access to the principal. With no money in hand and their annuities terminated, Utes grew understandably angry: "These goods are not given to us for nothing," protested Charles Buck, "But come from the sale of our lands." When payments were also withheld from parents who refused to send their children to school, Buck argued that the only criteria for receiving this money was "good conduct." Although interest payments were resumed, annuities were not, and the Judgment Fund money remained in IIAs where it was supposed to be used for an individual's "good"—or was garnished to pay debts.[31] But not all money was used wisely. One enthusiastic agent for the Ute Mountain Utes used tribal funds to purchase four thousand head of Hereford cattle; however, the waterless range was unsuitable, half the cattle died, and the rest were confiscated when owners could not prove they had sufficient graze or feed.[32]

The OIA also tried to teach some Utes the value of the goods they were receiving by instituting the Reimbursable Plan. Beginning in 1913, Southern Utes were required to purchase their farm implements, seeds, and supplies from the agency on credit. Those who failed to "reimburse" the tribe could have their IIAs garnished for the debt. Around the same time, officials also began to require labor—or workfare—in exchange for rations.[33]

Many OIA officials believed that the single greatest hindrance to Indian self-sufficiency was their reliance on the dole and their lack of motivation to work. Reformers were determined to encourage self-sufficiency by weaning Utes from this dependency. But the Utes angrily objected, viewing rations and annuities as payment for the *sale* of their land. Working for rations was the equivalent of being charged double for what the government owed them for their ceded land. But little changed and agents continued to insist on "working rations" and that Utes purchase goods with their government-controlled funds. As supplies, money, and land continued to dwindle, Utes were forced into a grinding poverty from which few escaped.[34]

THE TSENEGAT AFFAIR AND THE POSEY "WAR"

In the midst of these economic setbacks, racial, religious, economic, and band rivalries continued to muddy the waters in the Four Corners region. Conflict had simmered for years between southeastern Utah settlers and the "bronco" Utes and Paiutes who refused to tamely relocate on reservations. These people competed for graze and committed ongoing small-scale depredations. The situation came to a head in 1914 when a minor incident escalated into a vicious backlash by local Mormons seeking a final solution to a long-standing problem.[35]

The trouble began when Tsenegat (or Tse-quit),[36] a bronco Ute and notorious card shark and cheat, stalked and murdered a Mexican herder named Juan Chacón who refused to play cards with him. Three Ute Mountain Weeminuches witnessed Tsenegat disposing of the body but did not report it for fear of reprisals from his father, Poke, an influential and feared bronco leader. But details of the killing leaked out, and a grand jury in Denver indicted Tsenegat for the murder. As lawyers maneuvered in court, officials tried to apprehend the elusive Tsenegat. But Poke refused to cooperate, and Tsenegat continued to maintain his innocence despite mounting evidence of his guilt.[37] Authorities finally decided to raid Poke's camp and arrest Tsenegat by force.

United States marshal Aquila Nebeker set out to arrest the fugitive in February 1915. Though Nebeker was a prominent political figure from Utah, most Mormons refused to join him, claiming the Utes were peaceable and force unnecessary. So Nebeker assembled an enthusiastic posse from southern Colorado that was "composed chiefly of the rougher element of cowpunchers...[who] proceeded to tank up in anticipation of the coming fun with the Indians." Concerned citizens notified the commissioner of Indian Affairs that some of Nebeker's posse were "boozefighters, gamblers and bootleggers...[who] talked as though they were going rabbit hunting." A later investigation reported that the posse had indeed been "composed of the 'roughneck' or 'tinhorn' class, to whom shooting an Indian would be real sport!"

Poke and his San Juan Paiute brother-in-law, Posey, were camped only a few miles from Bluff, Utah. However, neither was aware of the quasi-military campaign being organized against them; rather, they had been assured no one would try to take Tsenegat by force. But Nebeker had other ideas, and his posse executed a surprise dawn attack on Poke's camp. When gun-carrying Utes rushed from their tipis, the posse opened fire without identifying themselves and without orders. The Utes fired back in self-defense as terrified women and children fled, several dying in the rain of bullets or drowned in a nearby river. Warriors from Posey's camp made a timely arrival, held off the posse, and both bands escaped.

The two bands fled 110 miles west, while the posse bivouacked in Bluff in order to "protect" the citizens and allow Nebeker's "war correspondent" to send a flurry of press dispatches relating a sensationalized and mostly falsified account of the campaign and the heroism of the cowboy fighters.[38] A few Ute

14.1. Ute prisoners being taken to Salt Lake City following the "Ute War," 1915; Aquila Nebeker (with binoculars), Posey, Poke, and Tsenegat. (Used by permission, Utah State Historical Society, #14609)

teens surrendered and were jailed, while the cowboys rooted out all nester Indians from their homesteads along the river bottoms. Then, to clear the potential battlegrounds, cowboys drove from their homes 160 noncombatant Indians—Utes, Paiutes, and Navajos—and forced them onto the Ute Mountain Ute Reservation. One journalist predicted this would

> result in the...ridding of the vicinity of Bluff of the troublesome reds. There is much fine farm land near Bluff that is open to entry and it will now probably be rapidly taken up by the settlers who like to dry farm. There is also a fine range close, which makes it good stock country.[39]

The article failed to note that the "reds" already held legal title to most of this fine land.

As a result of Nebeker's precipitous actions, a very real threat of war now loomed. While the outlaw Payuchis were few, the Navajos were a formidable force, and Washington could ill afford a full-fledged Indian war. The country was already wrestling with the serious international events leading toward World War I and needed neither the embarrassment nor military diversion of an Indian war. Brigadier General Hugh Scott was sent to Utah to resolve the affair. With the help of Navajo intermediaries and respected traders John and Louisa Wetherill, Scott met with Posey and Poke, after which Tsenegat and several others surrendered and voluntarily traveled to Salt Lake City. There Nebeker admitted he had failed to follow the due course of law in serving his warrant of arrest, and all were released except Tsenegat. The so-called "uprising" was over.[40]

Tsenegat's highly publicized murder trial began in Denver in July 1915. Indian rights proponents flocked to the trial, and officials, determined to give their Indian defendant a fair trial, appointed one of the finest lawyers available as defense attorney. San Juan residents were convinced of Tsenegat's guilt because physical and eyewitness evidence implicated him, and Poke himself later boasted that one of his sons had "killed a Mexican." However, witnesses were discredited, the prosecution's case foundered, and Tsenegat was acquitted.

San Juan County residents were disgusted and bitterly criticized the special treatment Poke, Posey, and Tsenegat had received, having been fed, housed, and paraded before photographers and a sympathetic public in Salt Lake City and Denver. One prosecution witness, Albert Lyman, angrily protested that the acquittal had been a miscarriage of justice that allowed "scoff-law" killers to go "scot-free" (including Posey and Poke). "Crack-brained" and "fanatical Indian Rights people" had come to Denver to be sure "the notorious murderer was released regardless of the evidence," and they would "not tolerate any word spoken against the 'poor Indian.'" This had encouraged Tsenegat to become "ten-fold more the child of hell," and "ignited coals among the smoldering, defiant Piute tribe" that led to more conflict. And in the wake of the trial, outlaw Utes and Paiutes did grow increasingly insolent and aggressive.[41]

Through it all, the peaceful Ute and Paiute homesteaders continued to suffer, for when they had been forcibly removed to the Ute Mountain Reservation, they had lost claim to their land. It would be another five years before the first of these displaced homesteaders dared venture back to file new claims in Allen Canyon.[42]

Even as the conflict in southeast Utah was contained, the United States was moving closer to its own international war. When World War I was finally declared in April 1917, American Indians were drawn into this struggle as well. American Indians had long been used by the U.S. military as allies and auxiliaries, including the Southern Utes who had allied to fight the Navajo and

Plains Indians, and northern Utes who had served as scouts in the 1879 Sioux campaign. Even after most Indian troubles had been subdued, some Indians continued to serve as regular soldiers in integrated units.

Beginning in 1891, the army began assembling several all-Indian units, one of which was a Sioux infantry unit briefly posted at Fort Douglas in Salt Lake City. However, the experiment in forming segregated units ended in 1893. Nevertheless, Indian service in integrated military units continued. Theodore Roosevelt's Rough Riders, for example, included a significant number of American Indians, and Indians also served in the Philippines and the Boxer Rebellion in China. For the most part, these soldiers came primarily from war-oriented tribes whose young men needed war deeds to gain standing or enter war societies. The Utes and their cultural cousins did not fit this profile, however, and military recruitment among the Utes, Shoshones, Bannocks, and Goshutes was singularly unsuccessful.[43]

As World War I approached, American Indians were included in the draft, and concerted efforts were made to recruit Indians at home and especially from boarding schools. Not surprisingly, the regimented boarding schools proved an excellent source for recruitment because many Indian students had learned useful vocational skills and were already familiar with uniforms, spit-and-polish behavior, and military-style drill.[44]

But recruitment was not without some resistance. Most American Indians were not citizens, so many questioned whether they had to register for the draft or if it was even legal for them to serve. And soldiers had to swear allegiance to the United States. Some feared this would negate their tribal enrollment and affect their tribal benefits. Utah's Goshutes were caught in the middle of this. Tribal leaders had already been protesting a corrupt superintendent, and when Goshute men also refused to register for the draft, the government took action. Troops from Fort Douglas staged an early-morning raid and arrested leaders for "inciting" a rebellion. Although other cases of draft resistance occurred elsewhere, including on the Southern Ute Reservation, most incidents were minor.[45]

Most Indians, however, heeded the call and served willingly and with distinction, primarily for patriotic reasons. But service also provided significant advantages financially and educationally, as well as opportunities to experience the world outside the reservation and interact with non-Indians.[46]

Meanwhile, Indian women at home became noted for their support of the war, especially of their own soldiers. They donated to the Red Cross and participated in liberty loan bond drives that netted millions of dollars for the war effort. One seventy-five-year-old Uintah Ute woman became a national celebrity when she contributed $500, all but emptying her savings. Like other Americans, Indian women also knitted clothing, planted victory gardens, and learned how to bottle food as part of war-effort food conservation programs.[47]

Although Ute participation in the war was minimal, they, like the majority of Native Americans, generally supported the United States and its war effort. A total of 10,000 to 12,000 Indian men served during World War I, which was at least twenty percent of the adult male population.[48] Among these servicemen were three Northern Utes and six Southern Utes. World War I veteran Julius Cloud became active in early tribal government, serving three times as chair of the Southern Ute tribe. Following World War I, a growing number of Utes participated in the U.S. military, with hundreds serving in subsequent United States conflicts.[49]

During their service, American Indian soldiers faced a number of issues, including language, education, ongoing racism, and enduring the stereotype of being "instinctive soldiers." They were painted as naturally bloodthirsty warriors with an inbred desire to fight, and with an inherited gift for camouflage and scouting. This served to enhance their reputations but also entailed expectations; they were often put into especially dangerous forward positions, which accounted for their high mortality rate in battle. On the other hand, Germans feared and respected them. Germans, too, had been steeped in the lore of the savage American Indian taken from dime novels and touring Wild West shows.[50] The stereotypes would continue to follow Indian soldiers into World War II.

When these Indian veterans returned from the war, they were treated as heroes at home, and tribes were feted by Washington. However, interest soon faded and reservations were left no better than they had been—and in some cases, worse. Land and herds were lost supporting the war effort, and enthusiasm for assimilation had been enhanced during the war, which led to accelerated policies to emancipate Indians from federal guardianship. This in turn hastened additional land loss by newly ordained "competent" Indians. And money earned with liberty loan bonds was also placed out of reach in IIA accounts. Nonetheless, the war effort helped some tribes who began farming for the first time, and it revived traditional ceremonies to send off and welcome home warriors. The war also helped accelerate citizenship; thousands of American Indians, even without citizenship, had fought for the United States. An increasing number of people felt Indians had earned that right.[51]

Life on the Utes' postwar reservations was little changed, but with increasingly desperate poverty, rampant diseases, and few jobs. And in southeastern Utah, conflict between non-Indians and Indians ignited once again.

The violence broke out in southeastern Utah in 1923 after a few inveterate Ute teenagers robbed a sheep camp, killed a calf, and burned a bridge. Both were arrested and went peaceably into Blanding for the trial. However, the aging Posey complicated the situation when he engineered a dramatic escape. Posey had a reputation for "troublemaking, arrogance, meanness, and thievery," and he was blamed for any mischief, proven or not.[52] Posey lived up to his reputation at the jail when blows were struck, guns were fired, and he and the defendants fled south with an ad hoc posse in hot pursuit. A massive manhunt ensued. Utes and Paiutes were rounded up en masse and held in a barbed-wire compound in Blanding, while others fled toward the wild Comb Ridge area west of Bluff.[53]

Once again, journalists sensationalized the new "Indian war" and claimed Blanding was terrorized and under siege by the "red fox." Meanwhile, a local posse grimly pursued the fugitives, determined to "dispose of the crisis before bungling outsiders could mess things up," and with orders to "shoot everything that looks like an Indian." The starving and freezing Utes were eventually cornered and then trucked and herded back to join their families in the barbed-wire compound. Resurrecting religious rhetoric, one settler exulted that it was "the first time these fellows have been stopped since the days of Gadianton." But Posey remained at large—and dying. Hidden in the rimrocks of Comb Ridge, the wounded chief died a slow and agonizing death from a festering wound, despite being secretly tended by occasionally furloughed relatives (who remained convinced the bullet had been poisoned).[54]

With the confirmation of Posey's death—first by a U.S. marshal who buried him, and then souvenir-hunting locals who twice disinterred his remains to have their pictures taken with him—the impounded Indians were allowed to go free.[55] But again, the Ute-Paiute mixed-bloods found themselves bereft of their belongings, their meager livestock, most of their land—and this time, even their children. Southern Ute Superintendent E. E. McKean had the children collected and taken to a new Indian boarding school at Towaoc, Colorado, an agency center replacing the Navajo Springs subagency near Sleeping Ute Mountain in 1918. Frantic, struggling children were caught and deloused, their hair cut, their clothing stripped off and burned, and new "civilized" clothing given in replacement.[56]

But the government was also forced to acknowledge the existence of these landless and destitute people, who had so determinedly remained off reservations. The remnants of Poke's small band was finally allotted land in Montezuma Creek, while Posey's people received land in the Allen Canyon area.[57]

However, bringing services to and educating this "most primitive and backward band of Indians" was an uphill battle. While there was some progress in cultivating small plots, only a small percentage of land was suitable for farming. Few roads existed for transporting goods; band members continued to live in tents or Navajo-style hogans; and parents were reluctant to send their children to a boarding school one hundred miles away. By 1930 officials were still trying to convince them to abandon their primitive homesteads and move to the Ute Mountain Reservation, but they steadfastly refused to leave their homes. Eventually, the Indian Office simply registered them on the Ute Mountain rolls, entitling them to the same benefits as other enrolled members.[58]

A NEW DEAL FOR INDIANS: NEW DEAL REFORMS AND THE INDIAN REORGANIZATION ACT

By the 1920s an era was ending. A number of prominent—or notorious—Utes died: Tsenegat of tuberculosis in 1922, Posey of gunshot wounds in 1923, and Poke and Chipeta of old age in 1924.[59]

Chipeta's final years help to illustrate the fluctuating attitudes of Euro-Americans toward Indians at the turn of the century, as well as native attitudes toward the changes being imposed on them. They also demonstrate the quiet resistance of many Utes caught in the shifting currents of change.

Chipeta, Ouray's widow, had been forced out of Colorado with the rest of the Uncompahgre in 1880. Although she begged to remain on her Montrose farm, it was sold (most of it to the manipulative Otto Mears), and the cash proceeds were given to her—which she promptly gifted to others. But the fine home she was promised at Ouray turned out to be an unfinished and unfurnished cabin, and she chose to live more traditionally in a tipi on barren Bitter Creek. Chipeta suffered from rheumatism in later years and eventually went blind. For her rheumatism, she occasionally sought treatments in the medicinal hot springs and vapor caves at Glenwood Springs, Colorado. However, despite her self-imposed poverty ("what is good enough for my people is good enough for me"), she achieved unwanted notoriety as an Indian folk heroine and "Queen of the Utes." Trailing remnants of traditions that an increasingly romantic public now ascribed to the pacified but once "noble" Indian, she was frequently visited by public figures, given many gifts by admirers, invited to participate in Colorado fairs, and feted and entertained in Colorado, even riding in a motorcade with President Taft. Some Coloradoans belatedly tried to raise funds for her, criticized her treatment, and called her an exile. When Chipeta died at the age of eighty-one, she was buried in a shallow grave. However, Superintendent McKean proposed raising a memorial to her and Ouray in Montrose, and her brother, McCook, agreed. A mausoleum was rushed to completion in 1925, and with much pomp and ceremony Chipeta's remains were reinterred at Ouray Memorial Park—near the homestead from which she had been expelled forty-five years earlier. But when promoters asked for Ouray's remains, Charles Buck refused. Instead, Ouray's bones (or someone's, at least) were ostensibly disinterred from their secret grave, and with great ceremony they were reburied in the Indian cemetery at Ignacio.[60]

By this time Indian lands were in tatters. However, attitudes toward Indian land rights were shifting, and attempts to usurp even more land were mostly unsuccessful. In 1923 non-Indians argued that an "unused" tract of Uintah-Ouray grazing land was more valuable as farming land and should therefore be opened to entry. The petition failed. Twenty years later, a non-Indian sheepherder again tested Ute land rights when he drove sheep onto unsold, open Uintah Ute range; the court upheld tribal rights to the land.[61]

Despite these small victories, the economic affairs of most Utes were in disarray. In 1925 delegations from all three reservations went to Washington to "demand an accounting" for the mismanagement, fraud, and corruption on the reservation and with their virtually inaccessible IIA funds. The OIA refused to recognize the delegation, but the delegation returned in 1926, and again in 1927, this time even more insistent. Southern Ute leaders complained that the superintendent E. E. McKean was "the worst enemy of the Utes...[and was] seeking [their] ruination...for his own financial benefit." They were being strangled economically, and "domestic bureaucratic tyranny" was turning Ute life into a "hideous dream." Financial and clerical errors drained tribal funds; the Reimbursable System was unfair; members were being forced to sell their allotments; and they were treated like children with no right to buy or sell their own property without the superintendent's permission—and then the negotiations were manipulated to their disadvantage.[62]

Representatives also met with an investigative committee where John Miller, the Ute Mountain chief who had succeeded Ignacio, repeated the common complaint that government payments should last forever. They were *owed* the money for the land they had "sold" to the United States, and to rescind payments for any reason abrogated their agreements. Many wanted their payments in cash, not livestock, for which they had neither feed nor water.[63] But by 1933, per capita payments and rations had already been eliminated as Washington prepared to revamp the political and economic structure of Ute life.

While no changes were made in response to the 1925, 1926, and 1927 protests, these attempts demonstrate a growing assertiveness by Ute leaders and "insurgent" tribal factions, as well as an increasing ability to maneuver within government bureaucracy and use the same legal weapons that were used against them. This was especially true of the Southern Utes, who for centuries had negotiated within a borderland culture where they had formed financial, social, and kinship alliances with non-Indians. Federal officials viewed Southern Utes as more progressive and cooperative, especially when compared with the Weeminuche, who, despite occasional dealings with local Euro-Americans, preferred the safety of isolation and remained entrenched in traditional lifeways at Ute Mountain.[64]

Unlike their Colorado cousins, however, the three northern Ute bands in Utah had not developed a strong centralized leadership that could successfully lead a fight. But this began to change after Uintah and Ouray leaders returned from their 1927 trip. Now they convened a tri-band council in their first attempt to work as a unified group. Though unofficial and with little actual power, this council did establish the first lineaments of a future tribal committee: six councilmen, with two representatives from each band, discussed tribal problems, made recommendations to the Indian Office, coordinated efforts with cousin tribes, and worked with attorneys.[65]

Major changes in most tribal governments would begin in the 1930s, when federal Indian policy was abruptly reversed. From the mid-1870s to the 1930s, Indian policy had firmly espoused agriculture, Christianity, and the assimilation of American Indians into the mainstream U.S. population—by force, if necessary. But the dismal 1928 Meriam Report had detailed the appalling failure of these programs.[66] Progressive idealism, coupled with a new romantic image of the West (including that of the defeated but brave Indian) and the appalling vision of their extinction as painted by the Meriam Report, led a new wave of reformers to review Indian policy. Although American Indians were not actually "vanishing Americans" by the 1930s (populations everywhere were rebounding), the image did help their cause. Abandoning the concept of total assimilation in favor of a more pluralistic view, a new Indian policy emphasized preservation of Indian culture and religion, protection of Indian land rights, and an increase in tribal self-determination.[67]

As the nation plunged into the Depression and Franklin D. Roosevelt assumed national leadership, American Indians were included in the economic and political reforms of the New Deal. Ironically, the Indians hit hardest by the Depression were those who had become the *most* assimilated—urban wage earners—while those who had remained on the reservations (already poverty-stricken, but with some subsistence farming) were buffered from the general economic distress. Nevertheless, some of Roosevelt's workfare programs targeted western reservations.

From 1933 to 1942, more than 25,000 Indians in fifteen western states were employed as part of the Civilian Conservation Corps—Indian Division (ICCC). Although some officials voiced concerns about the transitory nature of the cash wages provided by the ICCC, the cash brought a welcome economic windfall to reservations, as well as jobs, education, on-the-job training, and for many reservation Indians, their first encounter with a full-time wage-based economy. Additionally, after 1934 Johnson-O'Malley funds became available to subsidize off-reservation education for non-taxpaying Indians, and the OIA was allowed to contract out for health and social services.[68] The three Ute tribes were among those who benefited from the programs, as health, social, and educational benefits increased, fences and roads were built, and conservation projects were implemented on their reservations (although Ute Mountain Ute conservatives objected to building roads, which made their reservation refuge more accessible for non-Indians).[69]

And a number of new conservation measures significantly impacted some Indian tribes. The 1934 Taylor Grazing Act abolished unrestricted grazing on public lands and authorized the establishment of grazing districts allocated for use with grazing permits (resulting in forced stock reduction for some tribes, like the neighboring Navajo). The government also began to return land to tribes. In 1927 they restored 227,016 acres to the Southern Utes and a large chunk of the original Ouray Reservation to the northern Utes. Much of the original two-million-acre Ouray Reservation had not been claimed after it was opened. But a new policy had been instituted to return to tribes all land that remained unalloted and unclaimed after 1934. Despite concern over possible non-Indian mining and grazing rights, the land was restored to the Uintah and Ouray Reservation as the Hill Creek Extension in 1948.[70]

But the most significant change in Indian policy took place after Roosevelt appointed the controversial and zealous John Collier as commissioner of Indian Affairs. Collier was a Progressive reformer and the architect of the 1934 Wheeler-Howard Act, also known as the Indian Reorganization Act (IRA) or the Indian New Deal.[71] Controversial even today, Collier has been described as a man dedicated to the "romantic ideal" of Indians, a "brilliant, optimistic visionary," a "mystic, a philosopher, [and] a poet," but also "intellectually ruthless," "vindictive and overbearing," autocratic, abrasive, impatient, caustic, and a "gadfly" goading Congress (and tribes) into action. His policies put him at immediate odds with the Christian-based Indian Rights Association, who considered him to be "in league with the devil." To the association's horror, Collier attacked what he called the despotism of the Bureau of Indian Affairs (then the Office of Indian Affairs), and he advocated a retreat from the revered ideals of assimilation, individualism, and Christianization in favor of Indian communal ideals ("tribalism," "communism," and "socialism"). He seemingly suggested Indians "go back to the blanket" and revert to paganism, with his emphasis on the preservation of Indian cultures and religion.[72] Additionally, members of Congress who represented moneyed interests in the West—timber, cattle, minerals, and oil—grew concerned that if they gave land and resources back to the Indians, their constituents' interests would be seriously harmed from lost resources or from allowing Indian tribes to control leases rather than the federal government with whom they were on favorable terms.[73]

Although Collier was forward-thinking in his emphasis on diversity and pluralism, there were significant flaws in his vision and plans for Indian reorganization, especially in how his programs were implemented. He knew his time was limited before his enemies would successfully force him out of office, so he had to bulldoze his plans forward. The Wheeler-Howard Act had already been watered down by Congress before it was passed, but Collier felt something had to be done—or at least attempted—about the dismal conditions on Indian reservations. The IRA, even in its compromised form, seemed to offer the best solution; however, problems arose from its too-rapid implementation. For example, Indian Services personnel and tribal leaders were not adequately trained. And in the rush to create instant governments, many tribes were coached and pressured into simply adapting a templated constitution based on a corporate model provided by Collier. But constitutional government was foreign to most tribes; few truly understood the meaning of their new political structures; and the boilerplate constitutions failed to take into consideration the vast differences between tribal groups. Collier also overestimated the homogeneity within tribes; as factionalism was rife in all of them, including internal personal or political rivalries, differences in problem-solving, and disagreements between modernists and traditionalists.[74]

Notwithstanding the raging controversies and inherent flaws in the legislation, Congress returned a significant level of self-determination back to Indian tribes when it passed the Wheeler-Howard Act on June 18, 1934. Collier has since been accused of manipulating or strong-arming many of the tribes into accepting the IRA. Of the 258 tribes approached, 181 accepted the new-style governments, including the three Ute tribes. Regardless of this coercion, Collier's efforts did help validate authority for all tribes (with or without IRA constitutions) and gave them the recognition and resources needed to deal more successfully with federal and state governments. Historians and Indians alike hold varied opinions about Collier and his efforts, from the IRA being a "noble beginning" to the "Indian *Raw* Deal." However, some continue to argue it was important for Indian leaders to accept the promise of self-determination in theory if not in fact, and that without the IRA, today's tribal governments would probably not exist.[75]

The IRA also reinvigorated a sense of pride in American Indians for their cultural heritage. Because the IRA threw leaders from many different tribes together at meetings, a sense of pan-Indian unity began to develop as a result of their shared problems. Leaders realized they needed to take a more active and unified role in pressing for federal reforms. Particularly significant was the development in 1944 of the National Congress of American Indian (leaders), or NCAI, a pan-Indian organization that became increasingly influential.[76]

The main goals of the IRA legislation were to reverse land loss, create self-government, promote economic development, and encourage education. It was a direct repudiation of the failed allotment policy and an attempt to reverse the damage by abolishing allotment, extending trust restrictions, encouraging consolidation of fragmented reservations, providing money to acquire new (or restoring surplus) tribal land, and initiating conservation measures on reservations. Johnson-O'Malley funds helped public schools pay for an expected influx of non-taxpaying Indian students who were being transferred out of boarding schools, and funds were made available for scholarships, tuition, and educational loans.[77]

Meanwhile, the Office of Indian Affairs encouraged tribes to accept simplistic, business-oriented government structures and coached them in writing constitutions and bylaws based on a template they provided. Although these new constitutional governments were intended to be temporary, revisable "training wheels of democracy" by which Indians could be educated and assimilated into the American political process locally and nationally, most of these tribal governments solidified into permanent, sovereign, and often flawed systems.[78]

Because tribes were given access to money and resources, including a revolving credit fund, most constitutions were established on a corporate model that allowed tribes to manage their properties, resources, and new economic enterprises as businesses with elected boards of directors. While most tribes created a tribal council, including the Southern and Ute Mountain Utes, the Uintah-Ouray Utes bluntly called their governing body a business committee. Collier had originally envisioned constitutions that separated the legislative and executive functions from business concerns; however, most tribal governments preferred to keep the financial reins in the hands of their elected officials and consequently inherited a unilateral form of government without internal checks or a balance of power. The positive benefits of this arrangement were that business charters protected officials against suits but gave them the ability to sue; members could be given per capita "shares" of the "business"; and elected officials had the power to negotiate business deals, exploit natural resources, and develop economic enterprises. Unfortunately, it also led to the abuse of power, including nepotism (a natural outgrowth of the traditional ethos of helping family) and a rampant political spoils system. As council dominance and financial power grew, especially after the 1960s, political affairs needed no tribal consensus, and where chairs held veto power, that power often went unchecked.[79] Without a separate executive, legislative, and judicial system, there were similar abuses within the developing tribal court system as well.[80]

In the early years of the new tribal governments, constitutions and bylaws gave leaders some limited authority over tribal funds and allowed them to approve or veto the disposition of assets, although ultimate control remained with the Office of Indian Affairs. Tribal governments also had the right to negotiate with federal, state, and local governments; engage legal counsel (with the approval of the secretary of the Interior); and regulate law and order, tribal members, and other pertinent affairs regarding tribal lands.[81]

Although the new IRA governments were a step toward tribal self-determination, they did not solve all ongoing problems and in fact caused a few more. A common complaint was that while the new government organization had to be approved by a tribal ratification vote, it did not have to be a tribal majority. All that was needed was a majority vote of *those who attended* ratification meetings. Adding to the confusion, the language of the proposals was carefully written so that it could only be rejected if a simple majority of those voting voted against it. Consequently, most tribes who passed IRA reorganization passed it with a minority vote, as did the Utes when, in time-honored fashion, those who disapproved of the new governments simply did not attend the meetings and therefore did not vote. This experience reflected what happened among most tribes where typically 61 percent of those voting voted no or abstained.[82]

At first the Utes declined the new governments. They distrusted the federal government in general, were wary of an unknown system of governance, and preferred their existing system of chiefs and elected council. They were not, Charles Buck explained, "ready for the opportunities...of self-government." John Miller of the Ute Mountain Utes rejected the IRA government out of hand. He was convinced the federal government was only trying to trick the tribe and take away even more tribal rights and resources, so Miller told his people that a vote for Reorganization was like stealing from the tribe. All he wanted, he declared, was for the government to just live up to its old obligations to take care of the Utes with annuities and rations in perpetuity.[83]

But strong pressure was brought to bear by Collier and his agents. On many reservations voters were coerced, and balloting was sometimes manipulated, as happened with the Utes. Charles Buck was eventually convinced to support the measure, and on June 10, 1935, the Southern Ute voters accepted IRA reorganization with a 50 percent turnout and an eighty-five to ten vote. Two days later the Ute Mountain Utes also passed the IRA proposal with a "majority" vote of nine to three. In an attempt to defeat the proposal, Miller and subchief Jack House, who would succeed Miller as chief the following year, sat outside the polls, told members not to vote, and sent them away. But after both men went home for the night, twelve latecomers straggled in to vote. When their votes were counted, reorganization had passed.[84]

Like the Ute Mountain Utes, the more traditional Uintah and Ouray full-bloods strongly opposed political reorganization; however, enrolled mixed-bloods favored it. Haggling delayed approval of an IRA government until 1937, when it finally passed 213 to 8 in a minority-vote election. Only 30 percent of eligible members voted in a ratification meeting that had been carefully scheduled in the winter when travel was difficult. According to later accusations, officials rounded up pro-constitution voters in trucks and brought them to the meeting, while traditionalists who opposed ratification were ignored. Most of the collected voters were more assimilated Uintahs and Uintah mixed-bloods, a band whose long association, intermarriage, and incorporation of non-Indians, Paiutes, Shoshones, and other non-Ute Indians resulted in a substantial number of enrolled and politically savvy individuals. Disgruntled full-bloods later complained that many who voted were mixed-bloods interested in the reformation of leadership for their personal benefit.[85]

The political climate among the Uintah and Ouray Utes remained stormy, and resentment against mixed-bloods grew. For the next twenty years, political power remained in the hands of mixed-bloods (mostly Uintahs) and a few influential and educated Uncompahgres, while traditionalists remained opposed to the government and supported traditional leaders in defiance of the business committee. Although a few traditional chiefs and holy men were initially elected, they were functionally crippled by their lack of formal education and fluency in English; this muted their voices on the committee and hampered their ability to interact with non-Indian business advisors and BIA representatives. On the other hand, the mixed-bloods and one educated Uncompahgre dealt comfortably with and moved easily among non-Indians and seemed a model of Collier's new (and often malleable) governments. But many committee actions were not popularly supported, and leaders were accused of squandering tribal funds on unpopular projects, including the reacquisition of tribal land alienated during allotment and expensive community schemes like the Indian Irrigation Project. As early as 1946 the Uintah and White River bands tried to sue the tribal government for "wrongful and wasteful use of tribal trust funds" in paying for the unpopular irrigation project.[86] Antagonism against mixed-bloods continued to fester.[87]

With IRA governments approved, the next step was to write a constitution and bylaws for each tribe, a process carefully overseen by Indian Office officials. Once written, constitutions had to be ratified by a tribal vote and approved by the secretary of the Interior. Congress approved the Southern Ute constitution in November 1936, and the Uintah-Ouray constitution by 1938. With the aid of Southern Ute advisors, the reluctant Ute Mountain Utes finally drafted and ratified a constitution that Congress approved in May 1940.[88]

The northern bands retained the basic council format they had adopted in 1927 with their six-person council, now serving four-year terms and made up of two representatives from each band elected in two-year staggered elections. The Southern Utes also created a six-member council but with three-year terms, while the Ute Mountain Utes adopted a seven-member council, six with three-year terms and the seventh an annually elected representative of the Ute-Paiute band now settled predominantly in Allen Canyon (Allen Canyon Utes).[89]

Thus, the 1930s were a time of significant transition. Not only had the tribes been finagled into accepting a new governmental form, but the Colorado tribes would also lose two of their strong long-standing traditional chiefs: both the aging Charles Buck and John Miller died in 1936, before the new constitutions could be ratified. Charles Buck—Buckskin Charley—had led the Southern Utes for fifty-six years, while Miller had shepherded the Ute Mountain Utes for twenty-three. Buck was succeeded by his son, Antonio Buck Sr., while Miller's strong-minded and traditionalist subchief, Jack House, succeeded him. Both Antonio Buck Sr. and Jack House were elected to the first tribal councils, as were traditional northern Ute leaders like Pawwinnee and Red Cap.[90] This lent legitimacy to the new councils, but these traditional leaders held varying degrees of influence, and the divide between traditional chiefs and the newly elected tribal leadership began to widen.

The reclusive Ute Mountain Utes retained a stronger sense of traditional leadership and clung to it much longer than other tribes. Though never chair, Jack House was a member of the tribal council for twenty years. However, little was done without his approval. House remained the acknowledged chief, the most influential person in the tribe, the guiding hand in tribal affairs, and (according to agency personnel) head of the "reactionary element" until his death in 1971. Like his predecessors, John Miller and the earlier Ignacio, he was very traditional, isolationist, and originally fought cultural change and the imposition of white ways. But by the 1950s, journalists were beginning to describe him as progressive, having finally acknowledged the need to assimilate some non-Indian ways to survive.[91]

Ute Mountain Utes also preferred the strong leadership of a few prominent families who dominated tribal politics. Emphasizing the continuing significance of shamanic medicine men, the tribe's first tribal chair was George Mills, an influential religious leader and peyote chief, who held the position until 1955. Other prominent families included Scott Jacket Sr. (chair for much of his three decades on the council) and Albert Wing Sr., who alternated with Jacket as chair between 1955 and 1974. It would not be until the 1970s, when many veteran leaders either died or retired, that political agitation caused by financial crises and a temporary void in political power brought new faces to the fore. These included more progressive leaders like Earnest House, the grandson of Jack House, and the Knight family, descendants of Piah, including brothers Terry and Carl and their sister, Judy.[92]

Like the Ute Mountain Utes, Southern Ute leadership was also dominated by a few family dynasties, undoubtedly a continuation of the inherited chieftainships of influential families that had begun to develop among southern bands by the mid-1800s. Although the new tribal council originally elected John Burch as their head (chair of a pre-constitution council), Antonio Buck Sr. soon replaced him. Although Buck remained the titular chief of the tribe until his death in 1961, he only served on the tribal council for eight years and chaired it for only four. But over time the power of the tribal council grew, and political power increasingly fell into the hands of the council chair; as a result, Buck's significance as tribal chief waned. Instead, Southern Ute politics were soon dominated by three other families: the Clouds (kin of the Buckskin/Buck family and religiously influential), the Bakers, and the Burches. These families often dominated the tribal council, and tribal chairs from these families sometimes reigned for decades. Sam Burch and Julius Cloud dominated in the 1940s and 1950s, followed by John Baker Sr. in the 1960s. After 1967, Sam Burch's son, Leonard Burch, led the tribe for nearly thirty almost unbroken years.[93]

Uintah-Ouray politics remained much more fragmented and contentious. With the ratification of the new constitution, political control fell to the mixed-bloods and one Uncompahgre, while the White Rivers defiantly maintained their own succession of chiefs despite the existence of the Business Committee. Although full-bloods tried to elect hereditary leaders, factions split their votes and allowed the politically savvy mixed-bloods to remain in power. It was not long before most tribal business was being conducted without the knowledge or approval of most of the people.[94]

The fledgling IRA governments were, of course, strictly supervised by the Office of Indian Affairs, and tribal councils were at first little more than political waldos. The new Indian leadership was inexperienced with the new form of government, lacked confidence in their abilities to negotiate the new political system and procedures, and were used to being controlled by paternalistic agency personnel. Consequently, Indian Office employees coached the councils on procedures, initiated measures to be discussed, and suggested whether such measures should be passed or not—to which advice the councils usually acquiesced. The new tribal governments also had little tribal support. Many members refused to participate in elections and shared a perception that the OIA was still controlling tribal affairs (which in many ways they were), that members were being left out of political decisions, and that the tribal councils simply did not care about them.[95]

The new IRA leadership were neophytes, inexperienced, inefficient, and with little real power and fewer funds. But the groundwork had been laid, and in spite of the many imperfections, the first steps toward self-determination and a rebirth of sovereignty had begun. In time tribal councils would develop into powerful, if sometimes fractious, political entities, often headed by men—or women—with their own considerable power.

Chapter 15

The Struggle for Rebirth and Identity

1940–1970

Tribal reorganization ushered in the consolidation and development of political power for tribal governments and perpetuated the struggle to redefine racial and tribal identity. The Indian Reorganization Act (IRA) gave tribes experience in American legal and business techniques to function on a more equal footing within American society, and over the next years tribal leaders grew more comfortable with the political and economic reins of power. Another factor accelerating acculturation within tribes was the outbreak of war in 1941. Tens of thousands of American Indians—including more than two hundred Utes—left reservations to join the military or work in war-industry plants, railroads, and off-reservation agriculture.

With IRA and war-time experiences to energize them, tribes gained a new sense of legal, political, and cultural empowerment. Postwar America saw increased activism among Indian veterans and former war workers who fought legal battles for Indian rights. At the same time, a new sense of pan-Indian awareness developed as a growing population of urban Indians congregated in community centers or as reservation-based leaders united with allies in the fight for American rights for Indian Americans.[1]

AMERICAN INDIANS GO TO WAR

Thousands of American Indians were involved in the upheaval of World War II. Following World War I, military service had become increasingly attractive to American Indians for its financial and educational benefits, as well as an enhanced status at home. Indians also experienced less discrimination in the military. When Pearl Harbor was bombed in 1941, there were already over four thousand Indians serving in the military—including a number stationed at Pearl Harbor. Although some tribes resisted the compulsory draft when it was implemented in 1940 (citing sovereignty status), higher court decisions reiterated the legal reality that domestic law superseded any tribal treaties or agreements.[2]

But this resistance was isolated, and despite attempts by Nazi propagandists to link American Indians to the Nazi cause as a lost Aryan tribe, when Congress declared war in 1941 most Indians flocked to enlist—twice as many as were drafted. Before the end of the war, at least 44,000 Indians would serve, over 24,000 directly from reservations. Most served in the army, thousands served in the navy, some served in the Army Air Corps and Coast Guard, and over 800 served in the Marines, including the more than 400 Navajo Code Talkers. Indian women enlisted in women's volunteer corps as well, among them several Utes. More than 40,000 Indians, nearly half of them women, also found war-industry jobs in urban areas. It was a huge migration, with Indians traveling to populous industrial centers like Detroit, Chicago, Los Angeles, or San Francisco to work.[3]

On the front line, Indians served in all theaters from Europe to Asia, many fighting and dying in the bloodiest conflicts of the war. Like their fathers in the First World War, these "Chiefs" were assumed to be natural-born fighters with inbred scouting skills. As a result, they again had a very high mortality rate because they were more frequently given dangerous assignments. This was especially true in the later Vietnam War, where 64 percent of Indian veterans experienced heavy to moderate combat. Indians were often assigned to be point or to man listening posts because of their supposed abilities. This was especially dangerous in Vietnam, where the guerilla fighting meant the likelihood of stumbling into ambushes or falling victim to gruesome traps. Even more perilous, because they could pass as Vietnamese, Indians (along with Polynesians and Asians) were frequently assigned to "killer teams" and sent out in disguise on hit-and-run missions in enemy territory ("Indian Country").[4]

But World War II and subsequent conflicts also helped to erode the boundaries between the Indian "race" and their white counterparts, as Indians served in integrated units and shared the desire to wreak vengeance on America's enemies. Indian veterans brought home the higher social status they had earned as warriors. Veterans were, and continue to be, hailed as heroes, honored by their tribe and extended family. By the twenty-first century, all three tribes had raised major memorials to their veterans, inscribing their names on monuments and erecting statues in veterans' parks or plazas. Utes formed veterans' associations, honored them at all major tribal ceremonies and social events, and gave them a place of honor when marching in tribal and local parades.[5]

15.1. Color guard at the 2017 Denver Powwow was made up of Ute veterans from all three tribes. (Photo by Robert Ortiz, courtesy of the Southern Ute Drum)

During their service, many veterans gained an appreciation for education. This led not only to their own desire to complete their education via the GI Bill, but to demand better education for their children as well. Boarding schools were hopelessly inadequate for growing populations, and one response was to enroll as many Indian students as possible in public schools and legislate funding to subsidize them in lieu of the property taxes Indians did not pay. The demand for education was also a major factor in the Church of Jesus Christ of Latter-day Saints initiating an Indian Student Placement Program. From 1954 until 2000, this program provided for non-Indian Mormon families to foster Indian children during the school year. Among the fifty thousand children impacted by the program were Utes and Paiutes, especially in Utah.[6]

Emerging social, political, and vocational skills also propelled many veterans into positions of leadership within tribes. For example, among those who fought in World War II were forty-three Southern Utes, at least ninety-six Northern Utes, and a number of Ute Mountain Utes. Among these were veterans who would reach tribal prominence after the war, including the highly influential Southern Ute chiefs, John E. Baker Sr. (medical corps) and Anthony Cloud Burch, as well as Sunshine Cloud Smith, who joined the Women's Army

Corps as a nurse and later served on the tribal council and as vice chair for years. Eddie Box, a navy veteran, would become a highly respected Sundance chief. The highly regarded Leonard C. Burch, who served many years as tribal chair, was a veteran of the Korean conflict. In Utah, army veterans Francis McKinley and Stewart Pike were both active in tribal politics, while Fred Con-etah became tribal historian. Judy Knight-Frank, a Ute Mountain Ute who spent the war years working in California war industries, later chaired the Ute Mountain Utes and led the fight for Animas-La Plata water rights. By 2017, over 360 Northern Utes, 155 Southern Utes, and over 60 Ute Mountain Utes had served in all branches of the military. Utes not only served in peacetime, but they also fought in every foreign war from World War I on, including Korea (at least sixty-two), Vietnam (at least ninety), and the recent conflicts in the Middle East (at least forty).[7]

Returning veterans also found new sources of aid, helping them to break from their dependence on the BIA. The Veterans Administration (VA) helped them apply for benefits under the Servicemen's Readjustment Bill (GI Bill, 1944), allowed them to finish high school and attain vocational training or university experience. Indian veterans also became eligible for VA health benefits, although this was problematic because many reservations were often large and isolated, far from services. So many veterans suffering from physical and mental trauma turned back to traditional medicine men and curing rituals. Even Social Security and disability benefits became more accessible after veterans learned how to apply for them, and veterans helped lobby for the direct payment of these funds to individuals rather than deposited with the BIA or state.[8]

Reawakened to the plight of American Indians, many acculturated veterans became increasingly vocal proponents of racial equity. Wearing suits and ties, they were able to present their own cases in court, to congressional committees, and in legislatures, speaking for themselves, in English, and with supporting facts and figures. Veterans fought for the right to purchase liquor, a right they had exercised while in the military but were denied at home. They also fought for voting rights for Indians in Arizona and New Mexico. Although citizenship had been extended to all Indians in 1924, Indians in these states remained ineligible to vote because they were "wards" of the state (Arizona) or paid no property taxes (New Mexico). But through high-profile court cases, laws were changed, and by 1948 all Indians could vote. By 1953 they could also legally buy alcohol when off reservations. (Tribes were allowed the sovereignty to determine on-reservation laws, and many disallowed alcohol, including the Ute Mountain Utes.)[9]

But for many Indians, their improved status did not last long after the war. Income from military and war industry sources dried up. Without usable collateral, Indians could not secure loans to start businesses. Landholdings "belonged" to the tribe but were held in trust by the government, or lands were insufficient for profitable farming or ranching (lost, sold, or subdivided repeatedly). And an increasing number of veterans wanted patents in fee so they could simply sell what land they had and live off the reservation. Yet many who left the reservation found only short-term, low-paying, blue-collar jobs, were victims of racial discrimination, and were caught in a cycle of travel between living on reservations or in cities. Still, opportunities were better off-reservation than on, and many Indian veterans and war workers chose to remain in or return to cities, despite at times living in slum neighborhoods, holding poor jobs, and being alone.[10]

And matters were about to get even worse. As many veterans fought for their rights as Americans, a significant number of reformist politicians interpreted their struggle as the assimilationist aspirations of all Indians. Using this as justification, reformers ramped up their efforts to free all Indians from BIA or tribal control and allow them to integrate fully into American society.[11] But most Indians did not want to sacrifice their Indian identity or community to claim their rights as American citizens. War-time experiences had reinforced and often enhanced their unique identities as Indians. Thus, while activist Indian veterans did demand their constitutional rights as Americans, most were equally insistent that they were and would remain Indian and that their tribal rights should be restored as guaranteed in their treaties and agreements.[12]

But state and national politicians understood the Indian fight for civil rights in a very different light; for them, "freeing the Indian" meant freeing them from their special status with the federal government, terminating tribal organizations, and terminating the federal government's responsibility for them. It was a policy that would have disastrous long-term results for the Uintah Utes and sow the seeds of discord on the Uintah and Ouray Reservation for decades to come.

LAND ACQUISITION AND LAND CLAIMS

The formal move toward termination really began with the issue of lost land. John Collier's 1930s IRA policies had intended to move Indians toward self-sufficiency and independence. But to do this, they needed a solid land base from which to launch tribal enterprises, primarily understood at the time as

farming and ranching. Collier also encouraged the preservation of tribal traditions and culture. However, many Washington politicians disagreed with
the commissioner, arguing that his emphasis on reviving tribal traditions was
isolating and retrograde, and that the Office of Indian Affairs (OIA) should
instead encourage Indians to integrate and assimilate. Several attempts were
made to repeal the IRA, but all failed; however, officials were able to take
smaller steps toward weakening the OIA and encouraging detribalization.
During the war years, the OIA offices were moved from Washington to Chicago (not essential to the war effort), healthcare was shifted to federal and state
auspices, and tribes were encouraged to seek help from state and local social
workers rather than the OIA.[13]

Meanwhile, the OIA was helping tribes regain lost land. As a first step, the
federal government restored some tracts of land to tribal trust status, and then
tribes were encouraged to consolidate or purchase other pieces that had been
lost. But neither came without controversy. Tribal members resented having
to buy back their own land, while few non-Indians wanted public land (and
power) returned to Indians.[14]

In Utah, the first act of the new Business Committee of the Uintah and
Ouray Utes (now the Uintah-Ouray Utes) had been met with almost immediate criticism from members. Under the guiding hand of the OIA, the Business
Committee withdrew $100,000 from their trust funds to settle old debts and
redeem lost allotments. But members resented paying inflated prices for tribal
trust land lost when the reservation was opened for settlement. Even before
the Hill Creek Extension was restored, the Business Committee had purchased
large tracts of the former Ouray Reservation, while Utes and non-Indian cattlemen continued to wrangle over other grazing lands.[15]

About the same time, the first of the Uintah Irrigation Project (UIP) debts
against the tribe also came due. Members protested paying these assessments,
because they had opposed the project from the beginning and had derived
little benefit from it. Nevertheless, under OIA pressure, the Business Committee paid the debts.[16] Discontent continued to fester as members believed
the predominantly mixed-blood Business Committee was mishandling tribal
financial affairs.

Ute leaders again asked the government to return surplus land in Colorado. The IRA had authorized the return of surplus land that had been withdrawn from reservations and offered for sale but never sold. However, when
Secretary of the Interior Harold Ickes prepared to return land on Colorado's
western slopes, it created an uproar in the state. Senator Alva B. Adams (son

302

of former Governor Alva Adams) began crusading against the re-cession of the land. He successfully prevented the Utes from returning to Colorado when he attached an amendment to a minor congressional bill that prohibited the land's reversion to the tribe. Signed into law by Franklin D. Roosevelt on June 29, 1938, the Adams Amendment reaffirmed that 3.5 million acres of western Colorado land would remain public. However, specifically exempted and subsequently restored were 30,000 acres in Montezuma County, Colorado, and 222,016 acres southeast of Ignacio that was deemed useless for agriculture. (Large reserves of natural gas would later be found on these overlooked acres.)[17]

More importantly for Utes, the amendment gave tribes a legal justification to sue the United States over their lost land. The Agreement of 1880 had stipulated that ceded land would be paid for *as it was sold*, but because the surplus public land had never been sold, the tribes had never been paid for it. In refusing to return the land, the government had, in essence, "purchased" it themselves, and the Utes now wanted to be paid for it.

The biggest losers in the Adams Amendment were Utah's White River and Uncompahgre bands. During the early 1930s, Captain Raymond Bonin, the government-appointed attorney for the Uintah-Ouray tribe, began consulting with the new Washington-based firm of Moyle and Wilkinson concerning Ute claims against the government. Eventually rejoining the Southern and Ute Mountain Ute tribes, the three groups contracted directly with Ernest L. Wilkinson to represent the Confederated Ute Tribe in legal actions for the consolidated interests of all Utes, regardless of reservation, agency, or state, in claims against the government of the United States.[18]

The difficulty lay in the federal government's sovereign immunity. Although an early U.S. Court of Claims existed, an 1868 Congress had ruled that tribes could not bring suit against the U.S. government unless specifically authorized by Congress. Congress had already passed 133 separate pieces of legislation for tribal claims, one of which was the basis of successful Confederated Ute claims in 1910. Most suits had fared less well. Seventy-three percent of all Indian claims had lost, and those claims that did succeed averaged payments of only 2.2 percent of the amounts sued for.[19]

Wilkinson was reluctant at first to accept the Ute case because of his lack of experience with Indian law and the high odds against successfully litigating Indian claims (or of being paid). However, he accepted the case and devoted much of his law practice during the next sixteen years to pursuing Ute claims against the United States for seizure of Indian lands without just compensation.

15.2. Earnest Wilkinson represented the Confederated Ute Tribes in the "Big Ute Case," winning the tribes over $32 million. (L. Tom Perry Special Collections, Brigham Young University, Provo, Utah, UA909 Wilkinson s19-BB)

In the process, Wilkinson became a noted authority on Indian law, drafted significant legislation, served as an expert witness to Congress in many Indian claims cases, and his law firm (Wilkinson, Cragun, and Barker) ultimately represented more tribes than any other firm. By far his biggest action, the Ute land claims suit, included four separate claims, and the collective proceedings became known in Washington as "The Big Ute Case."[20]

Wilkinson's first task was to get the law changed that disallowed Indians from suing the government. In February 1936, Wilkinson initiated efforts to get legislation passed in Congress allowing the Utes to sue for redress. Fortunately for the Confederated Utes, his efforts fit into a growing interest in establishing an Indian claims court that could settle claims and allow the government to cut Indian tribes free of federal support. After unsuccessfully trying to work within existing laws, Wilkinson drafted his own legislative bill, taking the stance that the land had been taken by eminent domain, thus giving his clients the right to sue for surface, subsurface, and mineral rights. In August 1937, after eighteen months of lobbying, Congress finally passed the Ute Jurisdictional Bill, and in June 1938 Roosevelt signed it into law. It was one of only fifteen such bills that passed, out of nearly three hundred introduced. Over the next ten years, Wilkinson expanded the bill with five more amendments.[21]

On November 22, 1941, Wilkinson filed the most important of four Ute claims, asking compensation for the surface and subsurface value of over 4.4 million acres of Colorado land taken and retained by the United States government. Additional claims would be filed during the winter of 1945–1946.[22]

Wilkinson also testified before the House Committee on Indian Affairs, urging the creation of a temporary Indian claims commission with the authority to render final judgments without being overridden by Congress, as in the past. He presented a proposed bill to create such a claims commission. Not long after, he jointly redrafted the bill with Felix Cohen, the foremost authority on Indian law. Finally, after months of pressure from the recently organized National Congress of American Indians (NCAI), and from Wilkinson's lobbying, redrafting, and coaching, Congress approved H.R. 4497, and on August 13, 1946, authorized the Indian Claims Commission (ICC). For a limited period of time the ICC would hear grievances against the government on the question of broken treaties, unratified treaties, and other pertinent violations to the rights, dignity, or property of American Indians by the United States government. Because of the number and complexity of claims ultimately submitted, this "limited time" would be extended four times, and the court would not close until 1978.[23]

Congress created the ICC chiefly as a way to settle all outstanding Indian claims against the government and to rectify past injustices; but more importantly, to provide tribes with the means for self-sufficiency preparatory to the government severing all responsibilities to them.[24]

The first claim the new ICC heard was from the Confederated Ute Tribe, and in late 1946 Wilkinson won an interlocutory decree that determined his clients *were* entitled to damages. The next several years were spent determining how much Utes were owed through appraising the land and arguing its value in hearings. After 36,000 pages documenting prior ownership, another 10,000 pages of evidence, and over 35,000 pages of transcript from 180 witnesses, Wilkinson and his firm won. The ICC rendered judgment on March 17, 1950, and in July it awarded the Confederated Ute Tribe $31,938,473—the largest settlement by far for any tribe with the ICC and a massive victory for Wilkinson (most awards were less than $3 million).[25]

In addition to the monetary award, Wilkinson also won on behalf of the Utes restoration of over 600,000 acres of land valued at nearly $1.5 million. He

305

also saved an additional $7 million in offset expenses sued for by the government, and $12 million in "preserved rights to interest" as a part of just compensation. Thus, the total benefits accrued to the Confederated Utes—including the cash payment of almost $32 million—exceeded $54 million.[26]

The court battles had been difficult, with no guarantee the Utes would win. And the suit was expensive. Wilkinson had to pay for expert witnesses, researchers, and attorneys (over 62,000 attorney hours), 275,000 miles of air travel, over 500 telegrams, 1,200 long-distance phone calls, 35,000 local calls, and 10,000 pages of correspondence. The tribes often struggled to pay their legal fees, at times having to borrow from each other, as when the Uintah-Ouray were unable to pay their share of the litigation so southern tribes put up the money on condition of repayment.[27]

Not only did Wilkinson have to fight governmental bureaucracy and help legislators make significant legislative and policy changes in the original suit and during subsequent claims for lost lands in Utah, expert witnesses had to prove valid Ute identity with a demonstrable claim to the land taken. Witnesses had to show that Utes had inhabited very specific regions with well-known and recognized boundaries. During subsequent litigation on behalf of the Uintah Utes for land lost in Utah, it was also necessary to legally define which Indians *were* Ute. The Pahvant of central Utah were denied plaintiff status, which sparked heated discussion among Uintah-Ouray Utes. Expert witnesses also clashed over the identity of the Piedes of central Utah. Julian Steward, an eminent anthropologist, argued the undifferentiated pedestrian Indians of central Utah (including Piedes) were not Utes because they ate horses instead of riding them and maintained a subsistence pattern similar to the neighboring Southern Paiutes. However, anthropologists Anne Cooke Smith and Omer C. Stewart successfully testified in behalf of the Piede Utes and demonstrated inconsistencies in Steward's testimony. They argued that because these Piedes identified themselves as Utes, and others identified them as Utes, they were Utes, regardless of their diets. The central Utah Piede Utes were awarded plaintiff status.[28]

But even as Wilkinson labored on the case in Washington, internal divisions between and within the tribes threatened his efforts. Many Utes remained inherently distrustful of their attorney. The drawn-out case was time-consuming, and some believed it was taking too long "to get the money." Others feared attorney's fees and expenses would consume all their current funds or future awards: "He is going to keep asking for money and then our money will be gone.... This is all he wants—money. He has not gotten anything for us."[29]

And the tribes remained distrustful of each other, particularly the assertive Uncompahgres and the traditional Ute Mountain Utes. The latter had a long history of being cheated by the government; they had trouble understanding what was happening because few spoke English well; and they were especially unfamiliar with the need for land valuation and the process of litigation. Consequently, they grew angry and impatient. The Uncompahgre were also concerned over how long the case was taking and even terminated their attorney for a time (though his efforts continued as counsel for the Confederated Utes).[30]

The three tribes also argued over how to share the claims money, if and when they got it. The White River and Uncompahgre bands were entitled to two-thirds of the award, but the Southern and Ute Mountain Utes argued that it should be distributed by population. The courts ultimately divided the award sixty/forty, with a bit over $18 million going to the Uintah-Ouray Utes, specifically the White River and Uncompahgre bands. The Southern Ute and Ute Mountain tribes received approximately $6 million each.[31]

At first the Utes were jubilant: they had won an award greater than their attorney had hoped. The tribal chairs sent effusive thank you letters to him. George Mills thanked him "for getting this money. We never expected to receive that much." Sam Burch added, "I do not think that ever before has one man been entitled to so much credit as you are in the winning of the Ute judgment claims." Wilkinson's firm was awarded an 8.75 percent contingency fee (less than the standard 10 percent), or $2.8 million. Half of this amount paid the firm's seventy lawyers, and almost half to taxes. For his sixteen-year battle, Wilkinson netted only $700,000 personal income.[32]

But after the euphoria subsided, some began to reconsider their attorney and the multimillion-dollar fee his firm had been awarded, accusing him of having used them to enrich himself at their expense. The Big Ute Case did establish his firm as the premier advocate for Indian claims, a lucrative clientele during the claims-case heyday. However, once the Ute case was concluded, Wilkinson exited the stage when he was co-opted to serve as president of the Mormon Church–owned Brigham Young University (1951–1971). However, he did remain involved, as needed, in Ute legal affairs. Meanwhile, at the university, Wilkinson developed an active Indian Education Department, provided scholarship aid, and recruited hundreds of Native American students.[33]

Wilkinson's efforts on behalf of the Utes had a lasting effect on government relations with most Native Americans. As a result of the successful "Big Ute Case," other Indian tribes quickly initiated claims, receiving aggregate judgments of over $650 million. However, this sudden generosity came with a price tag: resolving long-standing claims gave Indian tribes money and allowed the government to justify terminating their relationships, withdrawing federal supervision and services, and launching them on the road to self-sufficiency, assimilation, and independence. Once Indians were "paid off," the government would no longer owe Indians anything.[34]

THE PUSH TO TERMINATE THE UTES

By 1945, policy attitudes in Washington were once again swinging back toward assimilation. During World War II and in the midst of the burgeoning Cold War, opinions shifted from the socialistic New Deal to a reemphasis on national unity and integration. Collier and his theories fell out of favor. In 1945 a disillusioned Collier retired as Congress moved to abandon his programs. Many viewed the reservation system as a tragic failure, while others, anxious to slash a bloated government bureaucracy, turned on the Office of Indian Affairs (in 1947 rechristened the Bureau of Indian Affairs) in an effort to minimize or abolish it entirely.[35]

Meanwhile, the integrationist attitudes of the country, coupled with obvious failures on reservations and an increasing push by tribes to divest themselves of the BIA's paternalistic control, led many reformers to urge the timely emancipation of Indians from their wardship status. Reservations were an outmoded anachronism, Collier's absurd policies had "forced the Indians back into Indianhood," and Congress needed to act quickly to remedy the "disaster of the Wheeler-Howard Act." Some argued that Indians had "outgrown the need for federal supervision," that the BIA was now hampering their development, and that Indians should not continue "as a baby" in the government's arms. Some journalists urged that Indians be freed "from the virtual slavery imposed upon him by the grasping greediness of the Indian Bureau," while congressmen urged that Indians no longer be sheltered but become Americanized as quickly as possible so that they should have all the rights, privileges, and responsibilities of any other American citizen.[36]

Most Indians were unaware that the House Resolution, which established the Indian Claims Commission in 1947, was only a prelude to termination and would encourage individual relocation. The Hoover Commission had begun examining the executive branch for waste, and by 1950 it had determined that both the current Indian policy and its administration were ineffective and costly, that American Indians should be integrated into the mainstream population, and that the BIA should be dismantled as quickly as possible. Reservations were causing a lower standard of living and creating an attitude of helplessness and patterns of dependency among Indians. The commission recommended reservations be eliminated, residents of overpopulated reservations be urged (or pressured) to relocate to urban centers, and redundant Indian welfare programs be transferred to other federal and state departments. Subsequently, Congress demanded the BIA account for its "maladjusted" performance. William Zimmerman, assistant commissioner of Indian Affairs and former Collier lieutenant, reluctantly ordered that programming plans be developed to help tribes prepare for withdrawal of federal control and funds. Among those targeted for early termination were the suddenly wealthy Utes.[37]

Reva B. Bosone, a concerned Representative from Utah, immediately proposed a congressional study be made to determine tribal preparedness for termination. Bosone's bill, premised on ultimate termination, was criticized by Harold Ickes and Collier, who called the policy of terminating tribes an attempt by the "administrative wizards...to whisk whole communities and tribes...toward economic and social confusion." On the other side, Utah's freshman senator Arthur V. Watkins, chairman of the Subcommittee on Indian Affairs and primary architect of the termination policy, argued against Bosone, claiming that any study would be a waste of time and money. Termination was the Indian's Emancipation Proclamation, and freeing the Indians from governmental wardship was a "universal truth, to which all men subscribe" and not "rightfully a subject to debate." Bosone's bill was defeated, although much of its language was incorporated into a later termination bill that was passed. Senator Watkins and Dillon Meyer (former director of the Japanese internment program and the BIA's new commissioner) moved forward with their plans to terminate as rapidly as possible those tribes deemed prepared for liberation.[38] By 1953 Congress passed both H.C.R. 108 and enacted P.L. 208, which began the process of terminating Indian tribes, transferring most legal jurisdiction over reservations to state governments, and shifting responsibility for health care out of the Indian offices.[39]

By 1950 Senator Watkins, a devout Mormon who had grown up near the Uintah and Ouray Reservation, had become a crusading power behind termination. A kind, mild-mannered, and soft-spoken man, he could be rock-hard when standing for his convictions. As chair of the Senate Select Committee, he withstood virulent attacks from Senator Joseph McCarthy when the committee recommended McCarthy be censured for his abusive conduct during the infamous Red Scare.[40] Watkins was equally convinced of the evils of the reservation system and the need to "help American Indians become independent and self-supporting American citizens."[41]

Imbued with the ideological wash of his Mormon religion, affected by the reservation border-town prejudices of his youth, and holding an "impenetrable belief in the rightness of his convictions," Watkins embraced the doctrine of Indians as a fallen people whose salvation lay in their self-sufficiency and rapid assimilation into the American mainstream.[42] As Watkins crusaded for terminating Indian wardship, he turned his attention particularly to the Indians of his home state. Not only had the Uintah-Ouray Utes received a windfall judgment of $18 million, making them perfect candidates for independence, they and the Northwestern Shoshones, Goshutes, and Southern Paiutes would make ideal models of termination for other states to follow.[43]

Unaware of the storm looming over them, the three Ute tribes remained exultant over their munificent land claims award, unaware that the money brought with it a whole new series of problems. The government had no intention of simply handing the Utes $32 million in cash. The purpose for the awards, in addition to rectifying past claims, was to help the tribes become independent so that government responsibility could be terminated. To do this, short- and long-range plans had to be made for tribal economic development, and Washington demanded that tribes create "permanent constructive plans" for economic rehabilitation detailing how they intended to use the money.[44]

These economic rehabilitation plans were quickly bogged down by arguments, and the three Uintah-Ouray bands immediately fell out over how to distribute the award. The White River and Uncompahgre bands argued that because the awards were for lost Colorado land, it was their money and Utah's Uintah band should have no share in it. However, the tribal attorneys urged them to share the funds equally. Their IRA government had merged the three bands into a single political entity, and they should pool their resources. If the White Rivers and Uncompahgres did not share their land claims money with the Uintahs, then the Uintahs wouldn't have to share their own promise of considerable wealth from future oil and mineral claims or land claims awards. In any case, if they did not resolve their differences and agree to function as one tribe, the attorney general would withhold all funds. The meeting dissolved in an uproar, and most Uncompahgres angrily stormed out. Regardless, an immediate vote was called, and the remaining members passed the proposal with a minority vote, binding the entire tribe to share all current and future revenues "without regard to band derivation." Senator Watkins promptly drafted the share-and-share-alike proposal into legislation that was quickly approved by Congress and became law, despite its opposition by the majority of the Uintah-Ouray Utes.[45]

While this solution was an administratively pragmatic decision, the manipulated results only widened the fissures between the three bands, particularly increasing Uncompahgre animosity toward Uintah and mixed-blood members.

Now arguments over how to use the money began in earnest. Leading proponents from the Uintah-Ouray Reservation, wanting less tribal development and larger individual payments, were predominantly Uintah mixed-bloods, especially the influential William Reed and Elizabeth Curry Bumgarner (married to a wealthy Euro-American farmer). They argued that communal projects encouraged a "socialist or communist" society rather than free enterprise. Among Southern Utes the key opposition leader was Sunshine Cloud Smith (a World War II veteran and daughter of religious leader Edwin Cloud), who contended that individual interests should supersede communal tribal interests; otherwise, the funds would end up in the hands of the BIA, as had the 1910 claims money. While individuals like William Reed (Uintah) and Southern Ute religious leader Eddie Box proposed per capita payments between $5,000 to $8,000—and Sunshine Smith urged total distribution—proponents of the tribal rehabilitation plans pushed for smaller individual shares and increased tribal development. Ultimately, the Uintah-Ouray Utes accepted an initial lump sum distribution of $1,000 of unrestricted cash, the Southern Utes $4,000, and the Ute Mountain Utes $3,500.[46]

TRANSFORMING IDENTITY ON THE UINTAH AND OURAY RESERVATION

Just as the 1887 Dawes Act had opened the debate about who was legally entitled to Indian land, so did the promise of windfall distributions of cash. Once again, tribes had to determine who was legally eligible for benefits from tribal development and reservation resources. Indian identity could no longer be based on self-identification, shared traditions, history, community bonds, ways of thinking, or "feeling" Indian. Instead, the restrictive legal definitions of blood quantum were reinforced to determine tribal and racial identity. With a new inheritance at stake, Indian tribes throughout the United States fell back on the European concept of lineal blood descent and genetic kinship, and anyone not enrolled in a recognized tribe—regardless of their Indian blood, cultural ties, or kinship links—were non-Indian.[47] To do this, Ute Mountain Utes used their IRA definition of one-quarter blood quantum for enrollment, as did the racially diverse Southern Utes after a failed experiment with raising the bar to 50 percent. On the Uintah-Ouray Reservation, however, control of the claims money divided members, resurrecting not only the heated question of who was an authentic Indian, but also who was an authentic Ute.

The Utes were not alone in their struggle to define "real" Indians and in fighting related battles over tribal resources; even today it continues to be a complex and controversial question throughout Indian America. Within the conflict are deeply embedded issues that embody the essence of what it means to *be* Indian. Much is at stake—from a sense of self and emotional attachment to the right to practice native religion, sell Indian arts and crafts, or access thousands of dollars in revenue and subsidies. The dispute over *Indianness* encompasses a complex body of arguments that has included political and legal definitions of identity that use the language of lineality and blood to codify racial Indianness, but it fails to address the heart and soul of Indianness that embody the community of *being* Indian. Consequently, Indian blood has become fetishized, as it unifies tribal groups within the symbolism of blood—while also dividing them. An Indian may have a Certificate of Degree of Indian Blood (CDIB), a pedigree chart proving that a biological ancestor appeared on an original Allotment roll or IRA census, or be able to prove quarter- or half-degree blood quantum. But no certificate can measure the sense of community felt when individuals participate in traditional ceremonials, engage in sweats, believe in the efficacy of peyote meetings, or travel the powwow circuit. Wearing native symbols as part of one's dress, being part of a healing ceremony, or understanding "Indi'n humor"—these cannot be measured with a CDIB or enrollment number.

Yet tribes have been understandably wary of self-identification alone as a criterion for tribal membership. After all, by the late twentieth century casino wealth, federal subsidies for minorities, ethnic pride and romanticism, as well as blatant native-identified fraud were generating too many unauthentic or marginal Indian wannabes. In response, tribal enrollment has become more restrictive. However, Indian writer Vine Deloria argues, "Who is to tell any group of any Indians that they must submit [to governments] and forfeit what they feel in their hearts is their personal and community identity?"[48]

The conflict has become a virulent standoff. On one extreme are a variety of "plastic medicine men" and their New Age religions, groupie copycats and "ersatz Indians," as well as authentic castoff mixed-bloods expelled from tribal membership rolls but whose kinship, sense of community, and heartstrings tell them they are *Indian.* On the other side of the divide stand the "real" blood Indians who are slamming shut their enrollment doors in order to protect the "integrity" of their genuine tribes. The fact that restricted membership also means fewer members with whom resources have to be shared is an added benefit few like to admit.[49]

This racial controversy was especially bitter on the Uintah-Ouray Reservation, where a simmering conflict between full-blood Utes and the "less authentic" mixed-bloods had chafed for years. With the added element of new money, "membership in the tribe became a sharply contested political battleground upon which the blood quantum argument merely [served] as a convenient excuse for fighting over the real issue—ownership of...money."[50] They were not alone. Similar battles took place among other tribes when they received claims money, and again after the arrival of Indian gaming in the 1990s.

The Termination Campaign

Competition over reservation resources had plagued Northern Ute bands since 1880, when the Uintahs had been forced to share their reservation with the White Rivers. The IRA tribal government only exacerbated affairs, and competition over claims money and the threat of termination in the 1950s further aggravated the bitter interband rivalries. As they argued over how the money should be distributed and who was entitled to share it, groups solidified into competing political entities—and eventually competing ethnic identities as well.

The antagonism between full-blood Utes (mostly Uncompahgres and White Rivers) and mixed-bloods (mostly Uintahs) had long simmered, boiling up whenever there was a question of money or resource distribution.[51] In part, it was a continuation of the underlying conflict initiated when the Colorado bands were relocated to Utah. The White Rivers and Uncompahgres blamed each other for their expulsion, and the Uintahs resented them both. The Uintah band also included a large number of mixed-blood members. The Uintahs had a long history of intermarriage with non-Utes and non-Indians. The White Rivers and Uncompahgres had remained more isolated than either the Western Utes who had been engulfed by Mormon colonization or the Southern Utes on the Hispanic frontier, and they were proud of their theoretically "pure" Ute ancestry. However, the reality was that all Utes had traditionally integrated oth-ers into their family bands, typically captives, as had most other Indian tribes. Some of the better-known mixed-heritage Utes included Nicaagat, a White River leader who was a Goshute runaway married into the tribe; Colorow, who was rumored to be Comanche; Chipeta, who was a Kiowa captive; and Ouray, who was half Apache and had been raised among Hispanics.[52]

But by the 1950s, most full-blood Utes—especially the Uncompahgres—no longer accepted mixed-bloods as real Indians, because the latter's Indian blood had been diluted and their racial, cultural, and educational background was predominantly non-Indian. Mixed-bloods were seen as shirttail relations who (with a few notable exceptions) had little involvement with the tribal government but were first in line to demand tribal benefits. The promise of a new influx of wealth had attracted even more mixed-blood Utes clamoring for enrollment. Fearing that their share of the money would be diminished, full-bloods regarded mixed-bloods with increased suspicion and resentment. Because the Uintahs had "let them in, in the first place," much of the antipathy was focused in their direction.[53]

On March 17, 1950, the same day they learned of the successful claims judg-ment, the Business Committee passed the first of several resolutions to restrict tribal enrollment. By July they had resolved to restrict membership to persons with one-half or more Uintah-Ouray Ute Indian blood, determined by whether a person's parents appeared on the IRA tribal rolls of the Uintah and Ouray Reservations in 1935. Within four years, negotiations with Arthur Watkins had altered this to a minimum of five-eighths Ute blood. Thus, a child with a full-blood Ute mother and a full-blood Sioux father might be an Indian and could enroll with the Sioux but was ineligible to enroll as a Uintah-Ouray Ute. By comparison, most other tribes as well as the federal government defined an Indian as a person with at least one-quarter blood quantum. (Some individual tribes added other requirements, such as provable lineal descent, patriarchal lineage, or residency.)[54] A census of the Uintah-Ouray tribe taken in March 1954 showed that while 75 percent of the Uncompahgres and 92 percent of the White Rivers claimed to be full-blood, only 34 percent of the Uintah band did; under the new blood-quantum requirements, nearly half the Uintahs were reclassified as non-Indians.[55]

The BIA had also been urging the Southern Utes to clean up their tribal rolls and limit enrollment. During the 1950s, tribal bylaws limited member-ship to 50 percent Ute blood, with adopted children needing at least a quarter Southern Ute blood to qualify. When individuals were expelled, some sued to be reenrolled—but civil courts repeatedly remanded their cases back to the tribe. Membership committees were set up to examine all enrollees to determine their right to membership based on the 1935 census. For a number of years, membership qualification vacillated between one-quarter and one-half blood quantum, but it soon became obvious that without extensively inbreeding within their limited population—which could result in increased birth defects—the tribe would be headed toward long-term disfranchisement. By the early 1960s, the council had settled on one-quarter blood quantum for membership. In any case, as one researcher wrote, the relevant factor for membership was "not what an individual's blood quantum 'really' [was], but what members of the tribe [thought] it was."[56]

Meanwhile, all three tribes began working on their constructive rehabilitation plans. Elbert Floyd, the Consolidated Ute Agency superintendent, guided the Southern and Ute Mountain Utes as they worked together to produce their first plan. However, they did not understand how carefully Washington wanted the tribes to steward their money—or as the *Washington Star* mockingly put it, to "waste no wampum." In April 1951, tribal chairs Julius Cloud and Jack House accompanied Floyd to Washington where they hand delivered their generalized three-page plan, which was promptly rejected. Shortly thereafter, the Southern Utes installed a new chair, Samuel Burch. He immediately recalled an original planning committee member, John E. Baker Sr., from Chicago where he was studying architecture and engineering at the Chicago Technical College. Baker's extended family was among the educated and acculturated Southern Utes; he had attended Sherman Indian School in California and was a veteran of World War II. Baker spoke little Ute, was not involved in traditional religion, and was a champion of modern economic development.[57]

Baker and his planning committee wrote a new comprehensive rehabilitation plan, this time entirely on their own, and presented it to the Southern Ute's General Tribal Council on September 28, 1951. It was immediately and angrily rejected, since it included no per capita cash distribution at all.[58] Baker wanted all of the money to be directed to socioeconomic development. In the long run, he argued, tribal development would be the best way to help members, and total distribution could lead to immediate termination. In any case, the BIA would never approve total distribution. But many members feared that if the money was not distributed, they would never see it. They wanted all of the money, immediately, with no strings attached.

But Baker argued his case, and as understanding grew, opposition leaders like Sunshine Smith, Julius Cloud, and Eddie Box guardedly swung behind it.

All three were veterans, were prominent in a concurrent revival of traditional religion and culture, and were resisting the move toward assimilation and termination (which full distribution might trigger). After a tempestuous three months of extensive negotiation, compromise, and threats that Baker would resign, the General Council finally approved a 110-page economic rehabilitation plan on December 27, 1951, with an immediate per capita distribution of $4,000. Federal approval came three years later in June 1954. It was a plan Baker could be justifiably proud of, and one that many other tribes would use as a prototype for their own rehabilitation programs.[59]

The Ute Mountain plan took longer to create but was less controversial. Working with Southern Ute advisors, their planning committee wrote an 88-page plan, which the tribe's General Council passed with little argument in February 1953 and Congress approved six months later.[60] The goals of both the Southern and Ute Mountain plans included the recovery of land, the development of agriculture, a tribal credit fund, and the creation and enforcement of a law and order code.

But the more contentious Uintah-Ouray Utes continued to drag their feet. Not only did they argue over how much money should be individually distributed, but they continually stalled over who was entitled to it. The tribe came under increasing pressure from Washington to create some type of economic plan if they were to receive any money at all. Eventually forced to compromise on the cash distribution question, the planning committee drew up a short-range three-year plan with the promise of a future long-range plan designed to help them assimilate into mainstream American life. The three-year plan, approved by Congress in August 1951, was a stopgap measure intended to allow the tribe access to some of their judgment money and demonstrate that they could use it wisely. It provided for an immediate $1,000 per capita distribution each year of the plan for a total of $5 million—used mostly for food, clothing, debts, and automobiles—and funds for a $1 million tribal loan program, $1.25 million for land acquisition, and $1.15 million for education and tribal resource development. The tribe purchased new grazing land, surveyed and improved existing land, initiated a housing rehabilitation plan, and began to prepare for the transfer of students from the Whiterocks boarding school to local public schools.[61]

As tempestuous as the initial planning had been, creating the long-range program was even stormier. The most influential men of this period were its only two college-educated members: Rex Curry and Francis McKinley. Tribal chair Rex Curry was an assimilated mixed-blood who had graduated from Brigham Young University, married a non-Indian, and lived in Roosevelt, where he had served as bishop of a local Mormon congregation and was raising his children outside Ute culture. Although he was proud of his heritage, he was an integrationist and believed members of the tribe should become contributing members of the greater American society. Although he distrusted the aims of termination, he was amenable to the advice of the tribe's attorneys Ernest Wilkinson and John Boyden, the state senator Arthur Watkins, and BIA program officer Robert Bennett. Francis McKinley, who was the tribal coordinating officer and head of the planning division, was a graduate of George Washington University. Like Curry, he was acculturated and supported tribal economic development. However, as an Uncompahgre full-blood he also represented the opinions of the Uncompahgre band, was a vocal opponent of termination, and was less trusting of the tribal attorneys and Senator Watkins.[62]

Developing any plan for the tribe was complicated by the bitter divisions that beset the contentious northern bands. The promise of wealth and benefits widened the rifts and set member against member as they squabbled over how much money they ought to get, how quickly they could get it, with whom they would have to share, and how the tribe would use it. This set full-blood White Rivers and Uncompahgres against mixed-blood Uintahs, and traditionalists against the most assimilated. Some disgruntled members even voiced their complaints directly to their tribal attorneys and congressional representatives. Unfortunately, this only made the problem worse. Officials grew impatient with the bickering, and Watkins and the BIA used some of what protesters said as justification to shove the tribe closer to termination.[63]

As early as 1949, some reactionary Uintahs had naively written to Senator Watkins to complain about the failure of the tribe's IRA government: they were not a tribe but three distinct bands, and sharing resources communally had never worked but had only caused contention and smacked of communism. In any event, the reservation belonged to the Uintahs and not the Colorado Ute interlopers. The letter struck a chord with Watkins. Not only was he anticommunist, but his personal goal was to revoke the IRA as part of termination, and it helped to have proof that Indians wanted to revoke it, too.[64]

Julius Murray, a traditional chief and Uintah opposition leader, complained directly to President Eisenhower about Utes being taxed (they were not), claimed the Uncompahgres and White Rivers were a threat to the business interests of the Uintah band, and argued that because they had always maintained themselves as a "separate, distinct and identifiable group" that they

317

should be separated and treated as such. The Uncompahgres were also agitating to establish themselves as a separate tribe, even as Sarah Hackford, a mixed-blood opposition leader on the Business Committee, sponsored a petition to abolish the IRA government entirely (only Congress had that authority).[65]

Further agitating the brew was the appearance of a man named Frank W. Kirk who specialized in duping Indians. Of mixed Afro- and Euro-American descent and with a passable knowledge of Indian law, he claimed he was a Cherokee named Frank Tom Pee-Saw who represented various Indian rights organizations, including the little-known and less influential "League of North American Indians." Linking up with Hackford, he took donations for his lobbying efforts and wrote a few accusatory letters to Washington. All this did was anger the BIA against the squabbling tribe, and the mixed-blood Uintahs in particular. The BIA sent Robert Bennett, a university-educated Oneida Indian and BIA–withdrawal-planning officer to investigate. Before he arrived, however, "Pee-Saw" prudently disappeared.[66]

Bennett delivered a letter from Senator Watkins threatening to withhold future money unless the tribe solved its internal problems and produced their plan for long-term tribal self-sufficiency. Copied and distributed around the reservation, the letter generated alarm as rumors of imminent termination ran rampant.[67]

In this highly charged atmosphere, the General Uintah-Ouray Council met in late May 1953 where the full-bloods of all three bands agreed to restrict tribal enrollment and define mixed-bloods out of the tribe. Although the new restrictions were meant to limit membership to future mixed-blood children and mend the rifts between factions, animosity only increased. Meanwhile, the inexperienced planning board tried to begin work in November 1953 but broke up almost immediately. The disgruntled Uncompahgres began writing their own plan and again lobbied to separate their assets from the other bands.[68]

Around this time Watkins also turned his attention to a less resistant Utah tribe: the Southern Paiutes. The underlying assumption about termination was that it should be rapid and completed, as Commissioner Dillon Meyer noted in 1952, "even though Indian cooperation may be lacking." Although H.C.R. 108 required tribes to have a significant degree of acculturation, economic resources, adequate educational levels, and a *willingness* to be terminated, many tribes were bullied, blackmailed, or simply manipulated into their emancipation from federal supervision and benefits. Watkins had targeted all Utah tribes to serve as models for termination; so while the Utes dragged their heels and the Northwestern Shoshones and Goshutes organized and obtained qualified legal counsel, the helpless and unorganized Southern Paiutes fell easy prey to Watkins and Bennett. After Bennett drafted their termination bill, he and Watkins skirted proper procedures and conveniently failed to provide them with funds to testify at their own withdrawal hearings. The Southern Paiutes were rapidly and summarily terminated, despite desperate attempts to protest through telegrams and letters. Included on the terminated Southern Paiute agency rolls were descendants of Utes who had refused to relocate on the Uintah Reservation and remained on titled land near Mormon settlements, including the Koosharem Utes and Kanosh Pahvants. (Sowoksoobet's Ute band, who had once homesteaded north of Fairview, had long since ceased to exist as a distinct people.)[69]

These nonreservation Utes, Pahvants, and Southern Paiutes already existed in grinding poverty, dependent on minimal government programs, field and domestic work, and Mormon largesse. Ironically, while potential economic independence was usually cited as a reason for termination—as in the case of the Utes—Watkins used poverty and government failures with the Paiutes, Pahvants, and Koosharem Utes as the reason *for* their termination. He (inaccurately) explained that since they were already receiving few government services, these benefits would not be missed; and after government supervision was withdrawn, the Mormon Church would be "more responsive" to their needs. Watkins was wrong. As happened with many other Indian groups who were subsequently terminated, the Southern Paiutes sank into a more dismal poverty when government programs for Indians were withdrawn.[70]

Some years later John Boyden, a member of Wilkinson's firm, undertook a Paiute land claims case and won a $7.3 million judgment in January 1965. The influx of money not only improved conditions for the Paiutes and Koosharem/ Pahvants, but it sparked an organizational awareness that led to the creation of the Utah Paiute Tribal Corporation in 1972. The Paiute tribe subsequently initiated a successful campaign to reverse termination and restore tribal recognition. Unfortunately, following the Paiute termination all of their previously reserved land had been appropriated. Now a variety of private ownership and public domain issues blocked all recommended land restoration. Ultimately, the government found a few very small pieces of property to act as a new land base for the reconstituted Southern Paiute Tribe.[71]

The mixed-blood Utes would not be so successful.

Terminating the Mixed-blood Uintahs

Watkins stepped up the pressure on the Uintah-Ouray Utes in February 1954, issuing an ultimatum that the tribe produce a rehabilitation plan within ninety days or lose all further legislative aid or assistance. He suggested their planning committee look to other termination bills then before Congress for the elements he expected to find in their plan, and he cautioned them to ignore the growing agitation against termination by Indian rights groups like the NCAI and Association of American Indian Affairs.[72]

Francis McKinley learned of Watkins's ultimatum while in Washington attending an emergency meeting of the NCAI. The NCAI was responding to the plethora of termination bills pending in Congress by drafting a "Declaration of Indian Rights" and demanding the United States honor treaty obligations and trust responsibilities. Now McKinley held his own emergency meetings with Robert Bennett. He had initially planned to present the Uncompahgres' resolution to withdraw from the Uintah-Ouray tribe, but now he and Bennett joined forces to subvert Watkins's plans to terminate all Uintah-Ouray Utes.[73]

Back on the reservation, McKinley and Bennett met secretly with Chairman Curry to develop a plan to divert Watkins's attention and address the Uncompahgres' desire for secession by partitioning the tribe. Meeting alone in a field, the three men developed a plan to jettison the mixed-bloods and provide for economic and political independence for each band. In their view, the tribe consisted of four distinct bands: the Uncompahgres, White Rivers, Uintahs, and the more acculturated mixed-bloods. Having sustained the primary loss of land in Colorado, the Uncompahgres also felt the claims money should have been apportioned between the two Colorado bands alone at a 75:25 ratio. However, knowing members would never approve this, they proposed a compromise plan: divide the reservation proportionally between the four bands, with the remaining money split between the three full-blood bands. The Uncompahgres would "loan" the Uintah band 41.6 percent of their share until the Uintahs received their own pending land-claims money for land ceded in the unratified 1865 Spanish Fork treaty. No provision was made for mixed-bloods. Once the land and money was distributed, the Business Committee would be abolished and the individual bands could create their own governing boards.[74]

But this proposal still generated significant opposition at a March planning meeting. White Rivers expressed fears that they were being kicked out of the tribe, too. So the plan was revised to expel just the mixed-bloods—a plan that united all full-bloods behind partition. Most believed this would also solve the persistent mixed-blood/full-blood conflict and serve the greater purpose of diverting Watkins. The acculturated mixed-bloods would be terminated immediately, temporarily satisfying the senator's agenda; in return, Watkins agreed to suspend his timetable for terminating full-bloods pending the success of their development program. The full-bloods argued that the better educated and acculturated mixed-bloods had benefited the most from the initial three-year rehabilitation program and were now "prepared" to withdraw from federal supervision.[75]

The General Council heard the plan on March 31, 1954. The official report of the meeting claims that the plan was received calmly and without serious opposition, and that the mixed-bloods favored partition and termination; however, recent studies argue convincingly that this was not true.[76] Rather, tribal attorneys Ernest Wilkinson and John Boyden, along with the BIA area director, arrived at the meeting unexpectedly. Wilkinson read the draft of the plan to a stunned audience and urged them to accept the proposal, which was "in the best interest of the tribe." The members responded in silence. Rex Curry urged discussion, but the only response was a single member's request to discuss it later, after it had been placed on the agenda and members had time to think about it. Many Uintahs simply walked out in silent protest. Keeping with the secret plan concocted with Bennett and McKinley (and perhaps playing to the full-blood crowd), Chairman Curry immediately moved for the vote by announcing, "Now is the time when you folks are going to get rid of the Mixed-bloods. We're getting rid of all of them... in here," indicating his heart and head. At this point, only twenty-one mixed-bloods remained present (including Curry), compared to well over 250 full-blood members. In the ensuing vote, all but eight voted for partition—some full-bloods raising two hands in their enthusiasm to be rid of the "half-breeds." The often contentious and resented mixed-bloods had become "sacrificial lambs" tossed to the wolves to buy the full-bloods more time to stave off termination.[77]

Most full-bloods were jubilant; many had long felt the mixed-bloods had been receiving the lion's share of tribal benefits and were monopolizing the tribal government. As Pawwinee, a full-blood Uncompahgre, put it, mixed-bloods were always "tell[ing] us what to do." Although they recognized mixed-bloods often had strong leadership skills, most believed mixed-bloods didn't understand the problems of the unacculturated and less-educated full-bloods. And many didn't consider mixed-bloods to be real Utes anyway. Some were also afraid that Watkins would use these more assimilated people to prove all Utes were ready for termination that would "prematurely and unwittingly thrust the full-blood Ute into a way of life for which they were not prepared."[78]

With the vote in, the next obstacle was how to word the partition bill. The BIA wanted to define Utes as those listed on official rolls based on a census to be taken in 1954, and to define all assets as noninheritable. But this would effectively freeze the rolls and disinherit all children born after 1954, implementing a backdoor termination. After intense lobbying by the tribe and their attorney, the 84th Congress amended the bill to allow future enrollment and allocate all noninheritable assets to the tribe as a corporate whole to be distributed among members (stockholders) as it saw fit.[79]

Meanwhile, the bewildered mixed-bloods tried to make sense of the new political and economic reality. One man protested later that "there are a lot of Indians that are mixed with a lot of [other] Indians here... [and] I can't figure out what it means to be full-blood." Most mixed-bloods had some Ute ancestry (on average, 28 percent) and others had a lot of Indian ancestry—just not from Utes. Some called the move to partition "a real snow job," complaining that most did not understand what it was or hadn't learned about it until after the resolution passed. In any case, the majority of those divested of tribal membership were children who had no say in the matter.[80]

But the BIA and Senator Watkins were satisfied, viewing partitioning as a solution to the troublesome "Ute Problem." The tribal attorneys, however, worried about what would happen to the mixed-bloods and their 27 percent share of tribal resources. Knowing the terminated Utes would need competent legal advice and ignoring possible conflicts of interest, tribal attorney John Boyden offered to represent both groups. As the partition legislation moved through Congress (P.L. 671), a new program committee quickly drafted a ten-year program with three main goals: the preservation and protection of Indian culture, the preservation of Indian resources, and an increase of technical and professional assistance from the federal government—all decidedly anti-assimilation and anti-termination. The plan was approved by Congress in November 1955. Official rolls were published six months later, identifying 490 mixed-bloods to be terminated and leaving 1,314 full-blood members of the Uintah-Ouray Ute tribe.[81]

As all three Ute tribes began to implement their new rehabilitation plans, the abandoned Northern Ute mixed-bloods began a rapid spiral into poverty and bitter recriminations. They joined nearly one hundred tribes who would be similarly terminated between 1953 and 1968. Having neither a political organization to protect them nor access to federal health or education programs, cash-strapped individuals began selling off their land, and many were urged to relocate to cities. With their cultural identity in shreds, the mixed-bloods—as with other terminated tribes—suffered the continuing effects of cultural isolation, poverty, dependence on welfare, and the frustration of being cut adrift.[82]

Even after the mixed-bloods were jettisoned from the tribe, the full-bloods continued to worry that they too would eventually be terminated. But Bennett, who felt the currents in Washington beginning to shift, assured them that attitudes were changing. And he was right. Within three years Watkins was not reelected, and the momentum for termination and relocation slowed. Terminated tribes had sunk into deeper poverty, and relocated Indians had not found adequate housing nor promised jobs. Instead, city dwellers had plummeted into urban poverty, this time without family or tribal organizations to support them. Secretary of the Interior Morris Udall's Task Force on Indian Affairs held hearings and in 1961 recommended termination be "terminated" as a goal. Consequently, the 1960s became a muddle of incomplete termination bills and the administrative problems inherent in shifting jurisdictional responsibility of Indians from the federal government to the states (P.L. 280, 1953). Indian policy again swung back toward the old IRA ideals of self-government. The Kennedy Administration pushed it forward first; it gained momentum under Lyndon Johnson; and by 1970 Richard Nixon formally repudiated termination when he asked Congress to affirm the right of tribal integrity and existence, urging the recognition of pluralism as "a source of national strength."[83] Over the next decades, dozens of terminated tribes applied for federal recognition and were reestablished as tribal entities. The mixed-blood Utes were not among them.

The Battle to Define an Indian Identity

The mixed-blood Utes remained adrift and economically pummeled. Conflicts of interest quickly arose for attorney John Boyden, as he tried to represent the interests of both the terminated mixed-bloods and the Uintah-Ouray Utes, now calling themselves the Northern Ute tribe. One historian has argued that Boyden's subsequent legal and financial actions were a deliberate and unethical manipulation of mixed-blood assets in such a way that the Northern Ute tribe regained most of their divisible assets, followed by the unethically orchestrated sale of the mixed-bloods' stock shares of indivisible assets. Parker M. Nielson, who eventually succeeded Boyden as the mixed-bloods' attorney, called this manipulation a "conspiracy" to deprive the mixed-bloods of their share of tribal assets and referred to these "shenanigans" as villainous.[84]

Certainly, this was the embittered perception of the terminated mixed-bloods, and their expulsion from the tribe left a long-lasting culture of litigation, shifting definitions of identity, and a virulent animosity between mixed-bloods, their full-blood neighbors, and the tribe. In time this hostility would drain them of even the desire to *be* Utes, and they would seek a new disassociated Indian identity. At the same time, full-bloods chose to believe (and still argue) that the mixed-bloods had asked to be terminated and had willingly agreed to the separation.[85]

Picking up the pieces, the mixed-blood Utes banded together in their common disfellowship.[86] They were still linked to the reservation community through kinship networks and geography, and they continued to participate in community activities, including powwows, Bear Dances, Sundances, sweats, and peyote meetings. Though no longer eligible to graze their cattle on tribal lands, vote in elections, or hold tribal jobs—and therefore quickly bereft of economic mainstays—they were still part of the community but not *of* the community.[87] Mixed-bloods were lineally, genetically, and culturally Indians, but not legally Indian. Worse, in the charged racist atmosphere of the Uintah Basin, they were still perceived to be Indians but without recourse to tribal or federal benefits and protection.

It was a bewildering status. Many continued to insist that despite their mixed descent, their entire *identity* remained not only Indian, but Ute. One mixed-blood who had been expelled from the tribe complained that

> My great grandparents, my grandparents, my father and I was born and reared on the Ute Reservation, so for me, my whole identity is tied in with the Ute tribe.... I may have been cut off from federal services, but I was never cut off from being an Indian, more particularly a Ute Indian...a Northern Ute Indian of the Uintah Band.[88]

Others identified themselves as Uintahs, not Utes, believing Uintah was an older and therefore more authentic identity. Some began to view the Ute identity as political, arguing that it had been mistakenly imposed on them by non-Indians. While this was not ethnologically logical, it made communal sense to these disfranchised Indians.

The Uintah "tribe" was actually an amalgamation of at least five different western bands who had identified themselves, even as late as the 1930s, as Utes or *Núu-ci*.[89] They recognized close cultural links with Utes in Colorado who "thought as they did" and had interacted frequently with the northern bands, as had the central Utah bands with the eastern Sheberetch. Pressured to cluster on the Uintah Reservation in the mid-1860s, these western bands had merged and unified as they intermarried, socialized, and suffered together on their poorly funded reservation.[90] Fifteen years later, when the Colorado Utes were thrust onto and near their reservation, the ensuing economic and political competition between bands hardened the previously porous boundaries between the Uintahs and their northern Colorado cousins. A resentful opposition to the "others" developed, uniting the Uintahs further in a common struggle to reach economic and political parity with their unwanted guests. The Uintahs' decades-long proximity to mountain men, traders, and Mormon colonizers, as well as their integration of Paiute, Goshute, and Shoshone captives, had resulted in a large number of mixed-heritage Indians and a significant amount of American acculturation. The cultural distance increased between the Uintahs and the more isolated and traditional Colorado Utes, and by the mid-twentieth century the Uintahs had come to see their community as politically and ethnically different.[91]

The continual rancor built solidarity and reinforced the differences between full-bloods versus mixed-bloods and Uintahs versus Colorado Utes, and it helped solidify the belief in a community of Uintah Indians that was different from the Ute Indians of Colorado.[92] "How can they make me a Ute?... I'm *still* a Uintah. I'm on the [pre-1937] Uintah roll!" Others argued that a Ute tribal identity had not existed until 1937, when the government created a new tribal organization that was illegal because of ratification irregularities, and which had no right to supersede their own Uintah identity.[93]

Following partition, the terminated mixed-bloods were given a temporary identity as Affiliated Ute Citizens of the state of Utah (AUC), with a constitution and bylaws written by Boyden. They were entitled to 27 percent of tribal assets, to be distributed as stock dividends through a newly created Ute Distribution Corporation, or UDC. In 1958 Boyden and a tribal committee determined the value of those assets, but due to a lack of qualified experts and under pressure to determine value quickly, these resources were undervalued. Where it had taken years of meticulous study by experts to assign values to land and resources during the Ute land claims cases, the value of the terminated mixed-bloods' divisible resources was accomplished within a few days and, according to one historian, in a slipshod "best guess" method.[94] AUC dividends included immediately divisible assets, future gas and oil royalties, and a share of the pending $7.7 million Spanish Fork judgment money that was supposed to compensate Western Utes for the loss of 5.7 million acres in Utah. Because the share-and-share-alike provisions on land claims money was still in effect, the tribe got a large share of the award, too.[95]

Bitterness increased as Affiliated Utes competed for access to reservation assets. The division of rangeland, for example, disrupted range conditions and crippled the cattle and sheep operations of the tribe. Rex Curry and acting chair Henry Cuch sought Boyden's help in buying out the Affiliated Utes to regain control of all the rangeland. Affiliated Ute range operations were being managed through newly created cattle companies and relied on private exchanges of individual range shares so that stockmen could accumulate sufficient range rights for viable operations. Individual shares provided only enough graze for two and a half head of cattle for six months or five sheep for one year, insufficient for a profitable enterprise. Despite earlier assurances that such private transactions were legal, Boyden now flipped and argued they were *not* legal; he claimed that if non-stockowners wished to sell or trade their shares, they had to offer them on the open market. However, even though Elizabeth Curry Bumgarner offered to buy up all Affiliated Ute shares at above the appraised value, Boyden blocked the sale by asserting that she was using non-Indian money to buy Indian land (her husband was not Indian). Ultimately, most of the Affiliated Ute rangeland was sold back to the tribe for a much lower price than Bumgarner had offered. In another questionable action, Boyden convinced the local bank that it was to the benefit of Affiliated Ute children to sell their shares too, and 87 percent of these were purchased by the tribe as well. Eventually, the AUC simply sold out and dissolved their two-stock operations. The thirty-eight mixed-blood shareholders who did not sell eventually traded their shares for several hundred acres of land (which is what they wanted in the first place).[96]

By 1963 most of the terminated Utes were desperate for money and began to sell their UDC stock as well. The local bank in Roosevelt charged with managing these accounts even set up a table in their lobby for brokering UDC stock, and stocks were sold for a fraction of their value at the very time their value had begun to rise rapidly. As a result, much of the UDC stock ended up in non-Indian hands, and eventually the UDC itself fell under the control of non-Indians. One unfortunate result was that when the Spanish Fork land-claims money was finally distributed, the Uintah mixed-bloods for whom it was intended saw very little of it. Because it was disbursed through UDC stock shares, most compensation for ceded Western Ute land ended up in the hands of non-Indian UDC stockholders.[97]

By 1963 the terminated mixed-blood Utes had become both "disowned and disinherited." However, they remained firmly embedded in an Indian identity that many began to reconstruct. Although the corporate identity of the AUC was dissolved in 1959, it had become much more than a financial entity, and some mixed-blood leaders decided to re-create a new unofficial Affiliated Ute Citizens association. It became a catalyst for unifying the mixed-bloods as a group and provided a social unit in which they could try to reconstruct who they were. Members shared an ethnic heritage as Uintahs and as Indians, and they shared a community of family and friends, a sense of culture and values, and an awareness of common tribulations. Thus, in the words of one historian, the new AUC became a "quasi-tribal economic association" created for the purpose of managing mixed-blood assets (cattle, sheep, and mineral rights) with a corporate structure similar to both the UDC and the Ute Tribal Business Committee.[98]

However, the courts refused to acknowledge this new AUC and continued to recognize the UDC as the only authorized representative of the terminated mixed-bloods to manage indivisible resources—despite the fact that the majority of stock had fallen into non-Indian hands. Regardless, many mixed-bloods continued to use the reorganized AUC as a community entity to demand mixed-blood rights, initiate numerous lawsuits, and assert their claims to reservation resources.[99]

The Affiliated Utes—and eventually other Uintah mixed-blood organizations—initiated an ongoing series of litigations and helped reconstruct a Uintah Indian identity in opposition to the Northern Ute "interlopers." Hundreds of lawsuits—many considered frivolous by court officials—were filed over asset management, hunting and fishing rights, legal jurisdiction, Indian identity, reenrollment, the unethical sale of shares, and so on. Despite a handful of favorable court decisions (e.g., the unethical sale of UDC stock by the bank), few tangible results were seen. The tribe continued to maintain that mixed-bloods were simply not Indians, regardless of genetics, culture, or quantity of Indian blood. Either an individual was an enrolled Northern Ute (with five-eighths or more Northern Ute blood), a non-Ute Indian (enrolled in another federally recognized tribe), or not an Indian at all.[100]

In the 1990s the Northern Ute Tribe was awarded another windfall award: a $295.5 million water settlement. Both the terminated mixed-bloods and the UDC (a mostly white corporation by then) immediately tried to garner a share by filing suit for the "right of joint management" of indivisible tribal water assets, and for their 27 percent of revenue resulting from either its management or any monetary settlement. But the U.S. District Court ruled the tribe had sovereign immunity and could not be sued, a decision reiterated in 1998 by the Tenth District Court. Two months later the assistant secretary of the Interior ruled that terminated mixed-bloods had already been given their water rights when they received their share of tribal land.[101] The tribe retained all management rights and the entire $295.5 million water settlement award.

While the conflict between the tribe and the terminated mixed-bloods existed, in part, because of the bitter history of interband feuding on the reservation after 1880, it was equally an aspect of modern Native American reality. As federal and tribal resources became more abundant beginning in the 1980s, shirttail relatives and Indian wannabes began emerging "from the woodwork" (as one Tohono O'odham secretary put it), and most tribes, as well as the BIA, began drawing stringent lines to determine enrollment and tribal funds entitlement. Subsequent Supreme Court rulings like the landmark *Santa Clara Pueblo v. Martinez* (1978) reinforced the right of Indian tribes to determine who was and who was not a member of their tribe—regardless of Indian blood quantum. Consequently, no person not enrolled in a federally recognized tribe could legally claim to be Indian and was not recognized by most government agencies or educational institutions.[102] It was a hardened position wholeheartedly subscribed to by the Northern Ute tribe in the face of ongoing mixed-blood attacks.

But it left the terminated mixed-bloods feeling resentful, "kicked to death in courts," and wondering how they got into such a "damn, sad situation." As more than one terminated mixed-blood complained, "We grew up believing we're Indians. To white people we're still Indians. We're caught in the middle."[103] Luke Duncan, Northern Ute tribal chair, demonstrated the ongoing antipathy in 1991 when Governor Norm Bangerter included a mixed-blood representative on a newly created Utah Indian Cooperative Council. In addition to representatives from the state's recognized tribes, Bangerter included representatives from Utah's urban Indians and mixed-blood Uintahs. An angry Duncan threatened lawsuits and opposed the seating of "non-Indians" on a council for *Indians*. Northern Ute representatives boycotted the first meetings, calling it "an affront to tribal rights" and accusing the state of "butting into tribal issues." Nevertheless, the mixed-bloods remained seated.[104]

Although they won this round, most mixed-blood attempts at recognition were less successful. Some campaigned for years to repeal the Partition Act and to be reinstated in the tribe, arguing that the act had been racially motivated and that Congress had enacted a racist law, a holocaust that stripped them of their ethnic identity and stole their land.[105] By the 1980s they were blaming both the government and the tribe (as a tool of the government). As one angry mixed-blood exclaimed in exasperation, "You sons of bitches... [you] fouled me up. You done this to me, tribe—Mr. Tribe. I don't even want to be part of your damn tribe."[106]

By the early 1990s some chose to deny their Ute heritage entirely, linking Uteness with their enemy, the tribe. At least two new mixed-blood groups emerged. One called itself the Uintah Band of Utah Indians (not to be confused with the Yuta Indians from Colorado); the other, the "Timpanogos Tribe, Snake Band of the Shoshone Indians," or alternatively, the "Timpanogos Band of the Shoshone Indians." By 2012 a new group was calling itself the Uintah Valley Shoshone Tribe of Utah Indians of the Uintah Valley and Ouray Reservation, aka Shoshone Tribe of Affiliated Ute Citizens. These groups claimed non-Indians had mistakenly identified them as Utes, and that the western Utes of Utah history were really Shoshone bands and their prominent leader, Wákara, a Shoshone war chief (an idea that would have surprised the war chief, who conducted many bloody raids against the Shoshones). President Lincoln had set aside the Uintah Reservation for Indians of Utah Territory, and the Timpanogos tribe had "exclusive lawful occupancy," had never "rescinded or ceded any of their rights," and the Utes from Colorado had illegally usurped their reservation and set up a "rogue government." The expulsion of the Timpanogos Indians from the tribe had been a "conspiracy of petroleum companies" and "dirty politics."[107]

Historical facts do not support these arguments. Neither did the courts, the federal government, nor the Northern Ute tribe. Nevertheless, the Timpanogos Tribe and the Uintah Valley Shoshone Tribe continue to assert their exclusive right to all reservation resources and hunting and fishing licenses, and they have sued for tribal recognition.[108] Their open hostility and bitterness in ongoing attempts to reestablish a unified Indian identity only highlights the long-standing conflict between these cast-off "breeds" and the corporately wealthy and increasingly influential Northern Ute tribe in the Uintah Basin.

With claims money and rehabilitation plans in hand, the three Ute tribes were prepared to press for increased autonomy to control their tribal resources, improve their prosperity through corporately controlled tribal assets, and reassert their identity as sovereign Indian nations with the rights of self-determination and government-to-government powers of negotiation.

Chapter 16

The Quest for Self-Determination and Sovereignty

Before looking at the changes that took place among Ute tribes during the final decades of the twentieth century, it is important to situate them within the larger context of Indian America at that time. Ground-shifting changes were taking place that impacted all Native Americans politically, economically, socially, and religiously. Many tribes were receiving land-claims money and were seeking to implement economic rehabilitation plans with the help of tribal members who were more educated and integrated with mainstream American culture due to their experiences during World War II. This helped, but did not eliminate poverty on reservations. But by the end of the 1960s, civil-rights protests by native activists shone a light on the dismal affairs on Indian reservations. Additionally, new funds became available to tribal leadership who not only took advantage of federal assistance to improve reservation infrastructures and social programs, but also encouraged their members to apply for a variety of welfare programs available to all Americans. Congress also passed a series of laws that placed more power into the hands of unicameral tribal governments and encouraged tribal self-reliance and sovereignty. Reservation politics became increasingly important, and, like politicians everywhere, tribal leaders had to pander to the demands of their constituency, with both positive and negative results. Leadership became less about the authority of age, wisdom, or skill than of power-brokering families and factions. Tribes also gained more control of their own resources as new laws protected Indian rights and increased their influence over reservation affairs. New gaming laws in the 1980s offered a significant source of new revenue for tribes. And improved communications technology and mass media threw open reservation doors and brought American culture directly into members' homes.

Thus, the last four decades of the twentieth and the first decade of the twenty-first centuries was a time of rapid change, and Utes became—by choice and opportunity—increasingly immersed in the physical, social, political, and economic culture of mainstream America. At the same time, some members continued to fight to maintain the essence of what it meant to be an Indian, and a Ute.

After 1958 the political climate began to change in Washington, as termination and relocation policies began to come under attack and government officials scrambled to repudiate them. With Arthur Watkins no longer leading the crusade in Congress (defeated in his bid for a third term), the postwar anti-collectivism hysteria waning, national prosperity increasing, and a more sympathetic Kennedy administration, Congress gradually abandoned the policies of termination and urban relocation.[1] Richard Nixon officially rang its death knell on July 8, 1970, during a message to Congress on Indian Affairs:

> Because termination is morally and legally unacceptable, because it produces bad practical results and because the mere threat of termination tends to discourage greater self-sufficiency among Indian groups, I am asking the Congress to pass a new concurrent resolution which would expressly renounce, repudiate and repeal the termination policy as expressed by the House Concurrent Resolution 108 of the 83rd Congress.[2]

At the same time, Nixon asked Congress to affirm the "integrity and rights to continued existence of all Indian tribes," reaffirm the government's commitment to their historic "treaty and trusteeship obligations" to Indian tribes, and to recognize the value of cultural pluralism.

Meanwhile, spurred by the attack on Indian identity, encouraged by the growing civil rights movement, and fueled by a growing availability of federal aid outside BIA channels, tribal governments increasingly moved toward self-determination and sovereignty. During this struggle both legal processes—and extralegal protests—helped propel Indian rights and support development.

In 1961 concerned Indian leaders convened a conference in Chicago, one of many urban centers of Indian relocation. Representing 142 tribes, the leaders of the National Congress of American Indians (NCAI) developed a "Declaration of Indian Purposes" in hopes of influencing the newly elected John Kennedy. But a number of young college-educated Indian leaders like Clyde Warrior and Melvin Thom were not content with the slow-moving petitioning of their elders, and they broke away to form the more aggressive National Indian Youth

Council (NIYC), through which they could express the growing Native American nationalism in a more politically active and militant manner. The NIYC staged "fish-in" demonstrations to preserve Indian fishing rights in the Northwest, coordinated the American Indian arm of the Poor People's Campaign, and in the 1970s helped file lawsuits on behalf of Indian communities fighting off environmentally devastating mining and milling on reservations. Media coverage increased as they attracted the support of celebrities like Marlon Brando and Jane Fonda, while eloquent Indian radicals like Vine Deloria Jr. published bitter indictments against the oppression of Indians, including his *Custer Died for Your Sins, God is Red*, and *Aggressions of Civilization*.[3]

Others were even more militant and aggressive in demanding Indian rights. Thirty years after the Meriam Report, Native Americans still constituted the poorest minority in the United States, most living with little hope, in inadequate housing, and with abysmal sanitation and poor health care; high unemployment and frustration continued to yield high rates of alcoholism, suicide, and homicide; and they suffered from high infant mortality rates, occasional forced sterilization, and a life expectancy of less than fifty years. Activists organized the American Indian Movement (AIM), or Red Power, and demanded self-determination and sovereignty, an end to the trustee-ward relationship, and the right to tribal traditions, justice, and improved living conditions.[4] In 1969, AIM protestors occupied a number of abandoned federal properties, including the vacated prison at Alcatraz during a nineteen-month standoff; in 1970 protestors organized a national day of mourning at Plymouth, Massachusetts, while others established a protest-settlement near Mount Rushmore in the sacred Black Hills. Two years later, eight American Indian groups organized a caravan of protesters from the west coast to Washington, D.C., calling it the Trail of Broken Treaties. In Washington, in an unplanned move, they took over, occupied, and then vandalized BIA headquarters. The following year members of AIM, in another unplanned incident, occupied Wounded Knee on the Pine Ridge Sioux Reservation and remained under siege during a ten-week confrontation and ultimate shootout with the FBI and a tribal "goon" squad, an incident later called Wounded Knee II.[5] Protestors staged The Longest Walk in 1977, another peaceful demonstration in which traditionally dressed Indians walked across the nation to protest legislation that continued to threaten tribes and reservations. A new generation of American Indian activists such as Dennis Banks, Clyde Bellecourt, Leonard Peltier, and George Miller promoted the International Indian Treaty Council and influenced the creation of the United Nations Working Group on Indigenous Populations, helping to draft the Universal Declaration of the Rights of Indigenous Peoples (contended by the United States); and in the 1990s they protested Columbus Quincentennial celebrations throughout the United States.[6] New national organizations were founded that addressed the need for jobs, leadership training, alcohol and drug abuse, and education. Urban Indian centers emerged to address the needs of the many relocated Indians who remained off reservations. All of these organizations helped fuel a rising pan-Indian awareness.[7]

Few Utes, however, were induced to participate in the militant protests of organizations like AIM. Perhaps comfortable in the promise of their newly acquired wealth, satisfied with the effectiveness of courtroom and negotiating tactics, and viewing the BIA as an ally rather than opponent, the tribal councils continued to rely on legal action and aggressive political lobbying to accomplish their goals. In step with many other tribes, they sued the government over land and resource use and abuse, and they supported a resurgence of traditionalism on reservations (in dress, ritual, and preservation of language and traditions). Nevertheless, whether or not Utes participated in protest movements, the actions of militant Indian activists focused media attention on the plight of Native Americans and was a factor that brought to congressional and executive attention (and sympathy) the issues of Indian poverty and their desire for tribal self-determination.

As Indian policy swung back toward tribal empowerment, advocates of Indian development found allies in Washington. Following the 1961 NCAI conference, Kennedy created a Task Force on Indian Affairs, which included Uncompahgre leader Francis McKinley. Lyndon Johnson subsequently established the National Council on Indian Opportunity, and Richard Nixon created an American Indian Policy Review Commission. Legislation was introduced in Congress, restoring back to federal recognition many tribes that had been terminated in the 1950s—including the Southern Paiute tribe, which administratively included the Koosharem Ute and the Kanosh Pahvant.

Ute tribes also benefited from a series of legislative, executive, and legal actions. One of the first was the 1968 Indian Civil Rights Act (ICRA), an attempt to guarantee Indians the same rights most Americans enjoyed in the Bill of Rights. However, this attempt was essentially negated by the Supreme Court decision in *Santa Clara Pueblo v. Martinez* (1978) when it ruled that tribes "as separate sovereigns preexisting the Constitution...have historically been regarded as *unconstrained by those constitutional provisions* framed specifically as limitations on federal or state authority"; that the ICRA "constitut[ed] an interference with tribal autonomy and self-government"; and that federal "forums" (i.e., courts) undermined tribal sovereignty and their ability to govern themselves and make their own laws.[8] Disgruntled Indians—including Utes—complained that this decision made the U.S. Constitution inapplicable on their reservations, because, under the ruling, Indians living on their own reservations had no civil rights as Americans, were subject only to the whims of tribal governments, and were now without judicial redress other than (often prejudiced) tribal courts.[9]

And the tribal courts were plagued with problems. Paralleling many other tribes, the Utes had a unicameral corporate model government with no separate or counterbalancing branches of government. Northern Ute tribal attorney, Stephen Boyden, referred to this as a "monolithic system of government" where the Business Committee held both executive and legislative authority, as well as supervisory control over tribal courts. This led to ongoing conflicts between courts and the governing tribal council, as when on one occasion the disagreements degenerated into a legal brawl accompanied by court injunctions against the Business Committee, the Committee firing the judge(s) and dissolving the court, and the intrusion of the BIA and BIA police.[10]

The Ute court systems were often in disarray in their early years, because judges and attorneys lacked training and experience, records were sometimes lost, standard legal procedures were often lacking, and it was difficult to empanel a court without conflicts of interest from the small, typically interrelated population. Those who found themselves at odds with the governing councils, whether individual or corporate, could not sue for redress due to sovereign immunity of the tribal government (although individual officials could be sued).[11]

Meanwhile, Indian education remained abysmal. Indian students—appallingly unprepared to succeed in mainstream schools—were tolerated, ignored, or taunted by school officials, teachers, and non-Indian students alike, and consequently retreated into academic apathy and failure. Most parents did not understand the educational system and remained uninvolved and typically unsupportive of one that taught their children failure. Johnson-O'Malley funds, intended to improve American Indian education, often disappeared into a school district's general fund. And there was little difference in how children were treated, whether they attended local schools or were bussed off the reservation. In 1969 a special Senate subcommittee issued a report on Indian education that called educational programs a "tragedy."[12]

In response, Congress passed the Indian Education Act in 1972, giving tribes and parents greater control over their children's education. It also provided competitive grant opportunities for children and adults, and subsequent amendments (1974, 1988, 1994, and 2001) included provisions for teacher training, the establishment of academic and culturally related programs, opportunities for gifted and talented funding, and later requirements for integration into George W. Bush's "No Child Left Behind" educational legislation.[13]

In 1975 Congress also passed the Indian Self-Determination and Education Assistance Act, which encouraged tribes to assume the responsibilities of managing many federal programs and services—including education, medical services, law enforcement, and construction—as part of making tribes more self-reliant. With this legislation, tribes could enter into "self-determination contracts" with the Secretary of the Interior and Health and Human Services so that they could administer the programs directly and utilize Indian contractors. One of these "educationally assisted" programs was Head Start, which tribes embraced wholeheartedly. However, they quickly found that there were hidden costs, including liability, for administering their own programs. The act was amended in 1988, 1989, and 1990 to require the federal government to provide liability insurance for tribes, tribal organizations, and tribal contractors. Any claims against tribal contractors would be deemed claims against the United States and covered by federal tort claims laws.[14]

Another program was the creation of tribal police forces. The Northern Ute foray into this arena, however, was less than successful. Within a few years, the cost and logistics of administering their own police brought a return to contracting with the BIA for law enforcement services, which ultimately served a long-term good. The BIA police and tribal wildlife officers were competent and drawn from among a diverse population of Native Americans from throughout the United States. These officials were trained at the Federal Police Academy, where training was similar to state or city police academies but with more stringent physical requirements. Another advantage of using BIA officers was the reduction in conflicts of interest that came from drawing Indian officers from a wider native background rather than from only the limited and interrelated reservation populations.[15]

Congress continued to pass legislation aimed at assisting tribes to regain rights. The Indian Health Care Act (1976, with subsequent amendments) sought to remedy deficiencies in Indian health care. The more controversial Indian Child Welfare Act (1978) sought to stop the removal of children for

335

adoptive or foster care without tribal consent and gave tribes jurisdiction over custody rights and child welfare services. Congress also passed the even more controversial 1990 Native American Graves Protection and Repatriation Act. NAGPRA protected and returned to identifiable tribes the thousands of remains and funerary objects that had been removed from burial sites by archaeologists, as well as thousands of native skeletal remains and skulls gathered from nineteenth-century battle sites or burials that were used to study human evolution and Darwinian typing. (The heads of a dozen Western Ute warriors had been removed for this purpose after the Provo uprising in 1850). Many of these remains now lay buried in museums or academic institutions.[16]

Unfortunately, NAGPRA led to significant legal conflicts over what constituted an ancestor of a tribe for the purposes of remanding remains into their custody for reburial. The most notable example was the controversy over the remains of a 9,000-year-old paleo-American hunter found in Kennewick, Washington, and claimed by local Paiutes—a tribe that had moved into the region less than a thousand years ago. Similar controversies arose over the handling of artifacts from Anasazi archaeological sites in the Four Corners area, over which both the Navajo and Ute tribes claimed some jurisdiction (though these pueblo remains were ancestors of neither tribe). Nevertheless, the law has generally worked to return and preserve the sanctity of Native American remains from what writers have referred to as the rampant graverobbing activities of early anthropologists and archaeologists.[17]

In 1978 Congress passed the Indian Religious Freedom Act to protect the rights of Indians to believe, express, and practice their traditional religions, including the right to worship through ceremonials and traditional rites, to possess and use sacred objects (including feathers from endangered or protected species), and to have access to religious sites. But conflict continued, including controversy over seizure and examination of medicine pouches, the use of peyote, and the protection of and access to sacred sites. Congress acted again in 1994, amending the act to increase protection of narrowly defined and authenticated religious sites on federal land, and passing the Religious Freedom Restoration Act, which reinforced the right of Indians—defined as enrolled members of federally recognized tribes—to use peyote (a controlled substance) when part of a religious ritual. By so doing, the law specifically excluded non-Indians and unenrolled individuals with blood-Indian heritage but who had become, by political definition, non-Indians.[18] However, after a series of high profile cases arguing religious freedom regardless of race, and a Supreme Court decision allowing—but not requiring—exemptions for religious use, Utah and

Colorado along with a number of other states reluctantly revised their restrictions and exempted peyote from controlled substance laws. Thus, the religious use of peyote became legal in Utah and Colorado, regardless of race or tribal affiliation. Other states were less lenient.[19]

An increasing number of federal aid programs also became available to tribes who scrambled for funding from the open coffers of Lyndon Johnson's Great Society programs. This included generous funding from the Office of Economic Opportunity (OEO), the offices of Housing and Urban Development (HUD), the Comprehensive Education and Training Program (CETA), and the Department of Health and Human Services' American Native Programs (ANA). The availability of this new money changed the face of tribal governments and Indian affairs. Tribes were no longer required to go hat in hand to the BIA; instead, grantsmanship became a requisite skill in tribal offices. As in other tribes, Ute leaders and tribal employees learned the art of writing successful grant proposals for federal funds while exploring how to lure private capital for mineral and agricultural development onto reservations as well.[20]

Tribes acquired money for office buildings and equipment, and they could travel to Washington at will or attend Indian affairs conferences. Until the OEO faded during the Jimmy Carter administration, it was the primary financial focus for tribes while the BIA declined in influence. With the new OEO funding, some of which Congress authorized to be paid directly to tribes, and armed with self-determination contracts, the federal government was forced to acknowledge tribal sovereignty and increasingly began working within a government-to-government relationship rather than treating tribes as little more than facilitators of government programs. Tribes were seen as legitimate and independent governments, similar to local and state governments, that could receive federal services beyond those particularly allocated for Indians.[21]

But with the new funding, tribal bureaucracies exploded as tribes were forced to develop administrative structures and systems of accountability. If, for example, a tribe wanted HUD money, they had to create their own tribal housing authority. Some tribes developed their own local offices of economic opportunity or education as well. Tribes became the dominant employers of their members, who in turn learned on-the-job administrative skills. A managerial class emerged, and many of the new native leaders apprenticed their governmental skills as OEO programs or enterprise administrators. Tribal councils and business committees, originally established to facilitate economic programs in the 1930s, took on more executive and legislative duties as they developed social and economic programs.[22]

But the influx of money did not solve the problems of poverty, and priorities varied. Many early tribal enterprises created under the first rehabilitation plans were mismanaged or poorly thought out. The Southern Utes, for example, used claims money to build a rodeo ground rather than work on health or sanitation problems. The Ute Mountain Utes began construction on a $350,000 community center in 1960 that included a gymnasium and swimming pool—even though Towaoc still lacked running water and culinary water had to be trucked in. Northern Utes developed range-fed cattle herds with no means to ship them to market. Tourist-oriented enterprises were developed just as national tourism plummeted due to the energy crisis and stagnant economy of the late 1960s and early 1970s. As a result, the Ute reservations became "graveyard[s] of failed economic-development projects"—as did most Indian enterprises throughout the United States.[23]

Meanwhile, dependence on OEO and HUD money left tribes in a boom-and-bust collapse when their programs were reduced and funding diminished in the early 1980s. Curtailed under Carter and then slashed under Ronald Reagan's stringent economies and "silent termination," a dearth of funding for health and education programs left many tribes in crisis. In a familiar refrain, Secretary of the Interior James Watt called American Indians "social misfits" and their reservations an example of "failed socialism." Despite landmark legislation favoring Indian sovereignty, the courts again grew hostile as they reacted to sovereignty with a growing fear of giving Indians too much jurisdiction, especially over non-Indians on reservations.[24]

But the 1990s brought a resurgence of self-determination and economic development. All three Ute tribes tapped into the energy resource industries and dealt directly with private companies, negotiated with federal and state governments over water rights and their cash value, and continued to avail themselves of ongoing, if reduced, social-welfare funding. Individuals also tapped into federal welfare and the Women, Infants, and Children (WIC) food and nutrition programs. Opportunities opened up for gaming income and renewed tourism with the Supreme Court decision in *California v. Cabazon Band of Mission Indians* (1987), which determined that gaming was legal on reservations if it was legal in the tribe's state. The subsequent 1988 Indian Gaming Regulatory Act confirmed the right of tribes to conduct gaming activities on reservations. Of 567 recognized tribes in 2015, 240 engaged in Class I or Class III gaming, generating thousands of jobs and millions in revenue.[25]

However, gaming also introduced a great deal of ongoing controversy, especially over what constituted an "authentic" Indian identity. In some cases, reconstituted tribes made up of lineal descendants with very little actual Indian blood used their status as Indians to invest in lucrative casino enterprises. For example, the Mashantucket Pequot, who ceased to exist as a people following the Pequot Massacre of 1637, eliminated their blood requirement to locate enough members to apply for federal recognition. Their membership doubled shortly after opening their *very* successful casino in 1995. Elsewhere, existing tribes began to comb their membership records and expel members with too-little blood quantum when they built casinos.[26]

Although not all tribes benefited from attempts at gaming, most did, among them the Southern and Ute Mountain Utes. With gambling legalized in Colorado at tourist destinations such as Cripple Creek, Black Hawk, and Central City, it opened the door for Indian gaming as well. Gaming would prove an economic windfall for the Utes in southern Colorado—and a source of envy for Northern Utes in nongaming Utah.[27]

Unearned income soared. With the 1950s land-claims money, Southern Utes' unearned income went from 20 percent in 1950 to 59 percent in 1962, Northern Ute unearned income reached 75 percent, while among the Ute Mountain Utes it jumped from 10 to 82 percent. Although these levels dropped abruptly when land-claims distribution ceased, tribal revenue from oil and gas leases began to bring in new per-capita income in the form of dividends. But as an increasing number of Utes on all three reservations became dependent on this unearned royalty income, fewer were motivated to work. Stock raising and farming diminished, and many made unrealistic demands on tribal governments to maintain per-capita cash distribution regardless of the international economic climate or success of tribal enterprises. Most achieved a higher standard of living but developed a lower standard of self-reliance. For the minority who did work, tribal and government programs continued to be the chief employer.[28]

Problems quickly developed, however, because most members viewed their unearned per-capita income as an *inheritance* from their dispossessed ancestors, rather than as *dividends* from communal business enterprises whose income fluctuated with the international market and financial cycles. Members instead viewed these payments as entitlements compensating them for their lost land and traditions. As early as the 1930s, Ute Mountain chief John Miller exemplified this when he resisted Indian Civilian Conservation Corps projects by protesting, "We do not want jobs for our young men, for if they learn to work you will say that they can earn their own living and we shall then never get rations" or other entitlements.[29]

All three tribes were located in economically depressed rural regions and in markets driven by agribusiness where members were unable to farm successfully. But neither were there jobs open for Indians off-reservation, where long-standing prejudice was rife. When members did obtain jobs, few maintained them, due to unreliability, tardiness, or absenteeism (sometimes caused by attendance at traditional events or rituals, and sometimes from despair-driven drunkenness). Because of increased unearned income and a reluctance to leave the safety of the reservation or family support networks, the motivation to work lessened and fewer farmed or hired out as part-time laborers. Unemployment or underemployment soared. As Judy Knight Frank noted in 1992 when the first Ute Mountain Ute casino opened, "Our people are reluctant to leave their homes so the tribe had to bring the employment to them." But in 1960 there was little employment on their reservation. While the average unemployment for U.S. Indians sat at 13 percent, Utes were experiencing between 50 to 80 percent.[30]

But unearned income quickly became a quagmire for all three tribes as members grew dependent on it, proving an economic and political tar pit. Tribal income depended on the fluctuating energy market because oil and gas leases provided the majority of tribal revenue, yet Ute politicians soon found per-capita dividends to be untouchable, and they skirted close to—and sometimes into—bankruptcy. And members refused to accept reduced payments when energy income dried up during economic bust cycles.[31]

The twentieth century saw the separated Ute tribes moving on divergent paths as they adapted to shifting federal programs, economic opportunities, as well as local issues and politics. Still, intertribal relations continued to reinforce a pan-Ute identity through extended family networks, while better transportation led to increased inter-reservation travel for popular communal events, including Sundances, powwows, and rodeos. However, politics and varying economic development also disconnected the respective tribes.

The final four decades of the twentieth century brought both financial crises and economic resurgence as all three Ute tribes explored new economic projects; tapped into new federal resources; fought court battles over jurisdictional and water rights issues; and fought for self-determination, sovereignty, and political potency. During this time the tribes wielded increasing political and economic power, much to the chagrin—and occasionally fear—of neighboring Euro-Americans. Some of these issues drove a wedge of prejudice more deeply between populations, at the same time highlighting the necessity of working together. By the end of the twentieth century, Ute economies began to soar, benefiting local non-Indian economies as well. Non-Indians grudgingly began to realize that they could no longer ignore—and could even work with—their Ute neighbors.

But even as members of the Ute tribes and their political machinery and economic bureaucracies began to look a lot like mainstream America, tribes continued to support those who enshrined their Ute heritage and identity. They established museums and language-learning programs, encouraged heritage programs, publicized Native American activities in tribal newspapers and websites, set up tribal Facebook accounts, and supported attendance at Indian rituals that gave the appearance of maintaining older traditions.

The final chapters will look more closely at the political, economic, and cultural changes and development of the Northern, Southern, and Ute Mountain Ute tribes.

Chapter 17

Uintah-Ouray Utes

1960 to a New Century

The second half of the twentieth century and the first decade of the twenty-first were marked by a dramatic upswing in economic, legal, and political power for the Uintah-Ouray Utes. It was also scarred by legal jurisdiction battles with neighboring non-Indians and bitter political discord within the tribe. While the tribe eventually reached a workable if sometimes uneasy accord with their non-Indian neighbors, fractious tribal politics continued to mar internal relations into the twenty-first century. Perhaps in part as a result of this discord, by the 1990s tribal leaders discarded the term Uintah-Ouray Utes in favor of band-blind names: first the Northern Utes and then the Ute Indian Tribe of the Uintah and Ouray Reservation. The new names were, among other things, a tool to help unify a still-disunited community. However, the Uncompahgres remained divided from the White River/Uintah factions. In part this was a result of the geographic-defining allotment pattern that placed the Uncompahgres in one section of the reservation while scattering the White Rivers and diminished Uintahs on the other; additionally, the relative population-driven power of the more numerous Uncompahgres continued to magnify internal differences between band factions. Consequently, the ongoing political clashes that plagued the tribe were often driven by band affiliation. Uintah-Ouray Utes they might be, but they also remained Uintahs, White Rivers, and Uncompahgres.

As these Utes approached the twenty-first century, the tribe became the focus of tribal life and identity, not only in managing tribal-wide social and religious activities, but also in assuming an increased responsibility for the social, physical, and economic welfare of its members. And because these concerns were the source of individual and tribal well-being, many increasingly savvy, often opinionated, and politically active members fought repeated battles for control of tribal affairs.

POLITICS AND ECONOMIC REHABILITATION, 1960–1980

In the midst of the 1950s uproar over termination and band parity, White River and Uintah members continued to agitate against their tribal government. The bylaws of the tribal constitution provided for equal representation in the governing Business Committee; however, White Rivers and Uintahs continued to elect influential spiritual advisors (*puwarat* or *puwágati*) to represent them. These members were steeped in older traditions and spoke English poorly. As a result, the acculturated mixed-bloods and a few educated Uncompahgres dominated the Business Committee and controlled policy-making decisions. The White Rivers also refused to recognize the legitimacy of the reorganized IRA government and instead supported independent but recognized chiefs within their own ranks. They were also more closely allied with the Uintahs because their individual allotments were intermixed, and by the 1950s many were linked by marriage and family ties. Because of this, the Uintah and White Rivers formed a loosely allied faction that began to move against the Uncompahgres and the Business Committee.[1]

In early June 1960 during a general council, the Uintah/White River faction made an unsuccessful motion to disband the Business Committee entirely. A few days later the faction, now calling themselves "True Utes," stormed the tribal offices, drove administrators out, and occupied the building. The True Utes wanted to end the Committee's reliance on non- Indian advice about how to spend Ute money—advice they thought did not further Ute interests. They also wanted to increase the distance between Utes and non-Utes politically, economically, and socially. Led by Julius Tahouy, an eloquent and intelligent political and religious leader, the faction held the building for four days before the siege ended and the insurgents were jailed. Within a short time, however, the prisoners were released so they could participate in the all-important July Sundance.[2] Charges and countercharges, suits and countersuits, and other legal actions flew between the Business Committee and the True Ute leadership throughout the next decade and beyond. The True Ute goals were never rewarded with anything but jail and ongoing legal fencing, and their issues faded into the background; however, it would not be the end of fractious politics.

Despite internal disagreements, the tribe's financial situation was improving. The initial payment from land claims was made in 1951. Funds had been trickling in from royalties on oil, phosphate, and Gilsonite leases, but the new land-claims money was a dramatic economic boost. From an average of $1,500 per household in the late 1940s, income briefly soared to over $6,500

17.1. Attempts to create successful tourist-oriented enterprises in the 1960s and 1970s were generally unsuccessful, as was the Bottle Hollow Resort on the Northern Ute reservation; later enterprises fared much better. (Photo: S. Jones 2007)

during the 1950s.[3] With the implementation of mandated rehabilitation programs, the development of tribal business enterprises, and the arrival of the Office of Economic Opportunity (OEO) and Community-based Anti-Poverty programs (CAP), tribal bureaucracies expanded and the federal and tribal government employed most members who chose to work. As a result, even employed members remained dependent on government funds in one form or another.[4]

Then in 1960 and 1962, the federal government refused to release land-claims payments, asserting that it was entitled to deduct costs for running the reservations. The three tribes sued and litigation continued until 1965, when the disputed monies were finally deposited in a trust fund and tribes were given the resulting interest to operate on.[5] But members had become dependent on the earlier per-capita distributions. Consequently, when the award money was not paid, incomes dropped dramatically. Some members took loans from the tribe, and they were advised to seek federal government welfare. Some were also exploited by local farmers who bailed them out of jail (usually on charges of drunkenness) in exchange for days of arduous farm labor to work off minimal fines. Adding to this financial crunch, the tribe's first ten-year rehabilitation plan was supposed to begin in 1960, and one provision was to gradually phase out all direct per-capita payments to individuals. It was expected that the Business Committee would eventually manage all communal monies for community programs, including education, recreation, and the administration of tribal business enterprises.[6]

Tribal enterprises were supposed to generate revenue for the tribe and create jobs for members. On recommendation from non-Indian advisors, the Uintah-Ouray Utes planned a monumental tourist and convention center midway between Roosevelt and Fort Duchesne on Highway 40. Called Bottle Hollow Resort (after the ditch where Major Randlett's soldiers had once thrown their liquor bottles after visiting The Strip), it was designed with hexagons and abstract tipis and included a convention center, museum, visitors' center, restaurant, and resort motel with a swimming pool, as well as boating, fishing, and camping facilities at a small reservoir nearby. In addition, the tribe established a cabinetry fabrication plant (UteFab), which supplied much of the furniture for the resort, and invested in a large cattle herd and a tannery. None proved to be long-term successes.[7]

The fate of these Uintah-Ouray and Southern Ute projects reflected similar disasters among other tribes who had also been advised to focus on tourism. The national closure rate for these new Indian enterprises was at least 25 percent in the 1960s. Bottle Hollow Resort, for example, had been built just as gas prices rose and tourism nosedived. The tribe's cattle enterprise foundered because Americans wanted grain-fed beef, not range-fed, nor did the tribe have a cost-effective means of shipping their cattle to market without a railroad. Poorly planned and ill-advised, Uintah-Ouray enterprises would languish in the red for years to come.[8]

Fractious Politics

Tribal politics on the Uintah and Ouray Reservation had been stormy since the 1880s, when the two resentful Colorado bands had been relocated into Utah. Politics became even more contentious after tribal reorganization in 1937. Controversies raged over management of tribal money, tribal services, and intergovernmental relations. The role of a chief had always been to ensure the prosperity of the people, and members expected their elected officials to do the same. They just differed—often sharply—on exactly what the political circumstances were, what power the Business Committee had, and how members should benefit. Often members assumed the Business Committee had greater powers under sovereign rule than they actually had, and members raged when leaders agreed to settlements that were less than members felt they were entitled to. Strong personalities and volatile emotions marked frequent power struggles between individuals and factions (often delineated by band membership). For the Uintah-Ouray Utes, the conflict usually centered on three political issues: who should run tribal affairs, how tribal affairs should be run, and how tribal money should be allocated.

Elections were often contested, and members circulated recall petitions against Committee members they didn't like or didn't agree with, and courts had the power to invalidate elections if they disliked the results. Sometimes new Committee members scuttled carefully developed financial or governmental agreements, while veteran committee members were accused of obstructionism when they tried to block such actions. Journalists began to refer to Ute politics as a "dirty game," while the politically active Ute leader Stewart Pike called them "Ute politics as usual."[9]

The competition for power was especially rancorous during the 1990s, when incumbent leaders were again accused of mishandling tribal funds and contributing to tribal poverty and unemployment (which in 1989 was 85 percent). At question was the control of the Central Utah Project (CUP) water and its monetary settlement. Angry members elected dissidents who promised to "call the shots" and "shake things up" as they asserted tribal power and challenged state and local governments. Their subsequent aggressive stance was a major factor in escalating tensions during a twenty-five-year battle over legal jurisdiction in the Uintah Basin. Not surprisingly, the new Ute administration, despite carrying out their election promises, became the new targets, accused of misusing tribal resources and power by squandering water settlement funds, decimating deer herds, developing questionable enterprises, and giving away the tribe's sovereign rights during a raging jurisdictional dispute.[10]

During this decade's highly emotional and heavily contested elections, opposing factions launched charges and countercharges against each other, while members accused officials of rigging elections or preempting the powers of the tribal court. Officials lodged criminal charges against committee members who opposed them, and tribal employees were dismissed or threatened with dismissal if they did not support reigning powers. For example, rumors accused committee member Curtis Cesspooch of junketing at tribal expense (although he argued he repaid the expenses). Feelings especially ran high against Committee chair Stewart Pike, who was accused of being "inefficient," "heavy-handed," a "manipulator," and a "bullheaded" tyrant trying to "run the reservation—by himself" and build his own empire. Politics became so fractious that one year newly elected members were locked out of the tribal offices

346

and forced to meet in a nearby auditorium; on another occasion dissidents elected an alternative governing council entirely. During one heated election the chief tribal judge swore in new candidates three different times, the tribal appeals court countered the judge, and a series of new elections were ordered, held, and then invalidated in turn. Eventually the brouhaha boiled down to what, exactly, was the constitutional governing authority over elections. When the dust finally settled, the newly constituted committee promptly amended tribal statutes to clarify the tribal power structure.[11]

The Utes had always been an individualistic people. However, by the twentieth century, those who disagreed with a leader's actions could no longer just pick up their outfit, move on, and shift band allegiances. Locked within the legal restrictions of tribal enrollment and controlling tribal governments, the Utes' new recourse was to become politically active and vocal. In this, both women and men excelled, voicing their concerns, their grievances, and their demands. Dissidents ran for office, opposition leaders were often elected, and women served as tribal chairs on all three reservations. In the latter decades, most Northern Utes were politically active in tribal politics, sometimes with as much as an 80 percent voter turnout. Varied, individualistic opinions continued to inform—and stir up—reservation politics, tribal policies, and new intergovernmental relations with local towns, counties, and state governments.

Interracial Relations and the Battle for Jurisdiction

One factor influencing political activity during the 1960s–1990s was the rise in tribal self-determination. With more money, improved education, access to legal expertise, and federally guaranteed sovereignty, tribes developed more political and legal clout. They were also imbued with a sense of entitlement and resentment for old injustices. But as they began to flex their political muscles, non-Indian neighbors responded predictably with anger, resentment, and jealousy over the tribes' enhanced control of resources.

Neighboring non-Indians continued to believe Utes ought to be poor and subservient. For centuries non-Indians had justified the appropriation of native resources on the basis of racial determinism that placed Indians in a lower social order. Few understood that the appropriation of native resources and the political strictures of Indian wardship had forced the Utes into this position of subservient poverty. Instead, the region continued to be an example of a political and social ordering that was the result of racial categorizing. Sociologists have noted that racism and racial prejudice have been used as ideological tools to help structure social relations for the purpose of reorganizing and redistributing resources. Thus, racial or ethnic subjugation is preeminently political as well as economic, and race or ethnicity has typically been used to restrict the political influence of some while enhancing the power of others by controlling who is subordinate. Because racial classifications easily become "common sense" when groups live with it long enough, once a people are "placed" within a social structure, they learn where they fit and everyone accepts it as the norm.[12] When subordinate people begin to question their position, conflict is inevitable. This was the situation in the Uintah Basin where, after many decades of subservience, the Utes began to reassert themselves. Non-Indians throughout the Uintah Basin responded with indignation and anger.

Armed with the tools of new tribal rights and money to fight their legal battles, the Uintah-Ouray Utes now reordered the power and economic relations between themselves and their non-Indian neighbors. During the final decades of the twentieth century, tribes had three major strategies for achieving self-determination: securing protection for the free exercise of religious and cultural rights, obtaining economic control of their land and resources, and gaining legal jurisdiction on reservations or tribal trust land, or "Indian country."[13] The Uintah-Ouray tribe would battle for over twenty-five years to gain the right to police their own people within the original exterior boundaries of their reservation. During this time the Utes and their neighbors learned how inextricably intertwined their economies were, and how important it was for them to learn to work together.

Throughout the 1960s and 1970s, tribal leaders had grown increasingly concerned over the mistreatment of Utes by non-Indian law enforcement officers and local courts. Leaders believed that Utes were being unnecessarily and unfairly harassed and abused by aggressive and racist non-Indian police. Charges included harassment, beatings, and an occasional wrongful death; in one instance, after being arrested for drunk driving, a man died in jail before police realized he was not drunk but only disoriented following a kidney dialysis treatment. In 1973 the tribe drafted its own Law and Order Code and, because the area was a complex checkerboard of Indian and non-Indian land, sought legal jurisdiction over all enrolled members living within the exterior boundaries of the original 1861 reservation—some 4.4 million acres.[14] Little was accomplished, so in 1985 the tribe sued the city of Roosevelt, the counties of Duchesne and Uintah, and the state of Utah, claiming civil and criminal jurisdiction over its members. The case ultimately made its way to the United States Tenth District Court of Appeals where, in 1985, the court determined that the reservation had never been *diminished*, only *opened* to settlement in 1905, and that therefore the exterior boundaries of the original reservation remained intact—along with Ute jurisdiction over it. Since the state of Utah had never been granted criminal jurisdiction over Indians who committed crimes within Indian country, this also meant neither state nor local authorities had jurisdiction over law-breaking Indians within these original boundaries.[15]

The tribe was elated and began to flex its political muscle over issues such as taxation, zoning, and liquor laws. Non-Indian residents of Duchesne and Uintah counties were angry and alarmed. They exchanged acrimonious epithets with the tribe, cried taxation without representation, argued that with sovereign immunity the tribe could enforce their own laws without reference to the U.S. Constitution and with a dual standard of justice, and expressed fears of minority tyranny in "Tehran, Duchesne County." At the same time, a legal loophole (quickly plugged) disallowed tribal courts to try non-Ute Indians. Non-Indian residents and Utes alike feared that the reservation could become a haven for lawless non-Ute Indians. Tension heightened. Roosevelt residents refused to allow Ute families to occupy vacant HUD homes, because residents feared having "lawless" Indians as neighbors against whom they could enforce no city laws. The tribal chair boasted that non-Indians "[hadn't] seen anything, yet," and that the tribe had not yet fully "practiced what we can do with our jurisdictional powers." Meanwhile, the assistant attorney general for Utah, Jan Graham, complained that Indians had become "a law unto themselves" because "state laws don't mean a whole lot to them." Local authorities waited for an appropriate test case to revisit the question of Ute jurisdiction.[16]

That test case came with the arrest and prosecution of Robert P. Hagen, a member of the Little Shell tribe of Chippewa, who lived in Myton, Utah. Hagen was arrested and convicted in tribal court for possession and distribution of a controlled substance (marijuana), but when Hagen was subsequently arrested on the same charge, the tribal court refused to hear the case on grounds that he was not a member of the Uintah-Ouray Ute tribe. So Hagen appeared in a local non-Indian court, where he pled guilty but then withdrew that plea, arguing that the local courts had no jurisdiction over him because he was an Indian living in Indian country. His argument was rejected because he was not a member of a federally recognized tribe (the Little Shell Chippewa had not yet been recognized but would be later), and that Myton was not located within a region defined as Indian country such that federal jurisdiction was exclusive.[17] Hagen appealed, and the state appellate court reversed the verdict. Basing its findings on the Tenth Circuit Court's 1985 decision that returned jurisdiction within the original exterior boundaries to the Ute tribe, it denied both state and local authorities criminal jurisdiction over any Indian who committed crimes within those boundaries.[18]

The decision stunned Basin residents and tied the region into a legal and jurisdictional snarl as non-Indians and the tribe tried to sort out their individual roles and new relationships. The tribe's original intent had been to simply gain criminal jurisdiction over its own members, but the implications of their new and poorly defined jurisdictional powers now raised a multitude of possibilities and questions. Non-Indians feared the tribe would abuse its newfound power, perhaps imposing taxes, closing hunting grounds, or arresting non-Indians with impunity; on the other side, the historically oppressed tribe gloated that non-Indians would "now know how our forebears felt when the Europeans came," and that the judicial shoe was now "on the other foot." As a result, the first meetings between the tribe and local officials were filled with bitter exchanges.[19]

Local police authorities, the tribe, and the BIA police attempted to negotiate a system of cross-deputization that would allow both Indian and non-Indian law enforcement officers to arrest offenders and remand nonmembers into state and local courts and Utes into tribal (misdemeanor) or federal courts (criminal). It would have been the first time the BIA Indian police ever had the power to do more than hold and detain non-Indian suspects on the fragmented reservation. However, many members of the tribe feared a return of non-Indian police abuse or of being forced into non-Indian courts; as a result, until the year 2000, members blocked every attempt by the Business Committee to ratify any cross-deputization pact, and by 2013 they had withdrawn from the pact, again.[20]

In 1992, another case involving jurisdiction also landed on the bench of the Utah Supreme Court. In 1983 Clinton Perank had pled guilty to the theft of rifles in Myton and was sentenced to prison. But in 1988 Perank appealed his case because the incident had occurred within the exterior boundaries of the Uintah and Ouray Ute Reservation and he was a Ute Indian. Perank based his claim on the fact that although he was not yet enrolled in the tribe, his father was a full-blood and his mother a mixed-blood, making him eligible for enrollment (he was enrolled later). Because he was not enrolled at the time of the crime, he was not, by tribal definition, a Ute. However, he did fit the federal definition of an Indian; *United States v. Rogers* (1846) had determined an Indian was any person who had "a significant degree of Indian blood and is recognized as an Indian by a tribe or society of Indians or by the United States government."[21]

After taking the case under advisement for four years, the Utah Supreme Court forced the issue of jurisdiction into the U.S. Supreme Court by ignoring the rulings of the Utah and federal courts of appeal and denying Perank's appeal. On the same day they revisited—and reinstated—Hagen's conviction. The Utah Supreme Court based their findings on a 1984 Supreme Court decision involving legal jurisdiction in Indian country (*Solem v. Bartlett*), arguing that because the original reservation had been specifically diminished in 1905, the exterior boundaries no longer existed, and local officers *did* have jurisdiction over law-breaking Indians off Indian trust land.[22]

Although chastised for its "opportunistic misuse" of the Perank case, Utah was able to force the issue into the U.S. Supreme Court and return several million acres of land and some towns back into public domain. Local officials hailed the state court's decision for simplifying the jurisdictional dispute and giving them a "second shot" at recovering control of the region. But almost immediately Judge Bruce Jenkins of the federal district court issued a temporary injunction on revoking Ute jurisdiction until the U.S. Supreme Court resolved the debate, and things remained in an uneasy status quo.[23]

When the U.S. Supreme Court finally rendered its decision in 1994, it agreed with Utah that both congressional and presidential intention had been to diminish the reservation; therefore, Myton was not in Indian country, and local officials had properly exercised criminal jurisdiction over Robert Hagen and Clinton Perank. Both the original language of the 1902 act to allot the Uintah reservation as well as a presidential proclamation opening the land for homesteading clearly stated that the unsold and unclaimed land should "be restored to the public domain." Tribal attorneys argued that the restoration language had been removed in the 1905 act that actually opened the reservation, but the court ruled that the "baseline intent to diminish" statement in the original 1902 act had never changed and had been retained in President Roosevelt's proclamation to open the reservation, and that contemporaneous understanding in 1905 had been that the reservation would be diminished.[24]

Among other evidence the court cited was James McLaughlin's explanation to Uintah-Ouray chiefs in 1903 that the "nails" that held down the exterior boundary were going to be "pulled up" by Congress, and that after 1904 there would "be no outside boundary line to this reservation." Within practical knowledge, the court argued, this diminishment had been accepted, because the population on opened land was 85 percent non-Indian, with the city of

Roosevelt at 93 percent, while tribal offices existed specifically on Ute trust land.[25] Jurisdiction was returned to local and state authorities except on Ute trust land; Roosevelt, though surrounded by Indian land, was specifically withdrawn from Ute jurisdiction and determined not to be Indian country. An immediate result was that Roosevelt officials attempted to reassert jurisdiction over Indians in Roosevelt. Ironically, the first Indian arrested following the Supreme Court decision was Robert Hagen, who pled guilty to drunk driving.[26]

But wrangling over jurisdiction continued and grew even more rancorous. The tribe threatened to retaliate, and bomb threats were made against the tribe and BIA. After the tribe curtailed hunting access across trust land, officials expressed fears that blood would flow.[27] Confusion and gaps in jurisdiction had law enforcement agencies and courts fuming and often left both in a frustrating legal limbo. The problem was exacerbated by the reluctance of Judge Jenkins to remove the temporary injunction that mandated the status quo of the Tenth Circuit Court's jurisdictional decision of 1985. Roosevelt police remained powerless, for example, to investigate an alleged sex crime involving a tribal member within city limits, while minor acts of violence by non-Ute Indians on tribal land went unprosecuted. In one incident a non-Ute Indian assaulted a BIA secretary, but tribal courts declined to prosecute because at the time they lacked jurisdiction over nonmembers, and the county also declined because they had no jurisdiction over Indians in Indian country.[28]

Salt Lake City journalists cynically referred to the ongoing wrangling as a game of "who's-in-charge-now." The tribe and local officials haggled over the definition of what was or was not Indian land. Non-Indians argued that anything not specifically Indian trust land was not Indian country, while the tribe continued to contend that any area within the original boundaries was Indian country except where specifically homesteaded or organized as town sites in 1902 and 1905. Meanwhile, Judge Jenkins refused to withdraw his injunction against civil or criminal jurisdiction by non-Indians over Indians within the old exterior boundaries, until the Tenth Circuit Court of Appeals determined the legal definition of Indian country. The legal hiatuses remained, especially in Roosevelt.[29]

Roosevelt business owners also complained about the tax-exempt status of Ute shoppers and worried about the considerable loss in tax revenue. Then, following the *Hagen v. Utah* decision in 1994, Roosevelt attempted to collect sales tax because the town was no longer part of the reservation.[30] But Judge Jenkins ruled that until the Tenth District Court made a final determination on the definition of Indian country, the Utes remained exempt from sales taxes in the reservation towns of Myton and Roosevelt—and the tribe continued to have legal jurisdiction over misdemeanor crimes committed by members off trust land.[31]

In 1997 the Tenth District Court finally ruled that the original boundaries had *not* been disestablished by the Supreme Court decision. This returned to the tribe all civil and criminal jurisdiction over Utes or other federally recognized Indians within the original exterior boundaries of the reservation— except in areas homesteaded or incorporated into town sites between 1902 and 1905. The two counties immediately appealed to the U.S. Supreme Court (the state refusing to become involved), the Supreme Court refused to revisit the boundary dispute, and Roosevelt remained a non-Indian doughnut hole in the midst of Indian country.[32]

Because the decision did not resolve the issues, the battle grew even more acrimonious. The tribe and the state signed agreements to no longer litigate over exterior boundaries, but attempts at negotiating friendly agreements between non-Indian officials and the Uintah-Ouray tribe were unsuccessful. Non-Indians continued to fear tribal power over non-Indians in Indian country, and Roosevelt demanded its right to collect sales tax and prosecute Indians who committed misdemeanors within city limits. The tribe offered to stipulate it would not impose governmental authority over non-Indians (i.e., taxes, zoning regulations, or hunting/fishing), on condition the county or state never again litigate the exterior boundaries. The tribe also reminded city officials that because Roosevelt was within the reservation's original exterior boundaries, it remained within Indian country, where Indians were tax-exempt.[33] But Roosevelt aggressively fought back, and in September 1997 officials finally convinced Judge Jenkins to lift his five-year injunction against Roosevelt exercising jurisdiction over Indians within the city limits. Jenkins would also lift it from the remainder of Uintah and Duchesne counties a year later. At the same time, however, he reaffirmed that Indians were sales-tax–exempt in Indian country.[34]

Roosevelt immediately began to prosecute Indians who committed crimes within city limits (e.g., theft or drunkenness), and in retaliation the tribe urged its members to boycott the town. The tribe also threatened to cut off access through Ute trust land to government-owned buildings or power lines and denied access to Sprouse Wells, an important future water source for Roosevelt.[35] But the city remained obdurate, persisting in exercising its right to arrest and prosecute law-breaking Indians within city limits. City officials feared the legal impotency of remanding lawbreakers into a tribal court, where they were likely to receive light penalties because of prejudice, nepotism, or a differing

353

law-and-order code. Business owners who did go to tribal courts complained that they received no justice or compensation because the courts were prejudiced against them.[36] But the tribe was determined to retain jurisdiction over its members, and the boycott remained. Retail sales dropped by 7 percent and local businesses suffered, especially those that had previously held contracts with the tribe. Hundreds of thousands of dollars in tribal purchases for vehicles, fertilizer, fuel, or propane now went to border-town Vernal. Squeezed, Roosevelt cried extortion, but remained unyielding.[37]

Finally, after thirteen months and numerous stormy city meetings, the city capitulated. In fall 1998 they agreed to negotiate jurisdiction with the tribe: because Roosevelt remained outside Indian country, it would retain the right to arrest and detain, but officials agreed to let Indians choose whether to be tried in local or tribal courts. The tribe agreed to lift their boycott and cooperate with Roosevelt over taxation, to not tax or regulate non-Indians living within "Indian Country," and to cooperate in developing Sprouse Wells.[38] Officials also resolved the thorny tax issue. Tribal members had remained tax-exempt for fourteen years if they made purchases anywhere within the boundaries of the original reservation. With the new agreement, they remained tax-exempt only if they purchased goods on or had them delivered to addresses on tribal trust lands.

The twenty-five-year dispute had cost the state and counties $1.8 million in legal costs and an unknown amount in lost revenue.[39] What both sides learned, however, was that their economies were intertwined and they needed to work together.

Throughout this same period, the Uintah-Ouray tribe's government and economy had expanded. The tribe haggled with the state over hunting and fishing rights off trust land but within exterior boundaries, ultimately issuing its own permits and initiating a new fish and game management program for the tribe. It battled over rights-of-way across Indian land and exercised sovereignty by occasionally closing bridges and roads. The tribe also questioned zoning laws and threatened to close all liquor distribution within exterior boundaries, including the state-controlled liquor stores.[40] Alcoholism had again become a serious problem on all three Ute reservations after the ban against selling alcohol to Indians was lifted in the 1950s. But following a local drug bust in 1992, the Uintah-Ouray tribe considered shutting down alcohol sales as well. The two counties protested, and journalists described tribal leaders "grin[ning] at the effectiveness of their bluff."[41] The Utes and neighbors may have agreed to a truce over jurisdiction, but political maneuvering continued.

354

POLITICS AND ECONOMIC DEVELOPMENT, 1980–2005

The ill-conceived business enterprises of the 1960s and 1970s had left the tribe in poor financial condition, and its members remained mired in poverty. But the tribe would soon receive a new source of income from valuable water rights in the Uintah Basin.

Uintah-Ouray Water Rights Settlement

The question of tribal water rights grew out of the competition in the West for Colorado River water. By the early twentieth century, the seven states that used water from the Colorado River and its tributaries foresaw serious wrangling over water rights if an agreement over equitable distribution could not be hammered out. By 1928 most of the states that used Colorado River water had signed onto the Colorado River Compact as a way to protect the future interests of upriver users against thirsty southern California. By 1949, upriver states had also developed plans for storage and delivery systems for their share of the water: the Upper Colorado River Basin Project. As part of this project, Utah organized the Central Utah Water Conservancy District, and Congress authorized the Central Utah Project (CUP) to help develop Utah's 23 percent share. For one part of the plan, the Bonneville Unit, leaders envisioned building dams and diverting water from the Uintah Basin to the heavily populated and industrialized Wasatch Front. Like the earlier Strawberry River Project (1906–1922), this was to be accomplished using a series of dams and tunnels. To compensate the Utes for this water, officials planned to place several water storage dams on the reservation as well.[42]

In 1965 Utah negotiated with the Uintah-Ouray tribe to allow the CUP to divert 60,000 acre-feet of water to the Wasatch Front in exchange for these future water projects, and by 1989 the Central Utah Water Conservancy District began to divert water to Utah's metropolitan areas. But the CUP bogged down as funding dwindled during the Vietnam War and as the country grew disenchanted with big water projects. Environmentalists began to protest and some claimed dam sites were unstable. At one point President Jimmy Carter placed the projects on his personal hit list, but under intense political pressure he restored them. Afraid of losing their water projects, CUP proponents quickly linked their needs to that of the Utes' treated water rights in order to press their case for the water storage and delivery systems. In so doing they "wrapped their project in an Indian blanket"—a phrase coined by antagonists of a similar fight going on in southern Colorado—a reference to the fact that so-called Indian law tacticians often used tribal water rights to gain ultimate access to Indian water rights for non-Indians. Regardless, reserved water rights were also, as legal authorities have noted, "the most potent force at the command of western tribes in their attempt to protect their lives, resources, and society."[43] Congress eventually reauthorized the CUP in 1992; by 1995 the Jordanelle Dam north of Heber City had been completed, along with several smaller dams within the Uintah Basin, including one on Ute trust land (though some disgruntled Ute and mixed-blood residents referred to the projects as "stealing Ute water" for Wasatch Front residents).[44]

But negotiations with the Uintah-Ouray tribe over CUP water foundered over jurisdiction issues, control of the water, and the amount of money the tribe should be paid for it. Based on the Winters Doctrine (*Winters v. United States*, 1908), tribes could claim prior independent water rights based not on "first use," but on the date their reservation was established, which for the Uintah-Ouray Utes was 1861. Unable to complete all of the promised Ute water projects in 1965, and recognizing that Indian water rights had to be met to avoid legal and political entanglements like those being fought by the Southern and Ute Mountain Utes, in 1989 Utah congressmen proposed the government simply pay the tribe for their water rights. Congressman Wayne Owens recommended the tribe be given $754 million to settle state and federal obligations for water diverted for non-Indian use. This was pared down to $614 million, and then to $514 million. A tribal referendum approved the agreement, and tribal officers signed a pact with Governor Norman H. Bangerter in which the state also guaranteed the tribe 498,000 acre-feet of water and certified Ute jurisdiction over their existing water rights within the limits of current Utah water law.[45]

But tribal politics flared as dissident candidates threatened to deep-six the compact—a campaign promise they promptly kept. Citing the Winters Doctrine, the newly elected dissidents argued that subjecting themselves to Utah's water law eroded self-determination and sovereignty. Within months the tribe threatened to withhold CUP water if they were not paid an immediate $100 million plus the right to lease out future water shares to downstream users at fair market value.[46] In 1991 Congress approved a new settlement with the Uintah-Ouray—now calling themselves Northern Utes—including annual payments, development money, and water storage projects, but the Business Committee was no more ready to accept this settlement than the 1989 one. They continued to demand the right to exercise jurisdiction and control of the water even after it left the reservation, as well as independent marketing rights for downstream users. However, the state continued to insist the tribe should be treated the same as any other water user.[47]

When Congress reauthorized the CUP in October 1992, they included a section that detailed how cash payments would be disbursed to reimburse the tribe for the government's default on the 1965 Deferral Agreement. For the first fifty years the tribe would receive $1.94 million a year for water already being diverted for industrial and municipal use; thereafter, they would be paid a percentage of fair market value for 35,500 acre-feet of water annually. The tribe would also receive $45 million in three installments for farm-related projects, including development of a farm/feedlot and reduction of the tribe's obligations on the old Ute Indian Irrigation Project. Money from this fund would also be available for individuals to upgrade personal farms. In addition, $28.5 million was authorized for specific projects for water storage and stream and habitat improvement. But like the 1950s land-claims money, the award came with strings attached. None of it could be distributed on a per-capita basis, and none of the $125 million earmarked for tribal economic development could be disbursed until the tribe produced a Tribal Development Plan, certified by an independent financial consultant. The strings also included a waiver of claims: once the money was distributed, the tribe could no longer claim or litigate over abandoned water projects like the Whiterocks or Taskeetch dams, which had been proposed for agriculturally marginal lands anyway. It was a total settlement of $295.5 million over fifty years, with $198.5 to be paid by 2005. By October 1993, the first of the "Bonneville Credits" had been deposited in the Northern Ute account.[48]

But the tribe protested. Most members were unhappy that they had not received the $514 million originally proposed, believing they had been "cheated" out of the $200 million difference and would have their sovereignty curtailed by yielding control and waiving litigation rights. The agreement became a heated political issue during subsequent tribal elections, and tribal leaders stubbornly refused to touch the settlement money lest they tacitly ratify the agreement and be accused by members of selling out the tribe. They held out for two and a half years until, desperate for money, leaders finally called a last-minute referendum where a minority of members (20 percent) ratified the compact so the tribe could start spending the water money.[49]

Still the controversy continued. As the state moved ahead on the Uintah Basin Replacement Project, tribal opposition to reservation projects snarled planning. Specifically under attack were the Upalco and Uintah units, two water storage projects on Ute land that would store water, provide recreation,

357

and beautify the environment. The projects allocated 22,000 acre-feet to the tribe for irrigation, 17,000 to non-Indian irrigators, and 3,000 to Roosevelt for municipal water. But the tribe began to question the projects, and environmentalists stepped up their opposition to damming Yellowstone Creek (Upalco) and the Uinta River, wanting to protect the last free-flowing stream on the south slope of the Uintas and four endangered fish species in the lower Duchesne: the humpback chub, bonytail chub, razorback sucker, and the Colorado pikeminnow.[50]

Still, plans appeared to be progressing until, in a surprise move, the tribe pulled the plug on the Uintah Basin projects. Tribal chair Ron Wopsock arrived at a June 1998 meeting with state and local officials and read a prepared speech in which he stated that neither project any longer provided the tribe with enough benefits to justify building them on the reservation, and that both were "untenable from the tribe's perspective." Then, without another word, he walked out. The planners were speechless since tribal leaders had, at one time, only agreed to support the projects if they were constructed *on* trust land. The tribe's opposition effectively scuttled plans to build either unit.[51]

The major bone of contention remained control of the water: secondary users (mostly non-Indian farmers) wanted water to irrigate their crops while the Utes wanted enough water stored to attract summer recreation. "It doesn't make sense for me to build a pond on your property," Wopsock argued, "if it doesn't benefit you."[52] Secondary users and the state contended that the tribe's 1861 water rights gave the Utes only "natural flow rights," but the tribe—supported by the federal government—responded that their water rights included storage. Blocked, planners had to search for alternative sites for water storage and delivery.[53]

Doing Business on the Reservation

Once tapped into the water settlement money, the Business Committee began using it to fund new economic and social projects. Thanks to previously unsuccessful business enterprises and their dependence on a boom-bust energy market, the Northern Utes had become financially pinched, and reservation poverty was rampant. Seventy percent of members had low or very low incomes; the median income for Northern Utes in 1999 was $14,500, which was higher than the $10,264 for Utah Indians in general, but lower than the average income in Utah of $18,185. The tribe also had a 50 to 77 percent unemployment rate. Federal and tribal government was still the major source of employment for those who did work, since jobs remained scarce in rural

Duchesne and Uintah Counties, and racial prejudice and discrimination had heightened during the jurisdiction feud.[54]

The financial downswing in oil and gas prices during the 1980s had significantly lowered tribal revenues, because 90 percent of tribal income came from oil leases. Indeed, the extractive industries remained an important source of income in all of Utah. By the late 1990s, the state was averaging $32.7 million per year for gas and oil lease income and ranked fifth in the nation for such revenue (Colorado ranked fourth). In Utah, the majority of this income came from the Uintah and Ouray regions.[55]

As the tribe began to search for new sources of income in the 1990s, one proposal was to impose a severance tax for oil and gas extracted from Indian trust land. This was well within their rights because the Supreme Court had found that "taxing power is an inherent attribute of tribal sovereignty." Taxes were part of a tribe's power to govern and pay costs of self-government, whether or not they also received rents or royalties for their gas and oil. However, Utah already imposed a severance tax on energy companies, and opponents feared this double taxation would kill the Uintah Basin's energy business. Regardless, the tribe sued Utah, arguing that *Merrion v. Jicarilla Apache Tribe* (1982) gave tribes the right to impose taxes, and that if gas and oil was taken from their reservation, the tribe should get the revenue. However, another Supreme Court decision in 1989 had also confirmed the right of states to tax energy production by non-Indians on Indian land (*Cotton v. New Mexico*). Because energy taxes constituted 20 percent of Utah's tax revenue, Utah was not willing to yield this income to the tribe, and the courts sided with the state.[56]

The tribe lost their case but decided to impose their own 4–10 percent sliding-scale tax anyway. But as opponents had predicted, the tribal tax boomeranged. Instead of raising revenue, energy companies closed operations and shifted off the reservation. A similar proposition to impose activity fees on non-Indians doing business on trust land became an equally controversial idea.[57]

Gas and oil companies grew reluctant to invest on the reservation because of the extra costs (tribal taxes), the slow processing time of permits (lack of personnel), and the high cost of drilling in a region with relatively low production. Operations in the Basin typically produced only 25 to 1400 barrels of oil per day, compared to oil-rich Kuwait, where operations were shut down if they produced fewer than 8,000 barrels per day.[58] Corporate investors also worried about the risk of long-term investments in an environment where "unstable" tribal government appeared to change policies at will and could

17.2. Ute Mini-mall near Fort Duchesne, Uintah and Ouray Reservation, 2007 (Photo: S. Jones)

claim "sovereign immunity" against suits for defaulted loans. As oil companies abandoned the Basin even as the cyclical price of oil continued to drop, so did tribal revenue. By 1994 the tribal budget was $1.6 million short of its expected oil and gas income, and leaders were forced to scramble to find ways to cut the budget without cutting salaries or jobs. It was at this juncture that desperate tribal leaders turned to the untouched water settlement money.[59]

Now the tribe began planning new business enterprises. Again, not all were successful. An attempt to develop a new manufacturing plant failed to pan out, and the Ute Indian Machine and Manufacturing Company closed in 1993 after defense budget cuts curtailed government contracts on which it depended. The tribe sold off the machining equipment four years later to cut its losses and reduce a loan it had taken from the BIA in an unsuccessful attempt to revive the ailing enterprise.[60] However, other enterprises were more successful.

Tribal leaders commissioned feasibility studies; hired or received grants for mentors in business, technology, and finance to help train personnel and offer guidance; and made plans to diversify their initiatives. Ute Tribal Enterprises (UTE) included projects to revitalize Bottle Hollow Resort, develop a cultural center, refill Bottle Hollow Reservoir, build tourist cabins near Stillwater Dam, develop big and small game hunting operations, build water-bottling facilities for natural spring water near Whiterocks, expand their cattle enter-prise, develop a feedlot and processing plant, and move Ute Petroleum—a tribally owned gas station—and its convenience store to a small mini-mall on Highway 40 near Fort Duchesne, where it would join an Associated Food franchised grocery store and a bank branch.[61] Many of the enterprises were linked, with the grocery store selling the tribe's own bottled water, ice, and less-expensive feedlot beef. The tribe also opened a bowling alley, offered guided tours of archaeologically rich Nine Mile Canyon, worked to develop a water delivery system on the west side of Uintah County, and started a garbage dis-posal company.[62]

The tribe also explored exchanging or selling elk. Herds had proliferated on the south slopes of the Uintas, crowding out deer and sometimes grazing in farmers' fields. After the state botched the roundup and removal of elk near Tridell in 1993, the tribe learned of the demand for live elk by elk breeders. Elk ranching was a growing industry, with a significant number of elk ranchers thriving in nearby Colorado where they raised elk for meat, breeding, and especially for elk antler velvet. During the 1990s, domestic pregnant cows were selling for $7,000–$10,000, breeding bulls for $8,000–$50,000, and elk breed-ers too could make as much as $300–$1,500 per animal, per year for the velvet, which was in high demand in the Asian holistic medicine market.[63]

In 1997 a Colorado elk rancher from Lone Cone Ranch approached the tribe, hoping to improve his herd by infusing a new gene pool. Having heard the tribe was having a problem with elk overpopulation, he offered $3,000 per live pregnant cow and $2,000 for calves and heifer cows. He set up holding facilities and handled inoculations for tuberculosis and stress, overseeing the required ninety-day quarantine. In turn, the tribe used a commercial helicop-ter firm to round up an initial 110 elk.[64]

All went well, and the rancher contracted with the tribe for another 280 elk the following year. Seeing potential for their own operations, the tribe requested the use of his facility to round up and hold additional elk to trade elsewhere for bison and other native game like wild turkeys, Rocky Mountain bighorn sheep, and antelope. The tribe was hoping to revive traditional Indian game animals, in part to develop a nutritious food source to help combat the obesity and diabetes epidemic that now plagued its members.[65]

However, rumors began to spread that the tribe was mishandling the round-ups. Exaggerated stories claimed "incompetents" were killing or crippling elk, that there were mass elk graves on Ute land, and that the tribe was trapping elk off-reservation. The tribe was accused of planning to sell thousands of elk to out-of-state brokers, and hunters complained the roundups so traumatized the remaining elk, their hindquarters were inedible. Additionally, because the state had signed a memorandum of agreement with the tribe in 1996 over hunting and fishing, the tribe was allowed to issue its own trust-land hunting permits. Now, with elk herds further depleted due to mass roundups, the Department of Wildlife Resources (DWR) withdrew all public hunting permits. This initiated a new flood of complaints from non-Indian hunters. Although the DWR publicly sympathized with the hunters, Governor Mike Leavitt insisted tribal sovereignty would be respected.[66]

Most of the rumors were unfounded, and the tribe and the helicopter company tried to counter the wilder stories. However, evidence suggests that some of the roundups were mishandled.[67] Worsening the situation was the lack of transparency in tribal affairs, and many non-Indians believed the air of secrecy suggested a coverup. The roundups ended within a few years, but Basin relationships remained roiled.

The tribe also attempted to lure big business back to the reservation, including new large-scale oil and gas leases as well as high-tech jobs.[68] In 1989 Bonneville Pacific Corporation signed an agreement to build a power-plant and greenhouse near Roosevelt, and in 1999 the tribe participated in the U.S. Department of Agriculture's Project BRAVO (Building Rural America with Venture Opportunities) and Utah's Smart Site program for developing technology-based businesses. In conjunction with this, the tribe signed an agreement with the Oracle software company for fiber optic cable to be installed in Fort Duchesne for developing jobs in internet and e-commerce. Both high school students and community members had access to technology education. Facilitated with mentoring from Affiliated Computer Services (ACS), the tribe opened the Uinta River Technology Company. Working with Oracle and ACS, the Fort Duchesne facility utilized more than two dozen networked computers and at least that many Ute employees to fulfill outsourcing contracts for data entry, forms processing, and data conversion and archiving. With the advantage of being a wholly minority-owned business with federal preference, Uinta River Technology garnered large contracts with the Illinois Department of Motor Vehicle Registration, Hill Air Force Base in Ogden (Utah), the Department of Immigration and Naturalization Service, and the BIA. At the same time, the website northernute.com provided an e-commerce routing site for online shoppers.[69]

In 2000, the tribe successfully negotiated the return of subsurface rights to the Naval Oil Shale Reserve No. 2, an 84,000-acre section of the Hill Creek

17.3. Tribal Enterprise Building, Ute Tribe of the Uintah and Ouray Reservation (Photo: S. Jones 2007)

Extension. Withdrawn from the Ouray Reservation in 1916 as a potential source of fuel for the Navy's oil-burning ships during World War I, the area was declared surplus in the 1990s, allowing the tribe to file a claim on it. With over two hundred oil and gas wells already drilled, it was a significant source of potential revenue. However, there was a catch. It included a 10.5-million-ton dump of uranium tailings near the Colorado River, left there after the 1956–1984 uranium boom. Water seeping through it was contaminating the river and angering downriver Californians. As part of the land-return deal, the tribe agreed to dedicate a percentage of their royalties to help pay for the $300 million cleanup. They did have some help from the federal government. Where the state and federal government had originally split the oil and gas royalties 50/50, now the federal government gave its royalties to the Utes and agreed to pay cleanup costs for the 56 percent share of the region's uranium that it had used. However, the cleanup itself was controversial; several plans were considered, including capping the radioactive tailings onsite or transporting them to different locations. A publicized plan to slurry the tailings through eighty-three miles of pipeline to a site only three miles away from the White Mesa Ute community in southeastern Utah (formerly the Allen Canyon Utes) met with strong resistance from the Ute Mountain Ute tribe; White Mesa had already fought a decades-long battle against the storage of radioactive waste near their small community.[70]

With subsurface rights in hand, the Northern Utes made plans to take an active part in the exploration and drilling for more gas and oil in the 83,000 acres, which held an estimated 17.5 billion cubic feet of natural gas, worth as much as $60 million. They developed a joint partnership with the Southern Ute's Red Willow Production Company and Contango Oil and Gas, and they signed a 50 percent exploration and development agreement with Dominion Exploration and Production, one of the country's largest energy producers.[71]

A new potential source of revenue appeared in 1988 with the passage of the Indian Gaming Regulatory Act (IGRA) and the expansion of gaming on Colorado reservations. The Northern Utes began to look into building their own casino on or near their reservation. However, under IGRA, Indians could only build gaming establishments in a state if that state had legalized gambling. Utah did not. But in 1991 Utah, one of only three states that did not allow gambling, voted on whether to allow pari-mutuel betting on horse-races in the state. If the measure passed, it would legalize gambling in Utah and open the door to Indian gaming. However, the bill did not pass, in large part because of the threat that Indians—especially the Northern Utes—might develop casinos on their reservation (which they would have).[72] The Northern Utes were left with only their low-stakes bingo at Bottle Hollow Inn (technically illegal, but to which the state turned a blind eye), and ongoing gambling on traditional games at tribal events. Wagering on hand games or rapid-paced games of Three-card Monte was a significant part of traditional Indian life to which most Utes felt entitled.[73]

With Utah closed to gaming, the tribe proposed building a high-stakes casino in tiny Dinosaur, Colorado, just across the border.[74] When this proposal failed, they offered to buy 18,000 acres near Steamboat Springs, Colorado, for the overt purpose of preserving sacred sites and burial grounds, but also to develop a winter sports area, a summer dude ranch, and grazing land for the tribe's cattle. However, hints of a possible casino and tribal assertion of sovereign rights killed the deal. An attempt in 1996 to acquire 40–80 acres of land in nearby Hayden failed when residents also rejected their offer, fearful that Ute plans to develop a small-stakes casino and resort hotel would pollute Hayden's "conservative and clean identity."[75] Gaming, as a source of income, was once again derailed.

ECONOMIC DEVELOPMENT IN A NEW CENTURY

The new century had arrived with ongoing political quarrels and a dramatic decline in cash flow. Tribal employees were furloughed and the tribe appeared to be on the brink of bankruptcy, again. In 2001 the tribe hired a new non-Indian financial advisor, John Jurrius, an investment banker who unashamedly delighted in making money for himself and his native clients. He boasted his salary was well worth it ($62,500 per month in 2006), because he helped tribes make money. "Do I make a lot of money? Sure. If they win, I make millions." He was, he explained, "an investment banker. I go in and make money and I leave." Fresh from a very successful—if controversial—tenure with the Southern Utes, Jurrius gave new promise to the Northern Utes' struggling finances.[76]

But some members of the tribe did not trust the "smooth-talking Texan," which was not surprising given the tribe's long history of lost wealth and betrayal from con men, well-meaning federal officials, and corrupt agents. Within a short time, charges and countercharges were filed against Jurrius, accusing him of dishonesty and mismanagement. Unfortunately, most members of the tribe were ill-equipped to understand the complexity of high-stakes banking investments and complained they were being kept in the dark. Ronald Wopsock and Luke Duncan, members of the Business Committee, accused Jurrius of raiding tribal funds and filed suit against the BIA for not watching out for the tribe's financial affairs. The Business Committee countered by expelling Wopsock and Duncan from the committee for gross misconduct and carrying their accusations beyond the committee and involving federal influence. Countersuits were filed against the Business Committee as well as federal officials, and the wrangling went on. As usual, elections grew contentious, recall petitions and lawsuits flourished against the new committee chair Maxine Natchees (who backed Jurrius), and members picketed as far away as Salt Lake City.[77]

Among the heated disputes that tore at tribal politics were questions over tribal management of their vast gas and oil reserves. This was especially true during the Persian Gulf War (1990–1991), and again in the years after 9/11 when conflicts in the Middle East pushed the price of oil to record highs. Because Jurrius recognized the value of these resources, his first advice to the tribe in early 2001 was to insist they take over management of their oil reserves rather than passively accept the 1 percent return from leases on their oil wealth. But as the tribe moved to control these resources, federal and state officials complained that tribal fees and restrictions were thwarting investment and driving oil companies out of the area. But as oil prices soared, Utah legislators and profit-minded investors began to again look at the Basin's oil shale and tar sand reserves, and speculators started exploring gas reserves. By 2012 the Basin was experiencing another boom in oil production, supplying 75 percent of all crude oil produced in the state of Utah.[78] A new "black-gold rush" to the Basin brought in thousands; property values soared, housing became scarce, unemployment almost nonexistent, and "man camps" blossomed as energy companies fought to house workers.[79]

As part of Jurrius's plan, the tribe made a detailed inventory of all tribal energy resources—owned or leased, past and present—with maps showing every gas and oil field and lists of all equipment, rights-of-way, and other resources, carefully plotted and computerized. Jurrius then created a new financial plan for the tribe and set up a venture fund for aggressive investments in energy and commercial development. Under his direction, the tribe withdrew $190 million of their water settlement money to be used for long-term investments. It was the maximum allowed, because the remaining money was required by law to remain in trust for agricultural projects, fisheries, and recreation enhancement on the reservation. Using the $190 million, and with Jurrius's advice, the tribe made several investments, including a 51 percent share of an energy development company called Ute Energy. When the energy boom occurred, they were already active partners with other companies drilling on Indian lease land, and they had sixty producing oil wells of their own with plans to drill a hundred more. By 2012, they were producing 7,800 barrels of oil equivalent (BOE) daily, making the tribe one of the largest oil producers in the Uintah Basin, with reserves of at least 38 million BOE and rights to massive deposits of oil shale.[80] That year Ute Energy was sold to an aggressive Canadian energy firm for $784 million cash and the assumption of $77 million of net debt. Investors anticipated that the company's innovative technology would be used in mining Uintah Basin oil shale. By 2016 other international firms were also showing interest, especially for strip mining in the Uintah Basin and northern Colorado—potential deals that had environmentalists up in arms.[81]

Not all tribal investments were in oil, and not all were wildly successful. Nevertheless, the economic well-being of the tribe was turning around. From near bankruptcy in 2002, the tribal worth had grown to over $100 million by 2006. New investments created new tribal jobs, and the tribe's workforce doubled from three hundred to six hundred. Under Jurrius's direction, the tribe developed a generous retirement fund, with proposals to lower retirement age to sixty and raise monthly dividends for all.[82] However, despite swelling coffers, improved finances did not solve tribal problems overnight, and not all investments proved profitable. Some members continued to complain that not enough tribal money was being shared, and others expressed fears that payments would cease if Jurrius left. And controversy swirled around Jurrius. Unhappy over his large salary and sometimes failed investments, members accused him of fraud, mismanagement, and profiteering at tribal expense. In 2008 the controversies peaked. The tribe severed relations with the Jurrius Group, firing and then suing Jurrius, who promptly countersued the tribe. All of the suits were settled within a few months, even as the intrepid consultant was forming a new investment company in Canada, where he partnered with Quantum Energy to establish Native American Resource Partners, LLC (NARP) and continued to advise and copartner energy companies for tribes (U.S.) and First Nations (Canada).[83]

SOCIAL ISSUES AT THE END OF THE CENTURY

All three Ute tribes continued to face social problems as they began the new century. Alcoholism remained a significant issue, and alcohol-related violence still plagued the reservations, from domestic abuse or neglect to several murders linked to its use. In response, in 1997 the Northern Ute tribe proposed building a residential drug and alcohol rehabilitation center in Fort Duchesne.[84]

Meanwhile, mirroring other Native American groups, the suicide rate remained three times—one in six—the national average.[85] Obesity, diabetes, and their complications also ravaged the tribe such that the average lifespan for Utes of forty-seven years was thirty years less than the average Utah resident.

During the second half of the twentieth century, type 2 diabetes had become prevalent among all Native Americans, for whom the "thrifty" survival gene of an earlier era expected feast-and-famine lifestyles accompanied by intensive physical activity. With neither, modern American Indians found themselves prey to poor diet (high in sugar, carbohydrates, and unhealthy fats, and low in fiber) and an inactive lifestyle. Where mountain men of the 1830s had described Utes as seldom corpulent, by the late twentieth century the Utes were experiencing an epidemic of obesity. But with typically low-income households and low educational levels, adjusting to a healthy lifestyle was difficult, especially with an inherent unwillingness to turn to outside influences and a distrust of non-Indian health services. Many refused early detection or blinded themselves with the philosophy that "If you don't know you have it, then you don't have it."[86] But by 2000, Northern Utes had a 53 percent diabetes rate and epidemic levels of obesity with all its complications, including pneumonia, influenza, and cardiovascular disease. Tribal leaders grew understandably concerned and sought outside studies and recommendations for educating members.[87] In 2006 the tribe opened the Painted Horse Diabetes Program, moving into a new building conveniently close to Indian Health Services, and offered exercise equipment and diet and cooking classes.[88]

In 1997 the tribe also signed an agreement to receive support, training, and technical assistance from the state for general social services, especially for women and children, and for help implementing the Indian Child Welfare Act (ICWA). In February 1998, the tribe opened a Ute Family Center, *Tahwe Towuhcheew*, and made plans to develop its own child welfare system and a program to train Ute foster families.[89]

Unfortunately, tribal social service programs on most reservations (including the Utes') were inadequate, with children often abused by both their parents and the system itself. Children were sometimes removed from non-Indian adoptive homes and relocated to reservation homes of less-than-enthusiastic birth relatives. Court judges were typically not trained in child welfare law, and at times courts ignored complaints, refused to prosecute cases, or suppressed evidence. Convicted abusers were sometimes given unsupervised visitation rights, and complainants were threatened to keep quiet lest the tribe be given a bad name.[90]

Questions over adoption were another important issue. ICWA gave tribal officials ultimate jurisdiction over members and had the power to reclaim Indian children placed for adoption with non-Indians. The purpose of ICWA was to stop the significant problem of traffic in Indian children through unregulated adoptions by non-Indian families. Children were, after all, the future of all tribes. Because relaxed abortion laws and birth control meant fewer adoptable white children, more non-Indian childless couples were turning to alternative sources, including Indian infants. But under ICWA, most tribes, including the Utes, chose to restrict adoptions outside culturally based homes. Among the Utes, tribal courts first sought homes within family networks, then within the tribe, and if necessary among other Ute tribes. Occasional fostering of Ute children by non-Indians was allowed but without the option of adoption.[91] Unfortunately, the intentions of the laws were sometimes abused by a few biological parents who reclaimed fostered or adopted children (sometimes after many years of foster care), for the purpose of gaining access to their tribal per capita and federal welfare payments. Tribes also had difficulty finding enough qualified homes for children.[92]

The problem of legally unrecognized Indian marriages was also resolved through the passage of Utah's H.B. 186 in 1996. As Utah courts went after non-Indian polygamous families, the definition of marriage became an issue, and laws were revised to reflect acceptable, if alternative, marriage patterns. Until 1996, couples who had nontraditional marriages "Indian way" (regardless of whether there had been a ceremony) were denied marriage benefits, including Social Security and insurance. But new Utah laws recognized Indian unions if couples obtained a marriage license, had a recognized Indian spiritual advisor perform the marriage, and recorded the marriage with the state. An Indian spiritual advisor was defined as a person who "leads, instructs, or facilitates a Native American religious ceremony or service, or provides religious counseling," and "is recognized as a spiritual advisor by a federally recognized Native American tribe." This included "a sweat lodge leader, medicine person, traditional religious practitioner, or holy man or woman." Marriage laws were similarly revised in Colorado.[93]

Public school education was another arena of conflict with local non-Indians. For decades the relations between the public school system and the tribe had been strained. In the 1920s, Indian agents had mainstreamed Ute students into public schools as a means of assimilation and terminating federal responsibilities. But Basin non-Indians retained a long-standing prejudice against Indians, claiming Indians did not want to progress, were willing to live in squalor, and carried harmful diseases. The Great Depression intensified hostility against publicly educating untaxed Indians, and many residents blamed Indians and their untaxed land base for local economic woes. Children were left standing at bus stops and teachers were openly prejudiced, often barely tolerating Ute children in classrooms ("seen but not heard")—when schools could not find a reason to jettison them entirely. Not surprisingly, Indian students responded sullenly and echoed their own and their parents' resentment against historic and ongoing wrongs.[94]

In the early 1950s, the Whiterocks boarding school was closed and Ute students were enrolled in public schools, straining classrooms and budgets. Appallingly unprepared, lacking academic skills, and simply passed through the system, Ute children languished in failure. Although federal funds for educating Indian students became available later, and despite attempts to open dialogues between the tribe and school districts, the educational environment remained hostile and the schools and their teachers openly discriminatory.[95]

But by the 1970s parents and the tribe grew more assertive. The tribe acquired Johnson-O'Malley funds for Indian education and established their own Head Start and early intervention programs. When in 1972 a number of Ute boys were expelled from a local junior high for wearing long hair (to conservative non-Indians, a symbol of rebellion and the drug culture), the issue ended up in court. A compromise was reached, and the students were allowed to wear their hair long if it was neatly groomed. Despite this success, Utes remained alienated from the educational system. For many, "white education" remained irrelevant: few wanted to abandon tribal identity for educated assimilation, and if they did want to work, the tribe (not local companies) would provide jobs. Not surprisingly, student achievement remained dismal.[96]

Nevertheless, tribal officials continued to battle for adequate education for their youth. When their Head Start program was threatened with probation if they did not correct problems—including deficiencies in curriculum, a high turnover rate of directors, the use of untrained teachers and staff, a lack of parental involvement, and failures in fiscal viability—the tribe implemented vigorous reforms and purchased a professionally developed curriculum.[97]

The University of Utah took an interest in the tribe's educational system as well, providing in-school counselors to help Ute students and directing graduate studies on Ute education. The tribe also sought more direct input into the public schools. Despite the significant population of Indian students, no Indian had ever been a member of the school board, as qualified Ute candidates were passed over when vacancies occurred. Concerned over low achievement scores, high dropout rates, and the failure to provide a relevant curriculum for Ute students, the tribe briefly boycotted the schools in 1997 over non-representation, and they created their own alternative charter school in 1998. Despite some greenhorn mistakes, the school graduated thirteen students in 2000. By 2004, however, the tribe was asking the state to create a government-funded public school district to specifically address the needs of American Indian students in the region.[98] By 2017, Ute children were faring much better; the tribe employed tutors, offered their children incentives for good attendance, and engaged a truancy officer who tracked attendance. Local educators were also willing to integrate diversity into their curriculum, and some schools offered classes in Ute arts and crafts or invited special visitors like Ute spiritual leader Larry Cesspooch and other native representatives to share traditional folklore and history.[99]

For Ute students in higher education, accommodations with various nearby universities helped provide tuition aid for Ute students; the University of Utah

17.4. Head Start building, Ute Tribe of the Uintah and Ouray Reservation (Photo: S. Jones 2007)

uses the name "Utes" with tribal permission and has guaranteed scholarships for Ute tribal members attending the university; Brigham Young University provided multicultural aid; and Colorado Mountain College, located in former Ute homelands, offered in-state tuition rates to Northern Ute students. Other innovative training included Oracle's Internet Academy for instructing youth in technology jobs, and the Ute Conservation Corps, where teens and at-risk youth worked in conservation, wildlife biology, and wilderness preservation.[100]

Meanwhile, a revival in traditionalism raised the issue of culture and language loss. Language and culture had declined dramatically, and the tribe was without a museum or cultural center after the Bottle Hollow enterprise closed and a leaking swimming pool damaged and closed the museum and its archives. Some worried the Northern Utes were becoming a "tribe without a heart." Grandparents, the keepers of tradition, had become segregated as elder programs improved, and more housing broke up extended families who had once lived together. Children spent their time watching television, playing video games, and hanging out with friends, and were less willing to sit down and listen to the old stories. As a result, traditions were no longer being passed on.[101]

However, by 2002 work progressed on developing a new cultural center at Bottle Hollow, reemphasizing tribal traditions and preserving the Ute language. The tribe produced short histories of the tribe and its government in the 1970s as well as short storybook collections of folklore. In 1982 the tribe published Fred Conetah's history of the Northern Utes. By the twenty-first century, Larry Cesspooch had taken his native storytelling on the road, using special props, music, and videos to retell Ute folklore and history through lecture, storytelling, and videos.[102]

372

Language loss was, of course, a major issue. By the end of the twentieth century, fewer than five hundred members spoke Ute fluently, and English had become the communicative norm. Ute was a difficult language to learn because it relied on oral transmission, and while consonants remained stable, vowels often varied by generation and band. Because language is such a powerful transmitter of culture, often holding the key to traditional concepts unexplainable in other languages, losing a language is a significant factor in culture loss. In response, and with the help of linguists, the tribe standardized the orthography and organized a Ute Language Revitalization Project to codify the language, create simple written texts, and provide means to preserve and teach the Ute language.[103]

Housing had also improved dramatically in the 1950s and 1960s with the influx of land-claims money and the help of Housing and Urban Development (HUD) funds; however, by the 1990s these buildings needed to be renovated, replaced, or enlarged. New HUD grants allowed the tribe to build new homes, with the tribe managing additional rental units. Still, as the Ute population increased, need outpaced building, and many families continued to share what housing was available, with some remaining homeless. To address this need, the tribe also began investigating additional creative mortgage options.[104]

As the Utes became increasingly integrated into mainstream America, they acquired new education, foods, dwellings, and dress; however, the Christian religion was a hat most still refused to don. Over the years, various Christian denominations had made sporadic efforts to Christianize Utes. The Mormons had proselyted in the mid-1800s, and Protestantism had arrived with Agent Critchlow in the 1880s. The 1890s saw the arrival of Episcopalian missionaries, and by the early 1900s their church had the only active proselyting in the region. Mormon interest revived briefly but died during the bitter jurisdiction battles. Despite this missionary work, few Northern Utes ever assimilated into mainstream Christianity. In the late 1990s, full-time Native American Episcopalian priests (a Bannock-Shoshone and a Sioux) attempted to revive their church's presence in Randlett and Whiterocks by incorporating elements of traditional religion into their liturgies with some success (e.g., drumming and sweetgrass or sage rather than traditional incense).[105] However, such religious melding was not without controversy and was rejected by Indians and non-Indians alike, who either objected to the theft of traditional religion or the adulteration of Christianity. Most Indians also resisted the appropriation of their ceremonials by New Age religionist or unaffiliated mixed-blood Indians.[106]

As the tribe increasingly assumed responsibility for community affairs and economics—from communal religious events, to childcare, to creating jobs—the tribe became the major focus of Ute life. By the end of the twentieth century, the Business Committee also moved toward helping its members think as a unified *tribe* rather than a confederation of disparate bands. The tribe also assumed an increasingly significant role in Utah affairs as its political clout grew through tribal wealth, corporate control of tribal resources, and insistence on tribal self-determination and political sovereignty. State and local governments could no longer ignore Utes as a marginal ethnic group but had to negotiate with them in the political arena, as Utes demonstrated during the controversies over jurisdiction, management of wildlife, and blocking the construction of CUP dams. And Utes became more involved within state bureaucracies; for example, Forrest Cuch would serve for an extended term as director of the Utah Division of Indian Affairs and was editor of the state's centennial publication, *A History of Utah's American Indians*, with Clifford Duncan writing a chapter on the Northern Utes.[107] With jurisdiction over its own members within the 4.4 million acres of the original Uintah and Ouray Reservations, Northern Utes now claimed the second-largest reservation in the United States.

373

As Northern Utes entered the twenty-first century, they were still struggling with issues of identity and the loss of traditional culture. While often contentious, most of their political and economic activity also served to assert the separateness of tribal identity as distinct from the "others" who neighbored them or who were not as "authentically" Ute. When the Utes fought for jurisdictional rights, it had been a battle waged to assert an Indian identity with Indian rights as opposed to those who were not Indian, or specifically not Ute Indian. The battle tightened and redefined ethnic boundaries, emphasizing the importance of being *Ute*.

Certainly, the jurisdictional issues had been born out of the blatant racism in the Basin that had long defined Indian from non-Indian, reinforcing their subservience within a racially hierarchical social order that left Utes with few rights. But federal legislation changed the power equation, and the jurisdiction controversy forced the courts to not only define Utes as a specific—and privileged—ethnic identity, but also to define them as distinct from other Indians.

Blood quantum would continue to define membership in the Ute tribe, and this racial and genetic identity became crucial, even as traditional religious and cultural forms changed. Because fewer people were speaking Ute, and folkloric wisdom was no longer being passed on, much of the essence of traditional Uteness was no longer being perpetuated, either. Language and folklore, essential for transmitting historical Ute mores and a *Núu-ci* ethos, were mostly left along the wayside as children immersed themselves in American culture by watching television or surfing the Internet. Young people abandoned the Ute language and no longer sought out elders whose traditional grandfather stories carried the older *Núu-ci* values. However, the tribe took on the role of conservator, codifying the Ute language and publishing tribal histories and collections of folktales. It also developed cultural, social, and educational programs for its members and attempted to exercise some control over the education of its youth. All of these activities helped reemphasize one kind of identity as members accepted these markers of a shared physical and emotional ethnicity.

And Northern Utes were assertively proud of their identity as Utes and as Indians. Though by the end of the twentieth century they ate, dressed, worked, played, lived, and politicked like mainstream Americans, they still shared a common history, ethnic identity, and a *sense* of Uteness. Inter-reservation competition refined that distinction as specific kinds of Utes, even as intra-reservation competition bolstered loyalties to Uintah, White River, or Uncompahgre identities. Tribal politics reinforced identity as the Business Committee continued to apportion representation equally between the three unapologetically political groups despite population disparities; in fact, as late as 2017, some Uncompahgres were still trying to spin off a separate political identity. The continuing legal battles with the expelled Uintah mixed-bloods also hardened the boundaries between "real" full-blood Utes and those who claimed to be Ute but whose genetic identity had been diluted through intermarriage.

Despite being entrenched in most aspects of American culture, the Northern Utes—by 2017 identifying themselves as the Ute Indian Tribe of the Uintah and Ouray Reservation—continued to cleave to and remain proud of their historical and racially defined identities as Utes.

Chapter 18

Southern and Ute Mountain Utes
1960 to a New Century

The decades after the southern Ute tribes received their land claims money were roller-coaster years of boom prosperity mixed with personal poverty and tribal bankruptcy. As Congress returned the rights to Utes to manage their own affairs, Ute leaders began rebuilding their tribal economies. In so doing they helped fashion an acculturated American identity for their members as well. However, even as the Utes grew more integrated into America's mainstream culture, they attempted to define their uniqueness as American Indians and as Ute Indians. The final decades between the twentieth and twenty-first centuries especially illustrate their struggle to grasp and master the intricacies of American law, legislation, and economics as tribal leaders jousted with federal lawmakers, local communities, and reservation factions. At the same time, leaders and members worked to find a balance between the demand to assimilate in order to raise their standards of living, a desire to be part of an exciting materialistic world, and a need to conserve an essence of their *Núu-ci* heritage that could anchor the boundaries of their unique ethnic identity.

Southern Utes had a long history of adapting to changing economies. In the eighteenth century it had been horses, European weaponry, commercial hunting, and skilled market trading. By the end of the twentieth century, and with their hands again untied, they were ready to exploit new financial opportunities. These included tapping into the burgeoning commercial tourist industry and the world of lucrative corporate investments. Much of the final story of the southern Ute bands can be told in terms of their battles within courtrooms and the halls of Congress as well as their developing ability to incorporate a new business acumen to exploit the economic advantages of being Native American.

POLITICS AND ECONOMIC DEVELOPMENT: 1950–2000

As had happened among the Northern Utes, the sudden influx of money from the land-claims settlement in the 1950s brought a fleeting prosperity as well as new problems for the Southern, Ute Mountain, and Allen Canyon Utes.

Politics and Interethnic Relations

As the Utes stepped from the shadows, friction with local communities increased. Some non-Indian businesses took advantage of local Utes with too much money and too little experience with financial management. Other communities tried to keep Indians out of town by targeting them for arrest and imposing heavy fines for any legal infractions. When the government legalized the use of alcohol by Indians in 1953, the problems only worsened due to the rapid upswing in alcohol-related problems. Non-Indians exploited the new market, and complaints about "drunken Indians" increased; residents of Cortez, for example, claimed they had no problems with Indians until after alcohol arrived.[1]

Meanwhile, relations with the BIA grew strained. During the 1940s and early 1950s, Southern Ute chair Julius Cloud was openly critical of government interference in tribal affairs, and the council argued with the dictatorial superintendent, Elbert J. Floyd; as a result, the council found themselves sitting on packing crates in the basement of the Consolidated Ute Agency for its tribal council meetings. After 1954, Robert L. Bennett replaced Floyd and the situation improved. Bennett was a college-educated Oneida who, as a planner for the BIA, had been intimately involved in the Utah termination issues, later serving as commissioner of Indian Affairs. As the Ute's agent, Bennett was less paternalistic and more cooperative. The Southern Ute council moved from the basement to a room next to the superintendent's office and eventually into offices in the agency's old hospital, which became the Tribal Affairs Building.[2] However, although Ute relations with the BIA became more amicable, Utes increased their verbal attacks against the BIA, and relations grew stormier again as the tribal council's confidence and assertiveness grew. Southern Ute leaders had not been afraid to challenge the government, suing for land claims in 1896; sending delegations to Washington in 1925, 1926, and 1938; and confederating with other Utes to sue for land claims again. As better-educated and well-traveled individuals began stepping into leadership roles, tribal assertiveness continued to increase. At the same time, internal conflicts escalated, in particular between traditionalist and modernist political rivals.[3]

This became a political and social contest between two very different perspectives. On the one hand the modernists in the tribe believed that in order to become sovereign, self-reliant, and fully functioning without BIA interference, members of the tribe—especially their leaders—needed to emphasize assimilation and arm themselves with a Western education and an understanding of the Euro-American legal, legislative, and economic systems. These modernists felt that to cling to old traditions—especially religion and superstition—would keep the Utes mired in poverty and dependent on (and therefore under the thumb of) the BIA. The tribal traditionalists, on the other hand, saw the preservation and practice of religion and traditional social gatherings critical for Utes to maintain a link to their ancestors and to the true essence of their Ute identity. They were concerned that full assimilation into mainstream America would strip them of their Uteness and make them little more than "red apples"—red on the outside and white on the inside.[4]

Sam Burch and John E. Baker Sr. became the dominant Southern Ute political leaders during the late 1940s and 1950s. In 1951 Burch recalled Baker from his college studies to help write the tribe's rehabilitation plan; the strong-willed and outspoken Baker was soon elected to the tribal council and in 1956 was elected chair. Baker's political activity continued for thirty years. Also active were his brother Christopher (1963–1987), as well as his cousin Clifford and son John Baker Jr. The Burch dynasty was similarly influential. Sam Burch's sons, Anthony and Leonard, were active on the tribal council, Anthony serving as chair in 1961 and Leonard—the "quiet warrior"—holding that seat in an unparalleled stint from 1967 through 1985, except for a short constitutionally mandated break when Chris Baker served as chair (1985–1987). Some have interpreted this as a continuation of the southern bands' trend toward hereditary leadership. Like the similarly long-termed Ute Mountain leaders, this continuity in leadership gave the Southern Utes a political stability that their more contentious relatives in the Uintah Basin failed to achieve.[5]

Ute women—in traditional culture known to be outspoken and a social force to be reckoned with—also grew active in Southern Ute politics. Pearl Casias was a frequent council member and was even elected chair in 2011. She became a familiar face in politics, as did other councilwomen like Marjorie Borst, Ramona Eagle, Vida Peabody, Joycelyn Dutchie, Euterpe Taylor, and Sunshine Cloud Smith. Euterpe Taylor, the mixed-blood daughter of a black army veteran, was the first woman to serve on the council (1949) and was followed by Sunshine Cloud Smith in 1952. From then on, there was almost always at least one woman on the seven-person council, and in later decades as many as three or four.[6]

377

18.1. Southern Ute Tribal Council, 1960-1961: Seated, Chairman Anthony Burch; L to R: Sunshine Smith, Anna Marie Scott, Euterpe Taylor, Martha Evensen, John E. Baker. (Neg. #F-41884, History Colorado)

The Baker family fell within the modernist camp. Despite their strong allegiance to their community and ancestral heritage, they believed the Utes needed to use the acculturative tools (and appearance) that gave them the power to work within the American legal and legislative system. John Baker Sr., the son of an educated farmer, was a World War II veteran, had attended college in Chicago, spoke little Ute, and had little use for traditional Ute culture, whose ceremonials he viewed as the activities of a private club. Both Baker Sr. and later chair Leonard Burch had similar political agendas: developing a strong, active, and assertive tribal government, emphasizing the tribe's long-range economic development, and asserting its distinct identity and sovereignty.[7]

The Baker family would come into direct political and philosophical competition with the traditionalist faction led by the Cloud family. Julius Cloud was a grandson of Buckskin Charley and the son of Edwin Cloud, the tribe's Sundance chief and most prominent holy man. The outspoken Julius, a veteran of World War I, was also an influential medicine man and, along with his uncle Isaac Cloud, became active on the tribal council during the 1940s and early

18.2. Leonard Burch, Southern Ute Chairman for
three decades, led his tribe to prosperity in the
1990s. (Used by permission of Fort Lewis College,
Center of Southwest Studies, T. B. Hetzel Collection,
SW-P003B5hF013Item05)

1950s. Many saw him as a champion of the people.[8] His sister, Sunshine Cloud
Smith, became Baker's chief rival during the 1960s. Like Baker Sr., she too
was well-educated and well-traveled. She had attended the University of New
Mexico, married a non-Indian, worked in a World War II land mine factory,
and served in the Women's Air Corps in New York as a surgical technician.
After the war she moved to Los Angeles, but like Baker she was recalled to
help write the tribe's rehabilitation plan. Unlike Baker, however, she proudly
embraced her cultural and religious Ute heritage and was a vocal advocate of
the people.[9] She was also a strong advocate of traditional Ute culture.

Following her father's death in 1946, Sunshine Smith joined with Eddie Box
Sr. to actively promote a revival of the Ute Sundance, sweat ceremonies, and
the Ute language. In addition to being active in tribal politics, Eddie Box, Julius
Cloud, and Sunshine Smith were also involved in the traditional activities the

Baker faction ignored. Box, a World War II navy veteran, became the tribe's leading spiritual leader after Edwin Cloud appointed him as Sundance chief in 1956. Box would lead the Southern Ute Sundance for forty-two years and the Bear Dance for thirty-eight years, and serve sixteen years on the tribal council.[10] The breach between the modernist and traditional nativist factions was not healed until Leonard Burch assumed leadership in 1966. The well-educated air force veteran vigorously promoted long-term economic development, while also embracing his heritage by participating in the Sundance and other traditional activities and lending his support to the preservation of culture and language.[11]

During the 1970s and 1980s, however, questions arose over the ultimate authority to schedule ceremonial activities as well as how to handle the logistics of large-scale community events like Sundances, Bear Dances, powwows, and fairs. The tribal council began to assume more responsibility for community events, including the administration of religious activities. The tribal council also began to coordinate major events with other tribes and took on scheduling, organizing, and financing them, as well as managing the logistics of police, sanitation, booths, and concessions.[12]

All three tribes experienced cultural revival in the 1970s, a period that saw an explosion of national Indian activism and a raised consciousness about Indian identity. Like the Northern Utes, the Southern and Ute Mountain Utes began to worry about the significant loss of culture and tribal language that was occurring. Because language is critical for encapsulating traditional culture, it is not surprising that elders grew alarmed at the loss and tribal councils discussed how best to preserve their culture. Museums were built, including one in Montrose near Ouray's old homestead, to house traditional artifacts and educate members and visitors about Ute culture.[13] In addition to publishing tribal histories and folklore, members and specialists studied the Ute language. In the late 1970s the Southern Utes formed a language committee of native speakers and collaborated with a linguist from the University of California, Los Angeles (UCLA) to publish a comprehensive Ute alphabet, grammar reference, and dictionary of the Ute language (1979). In 2016 the tribe announced that a new dictionary and grammar would be published. The White Mesa Utes in Utah hired a linguist in 2008 to help them develop their own dictionary and language lessons, and in 2013 a five-CD Ute language software program was released by the Ute Mountain Utes, *Kavia Naccie Nu-u-apa ga-pi* ("The Mountain Utes Language").[14]

18.3. Jack House (far right), the last chief of the Ute Mountain Utes, died 1971. (Denver Public Library, Western History Collection, X-30455)

Relations between the Ute Mountain Ute council and the BIA grew more placid during the 1970s, with politics still controlled by several prominent families. Ignacio had led the tribe for forty-two years, succeeded by John Miller in 1913 and Jack House in 1936. House would remain the recognized chief until his death in 1971 and an active member of the tribal council for over twenty years. Though never the chair, House wielded substantial power in the tribal council. Other veteran leaders included first council chair George Mills, who remained active in tribal politics for over fifteen years, as did Albert Wing Sr. and Scott Jacket Sr., who alternated with each other as tribal chairs from 1955 through the mid-1970s.[15]

Ute Mountain leaders were steeped in traditional Ute culture, and Ignacio, John Miller, and Jack House were all conservative isolationists who spoke little or no English, and were suspicious of and resisted federal plans to modernize the tribe. The move toward American-educated leaders occurred only gradually, and translators remained important in council meetings into the mid-1980s. The tribe's first chair, John Miller, was a Ute holy man and peyote road chief, and the council was dominated by the conservative Jack House. Albert Wing Sr., who chaired the council for much of the 1950s and 1960s, lived most of his life in a tent, and tended livestock for a living—his own and later the tribe's. During the 1950s it was Wing who urged the tribe to use their claims money to build a tribal racetrack, rodeo arena, and grandstand. However, he attended boarding schools through the mid-ninth grade in Ignacio and Santa Fe and worked with Roosevelt's Indian Civilian Conservation Corps. Scott Jacket Sr., who chaired the council from the mid-1950s into the tumultuous 1980s, had more education and was an army veteran and long-time tribal employee.[16]

By the 1970s, many of the veteran leaders retired or died, leaving a political void. When Jack House died in 1971, it ended tribal chieftainship as well. Meanwhile, new faces began to appear—younger, well-traveled, and better-educated. Jack House's grandson, Ernest House Sr., chaired the tribe for seven years in the 1980s and again during the early years of the twenty-first century. He was influential in developing the Ute Mountain Tribal Park in which the tribe offered guided tours.[17] Members of the Knight family rose to prominence in religious and political activities from the mid-1970s into the new century. The Knights were great-grandchildren of old Chief Piah (Peter Snow), the obstinate Northern Ute who joined Ignacio's band rather than relocate to Utah.[18] Brothers Terry and Carl and sister Judy Pinnecoose (later Judy Knight, and then Judy Knight-Frank) were all elected to the tribal council in the late 1970s. Judy was elected tribal chair and was succeeded by her brother Terry in 1981. Terry, an air force veteran, was a political activist and increasingly prominent religious leader. Judy, who had worked in California, returned to the reservation where she became an outspoken critic of the tribal council, among those demanding accountability for tribal funds. After three attempts, she was elected to the council and remained active through the new century, serving as vice chair from 1981–1988 and then as chair from 1989–1998. Defeated by Ernest House in 1999, Judy was reelected by one vote in 2001 but resigned following a tax-fraud conviction in 2004. Although women had been members of the first Ute Mountain Ute council, they had rarely been involved in direct tribal politics thereafter. This changed with Judy Knight-Frank. With degrees in accounting and business marketing, she dominated Ute Mountain leadership as the tribe embraced the expansion of energy production, tourism, and gaming. She also fought for unemployment compensation for tribal members and locked horns with the federal government over acquiring "wet" water from the proposed—but continually blocked—Animas-La Plata water storage and delivery project.[19]

18.4. The original Pino-Nuche motel and convention center was remodeled to include a moderate-sized casino; the motel and convention center was one of the first tourist-oriented enterprises Southern Utes attempted (Photo: S. Jones 2007)

Tribal Economic Development

During the 1950s, the southern tribes worked to develop new economic enterprises and regain additional lost land through new court actions. The Ute Mountain Utes sued the Navajos over 15,000 acres of grazing land and millions of dollars in subsidiary oil and gas revenues. However, conflicting surveys clouded title to the disputed land, and the Utes lost. In response, Utes appealed for redress "on the notion of elementary fairness" for the lost land and revenue; Congress agreed, but President Jimmy Carter vetoed the award as setting "a dangerous precedent for future relations with Indian tribes." However, Colorado congressmen reintroduced revised bills, and the tribe ultimately won its redress.[20]

In Utah the Allen Canyon Utes and Paiutes had also suffered from Navajo expansion into historic San Juan and Kaibab Paiute homeland and Weeminuche borderland. This area included the Monument Valley region west to Navajo Mountain and north to the lower San Juan. However, in the late 1800s an executive proclamation arbitrarily gave the area to the Navajo. Over the next years the region shifted status several times, as first gold and then oil prospectors deemed it valuable. Though at one point it was returned to the Paiutes, Navajo expansion again pushed them out, and eventually it was appended to the Navajo Reservations. However, a great deal of friction existed between the two people, with Ute/Paiute children bearing the brunt of open bullying. Allen Canyon Utes were also targets of racial and ethnic prejudice from Navajos, local Mormons, and even Ute Mountain Utes who considered them less authentically Ute because of their mixed heritage.[21]

The Ute Mountain and Southern Ute tribes began to implement their new rehabilitation plans in the early 1960s. Non-Indian advisors encouraged both tribes to develop tourist-oriented enterprises. The Southern Utes began by purchasing Lake Capote and stocking it with fish, adding a campground, and building a short-lived marina. They also constructed Pino Nuche Pu-Ra-Sa (meaning Pine River Utes), a motel and convention center, complete with swimming pool, restaurant, lounge, museum, arts and crafts store, and community center. In 1974 they also developed a horse training and conditioning facility at the tribal fairgrounds, which included a racetrack, heated indoor arena, and a hundred stalls, subsequently renamed Sky Ute Downs. But like the resort, it remained a financial failure until the arrival of gaming. In 1998 it was rejuvenated as the Sky Ute Events Center, and by 2013 it was billed as the Sky Ute Fairgrounds where it continued to host, among other events, the annual Southern Ute Tribal Fair and powwow. The Ute Mountain tribe also built a racetrack and rodeo grounds in the 1960s, and they began construction on an expensive community center with a gymnasium and swimming pool (although there would be no running water on the reservation until 1990). But tourism took a downturn in the 1970s as a result of an OPEC embargo and soaring gas prices. Consequently, all of these early enterprises fared poorly, draining tribal coffers rather than filling them. Making matters worse, what jobs *were* generated went to better-trained non-Indians, while only the low-paying menial positions remained available to Utes.[22]

Despite the failure of tribal enterprises, the 1960s also brought an influx of new federal money from various Great Society programs and antipoverty development grants. By this time revenues were also rising from oil and gas leases, especially for the Ute Mountain tribe. In 1938 the tribes had benefited from the Tribal Mineral Leasing Act, a law designed to help Indians develop their oil and gas reserves and allow energy companies to invest in operations on Indian land. Congress had originally passed laws in 1909 to help develop and distribute revenue from Indian mineral leases on allotted land. The 1938 and subsequent 1969 and 1982 laws for Indian mineral development were a boon to tribal development. However, tribes were not active participants in drawing up lease contracts, because the BIA and Department of Interior (DOI) considered Indians too incompetent to handle complicated business affairs. Consequently, although the tribes retained power of consent, the BIA and DOI negotiated directly with the oil and gas companies, as these government agencies, not the tribe, controlled the details of all leases. But these companies often took advantage of or cheated tribes, including the Utes. Theoretically, the BIA managed, collected, and audited the lease monies for the benefit of the tribes; however, the playing field was hardly level. Oil and gas companies shipped large amounts of deliberately undervalued oil and gas off the Southern Ute Reservation and then paid the tribe only a fraction of their worth. Nevertheless, as the energy industry boomed, these lease royalties began to generate significant income for the Utes, because all three Ute reservations held significant reserves of oil and gas, as well as coal and methane gas in Colorado. In 1939 tribal income for the Ute Mountain Utes was just under $40,000, while the Southern Ute tribe made over $80,000, and in 1946 the latter collected almost half a million dollars. It seemed a munificent amount; however, it was far less than the gas and oil were actually worth.[23]

Regardless of growing income, revenue continued to lag behind tribal budgets. Although the Ute Mountain tribe generated over $52 million in combined revenues between 1952 and 1969, it still faced bankruptcy in 1969, because annual expenditures always exceeded income, primarily because members continued to demand higher per-capita dividend payments. To keep up, the tribe repeatedly dipped into investment reserves. The situation was little different for Southern Utes. By the end of the 1950s, the council had begun to decrease the amount of per-capita payments in hopes of staving off their own bankruptcy.[24] The situation improved in the mid-1960s when Lyndon Johnson's generous antipoverty funds became available. This, added to a booming energy industry during the 1970s, led to increased tribal wealth and more generous per-capita payments to members. However, as members grew dependent on this unearned income, it undermined individual independence and wreaked havoc with tribal finances and politics.[25]

The problem was that members insisted on generous per-capita payments regardless of tribal finances. The initial plan had been that members would receive a share of profits generated from tribal enterprises, paid as per-capita corporate dividends. However, these early enterprises were not profitable and did not generate an income. But as oil and gas lease income increased, the tribe was able to pay increasingly higher dividends.[26] As members grew accustomed to receiving this income, they became dependent on it. Instead of seeing it as a fluctuating dividend based on the success of tribal enterprises, it became a paycheck to which they were entitled. Because tribal income was linked to the roller-coaster economy of the global energy industry, tribal income in turn fluctuated with it. However, tribal politicians dared not touch the sacred cow of per-capita payments if they hoped to retain their council seats—even if the tribe went bankrupt. When oil prices plummeted, per capita payments remained the same and became an increasingly large percentage of tribal expenses—sometimes consuming as much as half or more of the entire budget.[27]

As the two tribes dipped into dwindling reserves and populations grew, the BIA insisted payments be made only as dividends on enterprise income, and in the 1960s councils cut payments. But during the boom cycle of the 1970s, revenues increased and the appetite for per-capita paychecks rose again. Tribal fortunes were dangerously linked to this monocrop economy, however, and were dependent on international forces that were out of their control. When the energy industry plunged into a serious bust cycle during the 1980s, the price of oil and gas dropped precipitously, and with it, the economic well-being of all three tribes. Tribal revenues plummeted and budgets were shattered. Yet members still demanded the same high per-capita payments. By the 1980s most members had neither jobs nor land, and of those who had land, few had enough to be self-supporting. Unemployment rates ranged from 45 to 85 percent, and most members relied on per-capita income, tribal jobs, or both. And as budgets were trimmed, many of these tribal jobs disappeared as well.[28] Untrained in the international economics of the energy industry or the concept of dividends versus paychecks, few members understood the forces that were squeezing tribal revenue and balked at any attempt to reduce their incomes. For example, in the mid-1980s when the cash-strapped Southern Ute council attempted to reduce per-capita payments by as much as 88 percent, members demanded the council resign and dividends be increased instead. Ultimately forced to the wall, their coffers drained, and the tribe facing bankruptcy, the council slashed per-capita payments—and angry members forced a full-council recall election.[29]

The Ute Mountain Utes fared even worse. By 1975 the tribe had experienced fifteen years of budget deficits but continued to accede to member demands. In 1977 the tribe went bankrupt. By 1990 the tribal budget allowed dividends of only a few hundred dollars, yet the members insisted on eight times as much, an amount that would have liquidated the tribe's entire investment fund. Ultimately members compromised, which decimated but did not completely destroy the fund. However, the tribe was forced to cut costs elsewhere and laid off a third of its workforce. In response, members charged the council with mismanagement and abuse of their positions for personal gains. Accusations of nepotism, embezzlement, and witchcraft were flung about, and the FBI seized the tribe's financial records. No formal charges were ever brought, and there was no immediate change; however, members developed a new distrust of their leaders ("where is the money going?"). New voices, critical of the old leadership, entered the political arena.[30]

Politically unable to cut per-capita payments, both the Southern and Ute Mountain tribes began cutting other expenses instead, including operating funds and social programs. They tapped into investments (with penalties) and terminated tribal programs or returned them to federal oversight and financing—all a blow to self-sufficiency and self-determination.[31] Nevertheless, members continued to argue that the per-capita payments were not charity but compensation owed for their loss of land and culture; further, tribal money belonged to the people—earned or not. This somewhat socialistic viewpoint was decried by Southern Ute leaders like John Baker Sr. and Leonard Burch, who argued that reliance on tribal payments led to a lack of initiative and self-sufficiency. Yes, the standards of living were rising, but self-reliance had dropped. Fewer members were willing to work for wages or work their farms. By 1962, nearly 59 percent of Southern Ute income and 82 percent of Ute Mountain income was unearned, and by the 1970s fewer than 7 percent of Ute Mountain members owned or raised stock, with only 1 percent doing it full time. By the 1990s, less than 2 percent raised stock.[32]

Meanwhile, as individual Utes grew increasingly dependent on federal and tribal money and services, the tribes grew evermore independent of the BIA. Leaders and tribal officials learned to write grant requests and bypassed the BIA in favor of dipping into the free-flowing Great Society funds during the 1960s and 1970s. They assumed even more control after Congress passed the 1982 Indian Mineral Development Act, which allowed tribes to negotiate directly with companies for exploration and development of mineral and energy resources.[33]

Both the Southern and Ute Mountain Ute councils grew increasingly sophisticated in defining and developing energy resources during the boom cycle of the 1970s, and they were among the first tribes to join the knowledge-sharing Council of Energy Resource Tribes (CERT) formed in 1975. Ute leaders moved aggressively to make the Indian Mineral Leasing Act work to their advantage. In the early 1990s, the Southern Utes hired a former Exxon executive to help form Red Willow Production, an oil and natural gas exploration and production company through which the tribe was able to own and manage much of its energy resources. Seeking to affirm their subsurface rights to natural gas in the coal beneath the reservation, Southern Utes sued Amoco and other energy companies doing business on the reservation as well as non-Indian landowners; ultimately, Amoco settled out of court and relinquished to the tribe working interest in nearly a third of its wells on Indian land. Within a year the tribe owned and operated twenty-one active wells and held interest in another thirty; by 1995, they had quadrupled their production. By 2003 the Southern Utes controlled 1 percent of the U.S. supply of natural gas.[34] In 2000, Red Willow Production expanded beyond the borders of the reservation and partnered with the Northern Utes and two major energy industry companies, Contango Oil and Gas and Dominion Exploration and Production, to develop the vast oil and gas resources in the Hill Creek Extension.[35]

Ute Mountain leaders also negotiated a favorable contract with Wintershall Corporation, a Germany-based oil and gas exploration and development company, that not only agreed to help develop resources but also to train Ute employees and utilize a tribal construction company. The $7.7 million oil and gas deal with Wintershall helped jumpstart the Ute Mountain economy, and by the early 1990s the resource-rich tribe was managing over eighty oil and seventy gas wells on its reservation.[36]

As a result of this activity, all three Ute tribes had become heavily dependent on oil and gas revenues. Energy-resource income made up 97 percent of Southern Ute tribal revenues, while Ute Mountain Utes were almost totally dependent on their energy revenues. As a result, both tribes took serious financial hits during the dramatic slump in oil and gas prices during the 1980s, thus becoming anxious to find ways to diversify enterprises and stabilize their economy.[37]

However, because the tribes' earlier attempts to develop economic enterprises had fared poorly, and because the stagnant economy of the 1970s and the energy crisis of the 1980s slowed the tourist industry, few outside businesses were interested in investing with the tribe. So tribal officers began searching for better ways to develop their own businesses. Cattle ranching in the 1950s had been unsuccessful on the Ute Mountain Reservation because of the land's aridity, but it was more successful after the tribe purchased an 18,749-acre ranch between Montrose and Gunnison and trucked cattle there for summer grazing.[38]

About the same time, the Allen Canyon Utes established a cooperative livestock association and ran their cattle in Utah's Upper Comb Wash and

Arch Canyon region. But as tourism increased, environmental groups voiced objections to running cattle in these areas. In 1989 environmentalists filed lawsuits against the Ute Mountain Utes, the Bureau of Land Management (BLM), National Cattlemen's Association, local stockmen, Utah Farm Bureau, and the American Sheep Industry Association. Litigation persisted until 1993, when the court determined grazing could continue but would have to be limited. The Allen Canyon herds were diminished, and by 2000 the cooperative had sold out.[39]

The Ute Mountain tribe also established the Ute Mountain Tribal Park, a 125,000-acre region in Mancos Canyon that was rich with archaeological ruins, and tried to develop a tourist-oriented program of Ute-guided backcountry tours. Some isolationist members of the tribe vigorously opposed the idea of opening the reservation to outsiders. Though the project did go forward, it generated little income. However, the tribe discovered that a survey error had left a portion of Mesa Verde roads outside park boundaries but within the Ute Mountain Reservation. Hastily assembled stalls selling inexpensive Indian crafts quickly appeared at Soda Point. After some initial conflict with the National Park Service, the tribe negotiated a coexistence pact. But again, little income trickled in from these small-scale enterprises.[40]

The Ute Mountain tribe finally obtained water from the Dolores Water Project following the Colorado Ute Water Settlement Act of 1988—over a hundred years after the government had initially promised to provide water projects. Some of the water went to a new farm and ranch enterprise to develop commercial and experimental agricultural projects (alfalfa, field corn, wheat, and sunflowers), watered with central-pivot radio-controlled sprinkler systems utilizing state-of-the-art computerized links. It was later expanded to include over seven hundred head of Black Angus and Black Gelbvieh cattle. In June 2017, the tribe announced new plans to build a solar farm.[41]

An early enterprise that fared especially well was the Ute Mountain Ute Pottery business, established in 1970. Originally housed in the old clinic at Towaoc, it was moved to a new building near Highway 160, a major tourist route into the Four Corners region. The enterprise flourished, and sales increased after a major grocery chain began to sell the pottery in 1988. In 1992 another plant was opened at White Mesa, and the enterprise expanded its line of traditional painted Ute designs to include new painted and incised red pottery. While decorated pottery was not traditional (Utes were primarily basketmakers), it was popular with tourists. Some women also wove and sold traditional Ute baskets at regional trade fairs.[42]

One of the most successful Ute Mountain enterprises was the Weemi-nuche Construction Authority (WCA). Established in 1985, it had garnered $3 million in contracts by 1987 and by the mid-1990s employed hundreds of permanent nonunion employees and owned hundreds of pieces of heavy construction equipment. As a minority-owned business, the company won federal, state, and local contracts and worked on various water projects, including the Towaoc Irrigation Canal Project that brought water from McPhee Reservoir to the reservation. WCA also worked on road construction in Colorado and surrounding states, performed oil and gas field construction, made water system improvements in nearby Mesa Verde and Canyonlands National Parks, did home and infrastructure construction for the Ute Mountain Housing Authority, and built a welcome center for the city of Cortez.[43]

Although a non-Indian firm in Cortez managed the WCA, it still qualified as a minority business because it was owned and generally operated by the tribe and made "maximum use of Indian laborers and craftsmen." Because of this, it had an advantage when competing for federal contracts, since the Indian Self-Determination and Education Assistance Act (1975) required that tribal construction companies be given the right of first refusal for all federal construction projects that involved Indian tribes. When the Animas-La Plata water storage and delivery project was finally begun in 2000, the Southern Ute's new Sky Ute Sand and Gravel and the Ute Mountain's WCA were awarded substantial contracts. In addition to preliminary work, the WCA received a $17.8 million construction contract excavating the foundation for the Ridges Basin Reservoir, constructing some of the water-flow-management drop structures, and building permanent and hauling roads.[44]

However, like other tribal enterprises, the company attracted some discontent because it was managed by a non-Indian firm, and most Utes were employed for only the lowest-paying, labor-intensive jobs. The use of non-Indians for the highest paying jobs in tribal enterprises (or skilled craft workers from the region) became a continual source of irritation for members of both tribes in all of their major enterprises.[45]

With the passage of the 1988 Indian Gaming Regulatory Act, both tribes recognized the potential of a new source of income and the possibility of diversifying their investments beyond oil and gas. They took this opportunity after Colorado allowed limited-stakes gambling in three historic mining towns in 1990. However, introducing gaming was not without controversy, for although gambling was a deeply embedded cultural tradition, class III casino gambling was not, and some feared the influx of non-Indians and the negative

18.5. Sky Ute Casino and Resort on the Southern Ute reservation. (Photo by Scott D. W. Smith, Courtesy of the Sky Ute Casino)

influences of gambling and alcohol. Some Utes called gaming a vice, the devil's work, and a non-Indian intrusion. A few Southern Ute leaders argued a casino in Ignacio would be too close to schools and tribal offices, while Ute Mountain members, who had long since passed regulations banning alcohol on the reservation, feared reintroducing liquor, even though their casino would be built along Highway 160 on its far eastern border. (They would similarly ban marijuana cultivation or sale after it, too, became legal.) Opponents also argued that gaming would not solve the tribes' economic problems; however, both councils saw gaming as a panacea for their financial woes, and they very quickly began planning how to develop reservation casinos.[46]

In this, the Colorado Utes joined over eighty other Indian tribes that had, in the early 1990s, negotiated gambling compacts with their respective states for class II or class III casino-style gaming (by 2015, this number had risen to 242). The Ute Mountain tribe opened their first casino in September 1992, repurposing their old pottery plant near Route 160. The 30,000-square-foot facility housed hundreds of slot machines, blackjack and poker tables, keno, bingo, live entertainment, and a restaurant—but no alcohol. Operated by a non-Indian gambling company (as were most Indian casinos), it created hundreds of new jobs, half of which went to Native Americans, with 32 percent to tribal members (over 50 percent in later years, better than most tribes). The casino added a shuttle service between the casino and Cortez, and by 1997 the tribe was the second-largest employer in the Four Corners region. In 1994 it opened a full service RV park next to the casino. By 2007 a new and expanded Ute Mountain Casino and hotel complex was in full operation, with expansive upgrades by 2016.[47]

In 1993 the Southern Utes opened Sky Ute Casino in Ignacio, subsequently upgrading the old Pino Nuche resort into the Sky Ute Lodge, with rooms, conference center, and dining facilities. Smaller than the Ute Mountain casino, it employed over 170 people, with 50 percent of the jobs for Southern Utes. It took less than a year for the tribe to repay the $4.1 million loan they had given themselves. By 1995 the casino had so many visitors they had to make a $4 million expansion, tripling their slot machines and video poker, adding new gambling tables, and reviving bingo. By 1998 they had three casinos operating twenty-four hours a day, seven days a week and operated a free shuttle from Durango, the Purgatory ski resort, Farmington, and Pagosa. In 2012 they opened a large new casino-resort facility just outside Ignacio and were negotiating deals to take advantage of the new virtual gambling industry on the internet.[48]

As they had done with their energy resources, both southern Colorado tribes had been in the vanguard in developing their gaming resources. By 2006 American Indian gaming had become big business in the United States— enough so that accusations began to fly that monied non-Indian interests, corrupt influence peddling, and insider dealing in Washington were manipulating Indian identities and interests in order to cash in on the big gambling bonanza.[49] And bonanza it was: in 2002 the gross revenue nationwide from tribal government gaming was $14.5 billion; by 2018 this had risen to $32.4 billion, or 42.5 percent of the total gaming revenue for *all* of the United States. At the same time, Indian gaming generated over 600,000 jobs, up from 400,000 in 2002.[50]

However, not all the revenue went to sponsoring tribes. The Indian Gaming Regulatory Act (IGRA) required tribes to use most of the revenue for tribal development, but they were also required to share profits with local or state governments to recompense them for increased infrastructure needs. Strict regulations required tribes to use their gaming revenue to fund government operations or programs, promote tribal economic development, provide for the general welfare of the tribe and its members, or donate to charitable organizations. Only a fourth of the tribes with gaming enterprises distributed per-capita shares of revenue directly to their members (to help their "general welfare")—the Colorado Utes among them. Tribes were also required to execute revenue-sharing agreements with local non-Indian government agencies to help offset the increased burden on local economies (Indian enterprises

18.6. Ute Mountain Casino, 2007. (Photo: S. Jones)

remained tax-free if operated on reservations). Some tribes also made revenue-sharing agreements with states, which encouraged state approval of Indian gaming. Because of this, most neighboring communities welcomed Indian gaming due to the direct influx of shared revenue, as well as the new jobs that were created, and the increase in local tourism.[51] Indeed, in 2014 the Southern and Ute Mountain Utes, who made up just 1.6 percent of the state population, made a $1.5 billion impact on the state's economy. As the major employers in their respective counties, their enterprises generated 8,800 direct jobs and over 12,500 indirect jobs, with earnings from employment alone reaching more than $549 million.[52]

Of course, Indian gaming was just another idea in a long list of ideas for economic development for tribes in their quest for self-sufficiency. And on the surface, it appeared to be a spectacular success. The reality, however, has been uneven across tribes. Most American Indian gaming venues have remained small. About half the revenue and jobs boasted by the National Indian Gaming Association (NIGA) was generated by only a handful of extraordinarily successful, highly visible casinos owned by a few small tribes that were located near large cities in Connecticut, California, Minnesota, and Arizona or on major highways. Thus, despite the lure of gaming, most tribes continued to have high poverty rates. Some tribes shied away from gambling altogether. In

2005, the president of the National Congress of American Indians pointed out that "the success of a small handful of tribes does not translate into economic success for all Indian people." That the relatively remote Southern and Ute Mountain Utes were particularly successful in their gaming operations must be credited to their increasingly farsighted and regional planning, a skilled management team, their business acumen in using shuttles to bring tourists to their casinos, and their good fortune in the location of their reservations. While not near metropolitan centers, by the 1990s southwestern Colorado was boasting a revived and thriving tourist industry.[53]

NEW LEADERSHIP AND NEW ECONOMIC BATTLES

The 1980s brought a great deal more political activism for both the Ute Mountain and Southern Utes as a new generation of leaders entered the ring. Tribal officials and members argued issues of development, tribal economics, and traditionalism versus modernism. The tribes also faced a drawn out battle over a typical Western issue: water.

A Political New Guard

As tribal enterprises expanded, education and intercultural interaction increased, members obtained access to modern communication technology, and Utes grew increasingly integrated into mainstream America. Some leaders encouraged this evolution, while others grew concerned. For example, during the 1987 council elections on the Ute Mountain reservation, Arthur Cuthair voiced concerns over the cultural costs of development. How could Ute heritage be preserved, he asked, if the reservation was opened to non-Indians and job training redirected older lifeways? But members elected Judy Knight as tribal chair, preferring her platform of economic development, change, job training, and education. However, protest against development grew heated, and arsonists even struck the new tribal offices during construction.[54]

Southern Ute traditionalists like Eddie Box Sr., Sunshine Cloud Smith, and Julius Cloud had been locking horns with modernists like John Baker Sr. since the 1960s. They supported the perpetuation of traditional ceremonies like the Bear Dance, Sundance, sweats, and traditional gambling games, while modernists scorned such "amusements." Antagonism between full-bloods and mixed-bloods also surfaced among the Southern Utes, as money-rights issues grew with tribal prosperity.[55]

As a borderland people, the Southern Utes were a diverse group because of their long history of mingling, interacting, and intermarrying with Hispanics, Euro-Americans, non-Ute Indians, and some African Americans. As a consequence, membership requirements fluctuated between a 50 percent and 25 percent blood quantum, with the more isolated Ute Mountain Utes at 50 percent. As monetary dividends increased, Ute Mountain Utes argued the White Mesa/Allen Canyon Utes had too much Paiute and Navajo blood to be truly considered Utes. The Ute Mountain and White Mesa councils also quarreled over leadership and assets. A White Mesa Ute tribal council had been authorized by the Ute Mountain council to manage small business assets. But in 2004 tribal chair Arthur Cuthair dissolved the White Mesa council, ordered it out of its offices, and attempted to turn its assets over to Ute Mountain control. Instead the council, as a nonprofit organization, moved to Blanding and continued doing business.[56]

As tribal members became more actively involved in tribal politics, election scandals also struck in Colorado. Disgruntled and opinionated members lamented that tribal councils had become unassailable bastions of tribal power with dictatorial monopolies. They also leveled charges of voter intimidation, bribery, vote buying, and payoffs. Vocal opposition quickly stepped from soapbox to political platform as critics ran for office against the entrenched powers. Ray Frost, a severe critic of Leonard Burch, was elected to the Southern Ute council in 1993. In the late 1970s Judy Knight had taken her outspoken criticism to the polls and was elected to the Ute Mountain tribal council, where she served for the next twenty years as council member or tribal chair. Other critics like Tony Tallbird and Arthur Cuthair also gained office on the Ute Mountain council during the 1980s and 1990s.[57]

Exemplifying these contentious politics were Southern Ute recall elections in 1990. A political storm had roiled over the tribe's involvement in securing a large water storage project, as well as issues of mismanagement of funds, enrollment, reductions of per-capita payments, failures to amend the constitution, and—especially—the tribal chair's abuse of power and too frequent use of the veto. Critics contended that there was too much power concentrated among too few, resulting in the political oppression of members. Councils were accused of carrot-and-stick diplomacy by doling out benefits while punishing opposition. Many were afraid to oppose the council for fear of losing their jobs, because the council controlled most employment. Opponents like the outspoken Sage Remington, former council member Ray Frost, and others of

18.7. Leonard C. Burch Tribal Administration Building, Southern Ute Tribe, 2007. (Photo: S. Jones 2007)

18.8. Ute Mountain Ute Tribal Office Complex, 2007. (Photo: S. Jones)

the Southern Ute Grassroots Organization (SUGO) also criticized leaders for not listening to member concerns and being beholden to non-Indian advisors with economic ties to commercial or government interests outside the tribe.[58] When the recall vote was counted, the opposition had won by a narrow margin. However, charges of vote tampering and witchcraft were raised, and the tribal council nullified the elections and defeated the recall. This decision was immediately appealed to the tribal court, and then to the Southwest Intertribal Court of Appeals, which upheld the council—by an even narrower margin.[59]

Politics remained turbulent as the two tribes struggled to balance cultural preservation with economic development. Factions were vocal, and family feuds plagued politics. One of Leonard Burch's most vocal critics was his own sister, while John Baker Sr. was challenged by his brother Chris. Judy Knight-Frank's plans for economic development—in particular for the tribal casino—were opposed by a brother who ran against her for tribal chair.[60] During the 1990s the popular and progressive Knight-Frank survived accusations of slander, fraud, and FBI investigations to continue as tribal chair, although her margins of victory grew increasingly slender. But in 2002 her house of cards tumbled when she was indicted by a grand jury for tax fraud, embezzlement, and lying on loan applications after she failed to report or pay back over $350,000 in pay advances between 1996 and 1999. Facing over thirty years in prison and more than $1 million in fines, she plea bargained her conviction to one charge of tax fraud. The remaining charges were dropped, and she resigned as chair of the Ute Mountain tribe. As a convicted felon, she was barred in the tribal constitution from any further elected positions.[61]

Water Wars: The Animas-La Plata Water Project

The biggest controversy to beset the two southern Colorado tribes during the last decades of the twentieth century was a typically Western one: water. In 1889 when the Denver and Rio Grande Railroad promoted homesteading in the newly opened "Ute Strip," they misleadingly painted a glowing picture of a fictitious abundant water supply.[62] Successful farming demanded irrigation, and water rights became a highly contested battlefield. As miners, ranchers, and homesteaders inundated southwestern Colorado, and despite attempts by agents to establish prior water rights for their Ute wards, Euro-Americans appropriated the water from all seven rivers that flowed across the Ute reservations. Within fifty years all of the water had been apportioned and was being used by non-Indians. On the Ute Mountain Reservation, water remained almost nonexistent, and culinary water had to be hauled to Towaoc daily to fill buckets left on doorsteps. Because all of the water flowing through the Southern Ute Reservation had already been appropriated, Ute farmers remained last on the list to use it. Consequently, when there were droughts, Ute farmers received no water at all. In any case, many irrigation ditches did not reach Ute allotments, or when they did, headgates were not maintained.[63]

But in the pivotal 1908 Supreme Court decision, *Winters v. United States*, the court found that the establishment of a reservation implied the establishment of water rights necessary to fulfill the purposes of that reservation to advance civilization and "encourage habits of industry and thrift" (i.e., farming). This decision established senior rights to water dating to the establishment of a tribe's reservation, not its first use. This was reinforced in both the Colorado River Compact (signed in 1922 but passed as part of the Boulder Dam Project in 1928) and the 1948 Upper Colorado River Basin Project that specifically noted that nothing in the compacts would affect "the obligation of the U.S. of A. to Indian tribes."[64] The *Winters* decision, however, did not quantify Indian claims, nor did it provide for any type of delivery system. When the fight over water began in the mid-1900s, the Southern and Ute Mountain Utes based their claims on water rights dating from the Treaty of 1868, making theirs senior to any non-Indian claims.[65]

Residents of southwestern Colorado had been envisioning water storage projects for the region as early as 1904 when they first approached the Bureau of Reclamation about a project on the Animas River. The Utes' first attempts to claim water rights began in the 1930s after the Southern Utes were restored over 200,000 acres of land for which they needed irrigation water. Surface water rights on the Los Piños were subsequently adjudicated, and the Vallecito Reservoir was completed in 1942. This project provided irrigation and municipal water to La Plata County and parts of the Southern Ute Reservation, and Southern Ute claims to the Los Piños were eventually quantified to one-sixth of Vallecito's stored water.[66]

Then in 1968 the Colorado River Basin Act (P.L. 90-537) authorized a mammoth water storage and delivery project in southwestern Colorado. The Animas-La Plata project (A-LP) proposed three reservoirs, including one on the Animas (near Silverton) and miles of tunnels, canals, and pumping plants to deliver water to Durango and the nearby Ridges Basin. But by the 1970s, concerns over unjustifiably high costs and environmental damage had made this type of large water project unpopular. Armed with three new environmental protection acts—the 1969 *National Environmental Policy Act*, the 1973

Endangered Species Act, and the 1974 *Colorado River Salinity Control Act*—opponents of the A-LP project waged an all-out war to stop its implementation.[67]

With water projects stagnating, the United States filed suits on behalf of the Ute Mountain and Southern Ute tribes asserting *Winters* rights on the rivers flowing across their reservations. Since there was not enough water to satisfy the claims of both the Utes and local non-Indians (the rivers were already fully appropriated), this promised expensive litigation, and non-Indian farmers and communities feared it would wipe them out. Waving a big stick, attorneys called attention to a precedent-setting decision in which the Wind River Shoshones had successfully reclaimed water rights and left neighboring farmers high and dry. [68]

Throughout much of the 1980s, the two tribes huddled with local non-Indian users and water conservancy districts in an attempt to settle Ute water claims without taking water from non-Indian users. The tribes finally agreed they would not sue for their senior rights if the government agreed to build and develop water projects in the region, specifically the Animas-La Plata project. Ute leaders and interested non-Indian groups (including representatives from water conservancy districts, state and county officials, and federal entities) signed a final agreement in December 1986. Preliminary reports from the U.S. Fish and Wildlife Service suggested the project posed no serious danger to any endangered species, and Colorado's Congressman Ben Nighthorse Campbell and Senator Pete Domenici introduced bills in the House and Senate. Congress held extensive hearings and then reauthorized the A-LP and passed the Colorado Ute Indian Water Rights Settlement Act of 1988, including a comprehensive cost-sharing agreement with the tribes, which Ronald Reagan immediately signed into law (P.L. 100-585).[69]

The agreement successfully satisfied Indian water rights while meeting both Indian and non-Indian water needs (including a pipeline to finally deliver culinary water to Towaoc), and provided a $60 million development fund for the Southern and Ute Mountain tribes. Ute Mountain Utes would receive 1,000 afy (acre feet/year) of municipal water, 23,300 afy of irrigation water, and 800 afy for fish and wildlife management. Southern Utes were allocated 26,500 afy of municipal and industrial water and 3,400 afy for irrigation.[70]

All involved in the negotiations were elated. Leonard Burch called it a "darn good deal" and invited tribal members to come home to the new jobs it would create. The Southern Utes particularly hoped to use their water for farming and ranching, develop their vast coal reserves, and build slurry pipes to carry the coal to power-generating plants. They also hoped to sell the water rights to nearby towns, neighboring non-Indian farmers, or downstream users (a highly controversial and contested proposal).[71] However, opponents of the large water project immediately moved to block its implementation.

Adversaries asserted that the A-LP was fiscally unsound and environmentally and economically destructive. Grassroots taxpayer groups—including a vocal minority of Southern Utes—argued that the project was too expensive and that the tribes and taxpayers would be saddled with monumental debts from the cost-sharing agreements.[72] Calling it "Jurassic Pork," opponents claimed that it would cost millions to clean up the increased salinity downriver, while depleted rivers would cost power-generating dams like Glen Canyon millions in lost revenue.[73]

Others argued the project was ill-conceived and poorly thought out. The proposed pumping stations, for example, would use an excessive amount of electricity to pump water out of the Animas and up 1,000 feet to the Ridges Basin Reservoir (to pump the 100,000 afy of water to fill the reservoir would require the equivalent electricity needed to power a city of 63,000). The reservoir would provide four times the amount of water needed, even as it reduced the water in the Animas, killed the rafting and tourism industry, and desiccated the San Juan River. (Ironically, the controversy itself increased rafting by generating more interest in the Gold Medal Animas River.)[74]

Ultimately, the most convincing argument against the project was not cost, but the monumental environmental damage it would cause. Rivers would be depleted, elk and deer habitats flooded, a wildlife preserve destroyed, wetlands damaged, archaeological cultural sites and Indian burials destroyed, and eagles and some fish species endangered, including the Colorado squawfish, soon-to-be renamed the pikeminnow as a result of Judy Knight-Frank's complaints of sexist racism during her testimony in Congress.[75] Also at issue was increased salinity and fear that seepage from the heavily mined region would pollute the river. And if the Utes did develop their coal reserves and build a coal-powered electricity-generating plant, the resulting pollution and acid rain could be devastating.[76]

Opponents also argued the expensive A-LP would be of little actual benefit to the Utes because there were few agriculturally identifiable needs on the reservation, and besides, little of the Ute water would be used there since the delivery system stopped short of the reservation boundary. If they did want the water, the Southern Utes would have to pay for their own system using their own development funds. Meanwhile, the downriver Navajos might lose their Navajo-Gallup Pipeline Project and suffer from polluted water.[77] The

A-LP, they protested, was merely a non-Indian project "wrapped in an Indian blanket" to get "white guilt money" for a project non-Indians would use, or for "irresponsible illegal water speculation" (selling water) and "imaginary golf courses, dude ranches and coal-fired power plants" that the Utes might "one day fancy." Eighty-five percent of the water would provide irrigation for non-Indians, and 86 percent of the Indian water had not been earmarked for irrigation at all, but for municipal and industrial uses. Some opponents noted that the Utes' attorney, Sam Maynes, also represented the Animas Water Conservancy District, the San Miguel Water Conservancy District, and the La Plata Electrical Association.[78]

Controversy raged among the Southern Utes as well, and some members questioned the wisdom of the project, given the cost-sharing commitments that would obligate the tribe to contribute millions to access their water. Leading the opposition were Sage Remington and Ray Frost, with SUGO and their Committee to Improve Tribal Government. Frost complained loudly that the project was "not for our benefit," that "Anglos are just riding our shoulders," and that the tribe would be "saddled with a project that's going to cost us a lot of money." The controversy sparked a tribal recall election, but opponents were unable to unseat the long-standing Leonard Burch.[79]

Despite opposition, the involved parties signed contracts, authorized construction, and allocated money toward the A-LP. A pipeline was extended to Towaoc as part of the Dolores River project, and residents finally got running water in their homes. In 1992 a $32 million contract to build the thirty-four-mile Towaoc Canal was awarded to the Weeminuche Construction Authority to bring additional irrigation water to the tribe's Farm and Ranch program.[80] But the rest of the A-LP project remained embattled for another ten years.

When biologists discovered more endangered fish downriver, environmentalists immediately demanded new studies, and officials cancelled a scheduled groundbreaking. The Bureau of Reclamation (BOR) began working on alternative plans, and environmentalists and rafters organized a concerted public awareness campaign.[81] By 1994 even the Department of the Interior (DOI) was warning that the project was "neither financially feasible nor economically just" and that the A-LP water would be the most expensive in the Bureau of Reclamation's history. In 1995 the National Taxpayers Union and Friends of the Earth joined the fight, listing the A-LP as "one of the 10 most wasteful and environmentally harmful projects."[82]

In early 1996 the U.S. Fish and Wildlife Service finally issued its Final Supplement to the Final Environmental Statement (FSFES) for the A-LP and presented its recommendations for an alternative project—but the flurry of opposition just increased.[83] The Sierra Club joined the opposition and offered its own alternative plans; dissident Southern Utes petitioned the governor and sued the BOR; and the Environmental Protection Agency (EPA) was granted more time to study the project. By this time over $62 million had already been spent on the project, and no ground had been broken.[84]

At this point Colorado's governor Roy Romer and lieutenant governor Gail Schoettler intervened and attempted to negotiate a workable compromise. Since Indian claims to water had to be met, the Romer-Schoettler process produced structural and nonstructural alternatives. The nonstructural plan suggested that Indian claims be met by purchasing existing irrigated lands and associated water rights or by purchasing water from existing projects. The structural plan recommended building the FSFES's scaled-down version of the project.[85] But opponents remained adamant. They wanted no project at all.

In 1998 the secretary of the Interior Bruce Babbitt incorporated elements from both of the compromise plans and proposed a downsized A-LP, which was promptly dubbed the A-LP Lite. It was immediately endorsed by both Ute tribes. The A-LP Lite recommended only one off-stream reservoir at Ridges Basin, a pumping plant and inlet conduit that would deplete the Animas no more than the requisite 57,100 afy, pipelines to deliver water to the Utes and the San Juan Navajos and to remove the mostly non-Indian irrigation features to leave only municipal and industrial (M&I) water. Because the new project would be an Indian-water system, the cost-sharing elements were changed so that non-Indian water users would have to reimburse the government for any benefits they received, while all Indian elements would be at government expense and mostly nonreimbursable.[86]

But opposition continued, and tribal leaders fumed. Making matters worse, Senators Russ Feingold and Sam Brownback, along with Representatives Tom Petri and Peter DeFazio, introduced bills to deauthorize the A-LP entirely, calling it a "Pork Barrel Project," an expensive "boondoggle," and a "rotten deal." The Green Scissors Campaign placed the project on a "corporate welfare hit list," citing SUGO to prove that even the tribes did not want it. Taxpayers for Common Sense claimed it violated the Native American Graves Protection and Repatriation Act (by flooding cultural sites), the Clean Water Act, and the Endangered Species Act, and was just plain too expensive.[87]

By this time the project had become the most studied and most heatedly contested water project in U.S. history. Armed with Babbitt's reconciliation plan, Colorado congressmen introduced new bills into the Senate and House to amend the 1988 Settlement Agreement to reflect the A-LP Lite Reconciliation plans, now endorsed by both tribes, Colorado's Romer and Schoettler, New Mexico's governor Gary Johnson, and Secretary Babbitt. But diehard opposition grew even more vehement and again castigated the project as a "white elephant wrapped in an Indian blanket."[88] Tribal leaders testified again before Congress. Judy Knight-Frank argued passionately that her people needed the water and that "the squawfish—and I take offense at that name—seems to have more of a right to live than I do"; also that "we want wet water. We do not want paper money" (a reference to the Northern Ute's money settlement over water rights).[89] But Congress adjourned without acting.

Then the Clinton administration moved to kill the project entirely, and both tribes renewed threats to litigate. Politicians were accused of courting environmentally sympathetic voters and special interest groups. Editorialists lambasted the "theme-park environmentalists" and claimed the project had been a "target of a holy war by the Sierra Club...[who] see water projects as tools of Satan." But opponents lashed back, denouncing the proponents as "slick white conmen" who had tricked the Indians into supporting a wasteful project.[90]

Then the opposition switched to new arguments. First they claimed the Winters Doctrine referred only to domestic and agricultural water, not M&I water, so the amount the Indians could claim was limited. However, the Supreme Court decision hadn't limited tribal water to only agricultural projects; it had adjudged that reservation water rights were reserved for the purposes of "furthering and advancing the civilization and improvement of the Indians, and to encourage habits of industry and thrift." Although this had been agriculture and ranching in the early 1900s, by the 1990s "habits of industry" implied employment and included tribal enterprises, most of which were not agricultural.[91] Undeterred, opponents now argued the 1868 reservation had been extinguished, allotted, and then reformed under the Indian Reorganization Act in 1938, and therefore Ute water rights dated from 1938, not 1868.[92] And, they contended, the Utes had already been paid in full for all land and associated rights, including water, when they received their land-claims settlement in 1950.[93] However, there were significant flaws in all of the arguments, and Congress dismissed them.

Representatives and senators from Colorado continued to introduce compromise bills in Congress, and in 2000, construction was finally reauthorized. The scaled-down A-LP primarily served Southern and Ute Mountain Ute towns, removed irrigation for non-Indian farmers, retained the Ridges Basin

Dam and Reservoir, the Durango pumping station, and pipelines to deliver water to Ute and Navajo users. Because it was primarily an Indian project, lucrative construction contracts were also awarded to the Southern Utes' Sand and Gravel company and the WCA.[94]

Construction finally began in 2002; however, the controversy continued. Grassroots taxpayer organizations chorused an "I told you so" as, by 2003, the project had already gone well over budget, with its final expected costs estimated to be at least 50 percent more than anticipated. Cost overruns were attributed to deficiencies and omissions in design and construction estimates, higher-than-expected contracting costs, and increased security costs after the 9/11 terrorist attacks in 2001.[95]

That the construction finally did begin, despite years of controversy and powerful lobbies aligned against them, demonstrates the political power that the Southern and Ute Mountain Utes had developed by 2000. They had demanded their rights to treaty obligations and reserved water—and this time they had gotten them. It was a victory for tribal self-determination and sovereignty.

Economic Development and Entrepreneurial Triumph

In Utah the Allen Canyon Utes had long been treated like the Ute Mountain Utes' poor relatives, distant from the political center and disdained for their mixed heritage. Allen Canyon Utes had endured endemic poverty and entrenched racial prejudice from their non-Indian neighbors, and having been subjected to significant pressure to leave San Juan County and relocate closer to Towaoc. But they had stubbornly refused to relocate from the "land that owned them." Eventually, a long-standing dispute over allotments was resolved, and the Allen Canyon Utes were allowed to move to White Mesa in 1948. This location proved much better than their Allen Canyon homesteads, because it was less rocky, provided room to expand, allowed them to remain close to Blanding and its services and schools, and yet gave them distance from non-Indians, preserving a distinct social identity. While still living in Allen Canyon, this mixed band had formed a development council and hired an advisor to help manage a number of small economic enterprises. After their move, it was renamed the White Mesa Ute Council, an organization that functioned until the 1990s. By 2000 their cooperative cattle company was gone, but a uranium processing plant opened a few miles away from the small community: the White Mesa mill. At this point the White Mesa Utes remained mired in poverty, with a 57–80 percent unemployment rate. Because they were distant from the epicenter of Ute Mountain prosperity, the Ute Mountain Utes' wealth and opportunities had not spilled over to them. The mill offered a promise of economic relief for these impoverished people.[96]

However, despite the economic advantages, opinions about the mill were divided. The White Mesa Mill was the only conventional mill operating in the United States that processed uranium into yellow cake to be used in nuclear powerplant fuel rods and produced significant amounts of radioactive waste. Many Utes and non-Indian neighbors objected to it for fear it would contaminate the four springs and two aquifers lying below the proposed tailing pond, as well as desecrate sacred land or burials; others saw job opportunities. A proposal to bring in even more radioactive mill tailings reignited the controversy, as the opposition objected to using Indian land as a radioactive waste dump. Protests halted the project; however, by the early 2010s, the White Mesa Utes finally agreed to allow the waste in return for scholarships and employment. But by 2015 the controversy had exploded again, and activists were still protesting the mill in 2017.[97]

Meanwhile, in Colorado the Ute Mountain and Southern Utes were prospering. In 1997 the Southern Ute leaders hired John Jurrius, the non-Indian investment banker from Texas later hired by the Northern Utes. His job was to help the Colorado Utes diversify their investments. Leaders were concerned that tribal wealth would decline if it was based only on natural gas and oil. As the tribe's top financial advisor, Jurrius created a financial plan that included a Permanent Fund and a Growth Fund. Seventy-five percent of all energy royalties and casino profits were allocated to the Permanent Fund and were to be invested in securities. This would fund the tribal government and pay $520 per-capita payments to members each month. The tribe's profits from its energy and real estate holdings, along with the remaining 25 percent royalties, went into the aggressive Southern Ute Growth Fund. Ten percent of its profits were to be distributed to members under age sixty, pay for pensions for elders, and the remainder reinvested.[98]

The revolutionary financial plan was met—as usual—with strong opposition by conservative leaders, many wary of outside advisors or big business wheeling and dealing. Others continued to push for a more equal distribution of shares among the traditionally communalistic Utes. As one non-Indian director complained, his job was difficult because he was "a capitalist working for a bunch of socialists." And he was not alone in leveling the charge of socialism—the Ute governments owned tribal corporations as representatives of their people, and corporate profits were redistributed equally among them.[99]

18.9. Southern Ute Tribal Enterprise Building, 2007 (Photo: S. Jones)

Despite controversy, Jurrius's plan was adopted—and successful. The goal of the Growth Fund was an annual return of at least 15 percent or more. Instead, it averaged 30 percent annually, and its profits were plowed back into real estate and energy ventures from Hawaii (a $123 million cash purchase of an oil and gas company) to Kansas City real estate and to offshore drilling rights in the Gulf of Mexico. By 2006 the Growth Fund business investments were being managed out of a modern three-story Growth Fund building in Ignacio. Tribal investments included the Red Willow Production Company (oil and natural gas); Red Willow Offshore (drilling); Red Cedar Gathering Company (a natural gas processor and transporter) in conjunction with Kinder Morgan and the largest pipeline in Colorado; and AKA Energy Group, LLC (processor and transporter of natural gas and natural gas liquids). Among the tribe's real estate holdings were GF Properties Group, a commercial properties investment company; Tierra Group and Rocky Mountain Housing, which in turn did the construction for GF Properties, which built custom and semicustom homes and commercial office buildings; and Innovative Housing, another general building contractor specializing in manufactured buildings. By 2006 the tribe owned millions of dollars of real estate and owned ongoing projects in Kansas City (landlord to the Federal Aviation Administration), Denver, Houston, Albuquerque, and nearby Durango, where it was building a medical park and office buildings. Other business ventures were the Sky Ute Sand & Gravel Company that supplied construction materials, including the lucrative A-LP contract, and its own investment arm, the Private Equity Group.[100]

By 2000, both the Southern and Ute Mountain Utes reported less than 9 percent unemployment to census takers—the majority of employed linked to either tribal or tribally owned enterprises. The casinos, resorts, and service industries were providing nearly a third of all work for Ute Mountain Utes, and a fifth of Southern Ute employment. And with this influx of jobs came a dramatic rise in household incomes. In 2000, shortly after the casinos opened, Southern Ute household income rose to $36,000 and Ute Mountain Ute income to $19,000 (average state income, $47,000). By 2013, after the energy industry boomed, casinos expanded, the entrepreneurial Southern Utes diversified, and income shot up. Ute Mountain Ute households averaged over $26,000, and Southern Utes averaged over $61,000 (Colorado averaged $58,000). A 2009 economic survey in Colorado also noted that 15 percent of Indian households in Colorado (most of which were Ute) earned more than $70,000, with a small percent earning more than $100,000. One Southern Ute senior confided to an investigative journalist that in 2010 his dividend income alone was $77,500. It was a major income shift from the 1950s.[101]

By 2001 the energy-rich Southern Utes, with a population of little more than 1,300 people, had become one of the wealthiest tribes in the nation, with a net worth in excess of $1 billion and an AAA bond rating from Fitch and Moody—the first American Indian tribe ever to do so. By 2007, still with their AAA bond rating, the tribe's net worth had tripled to $3 billion. Despite the 2008 Great Recession, by 2010 it was reportedly between $3.5 and $14 billion, thanks to their investments in oil and gas. Credit for the tribe's success was variously assigned to the acumen of tribal leadership, especially Leonard Burch, as well as to the investment plans of financial advisor, John Jurrius.[102] However, in August of 2001 Jurrius left the Southern Utes amid a flurry of controversy and court actions and went to work for the Northern Utes. But by this time his Permanent Fund and Growth Fund were firmly in place, well run, and growing.

But sudden wealth did not solve all of the age-old problems overnight. While members now drove new Cadillacs, BMW convertibles, and late-model pickups, or sported diamond bracelets and cashed $10,000 checks at local banks, they still retrieved goods from pawn shops, lived in older homes, and struggled with the same health and social problems as before, including obesity, diabetes, and alcoholism. The wealth had also brought new issues of crime, as young people were murdered or assaulted for their money, gigolos courted rich husbands or wives, or a swarm of Indian wannabes suddenly "discovered" they had Ute blood and sought membership to claim a share of the family inheritance.[103]

Some members worried that the old saying was true: "Money is the root of all evil," while others observed increased contention and complained that "It seems like the more money we have, the less people get along." The allocation of the wealth and its management spawned occasional screaming matches and threats of assault in council and tribal meetings, recall petitions, and accusations of pocket-lining against tribal leaders and financial advisors. Dissidents complained the tribal government was "veiled in secrecy." And indeed, tribal officers grew reluctant to talk to journalists for fear of being misquoted, and their frustration with biased or inaccurate news reports that "emphasize[d] the pitfalls of wealth, including the political infighting," that suggested the Utes were "savages" who couldn't "handle money any better than they [could] handle liquor." Dissidents claimed the tribe was "being taken for a ride" by outsiders like Jurrius, who were making the reservation—in the words of conservative Sage Remington—a "nouveau riche banana republic." Adjusting to the new tribal wealth would take time.[104]

Addressing Tribal Social and Cultural Needs

As the Ute Mountain and Southern Ute tribes entered the new century, they faced new problems as well as old. A hundred years earlier, the issues had been too little money and too little freedom. By 2000 the issues were too much tribal money and too much freedom. Tribal councils had become, in the words of one social historian, socialistic "cradle-to-grave service organizations," providing income, services, and jobs, and acting as liaisons to the "outside" world,[105] while independence and self-reliance withered. Although some services like the Ute Mountain's law enforcement and court systems were returned to the BIA, the tribal councils retained many others (road maintenance, social services, housing, education, and for the Southern Utes, the courts) and expanded their control of economic development.[106] As tribal enterprises and income expanded dramatically, bureaucracies ballooned and grew complex. Tribes incorporated modern technology, the media, and the courts to demand tribal rights as a distinct ethnic group and control of their own resources.

But tribal power and wealth did not eliminate the same kinds of problems on Ute reservations as those plaguing most Indian tribes in the United States, and in some cases were worse within the three Ute tribes. More than a century of political, social, and economic oppression, as well as ongoing deprivation and dependency, had resulted in severe social dysfunction that played out in a multitude of antisocial behaviors and poor health.[107] Dietary changes along with an increasingly sedentary lifestyle led to an epidemic of obesity and type 2 diabetes, with over 25 percent of all Southern Utes over the age of forty-five suffering the effects of obesity and diabetes.[108]

409

Even more troubling was the rise in alcohol and drug abuse. Once alcohol became legal for Indians, life expectancy plummeted, acts of violence increased, and crime rates soared, with nearly all crimes being directly related to alcohol use. By the mid-1980s, 98 percent of all unnatural Ute deaths could be linked to alcohol. These trends reflected the rise of alcohol-related violence on all reservations; just in 1991–1992 the national reservation average for assault rose 25 percent, murder went up 60 percent, and suicide rates soared.[109] Alcohol was still a "curse...the *living death.*" As early as 1830, veteran mountain man Warren Ferris described the effects of alcohol on the Plains Indians; 160 years later the virulent effects of alcohol had changed little:

> They were gay and light hearted, but they are now moody and melancholy; they were candid and confiding, they are now jealous and sullen; they were athletic and active, they are now impotent and inert; they were just though implacable, they are now malignant and vindictive; they were honorable and dignified, they are now mean and abased; integrity and fidelity were their characteristics, now they are both dishonest and unfaithful; they were brave and courteous, they are now cowardly and abusive. They are melting away before the curse of the white man's friendship.[110]

The tribes responded by developing committees on alcoholism and establishing alcohol rehabilitation and treatment centers like the Southern Utes' "Peaceful Spirit Lodge" and a "Wellness Court" (*TüüCai* Court) for repeat offenders to direct them through multiagency community services. The Ute Mountain council banned alcohol on the reservation entirely, a measure heartily endorsed by most members, and some opposition over casinos on the reservation was rooted in their concern of reintroducing alcohol. On the other hand, the Southern Utes found such a ban impossible, given the checkerboard reservation and intermingling of cultural groups. To combat the pernicious effects of alcohol, both tribes supported the use of traditional spirituality and integrated ceremonial sweats into rehabilitation programs, and prominent spiritual advisors and religious leaders preached against its use. The Native American Church prohibited alcohol entirely, while some Sundance leaders, like Eddie Box (a reformed drinker himself), claimed the Sundance and alcohol were incompatible.[111]

Alcohol was also implicated in most cases of domestic abuse, but because of jurisdictional issues, only Indian-on-Indian incidents could be prosecuted. Because a 1978 Supreme Court ruling denied tribal courts the right to try non-Indians, the tribal police and its judicial system could do nothing about domestic abuse committed by non-Indians, and state and federal courts were reluctant to get involved. Yet according to one national report, nearly 50 percent of all American Indian or Alaska Native women were married to non-Indians, Indian women were two-and-a-half times as likely to experience sexual assaults as non-Indian women, and 33 percent of Indian women said they had been raped during their lifetime. This jurisdictional loophole was theoretically plugged in 2013 when President Barack Obama signed an expanded Violence Against Women Act, a heavily debated legislation that expanded tribal authority so that tribal police could finally arrest, and tribal courts could prosecute, reservation crimes linked to domestic violence, even if they were committed by non-Indians.[112]

One of the main witnesses before Congress on behalf of the new Violence Against Women Act was a Southern Ute woman, Diane Millich, whose non-Indian husband began beating her within days of their marriage. Throughout her ordeal, repeated calls to law officers led nowhere and her husband, who knew he could not be prosecuted, mocked her inability to get help. Although Millich ultimately divorced her husband, the violence did not stop. He was only arrested after he attempted to shoot her while she was at work (a felony)—and that charge was plea bargained down.[113]

Another major concern on all Ute reservations was how to retain traditional culture and values as members integrated into a world that incorporated individual capitalism, high technology use, international communications, and a demanding Euro-American work ethic. Western lifeways were sometimes antithetical to traditional egalitarianism, communalism, and a dependence on extended kinship relations. Ute employees who tended to family or ceremonial obligations were reprimanded for tardiness, unauthorized leaves of absence, and neglect of responsibilities.[114]

And much of their Ute culture and language were disappearing as children lost their once-extensive interaction with traditional transmitters of culture—grandparents and extended families. Grandparents now lived in their own homes and were encouraged to utilize elder care and senior center programs, while non-Indian social workers encouraged them to not let themselves be exploited as babysitters for employed children, though this was a role Ute grandparents had traditionally performed. Meanwhile, as the use of media and technology on the reservations increased, children no longer spent time with their elders: "They don't have time; they go watch T.V."[115]

411

The most apparent loss was of language, which most recognized as the core of Ute culture. This caused alarm and led to a coordinated effort to standardize the language and issue grammars, dictionaries, and language-learning programs.[116] Meanwhile, efforts to restore traditional activities were also revived. All three tribes attempted to incorporate bison herds (although short-lived on the arid Ute Mountain range), and by 2013 both tribes had successfully negotiated pacts with Colorado to allow enrolled members to hunt outside normal hunting season for a specified amount of big game and within much of their traditional hunting range—millions of acres northeast of their reservations.[117]

The most visible attempts by advocates of traditionalism, however, were to revive older religious perceptions and a renewed interest in native religious ceremonies. As healer medicine men died, a spiritual void had developed. At first some sought out expensive Navajo medicine men, but by the 1970s a new group of holy men were appearing who could offer spiritual advice and direction. However, few of these were "medicine" men in the traditional sense. Terry Knight, an influential advisor among the Ute Mountain Utes, claimed he was neither a "medicine man" nor a "spiritual" advisor. "I am not anybody. I'm just doing what I have to do...and [following] how I believe in the Creator." However, Knight was a significant religious leader; he not only held sweats but was a Sundance chief after 1980 and an important roadman in the Native American Church.[118]

By the 1970s sweat baths, once only an element of some healing ceremonies, became a ceremony unto itself and was used for doctoring, purification, rejuvenation, and spiritual enlightenment. Both the Ute Mountain and Southern Utes included sweats as part of their alcohol and drug rehabilitation programs, using them to transmit traditional values.[119]

The imported Native American Church also served as a rallying point for its practitioners. More than half of the Ute Mountain Utes participated in peyote ceremonies, with the tribe having nearly thirty active roadmen among its members in the 1990s. Although the Native American Church was a pan-Indian religion, the Ute Mountain Utes had adapted their traditional religious conceptions within the peyote meetings. This allowed them to continue to express traditional Ute mores even as they cemented their ethnic Indian identity. On the other hand, the Southern Utes generally rejected the peyote road, and only ten Southern Ute families were active members in the 1990s.[120]

A renewed interest in the important Sundance ritual arose as the century ended, still serving as a means of expressing Indian values, summoning individual and collective power, and for physical and spiritual doctoring. Religious leadership of the Sundance remained stable among both the Ute Mountain and especially the Southern Utes. Edwin Cloud had been the Southern Utes' only Sundance chief during early years, with Eddie Box assuming leadership when Cloud died in the 1940s. In 1994 an ailing Box turned these duties over to Neil Cloud, Edwin's grandson, who he considered the rightful chief. Neil Cloud relinquished this office to Kenny Frost, and by 2016, the dance was being led by Hanley Frost Sr. One of Kenny Frost's innovations was to introduce workshops to help teach members about the Sundance. Though there had been some resistance over tribal funding of religious community affairs in the 1950s and 1960s, by the final decades of the twentieth century the Sundance became one of the most important reservation activities, with timing coordinated for inter-reservation travel and tribes funding both the dance and the feast that followed.[121]

The revival of—or reemphasis on—traditional religion was linked to the concern over culture loss as increasing wealth and interaction with non-Indians wrapped most members in layers of Western culture and ideology. Ute elders voiced concern over the impact of this rising cultural displacement, the failure of youth to learn about the old ways, and the disappearance of their culture-laced language. Many lamented their former slower pace of life. The once quiet and isolated Towaoc became increasingly noisy and bustling, and some dreamt of escaping the clamor by retreating into the remote interior of the reservation. Other Ute Mountain Utes complained that the people had "too much money...People worship money...it has ruined the Ute people," and that "when we got this money, everything changed." Nearby, a Southern Ute elder reminisced that things were better "before the money...[when] everything was easier, simpler," when they could hunt and gather foods. "Now the young people could not live without luxuries like electricity."[122]

The shift into the economics and lifestyles of mainstream America was most dramatic for the once isolated and scattered Ute Mountain Utes, who leapt into the twentieth century within a few short decades. In 1953 there had only been six hundred enrolled members of the tribe; most could not speak

English and were illiterate, only thirty had even an elementary school education, while only five had graduated from high school. None were college graduates. But by the 1970s, their children were attending public schools in Cortez. In 2010, at least 60 percent had graduated from high school, and some had college degrees. They had also become a vigorous young tribe, with the majority of members under the age of thirty and living in Towaoc.[123]

However, the challenges of maintaining tribal wealth and using it wisely to improve the endemic social and physical problems of individual members remained the same for all three Ute tribes, along with the struggle to redevelop self-reliance in the face of continuing high levels of unearned income and the dampening effect of local prejudices that left non-Indians still reluctant to hire Native Americans. The challenge of balance between retaining traditional culture and mores with the expectations—and demands—of Western-style employment and management continued to raise significant issues for all Utes. One of the greatest challenges to twenty-first century Utes has been to adjust to a new culture of wealth and materialism, while continuing to incorporate traditional values and maintaining a strong ethnic identity, even in the face of social problems engendered by both.

413

Chapter 19

Epilogue

One day Coyote was out wandering around. He discovered a flock of chickadees laughing, talking, and playing in the willows. When he crept close he saw that they were tossing their eyes into willow branches, then shaking them down into their places again. Coyote thought that this looked fun and wanted to know how to do this trick too. But the chickadees did not like Coyote; they told him he would lose his eyes and wished him bad luck. But Coyote insisted on learning the trick. When he tried to toss his eyes into the willow branches they stuck fast and he could not shake them down again. Then he was blind and thought he would surely go crazy.

He covered his eyes with a piece of buckskin and wandered away. Soon he met two girls and joined up with them and took them to be his wives. But because he could not see he kept doing things wrong. When he went out to hunt buffalo he kept walking past his spent arrows without seeing them; when he finally killed a buffalo he did not know he had done it until his wives told him; when he skinned the beast he cut the skin all up and ruined it; when they cooked the meat he walked beyond the fire or sat on the meat; he disfigured the wickiup the wives made. Each time he made up excuses.

But finally the girls suspected something was wrong. So when Coyote went to sleep they peeked under the buckskin which covered his eyes and discovered that his sockets were filled with maggots and fly eggs. Then they decided to run away. But first they put his head on a log filled with red ants. When Coyote woke up with the ants all over him he called for his wives, but they were gone. Coyote followed them with his nose, picking up their scent. But when he drew close to them, one of the runaway wives threw her pouch which was covered with jingles over the edge of a cliff. Coyote followed the sound of the jingling and tumbled into the ravine, breaking his legs. When the girls peered over the edge they found him eating the marrow of his leg, thinking it was the bone of some succulent game animal. Despite his protestations, the girls recognized his shame.[1]

Once again Coyote, the bungling spoiler, reinforced the value of being content with who you are. He tried to imitate the behavior of another people, and it led only to injury and humiliation. Alien cultures (the chickadees) were engaged in something he thought would be fun and, despite warnings, he tried the new behavior but ended up blinding and shaming himself. Worse, when he tried to return to his own culture, his foray into foreign behavior had left him unable to see or function properly in a "Coyote" way.

This Eye-Juggler tale is just one of hundreds of grandfather stories that once transmitted important Numic mores, ethics, and values. Storytelling elders were a special asset to traditional Ute camps. They were entertainment on long winter evenings, but more importantly, they were transmitters of the collective moral conscience of the people.[2] This was particularly true of the fables about misbehavior and its consequences, especially those of the antisocial and maladroit trickster who was most often portrayed as Younger Brother Coyote (*Yukʷu-pi-ci*), as opposed to his wiser, more beneficent Elder Brother Coyote, or Wolf (*Siná-wavi*).[3]

The cultural fabric of these tales mirrored the world in which the Utes lived. The stories were about the People, and about the foibles of men placed in a mythical before-time in which animals spoke, things happened because a person thought them, and magic and supernatural powers were commonplace. While some tales simply explained the origins of everyday things or established sanctions, most were fables or parables that made an oblique point about a person's character flaws. They emphasized the dangers of misusing power, showed the results of greed, or emphasized the importance of community and the benefits of sociality and cooperation. Together, they shared the common anxieties shared by Numic people about survival in an uncertain world filled with ongoing and often unexplainable dangers.

While the tales were entertainment—a good story well told—they also carried the underlying morality of one's behavior. Coyote the Trickster was a metaphor for the evil within all men and the inner corruption that produced outer corruption, which was to be shunned or made the butt of gruesome jokes. He exemplified the maladjusted individual who, among making other mistakes, tries to imitate the behavior of a foreign people, rather than being satisfied with who he was and his own native way of being. The tales emphasized the dangers of trying to be something you were not.

The lessons inherent in these stories guided a people who lived in a world of constant change. And change was especially rapid after the Utes began to encounter non-Indian traders and colonizers and the new commodities they brought. But despite folkloric warnings not to imitate other people, the ever-pragmatic Utes have long demonstrated their ability to adopt and adapt to the new, and to integrate into their own culture what worked to enhance survival and improve their chances to prosper. But the metaphorical question has always been, could they learn to juggle their eyes, or were they doomed to suffer Coyote's fate of injury and humiliation? Change is, after all, a two-edged sword.

Physically, changes had been occurring for centuries, as these Numic people adapted to shifting environmental and social situations. Subsistence methods changed, from digging roots and catching rabbits in the Great Basin deserts to fishing, fowling, and hunting big game in the mountains. Survival toolkits shifted from digging sticks and rabbit nets to spears and arrows, and then to muskets and rifles. Social and political relationships transformed as well, depending on the availability of resources. Changing trade networks shifted from simple interband exchanges to commercial trading with non-Indians, and hit-and-run raiding was incorporated as new horses, weapons, and expanding territories increased contact and competition with other people.

Social and political relations shifted as well. The scattered family bands that eked out a subsistence from resource-poor regions coalesced into small, seasonal communal camps near lakes and rivers. As hunters acquired horses and more advanced weapons, their seasonal migration allowed family bands to cluster for communal hunting, for food and hide preparation, and for their mutual defense. As bands grew larger and more complex, leadership transformed, requiring influential and successful men to direct nomadic movements or represent the bands in negotiating with non-Utes.

Horses and new weapons transformed Ute physical culture as they traveled further and exploited new food resources and markets for furs, hides, meat, and slaves. Raiding and hunting increased and new tools, foods, clothing, shelters, and decorative accoutrements were incorporated into their world. The southern bands hunted on the Great Plains and traded on the Upper Rio Grande where they acquired a veneer of a Plains bison culture, accented by Pueblo, Navajo, and Spanish items. While the more isolated western bands retained many of their desert roots, they began to acquire more American goods as trade and colonization by non-Indians increased.

As contact with non-Indians increased, Ute chiefs were needed who could negotiate with the incoming strangers. Government officials demanded the Utes make treaties and provide recognized representatives with whom they could make them. But despite the chiefs' best efforts, by 1880 nearly all the Utes had been forced onto three restrictive reservations. And by the early twentieth century, they had lost much of this land as well.

Change was even more rapid on reservations, although most Utes tried to cling to an emotional essence of being Ute, of being *Núu-ci*. Canvas tents replaced tipis just as tipis had once replaced brush wickiups; textile clothing and blankets replaced buckskins, rabbit-skin blankets, and buffalo robes; government supplies supplemented berries and roots, and domestic sheep and cattle replaced the big game they had once hunted. Although these external trappings were changing, Utes still refused to completely abandon their traditional worldview, their general moral consciousness, or the right to express their own Indian spirituality, albeit within transforming ritual frameworks. Nomadism and hunting might be restricted, raiding nonexistent, employment difficult to find, and their dress, diet, and dwellings might resemble the non-Indians around them; nevertheless, Utes continued to *be Núu-ci* and were definitely not vanishing.

However, as the twentieth century dawned, most of The People had been reduced to a state of debilitating poverty and dependence, continually pressured to discard every vestige of Ute culture and custom in favor of a "civilized" assimilation (and absorption) into mainstream America. But many refused. Tents, tipis, and shade houses persisted as adjuncts to new housing; family networks remained important; and some hunting and gathering of traditional foods continued to supplement diets. While most clothing had changed, it could still be embellished with symbols of an Indian identity—beaded belts or hair clips, fancy belt buckles, Indian jewelry, or moccasins. Some western styles of clothing came to be associated with Indian identity as well: Levis, western shirts, and cowboy boots and hats. And the Utes defiantly continued to hold on to some traditional rituals, including shamanic healing and the spring Bear Dance (suitably renamed or rescheduled to appease agents), and they refused to abandon newly adopted religious rituals like the Sundance or peyote meetings that they had adapted and imbued with older *Núu-ci* beliefs.

Nevertheless, tribal communities remained tightly restricted, and their chiefs relatively powerless. However, when the Indian Reorganization Act

(IRA) finally untied their hands, Ute leaders were able to reassert themselves as representatives and negotiators for their tribes. Land-claims money combined with corporate rehabilitation plans and brought even more changes to the Utes' material, social, economic, and political cultures.

Tribal leaders were increasingly given the ability to control tribal affairs. But it took time for members and leaders to learn how to function successfully within their new economic and political world. The Utes had always been a fractious, independent people, highly mobile and flexible in their band associations. While no longer able to "vote with their feet" as Piah and Colorow had once done, members learned how to make their wishes known through protests and votes.

By the 1970s, all three tribes were pushing toward self-sufficiency through a corporate American model. Tribal leaders freely used the services of expert advisors and lawyers, incorporating their younger, educated, and more acculturated members to help transform tribal governments. Though a number of disastrous mistakes were made along the way and politics remained contentious, by the end of the twentieth century traditional tribal leadership had morphed into a capitalistic corporate mold. Tribal leaders and their advisors now brought prosperity to their people, not by guiding hunting or trading forays, but by managing successful, profit-generating tribal enterprises. And with these profits, tribes could develop reservation facilities, infrastructure, and community amenities; provide funding and administration for large-scale community events; and redistribute their growing wealth among members in a socialistic—but quite traditional—model of community sharing and support.[4]

The unabashed goal of tribal enterprises had always been to make the tribe prosperous and to create jobs *at home* on the reservation. Most Utes preferred to remain home where they were closer to supportive networks of family and friends and where they felt more comfortable among members of their own ethnic group. Families continued to pool resources in times of need, and pragmatic nepotism secured jobs for those who wanted to work. Families and tribal leaders also exerted their own significant pressure on wandering members, urging them to return home. Also factors were preferences for rural life, Indian sociality, and a general distaste for big cities. Although by 2000 half of all U.S. Native Americans were urban Indians, the majority of full-blood Utes were not.

Consequently, by the twenty-first century most Utes survived on a combination of earned and unearned income, both tied directly to various tribal and federal government resources. This impacted them culturally and, not surprisingly, reinforced some traditional worldviews. Broadly speaking, the Ute philosophy of living had always been an open expression of pragmatic hedonism in which life was enjoyed now rather than sacrificed for an amorphous heavenly reward. Utes were not inherently lazy or idle, as early non-Indians often complained; their precarious hunting-raiding-gathering subsistence required sustained and often desperately hard work followed by periods of recuperative idleness and a release of tension through playful sport and games. However, the loss of resources, imprisonment on reservations, the difficulty of farming, and the inability to nomadically hunt and gather left few viable alternatives.

Unlike the grinding work ethic that drives many Americans, Utes shared an easygoing acceptance of life. Life was not all work but was filled with a variety of experiences that included hard work, hard play, and a good amount of purely idle time in which stories and folklore were passed on, competitive games were played, and social relations strengthened. Many Utes rejected the day-in, day-out sustained labor pattern upon which the opulence of American society and its perception of physical and spiritual redemption were based. And the high priority given to the cares of religious or family obligations often interfered with inflexible daily work routines.[5]

Utes had a long tradition of interfamilial cooperation and collectivism as well. Most religious ritual encouraged a syndication of communal power to accumulate the *púwa* medicine power needed for specific healings or an overall communal good. Such syndications occurred in Sundances or Bear Dances, and on a smaller scale in sweats and peyote meetings. Utes had customarily shared their material prosperity through family networks as an important means of survival. However, as tribes and members gained greater financial independence, many of these bonds were broken, pulling family networks apart. Individuals looked to the tribe or federal welfare programs for assistance rather than extended family. But if tribal wealth decreased, federal programs cut back, or an individual lost a job, family networks could again pool resources—for family remained a Ute bedrock.[6]

But as financial independence unknotted family networks and media grabbed the attention of young people, the passing on of traditional lore, mores, and mystic tradition has grown more difficult. Medicine men have given way to spiritual advisors, children attend to electronic entertainment rather than storytelling by grandfathers, and Netflix and ESPN have replaced tale-telling around winter campfires for everyone. Assimilating the physical culture of America has inevitably included assimilating much of its worldview, too, and the emotional, spiritual, and physical health of Utes has suffered. Many younger members of the tribe no longer speak the Ute language, in which much of their Uteness is encoded. Some Utes echo the concerns of other American Indians, that the materialism fostered by gaming or other wealth has been inherently "antithetical to tribal culture and poses a threat to cultural values, practices, and traditions." Another concern is that "after a while, we'll all live like white men. We'll live in a square house and pay mortgages and live by the golden dollar."[7]

To counter these losses, tribal officials and concerned members have attempted to revive respect for traditional arts, crafts, and values through cultural education programs, language preservation, and an active support of traditional ceremonials, dance, music, and religion. Healing traditions and religious ceremonies have assumed an increased importance as an expression of Indian, and specifically Ute, identity, whether or not attendees subscribe to the religious beliefs they embody. Some have tried to emphasize a worldview that includes an "inbred" Indian spiritualism despite external trappings. Others have decried the loss of identity that the integration of non-Indian culture and an American work ethic have brought. One Northern Ute cynically observed in the 1980s that most Utes hung between the white and red worlds, many ceasing to be Utes except at ceremonials or when collecting benefits. Forty years earlier a Southern Ute had voiced similar concerns, worried that Ute identity was being changed as tribal officials adjusted to modern economic rhythms, such as shifting the traditional Bear Dance later in the spring—or even to the fall—to fit non-Indian work (and school) calendars. "It makes you wonder," he complained, "whether we are Utes or farmers." By the 1980s, tribes were no longer basing their Sundances on the lunar cycle (full moon), but coordinating their event calendars with the two other tribes.[8]

Meanwhile, factional politics, a century-long culture of poverty and dependency, traditional reserve, and a continual lack of knowledge or experience with a cash economy have combined with ongoing prejudice from non-Indians to hamper individual progress. Though personal income and standards of living have increased dramatically in the twenty-first century, some critics warned that large, unearned per-capita payments (dividends) were hampering personal development. And pockets of poverty remained, as did high mortality rates from suicide, alcoholism, heart disease, and diabetes. Many of the nouveau riche Utes of the new century continued to struggle with how to handle their new wealth because few had the financial literacy

420

necessary for a cash economy. In 2003 the *Wall Street Journal* described a seventy-nine-year-old Southern Ute woman, her diamond tennis bracelet resting on a handmade skirt, giving her opinion that too much money caused too much conflict.[9]

Nevertheless, most Utes have remained proud of their ethnic identity as *Núu-ci* Utes and as Indians. Although by the end of the twentieth century they ate, dressed, worked, played, lived, and politicked like mainstream Americans, they still shared a common history and racial identity with other Indians, and shared a sense of *Uteness* with other Utes. While internal politics and tribal economies have fostered some tribal splintering, including prejudice against mixed-heritage White Mesa Utes and the expulsion of mixed-blood Uintahs, most Utes share a strong sense of heritage and community.

And despite the miles that separate their reservations, all three Ute tribes still emphasize their linked ethnic identities. Early explorers clearly noted that while there were some distinctions between central Utah and Colorado Utes—including a distinct Timpanogos Ute accent—a unifying ethnic bond still existed between them. The mid-1900s found that all Utes—eastern or western, northern or southern, mounted or unmounted—still shared a basic Ute or *Núu-ci* identity, and "recognized that they were a *single* people," even though "there was no closer bond of unity nor any greater identity of interests beyond this general feeling of cultural similarity." They were the same people because they spoke the same language and shared a similar worldview. And they knew who were *not* Utes. As anthropologist and linguist James Goss pointed out when speaking of culture changes among the Utes, "A man may put on a new hat, but it doesn't necessarily change the way he *thinks*" or who he is.[10]

We can also learn something about how the genesis of ethnicity works by looking at what happened when one group of Utes were suddenly denied their Ute identity. After hundreds of mixed-heritage Uintahs were expelled from the tribe for having too little Ute "blood," their first response was to fight to be reincorporated into the tribe and be recognized as Utes. They identified themselves as Utes, they thought like Utes, they had Ute relatives, and they still attended Ute religious events. But after decades of being rebuffed for not being "real" Utes, they began to redefine themselves in opposition to the Ute Tribe, who they now viewed as genocidal interlopers and their foremost enemy.[11]

Instead, the mixed-heritage Uintahs turned their focus to their pre-1880 identity as Uintahs, and the pre-1800s presence of Shoshone hunters in the Uintah Basin. Many had developed marriage and social relationships with neighboring Shoshones, and harkened back a few Shoshone ancestors, including the wife of trader Jim Charboneau Reed. In any case, the neighboring Shoshones, once bitter enemies of the Utes, had grown closer through their common Numic ancestry and similar language, had shared similar tribulations of conquest and reservation life, and now shared a religious (and in some cases literal) kinship within the inter-reservation Sundance community.[12]

Thus, by the 1980s the terminated mixed-blood Uintahs, rejected at home by full-blood Utes, had begun to reconstruct their identity from the shards of an older identity that "belonged" in the Uintah Basin. They were not Utes at all and never had been. They were Shoshones, as had been all western "Utes."[13] To understand what happened, we must step back to a time when there were no tribal identities among the linguistically and culturally similar Numic people. The ethnic identities of Ute, Shoshone, Bannock, Goshute, or Paiute appeared only after competition and conflict developed over scarce resources, and especially after trade enriched and empowered some groups over others. A competition-induced genesis of specific ethnic groups—an *ethnogenesis*—spun out individual tribal identities and solidified ethnic boundaries as defined in opposition to "others"—that is, who was Ute and who was not, or more explicitly, who was Ute and who was an enemy.[14]

The modern competition over the Utah reservation's resources (natural and political) echoed this ethnic metamorphosis. Stripped of their Ute identity but still feeling Indian, and in a rancorous competition with "The Tribe," Uintah mixed-bloods searched for an identity that was uniquely theirs. If they were not Ute *Núu-ci* (which is what the tribe claimed), then they must be Shoshone *Newe*. Nineteenth-century officials and historians had mistakenly identified the Indians of central Utah as Utes when they were actually Shoshones. Though a well-documented and bloody historical enmity existed between the Shoshones and the central Utah Utes that testifies against this interpretation, it has been ignored. Court actions were initiated and reservation resources appropriated by mixed-blood groups with a variety of names, including the Timpanogos Tribe, Snake Band of the Shoshone Indians, or more recently, the Uintah Valley Shoshone Tribe of Affiliated Ute Citizens. Though the courts repeatedly dismissed such claims, these rechristened Uintahs continued defiant. As one woman summarized it, "I'm Shoshone and it don't never mind what anyone else says. I know who I am."[15]

Meanwhile, the enrolled members of all three tribes continued to deal with transformative cultural changes. As they more deeply integrated into mainstream America, the Utes, like other newly rich tribes, were faced with the problem of a "development-induced displacement" of their identity. New wealth caused tribal factionalism and fueled ongoing debates over how to use tribal money. Dissidents argued individual access to the money; complained about the transparency of tribal investments; and made accusations of mismanagement, corruption, self-aggrandizement, and nepotism. At the same time, members continued to worry about the rapid loss of culture and traditions.

At the prodding of concerned members, the tribes took an increasingly active role as conservators of their Ute heritage. While no one wanted to return to their hardscrabble life before horses, they remained proud of a romantic heritage as mounted nomads and their (idealized) relationship with nature and the land to which they "belonged." Tribes pushed to have hunting and fishing rights restored within the boundaries of earlier reservations, implemented conservation programs, and reintroduced healthier elements of an older diet.

But much of the essence of being Ute, the emotional identity as Utes, was contained within their language, their oral literature, and their religion, which was more difficult to retain. Leaders acted to conserve Ute history and traditions by building modern museums to hold relics and preserve the past, and they provided educational opportunities to remind members of their heritage. They created a written form of the Ute language and promoted its use and printed small collections of folklore, which was helpful but a long way from the hundreds of tales once told. They also promoted participation in traditional Ute events. All of these cultural preservation programs were implemented to counteract culture loss and reinforce pride in both an Indian and a Ute ethnic identity in the face of a rapidly changing physical and spiritual world.[16]

By the late twentieth century, few Utes viewed the integration of America's material culture as negating their inherent Indian or Ute identity. Simply adopting new "stuff" or participating in mostly nontraditional activities did not mean they were not still members of a distinct ethnic group. After all, they had been changing their material culture to accommodate new environments and new opportunities for centuries.[17]

Modern anthropologists have also argued that the boundaries defining an ethnic group are not the "cultural stuff" it encloses; rather, ethnic groups persist because people accept mutually agreed upon social boundaries that set them apart from others. Their identity is defined by who they believe themselves to be, and who others believe them to be. Members of the group accept criteria by which they signal to themselves and to others that they are members of a distinct community and not strangers; they feel that they are "playing the same game," or thinking the same way. So ethnic groups perpetuate themselves, not through an accumulation of physical things (which easily change over time and space) but through biological descent, by sharing fundamental cultural values, through social-community interactions (including family networks and common community activities), and by recognizing each other as members of the same group.[18]

Being Ute is more than just a legal membership in a distinct biologically defined community (blood quantum). Being Ute also comes from a sense of shared history, culture, and tribulations. This is why the disinherited Uintah mixed-bloods were able to re-create their oppositional identity in Utah. A group's identity is also reinforced through their participation in community events or group action, and particularly through their participation in religious activities that perpetuate more traditional perceptions and values. For those who do embrace Ute religious traditions, the rituals, symbols, music, and communal participation embody much of what they consider the heart of being Ute. Regardless of a person's belief in the spiritual efficacy of a traditional ritual, its very practices and symbols act to build cohesion, construct a distinct community, and reinforce the boundaries around the group.[19] Such events also provide space where they can socialize as Utes, don the traditional dress and accoutrements that symbolize their Ute Indian identity, and participate in traditional Ute activities, including camping in tents or tipis, using shade houses, playing traditional games of chance, and sharing a communal feast.

And reinforcing the Utes' greater Indian identity are the pan-Indian rodeos and powwows that have become a mainstay of community events. Reincorporating a pan-Indian musical sociality, such inter-reservation events have replaced the family-band gatherings of an earlier era, even as the modern powwow and rodeo circuits reflect an older seasonal nomadism. They have become a celebration of a participant's Indian heritage, a place where they can display traditional (and adopted) Indian skills, play traditional games, and participate in traditional social dances. It is a milieu wherein a pan-Indian identity and community continue to be encouraged.[20]

Over the past four hundred years, the Ute people have experienced massive cultural changes, during which they have exploited or accommodated their shifting circumstances. And as they did so, most of the external survival strategies, material culture, and social structures that once defined them have been transformed. But while most twenty-first-century Utes have adopted the material—and materialistic—culture of mainstream Americans, they have remained jealously protective of their heritage and historic identity as Ute. In part, this is a result of their shared conflict with outsiders who have battered at their identity, demanded they abandon their culture, and stolen their resources.

Today, to be Ute means to be enrolled in a federally recognized Ute tribe and to have a quantifiable measure of Ute "blood." But it is also an emotional sense of simply *being* Ute and being part of the Ute community. This is enhanced by the complex networks of family relations that stretch across reservation boundaries, encourages frequent cross-reservation visiting, and emphasizes their shared history and cultural heritage. Who the twenty-first-century Ute has become remains vastly different from who they were 500, 300, or even 100 years ago. But the sense of a common heritage, perpetuated by modern reservation activities, accoutrements, and attitudes, continues to reinforce the feeling of being Indian, especially of being a Ute Indian, a *Núu-ci*.

All of this has unified the Utes within a recognized ethnic and political identity, regardless of political infighting or American materialism. Utes may head to work in their modern, technologically up-to-date office buildings, dressed in a suit and tie or modish pant suits, but be found the next week suitably outfitted in traditional Sundance regalia, or jeans and ribbon-bedecked western shirt at a powwow, or even in fringed buckskin and feathers at a fancy-dance competition. Or they might eschew such demonstrations entirely. Regardless, both types of modern Ute recognize their ethnic kinship. At the very least, they recognize, are proud of, and support their ethnic heritage. Three decades ago, one elder touched the heart of this emotional and symbolic identity when he thumped his chest and reassured a worried grandson, "All that matters is that you remain Indian *here*."[21]

The story of the Ute people is not yet over. It continues as the Ute people, like everyone, continue to evolve and adapt to the ever-changing physical and social environments of modern America. While many tragic events have occurred in their history, the Ute story is not a tragedy. Rather than sinking into an oppressed oblivion as was once predicted, the Utes have demonstrated the resilience and dynamism possible among a determined American Indian people.

Appendix

Historical Nomenclature for Ute Bands

Modern Ute bands (and tribes) exist today as political entities because Euro-Americans needed to have distinguishing names for Ute groups for economic and administrative purposes. Early explorers did identify the local Indian groups they encountered and recorded these in diaries, memoirs, and reports. But by the 1850s, officially identifying these bands and tribes became politically important for the purpose of negotiating treaties or agreements with specific people with identifiable leaders in order to administer affairs through Indian agencies, and later reorganized corporate tribal organizations. However, traditional Ute bands were fluid, geosocial units. Although they were usually based on kin-and-clique relationships (family and friends), members could—and often did—shift allegiance and territory for a variety of reasons. Nevertheless, the nucleus of band membership usually remained relatively stable, as did the traditional nomadic circuit through which they traveled.

Because of the often amorphous nature of Ute bands, names and terms used for them are not always consistent in the historical and ethnographic literature. As a result, identifying exactly which group a record referred to can be problematic. In this study I have attempted to use the most easily identifiable references from the scholarly literature while still remaining as true as possible to traditional native identities. Since some of the names or origins of names may need more clarification than is possible within the text or notes of this book, the following list identifies most Ute bands, their names, and where they were usually located (within the constraints of seasonal nomadism). The list has been compiled from major historical, ethnographic, and native sources, and in some cases includes explanatory notes. It includes both native terms and those used by non-Indians, with differences often being little more than dialect and spelling variations, as non-Indians attempted to record unfamiliar words and names.

THE PEOPLE

"The People" or "The Real People" is the English translation of the term(s) Numic people used to refer to themselves. Variations include:

Núu-ci, Nutc, or the suffixes -nuch, -wach, meaning "The People" or "the people of" (Opler 1940; *Southern Ute Dictionary* 1979; Powell 1971)

Nooche, Nuche, or Noochew (tribal websites and resources)

Nu'-ints, nuints, nu'au, or the suffix 'nunts, meaning "an Indian" (Powell 1971; Stewart 1942, 1952)

Num, Numa, Nu'um-pats, or Numic People, meaning "an Indian" or nu'um-pats, meaning one who speaks Ute (Powell 1971)

Non-Indian names for Utes include:

Yutas, Yuttas, Yutaas, Youta (Escalante, and Chavez and Warner 1776/1995; Miera Map; Powell 1971; Fowler and Fowler citing Zarate Salmeron [1620s]; Stewart 1973; Tyler 1951; Ruxton 1950; Talbot 1931; Rivera, Leiby 1985). Spanish name, meaning and origin unknown.

Qusutus or Guaputa (Tyler 1951)

Eut, Ewte, Eutau, Eutaw, Eutah (Ferris 1940; Ruxton 1916, 1950; Brewerton 1993; Anderson 1967; Russell 1965; Yount 1966; O. Huntington, n.d.; Hafen and Hafen 1954)

Utacas, Utas, Utahs, or Utah Indians (J. Smith 1972; Potts letters 1824–1827; Hamilton 1960; Sage 1857; *ARCIA*; *Journal History*; Treaty 1849; Heap 1857; Gottfredson 1969; Scholes 1936; Stewart 1973) This spelling was used into the 1860s.

Ute became the predominate name after 1859, e.g., *ARCIA* (1856): "Utah Indians (commonly called Utes)."

Note: Eutah Lake, Uta's Lake, Utaw Lake and Utaw Mountains, Utah Lake, and Utah Valley (e.g., Potts letters 2000; Fremont 1966; J. Smith 1972; Russell 1965; *Journal History*; O. Huntington, n.d.)

WHITE RIVER UTES

Today's White River Utes are an amalgamation of Ute bands who ranged through northwestern Colorado, particularly along the Yampa, White, and

Grand Rivers, and were federally administered at the White River Indian
Agency. They were frequent visitors at Denver and the Denver subagency so
were sometimes referred to as Denver Utes. Today the amalgamated White
Rivers are one of three bands on the Uintah and Ouray Reservation. (Identified
in contemporary government documents, e.g., Agreement 1880 and Removal
Act 1880; *ARCIA*; Powell 1971; Stewart 1942, 1952; current tribal website.)

White River Utes (band)

Taviwadziu, Taviwatsiu, Tav-i-wot-su (Stewart 1942, 1952; Powell 1971; Lowie
    1924). Described as "those formerly west of Denver," and that "Den-
    ver was center of Taviwatsiu area"; some have confused this band with
    Escalante's Tabehuachis.
Parianuche or Parianuc, Parusanuch. From "west central Colorado," pah- or
    páa- meaning "water" or "river."

Yampa Utes

By 1800 this band had moved into the Yampa River Valley, an area that had
been vacated by Escalante's Yamparika Comanches. Yampa Utes occasionally
crossed the Uintah Basin to visit central Utah. Yamparkau means "Yampa eaters," a favorite tuberous food (*Perideridia gairdneri*) that grew plentifully in this
region. Utes called the river Yam'-pa-pa (river where yampa grows).

Yam-pa Kau-ru-ats, Yamparkau, Yamparka, Yamparika, Yamparica (Powell
    1971; Stewart 1942; Escalante, and Chavez and Warner, 1976/1995)
Yampa, Yampah, Yampai, Yampus, Yampaats, Jimpipas (Irish, Report on
    Spanish Fork Council; Treaties 1868, Agreement 1873; Powell 1971; Stew-
    art 1952)

Grand River Utes

These Utes ranged near the Grand (Colorado) River of west-central Colorado.

Win-ni-na-nau-ants-er Utes (Powell 1971)
Tabuats Utes (Powell 1971)
Grand River Utes (Treaty 1868, Agreement 1873; Stewart 1952; Powell 1971)

Denver Utes

In the mid-1860s an unofficial agency was established in Denver to administer
to the needs of (and complaints about) central and northwestern Colorado Ute

bands, who frequently passed through Denver on their way to and from the mountains to hunt bison on the Plains. Denver Utes included Yampa, White, and Grand River Utes, as well as the Tabeguache. Plains-hunting Mouache and Capote usually used mountain passes further south.

TABEGUACHE OR UNCOMPAHGRE UTES

These Utes ranged in west-central Colorado, from the Colorado or Grand River to the northern edges of Southern Ute territory and near Saguache, Colorado. Some historians have identified them as Rivera's (1675) and Escalante's (1776) Sabuagana/Seguaguana. In the mid-1800s they were known as Tabeguaches until their agency was relocated from the Los Piños to the Uncompahgre River. They were also referred to as Los Piños Utes in government documents (referring to their agency).

Yutas Tabehuachis, Tabeguachi, Taveguachis, Tobawaches (Rivera, Leiby 1985; Escalante, and Chavez and Warner 1976/1995, and Miera Map; *ARCIA* 1856)

Tabeguache or Tabeguache band of Utah Indians (Treaties and Agreements 1863–1873; *RSI* and *ARCIA*; Stewart 1952)

Taviwatsiu (Chavez and Warner 1979, the glossary suggests this is the modern name of Escalante's Tabehuachis Utahs)

Moĝwavaví?waa-ci or Mogwataviwaaci (Southern Ute Dictionary 1979). This Ute dictionary identifies these people as the modern Northern Utes; the word suggests "walking Utes," a possible reference to their long walk after banishment from Colorado or to their migrating northward; taví- means "stepping" or "walking."

Möwataviwatsiu or Möwatawiwadziu (Lowie 1924; Stewart 1942; Chavez and Warner 1976/1995, glossary). Stewart's informants identified these people as Uncompahgre; Chavez and Warner identify them as Escalante's Sabuagana Yutas.

Mogwá-ci or Mogwáche Ute (*Southern Ute Dictionary* 1979). A band that once lived on the northern edge of the Southern Ute Reservation.

Yutas Ancapagari, ?aká-páa-ĝarú-ri (*Southern Ute Dictionary* 1979; cf. Chavez and Warner 1976/1995, glossary). This refers to the Uncompahgre River and means "red water sitting," and is a reference to nearby sulfurous, red-colored hot springs.

Uncompahgre Utes (government documents, e.g., *ARCIA*; 1880 Agreement, 1880 Removal Act; Executive Orders 1882 [reservation established]; 1894 Allotments; Stewart 1952)

Sabuagana or Sabuagana Yutas (Escalante, and Chavez and Warner, 1976/1995; Stewart 1942). Chavez and Warner identify these Utes as modern Möwataviwatsiu; others have identified them as Uncompahgre. Escalante placed them near the Colorado (Grand) River and said they lived in "peaked brush houses"; Stewart places their home territory near Saguache, Colorado.

Seguaguanas or Seguaguanes (Rivera, Leiby 1985). These people were located near a river of the same name. Leiby locates this in southeastern Utah along the Colorado River.

SOUTHERN UTES

The Southern Utes are the reservation-identified merger of the Mouache and Capote bands. These Utes had acquired the horse by at least 1680, probably earlier. Also identified as pínu-nuu-ci, or Pine River Utes. As a borderland people, the Southern Utes traded and raided frontier Hispanic settlements and Pueblo villages in today's northern New Mexico and later San Luis Valley, Colorado. A symbiotic trade relationship also developed with Pueblo and Hispanic people.

Capote Utes

The Capote band ranged through southwestern Colorado and the northeastern parts of New Mexico.

Kapúuta, Kapota, Capota, Capote, Copote, Caporte (*Southern Ute Dictionary* 1979; Stewart 1942; government documents, e.g., *ARCIA*; Treaties and Agreements 1855, 1868, 1873; Legislative Acts 1879; Stewart 1952). Probably a borrowed Spanish name.

Mouache Utes

Mouache Utes ranged in south-central Colorado through the San Luis Valley as far north as Saguache, Colorado; traveled south through northern New Mexico, visiting Taos and Abiquiú; and hunted eastward on the Great Plains. Also known as Taos Indians (Sage 1857).

Möwatci, Möwats, Möwatsi, Mo-at-su (Lowie 1924; Stewart 1942). Ranged "around Cimarron."

Moache, Moaches, Muache, Mogwáche, Moĝuache, Mogache, Mo-at-su (Escalante, and Chavez and Warner, 1976/1995, Miera Map; Rivera, Leiby 1985; Treaty 1868, Agreement 1873; Sage 1857; Powell 1971; Stewart 1952)

Muhuachi, Mohuache, Muache, Muwac, Muachis, Nuhuachi (Rivera, Leiby 1985; Escalante, and Chavez and Warner notes 1976/1995; e.g., *ARCIA*; Treaty 1855; Agreement 1873; Legislative Acts 1879). Located near the Dolores River in 1765, later further east.

Monache, Menache, Mequache (1873 Cimarron Agreement; Stewart 1942, 1952; *ARCIA*)

Mowatei (Escalante, Chavez and Warner, notes and glossary, 1976/1995). Chavez and Warner say this is the modern name for Nuhuach.

Moĝwá-ci, Mogwách (*Southern Ute Dictionary* 1979). "A Ute person"; see Tabeguache or Uncompahgre.

UTE MOUNTAIN UTES

The La Sal Mountains were basecamp for the Weeminuche Utes (Stewart 1942). Relocated to the western end of the Southern Ute Reservation, this isolationist band was later allotted this area as an independent reservation. Sleeping Ute Mountain was the major geographic feature giving the band its reservation-based name. The Weeminuche traditionally ranged throughout the Four Corners region, especially in southeastern Utah, and shared more traits in common with the Western Utes and San Juan Paiutes than with the Capote and Mouache. Rivera (1765) and Escalante (1776) both identified the Indians in this region as Payuchis.

Yutas Payuchis, or Payuchis Yutas (Rivera, Leiby 1985; Escalante, and Chavez and Warner 1976/1995; Miera Map; Powell, and Fowler and Fowler notes 1971; Stewart 1942). Means Ute-Paiute (i.e., mixed-heritage people).

Payuchis Cimarrones or Simarrones, Cimarron Paiutes (Rivera, Leiby notes 1985). Leiby speculates that si-maroon referred to runaway slaves, possibly a reference to dark skin; he says these Utes were later associated with the Abiquiú agency.

Wiměnutci, Wimönuntci, Wimönumtci, Wimönunts, Wimönuntsi (Lowie 1924; Stewart 1942)

Wiminuche, Wiminuch, Wiminuchi, Wiminuc, Wimenutci (Stewart 1942, 1952; A. Smith 1974)

Wiminackes (probable misspelling by Powell 1973)

Win-ni-nu-nu-in-tsu, Winunuints, Wi-mi-nu-ints (Powell 1971, MS 1495 and MS 2264)

We-mau-uche (*ARCIA* 1863)

Weeminuche (government documents, e.g., Treaty 1868, Agreement 1873; legislative acts 1879; Ute Mountain Ute tribe website and tribal business names)

Wíi-núu-ci (*Southern Ute Dictionary* 1979). Suggests "The Old Utes" or "The Old People," meaning precontact Utes; possibly a reference to "old ways."

Weenuch, Weenuche (McPherson 1985, 1995, 2011; McPherson in Cuch 2000; and, e.g., Weenuche Smoke Signals Facebook page; White Mesa Ute histories online)

WHITE MESA UTES

Some of the borderland Weeminuche and San Juan Paiutes (many with Ute-Paiute-Navajo mixed heritage) refused to relocate on the Southern Ute Reservation and eventually homesteaded ancestral homelands in Allen Canyon, Utah (Allen Canyon Utes). Historical literature often refers to these people as Payuchis. Some sources also referred to them as "Bronco Utes" because they refused to relocate onto the reservation. In the twentieth century, after losing their Allen Canyon homesteads, they were given reserved land on nearby White Mesa. They are known as White Mesa Utes today and are registered as members of the Ute Mountain Ute tribe, with one seat on its governing committee (McPherson 1985, 1995, 2011; McPherson and Yazzie in Cuch 2000; and Lyman 1963).

UINTAH UTES

"Uintah Utes" refers to the amalgamated western Ute bands who were relocated from central Utah and concentrated on the Uintah Reservation after 1863. No Uintah band as such existed aboriginally, although children born during hunting expeditions in the Basin could be designated Uintahnunt or Uintahs. In 1776 the region was enemy country, used primarily by the Yamparica Comanches, and remained contested into the early 1800s. After an early fur trading fort was established near today's Whiterocks, a small band of Utes,

433

Shoshones, and mixed-heritage people settled nearby. Today the amalgamated Uintah Utes are one of three bands on the Uintah and Ouray Reservation, headquartered at Fort Duchesne, Utah.

Uinta, Uintah, Uintah-utes, Uintah Utes (government documents, e.g., *ARCIA*; treaties and agreements; Powell 1971; Stewart 1942, 1952; A. Smith, 1974). Informants told Smith the Basin had been a favorite wintering place; however, Stewart's informants said the Basin was only used for hunting until the early 1840s.

Uintahnunts, U'-in-tats (Powell 1971; Stewart 1942; Kelly 1964). Means people living in the Uintah Basin or on the Uintah Reservation.

Tuwinty, Yuwinta, Winta Valley (Kelly 1964; *ARCIA* 1855). Kelly said it meant Pine Valley.

Paĝwá-núu-ci (Southern Ute Dictionary 1979). The "Uintah Utes."

Timpanogos Utes

This band was centered in the well-watered Utah Valley near Utah Lake and its river tributaries. They hunted in the Strawberry and Uintah valleys and ranged southward through the San Pete and Sevier valleys and nearby mountains. Powell noted that *Tum-pwi'-tu-kich* meant "stony ground," while later sources translated the term to mean "rocky-bottomed river," a reference to the Provo River (Fremont 1844/1966). According to the *Southern Ute Dictionary* (1971), *tupúy-ci* means "rock" or "rocky" and *nukwí-ti* means "river." Powell (1971) listed Tum-pa-no'-ag or Tum-pwan'-o as the Ute names for the area near the mouth of the Provo River, where Provo City is now located.

Timopanogotzis or Timpanogitzes (Escalante 1976/1995; cf. Stewart 1942, 1952). These people were named for their home base near the lake, Timpa-nogó. The word for "lakes" was *pagariri* (*páa-* or *pah-* meaning "water").

Timpanogos or Timpanogoos, Tümpanagots, Timpanogs, Timpanoags, Tim-pa-na'-gats (Gottfredson 1969; *Journal History*; Wells 1933; Fremont 1844/1966; Irish at Spanish Fork Council 1865; Powell 1971; Steward 1938; Stewart 1952, 1942, and citing Steward 1937 *Linguistics*).

Timpanocuitzis (Escalante, and Chavez and Warner, 1976/1995; Stewart 1942)

Tumpanuwach, Tumpanuwac

Tipana-nuu-ci (Goss in A. Smith 1974)

Timpanois (Escalante, and Chavez and Warner, 1976/1995; Stewart 1942).
Escalante named nearby Mount Timpanogos, Sierra Blanca de los
Timpanois.

Timpanode Ute (Gottfredson 1969)

Tömpanöwöts or Tömpanöwötsnunts (Stewart 1942)

Tim-pai'-a-vats or Timpaiavats (Powell 1971; Stewart 1942)

Trimpannah Lake, Timpany or Timpeny Utes (Russell 1965; *Journal History*)

Pagwá-nuú-ci, Pagöwadziu, Paguwadziu or Pagönunts (Goss in A. Smith
1974; Lowie 1924; Stewart 1942). This literally means "water-edge Ute";
was used later to refer to a "Uintah-Ute person" or displaced Timpanogos Ute.

Pakwuna-nuu-ci, Pakianuc, Pakta (Goss in A. Smith 1974). Means "Fish Ute,"
pa-gu being "fish."

Lagunas (Escalante, and Chavez and Warner, notes and glossary, 1976/1995)

Lake Utes (Sage 1857)

Come-Pescado or Fish-Eaters (Escalante, and Chavez and Warner,
1976/1995). The name given by Sabuaganas Yutas because they subsisted
on the lake's abundant fish.

Spanish Fork Utes (Irish at Spanish Fork Council 1865)

Note: Timpanogos Lake, Lago de Timpanogos or Timpanogó; also known as
Eutaw, Utaw, or Utah's Lake (Escalante, and Chavez and Warner, 1976/1995 and
Miera Map; and various early mountaineer memoirs as noted)

San Pitch or San Pete Utes

Western Utes of central Utah who ranged primarily in the San Pete Valley and
nearby mountains. San Pete dwellers may have included some Timpanogos
and Moanunt Utes.

Sampeetches (Ferris 1940 citing Fr. De Smet)

Sam-pach, Sanpach, Uta's Sampach (J. Smith 1977; Morgan 1967)

Sam Pitc, Sampitch or Sampitches (Wells 1933; A.B.C. 1933; Stewart 1952)

Sanpitc or Sanpitcnunts (Stewart 1942, 1952)

Sann-Pitch, San Pitch or Sanpitch Band of Utahs, San puchi (Ferris 1940;
ARCIA; Stewart 1952)

San'-pits, Sanpete (Irish, Report of Council 1865; Powell 1971)

Ko'-sun-ats (Powell 1971)

Pi-ka-kwa'-na-rats, Pakwuna-nuu-ci (Powell 1971; Goss in A. Smith 1974)

Moanunts or Moavinunts

The Moanunts straddled the central Utah mountains, ranging through parts of southern San Pete valley, along the Sevier River, and into the Castle Valley region to the west. They also hunted in the Uintah Basin. Moavi means "pass in the mountain," referring specifically to Salina Canyon. A related Ute word, ?óa-vi means "salt," and according to Escalante, Salina Canyon was probably the source of salt for Indians in central Utah. This group was also known as the people of the Saline Pass and Sevier River People.

Moavi, Moavinunts, or Moanunts (Stewart 1942)

Pagönunts, Pagogowatsnunts, Pavogogwunsin, Pavogogwunsi (Stewart 1942, and citing Steward 1937, *Linguistics*)

Uintahnunts (Stewart 1942, referring to a Pagönunts child born in the Uintah Basin during hunting season)

Sheberetch or Elk Mountain Utes

Elk Mountain Utes is an indeterminate designation found in historical documents, and as a result there is some confusion—and controversy—about who these people were. There are three Elk Mountains: one in central Colorado, one in the La Sal Mountains of east-central Utah, and one near Elk Ridge in the Blue Mountains of southeastern Utah. Powell (1971) said the Utes specifically referred to the La Sal Mountains as the "Elk Mountains," or Pa-ri'-a-gaip (*pa'-ri-a* meaning "elk").

In Utah records, the Elk Mountain Utes were probably also known as the Sheberetch, who ranged along the Old Spanish Trail near the La Sal and who forced Mormon pioneers to abandon an early mission near today's Moab. Sheberetch Utes were the core of Black Hawk's raiders in 1865–1873, but they were virtually wiped out in an epidemic (smallpox?) c. 1871. Those who survived gravitated primarily to the Weeminuche and San Juan Paiute, with a few joining Uintah or Pahvant relatives. Being centrally located, they undoubtedly had kinship ties to both the Weeminuche and central Utah bands.

Sheberetch, Shiberetch, Shib-e-ritches (Powell 1971; Peterson 1993 and 1998; online sources including Southern Ute Tribe website; "Utah History to Go" online)

Cheveritts, Cheverets, Siverits, Sheverts, Ashivorits (early Utah documents, see Peterson 1998, footnotes)

Seuv-a-rits, Seuvarits, Sevarits (Stewart 1952; Powell 1971; A. Smith 1974)

Elk Mountain Indians (Stewart 1952; Peterson 1998)

Red Lake Utes (Powell 1971)

Piede Utes

Pied (French) or *pie* (Spanish) means "foot." The Piede Utes were small-band pedestrians who ranged south through Sevier County as far as Panguitch. Anthropologists who were expert witnesses for the Uintah Utes in their 1953 land claims case argued successfully that these people were Ute, regardless of whether they rode horses or ate them, and despite being poorer than most Utes (A. Smith 1974; Omer Stewart, personal communication, 1978). The anthropologists showed that identities were blurred because the culture and subsistence patterns of the Piede Utes and Southern Paiutes were similar. However, these people self-identified as Ute and were recognized as Ute—or at least "almost" Ute—by Southern Paiutes. Paiutes said Piede Utes dressed and wore their hair like Utes, and thought they were Utes (Kelly 1964). Early non-Indians typically mixed up "Paiute" and "Piede" and used the terms interchangeably for any unmounted Indian, which added to the confusion. There was similar confusion with the Weeminuche and San Juan Paiute, who were often lumped together as Piedes or Payuchis. Piede Utes included:

Koosharem Utes (Kelly 1964; Sapir 1930). Affiliated with Utes; Sapir refers
   to them as a Paiute band in Grass Valley; however, both Koosharem
   Utes and Panguitch Paiutes stole Paiute children from the Kanab region,
   making them "enemy people."
Panguitch Paiutes (Kelly 1964). "Some regarded [these people] as more Ute
   than Paiute." Most ethnographers, however, considered Panguitch Paiutes more Paiute than Ute (Sapir 1930).

PAHVANT

The Pahvant were located south of the Timpanogos Ute, along the lower Sevier River, near Sevier Lake and the desert valleys and mountains just west of this area. The Pahvants considered themselves neither Ute nor Paiute. In 1776 Escalante identified Indians in Pahvant homelands as Yutas Barbones (bearded Utes) and Tirangapui. Although Chavez and Warner (1976/1995) speculate Pahvants may have been Southern Paiute, it is more likely they were a borderland Ute-Paiute mix. Some have suggested possible early renegade Spanish heritage as well, giving them the bearded appearance neither Utes nor

Paiutes had. The Pahvant refused to join the Utes on the Uintah Reservation but remained on legally purchased lands near Fillmore, Utah. They were terminated in the 1950s, and a decade later they were re-recognized and incorporated into the organizational structure of the Southern Paiute tribe. However, Pahvants remained fiercely loyal to their identity as Pahvant, not Paiute.

Pahvantinunts, Pahvanduts, Pah-Vantes, Pa-vant, Pah-Vant, Pahvant or
  Pahvant Ute (*ARCIA*; *Journal History*; Powell 1971 and notes by editors,
  Fowler and Fowler; Kane 1874/1974; Wells 1933; Stewart 1942, 1952)
Kanosh Indians (Gottfredson 1969). Those led by Chief Kanosh.
Yutas Barbones (Escalante, and Chavez and Warner, 1976/1995). This means
  "bearded Yutas." With heavy beards and nose piercings, they were
  encountered near modern-day Levan.
Tirangapui (Escalante, and Chavez and Warner, 1976/1995; Stewart 1942).
  Self-identified as Tirangapui; Escalante associated them with the Yutas
  Barbones encountered earlier.

UTE NEIGHBORS

Southern Paiutes
The Southern Paiutes were Numic neighbors of the Utes, with whom the Utes frequently interacted, traded, intermarried (usually captives), and preyed upon. Numerous Paiute bands are named in the literature; in general, they were known as Paiutes, Piedes, or Digger Indians. The generalized names by which they were known to non-Indians suggest how closely they were identified as part of an ethnic and linguistic group that included Utes.

Payóo-ci, Pa-utch, Pa utch (*Southern Ute Dictionary* 1979; J. Smith 1977)
Py-Eut, Py-ute, Pey-ute (Ferris 1940; *ARCIA*)
Pa Ute, Pa-utahs, Pah Utes, Pau-Eutaw (e.g., *ARCIA* 1855; Sage 1857; Hamilton 1960; Brewerton 1993; Powell 1971)
Pi Utes, Piute, Pai-Ute (Peg Leg Smith in Yount 1966; Gottfredson 1969;
  Wells 1933; A. Smith 1974)
Pihede, Piede, Pi-edes, Pied (*ARCIA*; *Journal History*; Gottfredson 1969;
  Kane 1874/1974)
Yuta Cobardes (Escalante 1873). Means "timid or cowardly Utes." They were
  located in Southern Paiute territory.

Goshutes

The Goshutes were similarly associated with the Utes in non-Indian minds. Goshutes were related linguistically and culturally as Numic people but were actually more closely related to the Western Shoshones than the Utes.

Goshute or Gosh-utes, Go-sha-utes (*ARCIA*; Whitney 1892–1904; Gottfredson 1969; Cuch 2000; Stewart 1952)

Goshiute or Gosiute, Gosi-Ute, Go-si-utes of Utah (Powell 1873; Swanton 1952; and various encyclopedic and online sources as a variant for Goshute)

Ku-mo-i-gu-rum (Powell 1873). Self-identification.

Shoshones and Comanches

Shoshones neighbored the Utes to the north and west and included the Western, Northwestern, and Eastern Shoshone. They were known to the Utes as *kumá-ci*, "enemy people" or "left-handed relatives" (the left hand being the witching hand; see Goss in Clemmer, Mayers, and Rudden 1999). One band of Eastern Shoshones migrated southward, the Yamparica Comanches of Escalante's 1776 journal. The enemy Comanche would temporarily become allies of the southern Utes, but then their deadly enemies again.

Kumá-ci, Ku-muntsu, So-o-tsu (Powell 1971; Southern Ute Dictionary 1979; Fowler and Fowler 1971). Fowler and Fowler identify these with Washakie's nineteenth-century Eastern Shoshone.

Comanches/Cumanches Yamparicas, Yamparica Comanches (Escalante 1776, and Chavez and Warner, 1976/1995; Miera Map). These were a south-migrating band of Eastern Shoshone; their migrating descendants are today's Yampa-Rikani or Yapi tuhka Comanche band (Robinson and Armagost 1990).

Notes

1. Gregory Smoak expands on this in *Ghost Dances and Identity: Prophetic Religion and American Indian Ethnogenesis in the Nineteenth Century* (Los Angeles: University of California Press, 2006), 17–18.

2. Anne M. (Cooke) Smith, *Ethnography of the Northern Utes*, Papers in Anthropology, no. 17 (Albuquerque: Museum of New Mexico Press, 1974), 19–24, and quoting linguist James Goss, 21. See also Marvin K. Opler, "The Southern Ute of Colorado," in *Acculturation in Seven American Indian Tribes*, ed. Ralph Linton (New York: Harper & Son, 1940), 126.

3. Numerous studies discuss the development of the "blood-thirsty savage" stereotype. For additional insights, see Peter Silver, *Our Savage Neighbors: How Indian War Transformed Early America* (New York: W. W. Norton, 2008); and Jill Lepore, *The Name of War: King Philip's War and the Origins of American Identity* (New York: Vintage Books, 1999).

4. Smith, *Ethnography of the Northern Utes*, 19–24.

5. Jacquelyn Kilpatrick, *Celluloid Indians: Native Americans and Film* (Lincoln: University of Nebraska Press, 1990), 51–52.

6. For example, Alan Gallay, *The Indian Slave Trade: The Rise of the English Empire in the American South, 1670–1717* (New Haven: Yale University Press, 2002); Richard White, *The Middle Ground: Indians, Empires, and Republics in the Great Lakes Region, 1650–1815* (New York: Cambridge University Press, 1991); Alan Gallay, ed., *Indian Slavery in Colonial America* (Lincoln: University of Nebraska Press, 2009); Elliott West, *The Contested Plains: Indians, Goldseekers, and the Rush to Colorado* (Lawrence: University Press of Kansas, 1998), introduction, ch. 1–4; Ned Blackhawk, *Violence over the Land: Indians and Empires in the Early American West* (Cambridge, MA: Harvard University Press, 2006); and Smoak, *Ghost Dances and Identity.*

7. See, e.g., Smoak, *Ghost Dances and Identity*, 24–25, 38–39; and K. C. Tessendorf, "Red Death on the Missouri," *American West* 14 (January/February 1977): 48–53.

8. For the ripple effect of European encounters, see West, *Contested Plains*; Gallay, *Indian Slave Trade*; and Blackhawk, *Violence over the Land*. For disease, see Alfred W. Crosby, Jr., *Columbian Exchange: Biological and Cultural Consequences of 1492* (Westport, CT: Greenwood, 1972); Sheldon Watts, "Smallpox in the New World and the Old," in *Epidemics and History: Disease, Power, and Imperialism* (New Haven: Yale University Press, 1997); Tessendorf, "Red Death on the Missouri."

9. For theories of blood and race, see Joanne Barker, "Indian™ U.S.A.," *Wicazo Sa Review* 18 (Spring 2003): 28–30; Audrey Smedley, "'Race' and the Construction of Human Identity," *American Anthropologist* 100 (September 1998): 690–702.

10. See, e.g., Silver, *Our Savage Neighbors*; and Jill Lepore, *The Name of War*; Nancy Shoemaker, "How Indians Got to be Red" *The American Historical Review* 102 (June 1997): 625–44; Alexandra Harmon, *Indians in the Making: Ethnic Relations and Indian Identities around Puget Sound* (Los Angeles: University of California Press, 1998), esp. 9–10.

11. James Fenimore Cooper, *Last of the Mohicans* (1826). Michael Omi and Howard Winant discuss in *Race Critical Theories: Text and Context*, ed. Philomena Essed and David Theo Goldberg (Hoboken, NJ: Wiley-Blackwell, 2001), 123–45, how the concept of "race" developed as a political tool to reinforce social stratification. See also Howard Winant, "Race and Race Theory," *Annual Review of Sociology* 26 (2000): 169–85.

12. White, *Middle Ground*; Gallay, *Indian Slave Trade*. Cf. Smoak, *Ghost Dances*; James Brooks, *Captives & Cousins: Slavery, Kinship, and Community in the Southwest Borderlands* (Chapel Hill: University of North Carolina Press, 2002); and Fred Anderson, *Crucible of War: The Seven Years' War and the*

Fate of Empire in British North America, 1754–1766 (New York: Knopf, 2000), especially chapters on "Oswego" and "Fort William Henry."

The term *half-breed*, or *breed*, is a pejorative today. In this work the term mixed-blood will generally be used since it is used by most Utes today and reflects most native preference in the United States. *Métis*, used in the Great Lakes and U.S. southeast, means "half-blood," "half-caste," or "hybrid."

13. See, e.g., Smedley, "'Race' and the Construction of Human Identity"; and note the U.S. Census Bureau's struggle with defining race as a demographic category.

14. Gallay, *Indian Slave Trade*, 111–13, 139–44; White, *Middle Ground*, 214–15, 60–74, 189–92, and 230–31; Smoak, *Ghost Dances*, 18–20.

15. See, e.g., Smedley, "Race"; Fredrik Barth, "Introduction," in *Ethnic Groups and Boundaries: The Social Organization of Culture Difference* (1969; Long Grove, IL: Waveland Press, 1998); and Gallay, *Indian Slave Trade*, 9–10, 111–13. Some scholars argue that environmental determinism is also a factor, but not the *only* factor in culture development. See, e.g., Smoak, *Ghost Dances*, 17–18.

CHAPTER 2

1. Orthographic and dialect variations exist for this "identity" name: Nooche, Noochew, Nuche, Nuuciu, *núu-ci, nuutci, Nu'-ints*, or núu-ʔapáǧa-pi. James A. Goss, "Ute Lexical and Phonological Patterns" (PhD diss., University of Chicago, 1972); and Southern Ute Tribe, *Ute Dictionary and Ute Reference Grammar*, preliminary editions, 2 vol. (Ignacio, CO: Ute Press, 1979). See also John Wesley Powell, *Anthropology of the Numa: John Wesley Powell's Manuscripts on the Numic Peoples of Western North America, 1868–1880*, ed. Don D. Fowler and Catherine S. Fowler (Washington, D.C.: Smithsonian Institution Press, 1971), 168, 180; Julian Steward, *Ute Indians* (New York: Garland Publishing, 1974), 1:29–33, 63–66; Omer C. Stewart, "Ute Indians: Before and After," *Utah Historical Quarterly* 34 (Winter 1966): 42–45; Anne M. Smith, *Ethnography of the Northern Utes*, Papers in Anthropology, no. 17 (Albuquerque: Museum of New Mexico Press, 1974), 40–41; and Gregory Smoak, *Ghost Dances and Identity: Prophetic Religion and American Indian Ethnogensis in the Nineteenth Century* (Los Angeles: University of California Press, 2006), 16.

2. Julian H. Steward, "The Great Basin Shoshonean Indians," in *Theory of Culture Change* (Urbana: University of Illinois Press, 1955), 101–21; Jesse D. Jennings, "Early Man in Utah," *Utah Historical Quarterly* 28 (January 1960): 4–5; Omer C. Stewart, "The Basin," in Robert F. Spencer, et al, *The Native Americans: Prehistory and Ethnology of the North American Indians* (New York: Harper & Row, 1965), 273–82; Stewart, "Ute Indians: Before and After," 42–45.

3. See, e.g., David B. Madsen and James F. O'Connell, "Introduction," and Madsen, "Get It While the Gettin's Good: A Variable Model of Great Basin Subsistence and Settlement Based on Data from the Eastern Great Basin," in *Man and Environment in the Great Basin*, SAA Papers no. 2, ed. Madsen and O'Connell (Washington, D.C.: Society for American Archaeology, 1982): 207–26; David B. Madsen and Brigham D. Madsen, "One Man's Meat is Another Man's Poison: A Revisionist View of the Seagull Miracle," *Nevada Historical Society Quarterly* 30 (Fall 1987): 165–81; Richard O. Clemmer, L. Daniel Myers, and Mary E. Rudden, ed., *Julian Steward and the The Great Basin: The Making of an Anthropologist* (Salt Lake City: University of Utah Press, 1999); Mark Q. Sutton and David Rhode, "Background to the Numic Problem," in *Across the West: Human Population Movement and the Expansion of the Numa*, ed. David B. Madsen and David Rhode (Salt Lake City: University of Utah Press, 1994), 6–15; Smoak, *Ghost Dances and Identity*, 17–18.

4. For this view of Great Basin prehistory see especially Madsen and O'Connell, "Introduction," *Man and Environment in the Great Basin*; Madsen, "Get It While the Gettin's Good"; Madsen and Rhodes, *Across the West*; Ronald W. Walker, "Native Women on the Utah Frontier," *BYU Studies* 32, no. 4 (1992): 87–124. Earlier works include Steward, "Great Basin Shoshonean Indians," and *Ute Indians*, vol. 1; Stewart, "Utah Indians: Before and After," and "Western Utes"; Jennings, "Early Man in Utah"; Carling Malouf, "Ethnohistory in the Great Basin," in *The Current Status of Anthropological Research in the Great Basin: 1964*, ed. Warren L. d'Azevedo, et al. (Reno: Desert Research Institute, 1966), 4–5; Marvin K. Opler, "The Southern Ute of Colorado," *Acculturation In Seven American Indian Tribes*, ed. Ralph Linton (New York: Harper and Son, 1940).

5.   Fremont and Anasazi cultures are described in the classic *Southwestern Archaeology* by Alfred Vincent Kidder (New Haven: Yale University Press, 1962). Also J. Richard Ambler, *The Anasazi: Prehistoric People of the Four Corners Region* (Flagstaff: Museum of Northern Arizona, 1984); James H. Gunnerson and Steven R. Simms, *The Fremont Culture: A Study of Culture Dynamics on the Northern Anasazi Frontier* (Salt Lake City: University of Utah Press, 2009); Steven R. Simms, *Ancient People of the Great Basin* (Walnut Creek, CA: Left Coast Press, 2008); Linda Cordell, *Prehistory of the Southwest* (Orlando, FL: Academic Press, 1984). The Athabascan people include the Apaches and Navajos.

6.   For the conventional but contested view of who and where the Numic people first were and went, see Sidney M. Lamb, "Linguistic Prehistory in the Great Basin," *International Journal of American Linguistics* 24 (April 1958): 95–100; and C. F. Voegelin, F. M. Voegelin, and Kenneth Hale, *Typological and Comparative Grammar of Uto-Aztecan: Phonology, International Journal of American Linguistics*, Memoir no. 17 (1962), 1:144. See also James Goss, "Linguistic Tools for the Great Basin Prehistorian," in *Models and Great Basin Prehistory (A Symposium)*, Desert Research Institute Publications in the Social Sciences, no. 12, ed. Don D. Fowler (1972); and Madsen and Rhode, "Introduction," *Across the West.*

        Theories regarding an alternative migration from the north appear in Robert Delaney, *The Ute Mountain Utes* (Albuquerque: University of New Mexico Press, 1989), 5; Albert H. Schroeder, "Cultural Position of Hurst's Tabeguache Caves," *Southwestern Lore* 29 (1964): 4; and A. Irving Hallowell, "Bear Ceremonialism in the Northern Hemisphere," *American Anthropologist* 28 (January 1926): 2–175.

7.   Madsen and O'Connell, "Introduction," and Madsen, "Get It While the Gettin's Good"; David B. Madsen, "Mesa Verde and Sleeping Ute Mountain: The Geographical and Chronological Dimensions of the Numic Expansion," in *Across the West*, 24–31.

8.   Robert H. Lowie, "Shoshonean Tales: I—Southern Ute," *Journal of American Folk-Lore* 37 (January–June 1924): 2–4.

9.   "Old Bishop" Arrochis (traditional Northern Ute medicine man), conversation with author, summer 1979.

10.   Cultural information is drawn from John Wesley Powell, "Report on the Indians of the Numa Stock," in *Anthropology of the Numa*; Julian Steward, *Basin-Plateau Aboriginal Sociopolitical Groups* (1938; Salt Lake City: University of Utah Press, 1997); Julian Steward, "The Great Basin Shoshonean Indians: An Examples of a Family Level of Sociocultural Integration," in *Theory of Culture Change*, 101–21; Jennings, "Early Man in Utah," 4–5. See also Warren L. D'Azevedo, ed., *Handbook of North American Indians*, vol. 11, *Great Basin* (Washington, D.C.: Smithsonian Institution, 1986), especially Donald Calloway, Joel Janetski, and Omer C. Stewart, "Ute," 336–54; Omer C. Stewart, "The Western Ute" and "The Eastern Ute" (unpublished essays prepared for "Utes," in *Handbook)*, Omer C. Stewart Collection, 2nd Accession, box 5, Norlin Library Archives, University of Colorado, Boulder; Stewart, "The Basin," in *The Native Americans*, 273–82; Stewart, "Ute Indians: Before and After."

11.   Smith, *Ethnography of the Northern Utes*; Omer C. Stewart, "Culture Element Distributions: XVIII, Ute–Southern Paiute," *Anthropological Records* 6 (1942): 4:231–354; Stewart, "Western Ute," 1–29; Joel Janetski, *The Ute of Utah Lake*, Anthropological Papers no.116 (Salt Lake City: University of Utah Press, 1991); Madsen, "Get It While the Gettin's Good," 207–26; Albers and Lowry, "Index of Resources," in *Cultural Resources*, 33–97.

12.   For more on the structure of early Ute bands, see especially Steward, *Basin-Plateau Aboriginal Sociopolitical Groups*; Don D. Fowler, "Great Basin Social Organization," in *The Current Status of Anthropological Research in the Great Basin: 1964*, 37–73; Jorgensen, "Ethnohistory and Acculturation," 5–33; Malouf, "Ethnohistory," 1–38; Stewart, "Eastern Ute," 16–17 and "Western Ute," 16–21; Callaway, Janetski, and Stewart, "Ute," 352–54. Also cf. data in Omer Stewart's "Ute Chiefs List" which illustrate the fluidity of band membership even among prominent leaders: "Data on the Identification and Group Leadership of Ute Indian Chiefs" (Working paper prepared for Dockets 44–45, U.S. Indian Claims Commission, 1952), in the Omer C. Stewart Collection, 2nd Accession, box 1, Norlin Library Archives, University of Colorado, Boulder; also located in Omer Call Stewart Papers, Special Collections, Marriott Library, University of Utah. Hereafter "Ute Chiefs List." Note shifting band alliances in signatures on treaties/agreements.

443

13. On how complex, exogamous kin networks could blur definitions of band or tribal identity, see Alexandra Harmon, *Indians in the Making: Ethnic Relations and Indian Identities around Puget Sound* (Los Angeles: University of California Press, 1998), passim but esp. 8–9, 14, 37, 137–38.

14. For additional information, see Steward, *Aboriginal Sociopolitical Groups*, 238–42; Smith, *Ethnography of the Northern Utes*, 106, 128–52; Opler, "Southern Utes," 127–36; Stewart, "Culture Element Distribution," 296–97; Stewart, "Western Ute," 21–27; Walker, "Native Women," 95–104; Fowler, "Great Basin Social Organization," 58–64

15. See, e.g., Fowler, "Great Basin Social Organization," 59. See also Walker, "Native Women," 101–8; Peter Gottfredson, *Indian Depredations in Utah* (1919; Salt Lake City: Shelton Publishing Co., 1969), 317–18. Wákara, from the Ute, *ʔoá-qa-ri,* meaning yellow or brass. Cf. Utah's Oquirrh (yellow) Mountains. Southern Ute Tribe, *Ute Dictionary,* 195.

16. See Jacob Hamblin, "Journals and Letters of Jacob Hamblin" (typescript with original orthography), 28–31, 41, HBLL-SC, Brigham Young University, Provo, Utah. See also, "Home Correspondence" quoting Hamblin, *Deseret News,* April 4, 1855; Thomas D. Brown, *Journal of the Southern Indian Mission: Diary of Thomas D. Brown,* ed. Juanita Brooks (Logan: Utah State University Press, 1972), 104–5; cf. Stephen Van Hoak, "And Who Shall Have the Children? The Indian Slave Trade in the Southern Great Basin, 1800–1865," *Nevada Historical Society Quarterly* 41 (Spring 1998): 10.

17. Goss, "Lexical and Phonological Patterns," 14–15.

18. Infrequently brothers shared a wife's sexual favors, but this was probably not thought of as a polyandrous marriage. See Fowler, "Basin Social Organization," 59; cf. Steward, *Aboriginal Sociopolitical Groups,* 241.

19. Cynthia S. Becker and P. David Smith, *Chipeta: Queen of the Utes* (Montrose, CO: Western Reflections Publishing, 2003), 2.

20. Linguistic sources include Southern Ute Tribe, *Ute Dictionary,* vol. 2; Goss, "Ute Lexical and Phonological Patterns," 2:14–30; and Powell's various Southern Numic vocabularies in *Anthropology of the Numa,* esp. 164–83.

21. Jorgensen, "Ethnohistory and Acculturation," 33–67; Malouf, "Ethnohistory of the Great Basin," 4; Opler, "The Southern Ute," 133–46. For the double-edged sword of medicine power, see Goss, "Ute Lexical and Phonological Patterns," 35–36.

22. Ethnographic studies of Ute subsistence include Smith, *Ethnography of the Northern Utes*; Stewart, "Culture Element Distributions," 231–54; Stewart, "Western Ute," 1–29; Stewart, "The Basin," 273–82; Janetski, *The Ute of Utah Lake*; Callaway, Janetski, and Stewart, "Ute," 336–45; Powell, *Anthropology of the Numa,* 39–50; David B. Madsen, "Get It While the Gettin's Good"; Malouf, "Ethnohistory of the Great Basin"; Opler, "The Southern Ute of Colorado, 124–26; Patricia Albers and Jennifer Lowry, *Cultural Resource and Properties of the Northern Ute Tribe: A Technical Report on Sites under Possible Impact by the Uinta Basin Replacement Project* (Salt Lake City: American West Center, 1995), 33–97; and especially Steward, *Ute Indians,* vol. 1. Additional insights in Goss, "Ute Lexical and Phonological Patterns," 183, 279.

    Early travelers gave graphic descriptions of Ute diet and lifestyle. See, e.g., Warren Angus Ferris, *Life in the Rocky Mountains,* ed. Leroy R. Hafen (Denver: Old West Publishing, 1983), 344–48; Hamblin, "Journals," 8–9, 16, 20, 23; Brown, *Journal of the Southern Indian Mission,* 55–56; T. J. Farnham, *Travels in the Great Western Prairies,* in *Early Western Travels,* vol. 28, ed. Reuben Gold Thwaites (Cleveland: Arthur H. Clark, 1906), 249; James A. Little, "Biography of Lorenzo Dow Young," *Utah Historical Quarterly* 14 (1946): 99.

23. For subsistence, see Brigham Madsen, *The Shoshoni Frontier and the Bear River Massacre* (Salt Lake City: University of Utah Press, 1985), 12–15. For eastern band organization, see Jorgensen, "Ethnohistory and Acculturation," 12–15.

24. Goss, "Ute Lexical and Phonological Patterns," 45; Powell, *Anthropology of the Numa,* 85–86.

25. Crickets as food: Madsen, "One Man's Meat"; A. Smith, *Ethnography of the Northern Utes,* 50; Janetski, *Ute of Utah Lake,* 38; Stewart, "Western Ute," 8. Howard Egan, *Pioneering the West 1846 to 1878: Major Howard Egan's Diary* (Richmond, UT: Howard R. Egan Estate, 1917), 230–33; Little, "Biography of Lorenzo Dow Young"; April Holladay, "Mormon Crickets March 50,000 strong," in *USA Today* (online), July 23, 2004, accessed March 23, 2012, from usatoday.com; and Alexis Driggs, conversation with the author describing swarms on I-15 in western Utah, 2004.

26. Brown, *Southern Indian Mission* (June 1854), 44–45; and Egan, *Pioneering,* 228–30.

27. Janetski, *Ute of Utah Lake,* 27–29, 36–38; Angelico Chavez, trans., and Ted J. Warner, ed., *The Domínquez-Escalante Journal: Their Expedition through Colorado, Utah, Arizona, and New Mexico in 1776* (1976; Provo, UT: Brigham Young University Press, 1995), 57; Robert Leonard, archaeologist, personal communication to the author, June 2012; and presentations at The Old Spanish Trail Association conference, June 14–17, 2012, St. George, Utah.

28. George W. Bean's journal, quoted in Gottfredson, *Indian Depredations,* 20–22, 326–27. Solomon Nuñez Carvalho and George Douglas Breweton noted the abundance of good-tasting "salmon" trout in the "Provost" River. Carvalho, *Incidents of Travel and Adventure in the Far West with Colonel Fremont's Last Expedition* (New York: Derby and Jackson, 1856 and 1860); Breweton, *Overland with Kit Carson: A Narrative of the Old Spanish Trail in '48* (1930; Lincoln: University of Nebraska Press, 1993) 110–11, originally published in *Harper's New Monthly Magazine* in 1853.

29. Janetski, *Ute of Utah Lake,* 36–38, 79–89; Stewart, "Culture Element Distributions," 249; Smith, *Ethnography of the Northern Utes,* 61–64; Chavez and Warner, *Domínguez-Escalante Journal,* 57.

30. Janetski, *Ute of Utah Lake,* 29; Smith, *Ethnography of Northern Utes,* 58–60; Stewart, *Culture Element Distribution,* 243–44, 336–37.

31. Darrell Gardiner, personal communication with the author, summer 1980.

32. Smith, *Ethnography of the Northern Utes,* 58–59; Stewart, "Culture Element Distributions," 304, 333; Egan, *Pioneering,* 237, 245–46.

33. Egan, *Pioneering,* 235–40. Jack rabbit populations still explode about every seven years; antelope herds become harvestable every five to eight years.

34. For information on ubiquitous rabbit-skin blankets, see, e.g., Chavez and Warner, *The Domínquez-Escalante Journal,* 60, 64; and Egan, *Pioneering,* 237–38. See also Stewart, "Ute Indians," 38–61; Stewart, "The Basin," 277, 279, and "Culture Element Distributions," 242.

35. Bob Leonard, archaeologist, personal communication with the author, May 2012, provided information on mountain sheep. Lyman S. Tyler, "Before Escalante" (PhD diss., University of Utah, Salt Lake City, 1951), 52–57, 64–69, 159–60, mentions Ute bison hunters. Tyler argues that southern Ute bands were among the undifferentiated, pedestrian bison-culture Indians who hunted on the Great Plains, especially along the Rocky Mountain Front on the Yuta Plains. He cites Herbert E. Bolton (*Spanish Explorations in the Southwest,* 183, 250) who identified Coronado's *Querechos,* or bison-hunting people on the eastern borders of the Rockies, as "mountain people" (probably the Mouache Ute).

36. Elliott West, *The Contested Plains: Indians, Goldseekers, and the Rush to Colorado* (Lawrence: University Press of Kansas, 1998), 20–25; Van Hoak, "The Other Buffalo."

37. Egan, *Pioneering the West,* 235–40. See also Stewart, "Culture Element Distributions," 240; Stewart, "The Basin," 277.

38. Southern Ute Tribe, *Ute Dictionary,* 131. Sightings of these sprites were still being reported mid-twentieth century. See Earl Gardiner, "Water Babies," typescript interview, Northern Ute Museum, copy in possession of author.

39. Woman's-forward-stepping-dance, or *mamá-kwa-nhkwá-pu.* Hallowell, "Bear Ceremonialism"; Goss, "Ute Lexical and Phonological Patterns," 46–47; Smith, *Ethnography of the Northern Ute,* 51; Julian H. Steward, "A Uintah Ute Bear Dance, March, 1931," *American Anthropologist* 34 (1932): 263–73; Verner Z. Reed, "The Ute Bear Dance," *American Anthropologist* 9 (July 1896): 237–44; Stewart, "Western Ute," 28; Robert R. Jones, "Some Effects of Modernization on the Ute Indian Religion" (Master's thesis, University of Chicago, 1980), 19–23, and archived in Special Collections, Marriott Library, University of Utah.

40. See, e.g., Smith, *Ethnography of the Northern Ute,* 58; Stewart, "Culture Element Distributions," 304, 333.

41. For details of aboriginal dress see Smith, *Ethnography of the Northern Utes,* 17–23, 69–80, 262–63; J. Alden Mason, "Myths of the Uintah Utes" *Journal of American Folk-Lore* 23 (1910): 299–363; Stewart, "Culture Element Distribution," esp. 276–83, 342–43; Stewart, "The Basin," 273–82; Janetski, *Ute of Utah Lake,* 41–47; Calloway, Janetski, and Stewart, "Ute," 345–48; Madsen and O'Connell, *Man and Environment in the Great Basin.* For trade in tanned hides, see Frances Leon Swadesh [Quintana], *Los Primeros Pobladores* (Notre Dame, IN: University of Notre Dame Press, 1974), 47; Albert H. Schroeder, "A Brief History of the Southern Utes," *Southwestern Lore* 30 (1965), 59–60.

42. Stewart, *Culture Element* Distribution, 343; Stewart, "Western Utes," 15; Chavez and Warner, *Dominguez-Escalante Journal*, 60–63; Ferris, *Life in the Rocky Mountains*, 344–46.

43. For early observations, see Chavez and Warner, *Dominguez-Escalante Journal*, 60–62; Smith, *Ethnography of the Northern Ute*, 69–80, esp. 76–77; Ferris, *Life in the Rocky Mountains*, 344–46. Ute dress in Stewart, "Culture Element Distributions," 280–81; Janetski, *Utes of Utah Lake*, 42.

44. See, e.g., Smith, *Ethnography of the Northern Utes*, 72–70; Stewart, "Culture Element Distributions," 343.

45. Stewart, "Culture Element Distributions," 256–57.

46. Miera map in Chavez and Warner, *Domínguez-Escalante Journal*, 131. Detailed descriptions of construction and use of Ute tipis are found in Smith, *Ethnography of the Northern Ute*, 33–46; Stewart, "Culture Element Distributions," 257–59. For tipis in general, see Reginald Laubin and Gladys Laubin, *The Tipi*, 2nd ed. (Norman: University of Oklahoma Press, 1977).

47. Smith, *Ethnography of the Northern Utes*, 33–36; Stewart, "Culture Element Distributions," 257–58.

48. Stewart, "Culture Element Distributions," 261 (cf. Smith, *Ethnography of the Northern Utes*, 45–46); Steward, "A Uintah Ute Bear Dance," 263–73; Joseph G. Jorgensen, *The Sun Dance Religion: Power for the Powerless* (Chicago: University of Chicago Press, 1972). My observations are also based on personal observation at Sundance grounds, and interviews and conversations with Fred Conetah, 1978–1979; Darrel Gardiner, 1999, 2001; and Larry Cesspooch, March, 1999.

49. Malouf, "Ethnohistory of the Great Basin," 4. Traditional Ute shamanism discussed by most ethnographers and supplemented here by personal observations of modern curing rituals and conversations with practicing Indian doctors from the Northern and Southern Ute reservations ("Old Bishop" Arrochis, Eddie Box, Darrell Gardiner, 1978–1980, 1999–2003). See, e.g., Marvin K. Opler, "Dream Analysis in Ute Indian Therapy," in *Culture and Mental Health*, ed. Marvin K. Opler (New York: Macmillan Co., 1959); Opler, "Southern Ute," 133–46, 154–56, 171, 188–202; Stewart, "Culture Element Distributions, 231–354; Stewart, "Eastern Ute," 32–39, 50–57, and "Western Ute," 23–38; Calloway, Janetski, and Stewart, "Ute," 354–55; Smith, *Ethnography of the Northern Utes*, 152–228, 254–63; Gregory Smoak, *Ghost Dances and Identity*, 38–48; Jones, "Some Effects of Modernization."

50. Information in this section incorporates interviews and conversations, and personal observation of and participation in Ute rituals. Literature discussing Ute religion includes Jones, "Some Effects of Modernization"; Jorgensen, "Ethnohistory and Acculturation," 33–70, 139–56, 320–508; Opler, "Southern Ute," 133–46, 154–56, 171, 188–202; Stewart, "Culture Element Distributions, 231–354, "Eastern Ute," 32–39, 50–57, and "Western Ute," 23–38; Calloway, Janetski, and Stewart, "Ute," 354–55; Jorgensen, *Sun Dance Religion*; and Smith, *Ethnography of the Northern Utes*, 152–228, 254–63. See also Chapter 13, herein. For general Shoshonean shamanism, see Smoak, *Ghost Dances and Identity*, 48–58; Powell, *Anthropology of the Numa*, 53–61; Malouf, "Ethnohistory in the Great Basin," 4–5; and Opler, "Dream Analysis in Ute Indian Therapy," 97–117. Additional papers on the Bear Dance include Steward, "A Uintah Ute Bear Dance," 263–73; Reed, "The Ute Bear Dance," 237–44; and Albert B. Reagan, "The Bear Dance of the Ouray Utes," *Wisconsin Archaeologist* 9 (1931): 148–50.

51. See Goss, "Linguistic and Phonological Patterns," 33–37; Southern Ute Tribe, *Ute Dictionary*; and Opler, "Southern Ute," 133–46, 154–56, 171, 188–202. Orthographic representations of Ute language vary by dialect and collector; variants are not shown here.

52. Frances Densmore, "Songs Used in the Treatment of the Sick," in *Northern Ute Music*, Bulletin 75, Bureau of American Ethnology, 1922. Smoak, *Ghost Dances and Identity*, 48–58, uses the term "spirit tutor."

53. See Stewart, "Western Ute," 27, and quoting John Wesley Powell; Goss, "Ute Lexical and Phonological Patterns," 33.

54. See, e.g., Southern Ute Tribe, *Ute Dictionary*; Opler, "Southern Ute," 133–46, 154–56, 171, 188–202; E. E. White, *Experiences of a Special Indian Agent* (1893; Norman: University of Oklahoma Press, 1965), 94–96; Wilson Rockwell, *The Utes: A Forgotten People* (Denver: Sage Books, 1956), 212; Stewart, "Eastern Ute," 31–33.

55. Opler, "Dream Analysis in Ute Indian Therapy"; Arthur K. Shapiro and Elaine Shapiro, *The Powerful Placebo: From Ancient Priest to Modern Physician* (Baltimore, MD: Johns Hopkins University Press, 1997. One medical anthropologist estimated that more than 75 percent of all cures effected by physicians are psychosomatically induced faith healings, produced through the patient's confidence

in the efficacy of the doctor's ministrations; Jean Camaroff, personal conversation with R. Jones, fall 1979.

56. Smoak, *Ghost Dances and Identity*, 52; personal observation on the Navajo Reservation.

57. See, e.g., Powell, *Anthropology of the Numa*, 53–61.

58. Omer C. Stewart, *Ute Peyotism: A Study of a Cultural Complex* (Boulder, CO: University of Colorado Press, 1987). Note healing ceremonies in Jorgensen, *Sun Dance Religion*; and personal observation at Northern Ute Sundances and private curing ceremonies, 1978–1980 and 1999–2003.

59. Young, *Ute Indians of Colorado*, 67, 90–91; *Salt Lake Tribune*, October 10, 2000.

60. *Journal History of the Church, 1830–1972*, March 13 and 24, 1850, June 9, 1850 (Salt Lake City: Church History Library, Church of Jesus Christ of Latter-day Saints); B. H. Roberts, *A Comprehensive History of the Church of Jesus Christ of Latter-day Saints: Century One* (1930; Provo, UT: Church of Jesus Christ of Latter-day Saints, 1965), 3:464; Scott R. Christensen, *Sagwitch: Shoshone Chieftain, Mormon Elder, 1822–1887* (Logan: Utah State University Press, 1999); Frederick Quinn, "'To Elevate the Red Man': The Episcopal Church's Native American Policy in Utah," *Utah Historical Quarterly* 73 (Winter 2005): 44–63. See also *Salt Lake Tribune*, July 1, 1995; cf. P. David Smith, *Ouray, Chief of the Utes* (Ouray, CO: Wayfinder Press, 1986), 199.

61. Smith, *Ouray*, 35, 143–47, 179–82, esp. 3, and citing photographer W. H. Jackson, 133. See also agency wrangler Sidney Jocknick, *Early Days On the Western Slope of Colorado, 1870–1883, inclusive* (Glorietta, NM: Rio Grande Press, 1913), 143; and Richard K. Young, *The Ute Indians of Colorado in the Twentieth Century* (Norman: University of Oklahoma Press, 1997), 69–70; *Salt Lake Tribune*, July 1, 1995; Quinn, "To Elevate the Red Man."

CHAPTER 3

1. For Navajo and Apache origins and intercultural relations, see William B. Carter, *Indian Alliances and the Spanish in the Southwest, 750–1750* (Norman: University of Oklahoma Press, 2009), 23, 29–31; and James F. Brooks, *Captives & Cousins: Slavery, Kinship, and Community in the Southwest Borderlands* (Chapel Hill: University of North Carolina Press, 2002), ch. 3, esp. 80–88.

2. See, e.g., Duane Champagne, *Social Change and Cultural Continuity among Native Nations* (Chicago: University of Chicago Press, 2006); Edward H. Spicer, "Results of Contact: The Course of Cultural Change," "Paths to Civilization: The Processes of Cultural Change," in *Cycles of Conquest: The Impact of Spain, Mexico, and the United States on the Indians of the Southwest, 1533–1960* (1962; Tucson: University of Arizona Press, 1981); Spicer, *Perspectives in American Indian Culture Change* (Chicago: University of Chicago Press, 1961), esp. 517–43; Julian Steward, *Theory of Culture Change* (Urbana: University of Illinois Press, 1955); A. L. Kroeber, *Anthropology: Race, Culture, Psychology, Prehistory* (1923; New York: Harcourt, Brace, 1948), 344–85, 386–444.

3. Lyman S. Tyler, "Before Escalante" (PhD diss., University of Utah, Salt Lake City, 1951), 87–91, 98–99; Ned Blackhawk, *Violence over the Land: Indians and Empires in the Early American West* (Cambridge, MA: Harvard University Press, 2006), 25, and passim.

4. On Native movements, see Carter, *Indian Alliances*, 3–79; Elliott West, *The Contested Plains: Indians, Goldseekers, and the Rush to Colorado* (Lawrence: University Press of Kansas, 1996), 37–57; and cf. Tyler, "Before Escalante." For the Comanche, see Pekka Hämäläinen, *Comanche Empire* (New Haven: Yale University Press, 2008), 20–55. On trade markets, see Tyler, "Before Escalante," 110, and 107–9; Marvin K. Opler, "The Southern Ute of Colorado," in *Acculturation in Seven American Indian Tribes*, ed. Ralph Linton (New York: Harper & Son, 1940), 125; Brooks, *Captives & Cousins*, 45–79, 117–59

5. Tyler, "Before Escalante," 35–37, 43–46, 107–11, and citing Alonso de Posada's 1686 report and the *Relaciones* of Fray Gerónimo de Zárate Salmarón, written in 1626. On band names, see *Ute Dictionary and Ute Reference Grammar*, preliminary editions (Ignacio, CO: Ute Press, 1979).

6. Ramón A. Gutiérrez, *When Jesus Came the Corn Mothers Went Away* (Stanford, CA: Stanford University Press, 1991), 47–49. For known expeditions, see George P. Hammond and Agapito Rey, *The Rediscovery of New Mexico, 1580–1594: The Explorations of Chamuscado, Espejo, Castaño de Sosa, Morlete, and Leyva de Bonilla and Humaña* (Albuquerque: University of New Mexico Press, 1966). On the impact of European contact, see Carter, *Indian Alliances*, 118–37; Donald Cutter and Iris

Engstrand, *Quest for Empire: Spanish Settlement in the Southwest* (Golden, CO: Fulcrum Publishing, 1996), 54–55; Spicer, *Cycles of Conquest*; Hammond and Rey, *The Rediscovery of New Mexico, 1580–1594*; Marc Simmons, *The Last Conquistador: Juan de Oñate and the Settling of the Southwest* (Norman: University of Oklahoma Press, 1991).

7. West, *Contested Plains,* 48–53.

8. Ibid. For information on imperial rivalries, cultural interaction, and kinship linkages before and after Spanish colonization, see Brooks, *Captives & Cousins*; Brooks, "'This Evil Extends Especially…to the Feminine Sex': Negotiating Captivity in the New Mexico Borderlands," *Feminist Studies* 22 (Summer 1996): 279–309; and Carter, *Indian Alliances.*

9. Brooks, *Captives & Cousins,* 14, 33; West, *Contested Plains,* 42–44.

10. Carter, *Indian Alliances,* 68–79. See also Tyler, "Before Escalante," 95–101; and Brooks, *Captives & Cousins,* 26, 30.

11. Brooks, *Captives & Cousins,* 84.

12. Tyler, "Before Escalante," ii–iv, 26–27, 111, 124, and citing Valverde y Cosío's 1719 description of the Yuta plains, 148–51. On Ute aggression, see Tyler, "Before Escalante," 52–70, and citing Juan Amando Niel's "Apuntamientos que a las Memorias del Padre Fray Gerónimo de Zárate" (written 1626). The quote "brave men from the north" is cited in Tyler, "Before Escalante," and in A. F. Bandelier, "Report on the Ruins of the Pueblo of Pecos," in *Papers of the Archaeological Institute of America* (Boston: Williams and Co., 1881). See also Herbert E. Bolton, "Narrative of Antonio Espejo, 1582," in *Spanish Exploration,* 183; and John R. Swanton, *Indian Tribes of North America* (1952; Washington, D.C.: Smithsonian Institution Press, 1974), 343.

13. Tyler, "Before Escalante," quoting Nicholas de Lafora, *Relación del Viaje que Hizo a los Presidios Internos,* 102, 104–5; Charles W. Hackett, ed., *Historical Documents Relating to New Mexico, Nueva Vizcaya, and Approaches Thereto, to 1773,* collected by A. F. Bandelier and F. R. Bandelier (Washington, D.C.: Carnegie Institution of Washington, 1937), 3:486–87; Herbert E. Bolton, *Coronado, Knight of Pueblo and Plain* (1949; Albuquerque: University of New Mexico Press, 1991), 246–48.

14. On the spread of horse culture among the Utes, see Tyler, "Before Escalante," 43–44, 101–3; Albert H. Schroeder, "A Brief History of the Southern Utes," *Southwestern Lore* 30 (1965): 53–54; Frances Leon Swadesh [Quintana], *Los Primeros Pobladores* (Notre Dame, IN: University of Notre Dame Press, 1974), 38–51; Cutter and Engstrand, *Quest for Empire,* 43–44; West, *Contested Plains,* 48–53; Omer C. Stewart, "The Eastern Ute," 5, and "The Western Ute," unpublished essays, located in Omer C. Stewart Collection, 2nd Accession, box 5, Norlin Library Archives, University of Colorado, Boulder; and Omer Call Stewart Papers, Special Collections, Marriot Library, University of Utah; Stewart, "Ute Indians: Before and after White Contact," *Utah Historical Quarterly* 34 (Winter 1966): 49. See also Hämäläinen, *Comanche Empire,* 25, 346–47; and Escalante to the governor, December 31, 1779, in Ralph E. Twitchell, comp., *Spanish Archives of New Mexico,* Spanish Archives of New Mexico [SANM] (Cedar Rapids, MI: The Torch Press, 1914), 2:269, #779.

15. A. B. Thomas, trans. and ed., *Alonso de Posada Report, 1686: A Description of the Area of the Present Southern United States in the Late Seventeenth Century* (Pensacola: The Perdido Bay Press, 1982), 40; Tyler, "Before Escalante," 110, 107–9, and quoting Fr. Niels, "Apuntamientos" (1626).

16. Steward and Opler both believed that larger kin-clusters formed after the acquisition of the horse, but Tyler argues Plains Utes hunted in large kin-groups before the Spanish arrived ("Before Escalante," 43–46). Cf. Opler "Southern Ute," 156–63. On competition and Ute warfare, see Gregory E. Smoak, *Ghost Dances and Identity: Prophetic Religion and American Indian Ethnogenesis in the Nineteenth Century* (Berkeley: University of California, 2006), 32–35; West, *Contested Plains,* 20–25; and Anne M. Smith (Cook), *Ethnography of the Northern Utes,* Papers in Anthropology, no. 17 (Albuquerque: Museum of New Mexico Press, 1974), 237–39.

17. Opler, "Southern Ute," 156; Smith, *Ethnography of the Northern Ute,* 37–42, 46–51; Frances Leon Swadesh [Quintana], "Hispanic Americans and the Ute Frontier from the Chama Valley to the San Juan Basin" (Ph.D. Diss., University of Colorado, Boulder, 1966), 54, 233–44; Tyler, "Before Escalante," 90. For more on expanded language, see James A. Goss, "Ute Lexical and Phonological Patterns" (PhD diss., University of Chicago, 1972), 55–57; cf. Opler, "Southern Ute, 125.

18. Opler, "Southern Ute," 123, 101–3, 156–62; Hämäläinen, *Comanche Empire,* 25, 346–47.

19. Brooks, *Captives & Cousins,* 151.

20. On Utes trading Ute children for horses, see Smith, *Ethnography of the Northern Ute*, 26–32; Opler, "Southern Ute," 158–59; Stewart, "Eastern Ute," 4–5; and Stewart, personal communication, fall 1978. In 1970, Stewart saw a Ute woman in a bar attempt to trade away her newborn baby because it was interfering with her social life. See also Gottfried Otto Lang, *A Study in Culture Contact and Culture Change: The Whiterocks Utes in Transition*, Anthropological Papers, no. 15 (Salt Lake City: University of Utah Press, 1953), 3. For the trade of children in Utah, see Brian Q. Cannon, "Adopted or Indentured, 1850–1870: Native Children in Mormon Households," in *Nearly Everything Imaginable: The Everyday Life of Utah's Mormon Pioneers*, ed. Ronald W. Walker and Doris R. Dant (Provo, UT: Brigham Young University Press, 1998), 341–57. On eating horses, see Stewart, personal communication, fall 1978; and Smith, *Ethnography of the Northern Ute*, 18–22.

21. Brooks, *Captives & Cousins*; Brooks, "We Betray Our Own Nation," in *Indian Slavery in Colonial America*, 353–90; Hämäläinen, *Comanche Empire*, 247–59.

22. European colonialism and African-American slavery is but one example of this exploitation of labor. For Navajo slavery, see David M. Brugge, *Navajos in the Catholic Church Records of New Mexico, 1694–1875*, Research Report no. 1 (Window Rock, AZ: Navajo Tribe Parks and Recreation Department, 1968), 76; J. Lee Correll, *Through White Men's Eyes: A Contribution to Navajo History* (Window Rock, AZ: Navajo Heritage Center, 1969), 160–61; cf. Brooks, *Captives & Cousins*, 84–91; 108–9, 115–16. Navajos captured so many Mexicans that they developed a "Mexican clan," *Naakaii Dine'é* or "Mexican Navajos." On Comanche slavery, see Hämäläinen, *Comanche Empire*, 247–59.

23. See, e.g., John Wesley Powell, *Anthropology of the Numa: John Wesley Powell's Manuscripts on the Numic Peoples of Western North America, 1868–1880*, ed. Don D. Fowler and Catherine S. Fowler (Washington, D.C.: Smithsonian Institution Press, 1971), 50–51; cf. Carling Malouf, "Ethnohistory in the Great Basin," in *Current Status of Anthropological Research in the Great Basin: 1964*, ed. Warren L. d'Azevedo, et al. (Desert Research Institute, 1966), 1:1–38. *Conscience collective* describes the psychological undercurrent of cultural moral unanimity. See Emile Durkheim, *Elementary Forms of the Religious Life*, trans. Joseph W. Swain (New York: Free Press, 1915), and *Division of Labor in Society*, trans. George Simpson (New York: Free Press, 1933).

24. Stewart, "The Western Ute," 19–20; Stewart, "Culture Element Distributions: XVIII, Ute—Southern Paiute," *Anthropological Records* 6 (1942): 4:234, 299–302; Powell, *Anthropology of the Numa*, 50–51. See also Opler, "Southern Ute," 160–73; cf. Smith, *Ethnography of the Northern Utes*, 125–26; Smoak, *Ghost Dances and Identity*, 17–18. On different accounts of women in councils, see Stewart, *Element Distribution*; and E. E. White, *Experiences of a Special Indian Agent* (1893; Norman: University of Oklahoma Press, 1965), 113.

25. On *puwá* and prosperity, see John Alton Peterson, *Utah's Black Hawk War* (Salt Lake City: University of Utah Press, 1998), 95–100; cf. Opler, "Southern Ute," 160–73.

26. Opler, "Southern Ute," 160–73. See, e.g., Omer Stewart, "Eastern Ute," 16–17; Stewart, "Data on the Identification and Group Leadership of Ute Indian Chiefs" ("Ute Chiefs List"), working paper prepared for Dockets 44–45, U.S. Indian Claims Commission, 1952, located in the Omer C. Stewart Collection, 2nd Accession, box 1, Norlin Library Archives, University of Colorado, Boulder (also in Omer Call Stewart Papers, Special Collections, Marriott Library, University of Utah); and various treaties and agreements, 1863–1880, in Charles J. Kappler, comp. and ed., *Indian Affairs: Laws and Treaties*, vol. 2 (Washington, D.C.: Government Printing Office, 1902–1938).

27. Opler, "Southern Ute," 169–170. See also Southern Ute Tribe, *Ute Dictionary*, 2:96; and Goss, "Ute Lexical and Phonological Patterns," 33.

28. On wealth, see Tyler, "Before Escalante," 80–82, 98–100. On Spanish legends, see Tyler, "Before Escalante," 49, 62–75; Joseph P. Sánchez, *Explorers, Traders, and Slavers: Forging the Old Spanish Trail, 1678–1850* (Salt Lake City: University of Utah Press, 1997), 3–16, 9–21; and cf. Hämäläinen, *Comanche Empire*, 21.

29. Tyler, "Before Escalante," 80–82, 98–100, 166–70; Brooks, *Captives & Cousins*; Hämäläinen, *Comanche Empire*; David J. Weber, *The Spanish Frontier in North America* (New Haven and London: Yale University Press, 1992).

30. Tyler, "Before Escalante," 87; L. R. Bailey, *Indian Slave Trade*, 45.

31. Brugge, *Navajos In the Catholic Church Records*, 73, 81–92, 135; L. R. Bailey, *Indian Slave Trade in the Southwest* (Los Angeles: Westernlore Press, 1966), 100, 84–86, 177–78; and Brooks, *Captives & Cousins*, esp. 24–26. Cf. Alan Gallay, *The Indian Slave Trade: The Rise of the English Empire in*

449

the American South, 1670–1717 (New Haven: Yale University Press, 2002), 46–47; and Swadesh-Quintana, *Los Primeros Pobledores*.

32. On the slave trade, see Brooks, *Captives & Cousins*, 319–51; L. R. Bailey, *Indian Slave Trade*, esp. xiii–xvi, 25–33, and Galvez quote, 30, 66; Sondra Jones, *The Trial of Pedro León Luján: The Attack against Indian Slavers and Mexican Traders* (Salt Lake City: University of Utah Press, 1999), 19–52; Albert H. Schroeder and Omer C. Stewart, "Indian Servitude in the Southwest," n.d., typescript, esp. 5, 8, 11, Museum of New Mexico, Santa Fe; Leland Hargrave Creer, "Spanish-American Slave Trade in the Great Basin, 1800–1853," *New Mexico Historical Review* 24 (July 1949): 171–83; Carling Malouf and Arline Malouf "The Effects of Spanish Slavery on the Indians of the Intermountain West," *Southwestern Journal of Anthropology* 1 (Spring 1945): 378–91; William J. Snow, "Utah Indians and Spanish Slave Trade," *Utah Historical Quarterly* 2 (July 1929): 67–75. For information on trade fairs, see Eleanor B. Adams and Fr. Angélico Chávez, trans. and comp., *The Missions of New Mexico, 1776: A Description by Fray Francisco Atanasio Dominguez with other Contemporary Documents* (Albuquerque: University of New Mexico Press, 1955), 252–53; Hackett, *Historical Documents Relating to New Mexico*, 486–87; Brugge, *Navajos in the Catholic Church Records*, esp. 22 and frontispiece.

33. France V. Scholes, "Church and State in New Mexico," *New Mexico Historical Review* 11 (1936): 300–1; Brooks, *Captives & Cousins*, 50, 89; cf. Blackhawk, *Violence over the Land*, 23–25; Gov. Rosas quoted in Gutiérrez, *When Jesus Came*, 112–13.

34. C. W. Hackett and C. C. Shelby, "Revolt of the Pueblo Indians of New Mexico and Otermin's Attempted Reconquest, 1680–1682," *Coronado Cuarto Centennial Publications* (Albuquerque, N.M.: n.p., 1912), 206. See also Escalante to Governor Cavallero de Croix (Chihuahua), December 31, 1779, in SANM, doc. 779, 2:279–80.

35. Tyler, "Before Escalante," 25, 57, 59, 120–25, 170–71.

36. Schroeder, "Southern Ute," 56–57; J. Manuel Espinosa, *Crusaders of the Rio Grande* (Chicago: Institute of Jesuit History, 1942), 182–83, 193–97; and Espinosa, "Governor Vargas in Colorado," *New Mexico Historical Review* 11 (April 1936): 179–87. See also Hubert Howe Bancroft, *History of Arizona and New Mexico: 1530–1888* (San Francisco: History Company, 1889), 210.

37. Schroeder, "Southern Ute, 57–58; Tyler, "Before Escalante," 101–3, 110, 125–43; Blackhawk, *Violence over the Land*, 27–68; and Hämäläinen, *Comanche Empire*, 22–55. On the meaning of "Comanche," see Southern Ute Tribe, *Ute Dictionary*; Goss, "Ute Lexical and Phonological Patterns"; and Goss, "The Yamparica—Shoshones, Comanches, or Utes—or Does It Matter?" in *Julian Steward and the Great Basin: The Making of an Anthropologist*, ed. Richard O. Clemmer, L. Daniel Myers, and Mary E. Rudden (Salt Lake City: University of Utah Press, 1999), 74–84.

38. Tyler, "Before Escalante," 137–43; Schroeder, "Southern Ute," 58–59; Blackhawk, "Ute-Comanche Alliance," in *Violence over the Land*, 35–54; Opler, "Southern Ute," 161–62.

39. For French alliances, see Tyler, "Before Escalante," 137–54, and quoting from "Diary of the Campaign of Governor Antonio de Valverde against the Ute and Comanche Indians, 1719"; Blackhawk, *Violence over the Land*, 42; Brooks, *Captives & Cousins*, 121, 157; Weber, *Spanish Frontier*, 168–70.

40. Schroeder, "Southern Ute," 58–59; Tyler, "Before Escalante," 158–65; Swadesh-Quintana, *Los Primeros Pobladores*, 32–40, 47; Blackhawk, *Violence over the Land*, 48–52.

41. It is unclear today who the Sabuagana/Caguagua/Chapuapuas (aka Taguaganas or Aguaguanos) were. They guided Rivera and the later Dominguez-Escalante expeditions; modern scholars have identified them as Mowataviwatsiu. See Angelico Chavez, trans., and Ted. J Warner, ed., *The Domínguez-Escalante Journal: Their Expedition through Colorado, Utah, Arizona, and New Mexico in 1776* (Provo, UT: Brigham Young University Press, 1976; reprinted University of Utah Press, 1995); cf. Schroeder, "Southern Ute," 58–59; and Blackhawk, *Violence over the Land*, 48–52.

42. Schroeder, "Southern Ute," 58–59; Swadesh-Quintana, *Los Primeros Pobladores*, 35–39; Blackhawk, *Violence over the Land*, 48–52; Stanley F. L. Crocchiola, *The Abiquiú, New Mexico Story* in *New Mexico Stories*, vol. 1, n.d), 4.

43. Crocchiola, *The Abiquiú Story*; Swadesh-Quintana, *Los Primeros Pobladores*, 31–41; Brooks, *Captives & Cousins*, ch. 4, esp. 130, 139; "Petition for permission to remove," from residents of Abiquiú, Ojo Caliente, and Quemado, 1748, SANM, 1:25–26, #28. Génizaro is etymologically linked to janissary, elite soldiers among Ottoman Turkish troops, primarily drawn from Christian children who had been seized as tribute, converted to Islam, and trained for service.

44. Schroeder, "Southern Ute," 59–60; Stanley, *Abiquiú*; Brooks, *Captives & Cousins*, 151–52.

45. Schroeder, "Southern Ute," 59–60; Tyler, "Before Escalante," iv, 172–75; cf. Blackhawk, *Violence over the Land*, 52–56; Brooks, *Captives & Cousins*, 59–79; Hämäläinen, *Comanche Empire*, 49–55.

46. Schroeder, "Southern Ute," 59–60; Tyler, "Before Escalante," 172–75; Blackhawk, *Violence over the Land*, 52–56; Hämäläinen, *Comanche Empire*, 49–55.

47. Schroeder, "Southern Ute," 61; Tyler, "Before Escalante," 213–16. Alfred B. Thomas, ed. and trans., *Forgotten Frontiers: A Study of the Spanish Indian Policy of Don Juan Bautista de Anza, Governor of New Mexico, 1777–1787* (Norman: University of Oklahoma Press, 1932); and Weber, *The Spanish Frontier*, 230–31, 249–53.

48. Teodoro de Croix to Jose de Galvez, quoted in Alfred B. Thomas, *Teodoro de Croix and the Northern Frontier of New Spain, 1776–1783* (1941; Norman: University of Oklahoma Press, 1968), 75, 114; Tyler, "Before Escalante," 213–15. On the Navajo campaign, see Schroeder, "Southern Ute," 61–62; Brooks, *Captives and Cousins*, 150, 95n24; cf. Tyler, "Before Escalante," 95.

49. Schroeder, "Southern Ute," 61. Don Diego de Peñalosa Brizenos passed an early *Bando*, January 7, 1664, in SANM, 1:2, #3. The September 13, 1778, *Bando* in SANM 2:263, #740. See also L. R. Bailey, *Indian Slave Trade*, 141–44.

50. See, e.g., Pedro de Nava to Governor Chacón, July 14, 1797, in SANM, 2:383, #1390; Charles IV, Order, June 5, 1805, in SANM, 2:471, #1841a; and "Reports," SANM, 2:487, #1925, no. 32.

51. On the Old Spanish Trail and Utes, see Sánchez, *Explorers, Traders, and Slavers*; LeRoy R. Hafen and Ann W. Hafen, *Old Spanish Trail: Santa Fe to Los Angeles* (Glendale, CA: Arthur H. Clark Co., 1954); Joseph J. Hill, "The Old Spanish Trail: A Study of the Spanish and Mexican Trade and Exploration Northwest from New Mexico to the Great Basin and California," *Hispanic American Historical Review* 4 (1921): 444–73; and maps and commentaries posted on The Old Spanish Trail Association website, http://www.oldspanishtrail.org/learn/maps.php. See also Jones, *Trial of Don Pedro León*, 53–60. Pedro León was a militia commander from Abiquiú who fought the Navajo yet traded freely with the Utes.

52. Sánchez, *Explorers, Traders, and Slavers*, 19–21; Tyler, "Before Escalante," 165–66; Bolton, *Coronado*, 170–71.

53. Austin Nelson Leiby, "Borderland Pathfinders: The 1765 Diaries of Juan Maria Antonio de Rivera" (PhD diss., Northern Arizona University, 1985), 52–63, 178–222, and footnotes.

54. Leiby, "Rivera Diaries," 137–39, 162–72, 208–22. Cf. Sánchez, *Explorers, Traders, and Slavers*, ch. 2 and 3, and his translations, 137–57.

55. Leiby, "Rivera Diaries," 137–39, 198–200. Roland McCook, a Tribal Chair of the Northern Utes, an Uncompahgre raised in a very traditional household, related a similar story and insisted that the *Pituku-pi* were not the same as the *páa-?áapa-ci* water babies. McCook, telephone conversation with author, fall 1999.

56. See, e.g., Weber, *Spanish Frontier*, 242–56. California colonization began in 1769.

57. J. J. Hill, "Spanish and Mexican Exploration," 3–6. On Muñiz, see Chavez and Warner, *The Domínquez-Escalante Journal*, July 29, 1776, and fn., and August 27, 1776, and fn.; and Sánchez, *Explorers, Traders, and Slavers*, 55–80. Weber, *Spanish Borderlands*, 253–54. Chavez and Warner's *Domínguez-Escalante Journal* is the primary source for details related here. Cf. Herbert J. Bolton, *Pageant in the Wilderness: The Story of the Escalante Expedition to the Interior Basin, 1776* (Salt Lake City: Utah State Historical Society, 1950), and Cecil J. Alter, "Father Escalante and the Utah Indians," *Utah Historical Quarterly* 1 and 2 (1928–1929).

58. Chavez and Warner, *Domínguez-Escalante Journal*, August 28 and fns. See also Stewart, "Culture Element Distributions," 249; Smith, *Ethnography of the Northern Utes*, 61–64; Joel C. Janetski, *The Ute of Utah Lake*, Anthropological Papers no. 116 (Salt Lake City: University of Utah Press, 1991), 36–38, 79–89.

59. On the *Yamparica Comanches* (yampa-eater Comanches), see Chavez and Warner, *Domínguez-Escalante Journal*, August 29–September 1, and September 7, 1776; cf. Yamparika identification in James Mooney, *The Ghost Dance Religion* (1896; Chicago: University of Chicago Press, 1961), 280. The northernmost band of Comanches today is the *Yapi tuhka*, or Yapi-eaters (yampi-eaters), and were the last band to migrate south. See Lila Wistrand Robinson and James Armagost, *Comanche Dictionary and Grammar* (Arlington: University of Texas, 1990), 157–58.

60. Some historians suggest the Utes were setting up the explorers so they could steal their horses and blame the Comanches. However, the behavior of the frightened guides and later comments by

Silvestre to his Timpanogos relatives argue otherwise; so do the very real fears the Timpanogos had of Comanche/Shoshone raiders. See Chavez and Warner, *Domínguez-Escalante Journal*, August 19 to September 6, esp. September 1, 1776.

61. Chavez and Warner, *Domínguez-Escalante Journal*, September 13–23, 1776; cf. August 28, 1776, and fn.

62. Ibid., September 23–24, 1776.

63. Ibid., September 29, 1776.

64. Ibid., Oct. 2, 1776.

65. Ibid., October 2–November 7, 1776. See maps on The Old Spanish Trail Association website for the Armijo Route. On Mormon use of the crossing, see Todd Compton, *A Frontier Life: Jacob Hamblin, Explorer and Indian Missionary* (Salt Lake City: University of Utah Press, 2013).

66. Escalante to Governor de Croix, December 31, 1779, in SANM doc. 779, 2:279–80.

67. On prosperous traders, see Swadesh-Quintana, *Los Primeros Pobladores*, 42–43; and Hill, "Spanish and Mexican Exploration," 13, 17–19. On horse trading and raiding, see Mestas, 1804, in SANM, 2:478, #1881, no. 7; "War of the Yutas, Timpanogos, and Caiguas [Kiowas]," in SANM, 2:487, #1925, no. 27; SANM, 2:489, #1932, no. 1. On demand for the slave trade, see Arze and García testimony in the case against Miguel Thenorio, et al., Rio Arriba, September 6, 1813, "Trial for going without license to the Yutas," in SANM, 2:577, #2511. See also Sánchez, *Explorers, Traders, and Slavers*, 99–101; Swadesh-Quintana, *Los Pobladores*, 43, 47, 39–47. On tolls, see W. T. Hamilton, *My Sixty Years on the Plains: Trapping, Trading, and Indian Fighting* (Norman: University of Oklahoma, 1905; reprint, 1960), 75–82; John Charles Frémont, *Report of the Exploring Expedition to the Rocky Mountains* [1844] (Ann Arbor, MI: University Microfilms, 1966), 270; Gustive Larson, "Walker's Half Century," *Western Humanities Review* 6 (Summer 1952): 238; George Douglas Brewerton, *Overland with Kit Carson: A Narrative of the Old Spanish Trail in '48* (1930; Lincoln: University of Nebraska Press, 1993), 100; Gwinn Harris Heap, *Central Route to the Pacific*, ed. LeRoy R. Hafen and Ann W. Hafen (Glendale, CA: Arthur H. Clark Co., 1957), 195–97, 201; and Howard Louis Conard, *Uncle Dick Wootton: The Pioneer Frontiersman of the Rocky Mountain Region*, ed. Milo Milton Quife (Reprint, Chicago: R. R. Donnelley and Sons, 1957), 253–56, cf. 258–61. On horse raiding in California, see Paul Bailey, *Walkara: Hawk of the Mountains* (Los Angeles: Westernlore Press, 1954), and Gustive O. Larson, "Walker's Half Century," *Western Humanities Review* 6 (Summer 1952): 235–59. See also Chapter 4, herein.

68. September 13, 1778, *bando* in SANM, 2:263, #740. See also Bailey, *Indian Slave Trade*, 141–44.

69. Some traders were caught and tried. See Schroeder, "Southern Ute," 61; Bailey, *Indian Slave Trade*, 141–44; and, e.g., "Proceedings against [Marcelino Manzanares] for violations of the order relative to trading with the Yutes," April 10 and 26, 1785, in SANM, 2:297, #912; proceedings against Salvador Salazar, Santiago Lucero, and Francisco Valverde, April 22–May 9, 1785, in SANM, 2:297, #913; and against Vicente Serna, March 31 and April 29, 1785, in SANM, 2:298, #920; and "Trial for illegal trade in the Yutas' country" of Cristoval Lovato, et al., in SANM, 2:384, #1393.

70. SANM, 2:478, #1881, no. 7; SANM, 2:487, #1925, no. 27; 2:489, #1932, no. 1; and report filed by the governor in Santa Fe, quoted in Hill, "Spanish and Mexican Exploration," 16–17. See also Sánchez, *Explorers, Traders, and Slavers*, 99–101; Swadesh-Quintana, *Los Pobladores*, 43, 47, 39–47. Utes and Comanches were commonly confused with each other during this period.

71. See, e.g., Fred R. Gowans, *Rocky Mountain Rendezvous: A History of the Fur Trade Rendezvous, 1825–1840* (Salt Lake City: Gibbs-Smith, 1985), 11–13 and passim; and Gowans, personal communications, 1994.

72. Arze and García testimony in the case against Miguel Thenorio, et al., Rio Arriba, September 6, 1813, "Trial for going without license to the Yutas," SANM, 2:577, #2511. See also, Sánchez, *Explorers, Traders, and Slavers*, 101–2.

73. Warren Angus Ferris, *Life in the Rocky Mountains*, ed. Leroy R. Hafen (Denver: Old West Publishing, 1983), 344–46.

74. Stephen P. Van Hoak, "The Other Buffalo: Native Americans, Fur Trappers, and the Western Bison, 1600–1860," *Utah Historical Quarterly* 72 (Winter 2004): 4–18; cf. Karen D. Lupo, "The Historical Occurrence and Demise of Bison in Northern Utah," *Utah Historical Quarterly* 64 (Spring 1996): 168–80.

CHAPTER 4

1. David J. Wishart, *The Fur Trade of the American West, 1807–1840* (Lincoln: University of Nebraska, 1979), 207–8, 212–13, and citing Thomas Jefferson; cf. John R. Alley, "Prelude to Dispossession: The Fur Trade's Significance for the Northern Utes and Southern Paiutes," *Utah Historical Quarterly* 50 (Spring 1982); Ned Blackhawk, *Violence over the Land: Indians and Empires in the Early American West* (Cambridge, MA: Harvard University Press, 2006), 147–48, and 238–40.

2. For example, in Rufus B. Sage, *Rocky Mountain Life; Startling Scenes and Perilous Adventures in the Far West* (Chicago: Donohue, Henneberry, 1857), 223–28.

3. Dale L. Morgan, *Jedediah Smith and the Opening of the West* (1953; Lincoln: University of Nebraska, 1967), 196; Sage, *Rocky Mountain Life*, 222–25, 255–58; Osborne Russell, *Journal of a Trapper*, ed. Aubrey L. Haines (Oregon Historical Society, 1955), 120–21; Jerry Bagley, *Daniel Trotter Potts: First Known Man in Yellowstone Park* (Rigby, ID: Old Faithful Eye-Witness Publishing, 2000), appendices and "Daniel Potts Letters"; George C. Yount, *George C. Yount and His Chronicles of the West*, ed. Charles L. Camp (Denver: Old West Publishing, 1966), 79; George F. Ruxton, *Ruxton of the Rockies*, ed. LeRoy Hafen (Norman: University of Oklahoma Press, 1950), 198, 211, 236; John C. Frémont, *Report of the Exploring Expedition to the Rocky Mountains* [1844] (Ann Arbor, MI: University Microfilms, 1966), 271, 274–76. Modern geographic designations are used here, although New Mexico and Utah did not become territories until 1850 and Colorado until 1861.

4. See, e.g., Wishart, *Fur Trade*, 205–17; Alley, "Prelude to Dispossession."

5. Wishart, *Fur Trade*, 212–13. On the decline in beaver, see Warren Angus Ferris, *Life in the Rocky Mountains, 1830–1835*, rev. ed., ed. Leroy R. Hafen (Denver: Old West Publishing, 1983), 287; and George F. Ruxton, "The Beaver and His Trapper," in *Wild Life in the Rocky Mountains* (New York: The MacMillan Company, copyright 1916) and online; and cf. Blackhawk, *Violence over the Land*, 146.

6. Martha Knack, *Boundaries Between: The Southern Paiutes, 1775–1995* (Lincoln: University of Nebraska Press, 2004), 33–47; Todd Compton, *A Frontier Life: Jacob Hamblin, Explorer and Indian Missionary* (Salt Lake City: University of Utah Press, 2013), 348–56. For information on gifts, begging, and theft, see Benjamin Davies to Commissioner W. P. Dole, June 30, 1861, *Report of the Commissioner of Indian Affairs [RCIA]* (Washington, D.C., 1861), 129; Floyd A. O'Neil, "A History of the Ute Indians until 1890" (PhD diss., University of Utah, 1973), 48–50; Hubert Howe Bancroft, *History of Utah* (San Francisco: History Co., 1890), 629.

7. For more on the complexities of Indian slavery and bound servitude, see Sondra Jones, *The Trial of Don Pedro León Luján: The Attack against Indian Slavers and Mexican Traders* (Salt Lake City: University of Utah Press, 1999); and James F. Brooks, *Captives & Cousins: Slavery, Kinship, and Community in the Southwest Borderlands* (Chapel Hill: University of North Carolina Press, 2002).

8. See, e.g., Knack, *Boundaries Between*, 33–47; Compton, *A Frontier Life*, 348–56; Davies to Dole, June 30, 1861, in *ARCIA*, 129; Wishart, *Fur Trade*, 208–9.

9. Dale Morgan, *The West of William Ashley: The International Struggle for the Fur Trade…Recorded in the Diaries and Letters of William Ashley and his Contemporaries, 1822–1838* (Denver: Old West Publishing, 1964), 115, 281–82; Ferris, *Life in the Rocky Mountains*, 312; George Douglas Brewerton, *Overland with Kit Carson: A Narrative of the Old Spanish Trail in '48* [1853] (1930; Lincoln: University of Nebraska Press, 1993), 100; Sage, *Rocky Mountain Life*, 232, 250–54; W. T. Hamilton, *My Sixty Years on the Plains: Trapping, Trading, and Indian Fighting* (Norman: University of Oklahoma, 1905; reprint, 1960), 87.

10. "Expectant capitalists," in William H. Goetzmann, *Exploration and Empire: The Explorer and the Scientist in the Winning of the American West* (New York: Alfred Knopf, 1967), 180. See also Blackhawk, *Violence over the Land*, 146; Wishart, *Fur Trade*, 206, 209–11; Dale L. Morgan and Eleanor Towles Harris, "Étienne Provost," in *The Rocky Mountain Journals of William Marshall Anderson: The West in 1834*, ed. Dale L. Morgan and Eleanor Towles Harris (San Marino, CA: Huntington Library, 1967), 345, 349; Ruxton, *Ruxton of the Rockies*, 227–31; Fred R. Gowans, *Rocky Mountain Rendezvous: A History of the Fur Trade Rendezvous, 1825–1840* (Salt Lake City: Gibbs-Smith, 1985); Gowans, personal communication with author, 1993; "William Henry Ashley," in *Biographical Directory of the United States Congress*, at http://bioguide.congress.gov/ scripts/biodisplay. pl?index=A000315.

453

11. Jedediah S. Smith, *The Southwest Expedition of Jedediah S. Smith: His Personal Account of the Journey to California, 1826–1827,* ed. George R. Brooks (Glendale, CA: Arthur H. Clark, 1977), 43. Cf. Ferris, *Life in the Rocky Mountains,* 312; Theodore Talbot, *The Journals of Theodore Talbot, 1843 and 1849–52,* ed. Charles H. Carey (Portland, OR: Metropolitan Press, 1931), 42; Frémont, *Report of the Exploring Expedition,* 272–73; Brewerton, *Overland with Kit Carson,* 100; Howard L. Conard, *"Uncle Dick" Wootton: Pioneer Frontiersman of the Rocky Mountain Region* (Chicago: W. E. Dibble, 1890; reprint, 1950), 257; Ruxton, *Ruxton of the Rockies,* 213, 235–36.

12. Wishart, citing W. Zelinsky, in *Fur Trade,* 207.

13. See, e.g., Knack, *Boundaries Between,* 30–37.

14. On the eastern Ute child-exchange, see Anne Smith (Cooke), *Ethnography of the Northern Utes,* Papers in Anthropology, no. 17 (Albuquerque: Museum of New Mexico Press, 1974) 26–32; cf. Marvin K. Opler, "The Southern Ute of Colorado," in *Acculturation In Seven American Indian Tribes* (New York: Harper & Son, 1940), 158–59. See also Omer C. Stewart, "The Eastern Ute," unpublished essay written in preparation for "Utes" (1973), in *Handbook of North American Indians,* located in Omer C. Stewart Collection, 2nd Accession, box 5, Norlin Library Archives, University of Colorado, Boulder; and p. 4 in Omer Call Stewart Papers, Special Collections, J. Willard Marriot Library, University of Utah, Salt Lake City. As cultural mediators, see Brooks, *Captives & Cousins.*

   While Eastern Utes did sometimes trade their own children, there are few historical records of Western Utes trading theirs; see Brian Q. Cannon, "Adopted or Indentured, 1850–1870: Native Children in Mormon Households," in *Nearly Everything Imaginable: The Everyday Life of Utah's Mormon Pioneers,* ed. Ronald W. Walker and Doris R. Dant (Provo, UT: Brigham Young University Press, 1998), 341–57.

15. Jones, *The Trial of Don Pedro León*; Sondra Jones, "Redeeming the Indians: Enslavement of Indian Children in Utah and New Mexico," *Utah Historical Quarterly* 67 (Summer 1999): 220–41; Stephen P. Van Hoak, "Who Shall Have the Children?" *Nevada Historical Society Quarterly* 41 (Spring 1998): 3–25; Isabel T. Kelly, *Southern Paiute Ethnography,* Anthropological Papers, no. 69 (Salt Lake City: University of Utah Press, 1964), 86–87, 90–91, 95, 151–52, 174, 176, 188; Hamblin to the Deseret News, April 4, 1855. For information on the Paiute as middlemen, see Jacob Hamblin, "Journals and Letters of Jacob Hamblin," December 17, 1854, 15, 27–32, 44, typescript copy with original orthography, L. Tom Perry Special Collections, Brigham Young University [BYU-SC], Provo (original journals in the Church History Archives, Church of Jesus Christ of Latter-day Saints, Salt Lake City); Thomas D. Brown, *Journal of the Southern Indian Mission: Diary of Thomas D. Brown,* ed. Juanita Brooks (Logan: Utah State University Press, 1972), 40, 60, 100, 217. For slavery in New Mexico, see Brooks, *Captives & Cousins*; and Brooks, "'This Evil Extends Especially ... to the Feminine Sex': Negotiating Captivity in the New Mexico Borderlands," *Feminist Studies* 22 (Summer 1996), 279–309; David M. Brugge, *Navajos in the Catholic Church Records of New Mexico, 1694–1875,* Research Report no. 1 (Window Rock, AZ: Navajo Tribe Parks and Recreation Department, 1968); L. R. Bailey, *Indian Slave Trade in the Southwest* (Los Angeles: Westernlore Press, 1966). For Wákara's father, see Andrew Siler to George A. Smith, December 18, 1851, George Albert Smith Collection, CHA.

16. Knack, *Boundaries Between,* 30–37.

17. Daniel W. Jones, *Forty Years among the Indians* (Los Angeles: Westernlore Press, 1890; reprint, 1960), 47–48; Anne H. Abel, ed., *Official Correspondence of James S. Calhoun* (Washington: Government Printing Offices, 1915); LeRoy R. Hafen and Ann W. Hafen, "Slave Catchers: Traffic in Indian Women and Children," in *Old Spanish Trail: Santa Fe to Los Angeles* (Glendale, CA: Arthur H. Clark Co., 1954), 259–83; Bailey, *Indian Slave Trade,* 41–44, 84–87; Blackhawk, *Violence over the Land,* 70–80, 106–14, 133–44, 328n41; and Brugge, *Navajos in the Catholic Church Records,* 85.

18. See, e.g., James G. Bleak, "Annals of the Southern Utah Mission," TS, 17, BYU-SC; Hamblin, "Journals," 27, 39; Gwinn Harris Heap, *Central Route to the Pacific,* ed. LeRoy R. Hafen and Ann W. Hafen (Glendale, CA: Arthur H. Clark, Co., 1957; orig. published in Philadelphia, 1854), 99–100, 235; William J. Snow, "Some Source Documents on Utah Indian Slavery," *Utah Historical Quarterly* 2 (July 1929): 76–90; Hafen and Hafen, *Old Spanish Trail,* 267–68, 270–71; Thelma S. Guild and Harvey L. Carter, *Kit Carson* (Lincoln: University of Nebraska Press, 1984), 87, 135, 222.

19. William Palmer, cited in Hafen and Hafen, *Spanish Trail,* 281; Hamblin, "Journals," 28–29, 31, and Hamblin letter in *Deseret News Weekly,* April 4, 1855. For mountain men and the slave trade, see Harvey L. Carter, ed., *"Dear Old Kit:" The Historical Christopher Carson* (Norman: University of

Oklahoma, 1968), 94–95, n166; Heap, *Central Route*, 235; George F. Ruxton, *Life in the Far West* (Norman: University of Oklahoma, 1849/1951), 83–87, esp. 87.

20. Paiutes described in Hamilton, *My Sixty Years*, 229–30; Frémont, *Report of the Exploring Expedition*, 276; Yount, *George C. Yount*, 73; Bleak, "Annals of the Southern Utah Mission," 17; Hamblin, "Journals," 27, 39; Heap, *Central Route*, 99–100, 235.

21. See, e.g., Joel C. Janetski, *The Ute of Utah Lake*, Anthropological Papers no. 116 (Salt Lake City: University of Utah Press, 1991).

22. Janetski, *Ute of Utah Lake*; Ferris, *Life in the Rocky Mountains*, 345. Piede Ute identity was argued during the 1950s land claims cases. Anne M. Smith, in *Ethnography of the Northern Utes*, 49, and Omer Stewart, in personal communication, fall 1978, remained adamant on Piede identity. Julian Steward testified for the government and against Piede Ute claims. "Think they're Ute," in Isabel T. Kelly, *Southern Paiute Ethnography*, Anthropological Papers no. 69 (Salt Lake City: University of Utah Press, 1964), 33–34, 65, 145, 175.

23. Sources include Ray Allen Billington and Martin Ridge, *Westward Expansion: A History of the American Frontier*, 5th ed. (New York: Macmillan Publishing, 1982), 399–408; LeRoy R. Hafen, "A Brief History of the Fur Trade of the Far West," in *The Mountain Men and the Fur Trade*, 1:17–176.

24. David J. Weber, *Taos Trappers: The Fur Trade in the Far Southwest, 1540–1846* (Norman: University of Oklahoma, 1971), 48–49; Weber, *The Spanish Frontier in North America* (New Haven and London: Yale University Press, 1992), 292–94, 300; Elliott West, *The Contested Plains: Indians, Gold-seekers, and the Rush to Colorado* (Lawrence: University Press of Kansas, 1998), 153; Goetzmann, *Exploration and Empire*, 43–53, 57–64; and Goetzmann, *Army Exploration in the American West, 1803–1863* (New Haven: Yale University Press, 1959), 62.

25. See, e.g., Frémont, *Report of Exploring Expedition*, 284; Hamilton, *My Sixty Years*, 88; Ruxton, *Wild Life*, Ch. 6, "Into the Mountains." For information on cows and bison, see Southern Ute Tribe, *Ute Dictionary and Ute Reference Grammar* (Ignacio, CO: Ute Press, 1979), 122, 222, 228.

26. Many traders married local women; others brought Indian wives with them or purchased captives, e.g., Ruxton, *Wild Life*, Chap. 12, "Birds...at Bent's Fort"; cf. Sylvia Van Kirk, *Many Tender Ties: Women in Fur-trade Societies, 1670–1870* (Norman: University of Oklahoma Press, 1983).

27. West, *The Contested Plains*, 185–87; cf. Richard White, *Middle Ground: Indians, Empires, and Republics in the Great Lakes Region, 1650–1815* (Cambridge: University of Cambridge Press, 1991), 60–75; and Van Kirk, *Many Tender Ties*.

28. For the exploitation of women and attacks on forts, see Fred Gowans, telephone interview with author, 1990. See also Janet Lecompte, *Pueblo, Hardscrabble, Greenhorn: The Upper Arkansas, 1832–1856* (Norman: University of Oklahoma Press, 1978), 135–38.

29. For the early fur trade, see Hafen, "A Brief History of the Fur Trade," 1:35, 61–63; Hafen, "Etienne Provost," in *Mountain Men*, 6:371; LeRoy R. Hafen, "Mountain Men before the Mormons," *Utah Historical Quarterly* 26 (1958): 308–10; Weber, *Taos Trappers*, esp. 30–31, 43–49; Billington and Ridge, *Westward Expansion*, 405; Morgan and Harris, "Étienne Provost," in *William Marshall Anderson*, 343; Charles L. Camp, ed., "Trapping and Trading in the Southwest, 1815–1830," in *George C. Yount*.

30. Albert H. Schroeder, "A Brief History of the Southern Utes," *Southwestern Lore* 30 (1965)," 63. Similar impacts were felt on the California-Oregon Trail.

31. Weber, *Taos Trappers*, 12–31, 70–71. Details in LeRoy R. Hafen's classic ten-volume set, *The Mountain Men and The Fur Trade of the Far West*, esp. Hafen, "A Brief History of the Fur Trade," 1:65–67; Goetzmann, *Exploration and Empire*, 105–45.

32. Hafen, "A Brief History of the Fur Trade," 1:65–66; Weber, *Taos Trappers*, 70–73; Ruxton, "The Beaver and his Trapper," in *Wild Life*, ch. 7; Ferris, *Life in the Rocky Mountains*, 28; cf. Morgan, *Jedediah Smith*, 230–33; Hamilton, *My Sixty Years*, 76–77; Daniel Potts to Dr. Lukens, July 8, 1827, in Bagley, *Daniel Trotter Potts*, appendices, and "Potts Letters" online.

33. Goetzmann, *Exploration and Empire*, 101–3; Billington and Ridge, *Westward Expansion*, 400; Weber, *Taos Trappers*, 74–78; Hafen, "A Brief History of the Fur Trade," 1:75, 80–91; Hafen, "Mountain Men before the Mormons," 312–14; Gowans, *Rocky Mountain Rendezvous*, 12; Hafen, "Etienne Provost," in *Mountain Men*, 6:374–375; Morgan, "Étienne Provost," in *Rocky Mountain Journals*, 344; Ted J. Warner, "Peter Skene Ogden," in *Mountain Men*, 3:213–18; and Morgan, *The West of William Ashley*, 112, 278–79, 286, 290–91. For the economics of the trapper trade, see Morgan, *Jedediah Smith*, 230–34; Potts to Lukens, July 8, 1827; Potts to "Respectid Brother," July 8, 1827; and Potts to Robert

Montgomery Potts, October 13, 1828, in "Potts Letters" online and in Bagley, "*Daniel Trotter Potts*, appendices.

34. Gowans, *Rocky Mountain Rendezvous*, 15–16; Potts to Lukens, July 8, 1827, in "Potts Letters"; Ferris, *Life in the Rocky Mountains*, 272–73; Sage, *Rocky Mountain Life*, 232; Conard, *"Uncle Dick" Wootton*, 235, 253–56, 263; Hamilton, *My Sixty Years*, 29.

35. On tolls, see Hamilton, *My Sixty Years*, 75–82; Frémont, *Report of Exploring Expedition*, 270; and B. H. Roberts, *A Comprehensive History of The Church of Jesus Christ of Latter-day Saints* (1930; Provo, UT: The Church of Jesus Christ of Latter-day Saints, 1965), 3:463; Gustive Larson, "Walker's Half Century," *Western Humanities Review* 6 (Summer 1952): 238; Brewerton, *Overland with Kit Carson*, 100; Heap, *Central Route*, 195–97, 201; and Conard, *"Uncle Dick" Wootton*, 253–56, cf. 258–61.

36. See, e.g., Conard, *"Uncle Dick" Wootton*, 81, 102–5, 120; Frémont, *Report of the Exploring Expedition*, 280, 283–87; Ferris, *Life in the Rocky Mountains*, 273; Brewerton, *Overland with Kit Carson*, 137–38; Carter, *"Dear Old Kit*," 153; Ruxton, *Ruxton of the Rockies*, 213, 235–36.

37. For the 1826 treaty, see Smith, *Southwest Expedition*, 41–43. On conflicts of interest, see Charles Camp, ed., "Pegleg Smith," in *George C. Yount*, 235; Frémont, *Report of the Exploring Expedition*, 285–87; Howard A. Christy, "Open Hand and Mailed Fist: Mormon-Indian Relations in Utah, 1847–52," *Utah Historical Quarterly* 46 (1978), 228.

38. Yount, *George C. Yount*, 76–77; Hamilton, *My Sixty Years*, 33; Frémont, *Report of the Exploring Expedition*, 280, 283–87; Morgan and Towles, *Rocky Mountain Journals*, 291; Brewerton, *Overland with Kit Carson*, 96–100; Ruxton, *Ruxton of the Rockies*, 213, 235–36.

39. Gowans, *Rocky Mountain Rendezvous*; Hafen, "Mountain Men before the Mormons," 308–10; James P. Beckwourth, *The Life and Adventures of James P. Beckwourth, As Told to Thomas D. Bonner*, ed. Delmont R. Oswald (1856; Lincoln: University of Nebraska Press, 1972), 57–77; Delmont R. Oswald, "James Pierson Beckwourth," in *Mountain Men*, 6:37–60; Ruxton, *Wild Life in the Rocky Mountains*, ch. 7, "The Beaver and His Trapper."

40. Gowans, *Rocky Mountain Rendezvous*, esp. 12–23, 34–35, and Gowans to author, fall 1994; Potts to "Respectid Brother," July 8, 1827, in "Potts Letters"; cf. Morgan, *The West of William Ashley*, 168; Appendices in Bagley, *Daniel Trotter Potts*; Gerald C. Bagley, "Daniel T. Potts," in *The Mountain Men*, 3:254–58; Hafen, "Mountain Men before the Mormons," 308–10; Hafen, "A Brief History of the Fur Trade," 1:81–83.

41. Morgan, *The West of William Ashley*, 115.

42. Ibid., 114–15, 279–81; cf. Morgan, *Jedediah Smith*, 168.

43. Hafen, "A Brief History," 1:87; Hafen, "Mountain Men before the Mormons," 315–16; Gustive O. Larson, "Walkara, Ute Chief," in *Mountain Men*, 2:241. For more on Jed Smith, see Smith, *Southwest Expedition*; Morgan, *Jedediah Smith*, 195–97, 237–40. See also Hafen and Hafen, *Old Spanish Trail*, 109–29; "A brief sketch of accidents, misfortunes…," in Morgan, *The West of William Ashley*, 327–34, Appendix A. For the Utaw mountains, see Bagley, *Daniel Trotter Potts*, 178–79, and Potts to R. Potts, July 16, 1826, in "Potts Letters"; Oswald, "James Pierson Beckwourth," 58.

44. Morgan, *Jedediah Smith*, 237; Smith, *Southwest Expedition*, 41–43, Hafen, "Mountain Men before the Mormons," 315–16; Joseph P. Sánchez, *Explorers, Traders, and Slavers: Forging the Old Spanish Trail, 1678–1850* (Salt Lake City: University of Utah Press, 1997), 122–23. For more regarding Conmarrowap in Ferris, *Life in the Rocky Mountains*, 275–78; and W. M. Anderson, *Rocky Mountain Journals*, 290–91. Ferris says he was born a Timpanogos, but left to lead "Py-Euts."

45. William S. Wallace, "Antoine Robidoux," in *Mountain Men*, 4:264–71; Hafen and Hafen, *Old Spanish Trail*, 270; Frémont, *Report of Exploring Expedition*, 279.

46. Lecompte, *Pueblo, Hardscrabble, Greenhorn*; LeRoy R. Hafen and Ann W. Hafen, *Colorado: A Story of the State and its People* (Denver: Old West Publishing, 1952), 103–20; Weber, *Taos Trappers*, 68–69.

47. "Old Fort Utah" in B. H. Roberts, *History of the Church*, 3:461; Bancroft, *History of Utah*, 21. For more on Fort Uintah, see Wallace, "Antoine Robidoux," in *Mountain Men*, 4:262–63. For Charbonneau "Jim" Reed, see Henry Harris Jr. interview, July 19, 1967, 7–12, Doris Duke Oral History Collection, MLSC; and Oran F. Curry interview, July 20, 1967, 19–21, box 3, no. 48, Doris Duke Oral History Collection. The Reeds became prominent and vocal members of the mixed-blood faction in the Uintah Basin and claimed Shoshone and not Ute heritage.

48. Hafen, "A Brief History of the Fur Trade," 1:168–69; Hafen and Hafen, *Old Spanish Trail*, 94–95, 270. On the Utes at Fort Bridger, see Henry Harris Jr. interview, 24–25.

49. Hafen and Hafen, *Colorado*, 116; Wilson Rockwell, *The Utes: A Forgotten People* (Denver: Sage books, 1956), 59–60; LeRoy Hafen, "Fort Davy Crockett, its Fur Men and Visitors," *Colorado Magazine* 29 (September 1962).

50. Ruxton, *Ruxton of the Rockies*, 225–26.

51. Lecompte, *Pueblo, Hardscrabble, Greenhorn*, 135–38. See also Hafen, "A Brief History of the Fur Trade," 1:164; Wallace, "Antoine Robidoux," 4:271–72; O'Neil, "History of the Ute Indians," 21–22; Frémont, *Report of Exploring Expedition*, 279 fn. On the rendezvous, see Gowans, *Rocky Mountain Rendezvous*, 194–98.

52. See, e.g., Bagley, *Daniel Trotter Potts*, 283–84; and "Potts Letters," July 16, 1826, and July 8, 1827; Russell, *Journal of a Trapper*, 120.

53. Bagley, *Daniel Trotter Potts*, 283–84; Potts to Lukens, July 8, 1827, in "Potts Letters."

54. Ferris, *Life in the Rocky Mountain*, 353, 387–88 [1983 ed.] and 311–12 [1940 ed.]; Potts to Lukens, July 8, 1827, in "Potts Letters"; Jedediah Smith to Superintendent of Indian Affairs, William Clark, July 12, 1827, in Morgan, *Jedediah Smith*, 334–35; Sage, *Rocky Mountain Life*, 232.

55. Russell, *Osborne Russell's Journal*, 121–22; cf. Smith to Clark, in Morgan, *Jedediah Smith*, 334; Smith, *Southwest Expedition*, 41; Sage, *Rocky Mountain Life*, 232; Ferris, *Life in the Rocky Mountains*, 311.

56. Alfred Glen Humpherys, "Thomas L. (Peg-Leg) Smith," in *Mountain Men*, 2:312–14; Camp, "Pegleg Smith," in *George Yount*, 231.

57. Humpherys, "Thomas L. (Peg-Leg) Smith," in *Mountain Men*, 4:312–14, 323–28; Hafen and Hafen, *Old Spanish Trail*, 135–36, 230, 246; Hafen, "Mountain Men before the Mormons," 317. None of the Ute words for man (*ta?wá-ci*), one (*súúyis*), or foot (*nápa*) suggest Waketoco. See Southern Ute Tribe, *Ute Dictionary*; and James A. Goss, "Ute Lexical and Phonological Patterns" (PhD diss., University of Chicago, 1972).

58. Humpherys, "Thomas L. (Peg-Leg) Smith," in *Mountain Men*, 4:328. Camp, "Pegleg Smith," in *George C. Yount*, 234–35.

59. Hafen, *Old Spanish Trail*; and Sánchez, *Explorers, Traders, and Slavers*, 103–34.

60. Numerous studies of westward expansion exist, including Robert V. Hine and John M. Faragher, *The American West: A New Interpretive History* (New Haven: Yale University Press, 2000), 189–92; Billington and Ridge, *Westward Expansion*, 499; and West, *The Contested Plains*.

61. Humpherys, "Thomas L. (Peg-Leg) Smith," in *Mountain Men*, 4:329; Camp, "Pegleg Smith," in *George C. Yount*, 237–39.

62. Fred R. Gowans, *Fort Bridger: Island in the Wilderness* (Provo, UT: Brigham Young University Press, 1975); Cornelius M. Ismert, "James Bridger," in *Mountain Men*, 6:95–97; Hafen, "A Brief History," 1:168–69; Oran Curry, Doris Duke Interview, 16.

63. On rustling, see Hafen and Hafen, "Horse Thieves: Raiding California Missions and Ranchos," in *Old Spanish Trail*, 227–57.

64. Frederick H. Piercy, *Route from Liverpool to Great Salt Lake Valley*, ed. Fawn M. Brodie (1854; Cambridge: Harvard University Press, 1962), 278, and citing Dimick Huntington; Peter Gottfredson, *Indian Depredations in Utah* (1919; Salt Lake City: Shelton Publishing Co., 1969), 317–18.

    Wákara biographies include Paul Bailey, *Walkara: Hawk of the Mountains* (Los Angeles: Westernlore Press, 1954); Larson, "Walkara, Ute Chief," in *Mountain Men*, 2:339–50; and Larson, "Walker's Half Century," 235–59.

65. For the California horse raid, see Hafen and Hafen, "Horse Thieves: Raiding California Missions and Ranchos," in *Old Spanish Trail*, 227–57; Humpherys, "Thomas L. (Peg-Leg) Smith," in *Mountain Men*, 4:328; Oswald, "James Pierson Beckwourth," in *Mountain Men*, 6:50–52; cf. Blackhawk, *Violence over the Land*, 133–144, 328 n41.

66. The rustlers claimed they stole nearly 6,000 horses, which seems high. Oswald, "James Pierson Beckwourth," in *Mountain Men*, 6:52; Beckwourth, *Life and Adventures*, 474–76; Larson, "Walkara, Ute Chief," in *Mountain Men*, 2:343; Humpherys, "Thomas L. (Peg-Leg) Smith," in *Mountain Men*, 4:328–29; Camp, "Pegleg Smith," in *George C. Yount*, 236–37; Hafen and Hafen, *Old Spanish Trail*, 240–42.

67. Ruxton, *Life in the Far West*, 138–39 n7 and 8, 145, 173, 176; Beckwourth, *Life and Adventures*, 575–76, fn. See also Oswald, "James Pierson Beckwourth." On the extent of horse raiding, see Hafen and

457

Hafen, "Horse Thieves," in *Spanish Trail,* 227–58.; John Boessenecker, Gold *Dust & Gunsmoke: Tales of Gold Rush Outlaws, Gunfighters, Lawmen, and Vigilantes* (New York: Wiley & Sons, 1999), 58–68.

68. Oran F. Curry, Doris Duke interview, 1967, 20; Gottfredson, *Indian Depredations,* 317–18. See also Southern Ute Tribe, *Ute Dictionary,* 128, 155–56; cf. Goss, "Ute Linguistic and Phonological Patterns."

69. On the cattle industry, see John A. Peterson, "Mormons, Indians, and Gentiles and Utah's Black Hawk War" (PhD diss., Arizona State University, 1993); Stephen Van Hoak, "Waccara's Utes: Native American Equestrian Adaptations in the Eastern Great Basin, 1776–1876," *Utah Historical Quarterly* 67 (Fall 1999): 309–30.

70. See, e.g., Billington and Ridge, *Westward Expansion,* 408.

CHAPTER 5

1. On Wákara's complaints, see Ron W. Walker and Dean C. Jesse, "Chief Walker and Brigham Young," *Brigham Young University Studies* 32 (1993): 129, citing the minutes of a June 14, 1849, meeting with Young, 133–34 and notes. Cf., George F. Ruxton, *Wild Life in the Rocky Mountains* (New York: Macmillan, 1916), ch. 7.

2. Angelico Chavez, trans., and Ted. J Warner, ed., *The Domínguez-Escalante Journal: Their Expedition through Colorado, Utah, Arizona, and New Mexico in 1776* (Salt Lake City: University of Utah Press, 1995), September 23–24; cf. Osborne Russell, *Osborne Russell's Journal of a Trapper* (Portland: Oregon Historical Society, 1955; reprint, 1965). On the concept of a "middle ground," see Richard White, *Middle Ground: Indians, Empires, and Republics in the Great Lakes Region, 1650–1815* (Cambridge: University of Cambridge Press, 1991).

3. For Utes, all related persons of the same generation were older or younger brothers or sisters. Arapeen was likely a half-brother, while Sanpitch and Ammon were probably first, second, or even third cousins. See "Southern Numa Vocabularies," in *John Wesley Powell's Manuscripts on the Numic Peoples of Western North America, 1868–1880,* edited by Don D. Fowler and Catherine S. Fowler (Washington, D.C.: Smithsonian Institution Press, 1971), 129–210; and John W. Powell, "Uintah Ute Relationship Terms," mss.831-a, Ute, in Anthropology archives, Smithsonian, Washington, D.C. Cf., James Goss, "Ute Lexical and Phonological Patterns" (PhD diss., University of Chicago, 1972), kinship terms.

4. Joseph Smith, *History of the Church of Jesus Christ of Latter-day Saints* (Salt Lake City: Deseret Book, 1978), 5:85–86 and fn., 6:547–52.

5. Mormon pioneer history is widely published; see, e.g., B. H. Roberts, *A Comprehensive History of The Church of Jesus Christ of Latter-day Saints,* vols. 1–4 (Provo, UT: The Church of Jesus Christ of Latter-day Saint, 1930).

6. Brigham Young, et al., *Journal of Discourses* (London: Latter-day Saints' Book Depot, 1854–1886/1966), 4:41.

7. *JD,* 1:105.

8. *Journal History of the Church,* June 28, 1847, Church History Library, The Church of Jesus Christ of Latter-day Saints, Salt Lake City, Utah; *The Millennial Star* (Liverpool, England) 12 (1850): 243.

9. *JH,* July 21, 1847.

10. George Bean (for Walker) to Brigham young, May 1, 1854, quoted in Howard A. Christy, "Open Hand and Mailed Fist: Mormon-Indian Relations in Utah, 1847–52," *Utah Historical Quarterly* 46 (1978): 217.

11. Omer C. Stewart, ethnohistorian and expert witness in Ute land claims cases, personal conversation with author, 1978, regarding testimony about recognized traditional Ute territory in Utah. Several men appear in contemporary records as Wanship or Oneship, but the context of references suggest they were not always the same person.

12. James Amasa Little, "Biography of Lorenzo Dow Young," *Utah Historical Quarterly* 14 (1946): 98, 100.

13. 1 Nephi 12:23; cf. 2 Nephi 5:21–22.

14. Enos 1:20.

15. 2 Nephi 30:6; cf. 2 Nephi 5:21. The 1989 edition of the Book of Mormon was revised to say "pure and delightsome."

16. Doctrine and Covenants (D&C) 109:65; 49:24.

17. See, e.g., David Hurst Thomas, *Skull Wars: Kennewick Man, Archaeology, and the Battle for Native American Identity* (New York: Basic Books, 2000), 36–43, 49–51.

18. Nineteenth-century prejudices were bequeathed to the first generations of Utah historians; see, e.g., Edward W. Tullidge, *Tullidge's Histories*, 2 vol. (Salt Lake City: Press of the Juvenile Instructor, 1889); Orson F. Whitney, *History of Utah* (Salt Lake City: George Q. Cannon and Sons, Co., 1892–1904), 1:397–400, 420–32, 412–428, and 2:187–214; Leland H. Creer, *Utah and the Nation* (Seattle: University of Washington Press, 1929); Andrew Love Neff, *History of Utah, 1847 to 1869* (Salt Lake City: Deseret News Press, 1940), 364–409.

19. D&C 3:16–20; see also 2 Nephi 30:5–6.

20. Orson Pratt, July 15, 1855, in *JD* 9: 177–79.

21. There are numerous discussions of the federal assimilation policy. Thomas, *Skull Wars*, 64–76, 117–19, provides a short summary; cf. Francis Paul Prucha, *Indian Policy in the United States: Historical Essays* (Lincoln: University of Nebraska Press, 1981); Lyman S. Tyler, *A History of Indian Policy* (Washington, D.C.: United States Department of Interior, Bureau of Indian Affairs, 1973).

22. Orson Pratt, in *JD* 9:177–79. On Mormon Indian policy, see esp. Floyd A. O'Neil and Stanford J. Layton, "Of Pride and Politics: Brigham Young as Indian Superintendent," *Utah Historical Quarterly* 46 (1978): 236–50; and Lawrence G. Coates, "Brigham Young and Mormon Indian Policies: The Formative Period, 1836–1851," *BYU Studies* 18, no. 3 (Spring 1978): 428–52.

23. Ether 2:3.

24. See, e.g., Virginia Cole Trenholm and Maurine Carley, *The Shoshones: Sentinels of the Rockies* (Norman: University of Oklahoma Press, 1964), 142; James F. Brooks, *Captives & Cousins: Slavery, Kinship, and Community in the Southwest Borderlands* (Chapel Hill: University of North Carolina Press 2002), 27–32; Richard D. Kitchen, "Mormon-Indian Relations in Deseret: Intermarriage and Indenture, 1847 to 1877" (PhD diss., Arizona State University, 2002).

25. *JH*, June 23, 1854. See Peter Gottfredson, *Indian Depredations in Utah* (Salt Lake City: Shelton Publishing Co., 1919; reprint, 1969), 77–78; Paul Bailey, *Walkara: Hawk of the Mountains* (Los Angeles: Westernlore Press), 164; Gustive O. Larson, "Walkara's Half Century," *Western Humanities Review* 6 (Summer 1952), 255–57. See also Adelia Sidwell, "Reminiscences" in Manti Centennial Committee, *Song of a Century, 1849–1949* (Provo, UT: Community Press, 1949), 34–37; Daughters of Utah Pioneers, Sanpete County Company, *These—Our Fathers: A Centennial History of Sanpete County 1849 to 1947* (Springville, UT: Art City Publishing, 1947), 27–28; and Brigham Madsen, *The Shoshoni Frontier and the Bear River Massacre* (Salt Lake City: University of Utah Press, 1985), 86.

26. See, e.g., William R. Palmer, "Pahute Indian Homelands," *Utah Historical Quarterly* 6 (1933): 88–90.

27. On the usurpation of Paiute resources, see J. H. Holeman to L. Lea, September 21, 1851, microfilm, Letters Received, M-234, Office of Indian Affairs, Utah (OIA-UT), RG 75, National Archives and Records Administration; cf. Todd M. Compton, *A Frontier Life: Jacob Hamblin, Explorer and Indian Missionary* (Salt Lake City: University of Utah Press, 2013), 194, 237, 348–56, 443–48, and Hopis, 460–62.

28. Garland Hurt (Utah Superintendent), "Indians of Utah," Appendix O, in John H. Simpson, *Report of Explorations Across the Great Basin*, comp. by J. H. Simpson (Washington, D.C., 1876), 463.

29. Christy, "Open Hand and Mailed Fist," 234, and citing Brigham Young, 229; cf. Robert F. Berkhoffer, *Salvation and the Savage: An Analysis of Protestant Missions, and American Indian Response, 1787–1862* (Lexington: University of Kentucky Press, 1965), 159.

    Prejudice dies hard. As late as the 1950s, some Mormons still opposed giving Indians equal fellowship. One poisonous letter complained that, "I never dreamed I would live to see the day when the Church would invite an Indian buck to talk in the Salt Lake Tabernacle—an Indian buck appointed a bishop—an Indian squaw to talk in the Ogden Tabernacle—Indians to go through the Salt Lake Temple.... The sacred places desecrated by the invasion of everything that is forced on the white race." Spencer W. Kimball, "The Evil of Intolerance," *Official Report of the Annual General Conference of the Church of Jesus Christ of Latter-day Saints* (hereafter *LDS Conference Report*) (April 1954): 103–8.

459

30. Christy, "Open Hand and Mailed Fist," uses this term to describe Young's Indian policy of defense and conciliation. For information on the Nauvoo Legion, see Phillip M. Flammer, "Nauvoo Legion," in Daniel H. Ludlow, *Encyclopedia of Mormonism* (New York: Macmillan Publishing, 1992), 997–999; Richard C. Roberts, "Legacy: The History of the Utah National Guard from the Nauvoo Legion Era to Enduring Freedom" (National Guard Association of Utah, 2003).

31. *JH*, August 1, 1847. Kimball presided at this council because Young was sick. See also Roberts, *CHC*, 268–69.

32. Hurt to Brigham Young, September 30, 1855, in *Annual Report of the Commissioner of Indian Affairs, 1855* (Washington, D.C.), 200–20.

33. Colonization is described in general histories of Utah; see, e.g., Thomas G. Alexander, *Utah: The Right Place* (Salt Lake City: Gibbs Smith, 2003), ch. 4–8. See also Martha Knack, *Boundaries Between: The Southern Paiutes, 1775–1995* (University of Nebraska Press, 2004), 50–53.

34. Young to John M. Bernhisel, 1850, quoted in Christy, "Open Hand, Mailed Fist," 229 and fn.

35. Beverly Beeton, "Teach Them to Till the Soil: An Experiment with Indian Farms 1850–1862," *American Indian Quarterly* 3 (1977–1978): 311–13; Floyd A. O'Neil, "A History of the Ute Indians Until 1890" (PhD diss., University of Utah, 1973), 50.

36. See, e.g., Milton R. Hunter, *Utah in Her Western Setting* (Salt Lake City: Deseret News Press, 1943), 279–80.

37. Roberts, *CHC*, 3:465–66; Larson, "Walkara's Half Century," 235–59, esp. 241–43; Bailey, *Walkara: Hawk of the Mountains*, 58–61; *JH*, May 13, 1849.

38. Whitney, *History of Utah*, 1:397–98; Larson, "Walkara's Half Century," 240–41. Whitney reports this incident in Spanish Fork Canyon in 1847. Other sources place it outside Fort Utah, in the spring of 1850. See J. E. Booth, "A History of the Fourth Provo Ward, 1775–1858," unpublished manuscript, typed 1941, Special Collections, Harold B. Lee Library, Brigham Young University, Provo, Utah (BYU-SC), 9; and Gottfredson, *Indian Depredations*, 36.

39. Christy, "Open Hand and Mailed Fist," 220 and fn; Bruce Parry, interview with Howard A. Christy, April 1980, an unpublished article in author's possession. Parry, a Northwest Shoshone, was Utah State Director of Indian Affairs.

40. *JH*, August 22, 1847 (p. 197).

41. Brigham Young, "Manuscript History" [*BYMH*], 1847, 74, in CHL.

42. *JH*, March 1, 5, and 6, 1848; see also Christy, "Open Hand and Mailed Fist," 219. A significant amount of stock had been lost to "wolves and Indians" that first winter, angering the settlers. Some contemporary sources referred to Cone's band as Shoshone, possibly because the survivors sought refuge with Shoshones rather than Utes. However, their ties to kinsmen in Utah Valley argue their being Ute, or mostly Ute. Non-Indians often mixed up tribal identities.

43. *JH*, February 27 and 28, 1849, and March 10, 1849; Oliver B. Huntington, "Diary," 52–55, BYU-SC; Hosea Stout, "Diary," tms., 4:48–56, BYU-SC. The women and children were fed in Great Salt Lake City, and then sought refuge among the "Snake" Indians.

44. Opecarry was a "superior" chief, while Pariats led the band's war faction. Patsowett killed cattle and threatened Mormons thereafter, until he was arrested, tried, and summarily executed in 1850. *JH*, June 14, 1849; February 7–8, 1850, May 28–29, 1850. See also Huntington, "Diary," 52–53; Stout, "Diary," 4:48; Roberts, *CHC*, 3:459–60; and Walker and Jesse, "Chief Walker and Brigham Young," 125–26, 130, 134 and fn. Cf., Lawrence Coates, "Brigham Young and Mormon Indian Policies: The Formative Period, 1836–1851," *BYU Studies* 18 (Spring 1978): 437–38.

45. See, e.g., Akbar Nasir Khan, "The US Policy of Targeted Killings by Drones in Pakistan," *IBRI Journal* 11 (Winter 2011), 21–22, 31–30. According to terrorism studies, in cultures of revenge "killing insurgents usually serves to multiply enemies rather than subtract them."

46. Gottfredson, *Indian Depredations*, 25–29; Whitney, *History of Utah*, 2:423–26.

47. *JH*, March 17, 1849; Christy, "Open Hand and Mailed Fist," 221.

48. Gottfredson, *Indian Depredations*, 21, citing from George W. Bean's journal; Solomon Nuñes Carvalho, *Incidents of Travel and Adventure in the Far West with Colonel Fremont's Last Expedition* (New York: Derby and Jackson, 1856/1860), 184; Joel C. Janetski, *The Ute of Utah Lake*, Anthropological Papers no. 116 (Salt Lake City: University of Utah Press, 1991); D. Robert Carter, "Fish and the Famine of 1855–1856," *Journal of Mormon History* 27, no. 2 (2001): 92–124; Jared Farmer, *On*

Zion's Mount: Mormons, Indians, and the American Landscape (Cambridge: Harvard University Press, 2008), 54–104.

49. George W. Bean, "Autobiography," copy located in *CHL*; Moffitt, *Story of Provo*, 16–18, 31; Booth, "History of the Fourth Provo Ward," 1, 4–5; Hubert Howe Bancroft, *History of Utah* (San Francisco: History Co., 1890), 308–9; O'Neil, "A History of the Ute Indians," 27.

50. Ray E. Colton, "A Historical Study of the Explorations of Utah Valley and the Story of Fort Utah" (master's thesis, Brigham Young University, 1946), 138; Stephen A. Hales, "The Effect of the Rivalry between Jesse Knight and Thomas Nicholls Taylor on Architecture in Provo, Utah, 1896–1915" (master's thesis, Brigham Young University, 1991), 2–4.

51. February 7–8, 1850; Roberts, *CHC*, 3:465–69, citing John W. Gunnison. See also Howard Stansbury, *Exploration and Survey of the Valley of the Great Salt Lake of Utah* (Philadelphia: Lippincott, Grambo, 1852), 148–49; and Bancroft, *History of Utah*, 309–10.

52. *JH*, June 14, 1849.

53. Walker and Jesse, "Chief Walker and Brigham Young"; Frederick Hawkins Piercy, *Route from Liverpool to Great Salt Lake Valley*, ed. Fawn M. Brodie (1854; Cambridge: Harvard University Press, 1962), 277–78.

54. Whitney, *History of Utah*, 397–98, reports this incident in Spanish Fork Canyon in 1847; but Booth ("History of Fourth Provo Ward," 9) and Gottfredson (*Indian Depredations*, 36), both place it outside Fort Utah, in 1850.

55. "Report of Dimick Huntington on His Meeting with Chief Walker," May 14, 1849, in Brigham Young Collection, CHL; *JH*, June 13–14; Walker and Jesse, "Chief Walker and Brigham Young," 127–28.

56. *JH*, October 28 and November 22, 1849.

57. Geo. Bean journal, quoted in Gottfredson, *Indian Depredations*, 24; Bancroft, *History of Utah*, 278 and fn. "Virgin soil" diseases decimated America's native populations, killing between 85–90 percent of the native population. See William H. McNeill, *Plagues and Peoples* (New York: Anchor Books, 1976/1988), 135, 212–13; Sheldon Watts, *Epidemics and History: Disease, Power and Imperialism* (New Haven: Yale University Press, 1997), ch. 3.

58. *JH*, December 8, 1849, January 31, 1850, and February 20, 1850; Bailey, *Walkara: Hawk of the Mountains*, 91–98. On LDS ordinances, see *JH*, March 13 and 24, 1850, June 9, 1850; Roberts, *CHC*, 3:464.

59. *Panáqari Kwín'wáyke* or Pan-a-karry Quin-ker. See Dimmick B. Huntington, *Vocabulary of the Utah and Shoshone or Snake Dialects* (Salt Lake City: Salt Lake City Herald Office, 1872), 27; Piercy, *Route from Liverpool*, 278; Gottfredson, *Indian Depredations*, 317–18; and Southern Ute Tribe, *Ute Dictionary and Ute Reference Grammar* (Ignacio, CO: 1979), 128, 155.

60. *JH*, February 20, 1850; Coates, "Brigham Young and Mormon Indian Policies," 440–41, 445, quoting Morley to Wells, 29 February 29, 1850, UTMC; cf. Morley to Young, February 20, 1850.

61. Christy, "Open Hand and Mailed Fist," 223; BYMH, June 12, 1854, 1850:17–18, statement of Elder James Bean; and *JH*, January 31, 1850; cf. Bancroft, *History of Utah*, 309; Gottfredson, *Indian Depredations*, 22–23. James Bean told Young that while the murder occurred in January 1850, hostilities had begun earlier. George W. Bean remembered it occurring in early August 1849; see Gottfredson, *Indian Depredations*, 22–23.

62. *JH*, October 15, 1849, January 31, 1850; cf. *JH*, February 20, 1850.

63. *JH*, January 31, 1850; George W. Bean quoted in Gottfredson, *Indian Depredations*, 27–35, esp. 27; Booth, "History of Fourth Provo Ward," 6–8; and Stansbury, *Exploration and Survey*, 148–49. The reference to Pariats is from Coates, "Brigham Young and Mormon Indian Policies," 441–43.

64. Minutes of First Presidency Meeting, BYC, cited in Christy, "Open Hand and Mailed Fist," 224; Roberts, *CHC*, 3:466–69 and quoting from BYMH, June 12, 1854, addenda; cf. BYMH, February 1850, 17–18. See also Stansbury, *Exploration and Survey*, 148–49; John W. Gunnison, *The Mormons, or, Latter-day Saints, in the Valley of the Great Salt Lake* (Philadelphia: J. P. Lippincott, 1856), 146.

65. Brigham Young, February 10, 1850, BYC, quoted in Christy, "Open Hand and Mailed Fist," 226–27; cf. *JH*, June 28, 1847.

66. Stansbury, *Exploration and Survey*, 147–49.

67. *JH*, January 31, 1850, quoting marginal note, dated June 12, 1854, inserted in BYMH. See also Roberts, *CHC*, 3:466–71.

68. Coates, "Brigham Young and Mormon Indian Policies," 338, 437–38, 446–47; John A. Peterson, *Utah's Black Hawk War* (Salt Lake City: University of Utah Press, 1998); and Christy, "Walker War." See also *JH*, April 28–29, 1850.

69. Wells' Special Order No. 2; Young to Major Daniel H. Wells, February 14, 1850; both in reel 1, doc. 5, and reel 6, no. 1312, respectively, in Utah Territorial Military Correspondence, 1849–1863 [UTMC], Microfilm, ST-27 (Salt Lake City: Utah State Historical Archives). Cf. Christy, "Open Hand and Mailed Fist," 224; emphasis added.

70. Minutes of First Presidency Meeting, BYC, quoted in Christy, "Open Hand and Mailed Fist," 224.

71. Young to Wells, February 14, 1850, reel 6, no. 1312, UTMC. Emphasis in the original. There is considerable irony in the similarity of this order and the infamous 1838 extermination order issued by Governor Lilburn W. Boggs against Mormons in Missouri: "The Mormons must be treated as enemies, and must be exterminated or driven from the state if necessary for the public peace—their outrages are beyond all description." Roberts, *CHC*, 1:479.

72. *JH*, February 8 and 10, 1850.

73. Wells to Captain G. D. Grant, February 9, 1850, Special Orders No. 10, reel 4, UTMC. The reference to Opecarry is in *JH*, February 8, 1850.

74. Daniel H. Wells, "Daniel H. Wells Narrative," *Utah Historical Quarterly* 6 (1933): 126.

75. The "Provo War" is detailed in *JH*, February 7–28, 1850, and citing Tullidge's histories. See also Howland to Wells, February 8, 1850, reel 4, UTMC; and George W. Bean's version, in Gottfredson, *Indian Depredations*, 26–35.

76. Wells to Young, February 13–14, reel 3, no. 1309, UTMC; cf. Roberts, *CHC*, 3:471, and BYMH, February 1850, 22–23; *JH*, February 12, 1850; George W. Bean, in Gottfredson, *Indian Depredations*, 34–35; Christy, "Open Hand and Mailed Fist," 225; and Christy, personal conversation with author, 1985.

77. Thomas, *Skull Wars*, 36–63. Early American anthropologists collected and studied Native American skulls, acquiring thousands by robbing graves or collecting them from battle fields.

78. Christy, "Open Hand and Mailed Fist," 226 and fn. See also Peterson, *Utah's Black Hawk War*, 55–58.

79. On the Rock Canyon fight, see Wells to Young, February 18, 1850, reel 1, doc. 36, 44, 45, and reel 3, doc. 1312 in UTMC; Christy, "Open Hand and Mailed Fist," 226 and fn. Ambiguity in Well's report—"One squaw killed herself falling from a precipice"—may have given rise to romantic legends about Indian lovers' suicides on Squaw Peak. See BYU-SC Folklore collection re: "Squaw Peak"; and Susa Young, "The Courtship of Kanosh," 29–31.

80. *JH*, February 8 and 10, 1850; cf. May 14, 1850.

81. In his book, *Utah's Black Hawk War* (43–79), Peterson argues a revised belief that the Chief Black Hawk of the Provo War and the later Black Hawk of the Black Hawk War were one and the same; however, as he notes in his dissertation, most contemporary records described the later Atonga/Autanquer/Black Hawk as a surly teenager in 1850 who played with the Mormon boys. Regardless, Black Hawk would have been personally affected, whether youth or adult. Cf., Peterson, "Mormons, Indians, and Gentiles and Utah's Black Hawk War" (PhD diss., Arizona State University, 1993). The historian Edward W. Tullidge specifically notes that the Black Hawk during the Fort Utah affair was *not* the same Black Hawk as the later 1860s war (*JH*, February 10 1850).

82. Wells to Conover, March 21, 1850, UTMC; Stansbury, *Exploration and Survey*, 149; Roberts, *CHC*, 3:470–71; Booth, "History of Fourth Provo Ward," 8-9.

83. BYC, Microfilm 80, box 47, fd. 6; cf. 2 Samuel 11:15.

84. Coates, "Mormon Indian Policies," 338, 432–38, 445, 449, and quoting Wells to Eldridge, September 20, 1850.

85. Higbee and Peter W. Conover to Daniel H. Wells, as quoted in Juanita Brooks, ed., *On the Mormon Frontier: The Diary of Hosea Stout: 1844–1861* (Salt Lake City: University of Utah Press, 1964), 2:368.

86. Brooks, *On the Mormon Frontier*, 368–69.

87. Regarding raiders, see Carvalho, *Incidents of Travel and Adventure*, 193.

88. Christy, "Open Hand, Mailed Fist, 228.

89. Ibid. A.B.C.'s "Reminiscences of the Early Days of Manti," *Utah Historical Quarterly* 6 (October 1933): 117–18, suggests that if they were frightened by the display, they were not frightened for long.

90. Details vary, garbled through memory and multiple retellings. See Booth, "History of Fourth Provo Ward," 9–10; *JH*, May 14, 18, 20, and 31, 1850, and June 27, 1850; Christy, "Open Hand and Mailed

Fist," 228; Bailey, *Walkara: Hawk of the Mountains*, 107–12; Gottfredson, *Indian Depredations*, 36; Booth, "History of Provo Fourth Ward," 9–10; Edward W. Tullidge, "History of Provo," *Tullidge's Quarterly Magazine* 3 (July 1884): 240–41; Larson, "Walkara's Half Century," 244–45.

91. Christy, "Open Hand and Mailed Fist," 228; Coates, "Brigham Young and Mormon Indian Policy," 446–49, and quoting Wells to Eldridge, September 18, 1850, UTMC.

92. Tullidge, *Tullidge's Histories*, 2:83–84.

93. Christy, "Open Hand and Mailed Fist," 231. On the request for arsenic, see reel 3, doc. 1328, UTMC; cf. *Central City Miner's Register*, quoted in Al Look, *The Utes' Last Stand* (Denver: Golden Bell Press, 1972), 83. See also Edmund Morgan, *American Slavery, American Freedom* (New York: Norton and Company, 1975), 100; and Francis Jennings, *The Invasion of America* (Chapel Hill: University of North Carolina Press, 1975), 207–9.

94. Jacob Hamblin, *Jacob Hamblin: A Narrative of His Personal Experience As a Frontiersman, Missionary To the Indians and Explorer*, transcribed by James A. Little (Salt Lake City: *Deseret News* and *Juvenile Instructor*, 1881/1995), 29; Juanita Brooks, *On the Ragged Edge: The Life and Times of Dudley Leavitt* (Salt Lake City: Utah State Historical Society, 1978), 46–47.

95. Daniel H. Wells to George D. Grant, June 14, 1851, reel 1, docs. 123, 124, UTMC.

96. Brigham Young to Lorin Farr, July 11, 1851, BYC; Coates, "Brigham Young and Mormon Indian Policy," 449.

97. Roberts, *CHC*, 4:51.

98. See, e.g., Nicolay to Dole, November 10, 1863, in Office of Indian Affairs, *Report of the Secretary of the Interior, 1864* (Washington, D.C), 268; J. W. P. Huntington, Superintendent of Indian Affairs in Oregon, wrote in 1865 that it took ten "good" soldiers and $50,000 to kill or capture one Indian, as quoted in Utley, *Frontiersmen in Blue*, 227.

99. Henry R. Day to L. Lea, Commissioner of Indian Affairs, January 2, 1852, OIA-UT.

100. Young to Bernhisel, BYC, quoted in Christy, "Open Hand, Mailed Fist," 229 fn.; and BYMH, 108.

101. Carvalho, *Incidents of Travel*, 182–86.

CHAPTER 6

1. J. H. Holeman to Luke Lea, Commissioner of Indian Affairs, November 28, 1851, Letters received, Office of Indian Affairs, Utah Superintendency (OIA-UT), 1849–1880.

2. Henry R. Day to L. Lea, OIA-UT, January 2, 1852; Sowiette, in Peter W. Conover to Brigham Young, no date, doc. 329, reel 1, Utah Territorial Military Correspondence (UTMC), Utah State Historical Society, Salt Lake City.

3. See, e.g., W. Paul Reeve, *Making Space on the Western Frontier: Mormons, Miners, and Southern Paiutes* (Urbana: University of Illinois Press, 2006), 15, 25; Gary Tom and Ronald L. Holt, "The Paiute Tribe of Utah," in *A History of Utah's American Indians*, edited Forrest S. Cuch (Salt Lake City: Utah State Division of Indian Affairs/Utah State Division of History, 2000), 120–30; and Holt, *Beneath these Red Cliffs: An Ethnohistory of the Utah Paiutes* (Albuquerque: University of New Mexico Press, 1992), 22–23.

4. Elizabeth W. Kane, *Twelve Mormon Homes: Visited in Succession on a Journey through Utah to Arizona* (Salt Lake City: University of Utah Library, 1974), 66, 39; Joseph G. Jorgensen, *The Sun Dance Religion: Power for the Powerless* (Chicago: University of Chicago Press, 1972), 13–63. On Arapeen's band, see January 22, 1860, *Journal History of the Church (JH)*, 1860–1869, 1860 January–June, Church History Library (CHL), The Church of Jesus Christ of Latter-day Saints, Salt Lake City, Utah; Sowoksoobet (1865) qt. in John Alton Peterson, *Utah's Black Hawk War* (Salt Lake City: University of Utah Press, 1998), 81–82. Peterson notes the difficulty with estimating populations but suggests a drop from 13,000 (in Utah alone) to only 4,000 for all eastern and western bands by 1880 (see 360–61 and 361n48, 386–87).

5. *JH*, May 13, 1850; B. H. Roberts, *A Comprehensive History of The Church of Jesus Christ of Latter-day Saints: Century One (CHC)*(1930; Provo, UT: The Church of Jesus Christ of Latter-day Saints, 1965), 3:465–66; Gustive O. Larson, "Walkara's Half Century," *Western Humanities Review* 6 (Summer 1952): 241–43; Paul Bailey, *Walkara: Hawk of the Mountains* (Los Angeles: Westernlore Press, 1954), 58–61.

463

6. Stealing from "others" (non-Utes) was culturally acceptable; stealing from other Utes ("us") was not.

7. Virginia Cole Trenholm and Maurine Carley, *The Shoshones: Sentinels of the Rockies* (Norman: University of Oklahoma Press, 1964), 116–33; "Treaty of Fort Laramie," 1851, in Charles J. Kappler, *Indian Affairs: Laws and Treaties* (Washington, D.C.: Government Printing Office, 1902–1938), and available online.

8. Day to Lea, Commissioner of Indian Affairs, January 2, 1852, OIA-UT; and Trenholm and Carley, *Shoshones*, 127, 130–33.

9. Dennis L. Lythgoe, "Negro Slavery in Utah," *Utah Historical Quarterly* 39 (Winter 1971): 40–54; Christopher B. Rich, Jr., "The True Policy for Utah: Servitude, Slavery, and 'An Act in Relation to Service,'" *Utah Historical Quarterly* 80 (Winter 2012): 54–74. Legislative debates on bonded servitude in Utah, 1851 [full texts soon to be published], and Paul Reeve, personal conversation with author, January 2014. The LDS Church's position may be found in D&C, Official Declaration 2, 2013 edition; and "Race and the Priesthood," in LDS Gospel Topics, LDS Church website, https://www.lds.org/ topics/race-and-the-priesthood?lang=eng&query=racism. See also "Slave Schedule," United States Census, Utah, 1850 and 1860.

10. Indians as covenant people: Book of Mormon title page; and e.g. 2 Nephi 6:13; 3 Nephi 21:4; 3 Nephi 16:11.

11. See, e.g., Martha C. Knack, *Boundaries Between: The Southern Paiutes, 1775–1995* (Lincoln: University of Nebraska Press, 2004), 53–64.

12. Details of the Pedro León incident are found in Sondra Jones, *The Trial of Don Pedro León Luján: The Attack against Indian Slavers and Mexican Traders* (Salt Lake City: University of Utah Press, 1999), and Sondra Jones, "The Trial of Don Pedro León: Politics, Prejudice, and Pragmatism," *Utah Historical Quarterly* 65 (Spring 1997): 110–59, 178–204. For additional views on the impact of the Indian slave trade, see Frances Leon Swadesh [Quintana], "Hispanic Americans and the Ute Frontier from the Chama Valley to the San Juan Basin" (PhD diss., University of Colorado, Boulder, 1966), 88–90, 194–95; Swadesh-Quintana, *Los Primeros Pobladores* (Notre Dame, IN: University of Notre Dame Press, 1974), 218, n36; James F. Brooks, *Captives & Cousins: Slavery, Kinship, and Community in the Southwest Borderlands* (Chapel Hill: University of North Carolina Press, 2002).

13. Pedro Léon Luján's report to John Greiner, Acting Superintendent of Indian Affairs, New Mexico, subsequently forwarded to Luke Lea, Commissioner of Indian Affairs, May 19, 1852, in Anne H. Abel, ed., *Official Correspondence of James S. Calhoun* (Washington, D.C., 1915), 536–37.

14. Utah Territory, "Acts in Relation to Service," ch. 24, in *Acts, Resolutions, and Memorials, Passed at the Several Sessions of the Legislative Assembly of the Territory of Utah*, Salt Lake City, 1855 (passed January 31, 1852; approved March 7, 1852). "Slave Schedule," Utah, United States Census, 1860. See also Rich, "Utah Servitude, Slavery." Rich argues that chattel slavery was technically replaced by a form of gradual emancipation. Though official state documents referred to Black slaves as "servants," they were still listed as slaves on Utah's 1860 census, "Slave Schedule." Black children were given set years of bound servitude and were then freed, as were Indian children.

15. Daniel W. Jones, *Forty Years among the Indians* (Los Angeles: Westernlore Press, [1890], reprint, 1960), 50–51. Cf. Kane, *Twelve Mormon Homes*, 13, who was told it was Wákara who "whirled her in the air, dashed her down, and then, as she lay quivering out her life,... snatched his hatchet from his belt and chopped her into five pieces. 'Now, you can have her at no price.'"

16. Brigham Young Manuscript History (BYMH), May 13, 1851, 846, CHL.

17. Richard D. Kitchen, "Mormon-Indian Relations in Deseret: Intermarriage and Indenture, 1847 to 1877" (PhD diss., Arizona State University, 2002); Brian Q. Cannon, "Adopted or Indentured, 1850–1870: Native Children in Mormon Households," in *Nearly Everything Imaginable: The Everyday Life of Utah's Mormon Pioneers*, edited by Ronald W. Walker and Doris R. Dant (Provo, UT: Brigham Young University Press, 1998); Juanita Brooks, "Indian Relations on the Mormon Frontier," *Utah Historical Quarterly* 12 (1944): 1–48; Jones, "'Redeeming the Indian': The Enslavement of Indian Children in New Mexico and Utah," *Utah Historical Quarterly* 67 (Summer 1999).

18. Henry Lunt to George A. Smith, in *JH*, February 12, 1853. The Utes commonly traveled to the Hopi on the so-called Ute Trail over a favored crossing of the Colorado.

19. *JH*, April 23 and May 2, 1853; *Deseret News Weekly*, April 30 ("Proclamation by the Governor") and December 15, 1853; Jones, *Forty Years*, 54–55. See also Jones, *Trial of Don Pedro León Luján*, 104–5, and "Pedro León: Indian Slavers, Mexican Traders," 171–75.

20. Jones, *Forty Years*, 54–56; Jones, *Trial of Don Pedro León Luján*, 104–5, and "Pedro León: Indian Slavers, Mexican Traders," 171–75.

21. Brigham Young to William Wall, April 25, 1853, doc. 243, reel 1, UTMC; General Order No. 2, doc. 23, reel 1, UTMC. See also Jones, *Forty Years*, 55–56.

22. *JH*, April 27 and 29, May 2 1853; William Wall to Daniel H. Wells, April 11, 1853, doc. 243, reel 1, UTMC; and "Letter," *Deseret News Weekly*, May 31, 1853.

23. *JH*, April 27, 29, and May 2 and 12, 1853.

24. *JH*, May 2, 1853.

25. *JH*, May 8, 1853, conference address.

26. Brigham Young to Isaac Morley, May 7, 1853, box 13, folder 9, film 32, Brigham Young Collection (BYC), in CHL; and *JH*, May 8, 1853.

27. *JH*, Dimick Huntington to Daniel H. Wells, May 12, 1853; *JH*, July 2, 1853.

28. George McKenzie, cited in Peter Gottfredson, *Indian Depredations in Utah* (1919; Salt Lake City: Shelton Publishing Co., 1969), 43–47; Jones, *Forty Years*, 54. Most accounts say only one Ute died; others claim two. Only Ivie's one-sided (and justificatory) account of the incident exists.

29. George W. Bradley (Nephi), to Lt. General [Wells] Nauvoo Legion, July 19, 1853, doc. 256, reel 1, UTMC. Richard Ivie, James' son, was one of the three men who murdered Old Bishop, initiating the Provo War.

30. George McKenzie, cited in Gottfredson, *Indian Depredations*, 46.

31. Stephen C. Perry to James Hergerson (Ferguson), September 12, 1853, doc. 1304, reel 3, UTMC.

32. Ibid.

33. Ibid. Oneship or Wanship. He is also referred to in the document, confusingly, as the *son* of Oneship. It is also unclear whether this is the same Wanship mentioned in other documents of this era.

34. Orson F. Whitney, *History of Utah* (Salt Lake City: George Q. Cannon and Sons, 1892–1904), 1:514; Bailey, *Walkara: Hawk of the Mountains*, 141; and Peter W. Conover to Daniel H. Wells, July 19, 1853, doc. 257, reel 1, UTMC. Reports of the incident typically emphasize the unsuspecting nature of the Payson settlers whose hospitality was returned with cold-blooded murder. But Perry's party had been warned, and the negotiations and ride to Payson had been fraught with danger.

35. Howard A. Christy, "The Walker War: Defense and Conciliation as Strategy," *Utah Historical Quarterly* 47 (1979): 401.

36. Conover and Markham, Payson, Utah, to Wells, July 19, 1853, doc. 257, reel 1, UTMC.

37. See Whitney's *History*, 1:514; Canfield to G. A. Smith, July 24, 1853, doc. 286, reel 1, UTMC.

38. General Order No. 1, July 21, 1853, doc. 1335, reel 3, UTMC.

39. Special Order No. 1, July 19, 1853, doc. 258, reel 1, UTMC.

40. Special Order No. 2, July 19, 1853, doc. 259, reel 1, UTMC.

41. Conover to Wells, July 23, 1853, doc. 284, reel 1, UTMC.

42. Nelson Higgins to James T. S. Allred and Gardner G. Potter, July 20, 1853; and, G. G. Potter to James Ferguson, July 21, 1853, doc. 277 and 275, reel 1, UTMC; Conover to Wells, July 26, 1853, doc. 1339, reel 3, UTMC.

43. George A. Smith to Brigham Young, July 21, 1853, doc. 1336, reel 3, UTMC. Smith was also defense attorney for Pedro León Luján and his traders.

44. General Order No. 2, July 25, 1853, doc. 288, reel 1, UTMC.

45. Conover to Wells, July 26, 1853, doc. 1339, reel 3, UTMC; Whitney's *History*, 1:514. For information on Nowlen, see *JH*, February 9, 1850

46. G. A. Smith to Wells, August 25, 1853; Wells to Conover, August 25, 1853, doc. 356 and 353, reel 1, UTMC.

47. Christy, "Walker War," 405–8; *JH*, November 20, 1853.

48. Christy, "Walker War," 407–8; *JH*, November 20, 1853.

49. G. A. Smith to Brigham Young, July 28, 1853, doc. 299, reel 1, UTMC.

50. Young to Walkara, July 25, 1853, doc. 289, reel 1, UTMC.

51. Higgins to Ferguson, Conover, and Markham, July 29, 1853, doc. 305, reel 1, UTMC; George W. Bradley to Wells, August 1, 1853, doc. 1344, reel 3, UTMC; and Christy, "Walker War," 406. Wákara claimed he restrained the raiders from shedding blood; see Higgins to Ferguson, March 15, 1854, doc. 1386, reel 3, UTMC.

52. G. A. Smith to Brigham Young, July 28, 1853, doc. 299, reel 1, UTMC.

53. On the Sowiette incident, see Conover to Young, no date, doc. 329, UTMC. On Wyonah, see G. A. Smith to Wells, Aug. 27, 1853, doc. 357, UTMC. Chiefs sue for peace and Wákara goes south, as related in *JH*, September 10–12, and November 11, 1853. New Mexico Territory included today's New Mexico and Arizona.

54. Walker War details in Christy, "The Walker War." Special Order No. 13, August 16, 1853, doc. 1371, reel 1, UTMC. On Brigham Young's orders regarding trade, see *JH*, August 19, 1853. Military herders attacked at Clover Creek, as related in George W. Bradley to Wells, August 11, 1853 and Conover to Young, August 12, 1853, doc. 334 and 335, reel 1, UTMC. For the attack on men hauling timber in Parley's Park, see Whitney's *History* 1:517.

55. Joseph L. Heywood to Young, September 22, 1853, doc. 397, reel 1, UTMC.

56. Markham to Wells, October 5, 1853, docs. 395, 397, reel 1, UTMC.

57. George W. Bradley to Wells, October 2, 1853, doc. 396, reel 1, UTMC.

58. The official report of the incident claimed the militia was provoked when the Indians pulled weapons and attacked them; however, the two women eye-witnesses contradict this official version. The remains of these hastily buried Indians were discovered in 2006. Bradley to Wells, October 2, 1853, qt. in Christy, "Walker War," 412. Cf., BYMH, October 1, 1853; Adelia Almira Wilcox, "Memoirs," October 2, 1853, Utah State Historical Society, Salt Lake City. Wilcox was the wife of the guard killed earlier at Fillmore, making her testimony particularly poignant. See also the diary of Martha Spence Heywood, wife of territorial marshal, Joseph Heywood.

59. Bradley to Wells, October 2, 1853, qt. in Christy, "Walker War," 412.

60. Higgins to Wells, October 4, 1853, doc. 399, reel 1, UTMC; William McClellan to Markham, October 15, 1853, doc. 401, reel 1, UTMC.

61. On Young's statement, see *Millennial Star* 16 (1854): 563–65. Wells' orders are in UTMC, Special Order No. 21, October 5, 1853, reel 1, doc. 398; Young's plea to commanders in Young to Conover, Markham, and Bradley, October 16, 1853, BYMH.

62. On the Gunnison Massacre, see *JH*, November 26, 1853, which includes Beckwith's report, and extracts from Anson Call's journal. See also E. G. Beckwith, *Reports of Exploration for a Route for the Pacific Railroad by Capt. W. Gunnison,* Reports of Explorations and Surveys, Sen. Exec. Doc. 78, 33/2. Ser. 759: 75–76; and Solomon Nuñes Carvalho, *Incidents of Travel and Adventure in the Far West with Colonel Fremont's Last Expedition* (New York: Derby and Jackson, 1856 and 1860), 197–99, 243; Hubert Howe Bancroft, *History of Utah* (San Francisco: History Co., 1890), 467–70 and fn. 59; Josiah F. Gibbs, "Gunnison Massacre—1853—Millard County, Utah—Indian Mareer's Version of the Tragedy—1894," *Utah Historical Quarterly* 1 (1928): 70–75.

63. *JH*, November 26, 1852. Gibbs provides lively accounts in "Gunnison Massacre," 70–75, and "Moshoquop, the Avenger, as Loyal Friend," *Utah Historical Quarterly* 1 (1929): 6–7.

64. Bancroft, *History of Utah,* 493; Gibbs, "Gunnison Massacre," 74 esp. fn.; Brooks (*Captives & Cousins,* 310–13) notes that it was appropriate to offer expendable individuals as proxies to expiate tribal misdeeds.

65. Young to Sowiette, White Eye, Peteetneet, Arapine, and Teesharnosheegee, December 3, 1853, reel 92, box 57, folder 1, BYC.

66. Christy, "Walker War," 415.

67. *JH*, February 12, 1854; Brigham Young to E. A. Bedell, March 24, 1854, reel 93, box 58, folder 3, BYC. The federal government had to authorize the sale.

68. E. A. Bedell to Young, April 6, 1854, reel 93, box 58, folder 3, BYC; Young to Walkara, April 14, 1854, BYMH.

69. George Bean to Brigham Young, May 1, 1854, BYMH.

70. Carvalho, *Incidents of Travel,* 191–93.

71. Ibid., 191–93.

72. See Christy, "Walker War," and Floyd A. O'Neil, "A History of the Ute Indians until 1890" (Ph.D. diss., University of Utah, 1973), 30.

73. See, e.g., O'Neil, "History of the Ute Indians," 44–45; Bancroft, *History of Utah,* 477; Conway B. Sonne, *The World of Wakara* (San Antonio, TX: Naylor, 1962), 211–12; Roberts, *CHC,* 3:465.

74. Frederick Hawkins Piercy, *Route From Liverpool to Great Salt Lake Valley,* edited by Fawn M. Brodie (1854; Cambridge: Belknap Press of Harvard University Press, 1962), 278; Roberts, *CHC,* 3:465; and Kane, *Twelve Mormon Homes,* 14–15. Accounts of Wákara's burial differ, but all agree there was a

large amount of stock and personal wealth, which included captives. Human sacrifice was rare in Ute burials, but sending symbols of wealth and power was not. Also, Wákara had occasionally killed prisoners to appease bad spirits, as he had during a measles epidemic. See Carling Malouf and Arline Malouf, "The Effects of Spanish Slavery on the Indians of the Intermountain West," *Southwestern Journal of Anthropology* 1 (Spring 1945): 388.

467

CHAPTER 7

1. Janet Lecompte, *Pueblo, Hardscrabble, Greenhorn: The Upper Arkansas, 1832–1856* (Norman: University of Oklahoma Press, 1978), esp. 33–62, 74–97. See also, LeRoy R. Hafen, "The Fort Pueblo Massacre and the Punitive Expedition against the Utes," *Colorado Magazine* 4 (March 1927): 49–50; Francis T. Cheetham, "The Early Settlements of Southern Colorado," *Colorado Magazine* 5 (February 1928): 4.

2. Lecompte, *Pueblo, Hardscrabble, Greenhorn*, 13–24; Cheetham, "Early Settlements," 4; LeRoy R. Hafen and Ann W. Hafen, *Colorado* (Denver: Old West Publishing, 1952), 113–16.

3. On economic reforms in New Mexico after 1772, see James Brooks, *Captives & Cousins: Slavery, Kinship, and Community in the Southwest Borderlands* (Chapel Hill: University of North Carolina Press, 2002), 80, 88–89, 103–7; Frances Leon Swadesh [Quintana], *Los Primeros Pobladores* (Notre Dame, IN: University of Notre Dame Press, 1974), 50–51, 61–62; Ramón A. Gutiérrez, *When Jesus Came the Corn Mothers Went Away: Marriage, Sexuality, and Power in New Mexico, 1500–1846* (Stanford, CA: Stanford University Press, 1991), 318–27, esp. 327.

4. Albert H. Schroeder, "A Brief History of the Southern Utes," *Southwestern Lore* 30 (1965): 63.

5. Swadesh-Quintana, *Los Primeros Pobladores*, 62; Schroeder, "Southern Utes," 65; Lecompte, *Pueblo, Hardscrabble, Greenhorn*, 137.

6. Swadesh-Quintana, *Los Primeros Pobladores*, 62; Schroeder, "Southern Utes," 65; Lecompte, *Pueblo, Hardscrabble, Greenhorn*, 137.

7. Swadesh-Quintana, *Los Primeros Pobladores*, 61–62; Schroeder, "Southern Utes," 64, Lecompton, *Pueblo, Hardscrabble, Greenhorn*, 137–38.

8. See Sondra Jones, *The Trial of Pedro León Luján: The Attack against Indian Slavers and Mexican Traders* (Salt Lake City: University of Utah Press, 1999), 56–57; J. Lee Correll, *Through White Men's Eyes: A Contribution to Navajo History* (Window Rock, AZ: Navajo Heritage Center, 1969), 163, 167; reel 39, beginning f. 606, Mexican Archives of New Mexico (MANM), Santa Fe, NM; 1846 militia, reel 41, beginning f. 801, MANM; reel 26, f. 515–16, MANM; reel 85, f. 79–81, Territorial Archive of New Mexico (TANM), Santa Fe, NM; reel 87, f.115–47, 128–31,151–58, TANM; reel 88, f. 3, 2–22, TANM.

9. See, e.g., Swadesh-Quintana, *Los Primeros Pobladores*, 62–65; Ned Blackhawk, *Violence over the Land: Indians and Empires in the Early American West* (Cambridge, MA: Harvard University Press, 2006), 191–222; cf. Lecompte, *Pueblo, Hardscrabble, Greenhorn*, 237–45.

10. Kaniache or Coniach. Schroeder, "Southern Utes," 64. See also "William Gilpin," *New Perspectives on the West*, in The West Film Project, Public Broadcasting Services (PBS), 2001 [video].

11. Lecompte, *Pueblo, Hardscrabble, Greenhorn*, 237–39; cf. Blackhawk, *Violence over the Land*, 196–98. On the concept of ownership, see Lecompte, *Pueblo, Hardscrabble, Greenhorn*, 238, 243.

12. Beal to McClaws, March 13, 1850 (Military Dept.), in Anne H. Abel, ed., *Official Correspondence of James S. Calhoun* (Washington: Government Printing Office, 1915), 169–70; Lecompte, *Pueblo, Hardscrabble, Greenhorn*, 238; Robert M. Utley, *Frontiersmen in Blue: The United States Army and the Indians, 1848–1865* (Lincoln: University of Nebraska Press, 1967), 86; Thelma S. Guild and Harvey L. Carter, *Kit Carson* (Lincoln: University of Nebraska, 1984), 185–87.

13. Calhoun to Brown, November 15, 1849; Calhoun to Medill, October 1, 1849; Beall to McClaws, March 13, 1850; "Treaty," n.d.; all in Abel, *Official Correspondence*, 77, 30, 35, 127–32, 169–70. See also, "Treaty with the Utah, [December 30] 1849," in Charles J. Kappler, comp. and ed., *Indian Affairs: Laws and Treaties*, (Washington, D.C.: Government Printing Office, 1902–1938), 2:585–86. For information on Calhoun, see Utley, *Frontiersmen in Blue*, 88–89.

14. The Spanish name of Chico Velasquez does not appear on the treaty although in 1850 Mouaches told Maj. Beall he signed it. Beall to McClaws, March 13, 1850, in Abel, *Official Correspondence*,

169–70. See also Blackhawk, *Violence over the Land*, 196, 198; Lecompte, *Pueblo, Hardscrabble, Greenhorn*, 240–42; and James Hervey Simpson, "Foreword," in *Navaho Expedition: Journal of a Military Reconnaissance from Santa Fe… in 1849 by Lieutenant James H. Simpson*, edited and annotated by Frank McNitt (Norman: University of Oklahoma, 1964), xli–xlii.

15. "Treaty with the Utah, 1849," in Kappler, *Indian Affairs: Laws and Treaties*, 2:585–86; Calhoun to Orlando Brown, Commissioner of Indian Affairs, May 20, and June 12, 1850, in Abel, *Official Correspondence*, 127–32, 205, 208–9.

16. Lt. A. E. Burnside to Lt. J. N. Ward, May 23, 1850, and Burnside to Plympton, June 12, 1850, and Munro to McDowell, May 23, 1850, in Abel, *Official Correspondence*, 198–200; 207. See also Utley, *Frontiersmen in Blue*, 86.

17. Calhoun to Cyrus Choice (agent), May 10, 1850; Calhoun to Brown, May 20, 1850; Calhoun to Brown, June 12, 1850; all in Abel, *Official Correspondence*, 200–202, 205, 208–9.

18. See, e.g., Blackhawk, *Violence over the Land*, 191–222, esp. 204; cf. Lecompte, *Pueblo, Hardscrabble, Greenhorn*, 237–45.

19. Guild and Carter, *Kit Carson*, 200, 212; Thomas Dunlay, *Kit Carson and the Indians* (Lincoln: University of Nebraska, 2000), 210–19; Utley, *Frontiersmen in Blue*, 143. Inner bark of some trees was a nutritious and traditional end-of-winter food. See Anne M. Smith (Cooke), *Ethnography of the Northern Utes*, Papers in Anthropology, no. 17 (Albuquerque: Museum of New Mexico Press, 1974), 47, 65, 278.

20. Calhoun to Brown, March 16, June 12, July 30, and July 31, 1850, in Abel, *Official Correspondence*, 166–70, 229–31, 235–36.

21. Schroeder, "Southern Utes," 65–66; Beall to Lt. L. McClaws, March 13, 1850; John Greiner to Calhoun, October 20, 1851, in Abel, *Official Correspondence*, 170; Blackhawk, *Violence over the Land*, 204–5.

22. Calhoun to Governor Munroe, January 29, 1850; Calhoun to Brown, September 30, 1850; and Calhoun to Luke Lea, July 30, 1851; all in Abel, *Official Correspondence*, 122–23, 259, 393. See also Guild and Carter, *Kit Carson*, 198–214, and quoting from Kit Carson's *Memoirs*; Schroeder, "Southern Utes," 66–67; Robert Delaney, *The Ute Mountain Utes* (Albuquerque: University of New Mexico Press, 1989), 31,45–48.

23. "Colonel" Henry Inman, "Maxwell's Ranch," in *The Old Santa Fe Trail: The Story of a Great Highway* (1897; Topeka: Crane and Co., 1916), available online.

24. Greiner to Lea, April 30, 1852; Calhoun to Lea, February 29, 1852; Calhoun to Lea, July 30, 1851; all in Abel, *Official Correspondence*, 393, 438, 488, 530.

25. Meriwether to Manypenny, quoted in Utley, *Frontiersmen in Blue*, 143.

26. Schroeder, "Southern Utes," 66–67.

27. For more on the role of the frontier army, especially its noncombative activities, see Michael L. Tate, *The Frontier Army in the Settlement of the West* (Norman: University of Oklahoma Press, 1999), esp. 21, 231–36, 310–13.

28. George F. Ruxton, ch. 5, "Mexican Gratitude," in *Wild Life in the Rocky Mountains* (1847; New York: MacMillan, 1916). See also, *Ruxton of the Rockies*, edited by LeRoy Hafen (Norman: University of Oklahoma, 1950), 198.

29. Schroeder, "Southern Utes," 66–67; Hafen and Hafen, *Colorado*, 125–29; John Greiner to Calhoun, October 20, 1851, in Abel, *Official Correspondence*, 438.

30. Greiner to Calhoun, October 20, 1851; Calhoun to Daniel Webster, Secretary of War, October 29, 1851; Charles Beaubien to Calhoun, June 11, 1851; cf. Greiner to Lea, April 30, 1852; all in Abel, *Correspondence of Calhoun*, 357–58, 438, 441, 530.

31. On Beaubien settlements, see, e.g., Hafen and Hafen, *Colorado*, 128–30; Floyd A, O'Neil and Kathryn L. MacKay, *A History of the Uintah-Ouray Ute Lands*, American West Center Occasional Papers (Salt Lake City: University of Utah Press, n.d.), 9.

32. Gwinn Harris Heap, *Central Route to the Pacific*, edited and annotated by LeRoy R. Hafen and Ann W. Hafen (1854; Glendale, CA: Arthur H. Clark, Co., 1957).

33. Utley, *Frontiersmen in Blue*, 87; T. J. Sperry and Harry C. Meyers, "A History of Fort Union," Kansas University Heritage Project, Interactive Santa Fe Trail, online.

34. Schroeder, "Southern Utes," 65–67; O'Neil and MacKay, *History of the Uintah-Ouray*, 9; Wilson Rockwell, *The Utes: A Forgotten People* (Denver: Sage Books, 1956), 65; Cheetham, "The Early Settlements," 4–7.

35. Calhoun to Brown, July 30, 1850, in Abel, *Correspondence of Calhoun*, 229–31.

36. Schroeder, "Southern Utes," 69.

37. Utley, *Frontiersmen in Blue*, 143–45; Guild and Carter, *Kit Carson*, 199–200; Lawrence R. Murphy, "Cantonment Burgwin, New Mexico 1852–1860," *Arizona and the West* 15 (Spring 1973).

38. Utley, *Frontiersmen in Blue*, 143–45, and Garland to Col. Cooke (Ft. Union), April 7, 1854, as quoted in Utley; Guild and Carter, *Kit Carson*, 199–200. Murphy's history of Fort Burgwin adds detail.

39. Utley, *Frontiersmen in Blue*, 145–46; Guild and Carter, *Kit Carson*, 200–202.

40. Guild & Carter, *Kit Carson*, 199–204; Utley, *Frontiersmen in Blue*, 146; Murphy, "Cantonment Burgwin." TANM includes the military papers of Hispanic volunteers during this and the 1855 campaign, parts of which were fought by Abiquiú militias. See reel 85, frame 79; reel 87, frames 15–147; reel 88, frames 2–22; Apache campaign, 1st Brigade 2nd Division of Mounted Militia of New Mexico, May–August 1854, letter of December 12, 1857, and deposition December 12, 1857; all in TANM. See also Correll, *Through White Men's*, 1:163, 167.

41. Guild & Carter, *Kit Carson*, 204–25; and Carson's memoirs in Harvey L., Carter, ed., *"Dear Old Kit:" The Historical Christopher Carson* (Norman: University of Oklahoma, 1968), 142–43; P. David Smith, *Ouray, Chief of the Utes* (Ouray, CO: Wayfinder Press, 1986), 46–49, and quoting Carson to Meriwether. The accusation had precedence. See K. C. Tessendorf, "Red Death on the Missouri," *American West* 14 (January/February 1977); and Francis Jennings, *The Invasion of America* (Chapel Hill, NC: University of North Carolina Press, 1975), 207–9.

42. On the Fort Pueblo affair, see Lecompte, *Pueblo, Hardscrabble, Greenhorn*, 237, 245–553; Hafen, "Fort Pueblo Massacre"; Utley, *Frontiersmen in Blue*, 146–47. Howard Louis Conard, *Uncle Dick Wootton: The Pioneer Frontiersman of the Rocky Mountain Region*, edited by Milo Milton Quaife (1890; Chicago: R. R. Donnelley and Sons, 1957), 297–306. Blanco's scarring in Guild & Carter, *Kit Carson*, 211.

43. Utley, *Frontiersmen in Blue*, 147.

44. Carter, *"Dear Old Kit,"* 143–44.

45. Utley, *Frontiersmen in Blue*, 147–48; Hafen, "Fort Pueblo Massacre," 53–57; Lecompte, *Pueblo, Hardscrabble, Greenhorn*, 251–52.

46. Carson quoted in Guild and Carter, *Kit Carson*, 200, 204. On negotiations, see Schroeder, "Southern Utes," 67–68; "Treaty with the Capote Band of Utahs," August 8, 1855; and "Treaty with the Mohuache Band of the Utahs," September 11, 1855, in Kappler, *Indian Affairs*, 5:686–93. Both treaties were unratified.

47. Treaties with the Capote and Muhuaches Utes, August 8 and September 11, 1855, in Kappler, *Indian Affairs*, 5:686–93.

48. Schroeder, "Southern Utes," 68; O'Neil and MacKay, *History of the Uintah-Ouray*, 9; Hafen, "Fort Pueblo Massacre," 53–57.

49. Hafen and Hafen, *Colorado*, 138–45; Elliott West, *The Contested Plains: Indians, Goldseekers, and the Rush to Colorado* (Lawrence: University Press of Kansas, 1998), 98–108.

50. Hafen and Hafen, *Colorado*, 142–47, 150; cf. West, *Contested Plains*, 108–90.

51. Hafen and Hafen, *Colorado*, 147–51; West, *Contested Plains*, 98–190, 128; "William N. Byers," *Denver Characters*, online at Denver.gov.org/history.

52. Hafen and Hafen, *Colorado*, 151–56. These first finds were the Gregory and Jackson strikes near Central City and Idaho Springs.

53. See, e.g., Hafen and Hafen, *Colorado*, 154–57.

54. Schroeder, "Southern Utes," 69–71.

55. Hafen and Hafen, *Colorado*, 167–73.

CHAPTER 8

1. On Ute military alliances, see Ned Blackhawk, *Violence over the Land: Indians and Empires in the Early American West* (Cambridge, MA: Harvard University Press, 2006), 209–14.

2. Harvey L. Carter, ed., *"Dear Old Kit": The Historical Christopher Carson* (Norman: University of Oklahoma, 1968), 162–65; Calhoun to Carson, September 18, 1865, in "Doolittle Report," *Condition of the Indian Tribes: Report of the Joint Special Committee* (Washington: Government Printing Office, 1867), 197–98; Blackhawk, *Violence over the Land*, 208, 214.

3. Robert M. Utley, *Frontiersmen in Blue: The United States Army and the Indians, 1848–1865* (Lincoln: University of Nebraska Press, 1967), 88; Wilson Rockwell, *The Utes: A Forgotten People* (Denver: Sage Books, 1956), 65.

4. Albert H. Schroeder, "A Brief History of the Southern Utes," *Southwestern Lore* 30 (1965): 68–71; Robert Delaney, *The Ute Mountain Utes* (Albuquerque: University of New Mexico Press, 1989), 35, 39–40, 44–45; and Delaney, *The Southern Ute People* (Phoenix: Indian Tribal Series, 1974), 115–28.

5. Schroeder, "Southern Ute," 72–73; Delaney, *Southern Ute People*, 40.

6. Schroeder, "Southern Ute," 70–71; Floyd A. O'Neil and Kathryn L. MacKay, *A History of the Uintah-Ouray Ute Lands*, American West Center Occasional Papers (Salt Lake City: University of Utah Press, n.d.), 9; Floyd A. O'Neil, "A History of the Ute Indians until 1890" (PhD diss., University of Utah, 1973), 55; Rockwell, *The Utes*, 68–69; Luis Baca and Facundo Baca, "Hispanic Pioneer: Don Felipe Baca Brings His Family North to Trinidad," *Colorado Heritage* 1 (1982): 32.

7. Governor John Evans to S. G. Colley, in U.S. Department of the Interior, *Report of the Secretary of the Interior [RSI]* (Washington, D.C.: 1860–1875, 1863), 241–42; and Lyman S. Tyler, "Ute Indians along Civil War Communication Lines," *Utah Historical Quarterly* 46 (Summer 1978): 251–61. Details here are from Tyler's article.

8. Tyler, "Ute Indians along Civil War Communication Lines," 251–61; Utley, *Frontiersmen in Blue*, 282; Evans to commissioner, *RSI, 1864*, 241–43; and U.S. Department of War, *War of the Rebellion [WR]: A Compilation of the Official Records of the Union and Confederate Armies*, Series 1, Part II (Washington, D.C.: Government Printing Office, 1897), 50, 522, 362–63, 368–71, 404, 415, 443, 481, 492–95, 499–500.

9. United States Office of Indian Affairs, *Annual Report of the Commissioner of Indian Affairs [ARCIA]* (Washington, D.C.,: Government Printing Office, 1863), 121–22; Tyler, "Ute Indians along the Civil War Communication Lines," 259.

10. O'Neil, "History of the Ute Indians," 55–56; Tyler, "Ute Indians," 260; Joseph G. Jorgensen, *The Sun Dance Religion: Power for the Powerless* (Chicago: University of Chicago Press, 1972), 36, 42.

11. Evans to commissioner, *RSI, 1863–1864*, 243–44; O'Neil and MacKay, *History of the Uintah-Ouray*, 10; P. David Smith, *Ouray, Chief of the Utes* (Ouray, CO: Wayfinder Press, 1986), 59.

12. Evans to commissioner, *RSI, 1863–1864*, 241–42; Tyler, "Ute Indians on the Civil War Communications Lines," 260; J. G. Nicolay to commissioner, *RSI, 1863–1864*, 266–69.

13. Evans to commissioner, *RSI, 1863–1864*, 243–44, 246; S. Whiteley to Evans, *RSI, 1863–1864*, 250–52; O'Neil and MacKay, *History of the Uintah-Ouray*, 10; Schroeder, "Southern Ute," 71–72.

14. "Treaty with the Utah—Tabeguache Band, 1863," in Charles J. Kappler, ed., *Indian Affairs: Laws and Treaties* (Washington: Government Printing Office, 1902–1938), 2:856–59; P. D. Smith, *Ouray*, 59, 62–63. See also "Colorado Superintendency," in *ARCIA* (1863), 125–26, 148–51. Signatories included Gov. John Evans, Superintendent M. Steck, agents Simeon Whiteley and Lafayette Head, Uncowragut, Shawasheyet, Colorado (Colorow), Uray (Ouray), Novavetuquaret (Nevava), Sawawatsewich, Acamuchene, Mucuchop, Sapatch, and Cinche.

15. Ouray quoted in Robert Emmitt, *The Last War Trail: The Utes and the Settlement of Colorado* (Norman: University of Oklahoma Press, 1954), 269.

16. "Treaty Council with the Utahs," *ARCIA* (1863), 125–27, 149–50.

17. Treaty of 1863 in Kappler, *Laws and Treaties*, 2:856–59; "Treaty Council," *ARCIA* (1863), 126.

18. Thomas Jefferson, *Notes on the State of Virginia, 1743–1826*, edited by William Peden (Chapel Hill: University of North Carolina, 1955), 164–65.

19. The development of U.S. Indian policy is surveyed in a variety of sources, e.g., Lyman S. Tyler, *A History of Indian Policy* (Washington, D.C.: U.S. Department of Interior, Bureau of Indian Affairs, 1973); Francis Paul Prucha, *Indian Policy in the United States: Historical Essays* (Lincoln: University of Nebraska Press, 1981); and Robert M. Utley, *The Indian Frontier of the American West 1846–1890* (Albuquerque: University of New Mexico, 1984)

20. "Interview with Kit Carson," *New York World*, November 1866.

21. Forney to commissioner, *ARCIA* (1857), 210–11; Hurt to Forney, January 10, 1859, as quoted in Beverly Beeton, "Teach Them to Till the Soil: An Experiment with Indian Farms, 1850–1862," *American Indian Quarterly* 3 (1977–1978): 212.

22. Ely S. Parker biographies include William Armstrong, *Warrior in Two Camps* (1990); and Arthur C. Parker, *The Life of Ely S. Parker* (2010). For social evolution, see Louis Henry Morgan, *Ancient Society: Research in the Lines of Human Progress from Savagery through Barbarism to Civilization* (London: MacMillan, 1877). Morgan's theories are far more complex than presented here. They popularized Herbert Spencer's theory of Social Darwinism, ideas which prevailed until discredited by the events of World War II. See David Hurst Thomas, *Skull Wars: Kennewick Man, Archaeology, and the Battle for Native American Identity* (New York: Basic Books, 2000), 11–25, 44–51, 125.

23. "Treaty with the Utah—Tabeguache Band, 1863," in Kappler, *Indian Affairs*, 2:857.

24. "Kit Carson's Treaty" in Sidney Jocknick, *Early Days on the Western Slope of Colorado, 1870–1883* (1913; Glorietta, NM: Rio Grande Press, 1968), 341–43; Rockwell, *The Utes*, 69–70.

25. Smith, *Ouray*, 34–37, 43; Jocknick, *Early Days*, 232. See also "Chief Ouray Day," *Southern Ute Drum* (n.d.), Southern Ute Tribe webpage, 1998. Cynthia S. Becker and P. David Smith argue Ouray's *father* was Ute, his mother Jicarilla, and he a *nephew* of Guera Murah, a Jicarilla chief. See *Chipeta: Queen of the Utes* (Montrose, CO: Western Reflections, 2003), 11–16, 17n10. But contemporaries and friends claimed Ouray's father was Apache. See Thomas F. Dawson, "Major Thompson, Chief Ouray and the Utes," *Colorado Magazine* 7 (May 1930), 119. Eastern Utes sometimes "placed" their children (or poor relatives) into "indentures" in exchange for horses or weapons, expecting them to return later. Jocknick, who knew Ouray, said he was born in Taos, while Becker and Smith believe he was born near Abiquiú, though they offer no evidence for this (*Chipeta*, 13).

26. P. D. Smith, *Ouray*, 42, 45, 52, 140–41, 198–202; Becker and Smith, *Chipeta*, 12–16, 120–26; Jocknick, *Early Days*, 193–96, 228–32.

27. Nevava ("Snow" or "One that Slides Under the Snow") is variously identified as White River (1863), head chief of the Yampa (1865), Grand (1866), Tabeguache (1867), or Uintah (1868); he was kin-brother of Quinkent (Douglas), who succeeded him as chief of the White River band. Piah (aka Peter Snow), another chief, was his nephew but escaped relocation to Utah by joining Ignacio's Weeminuche. See Omer C. Stewart, "Data on the Identification and Group Leadership of Ute Indian Chiefs" ("Ute Chiefs List"), tms., working paper prepared for Dockets 44–45, U.S. Indian Claims Commission, 1952, in the Stewart Collection, Archives, Norlin Library, University of Colorado, Boulder.

28. Jocknick, *Early Days*, 116–20; Smith, *Ouray*, 52–55; and P. D. Smith, personal communication with author, 2001.

29. Smith, *Ouray*, 42–43, 49–50; Jocknick, *Early Days*, 233; Carter, *"Dear Old Kit,"* 170, 220–21.

30. Smith, *Ouray*, 49–50, 69, 108–9, 143–44; Jocknick, *Early Days*, 114–15, 120–22, 177–78, 229–35.

31. Carl Schurz, as quoted in Jocknick, *Early Days*, 228–29; cf. Smith, *Ouray*, 175.

32. Mr. Mathews (*Harper's Weekly*) to R. B. Townshend, as quoted in Smith, *Ouray*, 79.

33. See, e.g., Jocknick, *Early Days*; cf. Rockwell, *The Utes*, 72–87, 106–20.

34. See Guild and Carter, *Kit Carson*, 212; Thomas Dunlay, *Kit Carson and the Indians* (Lincoln: University of Nebraska, 2000), 199. U.S. troops had been sent to Utah Territory in 1857 to quell a supposed Mormon uprising.

35. Nicolay to commissioner, *RSI, 1864*, 268; cf. Utley, *Frontiersmen in Blue*, 227.

36. On the "Plains War" of 1864 and Evans' role in provoking hostilities, see Utley, *Frontiersmen in Blue*, 283–97; Donald J. Berthrong, *Southern Cheyennes* (Norman: University of Oklahoma, 1963), 241–44. Reference to the Sand Creek Massacre in "Appendix" to the "Doolittle Report," 52–55. On attitudes fighting Indians, see Brigham Madsen, *Glory Hunter: Encounter with the Northwestern Shoshoni at Bear River in 1863: Battle or Massacre?* (Ogden, UT: Weber State College Press, 1984), 121; and Connor to Evans, October 30, 1864, in *WR*, 50:1036–37.

37. Dunlay, *Kit Carson and the Indians*, 210–19.

38. Smith, *Ouray*, 55–56, 68; "Treaty with the Uintah and Yampa or Grand River Bands of Utah Indians" (August 29, 1866), Kappler, *Indian Affairs*, 2:705–6.

39. On reform movements, see Arrell Morgan Gibson, *The American Indian: Prehistory to the Present* (Norman: University of Oklahoma Press, 1980), 76–77.

471

40. Tyler, *Indian Policy*, 76–80; Gibson, *American Indians*, 392–94; "General Report on Indian Affairs," in *ARCIA* (1872), 3–14; and "Doolittle Report."
41. Gibson, *American Indians*, 394–95.
42. "Treaty with the Ute, 1868" (March 2, 1868, ratified July 25, amended treaty signed by individual bands, August–September 1868), Kappler, *Indian Affairs*, 990–96; Smith, *Ouray*, 72; Rockwell, *The Utes*, 72, 81–82, 110.
43. "Treaty of 1868." The reservation encompassed 14,784,000 acres. See *ARCIA* (1872), 89.
44. Jocknick's vivid descriptions of the "Denver Utes" in *Early Days*, 21–41.
45. "Treaty of 1868." John Lawrence to Commissioner of Indian Affairs, October 16, 1868, quoted in O'Neil and Mackay, *History of the Uintah-Ouray*, 10–11; cf. Rockwell, *The Utes*, 72, 81–82, 110.
46. O'Neil and MacKay, *History of the Uintah-Ouray*, 11.
47. "Treaty of 1868." Original commission included Oakes, Curtis, Kellogg, and Head, who witnessed the signatures, and other non-Indians known and trusted by the Utes, including Albert Pfeiffer, Manuel Lusero, and Juan Martine Martines. Sapowaneri signed as a Mouache but was later identified as subchief of the Tabeguache/Uncompahgres.
48. Jocknick, *Early Days*, 322; Rockwell, *The Utes*, 72–78.
49. Smith, *Ouray*, 84; Rockwell, *The Utes*, 83, 111.
50. Virginia Simmons, "When Opportunity Knocked on Saguache's Door," *Colorado Central Magazine* 75 (May 2000): 20+; Smith, *Ouray*, 54, 56, 61, 68, 83–85; Jocknick, *Early Days*, 344–45; "Report No. 4, F. W. Arny to commissioner, 1870," quoted in Delaney, *Ute Mountain Utes*, 35, 39–40, 44–45, and Delaney, *Southern Ute*, 115–28.
51. Arny to Parker, Special Report (1870), in Delaney, *Mountain Ute*, 35, 39–40, 44–45; Rockwell, *The Utes*, 72–81, 87.
52. Smith, *Ouray*, 75.
53. Arny to Parker, "Special Report No. 4," 1870, quoted in Delaney, *Ute Mountain Ute*, 42–43. Arny had been an agent at Maxwell's Ranch.
54. C. F. Roedel to N. Pope (New Mexico Superintendent), and Pope to commissioner, *ARCIA* (1871), 367–68, 395–98, esp. 397.
55. J. B. Hanson (agent) to Pope, *ARCIA* (1871), 405–8, esp. 406.
56. Roedel to Pope, *ARCIA* (1871), 395–98, esp. 397–98.
57. Smith, *Ouray*, 71. Regarding Colorow's shifting band affiliation, see Jocknick, *Early Days*, 326; and "Colorow" in Stewart, "Chief's List."
58. Dawson, "Major Thompson," 120; Jocknick, *Early Days*, 117–22, 177, 233; Smith, *Ouray*, 10, 52, 55, 143–44; Emmitt, *Last War Trail*, 12–20, 53; O'Neil, "History of the Ute Indians," 127–29.
59. See, e.g., Jocknick, *Early Days*, 99, 238–41; Smith, *Ouray*, 68, 83–85.
60. On Otto Mears, see Smith, *Ouray*, 83–85; Jocknick, *Early Days*, 99, 122–23, 204–5, 221–26, 235–42; Helen M. Searcy, "Otto Mears and the Utes," In *Pioneers of the San Juan*, vol. 1 (Colorado Springs: Out West Printing & Stationery Co., 1942). See also Simmons, "When Opportunity Knocked"; E. F. Kushner's *Otto Mears, His Life and Times* (Frederick, CO: Platte N. Press, 1979); Michael Kaplan, "Otto Mears: Colorado's Transportation King," *DAI, 1975* 35 (5): 3042-A. Numerous additional articles appear in the *Western States Jewish Historical Quarterly*.
61. Qt. in Smith, *Ouray*, 84, and Simmons, "Opportunity Knocked"; Jocknick to commissioner, *ARCIA* (1872), 262, and Trask to commissioner, *ARCIA* (1871), 554–55; and see "Treaty of 1868," Article 13.
62. Littlefield to commissioner, and Critchlow to commissioner, *ARCIA* (1872), 289, 291–93; John Alton Peterson, *Utah's Black Hawk War* (University of Utah Press, 1998), 364–68.
63. Jocknick, *Early Days*, 32–41; Smith, *Ouray*, 108; and Rockwell, *The Utes*, 84.
64. Jocknick to commissioner, September 30, 1871, 261–63; and Trask to commissioner, *ARCIA* (1871), 554–55; Jocknick, *Early Days*, 34–35.
65. Littlefield to commissioner, *ARCIA* (1871), 551–53, and *ARCIA* (1872), 287.
66. Thompson to commissioner, October 1, 1871, *ARCIA* (1871), 556–57; Jocknick, *Early Days*, 21–31.
67. Jocknick to commissioner, September 30, 1871, and Clum to C. Delano (Secretary of the Interior), *ARCIA* (1871), 263, 8; Adams to commissioner, *ARCIA, 1872*, 289–91; O'Neil and MacKay, *History of the Uintah-Ouray*, 11; P, D. Smith, *Ouray*, 94–99; Arny to commissioner, "Special Report No. 4, 1870," in Delaney, *Ute Mountain Ute*, 37, 41.

68. Gov. McCook's biennial message to the Colorado Legislature (January 3, 1872), and and Gov. Pitkin to Legislature, quoted in Smith, *Ouray*, 90–94, 149–50. Cf., commissioner's annual report to the Secretary of the Interior, in *ARCIA* (1872), 52.

69. Commissioner's annual report, in *ARCIA* (1872), 52.

70. Smith, *Ouray*, 93–94, 108. On the Ute opinion of Thompson, see Jocknick, *Early Days*, 22, 26; cf. Smith, *Ouray*, 81.

71. Gibson, *The American Indian*, 396–97; Tyler, *History of Indian Policy*, 84–85; and *The Cherokee Tobacco*, 78 US 616 (1870).

72. McCook, Lang, and McDonald, to commissioner, *ARCIA* (1872), 123–24; Smith, *Ouray*, 99–100; Simmons, "Opportunity Knocks."

73. Smith, *Ouray*, 100–113; Rockwell, *The Utes*, 96.

74. Smith, *Ouray*, 102–3.

75. McCook, Lang, and McDonald to commissioner, *ARCIA* (1872), 124; Smith, *Ouray*, 103–4.

76. *Boulder News* and *Denver Tribune*, March 26, 1873, quoted in Smith, *Ouray*, 91, 105–6.

77. Jocknick, *Early Days*, 115–16; Smith, *Ouray*, 113; "Agreement with the Ute Tribe," September 13, 1873 (ratified April 18, 1874); Kappler, *Indian Affairs*, 1:151–53.

78. "Proceedings of Negotiations with the Ute Indians," *ARCIA* (1873), 106–7.

79. Ouray quoted in Smith, *Ouray*, 52, 56–57, 108–9, esp. 109; cf. Jocknick, *Early Days*, 232–33.

80. Smith, *Ouray*, 108–9, 116–17.

81. Agreement of 1873," Kappler, *Indian Affairs*, 1:151–52; Smith, *Ouray*, 114–17; O'Neil and MacKay, *History of the Uintah-Ouray*, 11–12; Jorgensen, *Sun Dance Religion*, 44; Delaney, *Ute Mountain Ute*, 46. Jocknick describes San Juan wealth in *Early Days*, 161–70.

82. See Rockwell, *The Utes*, 98–99; Jorgensen, *Sun Dance Religion*, 44; Smith, *Ouray*, 106.

83. "Agreement of 1873"; Jocknick, *Early Days*, 110–13, 152–53; O'Neil and MacKay, *History of the Uintah-Ouray*, 11–12.

84. Jocknick, *Early Days*, 115–19; Smith, *Ouray*, 90. Assassins included Suckett, Dynamite, Jack of Clubs, Old Nick, and the Carlisle student, Hot Stuff (so named for an explosion he had caused in a science lab). Nicknames given by agency personnel.

473

CHAPTER 9

1. For an expanded discussion of Mormon-Indian relations, see Sondra Jones, "Saints or Sinners? The Evolving Perceptions of Mormon-Indian Relations in Utah Historiography," *Utah Historical Quarterly* 72 (Winter 2004): 19–46; cf. Todd M. Compton, *A Frontier Life: Jacob Hamblin, Explorer and Indian Missionary* (Salt Lake City: University of Utah Press, 2013), 194, 237, 348–56, 443–48.

2. *Journal History of the Church*, 1830–1972 [*JH*], January 1860, 22, Church History Library, Church of Jesus Christ of Latter-day Saints, Salt Lake City, Utah; F. H. Head to Commissioner, United States Office of Indian Affairs, *Annual Report of the Commissioner of Indian Affairs* [*ARCIA*] (Washington, D.C.: Government Printing Office, 1867), 175. A disease introduced to a people with no immunity because they have never before been exposed to it or any similar disease is called a "virgin soil" disease. See Alfred W. Crosby, *Ecological Imperialism: The Biological Expansion of Europe, 900–1900*, 2nd ed. (New York: Cambridge University Press, 2004); Crosby, *The Columbian Exchange: Biological and Cultural Consequences of 1492* (Westport, CT: Greenwood, 1972); Sheldon Watts, "Smallpox in the New World and the Old," ch. 3 in *Epidemics and History: Disease, Power, and Imperialism* (New Haven: Yale University Press, 1999); and William H. McNeill, "Transoceanic Exchanges, 1500–1700," ch. 5 in *Plagues and Peoples* (1977; New York: Random House, 1998).

3. *JH*, January 22, 1860; Elizabeth W. Kane, *Twelve Mormon Homes: Visited in Succession on a Journey through Utah to Arizona* (Salt Lake City: University of Utah Library, 1974), 66, 39; John Alton Peterson, *Utah's Black Hawk War* (Salt Lake City: University of Utah Press, 1998), 81. On fostered children, see Juanita Brooks, "Indian Relations on the Mormon Frontier," *Utah Historical Quarterly* 12 (1944): 1–48.

4. Exact numbers are difficult to determine. See, e.g., Joseph G. Jorgensen, *The Sun Dance Religion: Power for the Powerless* (Chicago: University of Chicago Press, 1972), 13–63; Peterson, *Black Hawk War*, 81–82, 104, 360–61, 361n48, 386–87.

5. Southern Ute Tribe, *Dictionary*, 154, 285, note *páa* (water) + *núu-cii* (Ute person).

6. For Puritan attitudes, see, e.g., "Colonial Indian Policy," in Arrell Morgan Gibson, *The American Indian: Prehistory to the Present* (Norman: University of Oklahoma Press, 1980), 186–91.

7. On perceptions in language, see James A. Goss, "Ute Lexical and Phonological Patterns" (PhD diss., University of Chicago, 1972), 40–44. For information on the ridicule of Uintah farmers, see J. J. Critchlow to Commissioner, *ARCIA, 1872*, 292; J. S. Littlefield to Walker, *ARCIA, 1872*, 288; cf. Compton, *A Frontier Life*, 194, 237, 348–56, 443–48.

8. Darrell Gardner, personal communication, 1980; and corroborated by ethnohistorians Omer C. Stewart, personal conversation with author, August 1977. Cf., Gary Lee Walker, "A History of Fort Duchesne, Including Fort Thornburgh: The Military Presence in Frontier Uinta Basin" (PhD diss., Brigham Young University, 1992), 188–91, 222–25, and personal communication with author, March 1998.

9. On intermarriage and indenturing, see Brooks, "Indian Relations," 1–48; Brian Q. Cannon, "Adopted or Indentured, 1850–1870: Native Children in Mormon Households," in *Nearly Everything Imaginable: The Everyday Life of Utah's Mormon Pioneers*, edited by Ronald W. Walker and Doris R. Dant (Provo, UT: Brigham Young University Press, 1998); Brian Q. Cannon and Richard D. Kitchen, "Indenture and Adoption of Native American Children by Mormons on the Utah Frontier, 1850–1870," in *Common Frontiers: Proceedings of the 1996 Conference and Annual Meeting*, edited by Donna R. Braden and Susan Gangwere McCabe (North Bloomfield, OH: Association for Living History Farms and Historical Museums, 1997); Kitchen "Mormon-Indian Relations in Deseret: Intermarriage and Indenture, 1847 to 1877" (PhD diss., Arizona State University, 2002); and Sondra Jones, "Redeeming the Indian: The Enslavement of Indian Children in Utah and New Mexico," *Utah Historical Quarterly* 67 (Summer 1999): 220–41.

10. "Peace Corps," in Lawrence G. Coates, "Brigham Young and Mormon Indian Policies: The Formative Period, 1836–1851," *BYU Studies* 18:3 (Spring 1978): 439–41. On the southern missions, see Thomas D. Brown, *Journal of the Southern Indian Mission: Diary of Thomas D. Brown*, edited by Juanita Brooks (Logan: Utah State University Press, 1972), 29–30; Jacob Hamblin, "Journals and Letters of Jacob Hamblin," Tms. in L. Tom Perry Special Collections, Harold B. Lee Library, Brigham Young University, Provo, Utah [BYU-SC], 19; Compton, *A Frontier Life*, esp. 45–90.

11. Hamblin, "Journals," July 15 and August 9, 1856, 43; Brown, *Southern Indian Mission*, 29–30; Compton, *A Frontier Life*, 194–95, 348–57, 443–48; cf. Eugene E. Campbell, *Establishing Zion: The Mormon Church in the American West, 1847–1869* (Salt Lake City: Signature Books, 1988), ch. 6 and 7, esp. 93–94, 111, 121.

12. Beverly Beeton, "Teach Them to Till the Soil: An Experiment with Indian Farms 1850–1862," *American Indian Quarterly* 3 (1977–1978): 299–320. Cf., Virginia Cole Trenholm and Maurine Carley, *The Shoshones: Sentinels of the Rockies* (Norman: University of Oklahoma Press, 1964), ch. 9; Scott R. Christensen, *Sagwitch: Shoshone Chieftain, Mormon Elder, 1822–1887* (Logan: Utah State University Press, 1999), ch. 3–5.

13. Brooks, "Indian Relations," 23–37; Beeton, "Teach Them to Till the Soil," 299–320.

14. Donald R. Moorman and Gene A. Sessions, *Camp Floyd and the Mormons* (Salt Lake City: University of Utah Press, 1992), 185–87.

15. The Utah War of 1857 will not be detailed here. One tragic fallout of the war hysteria that swept Utah Territory was the massacre of Arkansas emigrants by Mormons at Mountain Meadows, and initially blamed on Southern Paiutes.

16. Beeton, "Teach Them to Till the Soil," 299–320.

17. Ibid., Madsen, *Shoshoni Frontier*, 68, 70, 86, 91–93; Floyd A. O'Neil, "A History of the Ute Indians until 1890" (Ph.D. diss., University of Utah, 1973), 51.

18. For more on this power struggle, see Floyd A. O'Neil and Stanford J. Layton, "Of Pride and Politics: Brigham Young as Indian Superintendent," *Utah Historical Quarterly* 46 (1978): 236–50; cf. Peterson, *Black Hawk War*, 100–122.

19. Holeman to Luke Lea, Commissioner of Indian Affairs, December 28, 1851, Office of Indian Affairs, *Letters Received, Utah Superintendency, 1849–1880* [microfilm] (hereafter OIA-UT), rolls 897–98, M-234, Record Group 75, National Archives and Records Administration, Washington, D.C.

20. Hurt to G. W. Manypenny, Commissioner of Indian Affairs, May 2, 1855, OIA-UT.

21. August 31, 1856, in Church of Jesus Christ of Latter-day Saints, *Journal of Discourses* [*JD*] (London: Latter-day Saints' Book Depot, 1854–1886, reprint 1966), 4:41; and *JD*, 2:264.

22. J. Nicolay to W. P. Dole, November 10, 1863, in *Report of the Secretary of the Interior* [*RSI*] (Washington, D.C.: 1860–1875), 268. Other federal officials made similar statements.

23. G. Hurt to B. Young, *ARCIA, 1856*, 231–32; and G. Hurt, Appendix O, 463–64, in J. H. Simpson, comp., *Report of Explorations Across the Great Basin, etc.* (Washington, D.C., 1876). A southerner, Hurt's reports show him to be a decided racist, as were most Americans, including Brigham Young.

24. Holeman to Commissioner of Indian Affairs, November 28, 1851, OIA-UT, 897–98.

25. Solomon Nuñes Carvalho, *Incidents of Travel and Adventure in the Far West with Colonel Fremont's Last Expedition* (1856; New York: Derby and Jackson, 1860), 218.

26. Hurt to Manypenny, Commissioner of Indian Affairs, May 2, 1855, OIA-UT.

27. *Salt Lake Tribune*, September 28, 1877.

28. Report of Lt. Sylvester Mowry, under command of Lt. Col. Steptoe, July 23, 1855, typescript of letter, Utah Writers Project Collection, Utah State Historical Society (USHS), Salt Lake City.

29. Brigham Young to Wákara, July 25, 1853, doc. 289, reel 1, microfilm ST-27, Utah Territorial Military Correspondence (UTMC), Utah State Archives, Salt Lake City, Utah.

30. Quotes by Carvalho, *Travels and Adventures*, 187; Ronald W. Walker, "President Young Writes Jefferson Davis about the Gunnison Massacre Affair." *Brigham Young University Studies* 35:1 (1995): 147–49; and James F. Brooks, *Captives & Cousins: Slavery, Kinship, and Community in the Southwest Borderlands* (Chapel Hill: University of North Carolina Press 2002), 18; Brigham Madsen, *The Shoshoni Frontier and the Bear River Massacre* (Salt Lake City: University of Utah Press, 1985), e.g., 47–48, 55, 69, 79–91.

31. See, e.g., Brown (May 19, 1854), *Southern Indian Mission*, 25.

32. Brigham Young to Jacob Hamblin, August 4, 1857, letter book no. 3, 737–38, Brigham Young Collections (BYC), located in the CHL. See also Madsen, *Shoshoni Frontier*, 77–78.

33. John B. Floyd, to U.S. Congress (1858), and Buchanan to U.S. Congress (1857), both quoted in O'Neil and Layton, "Of Pride and Politics," 248–49.

34. Madsen, *Shoshoni Frontier*, 78–91. Substance was added to rumors when some Mormons did dress up as Indians during the Mountain Meadows massacre. See, e.g., Juanita Brooks, *Mountain Meadows Massacre* (Stanford, CA: Stanford University Press, 1962); Gary Tom and Ronald Holt, "The Paiute Tribe of Utah," 131–39, in *A History of Utah's American Indians*, edited by Forrest S. Cuch (Salt Lake City: Utah State Division of Indian Affairs and Utah State Division of History, 2000); and Richard Turley, Glen Walker, and Ronald Walker, *Massacre at Mountain Meadows: An American Tragedy* (New York: Oxford University Press, 2008); cf. the virulently anti-Mormon book by Will Bagley, *Blood of the Prophets* (2002).

35. O'Neil and Layton, "Of Pride and Politics," 247–48; cf. Madsen, *Shoshoni Frontier*, 12–20, 220–21, and passim.

36. Garland Hurt to John Elliott, October 4, 1856, OIA-UT.

37. Moorman and Sessions, *Camp Floyd and the Mormons*, 187–91; Madsen, *Shoshoni Frontier*, esp. ch. 5.

38. Moorman and Sessions, *Camp Floyd and the Mormons*, 197–203. See also Beeton, "Teach Them to Till the Soil," 307.

39. Garland Hurt to Jacob Forney, September 14, 1858, OIA-UT.

40. B. Davies to commissioner, *ARCIA, 1861*, 129; Humphreys to commissioner, *ARCIA, 1861*, 140; O'Neil, "History of the Ute Indians," 48–50.

41. Joseph G. Jorgensen, "The Ethnohistory and Acculturation of the Northern Ute" (PhD diss., Indiana University, Bloomington, 1964), 72–74; O'Neil, "History of the Ute Indians," 52–55.

42. Beeton, "Teach Them to Till the Soil," 311–12.

43. Brigham Young to Stephen Rose (subagent), July 21, 1851, OIA-UT; and O'Neil, "History of the Ute Indians," 51.

44. Humphreys to commissioner, *ARCIA, 1861*, 140; *Deseret News*, September 25, 1861; Floyd A. O'Neil and Kathryn L. MacKay, *A History of the Uintah-Ouray Ute Lands*, American West Center Occasional Papers (Salt Lake City: University of Utah Press, n.d.), 9. Cf., Andrew Love Neff's naively enthusiastic description in *History of Utah, 1847 to 1869*, edited by Leland H. Creer (Salt Lake City: Deseret News Press, 1940), 395.

45. "Executive Orders Relating to Reserves: Uintah Valley Reserve," approved May 5, 1864, Stats. 63 (June 13, 1878) 20 Stats. 165 (May 24, 1888) 25 Stats. 157; and in Charles J. Kappler, comp. and ed., *Indian Affairs: Laws and Treaties* (Washington, D.C.: Government Printing Office, 1902–1938), 1:900.

46. O'Neil, "History of the Ute Indians," 55.

47. Walker, "A History of Fort Duchesne, 188–91," 222–25, and personal communication with author, March 1998.

48. O'Neil, "History of the Ute Indians," 55, 86–89.

49. Because this conflict is best known as the Black Hawk War, this work uses the leader's more recognizable name, rather than Autanquer/Antonga. Note his name appears variously as Autanquer (contemporary documents and Peterson's dissertation) and Antonga (Peterson's book). See Peterson, *Black Hawk War*; and Peterson, "Mormons, Indians, and Gentiles and Utah's Black Hawk War" (PhD diss., Arizona State University, 1993); and Omer C. Stewart, "Identification and Group Leadership of Ute Indian Chief" ("Chiefs List"), working paper prepared for Dockets 44–45, U.S. Indian Claims Commission, 1952, Tms. in the box 1, Omer C. Stewart Collection, 2nd Accession, Archives, Norlin Library, University of Colorado, Boulder; and Omer Call Stewart Papers, Special Collections, J. Willard Marriot Library, University of Utah, Salt Lake City, Utah.

50. Madsen, *Shoshoni Frontier*, ch. 8–10; Madsen, *Encounter with the Northwestern Shoshoni at Bear River in 1863: Battle or Massacre?* Dello G. Dayton Memorial Lecture, May 11, 1983 (Ogden, UT: Weber State College Press, 1984); Robert S. McPherson, *Staff Ride Handbook for the Battle of Bear River, 29 January 1863* (Riverton, UT: Utah National Guard, 2000); Mae Perry, "The Northwestern Shoshone," in Cuch, *A History of Utah's American Indians*, 33–44; Utley, *Frontiersmen in Blue*, 223–24.

51. On Sand Creek, see Utley, *Frontiersmen in Blue*, 290–97; Depositions in the appendix (52–55), of James Doolittle, *Condition of the Indian Tribes: Report of the Joint Special Committee* ["The Doolittle Report"] (Washington: Government Printing Office, 1867), e.g., 51–54, 197–98. For Connor's correspondence, see Connor to Drum, October 30, 1864, in U.S. Department of War, *War of the Rebellion: A Compilation of the Official Records of the Union and Confederate Armies*, Series 1 [*WR*] (Washington, D.C.: 1897) 50 (pt. 2): 1036–37; Drum to Connor, December 17, 1864, 50 (pt. 2): 1101, in *WR*; Irvin McDowell to Adjutant-General of the Army [Washington, D.C.], December 17, 1864, 50 (pt. 2): 1100; Brigham Madsen, quoting a Chivington letter, in *Glory Hunter: A Biography of Patrick Edward Connor* (Salt Lake City: University of Utah Press, 1990), 121.

52. On the Navajos, see Thomas Dunlay, *Kit Carson and the Indians* (Lincoln: University of Nebraska, 2000); Thelma S. Guild and Harvey L. Carter, *Kit Carson* (Lincoln: University of Nebraska, 1984); Lynn R. Bailey, *The Long Walk: A History of the Navajo Wars, 1846–68* (Tucson, AZ: Westernlore Press, 1964); Johnson Broderick, *Navajo Stories of the Long Walk Period* (Tsaile, AZ: Dineh College, 1973).

53. Connor to Lieut. Col. R. C. Drum, April 13, 1863, 50 9 (pt. 2): 391–92; Connor to Drum, April 16, 1863, 50 (pt. 2): 404; Connor to Maj. J. W. Barnes, April 6, 1865, 50 (pt. 2): 658–59, Connor to J. W. Barnes [Asst. Adjutant-Genera;, Dept. of the Missouri], April 6, 1865, 50 (pt. 2): 1184–85; all in *WR*. See also Madsen, *Glory Hunter*, 94–96; Utley, *Frontiersmen in Blue*, 225; and Madoline Cloward Dixon who quotes "Bishop Thurber's Journal," in *These Were the Utes: Their Lifestyles, Wars and Legends* (Provo, UT: Press Publishing Co., 1983), 152–53.

54. Madsen, *Glory Hunter*, 94–96; Connor to Drum, April 6, 1863, 50 (pt. 2): 404, *WR*.

55. S. Lyman Tyler, "Ute Indians along Civil War Communication Lines," *Utah Historical Quarterly* 46 (Summer 1978): 253–61; Utley, *Frontiersmen in Blue*, 282; Gov. John Evans to S. G. Colley, *ARCIA, 1863*, 121–22.

56. Connor to Brig. Gen. Benjamin Alvord, June 10, 1863, in *WR*, 550 (pt. 2) (pt. 2): 479), Connor to Drum, July 18, 1863, in *WR*, 50 (pt. 2): 527–29; and April 28, 1863, *WR*, 50 (pt. 2): 415. See also Peterson, "Mormons, Indians, and Gentiles," 144–47, 266–69.

57. Connor to Drum, April 28, 1863 in *WR*, 50 (pt. 2): 415; and Connor Drum, June 24, 1863, *WR*, 50 (pt. 2): 492–95; and Phoebe Westwood to Dave Westwood, June 25, 1863, letter submitted by Connor, *WR*, 50 (pt. 2): 499–500.

58. Connor to Drum, June 24, 1863; April 28, 1863, *WR*, 50 (pt. 2): 415; December 20, 1862, *WR*, 50 (pt. 2): 257; June 11, 1863, *WR*, 50 (pt. 2): 481; and Connor to J. W. Barnes, April 6, 1865, *WR*, 50 (pt. 2):

1184–85. For information on being surrounded by enemies, see Connor to Westwood, June 25, 1863, *WR*, 50 (pt. 2): 499–500.

59. S. Whitely to J. Evans, *ARCIA, 1863,* 131; O'Neil, "History of the Ute Indians, 56; Jorgensen, *Sun Dance Religion,* 36; Peter Gottfredson, *Indian Depredations in Utah,* 2nd ed. (1919; Salt Lake City: Shelton Publishing Co., 1969), 121–29.

60. Whitely to Evans, *ARCIA, 1863,* 131–32.

61. Josiah F. Gibbs, "Black Hawk's Last Raid—1866," *Utah Historical Quarterly* 4 (1931): 103; cf. Daniel W. Jones, *Forty Years among the Indians* (1890; Los Angeles: Westernlore Press, 1960), 168–69.

62. Peterson, "Mormons, Indians, and Gentiles," 73–74; Peterson, *Black Hawk War,* 116–17; Bean, "Autobiography," 69–70. Cattle ranching, railroads, and centralized slaughterhouses in places like Kansas City and Chicago, financed by developing, vertically integrated monopolies, facilitated the growth of this important western industry.

63. Hyde to Bishop C. H. Bryan, April 26, 1865, BYC. On the growth of Mormon cattle ranching, see Peterson, "Mormons, Indians, and Gentiles," 66–70; and Peterson, *Black Hawk War,* 112–13, 116–17; Bean, "Autobiography" 69–70. Cf. Brigham Young to Brigham Young, Jr., May 23, 1866, BYC; and George Peacock, January 5, 1867, in "The Original Diary of Judge George Peacock," Ms. 2251, CHL.

64. Peterson, "Mormons, Indians, and Gentiles," 73–74; and Peterson, *Black Hawk War,* 116–17.

65. Bean, "Autobiography," 69.

66. Peterson, "Mormons, Indians, and Gentiles," 76–78; and Peterson, *Black Hawk War,* 120–21. Agency corruption was endemic throughout the West and is mentioned in most tribal histories.

67. None of Black Hawk's immediate family survived the war; only descendants of his brother, Quibets (Mountain), survive today.

68. Peterson, *Black Hawk War,* 16–17, 95–96; Peterson, "Mormons, Indians, and Gentiles," 55; Gottfredson, *Indian Depredations,* 321; Kate B. Carter, ed., *Heart Throbs of the West* (Salt Lake City: Daughters of the Utah Pioneers, 1939–1950), 6:480.

69. Bean, "Autobiography," 69–70; Peterson, "Mormons, Indians, and Gentiles," 18–20, 57–80; Peterson, *Black Hawk War,* 16–17; Gottfredson, *Indian Depredations,* 129–30.

70. Peterson, *Black Hawk War,* 105–6; cf. Carlton Culmsee, *Utah's Black Hawk War: Lore and Reminiscences of Participants* (Logan: Utah State University, 1973), 31–33; Carter, *Heart Throbs of the West,* 1:89–90; Kate B. Carter, *Our Pioneer Heritage* (Salt Lake City: Daughters of Utah Pioneers, 1958–1977), 3:423.

71. Peterson, "Mormons, Indians, and Gentiles," 18–20, 57–80; Peterson, *Black Hawk War,* 16–17, 100–101; Gottfredson, *Indian Depredations,* 129–30, 335–38; cf. Hubert Howe Bancroft, *History of Utah* (San Francisco: History Co., 1890), 633ff.; and Miles E. Johnson, "Miles Egar Johnson: The Life Review of a Mormon," Tms., ed. Rolla Virgil Johnson, 1930–1933, revised 1970, MS #1187, CHL; Culmsee, *Utah's Black Hawk War,* 34–35.

72. The war is detailed in Peterson's *Utah's Black Hawk War* and his dissertation, "Mormons, Indians, and Gentiles and *Utah's Black Hawk War.*" See also O'Neil, "History of the Ute Indians," 55–60, 70–85; R. Warren Metcalf, "A Precarious Balance: The Northern Utes and the Black Hawk War," *Utah Historical Quarterly* (Winter 1989): 24–35; Bancroft, *History of Utah,* 632–33; Kate Carter, "Black Hawk War," in *Our Pioneer Heritage,* 9:169–256; Orson F. Whitney, *History of Utah* (Salt Lake City: George Q. Cannon and Sons, 1892–1904), 187–214, 710–13; Neff's rather biased *History of Utah,* 393–409.

73. Peterson, "Mormons, Indians, and Gentiles"; cf. Peterson, *Black Hawk War,* esp. 16–41, 80–122, 335–38.

74. For Peterson's theories about the extent of Black Hawk's influence in stirring up pan-Indian hostilities, see *Black Hawk War,* 186–90, but compare to his dissertation, "Mormons, Indians, and Gentiles."

75. Peterson, *Black Hawk War,* 184–90. On Tabeguache's reluctance to cross the river, see R. McCook (an Uncompahgre/Tabeguache and former Northern Ute tribal chair), telephone conversation with author, 1998; cf. tales told Rivera, in Austin Nelson Leiby, "Borderland Pathfinders: The 1765 Diaries of Juan Maria Antonio de Rivera" (PhD diss., Northern Arizona University, 1985), 208–22.

76. Peterson, *Black Hawk War,* 186–90. For Paiute allies against the Navajo, see Leo Lyman, "Caught In Between: Jacob Hamblin and the Southern Paiutes during the Black Hawk-Navajo Wars of the Late 1860s," *Utah Historical Quarterly* 75 (Winter 2007): 22–43; and "Successful Sentinels: Southern

477

Paiutes and Jacob Hamblin Oppose Navajo Raiders, 1866–1870," paper presented at the Mormon History Association conference, May 26–29, 2001, St. George, Utah. For the Southern Paiute and Mormon conflict, see W. Paul Reeve, *Making Space on the Western Frontier: Mormons, Miners, and Southern Paiutes* (Urbana: University of Illinois Press, 2006), 68–72 and fn 16; cf. Compton, *A Frontier Life*, 239–40, 260–68, 283–93.

77. Peterson, *Black Hawk War*, 1–15, 229–34, 240–42, 262–63, 269.

78. On the impact of the war, see Peterson, *Black Hawk War*, 1–15.

79. Peterson, "Mormons, Indians, and Gentiles," 122–23, 161, and *Black Hawk War*, 171–74, 229–30. See Helaman 6 and 11; and 3 Nephi 1–4. Hyde's absolution is recorded in the "Journal of Jens Christian Andersen Weibye" (in Danish), August 3, 1865, CHL, and quoted in Peterson, *Black Hawk War*, 172. A number of militia men had been swept by guilt after killing women during the so-called "Squaw" fight.

80. Orson Hyde and Warren Snow quoted in Peterson, *Black Hawk War*, 233 and see 144–46, 171–73, 177.

81. Ibid., 144–46; Peterson, *Black Hawk War*, 93–95, and quoting Hyde; Carter, *Heart Throbs of the West*, 6:493–94.

82. Young to John D. Lee, March 6, 1866, MS 276, box 8, fd. 6, and letterbook, 1234 vol. 8, 169, in Brigham Young Manuscript History, CHL.

83. Brigham Young quoted in Peterson, *Black Hawk War*, 164, 172, and "Mormons, Indians, and Gentiles," 114–15, 123. See also, "Col. Snow on the Warpath," in BYC.

84. Peterson, "Mormons, Indians, and Gentiles," 123–24, 182–83, 192–93, 234–35, and *Black Hawk War*, 172–74, 260–61. See also Head to Cooley, June 21, 1866, in *ARCIA* (1866), 129–130.

85. Peterson, "Mormons, Indians, and Gentiles," 160–65, 169–70, 212–15, and *Black Hawk War*, 230–31, 235, 294–96; and quoting W. S. Snow to George A. Smith, March 14, 1866. Cf., Gottfredson, *Indian Depredations*, 181.

86. On hostage policy and events, see Peterson, *Black Hawk War*, 225–42, and "Mormons, Indians, and Gentiles," 164–67, 171–72. On Sanpitch as a target, see W. S. Snow to George A. Smith, March 18, 1866, reel 3, doc. 823, UTMC; Supt. F. H. Head to D. N. Cooley, 1866, in *ARCIA* (1866), 124–25. For Ute jail break(s), see Gottfredson, *Indian Depredations*, 187–89; Peterson, "Mormons, Indians, and Gentiles," 170–77, and *Black Hawk War*, 238–42; and Sanpete County Heritage, Manti-LaSal National Forest, and KBYU (producers), *Utah's Black Hawk War: Cultures in Conflict* [video recording], moderated by John Peterson and broadcast, April 19, 1998, including an interview with grandson of one of the men who pursued Sanpitch.

87. Peterson, *Black Hawk War*, 162–67, 381, and cf. "Mormons, Indians, and Gentiles," 113–16; Orange Seeley, Sr., "History of Orange Seeley, Sr., Told by Himself," mss. #9942, CHL. Other notes on this fight include Andrew Moffitt to Young, July 23, 1865, BYC; R. H. Allred to Stenhouse, July 20, 1865, BYC; and Reddick N. Allred, "Journal of R. N. Allred," mss. #8795, CHL. Southern Paiute oral history is cited in Peterson, *Black Hawk War*, 166–67.

88. General Orders No. 1 from the headquarters of the Nauvoo Legion issued by Gen. Daniel H. Wells, April 25, 1865, as cited in Peterson, *Black Hawk War*, 256–57.

89. Peterson, *Black Hawk War*, 243–48, and "Mormons, Indians, and Gentiles," 181–83. See also Winkler, "The Circleville Massacre," 4–21; Gottfredson, *Indian Depredations*, 144–46, 189–96; and, for a sanitized version, Carter, "Black Hawk Indian War," in *Our Pioneer Heritage*, 208–11. Sanpete Heritage and KBYU, "Black Hawk" [television special], interview with Circleville descendant.

90. See, e.g., massacres at Pipe Springs of local Kaibab Paiutes, and the Berry Massacre. Peterson, *Black Hawk War*, 178–81, 218–24, and "Mormons, Indians, and Gentiles," 130–34; Gottfredson, *Indian Depredations*, 169–80, 181–83. For a discussion of the Navajo front, see Peterson, "Mormons, Indians, and Gentiles," 149–60, and *Black Hawk War*, 209–24, esp. 217; Compton, *A Frontier Life*, 239–40, 260–70, 283–90, 336–39. On the Berry Massacre, see Compton, *A Frontier Life*, 268–70; cf., R. D. Covington to E. Snow, April 8, 1866, and postscript April 19, 1866, by George A. Smith, in reel 3, doc. 831, UTMC.

91. The Scipio raid and Ivie incident are related in Peterson, "Mormons, Indians, and Gentiles," 201–3, 212–15, and *Black Hawk War*, 267–70, 294–96; Gibbs, "Black Hawk's Last Raid," 99–106; Gottfredson, *Indian Depredations*, 201, 227–29. Young's sermon, July 28, 1866, *JD*, 11:263–66. Reinstated in the Idaho Falls Temple, November 21, 1965; F. Rees to L. Ivie, November 20 and 21, 1965; David O.

McKay, Hugh B. Brown, and N. Eldon Tanner [First Presidency] to Rees, ca. October 1965, photocopies in USHS. See also personal communication, 1999, Ivie descendant, name withheld.

92. Peterson, *Black Hawk War*, 17–22, 135–39, and "Mormons, Indians, and Gentiles," 84–85; W. S. Snow to Brigham Young, April 22, 1865, reel 58, box 30, fd. 4, BYC; Gottfredson, *Indian Depredations*, 129–32, 138–40; and Bancroft, *History of Utah*, 633ff. On Barney Ward, see Eugene E. Campbell and Fred R. Gowans, *Fort Supply: Brigham Young's Green River Experiment* (Provo, UT: Brigham Young University Press, 1976); LeRoy R. Hafen, "Elijah Barney Ward," in *The Mountain Men*, 7:343–51; Carter, "Indian Maiden, Orphaned, Has Stirring Life," in *Our Pioneer Heritage*, 6:451–52.

93. Peterson, *Black Hawk War*, 20–21, 135–39, 171, 328, and "Mormons, Indians, and Gentiles," 121–22; Gottfredson, *Indian Depredations*, 163–66.

94. See, e.g., G. A. Smith and Snow to B. Young, February 4, 1866, reel 57, box 42, fd. 8, BYC. On Isaac Potter, see G. A. Smith to John L. Smith, June 24, 1863, in George A. Smith, "G. A. Smith Collection," mss. #2736, box 27, fd. 2 (hereafter GAS), in CHL; A. F. McDonald to William B. Pace, May 24, 1866 in "William B. Pace Collection," mss. #10411, box 2, fd. 2, CHL. On arms trade and middlemen, see Peterson "Mormons, Indians, and Gentiles," 140–48. Alma Eldredge, "Diary, 1841–1925," July 1867, 97–109, mss. #5125, CHL, includes outlaw White men quote.

95. Young to H. S. Eldredge, October 4, 1870, Romney typescripts, mss. #2736, box 12, fd. 2, BYC.

96. Holeman to Lea, September 21, 1851, OIA-UT.

97. Peterson, "Mormons, Indians, and Gentiles," 73–74, and *Black Hawk War*, 116–17; Bean, "Autobiography," 69–70.

98. Connor, reported in O. Hyde to B. Young, April 15, 1865, in reel 71, box 40, fd. 2, BYC; on blind eye, in Woodruff to G. A. Smith, March 11, 1859, mss. #1322, box 6, fd. 2, GAS. For relations between Utah and federal officials during the Civil War, see O'Neil and Layton, "Of Pride and Politics"; and Thomas Alexander, *Utah: The Right Place*, 3rd ed. (Salt Lake City: Gibbs Smith, 2003), 140–42.

99. Peterson argues that Young deliberately suppressed news so the military would *not* get involved; however, Howard Christy argues (vehemently) that federal and military officials *all* knew about the situation and simply chose to do nothing about it, and that the idea of a *deliberate* "conspiracy" to suppress the war news is unfounded. See Christy, "Review of John Peterson's *Utah's Black Hawk War*," *Journal of Mormon History* 26 (Spring 2000): 282–89; and personal communication, spring 2001 and January 2003. For antipathy with the military, see Peterson, "Mormons, Indians, and Gentiles," esp. 35–39, 96, 112–13, 125, 158–59, 185–88; and *Black Hawk War*, 16–42 ("Beginnings" and "The Uneasy Triangle") and 101–22 ("Setting the Stage").

100. Kane, *Twelve Mormon Homes*, 91n48. See also Peterson, *Black Hawk War*, 296–301, 320–21, 368–71.

101. Details of the war in Peterson, *Black Hawk War* and "Mormons, Indians, and Gentiles." "Indian Rover," and "desperadoes," in Neff, *History of Utah*, 393–409; cf. Peterson, *Black Hawk War*, 396n60. For economic impacts, see W. Paul Reeve, "'Places That Can Be Easily Defended': A Case Study in the Economics of Abandonment during Utah's Black Hawk War," *Utah Historical Quarterly* 75 (Summer 2007): 220–37.

102. Peace negotiations are in Peterson, *Black Hawk War*, 148–55, and are based on official minutes and Brigham Young's personal papers.

103. O. H. Irish, report of the Treaty negotiations, letter of June 29, 1865, quoted in O'Neil, "History of the Ute Indians," 61.

104. O. H. Irish, report of the Treaty negotiations, letter June 29, 1865; and quoted (in part) in O'Neil, "History of the Ute Indians," 65–66; emphasis added.

105. Peterson, *Black Hawk War*, 148–58.

106. O'Neil, "History of the Ute Indians," esp. 60–68, 86–125, details the establishment and administration of the reservation from its inception to 1880; 69–85 detail the Black Hawk War period.

107. F. H. Head to D. N. Cooley, June 21, 1866, in *ARCIA* (1866), 129–30; S. Mackey (Acting Asst. Adj. Gen.) to Col. C. H. Potter, May 2, 1866, in *ARCIA* (1866), 130; MacDonald to Pace, May 24, 1866, in "Pace Collection."

108. O'Neil, "History of the Ute Indians," 67–68, 86–91; Peterson, "Mormons, Indians, and Gentiles," 169–74, 192–94. This was especially true by 1872.

109. Tabby and other chiefs (by L. B. Kinney) to Young, May 12, 1866, quoted in Peterson, "Mormons, Indians, and Gentiles," l94, and cf. 198; MacDonald to Pace, May 24, 1866, "Pace Collection."

479

110. Richard James noted in Head to Cooley, June 21, 1866, in *ARCIA* (1866), 129–30. On Black Hawk's enterprises, see Peterson, *Black Hawk War*, 203–5. On the uproar at Uintah, conciliation, and promises, see Head to Cooley, June 21, 1866, in *ARCIA* (1866), 125, 129–30, 175–79; Young to Chiefs, May 18, 1866, mss. #2736, BYC; O'Neil, "History of the Ute Indians," 70–76; Peterson, "Mormons, Indians, and Gentiles," 191–201, and *Black Hawk War*, 260–67; Gottfredson, *Indian Depredations*, 247–53.

111. Black Hawk's *puwá* and charisma in Peterson, *Black Hawk War*, 95–100. Details of raids in Peterson, "Mormons, Indians, and Gentiles," 202–8, 226–31, and *Black Hawk War*, 203–7, 271–76, 304–9; Gottfredson, *Indian Depredations*, 213–19. On the Battle of Gravely Ford, see Gibbs, "Black Hawk's Last Raid," 99–108.

112. Peterson, "Mormons, Indians, and Gentiles," 266–68, and *Black Hawk War*, 342–44. Alma Eldredge (arresting officer), in "Diary," July 3 and August 6, 1867, 102–9. One prisoner escaped; two were killed. Eldredge describes Potter being wounded but omits that he also slit his throat. Eldredge was later charged with murder.

113. F. H. Head to N. G. Taylor, August 22, 1867, in *ARCIA* (1867), 178.

114. Reported in the *Deseret News* (Salt Lake City), August 28, 1867; mourning customs, e.g., Omer C. Stewart, "Culture Element Distributions: XVIII, Ute—Southern Paiute," *Anthropological Records* 6 (1942): 312–14.

115. Gottfredson, *Indian Depredations*, 270–76, 278–85; Peterson, "Mormons, Indians, and Gentiles," 206, 272–74; cf. *Black Hawk War*, 348–50. Shena- or *Siná-wa* or *shinawob* (god, power). See Southern Ute Tribe, *Ute Dictionary and Ute Reference Grammar* (Ignacio, CO: Ute Press, 1979), 242.

116. Peterson, "Mormons, Indians, and Gentiles," 274–75, and *Black Hawk War*, 351; O'Neil, "History of the Ute Indians," 80–81; Gibbs, "Black Hawk's Last Raid," 100–108.

117. F. H. Head to N. G. Taylor, 22 August 1867, in *ARCIA* (1867), 179.

118. O'Neil, "History of the Ute Indians," 79, 92–93; and M. J. Shelton to J. E. Tourtellotte, Supt. Indian Affairs, February 28, 1870, quoted in Peterson, "Mormons, Indians, and Gentiles," 277.

119. Peterson, "Mormons, Indians, and Gentiles," 277–79, and *Black Hawk War*, 352–58, 395–97; Gottfredson, *Indian Depredations*, 227–78.

120. Brigham Young in O. H. Irish's report of the Treaty negotiations, letter June 29, 1865, and quoted in O'Neil, "History of the Ute Indians," 65–66; cf. July 28 1866, *JD*, 11:263–66.

121. Peacock, "Diary," June 15–27, 1870; D. W. Jones, *Forty Years*, 173; Peterson, "Mormons, Indians, and Gentiles," 278–80, and *Black Hawk War*, 354–58.

122. Comments regarding identity and power loss in Peterson, *Black Hawk War*, 89–95, 155–58, and "Mormons, Indians, and Gentiles," 108–10.

123. Head to Commissioner of Indian Affairs, July 31, 1867, in *ARCIA* (1867), 181; J. E. Tourtellotte to Parker, September 20, 1870, in *ARCIA* (1870), 143–44 and *RSI* (1870), 606–7. On visiting other agencies, see Jocknick, "Special Report," September 30, 1871, in *ARCIA* (1871), 260; Thompson to H. R. Clum, October 1, 1871, in *ARCIA* (1871), 556–57; Critchlow to Walker, September 1, 1872, in *ARCIA* (1872), 293–94; Stewart, "Antero," in "Chief's List," quoting Hunt to Commissioner of Indian Affairs, November 11, 1868, in *ARCIA* (1868); Graffam to Post Adjutant at Fort Bridger, April 1, 1870; and *Deseret News*, June 4, 1870. See also O'Neil, "History of the Utes," 104–5; and Jorgensen, *Sun Dance Religion*, 38–39.

124. See Chapter 13 for additional discussion. Ghost Dance classic sources include James Mooney, *The Ghost-dance Religion* (1896; Chicago: University of Chicago Press, 1965), esp. 2–59; Weston LaBarre, *The Ghost Dance* (Garden City, NY: Doubleday, 1970).

125. *Salt Lake Herald*, May 7, 12, 18, and 29, 1871, and June 15, 1871.

126. Jones, *Forty Years*, 168–73, 184–86.

127. Ibid., 168–69, 184–86; cf. Peterson, *Black Hawk War*, 203–8, 336–37, and regarding Supt. F. H. Head's possible collusion.

128. Critchlow to Commissioner F. A. Walker, September 1, 1872, in *ARCIA* (1872), 292; J. S. Littlefield to Walker, September 30, 1872, in *ARCIA* (1872), 288.

129. Littlefield to Walker, September 30, 1872, in *ARCIA* (1872), 288; Peterson, "Mormons, Indians, and Gentiles," 287, and *Black Hawk War*, 362.

130. John Wesley Powell and G. W. Ingalls. "Report of J. W. Powell and G. W. Ingalls," in *RSI* (1873), 415.

131. Peterson, "Mormons, Indians, and Gentiles," 292, and *Black Hawk War*, 366–67; and quoting letters from George Halliday to W. B. Pace, August and September 4, 1872.

132. Gottfredson, *Indian Depredations*, 296–312; *Deseret News*, August 9, 1872; Critchlow to Walker, September 1, 1872, in *ARCIA* (1872), 293; O'Neil, "History of the Ute Indians," 97; Peterson, "Mormons, Indians, and Gentiles," 292–93, and *Black Hawk War*, 364–68.

133. Gottfredson, *Indian Depredations*, 324–30.

134. Peterson, *Black Hawk War*, 310–34, and "Mormons, Indians, and Gentiles," 231–38. See also, e.g., Nethella G. Woolsey, *The Escalante Story: A History of the Town of Escalante…1875–1964* (Springville, UT: Art City Publishing, 1964), 19; Jerry C. Roundy, *"Advised Them to Call the Place Escalante"* (Springville, UT: Art City Publishing, 2000).

135. Peterson, *Black Hawk War*, 313; Gottfredson, *Indian Depredations*, 221–27; Woolsey, *Escalante Story*, 26–27.

136. J.J. Critchlow to Clum, September 22, 1871, in *ARCIA* (1871), 545.

137. O'Neil, "History of the Ute Indians," 106.

138. Ibid., 106–7.

139. "An Act to Vacate and Sell the Present Indian Reservations in Utah Territory, and to Settle the Indians of said Territory in the Uinta Valley," Chap. 77, 38th Congress, sess. 1 (1864), 63. Cf., Lincoln's executive order, October 3, 1861, "Uintah Valley Reserve. (emphases added)

140. In Powell and Ingalls, "Report," 415–16. See also Reeve, *Making Space on the Western Frontier*, 60–62.

141. O'Neil, "History of the Ute Indians," 115.

142. John J. Critchlow to Commissioner F. A. Walker, September 1, 1872, in *ARCIA* (1872), 292; *RSI* (1872), 678; O'Neil, "History of the Utes," 105.

143. Critchlow to Commissioner, August 25, 1877, in *ARCIA* (1877), 182–83.

144. See O'Neil, "History of the Ute Indians," 115–19; Gottfredson, *Indian Depredations*, 338–43.

145. "Mormon Land Grab," report of the Grand Jury, Third Judicial District, Utah Territory, September 26, 1877, *OIA-UT*; and in *The Salt Lake Tribune*, September 29, 1877. O'Neil, "History of the Ute Indians," 118–19.

146. Critchlow to E. Hayt, Commissioner of Indian Affairs, October 26, 1877, M-234, RG-75, *OIA-UT*.

147. Critchlow to E. Hayt, Commissioner of Indian Affairs, September 26, 1877, *OIA-UT*; Critchlow to Commissioner, August 31, 1880, in *ARCIA* (1880), 150–51; O'Neil, "History of the Ute Indians," 118–19. Pardon Dodds, first Uintah agent, retired to Ashley Creek in 1868, as did two agency employees. The first family arrived in 1878. Doris K. Burton, *Utah History Encyclopedia* (online).

CHAPTER 10

1. E. H. Danforth to Commissioner of Indian Affairs, United States Office of Indian Affairs, *Annual Report of the Commissioner of Indian Affairs [ARCIA]*, (Washington, D.C.: Government Printing Office, 1887), 46; W. D. Wheeler to commissioner, *ARCIA*, 1877, 43–44. The settlement was later named Ouray.

2. For comments on Evans' campaign to rid Colorado of Indians, see Robert M. Utley, *Frontiersmen in Blue: The United States Army and the Indians, 1848–1865* (Lincoln: University of Nebraska Press, 1967), 283–97; cf. Donald J. Berthrong, *Southern Cheyennes* (Norman: University of Oklahoma, 1963), 241–42.

3. Sidney Jocknick, *Early Days on the Western Slope of Colorado, 1870–1883, inclusive* (Glorietta, NM: Rio Grande Press, 1913), 115–19; cf. Wilson Rockwell, *The Utes: A Forgotten People* (Denver: Sage Books, 1956), 104.

4. Jocknick, *Early Days*, 81–86, 103–8; P. David Smith, *Ouray, Chief of the Utes* (Ouray, CO: Wayfinder Press, 1986), 131–37.

5. Jocknick, *Early Days*, 82–86, 105–8; Smith, *Ouray*, 137.

6. Robert Delaney, *The Ute Mountain Utes* (Albuquerque: University of New Mexico Press, 1989), 32, 47–48; Delaney, *The Southern Ute People* (Phoenix: Indian Tribal Series, 1974), 52–58; "Report of the Ute Commission," *ARCIA*, 1879, 170–81 (including "Agreement with the Capote, Muache, and Weeminuche Utes," 178–81); and Acts passed March 3, 1875 (18 Stat. 420) and March 3, 1879 (20

Stat. 377), in Charles J. Kappler, comp. and ed., *Indian Affairs: Laws and Treaties* (Washington, D.C.: Government Printing Office, 1902–1938), 1:157, 1:176.

7.   Jocknick, *Early Days*, 23–24, 321; J. Thompson to commissioner, *ARCIA*, 1874, 272.

8.   On the lack of a developed war ethic, see Marvin K. Opler "The Southern Ute of Colorado," in *Acculturation in Seven American Indian Tribes*, ed. Ralph Linton (New York: Harper & Son, 1940), 123, 162–63.

9.   See, e.g., William Vickers, *Denver Republican*, quoted in Smith, *Ouray*, 150–53.

10. Dee Brown, *Bury My Heart at Wounded Knee* (New York: Bantam Books, 1972), 351, 356–58; Marshall Sprague, *Massacre: The Tragedy at White River* (Boston: Little, Brown & Co., 1957), 92, 157, 176; Jason Brockman, preface, "The Governor Frederick W. Pitkin Collection," Colorado State Archives website, retrieved 2004.

11. Pitkin to the Colorado legislature, 1876, quoted in Smith, *Ouray*, 149–50.

12. William Vickers, *Denver Republican* and *Denver Tribune*, quoted in Smith, *Ouray*, 150–53.

13. Floyd A. O'Neil, "A History of the Ute Indians until 1890" (PhD diss., University of Utah, Salt Lake City, 1973), 120; Brown, *Bury My Heart*, 364; and comments in Robert Emmitt, *The Last War Trail: the Utes and the Settlement of Colorado* (Norman: University of Oklahoma Press, 1954), 12–20.

14. Thomas F. Dawson, "Major Thompson, Chief Ouray and the Utes: An Interview, 23 May 1921," *Colorado Magazine* 7 (May 1930): 119–20; Emmitt, *Last War Trail*, 250–53; Smith, *Ouray*, 133–41.

15. *Report of the Superintendent of Indian Affairs [RSI] 1873* (Washington D.C., Government Printing Office), 465–79. Schurz quoted in Jocknick, *Early Days*, 229, 232.

16. Quoted in Brown, *Bury My Heart*, 350; cf. Sprague, *Massacre*, 92.

17. J. J. Critchlow to Walker, *ARCIA*, 1872, 292–93. Jocknick, *Early Days*, 40, 179–80, 324–25.

18. Danforth to commissioner, *ARCIA*, 1877, 46; Emmitt, *Last War Trail*, 12–20, 53; O'Neil, "History of the Ute Indians," 127–29.

19. Much literature exists regarding Nathan Meeker, the White River incident, and Ouray's role. Their research will not be duplicated here, though illustrative quotations from these sources are used, as noted. Some sources on Meeker include Sprague, *Massacre*, and Emmitt, *Last War Trail*. On Meeker, see Mark W. T. Harvey, "Misguided Reformer: Nathan Meeker among the Ute," *Colorado Heritage* (1982): 36–44; Mike Peters, "The Obituary of Nathan Meeker: Written as it Would Appear Today," *Greeley Tribune* [online], July 2, 2001; Brandi Denison, "Plowing for Providence: Nathan Meeker's Folly," in *Ute Land Religion in the American West, 1879–2009* (Omaha: University of Nebraska Press, 2017), ch. 1.

20. Nathan C. Meeker, *The Adventures of Captain Armstrong* (New York, 1856); O'Neil, "History of the Ute Indians," 129; David Boyd, *History of Greeley and the Union Colony of Colorado* (Greeley, CO, 1890); Brown, *Bury My Heart*, 354.

21. Testimony of Nicaagat, in *Ute Commission Investigation*, quoted in Brown, *Bury My Heart*, 354.

22. Meeker to commissioner, *ARCIA* (1879), 18.

23. N. C. Meeker to commissioner, *ARCIA* (1879), 19; and Meeker to Sen. Henry M. Teller, quoted in Brown, *Bury My Heart*, 355.

24. Meeker, quoted in Sprague, *Massacre*, 92.

25. Vickers, quoted in Sprague, *Massacre*, 163. Cf. Jocknick comments, in *Early Days*, 103–4. Communism had become a significant bogeyman to the free-wheeling capitalism of this period.

26. Pitkin to commissioner of Indian Affairs, *RSI* (1879), 84.

27. At Los Piños, for example, Agent Bond resorted to weekly rations in 1877, although his successor expanded the interval so rations could be supplemented with short hunts. Wheeler to commissioner, in *ARCIA* (1877), 43–45.

28. The Thornburgh and Meeker incidents are well known and remain controversial. It was highly publicized, survivors went on lecture tours, and many books and articles have been written detailing the events leading up to and the investigation following the incidents. Sources used in this summary include Emmitt, *Last War Trail*; Sprague, *Massacre*; Brown, *Bury My Heart*, 349–67; Denison, *Ute Land Religion*, ch. 1–3, and attempted reconciliation, 5–6; O'Neil, "History of the Ute Indians," 127–35; Jocknick, *Early Days*, 179–202; Robert M. Utley and Wilcomb E. Washburn, *Indian Wars* (1987; Boston: Houghton Mifflin, 2002), 270–74. Some new sources not used here include Peter Decker, *The Utes Must Go* (2004); and Robert Silbernagel, *Troubled Trails: The Meeker Affair and the Expulsion of Utes from Colorado* (2011).

Primary source documents include testimonies given in U.S. House, Ute Commission, *White River Ute Commission Investigation*, 46th Cong., 2nd Sess., H. Ex. Doc. 83, 84, and H. Misc. Doc. 38 [hereafter *Ute Commission Investigation*], and Jocknick, *Early Days*. Many sources are highly biased. For example, Hafen and Hafen, in *Colorado*, 248–50, accept the reports of Utes rampaging, setting fires, and burning farms, and slant the story to emphasize Meeker's kindly attempts to befriend and teach the Indians, their obdurateness, and his sense of danger, which "naturally" led to his requesting military aid. Others (e.g. Emmitt, *Last War Trail*) suggest the entire incident was a deliberate setup so the Utes could be expelled. Harvey, in "Misguided Reformer," suggests Meeker was simply a tragic idealist caught up in Western forces for change that no single man could control.

29. Cynthia S. Becker and P. David Smith, *Chipeta: Queen of the Utes* (Montrose, CO: Western Reflections, 2003), 96–99; Brandi Denison, *Ute Land Religion in the American West, 1879–2009* (Lincon: University of Nebraska Press, 2017), ch. 1–2. Piah led the Middle Park Utes who were among the northern Ute bands that frequented the White River agency.

30. Mary Lyons Carins, *The Pioneers* (Denver: World Press, 1946), 45–55; Danforth to commissioner, in *ARCIA* (1877), 46–48; Dawson, "Major Thompson," 121–22.

31. See, e.g., Meeker to commissioner, *ARCIA* (1879), 17–19. In an interesting interpretation, a scholar of religious studies has suggested that horses were linked to a "Ute warrior masculinity" and that farming was connected to servitude; she also argues that like British aristocracy, Utes found manual labor demeaning. See Denison, *Ute Land Religion*, 31–34, 60–61.

32. Emmitt, *Last War Trail*, 132–46, 150–54.

33. Meeker to L. A. Hayt, September 8, 1879; *RSI* (1879), 91.

34. Meeker to Pitkin, quoted in Emmitt, *Last War Trail*, 157.

35. Meeker to W. M. Byers, quoted in Emmitt, *Last War Trail*, 157–58; "William N. Byers," Denver-gov.org biographies, online. Byers founded the *Rocky Mountain News* and published a guide for Colorado-bound emigrants.

36. "T. T. Thornburgh," Arlington National Cemetery Web site, posted June 28, 2003.

37. Governor John Evans to commissioner, in *ARCIA* (1863), 121–22.

38. Meeker to Thornburgh, September 27, 1879, *RSI* (1879), 92–93; Meeker to Hayt, September 29, 1879, *RSI* (1879), 93; and *Deseret Evening News*, October 13, 1879.

39. Thornburgh to Meeker, September 28, 1879, *RSI* (1879), 93.

40. Meeker to Thornburgh, September 29, 1879, *RSI* (1879), 93; *Deseret Evening News*, October 13, 1879.

41. *Deseret Evening News*, October 7 and 9, 1879.

42. Payne to Gen. Phillip Sheridan, September 29, 1879; and James France in Rawlins to Commissioner Hayt, Washington, D.C., October 1, 1879, both quoted in *Deseret Evening News*, October 1, 1879.

43. *Denver Tribune* and the *Washington Herald*, quoted in *Deseret Evening News*, October 13 and 24, 1879.

44. Critchlow to commissioner, *ARCIA* (1880), 150–51.

45. Pitkin quoted in Smith, *Ouray*, 165.

46. *Washington Herald*, quoted in *Deseret Evening News*, October 4, 1879; cf. Brown, *Bury My Heart*, 366.

47. *RSI* (1879), 94.

48. Emmitt, *Last War Trail*, 227.

49. *Deseret Evening News*, October 8, 1879.

50. Smith, *Ouray*, 163–64; Jocknick, *Early Days*, 193–95. Becker and Smith (*Chipeta*, 105–8) argue that Chipeta did not go personally. On romantic memorialization, see Denison, "She-towitch [Tsashin] and Chipeta: Remembering the 'Good' Indian," *Ute Land Religion*, ch. 3.

51. *Denver Daily News*, October 13, 1879; *Deseret Evening News*, October 13, 1879.

52. Josephine Meeker, *Ute Massacre: Brave Miss Meeker's Captivity, and Her Account of It* (Philadelphia: Old Franklin Publishing, 1879). Captivity narratives were popular at this time. For the commercialization of captive experiences, see, e.g., Victoria Smith, *Captive Arizona, 1851–1900* (Lincoln: University of Nebraska Press, 2009). Also see Denison, "Of Outrageous Treatment: Sexual Purity, Empire, and Land," ch. 2. Denison (65–66) suggests the women were urged to fabricate the sexual assault in order to justify Ute removal.

53. See O'Neil, "History of the Ute Indians," 136; Brown, *Bury My Heart*, 366–67; *Deseret Evening News*, October 4, 1879, quoting *New York Herald Tribune*.

54. O'Neil, "History of the Ute Indians," 136; Brown, *Bury My Heart*, 366–67; *Deseret Evening News*, October 4, 1879.

55. *Deseret Evening News*, October 4, 1879, and quoting *New York Herald Tribune*.

56. *New York Herald, New York Times, Sacramento Record Union, San Francisco Chronicle, Washington Post* all quoted in *Deseret Evening News*, October 14, 1879.

57. Crook quoted in *Deseret Evening News*, October 16, 1879.

58. Stanley to commissioner Hayt, quoted in Emmitt, *Last War Trail*, 237, and Smith, *Ouray*, 165, 168.

59. Quoted in *Deseret Evening News*, October 8, 1879.

60. Ouray, quoted in Smith, *Ouray*, 172–73.

61. Smith, *Ouray*, 109, 168. The Ute hunters were killed for having guns, which was illegal at this time.

62. Smith, *Ouray*, 171; Jocknick, *Early Days*, 195–217.

63. Smith, *Ouray*, 171, and citing *The Solid Muldoon* (Ouray, CO), December, 1879.

64. Jocknick, *Early Days*, 195–217, Ute Commission reports detailed in Emmitt, *Last War Trail*, 1879; and as reported in *Deseret Evening News*, December 9, 1879.

65. *Deseret Evening News*, December 20, 1879.

66. Emmitt, *Last War Trail*, 282–84; Smith, *Ouray*, 174–76; Jocknick, *Early Days*, 195–217. Emmitt says Quinkent was jailed for two years; P. D. Smith says 348 days.

67. *Deseret Evening News*, January 2, 1880.

68. *Deseret Evening News*, December 24, 1879.

69. *Deseret Evening News*, January 2, 1880.

70. Pros and cons quoted in *Deseret Evening News*, January 2, 1880. "Atonement" in Jocknick, *Early Days*, 203–7.

71. "An act to accept and ratify the agreement submitted by the confederated bands of Ute Indians in Colorado, for the sale of their reservation, etc." ("Agreement of 1880"), in Kappler, *Indian Affairs*, 1:180–86; *Deseret Evening News*, January 10 and 11, 1880; Floyd A. O'Neil and Kathryn L. MacKay, *A History of the Uintah-Ouray Ute Lands*, American West Center Occasional Papers (Salt Lake City: University of Utah Press, n.d.), 12–13.

72. Lyman S. Tyler, *A History of Indian Policy* (Washington, D.C.: United States Department of Interior, Bureau of Indian Affairs, 1973), 95–105. Comments regarding allotment, e.g., O'Neil and MacKay, *History of the Uintah-Ouray*, 12–13; and Jocknick, *Early Days*, 207.

73. Comments on the Board of Indian Commissioners (1888), in Tyler, *History of Indian Policy*, 95.

74. Agreement of 1880; O'Neil and MacKay, *History of the Uintah-Ouray*, 12–13. Signatories included Shavano (Chavanaux), Ignacio, Alhandra, Veratzitz, Galota, Jocknick, Wass, Sowawick, and Ouray. Witnesses included W. H. Berry, Otto Mears, Henry Page (Southern Ute agent), and Charles Adams (Special Agent).

75. Smith, *Ouray*, 143–44, 175, 179–85.

76. Re-burial in 1925. Smith, *Ouray*, 183–86, 204–7; C. W. Wiegel, "The Re-burial of Chief Ouray, *Colorado Magazine* 5 (1928): 165–73.

77. *Frank Leslie's Illustrated Newspaper*, special, August 25, 1880; *Denver Tribune*, August 25, 1880; and Ouray's obituary in *Denver Tribune*, August 25, 1880, all quoted in Smith, *Ouray*, 182, 184–85, 209, cf. 108 and 168–69.

78. Smith, *Ouray*, 185–89; Jocknick, *Early Days*, 215–16; Emmitt, *Last War Trail*, 292–95; O'Neil, "History of the Ute Indians," 137–38.

79. Smith, *Ouray*, 185–89; Samuel Kirkwood quoted in Jocknick, *Early Days*, 215–16.

80. Agreement of 1880, in Kappler, *Indian Affairs*, 1:181.

81. Evidence of ongoing small-group visits, in Curtis Martin, *Ephemeral Bounty: Wickiups, Trade Goods, and the Final Years of the Autonomous Ute* (Salt Lake City: University of Utah Press, 2016). Piah and his descendants were later prominent among the Ute Mountain Utes.

82. U.S. Congress, *Ute Indians, A Special Report to the Congress*, vol. 2; Agreement of 1880; O'Neil, "History of the Ute Indians," 148–51.

83. Agreement of 1880, emphasis added. See also Emmitt, *Last War Trail*, 292–95; O'Neil, "History of the Ute Indians," 137–38, and 148–51 citing the *Ute Commission* report (1880).

84. *Ute Commission* report (1880), in O'Neil, "History of the Ute Indians," 148–51. Mears's defense in Smith, *Ouray*, 189–90; and see Jocknick, *Early Days*, 218–21. Andrew Jackson justified Indian removal in 1830, using a similar rationale.

85. O'Neil, "History of the Ute Indians," 150–51; Rockwell, *The Utes: A Forgotten People*, 171–72; Jock-nick, *Early Days*, 210–11, 218–21.

86. McKenzie, quoted in Emmitt, *Last War Trail*, 292–93.

87. Quoted in Emmitt, *Last War Trail*, 292–95; cf. Jocknick, *Early Days*, 221–26.

88. Jocknick, *Early Days*, 219, 258. This included various irrigation projects. See "Grand Valley Project," Bureau of Reclamation, https://www.usbr.gov/ projects/index.php?id=464; and "Gunnison Tunnel," Bureau of Reclamation Historic Dams and Reclamation Projects, https://www.nps.gov/nr/testing/ ReclamationDamsAndWaterProjects/Gunnison_Tunnel.html.

89. *Ute Commission* report (1880), in O'Neil, "History of the Ute Indians," 151; and Smith, *Ouray*, 192–93.

90. Quoted in Smith, *Ouray*, 193.

91. See, e.g., Jocknick, *Early Days*, 262–68, 282–88, 299–303, 326–28.

485

✿

CHAPTER 11

1. H. P. Myton to commissioner of Indian Affairs, in United States Office of Indian Affairs, *Annual Report of the Commissioner of Indian Affairs* [*ARCIA*] (Washington, D.C.: Government Printing Office, 1899), 352.

2. See, e.g., Louise Lamphere, "The Problem of Membership in the Southern Ute Tribe," Research report #41, Tri-Ethnic Research Project (University of Colorado, 1963); Southern Ute Tribe website, home.

3. On the removal from New Mexico, see "Report of the Ute Commission," *ARCIA* (1879), 170–81, including "Agreement with the Capote, Mouache, and Weeminuche Utes" (178–81); and Acts passed March 3, 1875 (18 Stat. 420) and March 3, 1879 (20 Stat. 377), in Charles J., Kappler, comp. and ed., *Indian Affairs: Laws and Treaties* (Washington, D.C.: Government Printing Office, 1902–1938), 1:157, 176; cf. New Mexico Ute agency reports in *ARCIA*, 1873–1878. See also Robert Delaney, *The Ute Mountain Utes* (Albuquerque: University of New Mexico Press, 1989), 32, 47–48; Delaney, *The Southern Ute People* (Phoenix: Indian Tribal Series, 1974), 52–58.

4. See, e.g., H. Page to commissioner, *ARCIA* (1881), 22–23; Stolltsteimer to commissioner, *ARCIA* (1887), 50.

5. Robert S. McPherson, *As If the Land Owned Us: An Ethnohistory of the White Mesa Utes* (Salt Lake City: University of Utah Press, 2011), 151–53, 164, 167–69.

6. Robert S. McPherson, *A History of San Juan County: In the Palm of Time* (Salt Lake City: Utah Historical Society and San Juan Commissioner, 1995), 49–72, and 145–69; McPherson, *As If the Land Owned Us*. Cf. Albert Lyman, *Indians and Outlaws: Settling of the San Juan Frontier* (Salt Lake City: Bookcraft, 1962); and Lyman, *The Outlaw of Navaho Mountain* (Salt Lake City: Deseret Book, 1963).

    Although McPherson argues the term *Weenuche* Ute is most correct, because *Weeminuche* was used in contemporary literature and is currently used by the Ute Mountain Ute tribe, it is used here.

7. McPherson, *As If the Land Owned Us*, 151–52.

8. Sheberetch and Weeminuches appear to have been closely related, undoubtedly interrelated through complex networks of intermarriage and territorial overlay. See comments in McPherson, *As If the Land Owned Us*, 84–85.

9. Duane A. Smith, "A Last Rush to Eden: The Settlement of Colorado's Ute Strip," *Our Public Lands* 30 (Spring 1980): 18–19; Lyman, *Indians and Outlaws*; Rusty Salmon and Robert S. McPherson, "Cow-boys, Indians, and Conflict: The Pinhook 'Draw' Fight, 1881," *Utah Historical Quarterly* 69 (Winter 2001): 8–9; McPherson, *History of San Juan County*, 146–50; and stock numbers in *As If the Land Owned Us*, 154.

10. See Margaret Bearnson's "Moab," Robert S. McPherson's "Monticello" and "Blanding," in *Utah History Encyclopedia*, ed. Allan Kent Powell (Salt Lake City: University of Utah Press, 1994) [online versions], at http://www.uen.org/utah_history_encyclopedia/; Leonard J. Arrington and Davis Bit-ton, *Saints Without Halos* (Salt Lake City: Signature Books, 1981), 95; and Lyman's colorful account of the Mormon "Peace Mission," in *Indians and Outlaws*.

11. "Crucified," in Lyman, *Indians and Outlaws*, 37; Salmon and McPherson, "Cowboys, Indians, and Conflict," 9–10; and quoting *Dolores News*, May 22, 1880, and May 29, 1880. See also McPherson, *History of San Juan County*, 146–51, and *As If the Land Owned Us*, 151–85.

12. Salmon and McPherson, "Cowboys, Indians, and Conflict," 10–11 and notes; Forbes Parkhill, *The Last of the Indian Wars: The Final, Heroic Fight of the American Indian for Independence* (New York: Collier Books, 1961), 31; Charles S. Peterson, *Look to the Mountains: Southeastern Utah and the La Sal National Forest* (Provo, UT: Brigham Young University Press, 1975), 58, 66–67.

13. Platte D. Lyman, "Journal" [microfilm], May 6 and 15, 1881, L. Tom Perry Special Collections, Brigham Young University, Provo, Utah.

14. "Whip cowboys" in McPherson, *As If the Land Owned Us*, 195. See also Salmon and McPherson, "Cowboys, Indians, and Conflict," 12–13; Lyman, *Indians and Outlaws*, 39–42.

15. Lyman, "Journal," May 6 and May 15, 1881; Salmon and McPherson, "Cowboys, Indians, and Conflict," 12–13; McPherson, *As If the Land Owned Us*, 136–51; Lyman, *Indians and Outlaws*, 39–42.

16. Details in Salmon and McPherson, "Cowboys, Indians, and Conflict," 10–27, esp. 14; and McPherson, *As If the Land Owned Us*, 136–51.

17. Salmon and McPherson, "Cowboys, Indians, and Conflict," 15–17; and McPherson, *As If the Land Owned Us*, 142–43, 159.

18. Details vary in different accounts. See Salmon and McPherson, "Cowboys, Indians, and Conflict," 18–25; and McPherson, *As If the Land Owned Us*, 144, 148. Also killed were two Moab herdsmen who stumbled into the attack.

19. Salmon and McPherson, "Cowboys, Indians, and Conflict," 25–26; Parkhill, *Last of the Indian Wars*, 31–33.

20. Salmon and McPherson, "Cowboys, Indians, and Conflict," 18–25. The 9th and 10th Cavalries were made up of African American soldiers with white officers.

21. Salmon and McPherson, "Cowboys, Indians, and Conflict," 27–28; Lyman, *Indians and Outlaws*, 39–42, and *Outlaw of Navaho Mountain* (Posey).

22. McPherson, *As If the Land Owned Us*, 155–57. Cf. other versions in Parkhill, *Last of the Indian Wars*, 33–34; Peterson, *Look to the Mountains*, 69–71; Wilson Rockwell, *The Utes: A Forgotten People* (Denver: Sage Books, 1956), 225–28; and Lyman, *Indians and Outlaws*, 65.

23. McPherson, *As If the Land Owned Us*, 158–62; Peterson, *Look to the Mountains*, 70, and citing Sam Todd, "A Pioneer Experience"; cf. a biased but colorful account in Lyman, *Indians and Outlaws*, 65–68. Graves mark the site of the fight.

24. Parkhill, *Last of the Indian Wars*, 33–34.

25. Petition quoted in Parkhill, *Last of the Indian Wars*, 36; "Joint Memorial to Congress for the Removal of the southern Ute Indians from Colorado," quoted in its entirety in Delaney, *Ute Mountain Utes*, 63–64. See also Smith, "A Last Rush to Eden," 18–20.

26. McPherson, *As if the Land Owned Us*, 165–66; Parkhill, *Last of the Indian Wars*, 38–42. For Weeminuche oral traditions, see McPherson (above) and Delaney, *Ute Mountain Utes*, 65–68.

27. Parkhill, *Last of the Indian Wars*, 38.

28. Stollsteimer to commissioner, *ARCIA* (1885), 15.

29. McPherson, *As If the Land Owned Us*, 166.

30. Sidney Jocknick, *Early Days On the Western Slope of Colorado, 1870–1883* (Glorietta, NM: Rio Grande Press, 1913), 378–80; Frances Leon Swadesh, "The Southern Utes and Their Neighbors, 1877–1926" (master's thesis, University of Colorado, Boulder, 1962), 14–16; and Frances Leon [Swadesh] Quintana, *Ordeal of Change: The Southern Utes and their Neighbors* (Walnut Creek: AltaMira Press, 2004; Gregory C. Thompson, "The Unwanted Indians: The Southern Utes in Southeastern Utah," *Utah Historical Quarterly* 49 (Spring 1981): 193–94.

31. "Not for nothing" in McPherson, *As If the Land Owned Us*, 179–80; cf. Quintana, *Ordeal of Change*, 21–22, 107–8. For regimentation, see Thomas A. Britten, *American Indians in World War I: At War and At Home* (Albuquerque: University of New Mexico Press, 1997), 65–66; Craig H. Blackman, "The Story of the Ute and the Grand Junction Indian School," *Whispering Wind* (Cengage Learning, 2008), available online from The Free Library.

32. See, e.g., see agency reports for the Southern Ute agency, in *ARCIA* (1887), 14–15; (1888), 23–24; (1889), 127–29. See also Meyer to commissioner, *ARCIA* (1898), 139–40, when agent William Meyer recommended sending Ute students to the Fort Lewis boarding school.

33. Indian Homestead Act of 1875 and Dawes Severalty or General Allotment Act of 1887 are in Kappler, *Indian Affairs: Laws*, 1:23 and 1:33–36.

34. Parkhill, *Last of the Indian Wars*, 20; Richard K. Young, *The Ute Indians of Colorado in the Twentieth Century* (Norman: University of Oklahoma Press, 1997), 60–61, 300.

35. G. A. Cornish to commissioner, in *ARCIA* (1898), 295.

36. David Hurst Thomas, *Skull Wars: Kennewick Man, Archaeology, and the Battle for Native American Identity* (New York: Basic Books, 2000), 44–51; Lyman S. Tyler, *A History of Indian Policy* (Washington, D.C.: United States Department of Interior, Bureau of Indian Affairs, 1973), 95–107, esp. 99, 104, and quoting Senator John Pendleton of Ohio and Theodore Roosevelt (1901), arguing for individualization of money disbursements, too. See also Floyd O'Neil, in *Indian Self-Rule: First Hand Accounts of Indian-White Relations from Roosevelt to Reagan*, ed. Kenneth R. Philp (Salt Lake City: Howe Brothers, 1986), 31–32.

37. Frances E. Leupp, *The Latest Phase of the Southern Ute Question: A Report* (Philadelphia: Indian Rights Association, 1895), 4–6, 27–29; Thompson, "The Unwanted Indians," 196–98; Smith, "Last Rush to Eden," 18–20.

38. Leupp, "The Southern Ute Question," 4–7, esp. 6–7; Thompson, "The Unwanted Indians," 196–98; Quintana, *Ordeal of Change*, 17–23; Delaney, *Ute Mountain Utes*, 70–71; McPherson, *As If the Land Owned Us*, 181–84.

39. Leupp, *The Southern Ute Question*, 11–12; McPherson, *As If the Land Owned Us*, 184–93; Quintana, *Ordeal of Change*, 15, 21.

40. Thompson, "The Unwanted Indians," 200–202. McPherson, *As If the Land Owned Us*, 184, 195. Regarding America's growing cattle industry, see Lewis Atherton, *The Cattle Kings* (1961; Lincoln: University of Nebraska Press, 1972).

41. McPherson, *History of San Juan*, 152; McPherson, *As If the Land Owned Us*, 186–99; Lyman, *Indians and Outlaws*, 133–34.

42. "An act to disapprove the treaty…with the Southern Ute Indians to be removed to the Territory of Utah…[and] providing for settling them down in severalty, etc." *Hunter Bill* (1895), in Kappler, *Indian Affairs: Laws*, 1:555–57. See also Thompson, "The Unwanted Indians," 200–203; McPherson, *As If the Land Owned Us*, 198.

43. Leupp, *The Southern Ute Question*, 7–21, 37–39, and passim; Thompson, "The Unwanted Indians," 198–203.

44. Francis Leupp, *Southern Ute Question*, 17, 37. Regarding Ignacio, see esp. Delaney, *Ute Mountain Utes*, 75.

45. Jocknick, *Early Days*, 378–80; Swadesh, "Southern Utes," 20–24; Quintana, *Ordeal of Change*, 22.

46. *Hunter Bill* (1895), Sec. 3, in Kappler, *Indian Affairs*, 1:556. See also Leupp, *Southern Ute Question*, 20, 29–33, 36–37; McPherson, *As If the Land Owned Us*, 199–202.

47. Quintana, *Ordeal of Change*, 29–31. On attempts at irrigation, see, e.g., Southern Ute agency, *ARCIA* (1887), 14–15; (1888), 23; (1889), 127, 139–40.

48. Quintana, *Ordeal of Change*, 23–25; Smith, "A Last Rush to Eden," 20–22; Young, *Ute Indians of Colorado*, 36–38. "Fertile portions" in "A Wild Rush for Ute Lands," *Denver Times*, May 4, 1899.

49. Jorgensen, *Sun Dance Religion*, 62–64; Swadesh, "Southern Utes," 16–18; and Quintana, *Ordeal of Change*, 19–20, 23–25, 109. "Ennobling," in Myton to commissioner, *ARCIA* (1889), 351; "burn crops," in Stollsteimer to commissioner, *ARCIA* (1887), 16.

50. Swadesh, "Southern Utes," 41–49; cf. Quintana, *The Ordeal of Change*, 27–42; Jorgensen, *Sun Dance Religion*, 63. On the assimilation campaign, see Frederick E. Hoxie, *A Final Promise: The Campaign to Assimilate the Indians, 1880–1920* (Lincoln: University of Nebraska, 1984); and Thomas, *Skull Wars*, 44–51.

51. Mesa Verde created June 29, 1906 (*U.S. Statutes at Large*, 34:616); compensatory acreage given to the Weeminuche on June 30, 1913. U.S. Congress, House Appropriations for 1914, 63rd Cong., 1st Sess., June 30, 1913, H.R. 1917, both in Kappler, *Indian Affairs*, 3:566–68. See also McPherson, *As If the Land Owned Us*, 206–7.

487

CHAPTER 12

1. Thompson to commissioner of Indian Affairs, in United States Office of Indian Affairs, *Annual Report of the Commissioner of Indian Affairs [ARCIA]* (Washington, D.C.: Government Printing Office, 1874), 271–73; and J. B. Thompson to commissioner, in *ARCIA* (1871), 555–57. Ute views reported by Jocknick in *Early Days*, 21–25. Thompson later moved to Hayden on the Yampa and was involved in helping to resolve the Meeker incident.

2. See, Judy Knight-Frank (Piah's great-granddaughter), excerpts of testimony before Senate, 24 June 1998, in "What Others Are Saying," Animas-La Plata Web Site, maintained by the Ute Mountain and Southern Ute Tribes; signatures on the "Treaty of 1868," and unratified "Agreement of 1879." See also Omer C. Stewart, "Piah," in his working notes, "Data on the Identification and Group Leadership of Ute Indian Chiefs ["Ute Chiefs List"], tms., prepared for Dockets 44–45, U.S. Indian Claims Commission, 1952, in the Omer C. Stewart Collection, Norlin Library Archives, University of Colorado, Boulder, and in Special Collections, Marriot Library, University of Utah, Salt Lake City.

3. J. F. Minnis to commissioner, *ARCIA* (1882), 292; Southern Ute agents said much the same.

4. P. H. Sheridan to commissioner, in *ARCIA* (May 1, 1882).

5. "It is hereby ordered that the following tract of country, in the Territory of Utah, be…withheld from sale and set apart as a reservation for the Uncompahgre Utes…" Signed Chester A. Arthur, January 5, 1882.

6. Gary Lee Walker, "A History of Fort Duchesne, Including Fort Thornburgh: The Military Presence in Frontier Uinta Basin" (PhD diss., Brigham Young University, 1992), 40–139. See also Floyd A. O'Neil, "The Reluctant Suzerainty," *Utah Historical Quarterly* 39 (1971): 187; and O'Neil, "A History of the Ute Indians until 1890" (PhD diss., University of Utah, 1973), 159.

7. Walker, "History of Fort Duchesne," 204–9; O'Neil, "Reluctant Suzerainty," 134; and An Act Granting the Utah Midland Railway Company the Right of Way, etc., 49th Cong., 2nd sess., March 3, 1887, in Kappler, *Indian Affairs: Laws and Treaties*, 1:255–56.

8. J. J. Critchlow to commissioner, *ARCIA* (1881), 157.

9. United States, Annual *Report of the Secretary of the Interior (RSI)* (Washington, D.C.: Government Printing Office), October 24, 1881, 2. Cf. similar situations with southern Ute bands in 1857 and 1873; e.g., McPherson, *History of San Juan County*, 60–61; Thelma S. Guild and Harvey L. Carter, *Kit Carson* (Lincoln: University of Nebraska Press, 1984), 212; and Thomas Dunlay, *Kit Carson and the Indians* (Lincoln: University of Nebraska Press, 200), 199.

10. E. Davis to commissioner, *ARCIA* (1885), 180–81; Critchlow to Commissioner, *ARCIA* (1882), 149–50; Jorgensen, *Sun Dance Religion*, 49–50; and esp. R. Warren Metcalf, *Termination's Legacy: The Discarded Indians of Utah* (Lincoln: University of Nebraska Press, 2002), and Metcalf, "Lambs of Sacrifice: Termination, the Mixed-Blood Utes, and the Problem of Indian Identity," *Utah Historical Quarterly* 64 (Fall 1996): 322–43. Uncompahgre band has repeatedly argued that they should be a separate tribe with a separate tribal council, most recently in 2017. See "Uncompahgre Band's Petition to Pursue Certain Claims," *Ute Bulletin* 52, no. 2 (October 20, 2017).

11. Jorgensen, *Sun Dance Religion*, 49; Walker, "History of Fort Duchesne," 157–62; and, e.g., Davis to commissioner, *ARCIA* (1885), 179; Byrnes to commissioner, *ARCIA* (1887, 1888, 1889); and *RSI* (1886), 128. This was the Meeker Pension Fund.

12. E. E. White, *Experiences of a Special Indian Agent* (1893; Norman: University of Oklahoma Press, 1965), 91–94; cf. *RSI* (1886), 127–29; White remembered the number as 360 names. See also White to commissioner, in *ARCIA* (1886), 201; McKewan (clerk) to White, in *ARCIA* (1886), 228–29.

13. T. A. Byrnes to commissioner, in *ARCIA* (1887), 201; W. A. McKewan (clerk) to White, in *ARCIA* (1886), 228–29.

14. Agents lodged increasingly serious complaints about the whiskey trade. See, e.g., Critchlow to commissioner, in *ARCIA* (1881), 157; G. A. Cornish to commissioner, in *ARCIA* (1898), 293.

15. *RSI* (1886), 127–29; and Report of Major E. G. Bush to Adjutant General's Office, War Department, "Report of Investigation of Ouray Indian Agency," June 12, 1886, Records of United States Army Continental Command, 1871–1945, RG 394, National Archives and Records Administration, Washington, D.C. See also McKewan to White, regarding shamanism and killings, in *ARCIA* (1886), 226–27.

16. *RSI* (1886), 127–29; Bush, "Report of Investigation."

17. Special Orders No. 99, Department of the Platte, August 7, 1886, RG 394; location of the fort requested August 31, 1887, and approved by Grover Cleveland, September 1, 1887. Executive orders pertaining to the Uintah reservation in Kappler, *Indian Affairs,* 1:900–901. For more details, see Walker, "History of Fort Duchesne," 165–73; O'Neil, "History of the Ute Indians," 173, 175–76; and O'Neil, "Reluctant Suzerainty," 137.

18. White, *Experiences of a Special Indian Agent,* 122–28.

19. Ibid., 138–39.

20. Walker, "History of Fort Duchesne," 140–42; White, *Experiences of a Special Indian Agent,* 147–48. For more on the 9th and 10th Cavalries, see William H. Leckie, *The Buffalo Soldiers: A Narrative of the Negro Cavalry in the West* (Norman: University of Oklahoma Press, 1967); William A. Dobak and Thomas D. Phillips, *The Black Regulars: 1866–1898* (Norman: University of Oklahoma Press, 2001); Ronald G. Coleman, "The Buffalo Soldiers: Guardians of the Uintah Frontier 1886–1901," *Utah Historical Quarterly* 47 (Fall 1979), 421–39. Note: black (*túu*) nigger (*nigíci*), or *túu-mericats,* "black American." See Southern Ute Tribe, *Ute Dictionary and Ute Reference Grammar* (Ignacio, CO: Ute Press, 1979), 2:192, 220, 258.

21. Walker, "History of Fort Duchesne," 165–80, 288; *RSI* (1886), 128.

22. Walker, "History of Fort Duchesne," 180–84, 210–13.

23. See Ibid., 193–201.

24. Ibid., 244, 307–8, 321–22; Walker, personal communication with author, December 1997.

25. Walker, "History of Fort Duchesne," 288–308, 315–22, and quoting from *The Vernal Express,* December 1 and 29, 1892; Waugh to T. J. Morgan, commissioner of Indian Affairs, October 13, 1892, RG 394; Randlett to Asst. Adjutant General, Department of the Platte, October 18, 1892, RG 394; and Walker, personal communication with author, December 1997. The secret agent was never named in Nutter's correspondence.

26. Details of this intrigue are in Walker, "History of Fort Duchesne," 288–308, 315–22, and quoting from the Nutter papers; Walker, personal communication with author, spring 1998.

27. Military reserve approved September 1, 1887. See Kappler, *Indian Affairs: Laws,* 1:900–901.

28. Walker, "History of Fort Duchesne," 227–229; Robert L. Foster, "The Duchesne Strip: Part I, The Whiskey Tent Treaty," *True West* (August 1988), 26–29; Mile P. Romney, "Utah's Cinderella Minerals: The Nonmetallics," *Utah Historical Quarterly* 31 (July 1963): 220–34; Byrnes to commissioner, in *ARCIA* (1889), 280.

29. See, e.g., J. F. Randlett to commissioner, in *ARCIA* (1897), 285; Cornish, in *ARCIA* (1898), 293; Myton, in *ARCIA* (1899), 351; W. A. Mercer, in *ARCIA* (1903), 328; and Walker, "History of Fort Duchesne," 227–37. Tabby Weep, in Robert L. Foster, "The Duchesne Strip: Part II, A Lawless Land," *True West* (September 1988): 52–56.

30. Byrnes to commissioner, *ARCIA* (1888), 218–19, and *ARCIA* (1889), 279–80; Floyd A. O'Neil and Kathryn L. MacKay, *A History of the Uintah-Ouray Ute Lands,* American West Center Occasional Papers (Salt Lake City: University of Utah Press, n.d.), 15–16, 23–25.

31. O'Neil and MacKay, *History of the Uintah-Ouray,* 24; Kathryn L. MacKay, "The Strawberry Valley Reclamation Project and the Opening of the Uintah Indian Reservation," *Utah Historical Quarterly* 50 (Winter 1982): 68–89.

32. Robert S. McPherson discusses commercial overhunting by pre-reservation Utes and Navajos in *The Northern Navajo Frontier: 1860–1900: Expansion through Adversity* (Albuquerque: University of New Mexico Press, 1988), 60–62. See also McPherson, *History of San Juan County,* 148, 151; and McPherson, *As If the Land Owned Us,* 171–73.

33. The Colorow incident is detailed in Byrnes to commissioner, in *ARCIA* (1887), 200–204; Byrnes to commissioner, in *RSI* (1887), 201–4; and Byrnes to commissioner, in *RSI* (1888), 221. See also John H. Nankivell, "Colorado's Last Indian War," *Colorado Magazine* 10 (1933): 222–34; P. D. Smith, *Ouray, Chief of the Utes* (Ouray, CO: Wayfinder Press, 1986), 196–97. The camp was that of Enny Colorow, Colorow's son.

34. Nankivell, "Colorado's Last Indian War," 222–34; Smith, *Ouray,* 196–97.

35. Byrnes to commissioner of Indian Affairs, in *RSI* (1887), 201–4; Byrnes to commissioner, August 15, 1888, in *RSI* (1888), 221; Byrnes to commissioner, in *ARCIA* (1887), 203–4; "shot on sight" in Byrnes to commissioner, in *ARCIA* (1889), 281–82. On continuing requests for restitution, see Byrnes to commissioner, in *ARCIA* (1888), 221; and *ARCIA* (1889), 282.

36. "War of 1897," in J. Monaghan, *Moffat County Interviews, Book I, 1933–34*, Pamphlet 356, Doc. 1–73 (Denver: State Historical Society of Colorado, 1934), 180–92, 261–66, 174–79. Game laws, *Ward vs. Race Horse*, 163 U.S. 504 (1896).

37. "War of 1897," 180–92, 261–66, 174–79. Note that some covert, small-scale hunting and family visits did continue, as evidenced by numerous small hunting or medicine camps dated after 1897. See Curtis Martin, *Ephemeral Bounty: Wickiups, Trade Goods, and the Final Years of the Autonomous Ute* (Salt Lake City: University of Utah Press, 2016).

38. Brandi Denison, *Ute Land Religion in the American West, 1879–2009* (Lincoln: University of Nebraska Press and American Philosophical Society, 2017), 222–27, 235–44. Note that Southern Utes were able to negotiate with Colorado for these rights. See ch. 18, herein.

39. Jorgensen, *Sun Dance Religion*, 56–57; and see Byrnes to commissioner, in *ARCIA* (1887), 199; *ARCIA* (1888), 219–20; "squatted" in Cornish to commissioner, *ARCIA* (1898), 296.

40. Fanny Weeks to Agent Byrnes, in *ARCIA* (1888), 219–20; Byrnes to commissioner, in *ARCIA* (1887), 199; Cornish to commissioner, in *ARCIA* (1898), 293, and "fight first," 296; O. M. Waddell to C. G. Hall, acting agent, in *ARCIA* (1904), 348–49.

41. Byrnes to commissioner of Indian Affairs, September 1889, 282; Blackman, "Grand Junction Indian School" (2008).

42. Byrnes to commissioner, in *ARCIA* (1887), 199; *ARCIA* (1888), 219–20; *ARCIA* (1889), 280; and see Jorgensen, *Sun Dance Religion*, 56–57.

43. Cornish to commissioner, in *ARCIA* (1898), 293–95; Superintendent E. O. Hughes to commissioner, in *ARCIA* (1901), 382; Jorgensen, *Sun Dance Religion*, 56–57; Waddell to C. G. Hall, acting agent, in *ARCIA* (1904), 348–49.

44. See, e.g., Byrnes to commissioner, in *ARCIA* (1887), 199–200; *ARCIA* (1888), 218; and *ARCIA* (1889), 281. Byrnes did recognize they had little else to do.

45. See, e.g., H. J. Curtis (Uintah School) to E. Reel, Superintendent of Indian Schools, in *ARCIA* (1898), 296; E. O. Hughes (Uintah School) to commissioner, in *ARCIA* (1901), 382–83; Charley Wyàskex, personal communication, 1979. If students at Whiterocks students spoke Ute, teachers washed their mouths out with lye soap.

46. Randlett to commissioner, in *ARCIA* (1897), 286–87; H. P. Myton to commissioner, in *ARCIA* (1902), 353; Jorgensen, *Sun Dance Religion*, 54.

47. See, e.g., Randlett to commissioner, in *ARCIA* (1897), 286–87; Cornish to commissioner, in *ARCIA* (1898), 294–95; H. P. Myton, in *ARCIA* (1899), 351.

48. Theodore Roosevelt, "A Proclamation" adding and reserving Uintah Reservation lands to the Uintah Forest Reserve, in Kappler, *Indian Affairs*, 3:602–3.

49. "1880 Agreement," in Kappler, *Indian Affairs: Laws*, 1:181. O'Neil and MacKay, *History of the Uintah-Ouray*, 19; and U.S. Congress, House, *Changing the Boundary of the Uncompahgre Reservation*, 51st Cong., 1st and 2nd sess., 1890. H. Rept. 3305 and 3395, 3.

50. O'Neil and MacKay, *History of the Uintah-Ouray*, 19–21, and quoting U.S. Congress, *Changing the Boundary* (1890).

51. On Uncompahgre allotments, see U. S. Congress, *Appropriations for Fiscal Year, 1895*, 53rd Cong., 2nd Sess., August 15, 1894, and U.S. Congress, *Appropriations for Fiscal year, 1898*, 55th Cong., 1st Sess., June 7, 1897, both in Kappler, *Indian Affairs*, 1:546, 1:621; O'Neil and MacKay, *History of the Uintah-Ouray*, 19–21; and Cornish to commissioner, in *ARCIA* (1898), 294.

52. U.S. Congress, 1897, *Appropriations, 1898*, in Kappler, *Indian Affairs: Laws*, 1:621. See "An Act to Disapprove [a] Treaty," in Kappler, *Indian Affairs: Laws*, 1:55.6; Cornish to commissioner, in *ARCIA* (August 1898), 294.

53. O'Neil and MacKay review the allotments in *History of the Uintah-Ouray*, 20–21. See also Jorgensen, *Sun Dance Religion*, 52–53.

54. O'Neil and MacKay, *History of the Uintah-Ouray*, 20–23; Cornish to commissioner, in *ARCIA* (1898), 294–95, and personal communication with members of the Uncompahgre and White River bands, summer 1979.

55. "An Act for the Appointment of a Commission to Make Allotments...upon the Uintah Indian Reservation," 55th Cong., 2nd Sess., June 4, 1898, in Kappler, *Indian Affairs: Laws*, 1:642–43; Cornish to commissioner, in *ARCIA* (1898), 294; H. P. Myton to commissioner, in *ARCIA* (1899), 351.

56. Ross Griffin to commissioner, January 7, 1899, quoted in O'Neil and MacKay, *History of the Uintah-Ouray*, 26; Myton to commissioner, in *ARCIA* (1899), 351.

57. Comment of Indian Commissioner to W. A. Jones during Senate hearings, quoted in O'Neil and MacKay, *History of the Uintah-Ouray*, 26.

58. U.S. Congress, Senate, *Leasing of Indian Lands* (1902), quoted in O'Neil and MacKay, *History of the Uintah-Ouray*, 26–29. Also see O'Neil, "Reluctant Suzerainty," 138–39; and MacKay, "The Strawberry Valley Reclamation Project."

59. "Act for the Appointment of a Commission to Make Allotments" (1902); O'Neil and MacKay, *History of the Uintah-Ouray*, 29.

60. *Lone Wolf v. Hitchcock*, 187 U.S. 553 (1903), and in Kappler, *Indian Affairs: Laws*, 1:1058–65.

61. O'Neil and MacKay, *History of the Uintah-Ouray*, 29; "Appropriations for Fiscal Year, 1902," 57th Cong., 1st Sess., May 27, 1902, with amendments providing for grazing lands, June 19, 1902, in Kappler, *Indian Affairs: Laws*, 1:753, and 1:799–800.

62. McLaughlin, Minutes of Councils, May 18–23, 1903, quoted in O'Neil and MacKay, *History of the Uintah-Ouray*, 30; *Laws Relating to Indian Affairs, Public Acts [1903]*, 57th Cong., 2nd Sess., 1903, in Kappler, *Indian Affairs*, 3:17–19.

63. U.S. Congress, House, "Grant of Lands for Use of Certain Indians," 58th Cong., May 30, 1903; Happy Jack quoted in O'Neil and MacKay, *History of the Uintah-Ouray*, 30.

64. O'Neil and MacKay, *History of the Uintah-Ouray*, 29–31; Jorgensen, *Sun Dance Religion*, 54–55. The commission began making allotments April 3, 1905; Hall to commissioner, in *ARCIA* (1905), 353–54.

65. "Act for the Appointment of a Commission to Make Allotments" [1902], also various laws, appropriations, and modifications by the 55th and 57th Cong. [1898, 1902, 1903], in Kappler, *Indian Affairs*, 1:686, 753, 799–800, and 3:17–19.

66. Porter J. Preston and Charles A. Engle, "Report of Advisors on Irrigation on Indian Reservations," June 8, 1928, and U.S. Congress, Senate, *Survey of Conditions in the United States* (1930), both quoted in O'Neil and MacKay, *History of the Uintah-Ouray*, 32.

67. O'Neil, "Reluctant Suzerainty," 140.

68. MacKay, "The Strawberry Valley Reclamation Project"; O'Neil and MacKay, *History of the Uintah-Ouray*, 33; Theodore Roosevelt, "A Proclamation by the President," withdrawing land for the reservoir site, August 3, 1905, in Kappler, *Indian Affairs*, 3:610–12. See also Uintah-Wasatch-Cache National Forest, "A Century of Stewardship: Strawberry Valley Management Area," Forest Service Web site, http://www.fs.usda.gov/detail/ uwcnf/learning/history-culture/?cid=stelprdb5052907 (March 16, 2013). On the race to build reclamation projects, see Marc Reisner, *Cadillac Desert: The American West and its Disappearing Water* (New York: Penguin Books, 1986).

69. O'Neil and MacKay, *History of the Uintah-Ouray*, 33–35.

70. O'Neil and MacKay, *History of the Uintah-Ouray*, 33–35; Fiscal appropriation bill, 59th Cong. 1st sess., June 21, 1906 (and continuing appropriation bills thereafter), in Kappler, *Indian Affairs*, 3:243.

71. Coulson Wright and Geneva Wright, "Indian-White Relations in the Uintah Basin," *Utah Humanities Review* 2 (1945): 334; Jorgensen, *Sun Dance Religion*, 147. Agent Myton reported the 1899 requests by "Utes," undoubtedly Uintahs.

72. Floyd A. O'Neil, "The Anguished Odyssey: The Flight of the Utes, 1906–1908," *Utah Historical Quarterly* 36 (1968): 315–37; Jeffrey D. Nichols, "Ute Trek to South Dakota in 1906 Ended in Disappointment," *History to Go* website, maintained by the State of Utah, posted June 1995.

73. Much literature has been published on various aspects of "Indian" identity. Some of the sources used here include Circe Sturm, "Blood Politics, Racial Classification, and Cherokee National Identity," *American Indian Quarterly* 22 (Winter/Spring 1998): 230–57; and Sturm, *Becoming Indian: The Struggle over Cherokee Identity in the Twenty-first Century* (Santa Fe: School for Advanced Research Press, 2010); Joanne Barker, "Indian™ U.S.A.," *Wicazo Sa Review* 18 (Spring 2003): 36–42; Eva Marie Garroutte, "The Racial Formation of American Indians: Negotiating Legitimate Identities within Tribal and Federal Law," *American Indian Quarterly* 25 (Spring 2001): 224–39; David L. Beaulieu, "Curly Hair and Big Feet: Physical Anthropology and the Implementation of Land Allotment on the White Earth Chippewa Reservation," *American Indian Quarterly* 18 (Autumn 1984): 281–82, 286–89.

74. Beaulieu, "Curly Hair," 288–89; James A. Clifton, "Alternate Identities and Cultural Frontiers," in *Being and Becoming Indian: Biographical Studies of North American Frontiers*, ed. James A. Clifton (Chicago: Dorsey Press, 1989), 23–27.

491

75. See, e.g., Barker, "Indian™ U.S.A.," 28–30; and Chapter 1, herein.
76. See, e.g., George Pierre Castile, "The Commodification of Indian Identity," *American Anthropologist, New Series* 98 (December 1996): 200–220. *Santa Clara Pueblo v. Martinez*, 436 U.S. 49 (1978). See also Sturm, "Blood Politics," para. 24 in section "Breaching the Dawes Rolls"; Metcalf, *Termination's Legacy*, 69–72, 134, 161–62. Indian sovereignty was determined with *The Self-Determination and Education Assistance Act* (PL 93–638) (1975). The Santa Clara Pueblo, a matriarchal society, used patrilineal descent to determine tribal membership for the purpose of preventing white gigolos from fraudulently gaining access to tribal land, benefits, or money.
77. See, e.g., Garroutte, "The Racial Formation of American Indians"; Barker, "Indian™ U.S.A.," 30–31; Castile, "Commodification of Indian Identity," 744.
78. Quoted in Pauline Turner Strong and Barrik Van Winkle, "'Indian Blood': Reflections on the Reckoning and Refiguring of Native North American Identity," *Cultural Anthropology* 11, *Resisting Identities* (November 1996): 560–63. Some have argued Momaday's "blood" imagery was racist.
79. Clifton, "Alternate Identities," 23; Peter Beinart, "Lost Tribes: Anthropologists Feud over Indian Identity," *Lingua Franca* (May/June 1999): 35–37; Angela Gonzales, "Gaming and Displacement: Winners and Losers in American Indian Casino Development," *International Social Science Journal* 55 (March 2003): 128–31.

CHAPTER 13

1. On unifying and identity-enhancing power, see Gregory Smoak, *Ghost Dances and Identity: Prophetic Religion and American Indian Ethnogenesis in the Nineteenth Century* (Berkeley: University of California, 2006), esp. 134–35, 142, 147, 150–51, 170–71, 193–205; James Mooney, *The Ghost-dance Religion and the Sioux Outbreak of 1890*, edited and abridged by Anthony Wallace (1896; Chicago: University of Chicago Press, 1965); and Anthony Marshall's introduction, ix–x.
2. See Chapter 2, "Medicine and Power," where precontact religion and shamanism is discussed. Sources on post-reservation religion include, e.g., Eddie Box., Sr., "Sun Dance," original in Southern Ute Drum, reprinted on Southern Ute Indian Tribe webpage: "Culture," accessed October 12, 2016. Box was a Southern Ute Sundance chief, aka Red Ute or *Aka Nuche*. See also Smoak, *Ghost Dances and Identity*, 48–80; Robert R. Jones, "Some Effects of Modernization on the Ute Indian Religion" (master's thesis, University of Chicago, 1980); Joseph G. Jorgensen, "The Ethnohistory and Acculturation of the Northern Ute" (PhD diss., Indiana University, 1964), 33–67, 139–56, 320–508. Ethnographic descriptions of religion include Anne M. (Cooke) Smith, *Ethnography of the Northern Utes*, Papers in Anthropology, no. 17 (Albuquerque: Museum of New Mexico Press, 1974), 152–228, 254–63; Marvin K. Opler, "The Character and History of the Southern Ute Peyote Rite," *American Anthropologist* 42 (1940):133–46, 154–56, 171, 188–202; Omer C. Stewart, "Culture Element Distributions: XVIII, Ute—Southern Paiute," *Anthropological Records* 6 (1942): 231–354; Stewart, "The Eastern Ute," 32–39, 50–57, and "Western Ute," 23–38, unpublished essays written in preparation for co-written *Utes*, in *Handbook of North American Indians*, vol. 11, 354–55, and located in box 5, 2nd Accession, Omer C. Stewart Collection, Archives, Norlin Library, University of Colorado, Boulder; and Joseph G. Jorgensen, *The Sun Dance Religion: Power for the Powerless* (Chicago: University of Chicago Press, 1972).
3. Omer C. Stewart and David F. Aberle argued that because the ritual framework was the same from tribe to tribe, Peyotism was a pan-Indian religion. Others disagreed. Marvin K. Opler and Jorgensen both described how peyote meetings were being used to express *Ute* perceptions and perpetuate *Ute* healing ceremonies. See Aberle and Stewart, *Navaho and Ute Peyotism: A Chronological and Distributional Study*, Series in Anthropology, no. 6 (Boulder: University of Colorado Press, 1957); Stewart, *Ute Peyotism: A Study of a Cultural Complex*, University of Colorado Studies, Series in Anthropology, no. 1 (Boulder: University of Colorado Press, 1948); Opler, "Southern Ute Peyote Rite," 391–95; Jorgensen, "The Ethnohistory of the Northern Ute," 379–90; Smoak, *Ghost Dances and Identity*.
4. Richard K. Young, *The Ute Indians of Colorado in the Twentieth Century* (Norman: University of Oklahoma Press, 1997), 95, 274–75; personal observation on the Uintah and Ouray Reservation,

1980; Larry Cesspooch, tribal liaison, spiritual advisor, and storyteller, interview with author, March 1999. Examples of his storytelling are now available on YouTube.

5. Personal observation of blessings at the Sundance and during several private curing ceremonies on the Northern Ute Reservation, summers 1978–1980 and 1999–2003. Healing rituals varied. On one occasion a patient—a non-Indian agnostic—came into a healing ceremony (using both ritual and herbs) as an unbeliever, but was overcome, nearly collapsed, and is today a participant and leader in open, non-Ute Sundances and a vocal advocate of sweat lodge ceremonies. Jeannette Harrison, personal communication and observation.

6. Young, *The Ute Indians of Colorado*, 95, 274–75; Cesspooch, interview with author, March 1999

7. General sources on the Ghost Dance include Mooney, *Ghost-dance Religion*, esp. 2–59, 19–35; Weston LaBarre, *The Ghost Dance* (Garden City, NY: Doubleday & Co., 1970); Alice Beck Kehoe, *The Ghost Dance: Ethnohistory & Revitalization*, 2nd ed. (Long Grove, IL: Waveland Press, 2006), esp. 4–12, 27–42; Kehoe, "Where were Wovoka and Wuzzie George?" in Richard O. Clemmer, L. Daniel Myers, and Mary E. Rudden, *Julian Steward and the Great Basin: The Making of an Anthropologist* (Salt Lake City: University of Utah Press, 1999); and Michael Hittman, *Wovoka and the Ghost Dance*, edited by Don Lynch (Lincoln: University of Nebraska Press, 1990), esp. 29–34, 63–100. Specific Ute impact is detailed in John A. Peterson, *Utah's Black Hawk War* (Salt Lake City: University of Utah Press, 1998), 361–65.

8. Smoak, *Ghost Dances and Identity*, 48–80; Hittman, *Wovoka*, 29. Wodziwob (Grey Head or "Fish Lake Joe"); Täivo/Tävibo or *Numu-tiboʼo* meaning "Northern Paiute-Whiteman."

9. Neolin rose in prominence in the 1760s, Handsome Lake after 1799, and Tenskwatawa in the 1830s, in conjunction with his brother, Tecumseh. The Code of Handsome Lake is still influential among the Iroquois.

10. Mooney especially emphasized this link with Mormon beliefs in *Ghost-dance Religion*, 4–5, and esp. 34–37; cf. Lawrence G. Coates, "The Mormons and the Ghost Dance," *Dialogue: Journal of Mormon Thought* 18 (Winter 1985): 89–111; Garold Barney, *Mormons, Indians, and the Ghost Dance Religion of 1890* (Lanham, MD: University Press of America); Smoak, *Ghost Dances and Identity*, e.g., 71–80, 113–33, 166–71.

11. Commentary in Mooney, *Ghost-dance Religion*, 19; Hitman, *Wovoka*, 63.

12. Quoted in *Millennial Star* (Liverpool, England, 1850–1945) 32 (1870):25; cf. John A. Jones, *The Sun Dance of the Northern Ute*, Bureau of American Ethnology, Bulletin no. 157 (Washington, D.C.: Smithsonian Institution, 1955), Anthropology Paper 47:239–40.

13. *Salt Lake Herald*, May 7, 12, 18, and 29, 1871, and June 15, 1871.

14. Mooney, *Ghost-dance Religion*, 49–50; Smoak, *Ghost Dances and Identity* (passim); and Richard W. Stoffle, et al., "Ghost Dancing the Grand Canyon: Southern Paiute Rock Art, Ceremony, and Cultural Landscapes," *Current Anthropology* 41 (February 2000): 11–38.

15. Mooney, *Ghost-dance Religion*, 50; Smith, *Ethnography of the Northern Utes*, 154, 216–20, and citing oral communication from Joseph Jorgensen. See also Jones, *The Sun Dance of the Northern Ute*, 47:240.

16. Sources for the Sundance include Jorgensen, *Sun Dance Religion*; Jones, *The Sun Dance of the Northern Ute*; Robert H. Lowie, *The Sun Dance of the Shoshone, Ute, and Hidatsa*, American Museum of Natural History Anthropological Papers 16 (1919):387–431; Demitri B. Shimkin, *The Wind River Shoshone Sun Dance*, Bureau of American Ethnology, Bulletin no. 151, Anthropology Paper 41:397–484 (Washington, D.C.: Smithsonian Institution, 1953); Smith, *Ethnography of the Northern Utes*, 174–216; Lowie, *Sun Dance*; Eddie Box., Sr., "Sun Dance"; Jones, "Some Effects of Modernization." Sources supplemented by author's field work and collaboration with R. R. Jones, personal communication with participants from the northern and Southern Ute Reservations, personal participant-observation of Sundances on the Uintah and Ouray Reservation, 1979–1983, and 1999–2000, and visits to the Southern Ute and Ute Mountain Ute Sundance grounds (located five miles up into the mountain). Here we incurred a punctured gas tank on the rough road and subsequently experienced the helpful nature of being part of the Sundance community—despite not being Ute—when members of the tribe helpfully towed and repaired the tank.

17. *Tagúy-narúʔay* (thirsty); *tagú-pu* was the spiritual *puwá* power sought by the *tagú-wuní* or Sundancer ("one who stands for Sundance power" or, literally, "standing thirsty"). Southern Ute Tribe, *Ute Dictionary and Ute Reference Grammar*, preliminary editions (Ignacio, CO: Ute Press, 1979),

493

2:183; James A. Goss, "Ute Lexical and Phonological Patterns" (PhD diss., University of Chicago, 1972), 303. Goss renders *takᵂu=nu-kaa=pi*, literally, as "thirst-dance."

18. Because the Ute "standing thirsty" dance differs from the Plains Sun Dance or the Utes aboriginal Sun Dance, and because they do not refer in their own language to the dance as a *Sun* Dance (though they do in English), the orthographic term *Sundance* is used here to distinguish the Ute/Shoshone ceremony from the Plains Indian ceremonial. Eddie Box, Southern Ute Sundance chief, referred to the Sun Dance as the Sundance in his *Southern Ute Drum* article, "Sun Dance."

19. Jorgensen, *Sun Dance Religion*, 17–26. As Jorgensen's title notes, "Power for the Powerless." Cf. Jones, *Sun Dance*, 228–29.

20. Statistics in Jorgensen, *Sun Dance Religion*, 13–63, esp. 37–38, 91; cf. Peterson, *Utah's Black Hawk War*, 81–82, 104, 360–61 and fn. 48, 386–87. Populations have rebounded; the 2016 tribal census was at least 3,500 on the Uintah and Ouray Reservation, not counting several thousand unenrolled mixed-bloods who claimed to be Indian.

21. Jorgensen, *Sun Dance Religion*, 17–26.

22. Ibid., 17–26, 228–29; Box, "Sun Dance."

23. John Wesley Powell, *Anthropology of the Numa: John Wesley Powell's Manuscripts on the Numic Peoples of Western North America, 1868–1880*, edited by Don D. Fowler and Catherine S. Fowler (Washington, D.C.: Smithsonian Institution Press, 1971); Sidney Jocknick, *Early Days on the Western Slope of Colorado, 1870–1883* (Glorietta, NM: Rio Grande Press, 1913); Marvin K. Opler, "The Southern Ute of Colorado," in *Acculturation in Seven American Indian Tribes*, edited by Ralph Linton (New York: Harper & Son, 1940), 155; Box, "Sun Dance." Note that the Aztec of Mexico and the Hopi of Arizona, both linguistic relatives of the Shoshonean people, incorporated sun reverence or sun worship.

24. Jorgensen, *Sun Dance Religion*, 253–54; Young, *Ute Indians of Colorado*, 278–79. A number of independent, pan-Indian versions of the Sun Dance have appeared from Texas to California, in which women do dance and hold leadership roles. Jeanette Harrison, personal communication.

25. Descriptions of the Sundance include personal observation, Uintah and Ouray Sundances, 1978–1993, 1999–2000, and visits to Southern and Ute Mountain Sundance grounds. Cf. Smith, *Ethnography of the Northern Utes*, 174–216; Jorgensen, *Sun Dance Religion,* 177–205.

26. Exhaustion and hyperventilation from blowing their whistle and extreme hunger combine to produce a semi-hypnotic state not unlike that experienced by long-distance runners. Leona Holbrook, physical education specialist, personal communication with author, fall 1979.

27. Box, "Sun Dance."

28. Utes were noted for their knowledge of healing plants. See, e.g., Smith, *Ethnography of the Northern Utes*, 162–64. Smith collected botanical samples in the 1930s but lost them in a car accident. C.f. Patricia Albers and Jennifer Lowry's compilation of plants still gathered by Utes and used for food and medicinal specifics in *Cultural Resource and Properties of the Northern Ute Tribe: A Technical Report on Sites under Possible Impact by the Uinta Basin Replacement Project* (Salt Lake City: American West Center, 1995).

29. On Peyote religion, see Aberle and Stewart, *Navaho and Ute Peyotism*; Stewart, *Ute Peyotism*; Omer C. Stewart, *Peyote Religion: A History* (Norman: University of Oklahoma Press, 1987); Stewart, "Friend to the Ute: Omer C. Stewart Crusades for Indian Religious Freedom," *Colorado Heritage* 2 (1982): 45–52; Weston La Barre, *The Peyote Cult*, 4th ed., enl. (New York: Schocken Books, 1975); Opler, "The Character and History of the Southern Ute Peyote Rite," 463–78; and Young, *Ute Indians of Colorado*, 69, 95–98, and fn 302. See also Richard Evans Schultes and Albert Hoffman, *Plants of the Gods: Their Sacred Healing and Hallucinogenic Powers* (Rochester, VT: Healing Arts Press, 1992).

30. Darrell Gardiner (Sundancer and mixed-blood medicine man), personal communication, 1978.

31. Stewart, *Ute Peyotism*, 28. LeBarre (*Peyote Cult*) and Opler (*Southern Peyote Rite*) contest Stewart's claim for religious syncretism.

32. Stewart, "Friend of the Ute," 46–47.

33. LaBarre, *Peyote Cult*, 199.

34. Stewart, "Friend to the Ute," 51; Aberle and Stewart, *Navajo and Ute Peyotism*.

35. For details of Ute peyote ceremonies, see, e.g., Stewart, *Ute Peyotism*; Stewart, "Friend of the Ute"; and Aberle and Stewart, *Navajo and Ute Peyotism*.

36. Urban settings were more difficult but possible. See Scott Momaday, *House Made of Dawn* (New York: Harper Row, 1968).

37. Jorgensen, "Ethnohistory and Acculturation," 379–82.

38. Young, *Ute Indians of Colorado*, 95–98; Aberle and Stewart, *Navajo and Ute Peyotism*, 17; Opler, "The Character and History of the Southern Ute Peyote Rite," 466–67.

39. Young, *Ute Indians of Colorado*, 95, 98, 275.

40. Stewart, *Culture Trait Distribution*, 259–61; Raymond Wissiup (Uncompahgre), personal communication, March 18, 1999 (Uintah and Ouray Reservation); "Old Bishop" Arrochis, personal communication, 1980.

41. Darrel Gardiner, Larry Cesspooch, and Raymond Wissiup, separate personal communications, March 18–19 and August 1999; Terry Knight, cited in Young, *Ute Indians of Colorado*, 272–74. Cesspooch and Knight were Ute spiritual advisors; Gardiner was a mixed-blood Uncompahgre, and an Indian doctor. Gardiner sued the state of Utah over holding sweats in prison. See, e.g., *Deseret News*, November 16, 1988, December 4, 1988, February 29, 1999, and April 29, 2000; *Salt Lake Tribune*, February 5, 1999; personal observations, summer 1979, and personal communication with "Old Bishop" Arrochis, 1979–1980, and with Gardiner, 1999.

42. See, e.g., Jessica Ravitz, "Sweat Ceremonies Offer Patients an Enigmatic Way to Look for Healing," *Salt Lake Tribune*, November 10, 2006; Taki Telonidis, "In Sweat Lodge, Vets Find Healing," May 28, 2012, National Public Radio, npr.org; Ken Olsen, "Spiritual Pathways," *American Legion*, April 1, 2008; U.S. Department of Veterans Affairs, "Chaplain Service Guidelines Concerning Native American Indian/Alaskan Native Traditional Practitioners"; Patty Murray (Senator from Washington), "Murray Stands Up For Native American Veterans in Health Care Battle," Press Release, April 12, 2004, at http://murray.senate.gov /news.cfm?id=220410. Veteran rehabilitation occurred at Walla Walla Medical Center's "Sweats for Vets," the Ft. Meade Black Hills Veteran's Medical Center and Clinic, the VA Southern Oregon Rehabilitation program, the Salt Lake City Veterans Medical Center, Denver Veterans Administration Medical Center, and the veteran's centers in Albuquerque (NM), and Prescott and St. Cloud (AZ), to name but a few.

43. "Old Bishop" Arrochis, personal communication, 1980; Eddie Box, Sr., personal communication with author and R. R. Jones, 1978, 1979; and personal observation. Terry Knight (Ute Mountain) and Larry Cesspooch (Uintah/White river) were spiritual advisors in 2000. Darrell Gardiner, though an unenrolled mixed-blood Uncompahgre, was a practicing medicine man in Utah and Canada; however, not being on any tribal rolls, the tribe did not recognize him as an "Indian" medicine man.

44. Jorgensen, *The Sun Dance Religion*, 255; Gardiner, personal communication, July 18, 1999; personal observation, July 1999.

45. Young, *Ute Indians of Colorado*, 275–76, 278–79; Jorgensen, *Sun Dance Religion*, 259.

46. Jorgensen, *Sun Dance Religion*, 259; and Baker, minutes of the 1961 Southern Ute tribal council meeting, cited in Young, *Ute Indians of Colorado*, 279.

47. Larry Cesspooch, spiritual advisor and tribal liaison, interview with author, March 18–19, 1999; Gardiner, personal communication, March and July 1999; personal observation of healing ceremonies, 1978–1982, 1999.

48. Stewart "Friend to the Ute; *Denver Rocky Mountain News*, June 28, 1967; Amendment to the American Indian Religious Freedom Act [U.S.C. 42 Sec 1996a, P.L. 103–344], 103rd Cong., H.R. 4230, October 6, 1994.

49. American Indian Religious Freedom Act, U.S. Code, Title 42, Chapter 21, Sec 1996 (1978); and U.S. Congress, Amendment to the American Indian Religious Freedom Act, 1994.

50. Personal observation, Darrel Gardiner home, summer 1980.

51. *Deseret News*, July 8, 1993; Amendment to the American Indian Religious Freedom Act, 1994. Arizona, Colorado, Idaho, Texas, Minnesota, Nevada, New Mexico, Oregon, and Utah allow sacramental peyote use, regardless of race (as of 2016).

52. U.S. Supreme Court Decision, *Employment Div., Ore. Dept. of Human Res. v. Smith et al.*, 494 U.S. 872 (1990).

53. Young, *Ute Indians of Colorado*, 279; Religious Freedom Restoration Act of 1993, 107 Stat. 1488, U.S. Code Title 42, Chap. 21B, sec. 2000bb; nullified by *City of Boerne v. P. F. Flores, Archbishop of San Antonio, and United States*, 521 U.S. 507 (1997).

54. Indian Religious Freedom Act Amendments of 1994; cf. U.S. Code, Title 42, Chap. 21, sub. I § 1996a, "Traditional Indian Religious Use of Peyote," July 24, 2003. *U.S. v. Boyll*, 774 F.Supp. 1333 (D.N.M. 1991); *Deseret News*, June 23, 2004, July 12, 2004, August 28, 2004; David Hamblin, *Deseret News*, February 22, 2005.

55. *Deseret News*, June 23, 2004, July 12, 2004, August 28, 2004; David Hamblin, *Deseret News*, February 22, 2005; "Peyote Advocate Charged," *Salt Lake Tribune*, June 24, 2005; "Utah High Court OKs Non-Indian Peyote Use," Associate Press, 2004; *Utah v. Moony et al.*, Utah Supreme Court, June 22, 2004; "Peyote Legal Status," Vaults of Erowid website (2016), https://www.erowid.org.

56. *Deseret News*, December 8, 1991.

57. *Deseret News*, September 8, 1992, December 8, 1991.

58. *Deseret News*, December 8, 1991, September 8, 1992. Suit was brought in behalf of James Gardiner. After his release, James became a road man, a Sundance leader, and holy man. J. Gardiner, personal communication with author, 2008–2010; Colleen Gardiner, personal communication with author, 2009; and Larry Cesspooch (Uintah-Ouray Ute Tribal liaison), personal communication with author, March 1999.

59. *Deseret News*, January 29, 1995; U.S. Congress, Religious Freedom Restoration Act of 1993.

60. *Deseret News*, July 2, 1989, September 8, 1992. On the national push, see NBC, "Prison Offers Sweat Lodges to Indian Inmates," May 29, 2007 (online). Officials reported the ceremonies seemed to help improve the behavior of most participants.

61. D. Gardiner, personal communication with author and observation, 1979–1983 and 1999–2000. Gardiner combined traditional healing ceremonies and traditional medicinal plants.

62. *Deseret News*, February 29, 1999, April 29, 2000; D. Gardiner, personal communication, March 1999.

63. *Deseret News*, February 29, 1999; *Salt Lake Tribune*, February 5, 1999; D. Gardiner, personal communication with author, March 1999. The disgruntled Gardiner *claimed* that most of those qualified to conduct sweats had legal issues that disallowed them from entering the prisons.

64. Young, *Ute Indians of Colorado*, 245, 250; cf. Jorgensen, *Sun Dance Religion*.

65. Alice B. Kehoe, "Primal Gaia: Primitivists and Plastic Medicine Men," in James A. Clifton, *The Invented Indian: Cultural Fictions and Government Policies* (1990; New Brunswick, NJ: Transaction Publishers, 2007), 193–209; *Deseret News*, May 5 1994, June 4, 1994, July 8, 2005; *Salt Lake Tribune*, July 22, 1997.

66. *Salt Lake Tribune*, July 22, 1995; Larry Cesspooch, interview with author, March 18–19, 1999; D. Gardiner, personal communication with author, March 19, 1999.

67. "Peyote Legal Status," Vaults of Erowid website (2016); Eric Tsetsi, "Remote Arizona Church," *New Phoenix Times*, January 9, 2014.

68. Larry Cesspooch, interview with author, March 18–19, 1999.

CHAPTER 14

1. On developing ethnic boundaries, see, e.g., Duane Champagne, *Social Change and Cultural Continuity among Native Nations* (Chicago: University of Chicago Press, 2006); James A. Clifton, ed., *The Invented Indian, Cultural Fictions and Government Policies* (1990; New Brunswick: Transaction Publishers, 2007); James A. Clifton, *Being and Becoming Indian* (Prospect Heights, IL: Waveland Press, 1989); Pauline Turner Strong and Barrik Van Winkle, "Resisting Identities," in "'Indian Blood': Reflections on the Reckoning and Refiguring of Native North American Identity," *Cultural Anthropology* 11 (November 1996): 547–76; Kimberly TallBear, "DNA, Blood, and Racializing the Tribe," *Wicazo Sa Review* 18 (Spring 2003): 81–107; Eva Marie Garroutte, *Real Indians: Identity and the Survival of Native America* (Berkeley: University of California Press, 2003).

2. Frances Leon [Swadesh] Quintana, *Ordeal of Change: The Southern Utes and their Neighbors* (Walnut Creek: AltaMira Press, 2004), 43–44; cf. Katherine M. B. Osburn, *Southern Ute Women: Autonomy and Assimilation on the Reservation, 1887–1934* (Albuquerque: University of New Mexico Press, 1998), 113.

3. Kenneth R. Philp, ed., *Indian Self-Rule: First Hand Accounts of Indian-White Relations from Roosevelt to Reagan* (Salt Lake City: Howe Brothers, 1986), 31; Frances Leon Swadesh [Quintana], "The

Southern Utes and Their Neighbors, 1877–1926" (master's thesis, University of Colorado, Boulder, 1962), 38–39; Quintana, *Ordeal of Change*, 49–50. On the reference to Uintah equipment, see Byrnes to commissioner, United States Bureau of Indian Affairs, *Annual Report of the Commissioner of Indian Affairs* [*ARCIA*] (Washington, D.C., 1887), 199–200; and *ARCIA* (1889), 279.

4. Max Weber, *Protestant Ethic and the Spirit of Capitalism*, trans. Talcott Parsons (New York: Charles Scribner's Sons, 1958); David Hurst Thomas, *Skull Wars: Kennewick Man, Archaeology, and the Battle for Native American Identity* (New York: Basic Books, 2000). Compare the cultural and racial hierarchies of Social Darwinism with Lewis Henry Morgan's 1880s anthropological theories of unilinear cultural development. Morgan posited that all societies inevitably progressed from savagery (hunter-gatherer) through barbarism (early agriculture and simple metal-work) to civilization (beginning writing).

5. On details of the conflicts of interest, see Quintana, *Ordeal of Change*, 34–42, 46.

6. Ibid., 34–42, 46.

7. Thomas A. Britten, *American Indians in World War I: At Home and at War* (Albuquerque: University of New Mexico Press, 1999), 141–49, 157.

8. Ibid.

9. Omer C. Stewart, "Southern Ute Adjustment to Modern Living," in *Acculturation in the Americas*, edited by Sol Tax (Chicago: University of Chicago Press, 1952), 2:80; Joseph G. Jorgensen, *The Sun Dance Religion: Power for the Powerless* (Chicago: University of Chicago Press, 1972), 148.

10. Jorgensen, *Sun Dance Religion*, 91–100; Richard K. Young, *The Ute Indians of Colorado in the Twentieth Century* (Norman: University of Oklahoma Press, 1997), 51, 55; Swadesh, "Southern Utes," 38–49; and Quintana, *Ordeal of Change*, 27–42; *ARCIA* (1914), 59–61.

11. Quintana, *Ordeal of Change*, 42, 46–47.

12. Agency correspondence is quoted in Quintana, *Ordeal of Change*, 62–63.

13. Jorgensen details Ute land loss and poverty in "Neocolonial Reservation" and "Deprivation of the Utes," in *Sun Dance Religion*, 89–173, esp. 92–116. Cf. Quintana, "Crisis: Self-Support," in *Ordeal of Change*, 43–66, 108; Osburn, *Southern Ute Women*, 117–18.

14. Young, *Ute Indians of Colorado*, 54–55, 81–82; Swadesh, "Southern Ute," 58–59, 69–72, 89, 96–98, 149; Quintana, *Ordeal of Change*, 43–73, 118–19. For women's political activism, see Osburn, *Southern Ute Women*, 21–68, 113–15; and, e.g., *ARCIA* (1914), 59–61.

15. Jorgensen, *Sun Dance Religion*, 101, 111; Young, *Ute Indians of Colorado*, 47–75; and, e.g., E. E. White to commissioner, in *ARCIA* (1886), 226–27; T. A. Byrnes to commissioner, in *ARCIA* (1887), 200; *ARCIA* (1889), 279; G. A. Cornish to commissioner, in *ARCIA* (1898), 293.

16. See, e.g., Jorgensen, *Sun Dance Religion*, 101, 111; Young, *Ute Indians of Colorado*, 47–75.

17. Quintana, *Ordeal of Change*, 53–61, 108. For inter-reservation visits and shamanic healing, see Jorgensen, *Sun Dance Religion*. On continuing shamanism, see, e.g., *ARCIA* (1880), 17; *ARCIA* (1887), 199; *ARCIA* (1888), 219–20; *ARCIA* (1889), 280; and *ARCIA* (1901), 381; and personal observation of Sundance and individual shamanic doctoring on the Northern Ute Reservation, 1979–1982 and 2000–2002.

18. Brookings Institute, *The Problem of Indian Administration: Summary of Findings and Recommendations* ["Meriam Report"] (Washington, D.C., 1928); Arrell Morgan Gibson, *The American Indian: Prehistory to the Present* (Norman: University of Oklahoma Press, 1980), 535–37.

19. See, e.g., Robert Delaney, *The Ute Mountain Utes* (Albuquerque: University of New Mexico Press, 1989), 36, 39, 48–51; cf. Delaney, *The Southern Ute People* (Phoenix: Indian Tribal Series, 1974); Young, *Ute Indians of Colorado*, 49; Robert S. McPherson, *As If the Land Owned Us: An Ethnohistory of the White Mesa Utes* (Salt Lake City: University of Utah Press, 2011), ch. 10–12; David Rich Lewis, "Reservation Leadership and the Progressive-Traditional Dichotomy: William Wash and the Northern Utes, 1865–1928," *Ethnohistory* 38 (Spring 1991): 124–48. Wash was a cattle-owning Uintah. Statistics of livestock ownership for Southern Utes in Quintana, *Ordeal of Change*, 58, 70–71.

20. Note gender-linked linguistics in James A. Goss, "Ute Lexical and Phonological Patterns" (PhD diss., University of Chicago, 1972), 40. See also Quintana, *Ordeal of Change*, 28; and cf. Omer C. Stewart, "Culture Element Distributions: XVIII, Ute—Southern Paiute," *Anthropological Records* 6 (1942): 4:250, 254–56. Cf. Robert McPherson, "Homes on the Range: Settling the Great Sage Plain of Southeastern Utah," in *Life in a Corner: Cultural Episodes in Southeastern Utah, 1880–1950* (Norman:

497

University of Oklahoma Press, 2015), 221–45, for difficulty of farming in arid Weeminuche territory.

21. Swadesh, "Southern Utes," 64, Quintana, *Ordeal of Change,* 19–20, 109.

22. Floyd A. O'Neil and Kathryn L. MacKay, *A History of the Uintah-Ouray Ute Lands,* American West Center Occasional Papers (Salt Lake City: University of Utah Press, n.d.), 32, 34–35; cf. Quintana, *Ordeal of Change,* 29–31.

23. Quintana, *Ordeal of Change,* 29–31. See also John Shurts, *Indian Reserved Water Rights: The Winters Doctrine in its Social and Legal Context, 1880s–1930s* (Norman: University of Oklahoma Press, 2000).

24. O'Neil and MacKay, *History of the Uintah-Ouray,* 32.

25. See, e.g., Cornish to commissioner, in *ARCIA* (1898), 293; J. Randlett to commissioner, in *ARCIA* (1897), 285.

26. Gary Lee Walker, "A History of Fort Duchesne, Including Fort Thornburgh: The Military Presence in Frontier Uinta Basin" (PhD diss., Brigham Young University, 1992), 328–32; Cornish to commissioner, in *ARCIA* (1898), 293; and Randlett to commissioner, in *ARCIA* (1897), 285. For ongoing complaints, see *ARCIA* (1887–1905).

27. Walker, "History of Fort Duchesne," 332–34; e.g., W. A. Mercer to commissioner, in *ARCIA* (1903), 323; Myton to commissioner, in *ARCIA* (1901), 381, and *ARCIA* (1899), 351.

28. Quintana, *Ordeal of Change,* 79–80, 108.

29. Swadesh, "Southern Ute," 153; Quintana, *Ordeal of Change,* 96–100; McPherson, *As If the Land Owned Us,* 207–8; Young, *Ute Indians of Colorado,* 6–7, 21, 99, 105–6.

30. *Confederated Bands of Ute Indians. v. U.S.,* May 23, 1910, case no. 30360. Also see Young, *Ute Indians of Colorado,* 55, 74; Quintana, *Ordeal of Change,* 53–55, 98–100; Uintah-Ouray Ute Tribe, *Ute System of Government* [pamphlet] (Fort Duchesne: Uintah-Ouray Tribe, 1977), 17; Jorgensen, *Sun Dance Religion,* 98. On Uintah-Ouray claims, see Cornish to commissioner, in *ARCIA* (1898), 294; Myton to commissioner, in *ARCIA* (1902–353).

31. Young, *Ute Indians of Colorado,* 54–55, 81–82; Swadesh, "Southern Ute," 69–71, 89, 97–98, 149; Quintana, *Ordeal of Change,* 54–58; Osburn, *Southern Ute Women,* 114.

32. Delaney, *Ute Mountain Ute,* 85–86.

33. Young, *Ute Indians of Colorado,* 54–55; Swadesh, "Southern Utes," 71–72; Quintana, *Ordeal of Change,* 56–63.

34. Young, *Ute Indians of Colorado,* 54–55; cf. Jorgensen, *Sun Dance Religion,* 91, 147; Swadesh, "Southern Ute," 72, 96, and citing Runke to Indian Office, 95; Quintana, "Crisis: 'Self-Support,'" in *Ordeal of Change,* 43–66, esp. 51–62.

35. Forbes Parkhill calls these incidents a "last Indian war," while McPherson calls it a last *White* uprising. See Parkhill, *The Last of the Indian Wars: The Final, Heroic Fight of the American Indian for Independence* (New York: Collier Books, 1961), 54–57, 111; McPherson, *As If the Land Owned Us,* 203–45; and cf. Albert R. Lyman, *Indians and Outlaws: Settling of the San Juan Frontier* (Salt Lake City: Bookcraft, 1962), 150–52, 159–65. Lyman was personally involved in the events, and his colorful book is a memoir. Sources for the events noted here include (passim): McPherson, Albert Lyman, and Parkhill (who cites extensively from Colorado's *Montezuma Journal,* 1915, and *Outlook Magazine,* March 31, 1915).

36. Parkhill claims Tsenegat meant "Cry-Baby" a name his father gave him as an infant, and which he refused to use as an adult. McPherson says that Tsenegat (Činigat) actually means silver-earring. See *As If the Land Owned Us,* 203–45, and "Paiute Posey and the Last White Uprising," *Utah Historical Quarterly* 53 (Summer 1985): 248–67.

37. Lyman argues that Tsenegat was unquestionably guilty. See *Indians and Outlaws,* 159–60.

38. Note comments regarding this publicity in Parkhill, *Last of the Indian Wars.*

39. In Parkhill, *Last of the Indian Wars,* and quoting *Montezuma Journal* (Cortez, CO, 1915).

40. Lyman, *Indians and Outlaws,* 163–64; and cf. McPherson, 218–23. More about John and Louisa Wetherill in Harvey Leake, at http://wetherillfamily.com/john_wetherill.htm.

41. Lyman's opinions are in *Indians and Outlaws,* 163–65. McPherson, *As If the Land Owned Us,* 218–28, agrees that the acquittal led to increased trouble.

42. Parkhill, *Last of the Indian Wars,* 114.

43. Britten, *American Indians in World War I,* 19–27.

44. Ibid., 61–67; "The Indian and War," Report of the Commissioner of Indian Affairs, in *ARCIA* (1917), 5.

45. Britten, *American Indians in World War I*, 61–67.

46. Ibid.

47. Britten, *American Indians in World War I*, 58–60, 132–139; "Liberty Loan Bonds," in Report of the Commissioner, *ARCIA* (1917), 7–8; and "Pe-retta's Gift," in *The Indian's Friend* 31 (November 1918): 5.

48. Britten, *American Indians in World War I*, 58–60.

49. Southern Ute Tribe, "Veterans," Southern Ute Veterans Association. Site lists the names off veterans inscribed on the Tribe's Veterans Memorial monument. See Southern Ute Tribe website, "Veterans," retrieved November 2017 from https://www.wouthernute-nsn.gov/va/. On the Uintah and Ouray Reservation, Ute Tribe, "Veterans Day in the United States," *News from Ute Country: Ute Bulletin* 52, no. 3 (November 3, 2017): 6–8. Article lists all veterans from the Uintah and Ouray Reservation, from World War I to present. List does not include nonmember mixed-blood Utes.

50. Britten, *American Indians in World War II*, 45–46, 82, 99–111.

51. Ibid., 144–58.

52. McPherson, "Paiute Posey," 251–52; Albert R. Lyman, "A Relic of Gadianton: Old Posey as I Knew Him," *Improvement Era* 26 (July 1923): 793; and Lyman, *Outlaw of Navaho Mountain* (Salt Lake City: Deseret Book, 1963), a biographical novel about Posey.

53. Details in McPherson, "Paiute Posey," 253–57, and *As If the Land Owned Us*, 226–45, 236–37; J. M. Redd, "Last American Indian War," *Deseret News*, January 1, 1979; Young, *Ute Indians of Colorado*, 63.

54. McPherson, "Paiute Posey," 257–65, quote 258; Lyman, *Indians and Outlaws*, 173–95, quote 173. See also McPherson, *As If the Land Owned Us*, 237–44. Gadianton quote from an unpublished Lyman manuscript, 244, copy in author's possession.

55. McPherson, "Paiute Posey," 264–65; Lyman, *Indians and Outlaws*, 193–95.

56. McPherson, "Paiute Posey," 266, and *As If the Land Owned Us*, 244–45; Young, *Ute Indians of Colorado*, 38, 59.

57. Young, *Ute Indians of Colorado*, 61–63.

58. McPherson, *As If the Land Owned Us*, 246–68; Young, *Ute Indians of Colorado*, 61–63.

59. Parkhill, *Last of the Indian Wars*, 116, 118.

60. P. D. Smith, *Ouray, Chief of the Utes* (Ouray, CO: Wayfinder Press, 1986), 194–204; cf. Cynthia S. Becker and P. David Smith, *Chipeta: Queen of the Utes* (Montrose, CO: Western Reflections, 2003), 202–49; Brandi Denison, "She-towitch and Chipeta: Remembering the 'Good' Indian," in *Ute Land Religion in the American West, 1879–2009* (Lincoln: University of Nebraska Press and American Philosophical Society, 2017); Albert Reagan and Wallace Stark, "Chipeta, Queen of the Utes," *Utah Historical Quarterly* (April 1933): 791–97; and C. W. Wiegel, "The Re-burial of Chief Ouray," *Colorado Magazine* 5 (1928): 165–73.

61. O'Neil and Mackay, *History of the Uintah-Ouray*, 35–36.

62. Ute delegation quoted of Young, *Ute Indians in Colorado*, 74–76, 131–35; and cf. Quintana, *Ordeal of Change*, 34–42, 46.

63. Young, *Ute Indians of Colorado*, 82, 100–103.

64. Quintana, *Ordeal of Change*, 99–100, 107.

65. Uintah-Ouray Ute Tribe, *Government*, 13–15.

66. Brookings Institute "Meriam Report"; Felix Cohen, *Handbook of Federal Indian Law* (Washington: Government Printing Office, 1942), 26–27; and Philp, *Indian Self-Rule*, 37–38, 103.

67. Philp, *Indian Self-Rule*, 16, 33–40, 80–81, 93, 99, 133–34; Francis Paul Prucha, *Indian Policy in the United States: Historical Essays* (Lincoln: University of Nebraska Press, 1981), 32–35; cf. Wilcomb E. Washburn, "A Fifty-Year Perspective on the Indian Reorganization Act," *American Anthropologist* 36 (June 1984): 279–89.

68. Philp, *Indian Self-Rule*, 16–18, 39–40; Young, *Ute Indians of Colorado*, 84; Lyman S. Tyler, *A History of Indian Policy* (Washington, D.C.: U.S. Department of Interior, Bureau of Indian Affairs, 1973), 125–29, 133.

69. Young, *Ute Indians of Colorado*, 84, 122.

499

70. O'Neil and MacKay, *History of the Uintah-Ouray*, 36–37; Delaney, *Southern Ute People*, 79; John A. Jones, *The Sun Dance of the Northern Ute*, Bureau of American Ethnology, Bulletin no. 157 (Washington, D.C.: Smithsonian Institution, 1955), 47:203–64, esp. 232–34.

71. Numerous works have been published about the Indian Reorganization Act; especially see Philp, *Indian Self-Rule*; Philp, *John Collier's Crusade for Indian Reform, 1920–1954* (Tucson: University of Arizona Press, 1977); and Graham D. Taylor, *The New Deal and American Indian Tribalism: The Administration of the Indian Reorganization Act, 1934–45* (Lincoln: University of Nebraska Press, 1980).

72. Philp, *Indian Self-Rule*, 28–29, 33–37, 40–44, 53, 58–59, 86, 92–93; Tyler, *Indian Policy*, 135–36; Lawrence C. Kelly, "The Indian Reorganization Act: The Dream and the Reality," *Pacific Historical Review* 44 (August 1975): 291–312; Washburn, "A Fifty-Year Perspective"; Taylor, *New Deal and American Indian Tribalism*, x–xii, 139–50, esp. 140–41 on accusations of Collier being a communist.

73. Taylor, *New Deal and Indian Tribalism*, 140–43.

74. Philp, *Indian Self-Rule*, 51, 77–78, 83–84, 146; Tyler, *Indian Policy*, 131–33; and Taylor, *New Deal and Indian Tribalism*, xi, 139–50, esp. 143.

75. On Collier's "saint or sinner" status, see Philp, *Indian Self-Rule*, 27–110, esp. 73–74, 87, 91, 104. For varying attitudes, statistics, and non-IRA tribal success, see Philp, *Indian Self-Rule*, 41, 47, 49, 71–72, 88–91, 101, 146. See also Washburn, "Fifty-year Perspective," esp. 279, 287–88; and Taylor, *New Deal and Indian Tribalism*, 150.

76. Taylor, *New Deal and Indian Tribalism*, 139–40, 144–50.

77. Philp, *Indian Self-Rule*, 10, 17, 71, 74–75. Johnson-O'Malley funds were sometimes placed in general funds. See, e.g., Clifford Duncan, "The Northern Utes of Utah," in *A History of Utah's American Indians*, edited by Forrest S. Cuch (Salt Lake City: Utah State Division of Indian Affairs and Utah State Division of History, 2000), 216.

78. Philp, *Indian Self-Rule*, 17, 83–85, 89.

79. Ibid., 17, 75, 85, 91, 97, 103, 254–55.

80. For example, see Chapter 17, which details judicial issues on the Uintah and Ouray Reservation.

81. See, e.g., Jorgensen, *Sun Dance Religion*, 98.

82. Young, *Ute Indians of Colorado*, 112.

83. Ibid., 108–10.

84. Young, *Ute Indians of Colorado*, 110–12.

85. Jorgensen, *Sun Dance Religion*, 138–39, 149–50; Utes described the voter chicanery to J. A. Jones. See *Sun Dance of the Northern Ute*, 229–31; and R. Warren Metcalf, *Termination's Legacy: The Discarded Indians of Utah* (Lincoln: University of Nebraska Press, 2002), 130, 133–37.

86. Jorgensen, *Sun Dance Religion*, 148–49; U.S. Congress, House, Committee on Interior and Insular Affairs, *Investigation of the Bureau of Indian Affairs*, 82d Cong., 2d sess., 1953, H. Rept. 2503, 636.

87. Metcalf, *Termination's Legacy*, 154–56, and "Lambs of Sacrifice: Termination, the Mixed-Blood Utes, and the Problem of Indian Identity," *Utah Historical Quarterly* 64 (Fall 1996): 332–37; Jorgensen, *Sun Dance Religion*, 138–39, 149.

88. Young, *Ute Indians of Colorado*, 110–17; Uintah-Ouray Ute Tribe, *Government*, 16.

89. Uintah-Ouray Ute Tribe, *Government*, 13–15; Young, *Ute Indians of Colorado*, 117–18; McPherson, *As If the Land Owned Us*, 282.

90. Young, *Ute Indians of Colorado*, 6–8, 106, 115, 118, 121, 170; Uintah-Ouray Ute Tribe, *Government*, 16–19, 27.

91. Young, *Ute Indians of Colorado*, 6–8, 99, 106, 114–15, 118, 173.

92. Ibid., 118, 126, 170–71,177, 185, 195, 226–29, 268.

93. Ibid., 117–18, 157, 177, 204, 217, 223–25, 268; John Burch's election, 312n27. The Southern Ute Tribe web site lists all chairs and council members from 1936–1998. Julius Cloud, John Baker, Anthony Cloud Burch, and Leonard Burch were all military veterans. See "Veterans," on the Southern Ute webpage.

94. Jorgensen, *Sun Dance Religion*, 138–39; Jones, *Sun Dance of the Northern Ute*, 229–31.

95. Young, *Ute Indians of Colorado*, 120–25, 174–75; Jorgensen, *Sun Dance Religion*, 146–59; Philp, *Indian Self-Rule*, 40–41, 83, 89, 108. A waldo is a mechanical or electronic manipulator that is operated remotely.

CHAPTER 15

1.   Alison R. Bernstein, *American Indians and World War II: Toward a New Era in Indian Affairs* (Norman: University of Oklahoma Press, 1991), 159–75.

2.   Ibid., 31–33, 40; Selective Training and Service Act of 1940, P.L. 76–783, 54 Stat. 885. Decisions regarding sovereignty based, in part, on *Ex Parte Green 286 U.S. 437 (1932)*.

3.   Bernstein, *Indians and World War II*, 22–39. Numbers are based on tribal reports and may not reflect off-reservation Indians. The military did not have a racial category for Indians and therefore could not accurately track their numbers, and some Indians were misclassified as other races. For Nazi propaganda and Aryan link, see Kenneth W. Townsend, "Nazi propaganda among American Indians," *World War II and the American Indian* (Albuquerque: University of New Mexico Press, 2000), 31–60; Tom Holm, "Forgotten Warriors: American Indian Service Men in Vietnam," *Vietnam Generation* 1, no. 2 (1989), Article 6 (56–68), available at http://digitalcommons.lasalle.edu/vietnamgeneration/volt/iss2/6. See also Forest Country Potawatomie, "Native Americans in the Military," *Keeper of the Fires*, February 15, 2015, online publication retrieved November 2017 from https://www.fcpotawatomi.com/news/native-americans-in-the-military-world-war-ii/; and Vincent Schilling, "By the Numbers: A Look at Native Enlistment during the Major Wars," *Indian Country Today*, February 6, 2014, online publication retrieved November 2017 from https://indiancountrymedianetwork.com/news/veterans/by-the-numbers-a-look-at-native-enlistment-during-the-major-wars/.

4.   Bernstein, *Indians and World War II*, 40–63, esp. 41–42, 46, 53–55; Tom Holm, "Forgotten Warriors: American Indian Service Men in Vietnam," *Vietnam Generation* 1, no. 2 (1989): 61–66.

5.   Bernstein, *Indians and World War II*, 38, and, e.g., 42–46, 54–57. Southern Ute website, and news articles about veterans and veteran's memorials in *The Journal*, the *Ute Bulletin*, and *The Southern Ute Drum*. See also Robert Jones, conversation with author regarding his experience in several Sundances.

6.   Bernstein, *Indians and World War II*, 146–52; Genevieve DeHoyos, "Indian Student Placement Services," in *Encyclopedia of Mormonism* (New York: Macmillan, 1992), 2:679–80; Matthew Garrett, *Making Lamanites Mormons: Native Americans and the Indian Student Placement Program* (Salt Lake City: University of Utah Press, 2016). The program was phased out as more public schools were built on and near reservations. Personal communication via telephone with author, to the LDS Church offices, Indian Placement department.

7.   Southern Ute Veterans Association, "Southern Utes: Veterans of Foreign Wars," retrieved November 2017, www.southernute-nsn.gov/va/; Ute Tribe of the Uintah and Ouray Reservation, "Veterans Day in the United States," *Ute Bulletin* (online) 52, no. 3 (November 3, 2017): 6–8; *Uintah Basin Media* (*UB Standard*, online), July 1, 2016; and "New Memorial Dedicated," September 26, 2013, KSL.com. Ute Mountain Ute information from photo (one side of memorial only) of Veterans Memorial, Towaoc, in "Bikers Honor Ute Vets," *The Journal* (online), May 21, 2015. A breakdown of which specific foreign conflicts Ute Mountain Utes fought in is unavailable.

8.   Bernstein, *Indians and World War II*, 145–48, 159; Holm, "Forgotten Warriors," 65–66.

9.   For postwar impact on American Indians, see Bernstein, *Indians and World War II*, ch. 6–8; and Townsend, *World War II and the American Indian*, ch. 8–9.

10.   Bernstein, *Indians and World War II*, 131–58.

11.   See, e.g., Kenneth R. Philp, ed., *Indian Self-Rule: First Hand Accounts of Indian-White Relations from Roosevelt to Reagan* (Salt Lake City: Howe Brothers, 1986), 21, 63; R. Warren Metcalf, *Termination's Legacy: The Discarded Indians of Utah* (Lincoln: University of Nebraska Press, 2002), 9, 19. On the impact of World War 2, see Bernstein, *Indians and World War II*; and Townsend, *World War II and the American Indian*.

12.   See, e.g. Bernstein, *Indians and World War II*, 122–28; Holm, "Forgotten Warriors," 60–61, 66.

13.   Bernstein, *Indians and World War II*, 89–111.

14.   Philp, *Indian Self-Rule*, 118–19.

15.   Floyd A. O'Neil and Kathryn L. MacKay, *A History of the Uintah-Ouray Ute Lands*, American West Center Occasional Papers (Salt Lake City: University of Utah Press, n.d.), 34–37.

16.   Joseph G. Jorgensen, *The Sun Dance Religion: Power for the Powerless* (Chicago: University of Chicago Press, 1972), 146–59.

501

17. Richard K. Young, *The Ute Indians of Colorado in the Twentieth Century* (Norman: University of Oklahoma Press, 1997), 134–35; Robert Delaney, *The Southern Ute People* (Phoenix: Indian Tribal Series, 1974), 79.

18. *Confederated Bands of Ute Indians v. United States*, nos. 45585, 46640, 47564, 47566, in the Court of Claims of the United States, March 17, 1950. See also affidavit of Ernest L. Wilkinson respecting attorneys' services rendered in above cases; and Wilkinson, "Ute Claims," Wilkinson Collection, Special Collections, Harold B. Lee Library, Brigham Young University, Provo, Utah; Young, *Ute Indians of Colorado*, 136; Metcalf, *Termination's Legacy*, 50–51.

19. *Confederated Bands of Ute Indians v. United States*, Nos. 45585, 46640, 47564, 47566, in Ernest L. Wilkinson, *In the Court of Claims of the United States* and in J. Reuben Clark, Jr. Collection (United States: Court of Claims, 1950), 449–50, located in HBLL.

20. Metcalf, *Termination's Legacy*, 51–54, 56, 61; *Confederated Bands of Ute Indians v. United States*, Nos. 45585, 46640, 47564, and 47566, in Wilkinson, *Court of Claims*.

21. Bernstein, *Indians and World War II*, 159–64; Metcalf, *Termination's Legacy*, 52–53; and, e.g., H.R. 4399, "To adjudicate claims of certain Ute Indians."

22. Metcalf, *Termination's Legacy*, 57. Details in Wilkinson, "Ute Claims," and Wilkinson, *Court of Claims*.

23. Metcalf, *Termination's Legacy*, 54–55; Charles J. Kappler, comp. and ed., *Indian Affairs: Laws and Treaties* (Washington, D.C.: Government Printing Office, 1902–1938), 6:322–23; Bernstein, *Indians and World War II*, 159–62.

24. See, e.g., Philp, ed., *Indian Self-Rule*, 118–19; Metcalf, *Termination's Legacy*, 55–56, 62.

25. Wilkinson, *Court of Claims*, 450–61; Metcalf, *Termination's Legacy*, 57–58.

26. Wilkinson, *Court of Claims*, 450–61.

27. Ibid., 158–59, 445–48. Wilkinson presented these figures to justify being paid.

28. Piede simply means pedestrian, and was used to describe most nonequestrian Indians in Utah in the nineteenth century. On testimonies, see Wilkinson, *Court of Claims*, 461; Anne M. (Cooke) Smith, *Ethnography of the Northern Utes*, Papers in Anthropology, no. 17 (Albuquerque: Museum of New Mexico Press, 1974), 18–19; Isabel Kelly on Paiute/Ute identity in *Southern Paiute Ethnography*, University of Utah Anthropological Papers, no. 69 (Salt Lake City: University of Utah Press, 1964), 33–34, 91, 145, 175; and Omer C. Stewart, personal communication with author, September 1977.

29. Young, *Ute Indians of Colorado*, 137–39, esp. 139, and quoting notes from a joint meeting of Southern and Ute Mountain Utes.

30. Ibid., 137–39.

31. Ibid., 137; Metcalf, *Termination's Legacy*, 58.

32. Wilkinson, *Court of Claims*, 463–65. Wilkinson quoted tribal endorsements in his formal report and request for fees. See also Metcalf, *Termination's Legacy*, 253n24.

33. The bitterness against Wilkinson is based on personal communications from various members of the Northern Ute tribe, summers of 1978–1979, and again in 1998–1999. The belief Wilkinson personally made millions was a general consensus. See also Metcalf, *Termination's Legacy*, 49, 61, 253n24. Wilkinson as university president: e.g. Spencer W. Kimball, "The Expanding Indian Program," *Ensign*, October 6, 1956; Woodruff J. Deem and Glenn Bird, *Ernest L. Wilkinson—Indian Advocate and University President* (Provo, UT: Alice Wilkinson).

34. See, e.g., Philp, *Indian Self-Rule*, 58–59, 80–81, 118–21; Metcalf, *Termination's Legacy*, 59–62. For more on termination, see, e.g., Bernstein, *American Indians and World War II* (ch. 8); Donald Fixico, *Termination and Relocation: Federal Indian Policy, 1945–1960* (Albuquerque: University of New Mexico Press, 1986); Kenneth Philp, *Termination Revisited: American Indians on the Trail to Self-Determination, 1933–1953* (Lincoln: University of Nebraska Press, 1999); and U.S. Congress, *Termination of Federal Supervision over Certain Tribes of Indians, Joint Hearings before the Subcommittees on Interior and Insular Affairs, 83rd Cong., 2nd sess., on S. 2670 and H.R. 7674*, part 1, "Utah" (1954).

35. See, e.g., Philp, *Indian Self-Rule*, 21–22, 45, 58–59, 80–81, 119, 124, 134–36; Metcalf, *Termination's Legacy*, 2–5, 11, 82, 38–39. Bernstein, *American Indians and World War II*, 89–111.

36. Metcalf, *Termination's Legacy*, 5, 19, 43–46, 63, 75, 82, 112, and quoting Ernest Wilkinson, Rep. James G. Donovan [NY], Rep. O. K. Armstrong [MO], Sen. Arthur V. Watkins [UT], and Rep. Reva B. Bosone [UT] in the *Los Angeles Herald*.

37. Metcalf, *Termination's Legacy*, 43–45, 55, 83; Fixico, *Termination and Relocation*.

38. Metcalf, *Termination's Legacy*, 5–6, 78–81; cf. Bernstein, *Indians and World War II*, 159–75.

39. Metcalf, *Termination's Legacy*, 15, 46, 76–78.

40. Thomas G. Alexander, *Utah, The Right Place*, rev. ed. (Salt Lake City: Gibbs Smith, 2003), 379–80; and cf. Brigham Young High School (BYH) Alumni Web site, "Arthur V. Watkins & the Law of Unintended Consequences: Attorney, U.S. Senator, Historian," BYH biographies (Class of 1906), at http://www.byhigh.org/Alumni_U_to_Z/Watkins/ArthurV.html.

41. Robert Bennett, quoted in Metcalf, *Termination's Legacy*, 144.

42. Metcalf, *Termination's Legacy*, 2–5, 15, 22–37; Ronald L. Holt, *Beneath These Red Cliffs: An Ethnohistory of the Utah Paiutes* (Albuquerque: University of New Mexico Press, 1992), 63–64, 72, 78–79; Philp, *Indian Self-Rule*, 177; "Arthur V. Watkins," BYH alumni page (online).

43. Metcalf, *Termination's Legacy*, 95, 101, 122; Holt, *Beneath These Red Cliffs*, 65–68, 72; Alexander, *Utah*, 382–84.

44. Young, *Ute Indians of Colorado*, 153, 178; Metcalf, *Termination's Legacy*, 87.

45. Metcalf, *Termination's Legacy*, 65–74 147.

46. Young, *Ute Indians of Colorado*, 143–50; Metcalf, *Termination's Legacy*, 87–91.

47. See comments in Metcalf, *Termination's Legacy*, 210–17. See also Larry Cesspooch, personal communication with the author, March 18, 1999.

    Much literature exists on the controversial topic of blood quantum, tribal enrollment, and Indian identity. A sample includes James A. Clifton, "Alternate Identities and Cultural Frontiers," in *Being and Becoming Indian: Biographical Studies of North American Frontiers* (Chicago: Dorsey Press, 1989); Eva Marie Garroutte, "The Racial Formation of American Indians: Negotiating Legitimate Identities within Tribal and Federal Law," *American Indian Quarterly* 25 (Spring 2001): 224–39; David L. Beaulieu, "Curly Hair and Big Feet: Physical Anthropology and the Implementation of Land Allotment on the White Earth Chippewa Reservation," *American Indian Quarterly* 18 (Autumn 1984): 281–314; Circe Sturm, "Blood Politics, Racial Classification, and Cherokee National Identity," *American Indian Quarterly* 22 (Winter/Spring 1998): 230–57; and Sturm, *Blood Politics: Race, Culture, and Identity in the Cherokee Nation of Oklahoma* (Berkeley: University of California Press, 2002), esp. 202–12; Terry P. Wilson, "Blood Quantum: Native American Mixed Bloods," in *Racially Mixed People in America* (Thousand Oaks, CA: Sage Publications, 1992), 108–25

48. "Fetishized" in Sturm, *Blood Politics*, 230–57. See also Kenneth Lincoln, *Indi'n Humor: Bicultural Play in Native America* (New York: Oxford University Press, 1993); Pauline Turner Strong and Barrik Van Winkle, "'Indian Blood': Reflections on the Reckoning and Refiguring of Native North American Identity," *Cultural Anthropology* 11 (November, 1996): 547–76; Garroutte, "Racial Formation," 224–39; George Pierre Castile, "The Commodification of Indian Identity," *American Anthropologist*, New Series 98 (December 1996): 743–49; Joane Nagel, *American Indian Ethnic Renewal: Red Power and the Resurgence of Identity and Culture* (New York: Oxford University Press, 1996), 140–41, 237–48; Clifton, "Alternate Identities," 17; and Vine Deloria, quoted in Metcalf, *Termination's Legacy*, 216, from a rebuttal review of James A. Clifton's *The Invented Indian: Cultural Fictions and Government Policies*.

49. See, e.g., Joanne Barker, "Indian™ U.S.A.," *Wicazo Sa Review* 18 (Spring 2003): 25–79; Alice B. Kehoe, "Primal Gaia: Primitivists and Plastic Medicine Men," in Clifton, *The Invented Indian*; Sturm, *Blood Politics*, 139; Clifton, "Alternate Identities," 17–18, 23; Castile, "The Commodification of Indian Identity"; Angela A. Gonzales, "Gaming and Displacement: Winners and Losers in American Indian Casino Development," *International Social Science Journal* 55 (March 2003): 123–33; Peter Beinart, "Lost Tribes: Anthropologists Feud over Indian Identity," *Lingua Franca* (May/June 1999): 35–37; William T. Hagen, "Full Blood, Mixed Blood, Generic, and Ersatz: The Problem of Indian Identity," *Arizona and the West* 27 (Winter 1985): 309–26.

50. Metcalf, *Termination's Legacy*, 138. Cf. Jorgensen, *Sun Dance Religion*, 151–52; and Parker M. Nielson (attorney for the terminated Utes), *The Dispossessed: Cultural Genocide of the Mixed-Blood Utes* (Norman: University of Oklahoma Press, 1998). Metcalf covered this issue in the most depth and is cited extensively here, supplemented by personal observations and conversations with full- and mixed-blood Utes.

51. Conflict between "full-bloods" and mixed-heritage members is endemic on all reservations; see, e.g., Devon A. Mehesuah, "Too Dark to be Angels: The Class System among the Cherokees at the Female Seminary," *American Indian Culture and Research Journal* 15, no. 1 (1991): 29–52.

503

52. Nicaagat: Robert Emmitt, *The Last War Trail: The Utes and the Settlement of Colorado* (Norman: University of Oklahoma Press, 1954), 39–40. His sources included personal interviews with Saponise Cuch, who knew Nicaagat personally. On Chipeta, see Cynthia S. Becker and P. David Smith, *Chipeta: Queen of the Utes* (Montrose, CO: Western Reflections, 2003), 2. For more on Ouray, see Becker and Smith, *Chipeta*, 11–12, 17; Thomas F. Dawson, "Major Thompson, Chief Ouray and the Utes: An Interview, May 23, 1921," *Colorado Magazine* 7 (May 1930): 113–22; and cf. P. David Smith, *Ouray, Chief of the Utes* (Ouray, CO: Wayfinder Press, 1986).

53. Metcalf, *Termination's Legacy*, 69–73, 148.

54. See, e.g., Castile, "Commodification of Indian Identity," 200–220; *Santa Clara Pueblo v. Martinez*, 436 U.S. 49 (1978); Sturm, *Blood Politics*, esp. 105–7, 201–12; Alexandra Harmon, *Indians in the Making: Ethnic Relations and Indian Identities around Puget Sound* (Berkeley: University of California Press, 1998); and Harmon, "Tribal Enrollment Councils: Lessons on Law and Indian Identity," *Western Historical Quarterly* 32 (Summer 2001): 175–200; and Kimberly TallBear, "DNA, Blood, and Racializing the Tribe," *Wicazo Sa Review* 18 (Spring 2003): 81–107.

55. Metcalf, *Termination's Legacy*, 69–72, 134, 161–62.

56. Louise Lamphere, "The Problem of Membership in the Southern Ute Tribe," Research report #41, Tri-Ethnic Research Project (University of Colorado, 1963). Fear of birth defects was also expressed among members of the Uintah-Ouray Tribe in personal communications with the author, 1979.

57. Young, *Ute Indians of Colorado*, 3–5, 22, 142–43; *Washington Star* cited in Metcalf, *Termination's Legacy*, 87.

58. Young, *Ute Indians of Colorado*, 142–55.

59. Ibid., 143–49; Eddie Box, spiritual leader, personal communication with Robert Jones, 1979, notes in author's possession.

60. Young, *Ute Indians of Colorado*, 149–50.

61. Metcalf, *Termination's Legacy*, 87–88, 91.

62. Ibid., 12, 85, 93–96.

63. Ibid., 46–47, 68, 72–74, 88–89.

64. Ibid., 46–48, 57. Mixed-blood organizations continue to use the "interloper" arguments today. See, e.g., Affiliated Ute Citizens website at http://affiliatedutecitizens.org/and associated links (retrieved 2007).

65. Metcalf, *Termination's Legacy*, 125–30. On the Uncompahgre's continued desire to separate, see "Uncompahgre Band's Petition" (to separate itself from the other bands of Ute Indian Tribe), *Ute Bulletin*, October 20, 2017.

66. Metcalf, *Termination's Legacy*, 125–30; cf. Steven Crum, "Almost Invisible: The Brotherhood of North American Indians (1911) and the League of North American Indians (1935)," *Wicazo Sa Review* 21, no. 1 (Spring 2006): 43–59; Stewart Rafert, *The Miami Indians of Indiana* (Indiana Historical Society, 2016), 234.

67. Metcalf, *Termination's Legacy*, 98–99, 127, 130–31, 139.

68. Ibid., 127–31, 140–42. Some Uncompahgre's were still trying to do this as late as 2017.

69. Holt, *Beneath These Red Cliffs*, esp. 61–87; Metcalf, *Termination's Legacy*, 102–23, 141, 196.

70. Holt, *Beneath These Red Cliffs*, 98–147; and Metcalf, *Termination's Legacy*, 122–23.

71. Holt, *Beneath These Red Cliffs*, 98–147; and Metcalf, *Termination's Legacy*, 122–23.

72. Metcalf, *Termination's Legacy*, 99–100.

73. Ibid., 143–46, and "Lambs of Sacrifice," 332.

74. Metcalf, *Termination's Legacy*, 143–46, and "Lambs of Sacrifice," 332–33.

75. Metcalf, *Termination's Legacy*, 146–65, 180, and "Lambs of Sacrifice," 332–37.

76. See evidence presented in Metcalf, *Termination's Legacy*, and "Lambs of Sacrifice."

77. Metcalf uses this term; see "Lambs of Sacrifice," 323, 334–35, 342–43, and *Termination's Legacy*, 154–56, 178–79. See also commentary on tribal enrollment issues in Harmon, "Tribal Enrollment Councils," 175–200; and Harmon, "When is an Indian not an Indian? The 'Friends of the Indian' and the Problems of Indian Identity," 18 *Journal of Ethnic Studies* (Summer 1990): 95–123.

78. Metcalf, "Lambs of Sacrifice," 132, 135, 327–34, and *Termination's Legacy*, 148.

79. Metcalf, *Termination's Legacy*, 164–66.

80. Ibid., 134–35, 157, 204–5, 222, 227–29, and quoting Hugh Sesswich, Sonny Van, Smiley Denver, and other terminated mixed-bloods. Cf. Nielsen, *The Dispossessed;* and personal conversations with mixed-blood Reed and Gardiner families, March 1999 and spring 2003.

81. Metcalf, *Termination's Legacy*, 157, 159, 189, 167–80.

82. Fixico, *Termination and Relocation*; Metcalf, *Termination's Legacy*.

83. Philp, *Indian Self-Rule*, 22–23, 125–28, 138; Fixico, *Termination and Relocation*; Metcalf, *Termination's Legacy*; Richard Nixon, July 8, 1970, "Special Message to the Congress on Indian Affairs," *Senate Committee on Indian Affairs Briefing Booklet: The Enduring Validity of Indian Self-Determination*, Presidential Policy Papers (online at senate.gov).

84. Metcalf, *Termination's Legacy*, 168–214, and ch. 7. Metcalf details this manipulation, as does Nielson in *The Dispossessed: Cultural Genocide of the Mixed-Blood Utes*. Holt, in *Beneath These Red Cliffs*, presents similar jaded views of Boyden's relations with the Southern Paiutes.

85. Nelson, *The Dispossessed*; personal conversations (1999) with mixed-blood Reed and Gardiner families, and full-blood members, including Larry Cesspooch (public relations) and Fred Conetah (tribal museum director and historian), summers 1979, 1980. Cf. Jorgensen, *Sun Dance Religion*, 152; and Jorgensen, "The Ethnohistory and Acculturation of the Northern Ute" (PhD diss., Indiana University, Bloomington, 1964), 248. Regarding current issues, see, e.g., "Mixed Blood Group Prosecuted…for Wire Fraud," *Ute Bulletin*, November 3, 2017.

86. Metcalf, *Termination's Legacy*, 232; cf. Jorgensen, *Sun Dance Religion*, 152; and Jorgensen, "Ethnohistory and Acculturation," 248.

87. Nielsen, *The Dispossessed,* 45, 160–83; Metcalf, *Termination's Legacy,* 181–203. See also Melissa Meyer, "American Indian Blood Quantum Requirements: Blood is Thicker than Family," in *Over the Edge: Remapping the American West* (Berkeley: University of California Press, 1999), 231–44.

88. Quoted in Metcalf, *Termination's Legacy*, 227–28.

89. As noted in Chapter 2, Yuta was the Spanish name for the Núu-ci (or Nuche). Núu-ci simply means "the people," and all of the Numic tribes used linguistic variants of this term. However, those who identified as Yuta Núu-ci recognized themselves as one people, separate from the other Numic tribes. See Chapter 2, herein.

90. Testimony of historian Floyd O'Neil regarding the identity of Uintah and Timpanogos Indians, in *Timpanogos Tribe, Snake Band of Shoshone Indians v. Conway and Leavitt*, 10th Circuit Court of Appeals, April 15, 2002, decided 2005; Floyd O'Neil, personal communication with author, March 2011; and Omer Stewart, personal communication with author, fall 1978. Stewart and Smith argued Ute identity in the Uintah land claims case. See Smith, *Ethnography of the Northern Utes*, 18–19; and cf. Kelly, *Southern Paiute Ethnography*, 33–34, 91, 145, 175.

91. See, e.g., Mixed-Blood Uintas website, at http://www.undeclaredutes.net/ProfileOranna.html, retrieved 2008; Oran F. Curry, interview, July 20, 1967, 19–21, no. 48, box 3, Doris Duke Oral History Collection, and Henry Harris, Jr., interview, July 19, 1967, 7–12, Doris Duke Oral History.

92. Floyd O'Neil, testimony, in *Timpanogos Tribe, Snake Band of Shoshone Indians v. Conway and Leavitt*; and O'Neil, personal communication with author, March 2011.

93. See Metcalf, *Termination's Legacy*, 130, 133–37, and quotes 231–33; Jorgensen, *Sun Dance Religion*, 138–39; personal conversations with members of the Reed and Gardiner families, 1979–1981, 2009, and 2011; J. A. Jones, *The Sun Dance of the Northern Ute*, Bureau of American Ethnology, Anthropology Paper 4, Bulletin no. 157 (Washington, D.C.: Smithsonian Institution, 1955), 229–31. Uintah-Ouray Utes told J. A. Jones about the ratification chicanery.

94. Metcalf, *Termination's Legacy*, 186–90.

95. Ibid., 180–217.

96. Ibid., 194–202.

97. Ibid., 202–3; Larry Cesspooch, personal communication with author, March 18, 1999.

98. Metcalf, *Termination's Legacy*, 211–12. Cf. Nielsen, *The Dispossessed*.

99. *Ute Distribution Corporation v. Ute Indian Tribe*, 10th U.S. Cir. Ct. of App. (1998) #96-4194; and *Ute Distribution Corporation v. Norton et al.* (2002), #01-4020. On attitudes toward the UDC, see Metcalf, *Termination's Legacy*; similar attitudes were shared by Colleen Gardiner and sister, Mrs. Reed, in conversations with author, summer 1999 and April 2009.

  On fraudulent sales, see Metcalf, *Termination's Legacy*, 192–203; Nielsen, *The Dispossessed,* 140–211, esp. 184–211; and see *Ute Distribution Corporation v. Norton* (2002); *Ute Distribution*

505

Corporation v. Ute Indian Tribe, "Background" and "Opinion," #95-CV-37-W (1998); *Affiliated Ute Citizens of Utah v. United States,* 406 U.S. 128 (1972).

100. Larry Cesspooch, tribal public relations, personal communication with author, March 18, 19, 1999. To be enrolled with the Northern Utes, a member had to be five-eighths Northern Ute. Being Southern or Ute Mountain Ute did not qualify one. For more, see Metcalf, *Termination's Legacy,* 205–10. *The Deseret News* and *Salt Lake Tribune* often report on prominent litigation or conflict between the mixed-blood Uintahs and the Ute Tribe. The tribe's *Ute Bulletin* now publish detailed articles on current legal battles as well. For one 2017 example, see "Mixed Blood Group Prosecuted…for Wire Fraud…sale of Invalid Hunting and Fishing Licenses," *Ute Bulletin,* October 25, 2017. See typical arguments about mixed-blood identity and rights in *State v. Reber,* 171 P.3d 406 (2007 UT 36); *State v. Gardner,* 827 P.2d 980, 981 (Ut. Ct. App. 1992); and *Gardner and Kozlowiecz v. United States et al.,* 25 F.3d 1056 (10th Cir. 1994).

101. *Ute Distribution Corporation v. Ute Indian Tribe,* D.C. (1998); and reports in *Deseret News,* October 14, 1989, March 30, 1991, February 2, 1996, June 26, 1997, January 4, August 2, September 9, October 19, 1998.

102. On identity and the use of blood quantum as a legal fiction to manage tribal resources and determine preferential treatment by the federal government, see e.g., Metcalf, *Termination's Legacy,* 210–17. Also, *Santa Clara Pueblo v. Martinez.* Also, personal communication with mixed-blood Gardiner family, Mrs. Reed, and Tribal Public Relations officer, Larry Cesspooch, March 18–19, 1999, and telephone conversation with unidentified secretary, Tohono O'odham Tribe, winter 1993.

103. Quoted in Metcalf, *Termination's Legacy,* 205–10; *Salt Lake Tribune,* August 1, 1993; and Darrel and Colleen Gardiner, summers 1979 and 1980, 1998.

104. *Salt Lake Tribune,* April 7, September 14, 1991.

105. See, e.g., The mixed-blood Uintas website, http://www.undeclaredutes.net (retrieved 2007), and especially "Why a Lawsuit" and "U.S. Government Holocaust against Terminated Utah Uinta Ute Indians Continues," documents posted online.

106. Maxie Chapoose (full-blood Uintah), quoted in *Termination's Legacy,* 233; similar sentiments from Darrell Gardiner, conversation with author, summer 1979.

107. *Timpanogos Tribe v. Conway,* No. 01-4056, 10th Circuit Court of Appeals, April 2002; The mixed-blood Uintas website, http://www.undeclaredutes.net/ (retrieved 2007); Uinta Valley Shoshone Tribe website at http://www.uintavalleyshoshonetribe.com. See also various court cases as reported in *Deseret News,* June 7, 1988, November 9, 20, 30, 1999, September 8, 16, 23, 2000, October 12, 2002, March 23, 2004, and *Ute Bulletin,* November 3, 2017; Colleen (Reed) Gardiner and sister, Mrs. Reed, conversations with author, March 19, 1999.

108. Prominent court cases involving the Timpanogos tribe include *Timpanogos Tribe v. Conway* (2002); *Ute Distribution Corporation v. Norton* (2002); *State v. Gardner, 827 P.2d. 980, 981* (Ut. Ct. App. 1992); *Gardner v. United States, et al.,* 25 F.3d 1056 (10th Cir. 1994); *State v. Reber,* 171 P.3d 406 (2007 UT 36). See also "Mixed Blood…Wire Fraud," *Ute Bulletin,* November 3, 2017; and, e.g., *Deseret News,* June 7, 1988, November 9, 20, 30, 1999, September 8, 16, 23, 2000, January 8, 2001, October 12, 2002, March 23, 2004.

CHAPTER 16

1. Donald Fixico, *Termination and Relocation: Federal Indian Policy, 1945–1960* (Albuquerque: University of New Mexico Press, 1986).

2. Richard Nixon, July 8, 1970, "Special Message to the Congress on Indian Affairs," *Senate Committee on Indian Affairs Briefing Booklet: The Enduring Validity of Indian Self-Determination,* Presidential Policy Papers, online at senate.gov and at http://www.presidency.ucsb.edu/ws/?pid=2573; Robert T. Anderson, "Blurring the Boundaries on Tribal and State Jurisdiction," *Washington State Bar News,* November 2002, online.

3. NCAI was formed in November 1944 and had become increasingly influential. See Thomas Cowger, *The National Congress of the American Indians: The Founding Years* (Lincoln: University of Nebraska Press, 1999). "National Indian Young Council—History," University of New Mexico e-library regarding NIYC Records, Center for Southwest Research, General Library, University of New

Mexico; and, e.g., Robert Allen Warrior, "Clyde Warrior [Ponca]," in *Encyclopedia of Native American Indians* (online) (Houghton-Mifflin, March 2004); Ward Churchill, "Radicals and Radicalism, 1900 to Present," *Encyclopedia of Native American Indians* (online) (Houghton-Mifflin, retrieved March 2004); Alexandra Harmon, *Indians in the Making: Ethnic Relations and Indian Identities around Puget Sound* (Los Angeles: University of California Press, 1998), 213–14, 232–35.

4. See, e.g., Dennis Banks, *Ojibwa Warrior: Dennis Banks and the Rise of the American Indian Movement* (Norman: University of Oklahoma Press, 2004); Mary Crow Dog and Richard Erdoes, *Lakota Woman* (New York: Harpers, 1990). Sherman Alexie mentions his mother's forced sterilization in *The Absolutely True Diary of a Part-Time Indian*; Johanna Schoen describes coercive sterilization among low-status women, including Indians, in *Choice and Coercion: Birth Control, Sterilization, and Abortion in Public Health and Welfare* (Chapel Hill: University of North Carolina Press, 2005).

5. Dennis Banks, *Ojibwa Warrior*; Churchill, "Radicals and Radicalism"; Joseph M. Marshall, III, "Wounded Knee Takeover, 1973," in *Encyclopedia of North American Indians* (online); Crow Dog, *Lakota Woman*; Joan Rapczynski, "Native American Culture in Crisis" (Yale-New Haven Teacher's Institute: Yale University), online; "America in Ferment: The Tumultuous 1960s—The Native American Power Movement" in Digital History, *Online American History Textbook* (University of Houston, retrieved March 2004).

6. Dennis Banks, *Ojibwa Warrior*; Churchill, "Radicals and Radicalism"; Joseph M. Marshall, III, "Wounded Knee Takeover, 1973," in *Encyclopedia of North American Indians* (online); Crow Dog, *Lakota Woman*; Joan Rapczynski, "Native American Culture in Crisis" (Yale-New Haven Teacher's Institute: Yale University), online; "America in Ferment: The Tumultuous 1960s—The Native American Power Movement" in Digital History, *Online American History Textbook* (University of Houston, retrieved March 2004). For specific and in-depth details and statistics on the economic status of Ute Indians in the 1940s, 1950s, and early 1960s, see Joseph G. Jorgensen, *The Sun Dance Religion: Power for the Powerless* (Chicago: University of Chicago Press, 1972), ch. 4–5.

7. Kenneth R. Philp, ed., *Indian Self-Rule: First Hand Accounts of Indian-White Relations from Roosevelt to Reagan* (Salt Lake City: Howe Brothers, 1986), 113; Richard K. Young, *The Ute Indians of Colorado in the Twentieth Century* (Norman: University of Oklahoma Press, 1997), 230.

8. Indian Civil Rights Act, 25 U.S.C. §§ 1301–3 (1968), emphasis added; *Santa Clara Pueblo v. Martinez*, 436 U.S. 49, 1978.

9. See, e.g., *Deseret News*, January 11, 1989, November 9, 1994.

10. *Deseret News*, February 4, March 2, 4, 5, 9, 1989.

11. Larry Cesspooch (Northern Ute public relations), personal communication, March 18–19, 1999; *Deseret News*, March 2, 23, 1989, November 9, 1994; and, e.g., *Ute Distribution Corporation v. Ute Indian Tribe*, United States 10th Circuit Court of Appeals, D.C. No. 95-CV-37-W (1998).

12. U.S. Congress, Senate, Committee on Labor and Public Welfare, Special Subcommittee on Indian Education, *Indian Education: A National Tragedy—A National Challenge*, 91st Cong., 1st Sess. (1969), S. Rept. 91–501. See also U.S. Department of Education, "History of Indian Education: Legislative History," available online; Kim M. Gruenwald, "American Indians and the Public School System: A Case Study of the Northern Utes," *Utah Historical Quarterly* 64 (Summer 1996): 253–57.

13. Indian Education Act, U.S.C. 25, chap 27, and PL 93-380 (1974), PL 100-297 (1988), PL 103-382 (1994), and PL 107-10 (2001).

14. Self-Determination and Education Assistance Act, 25 U.S.C. Chap. 14, PL 93-638 Stat. 2203 (1975).

15. L. Cesspooch, personal communication, March 18–19, 1999; Raymond Wissiup (asst. director, tribal Fish and Wildlife, and director of conservation officers), personal communication, March 18, 1999.

16. Indian Health Care Act, 25 U.S.C. Chap. 18; Indian Child Welfare Act, 25 U.S.C. Chap. 21; Native American Graves Protection and Repatriation Act (NAGPRA], 25 U.S.C. Chap. 32.

17. Numerous press and journal articles have addressed the question of who "owns" Indian remains. See, e.g., David Hurst Thomas, *Skull Wars: Kennewick Man, Archaeology, and the Battle for Native American Identity* (New York: Basic Books, 2000), xix–xxvi, 29–63, 232–34, 241–43. *Anasazi* is a Navajo word meaning "enemy" or "non-Navajo ancestor."

18. Indian Religious Freedom Act (1978), 42 U.S.C. Chap. 21 (civil rights), subchap. I, sec. 1996a; Religious Freedom Restoration Act (1993), Chap. 21B, 107 Stat. 1488, 42 U.S.C. Sec. 2000bb.

19. Laws vary from state to state. See Chapter 13, here; Robert Gehrke, "Utah Case Tests American Indian Peyote Law," *Cannabis News*, retrieved January 8, 2001 from www.cannabisnews; Omer C.

507

Stewart, "The Native American Church and the Law, with Description of Peyote Religious Services," reprint from *Westerners Brand Book* 17 (1961); and *Employment Div., Ore. Dept. of Human Res. V. Smith*, 494 U.S. 872 (1990).

20. Philp, *Indian Self-Rule*, 189–90, 194, 221; U.S. Department of Justice, "Department of Justice Policy on Indian Sovereignty and Government-to-Government Relations with Indian Tribes," available online.

21. Philp, *Indian Self-Rule*, 194–200; Young, *Ute Indians of Colorado*, 198–201.

22. Philp, *Indian Self-Rule*, 198–200, 221.

23. Young, *Ute Indians of Colorado*, 179, 183, 198–201; Philp, *Indian Self-Rule*, 199, 209–10, and referencing Robert Bennett; Jorgensen, *Sun Dance Religion*, 121–24; *Salt Lake Tribune*, November 19, 1998; "Graveyard," in Kenneth Y. Tomlinson, "Scalping at Crow Creek," *Reader's Digest* (October, 1979): 199–200. Adding to the problems, OPEC imposed an oil embargo in 1973, significantly impacting tourism nationwide.

24. Philp, *Indian Self-Rule*, 12, 24; Anderson, "Blurring the Boundaries"; Peter d'Errico, "Sovereignty: A Brief History in the Context of U.S. 'Indian Law'" (posted online), article prepared for inclusion in *The Encyclopedia of Minorities in American Politics* (Amherst, MS: University of Massachusetts Legal Studies Department).

25. On the National Conference of State Legislatures, see "Federal and State Recognized Tribes," online. *California v. Cabazon Band of Mission Indians*, 480 U.S. 202 (1987); Indian Gaming Regulatory Act, 25 U.S.C. sec. 2701 (PL 100-497) (1988); National Indian Gaming Association (NIGA), "Indian Gaming Facts" (online).

26. NIGA, "2005 Economic Impact of Indian Gaming" (online); Patricia L. Janes, and Jim Collison, "Community Leader Perceptions of the Social and Economic Impacts of Indian Gaming," *University of Las Vegas Gaming Research & Review Journal* 8 (2004): 13–30. On controversies, see Peter Beinart, "Lost Tribes: Anthropologists Feud over Indian Identity," *Lingua Franca* (May/June 1999): 35–37; Angela Gonzales, "Gaming and Displacement: Winners and Losers in American Indian Casino Development," *International Social Science Journal* 55 (March 2003): 128–31; James A. Clifton, "Alternate Identities and Cultural Frontiers," in *Being and Becoming Indian: Biographical Studies of North American Frontiers*, edited by James A. Clifton (Chicago: Dorsey Press, 1989), 23.

27. Janes and Collison, "Economic Impacts of Indian Gaming," 13–30; *Deseret News*, July 19, 1992; L. Cesspooch, personal communication, March 18–19, 1999.

28. Young, *Ute Indians of Colorado*, 109–10, 157–58, 163, 185–86; Jorgensen, *Sun Dance Religion*, 115, 123–27.

29. Miller, as quoted in Young, *Ute Indians of Colorado*, 286, 260–62.

30. Ibid.; Jorgensen, *Sun Dance Religion*, 123–27, 170–72; *Deseret News*, January 1, 2000.

31. Jorgensen, *Sun Dance Religion*, 159–67; Young, *Ute Indians of Colorado*, 186, 190–92, 236–38.

CHAPTER 17

1. Joseph G. Jorgensen, *The Sun Dance Religion: Power for the Powerless* (Chicago: University of Chicago Press, 1972), 152

2. Jorgensen, *Sun Dance Religion*, 155; personal conversations with various Uintah and Uncompahgre mixed-blood Utes and members of the Whiteriver and Uintah bands, summer 1979 and 1980.

3. Jorgensen, *Sun Dance Religion*, 159–60.

4. Ibid., 111–15, 163–65.

5. Ibid., 156–57.

6. Ibid., 159–73.

7. Ibid., 111, 163–64.

8. Ibid., 121–24; *Salt Lake Tribune*, November 19, 1998; and, e.g., Kenneth Y. Tomlinson, "Scalping at Crow Creek," *Reader's Digest* (October 1979): 199–200.

9. Salt Lake City newspapers covered the political brouhahas on the Northern Ute Reservation in depth. See, e.g., *Deseret News*, February 4, 7, March 3, April 18, 19, May 1, June 11, 17, July 12, and November 1989, September 5, 1994, June 3, 25, and August 24, 1995, April 23, 1997, December 20,

1998; *Salt Lake Tribune*, May 26, September 7, November 16, December 27, 1995, and December 15, 1998.

10. *Deseret News*, June 11, 17, July 12, 1989; and *Deseret News*, April 23, 1997, December 20, 1998; *Salt Lake Tribune*, September 7, November 16, and December 27, 1995, and December 15, 1998.

11. *Deseret News*, April 3, May 17, 1991, May 16, 1992, January 7, 13, 19, February 4, 23, March 27, 29, June 3, 14, July 13, 24, August 13, 24, September 5, 19, 29, 1995, April 23, 1997, December 20, 1998; and *Salt Lake Tribune*, June 13, September 7, November 16, and December 27, 1995, December 15, 1998.

12. Michael Omi and Howard Winant, "Racial Formations," in *Race Critical Theories: Text and Context*, edited by Philomena Essed and David Theo Goldberg (Hoboken, NJ: Wiley-Blackwell, 2001), 123–45; cf. Howard Winant, "Race and Race Theory," *Annual Review of Sociology* 26 (2000): 169–85. On the discussion of non-Indian reaction to Indian wealth, see Alexandra Harmon, *Rich Indians: Native People and the Problem of Wealth in American History* (Chapel Hill: University of North Carolina, 2010), and esp. "Gambling Money," 249–79.

13. Raymond Cross, "Tribes as Rich Nations," *Oregon Law Review* 79 (Winter 2000): 896, 922–23.

14. Larry Cesspooch, Northern Ute Public Relations officer and spiritual advisor, interview with author, March 18–19, 1999; *Deseret News*, May 11, 1997.

15. *Deseret News*, December 3, 1989, May 11, 1997; L. Cesspooch, interview, March 18–19, 1999; *Ute Indian Tribe v. State of Utah*, 773 F. 2d 1087 (CA 10) [1985].

16. L. Cesspooch, interview, March 18–19 1999; *Deseret News*, November 30, 1989, May 15, 1991, July 19, 1992; *Salt Lake Tribune*, April 25, 1993.

17. *Hagen v. Utah*, U.S. 510-399 (1994); L. Cesspooch, interview, March 18–19, 1999.

18. *Hagen v. Utah*; *Ute Indian Tribe v. State of Utah*, 773 F. 2d 1087 (CA 10) (1985).

19. *Deseret News*, October 9, 1988; cf. L. Cesspooch, interview, March 18–19, 1999.

20. *Deseret News*, October 9, December 18, 1988, February 2, 18, 1989; L. Cesspooch, interview, March 18–19, 1999; Bob Martin, personal communication with author, July 2013.

21. Court Opinion, in *State of Utah v. Clinton Perank*, 858 P. 2nd 927, No. 860243, Supreme Court of Utah, July 17, 1992.

22. *Deseret News*, July 22, 30, 1992, and February 2, 1994; *Salt Lake Tribune*, July 21, 1992; *Solem v. Bartlett*, 465 U.S. 463, 467 (1984), cf. *Hagen v. Utah*.

23. *Deseret News*, July 30, 1992, November 2, 1993; *Salt Lake Tribune*, March 6, 1992, April 20, 25, November 1, 1993.

24. John D. Barton and Candace M. Barton, "Jurisdiction of Ute Reservation Lands," *American Indian Law Review* 26 (2001): 133–287; *Hagen v. Utah*. For reaction in Utah, see *Deseret News*, February 23, 24, and August 11, 1994.

25. John D. Barton and Candace M. Barton, "Jurisdiction of Ute Reservation Lands," *American Indian Law Review* 26 (2001): 133–287; *Hagen v. Utah*. For reaction in Utah, see *Deseret News*, February 23, 24, and August 11, 1994.

26. *Deseret News*, November 9, 1994.

27. *Deseret News*, February 24, 26, 27, 1994.

28. *Salt Lake Tribune*, May 10, 23, September 13, 1994; *Deseret News*, May 9, June 4, August 11, and September 13, 1994, October 5, 1995.

29. *Deseret News*, March 26, April 19, (Supreme Court refuses to review case), June 4, September 13, 1994, September 19, 1995, April 9, August 23, 1996.

30. *Deseret News*, May 27, 1992, March 27, 1994, June 22, 1995; *Salt Lake Tribune*, April 25, 1993.

31. *Deseret News*, September 19, 1995, April 9, 26, and August 23, 1996.

32. *Deseret News*, May 9, 11, October 27, November 28 (county appeals), and December 9, 1997; *Salt Lake Tribune*, February 24, 1998.

33. *Deseret News*, June 21, August 10, and December 9, 1997. Regarding taxation, see Native American Rights Fund and the Department of Human Resources, "FAQs," http://www.narf.org/pubs/misc/faqs.html; and http://aspe.hhs.gov/SelfGovernance/faqs.htm.

34. *Deseret News*, September 9, 20, 1997, August 2, 10, 1998.

35. *Deseret News*, September 20, October 13, 27, 1997, August 2, and October 10, 1998.

36. Cross, "Tribes as Rich Nations," 927–28. Cf. opinion, Justice William Rehnquist, *Oliphant v. Suquamish Tribe* (1978), regarding injustice of trying non-Indians in Indian tribal courts. See also L. Cesspooch, interview with author, March 18, 1999.

509

37. *Salt Lake Tribune*, May 31, 1998; *Deseret News*, August 2, 1998.

38. *Deseret News*, September 9, October 3, 10, and 26, 1998; *Salt Lake Tribune*, September 25, 1993, September 10, 1998, March 14, 2000.

39. *Salt Lake Tribune*, February 24, 1998, March 14, 2000; *Deseret News*, February 3, 1998, May 26, 2000.

40. On disputes, see, e.g., *Deseret News*, July 2, 1989, September 23, 1993, February 23, September 25, 28, 1994, April 6, 1995, September 10, 1996.

41. *Deseret News*, May 2, 1992, July 8, 1993.

42. Thomas Alexander, *Utah, The Right Place*, rev. ed. (Salt Lake City: Gibbs Smith, 2003), 303–7, 385–88, 413–14. For western water issues and arguments over the Colorado River, see Marc Reisner, *Cadillac Desert: The American West and Its Disappearing Water* (New York: Penguin, 1986), esp. "American Nile I" (125–264) and "American Nile II" (264–316); Michael Wines, "Colorado River Drought Forces a Painful Reckoning for States," *New York Times,* January 5, 2014.

43. On Indian water rights, see David H. Getches, "The Unsettling of the West: How Indians Got the Best Water Rights," *Michigan Law Review* 99 (May 2001): 1473–99, 1498–99, and John Shurts quoted on 1474. This article is an extensive review of Shurts' *Indian Reserved Water Rights: The Winters Doctrine in Its Social and Legal Context, 1880–1930s* (2000), as well as a discussion of how water rights developed.

44. *Central Utah Project Completion Act*, P.L. 102–575, 102nd Cong. (October 30, 1992), especially Title V: *Ute Indian Rights Settlement*, sec. 501-07; Alexander, *Utah, The Right Place*, 387–88; *Deseret News*, October 9, 1988; Getches, "The Unsettling of the West"; Coleen Gardiner, personal communication, summer 2000.

45. *Winters v. United States*, 207 U.S. 564 (1908); *Deseret News*, October 9, 1988, March 17, 19, and May 1, 1989.

46. *Deseret News*, May 1, and November 30, 1989.

47. *Deseret News*, November 30, 1989, February 7, 1994.

48. *Deseret News*, February 12, 1993, February 28, and October 27, 1995.

49. Ratification passed with 138–46. *Deseret News*, October 27, 1995, February 16, 1996; *Salt Lake Tribune,* February 11, 1993; *High Country News* (online), June 27, 1994, at *www.hcn.org.*

50. *Deseret News*, March 14, 1996, February 2, May 17, 1997, April 5, 1998. Colorado pikeminoow aka Colorado squawfish.

51. *Deseret News*, June 27, 1998, May 11, 1999; *Salt Lake Tribune,* May 8, 1999.

52. Quoted in *Salt Lake Tribune*, July 8, 1998.

53. *Deseret News*, May 11, June 15, 1999; *Salt Lake Tribune,* July 5, 1999.

54. *Deseret News*, January 1, 2000. See also "Utah Data Guide," Fall 2002, Utah State Data Center, Governor's Office of Planning and Budget; U.S. Census Bureau, Census 2000, "Quickfacts" (online); and Utah Division of Indian Affairs: Ute Tribe (online data, 2004).

55. *Deseret News*, April 27, 1993; Bureau of Land Management, "Production and Revenue Statistics," updated December 3, 2002, retrieved June 22, 2004 from BLM (Vernal Office) website.

56. On the right to tax, see *Merrion v. Jicarilla Apache Tribe*, 455 U.S. 130 (1982). Other cases also argued the state's right to tax extracted minerals had been preempted by the Indian Mineral Leasing Act (1938), 25 U.S.C. Sec 396a–396g). See, e.g., *Montana v. Crow Tribe*, 484 U.S. 997 (1998); *Montana v. Blackfeet Tribe*, 471 U.S. 759 (1985); and *Cotton v. New Mexico,* 490 U.S. 163 (1989).

57. *Deseret News*, April 26, November 30, and March 30, April 9, 1991, April 27, 1993, June 10, October 13, 1994, October 9, 2000; *Salt Lake Tribune,* June 20, 1998.

58. *Deseret News*, April 9, 1991, April 7, 1992; cf. "Kuwait Facts and Figures," OPEC website, http://www.opec.org/opec_web/en/about_us/165.htm.

59. *Deseret News*, April 26, 1989, March 30, 1991, April 27, 1993, June 10, 1994, October 9, 2000; *Salt Lake Tribune,* June 20, 1998.

60. *Deseret News*, March 6, 1991, March 6, 1992, April 17, 1996, March 13, 1997.

61. *Deseret News*, May 7, 1992, March 10, April 9, 1994, November 8, 1997, November 17, 23, 1998, May 2, 1999; *Salt Lake Tribune,* November 19, 1998.

62. L. Cesspooch, interview, March 18–19, 1999; Chapoose Canyon Adventures, Internet brochure, retrieved June 2004 from sidecanyon.com.

63. *Deseret News*, February 13, 1993. On the Tridell incident, see Steven McKee, telephone interview with author, January 1999. The Elk velvet industry is described in Elk Breeders home page, *http://*

510

wapiti.net (retrieved February 1999) and links to Colorado Elk and Game Breeders Association [CEBA], posted 1996; Mountain Velvet, Ltd. (one of many Colorado ranches), retrieved February 1999 from http://www.elkusa.com/Elk_Farming.htm; "Setting up Your Own Ranch," Elk Breeders Home Page, retrieved February 5, 1999 from Wapiti.net.

64. Purchaser for the Lone Cone Ranch (name withheld), telephone interview with author, February 10, 1999; and Elk Breeders, "Setting up Your Own Ranch" (online).

65. *Deseret News*, May 27, June 13, 1998; *Salt Lake Tribune*, October 10, 2000.

66. *Deseret News*, January 7, May 27, June 13, 1998; Raymond Wissiup, assistant director, Northern Ute Fish and Wildlife, interview with author, March 18, 1999; Lone Cone Ranch, telephone interview, February 10, 1999.

67. Wissiup, interview with author, March 18, 1999; Lone Cone Ranch, telephone interview, February 10, 1999. On the Utah state elk trade, see *Deseret News*, May 27, 1998, February 9, 1999.

68. *Deseret News*, December 20, 1991, March 25, 1994.

69. *Deseret News*, March 24, November 23, 1999, March 31, 2000, March 8, 2001; press releases and information links, Uinta River Technology website, www.uintarivertech.com (as of June 2004), northernute.com (June 2004), and utetribe.com (2017).

70. See, e.g., *Deseret News*, December 17, 1999, January 22, April 4, 2000; *Salt Lake Tribune*, February 6, 2000; *Cortez Journal*, December 2, 2003, June 8, 2015, May 3, 2016, May 13, 2017; Robert S. McPherson, *As if the Land Owned Us: An Ethnohistory of the White Mesa Utes* (Salt Lake City: University of Utah Press, 2011), 351–52.

71. *Dominion News* Press Releases, June 1, 2001 (online); *Business Wire* (online), May 18, 2001; *Indianz. com,* in print (online), May 21, 2001.

72. *Deseret News*, July 19, 1992; L. Cesspooch, interview with author, March 18–19, 1999. By 2015, Utah was one of only two states that did not allow gambling.

73. *Deseret News*, July 19, 1992; L. Cesspooch, interview, March 18–19, 1999; and personal observations at Sundances, 1978–1981, 1999.

74. *Deseret News*, July 19, 1992; L. Cesspooch, interview, March 18–19, 1991.

75. *Deseret News*, July 11, 28, September 20, 1999; *Salt Lake Tribune*, June 20, 1998. See also Alexandra Harmon, "Gambling Money," in *Rich Indians*, 249–79. Steamboat Springs and Hayden are both located on the Yampa River and were home to the Yampa Ute band.

76. Jurrius tenure (2001–2008) sparked significant interest in the news media. See, e.g., *Deseret News*, July 6, September 24, 2006; *Durango Herald*, December 6, 2000; and cf. *Wall Street Journal*, June 13, 2003. Quotes in "A New Day," and "Utes Thriving," *Deseret News*, September 24, 2006. See also "Our Team," at Native American Resources Partners, LLC Web site, http://narpllc.com.

77. See, e.g., *Salt Lake Tribune*, October 24, 2003; *Deseret News*, April 22, October 25 (editorial), 2003, December 6, 2005; and *Vernal Express*, April 20, 2005; *Wopsock, Duncan, and Kochamp v. Natchees et al. and Kepthorne et al.,* 05-1494, U.S. Court of Appeals for the Federal Circuit, July 11, 2006; *Wopsock v. Millicent Maxine Natchees*, Fed. Cir. 05-1494 (2006).

78. *Salt Lake Tribune*, November 12, 2003, August 18, November 30, 2012; *Deseret News,* March 4, 2005, July 6, September 24, 2006. On development of oil shale and tar sands, see *Deseret News*, August 11, 18, 26, 2006; and personal observation at earlier Basin planning meetings, 1980; cf. "Oil Boom," *Salt Lake Tribune*, November 30, 2012.

79. "Some Rich" and "Energy Fever Burns," in *Salt Lake Tribune*, October 8, 2006.

80. "Utes Thriving" and "A New Day," in *Deseret News*, July and September 24, 2006; "How Long Will Energy Boom Last?" and "Oil Boom," *Salt Lake Tribune*, October 8, 2006, November 30, 2012; "Ute Energy Corporation," at www.answers.com/topic/ute-energy-corporation; and Rebecca Penty, "Crescent Point to Buy Ute Energy for $784 Million," *Bloomberg*, web news at www.bloomberg.com/news/2012-11-01.

81. "Ute Energy Corporation," at Answers.com; "Crescent Point to Buy Ute Energy," and "Crescent Point Ups Ante in Uinta Basin," news releases at www.shaleexperts.com/articles. The other 49 percent of Ute Energy was owned by Quantum Energy Partners, which also partnered with John Jurrius' Canadian firm, Native American Resource Partners (NARP). International interests included Estonian-owned Eesti Energia and affiliate, Enefit American Oil. See "Oil Shale Extraction: Worse than Fracking," *Indian Country Today*, August 22, 2016, retrieved November 2016, from

indiancountryonlinemedia.com; and "Tar Sands in Utah?" *Indian Country Today*, August 27, 2016; and "Don't Let Estonian…," editorial, *Salt Lake Tribune*, June 12, 2016.

82. Reported in *Deseret News*, September 24, 2006; and, e.g., Ute Tribe, "Ute Bulletin," April 11, 2013.

83. *Deseret News*, April 19, 1989, January 1, 2000, October 27, 2005, July 6, September 24, 2006; *Salt Lake Tribune*, June 2, 2009, October 10, 2000; Jonathan Thompson, "The Ute Paradox," *High Country News*, July 19, 2010. Jurrius in Canada is in "Our Team," at Native American Resources Partners, LLC website. On data for income, see U.S. Census Bureau (2000) released August 13, 2002, also presented in "Utah Data Guide," fall 2002, in Utah State Data Center, Governor's Office of Planning and Budget; U.S. Census, "Quickfacts," for Utah. The "Utah Tribes Today: Ute" website was still citing out-of-date 1990 census statistics for individual Ute income in 2006. See also 2000 census statistics for Uintah and Duchesne County, Utah State Census 2000 Census Files, compiled by the University of Utah Bureau of Economic and Business Research for Uintah and Duchesne Counties, retrieved October 2006.

84. *Deseret News*, January 30, 1997. For examples of violence, see *Deseret News*, August 28, 1994, June 1, 1995 (Manning murder); *Deseret News*, December 6, 7, and 14, 1995 (Tapoof murder); *Deseret News*, July, October 2, November 3, 1997 (Murray murder).

85. *Deseret News*, March 27, 1997. For suicide risk among Indian youth, see, e.g., Angela A. Gonzales, "American Indians: Their Contemporary Reality and Future Trajectory," in *Challenges for Rural America in the Twenty-First Century* (University Park: University of Pennsylvania Press, 2003), 48; cf. David C. Grossman, B. Carol Milligan, and Richard Deyo, "Risk Factors for Suicide Attempts among Navajo Adolescents," *American Journal of Public Health* 81 (July 1991): 870–74.

86. Warren Ferris, *Life in the Rocky Mountains*, rev. ed. (Denver: Old West Publishing, 1983), 353. On the diabetes epidemic, see James Thalman, "Diabetes Ravaging Ute Tribe," *Salt Lake Tribune*, October 10, 2000, and citing tribally contracted study by Nedra Christiansen of Utah State University. See also National Diabetes Information Clearinghouse (NDIC), "Diabetes in American Indians and Alaska Natives," online report from the National Institute of Diabetes and Digestive and Kidney Diseases, National Institutes of Health, retrieved May 29, 2004, http://www2.niddk.nih.gov/; Noah T. Boaz, "Diabetes Mellitus and the 'Thrifty Genotype,'" ch. 9 in *Evolving Health: the Origins of Illness and How the Modern World is Making Us Sick* (New York: Wiley, 2002). And see Chapter 18, herein, for more information on diabetes.

87. *Salt Lake Tribune*, October 10, 2000, citing Nedra Christiansen; and Indian Health Services nurse, conversation with author in Roosevelt, 1979.

88. *Ute Bulletin*, September 20, 2006.

89. *Deseret News*, February 28, 1998.

90. *Deseret News*, February 23, April 13, 1989, March 31, 1991; *Salt Lake Tribune*, March 23, 1991; Darrel and Colleen Gardiner shared personal experiences with author, March 18, 1999. For child abuse examples, see *Salt Lake Tribune*, March 20, 2005, September 13, 2004. See also "Utah Tribe to Investigate Placement of Children," *Indianz.com*, October 11, 2004; cf. *Deseret News*, December 2, 2005.

91. L. Cesspooch, interview, March 18–19, 1999; *Salt Lake Tribune*, January 29, 1983; *Deseret News*, April 30, 1988. Significant examples of issues raised by the ICWA include highly publicized cases among the Navajo and the Cherokee. See U.S. *Adoptive Couple v. Baby Girl*, 570 U.S. ___ (2013) aka "Baby Veronica" case; Nina Totenberg, "Adoption Case Brings Rare Family Law Dispute to High Court," National Public Radio, April 2013, npr.org; Gene Demby, "Repealing Law in 'Baby Veronica,'" NPR, April 16, 2013 at npr.org/codeswitch/2013/04/16; Adam Liptak, "Justices Take Case on Adoption of Indian Child," *New York Times*, January 4, 2013; Troy R. Johnson, "The State and the American Indian: Who Gets the Indian Child?" *Wicazo Sa Review* 14 (2012).

92. See, e.g., *Salt Lake Tribune*, January 23, 1993; *Deseret News*, April 30, May 26, 1988.

93. *Deseret News*, November 20, 1996, January 25, 1997; *Marriage*, Utah Code, Title 30, Chap. 1, sec. 6 and 7, amended 2004. See "Colorado Marriage Laws: Common Law Marriages," Larimer County Virtual Courthouse website; and "Marriage Codes," Denver.gov Web site, City and County Recorder.

94. Kim M. Gruenwald, "American Indians and the Public School System: A Case Study of the Northern Utes," *Utah Historical Quarterly* 64 (Summer 1996): 246–63.

95. Gruenwald, "American Indians and the Public School System."

96. Ibid.

97. *Deseret News*, February 28, 1998, October 14, 1999.

98. On university involvement, see Gruenwald, "American Indians and the Public School System," 254–55, and on the school board, see *Deseret News*, February 4, 2000; *Salt Lake Tribune*, March 28, 1997, February 8, 2000, May 17, 2004; *Vernal Express*, April 2, 1997.

99. "School Attendance," *Ute Bulletin*, September 25, 2017; "Knowing the Name You Carry," *Ute Bulletin*, September 22, 2017.

100. *Deseret News*, November 23, 1999, June 2000; "Tribal Leaders Negotiate... Future Use of Ute Name," *Deseret News*, November 11, 2013, cf. April 15, 2014; Rocky Mountain Youth Corps program for teens and at-risk youth, Steamboat Springs, Colorado (online press release).

101. L. Cesspooch, interview, March 18–19, 1999. Cesspooch is a Vietnam veteran, one-time public affairs liaison, spiritual leader, and public storyteller.

102. *Salt Lake Tribune*, May 30, 2000; *Deseret News*, February 24, 2002; L. Cesspooch, interview, March 18–19, 1999; and see *Through Native Eyes* website (Larry Cesspooch director and producer), at https://www.throughnativeeyes.net/; and various online Youtube videos. Early published works by the tribe included *The Ute System of Government* (1977); and *The Ute People* (1977). See also June Lyman and Norma Denver, *Ute People: An Historical Study*, edited by Floyd A. O'Neil and John D. Sylvester (1970); *Weenoocheeyoo Peesaduehnee Yak:Anup: Stories of our Ancestors* (1974); and *Stories of our Ancestors: A Collection of Northern Ute Indian Tales* (1974), both illustrated by Clifford Duncan; and Fred Conetah (with Kathryn MacKay and Floyd A. O'Neil), *A History of the Northern Ute People* (Uintah-Ouray Tribe, 1982). Conetah had been director of the tribal museum.

103. *Salt Lake Tribune*, May 30, 2000; *Deseret News*, February 2002; L. Cesspooch, interview March 18–19, 1999.

104. *Salt Lake Tribune*, September 29, 1992; *Deseret News*, October 7, 2000.

105. *Salt Lake Tribune*, July 1, 1995; Frederick Quinn, "To Elevate the Red Man': The Episcopal Church's Native American Policy in Utah," *Utah Historical Quarterly* 73 (Winter 2005): 44–63.

106. *Deseret News*, December 8, 1991, September 8, 1992, May 5, June 4, 1994, January 29, 1995, April 29, 2000; *Salt Lake Tribune*, May 16, 1992, July 22, 1997, February 5, 1999; Darrell Gardiner, conversations with author, March 18, 1999, and July 18, 2000. See Chapters 13 and 15, herein, on mixed-blood religious controversy.

107. Cf. Harmon, *Rich Indians*, 249–79, esp. 268–72. See Forrest Cuch, ed., *A History of Utah's American Indians* (Salt Lake City: Utah State Division of Indian Affairs, 2000).

CHAPTER 18

1. Richard K. Young, *The Ute Indians of Colorado in the Twentieth Century* (Norman: University of Oklahoma Press, 1997), 167; Robert Delaney, *The Ute Mountain Utes* (Albuquerque: University of New Mexico Press, 1989), 100–101, 107; Frances Leon [Swadesh] Quintana, *Ordeal of Change: The Southern Utes and their Neighbors* (Walnut Creek: AltaMira Press, 2004), 79–80, 108.

2. Oneida Tribe of Indians of Wisconsin, "Robert L. Bennett," Oneida Nation website, http://www.oneidanation.org/museum/page.aspx?id=8492; Young, *Ute Indians of Colorado*, 131–32, 178–79.

3. Young, *Ute Indians of Colorado*, 172; Jonathan Thompson, "The Ute Paradox," *High Country News*, July 19, 2010.

4. Young, *Ute Indians of Colorado*, 3–4, 176–77, 204, 217, 222–25.

5. "Southern Ute Tribe: Council Members," and "Chairmen," retrieved 2013 from www.southernute-nsn.gov; Young, *Ute Indians of Colorado*, 3–4, 176–77, 204, 217, 222–25; Thompson, "The Ute Paradox."

6. Southern Ute Tribe, "Council Members," and "Veteran's Association," retrieved December 2017 from www.southernute-nsn.gov. On Euterpe Taylor, see Quintana, *Ordeal of Change*, 46–47; and cf Kathryn M. B. Osburn, "Women and Public Leadership," in *Southern Ute Women: Autonomy and Assimilation on the Reservation, 1887–1934* (Albuquerque: University of New Mexico Press, 1998), 21–35.

7. Southern Ute Tribe, "Tribal Council Members" and "Chairmen"; Young, *Ute Indians of Colorado*, 3–4, 176–77, 204, 217, 222–25, 275–79.

8. Young, *Ute Indians of Colorado*, 98, 125–26, 144, 168–69, 176–77.

513

9. Ibid., 144–45, 176–7; Southern Ute Veteran's Association, at www.southernute-nsn.gov/va/; "Sunshine Cloud Smith Dies," *Native News Online* archive, December 25, 2002, https://www.mail-archive.com/natnews@nativenewsonline.org/msg00002.html.

10. Young, *Ute Indians of Colorado*, 168, 144–45, 176–77; Southern Ute Tribe, "Tribal Council Members"; and Edward Bent "Red Ute" Box memorial notice, September 18, 2012, Ashville Mortuary (online).

11. Young, *Ute Indians of Colorado*, 176–77, 204, 217, 223–26.

12. Ibid., 132; Eddie Box, interview with Robert Jones, 1979; Larry Cesspooch, interview with author, March 18–19, 1999; Darrell Gardiner, conversations with author, March and August, 1999.

13. Personal observation, Northern and Southern Ute Reservations, 1980s and 2012; "New Museum," Cortez *Journal*, September 28, 2017. The museum in Montrose was to be directed by a Ute Mountain woman and member of the tribal council.

14. James A. Goss, "Ute Lexical and Phonological Patterns"(PhD diss., University of Chicago, 1972); Southern Ute Tribe, *Ute Dictionary and Ute Reference Grammar*, 2 vols., preliminary editions (Ignacio, CO: Ute Press, 1979); New dictionary and grammar announced, *Southern Ute Drum* (online), June 2016; "D'Wolf Launches Ute Language Software," *Southern Ute Drum*, April 20, 2013. See also Young, *Ute Indians of Colorado*, 269; Robert S. McPherson, *As If the Land Owned Us: An Ethnohistory of the White Mesa Utes* (Salt Lake City: University of Utah Press, 2011), 361.

15. Young, *Ute Indians of Colorado*, 6–8, 115, 118, 126, 177, 170–73, 222, 226–27.

16. Ibid., 6, 99, 106, 126, 171, 226–28.

17. Ibid., 195, 222, 227–29; Ute Mountain Ute Tribe website, data retrieved 2002 and 2013; Ernest House, testimony submitted to the Senate Committee on Indian Affairs, June 7, 2000, regarding S. 2508, Colorado Ute Water Settlement Act Amendments of 2000 (106th Cong., 2nd Sess., May 4, 2000). See also "Tourist Attractions," Ute Mountain Ute Tribe website at www.utemountainute.com.

18. Piah (Peter Snow), a Whiteriver Ute, was Chief Nevava's ("Snow") nephew. Identified on documents as a Uintah, Grand River, White River, or "Denver" Ute. See Omer C. Stewart, "Data on the Identification and Group Leadership of Ute Indian Chiefs" ("Ute Chiefs List"), working paper prepared for Dockets 44–45, U.S. Indian Claims Commission, 195, located in the Omer C. Stewart Collection, Archives of the Norlin Library, University of Colorado, Boulder, and in Special Collections, Marriot Library, University of Utah, Salt Lake City.

19. Young, *Ute Indians of Colorado*, 228–29; Judy Knight-Frank, "Excerpts of Testimony," posted on Ute Mountain and Southern Ute Tribes, Animas-La Plata website, accessed variously 1999–2005 from www.animaslp.com; Testimony of Earnest House and "What Others Are Saying," Animas-La Plata website; *Rocky Mountain News*, March 23, 2004; and Press Release, U.S. Dept. of Justice, March 22, 2004; *Durango Herald*, March 24, 2004.

20. Delaney, *Ute Mountain Utes*, 101–6.

21. McPherson, *As If the Land Owned Us*, 279, 274–76.

22. Young, *Ute Indians of Colorado*, 179, 197–201; Robert Delaney, *The Southern Ute People* (Phoenix: Indian Tribal Series, 1974), 82–98. On the definition of Pino Nuche (*pínu-núu-ci*), see Southern Ute Tribe, *Ute Dictionary*, 163. For Pino Nuche Resort and Sky Ute Arena/Fairgrounds, see Southern Ute Tribe Tribe website at http://www.southernute-nsn.gov and www.skyutefairgrounds.com (retrieved 1998, 2013); personal observation, 1978 and 2012–2014. OPEC is the Organization of Petroleum Exporting Countries.

23. Young, *Ute Indians of Colorado*, 132–206, 132, 156–57, and citing Sam Maynes, attorney; Mineral Leasing Act for Allotted Land (1909) 25 U.S.C. 396 25 CFR; Tribal Mineral Leasing Act (1938), U.S. Code. 25, Sec 396a–396g; Omnibus Tribal Leasing Act of 1969 25 U.S.C. 396, 396a–396d; and Indian Mineral Development Act (1982) 25 U.S. C. para. 2101–2108; cf. commentary in Thompson, "The Ute Paradox."

24. Young, *Ute Indians of Colorado*, 156–57 (Southern Ute), 189–90 (Ute Mountain Ute).

25. Ibid., 181–86, 190–92, 236–38.

26. Ibid., 156–57, 188–90; Delaney, *Ute Mountain Utes*, 100–101.

27. Young, *Ute Indians of Colorado*, 137–38, 156–57, 186, 236–37, 192.

28. Ibid., 158, 186–89.

29. Ibid., 158, 186, 190, 237–38, 260.

30. Ibid., 191–92, 242–44.

31. Ibid., 192.

32. Ibid., 57, 158, 164; Joseph G. Jorgensen, *The Sun Dance Religion: Power for the Powerless* (Chicago: University of Chicago Press, 1972), 115.

33. Indian Mineral Development Act (1982).

34. *Wall Street Journal*, June 12, 2003; *Durango Herald*, December 3, 2001; Young, *Ute Indians of Colorado*, 191, 205–8.

35. *Dominion News* release, June 1, 2001 (online); *Business Wire*, May 18, 2001 (online); *Indianz.com* (online), May 21, 2001; *Deseret News*, December 17, 1996, January 22, April 4, 2000; *Salt Lake Tribune*, February 6, 2000.

36. Young, *Ute Indians of Colorado*, 191, 205–8; U.S. Department of Commerce, Economic Development Administration (EDA), "Colorado: Ute Mountain Reservation," online fact sheet, 314, retrieved June 24, 2004; Thompson, "The Ute Paradox." Regarding boom-bust cycle, see David Yager, "Why Today's Oil Bust Pales in Comparison to the 1980s," OilPrice.com (online), February 11, 2016, retrieve November 2016 from http://oilprice.com/Energy/Energy-General/Why-Todays-Oil-Bust-Pales-In-Comparison-To-The-80s.html.

37. Young, *Ute Indians of Colorado*, 187.

38. Ibid., 183.

39. Details in McPherson, *As If the Land Owned Us*, 342–45; Young, *Ute Indians of Colorado*, 193–96. Today the region remains controversial as part of the established and then disestablished Bears Ears National Monument.

40. Young, *Ute Indians of Colorado*, 193–96; Ute Mountain Ute webpage, retrieved 1999, 2004, 2013.

41. Young, *Ute Indians of Colorado*, 197; Ute Mountain Ute Tribe website, retrieved 2010 at www.utemountainfarmandranch.com; Cortez *Journal*, June 29, 2017; Southwestern Conservation District (Durango), "Water Information Programs: Colorado Ute Water Rights Settlement Agreement" (condensed, online), retrieved June 25, 2004.

42. Young, *Ute Indians of Colorado*, 194; "Tourist Attractions," Ute Mountain Ute Tribe website at www.utemountainute.com; McPherson, *As If the Land Owned Us*, 360–61.

43. Young, *Ute Indians of Colorado*, 196–97, 201; Economic Development Authority, "Colorado: Ute Mountain Reservation"; "Weeminuche Construction Authority," Ute Mountain Ute Tribe website at www.utemountainute.com and http://wcacontracting.com.

44. Cortez *Journal*, June 25, 2004; U.S. Department of the Interior (DOI) and Bureau of Reclamation (BOR), news release (online), December 12, 2003, retrieved June 25, 2004.

45. EDA, "Ute Mountain Ute Reservation"; U.S. DOI and BOR, news release, December 12, 2003; Young, *Ute Indians of Colorado*, 196–97.

46. Young, *Ute Indians of Colorado*, 208, 282; Thompson, "The Ute Paradox"; and cf. *Deseret News*, July 19, 1992, an investigative article on the effects of reservation gaming in general. See *Indian Gaming Regulatory Act*, U.S. Code 25 sec. 2701 (P.L. 100-497) (1988). On marijuana, see Cortez *Journal*, April 6, 2015.

47. Young, *Ute Indians of Colorado*, 208–9, 282–84; *Deseret News*, July 19, 1992; *Durango Herald*, March 23, 2004; Ute Mountain Ute Tribe website, "Tourist Attractions," retrieved 2005 from www.utemountainute.com/overview_statistics; "Ute Mountain Casino Unveils $5.5 Million Upgrade," Cortez *Journal*, December 30, 2016. See also National Indian Gaming Association (NIGA), "Indian Gaming Facts" and "2005 Economic Impact of Indian Gaming," online; "2014 Indian Gaming Revenues Increase," National Indian Gaming Commission press release, July 23, 2015, retrieved December 2017 from https://www.nigc.gov/news/detail/2014-indian-gaming-revenues-increase; Patricia L. Janes, and Jim Collison, "Community Leader Perceptions of the Social and Economic Impacts of Indian Gaming," *University of Las Vegas Gaming Research & Review Journal* 8 (2004): 13–30. "Ute Mountain Casino Unveils $5.5 Million Upgrade," Cortez *Journal*, December 30, 2016.

48. Southern Ute Tribe website, retrieved June 2005 and 2013; Sky Ute Casino website, at www.skyutecasino.com; Young, *Ute Indians of Colorado*, 209–10; personal observation, 2003, 2012.

49. See Peter Beinart, "Lost Tribes: Anthropologists Feud over Indian Identity," *Lingua Franca* (May/June 1999): 35–37; Angela Gonzales, "Gaming and Displacement: Winners and Losers in American Indian Casino Development," *International Social Science Journal* 55 (March 2003): 128–31; James A. Clifton, "Alternate Identities and Cultural Frontiers," in *Being and Becoming Indian: Biographical Studies of North American Frontiers* (Chicago: Dorsey Press, 1989), 23.

50. "2014 Indian Gaming Revenues Increase 1.5 Percent," NIGC press release, July 23, 2015, retrieved December 2017 (online); American Gaming Association Survey of Casino Industry report, 2015 and 2017 (online). "U.S. Gaming Market Revenue from 2004–2017," www.statista.com (online). U.S. casino industry revenue was $70.16 billion.

51. NIGA, "Report on Economic Impact of Gaming, 2005" and "Indian Gaming Facts"; Jason Lee Ste-orts, "Tribal Loyalties: The BIA—A Washington Disgrace," *National Review* (August 8, 2005): 39–41; Judy Zeilo, "Tribes Bet on Gaining," *State Legislatures* 31 (March 2005): 26–28; Angela A. Gonzales, "American Indians: Their Contemporary Reality and Future Trajectory," in *Challenges for Rural America in the Twenty-First Century* (University Park: University of Pennsylvania Press, 2003), 49–53.

52. "Ute Tribes Impact Colorado's Economy," *Durango Herald (Journal, Denver Bureau)*, July 30, 2015 (online).

53. Zeilo, "Tribes Bet on Gaining," and quoting Tex Hall; Ronald A. Nykiel, "A Special Look at Indian Gaming," *UNLV Gaming Research & Review Journal* 8 (2004): 51–56; Gonzales, "American Indians: Their Contemporary Reality," 49–53; Matthew Miller, "Off the Reservation," *Forbes*, June 2005, 152–53; "Indian Tribes Cashing in Big on their Casinos," *Durango Herald*, December 3, 2001, and citing a 1998 study; "Ute Tribes Impact Colorado's Economy"; cf. AGA Survey of Casino Industry report; Thompson, "The Ute Paradox"; Raymond Cross, "Tribes as Rich Nations," *Oregon Law Review* 79 (Winter 2000): 949–51.

54. Young, *Ute Indians of Colorado*, 242, 250–51, 257.

55. Ibid., 168–69, 245–46. Cf. mixed-blood controversy among Northern Utes, Chapter 17, herein.

56. Thompson, "The Ute Paradox"; McPherson, *As If the Land Owned Us*, 354–56.

57. Young, *Ute Indians of Colorado*, 251–55, and quoting Arthur Cuthair, interview and a letter to the editor of a local newspaper; also *Durango Herald*, March 24, 2004; *Rocky Mountain News*, March 23, 2004. Cf. Southern Ute Tribe webpage, "Tribal Council." African American members of the 9th Cavalry were posted at Fort Lewis; some veterans remained in the area.

58. Young, *Ute Indians of Colorado*, 245–50; Lisa Jones, "Animas-La Plata Still Flawed," *High Country News* (online), December 17, 1990; "SUGO Ute Legacy," Southern Ute Grassroots Organization (online), retrieved June 1998; "Sage Remington," *Westward*, January 29, 1998 retrieved 2017, from http://www.westword.com/news/sage-remington-5058266; Southern Ute Tribe website, "Council Members."

59. Young, *Ute Indians of Colorado*, 245–50.

60. Ibid., 245–47.

61. Ibid., 252–53 (allegations); U.S. DOJ, Press Release, May 7, 2002, and March 22, 2004; *Durango Herald*, March 24, 2004; *Rocky Mountain News*, March 23, 2004. On the Judy Knight-Frank conviction, see *KUTV News* (online), June 21, 2004.

62. Duane A. Smith, "A Last Rush to Eden: The Settlement of Colorado's Ute Strip," *Our Public Lands* 30 (Spring 1980): 20–22.

63. Young, *Ute Indians of Colorado*, 52–53, 201; U.S. Congress, House, Committee on Interior and Insu-lar Affairs, *Animas-La Plata Water Rights Settlement: Hearings on H.R. 2642*, 100th Cong., 1st sess., September 16, 1987, 30, 33, 357, 430; L. Jones, "Animas-La Plata: Still Flawed."

64. *Winters v. United States*, 207 U.S. 564 (1908). The joint statement by the Ute Mountain and South-ern Ute Tribes is in *Animas-La Plata Water Rights Settlement Hearings* (H.R. 2642), 416. David H. Getches, "The Unsettling of the West: How Indians got the Best Water Rights," *Michigan Law Review* 99 (May 2001): 1473–99.

65. *Winters v. United States*; "Indian Water Wars," *Newsweek*, June 13, 1983, 80–82.

66. L. Jones, "Animas-La Plata Still Flawed"; Southwestern Conservation District, "Water Information Programs: Settlement Agreement"; Young, *Ute Indian of Colorado*, 53.

67. James Brooke, "Battle of What May Be the West's Last Big Dam," *New York Times*, September 20, 1997; L. Jones, "Animas-La Plata Still Flawed"; testimonies of Judy Knight-Frank, June 24, 1998 (before the Senate) and Earnest House, June 7, 2000 (before the Committee on Indian Affairs); and "Animas-La Plata Timeline," retrieved March 1999 and April 2004 from the Ute Mountain and Southern Ute Tribes, Animas-La Plata website at www.animaslp.com; Taxpayers for Common Sense (TCS), "Campaign to Stop Animas-La Plata," retrieved April 1999 from www.taxpayer.net/TCS/States/co.html.

68. Dan Israel and Mr. McElroy, attorneys for the Ute tribes, in *Animas-La Plata Water Rights Hearings* (H.R. 2642), 33–34, 337–38, 430, and esp. 332. See also Young, *Ute Indians of Colorado*, 201.

69. Young, *Ute Indians of Colorado*, 201; U.S. Congress, Colorado Ute Indian Water Rights Settlement Act of 1988, 100th Cong., 2nd sess. (P.L. 100-585), November 3, 1988, including the "Agreement in Principle Concerning the Colorado Ute Indian Water Rights Settlement and Binding Agreement for Animas-La Plata Project Cost Sharing" (signed June 30, 1986); "Colorado Ute Indian Water Rights Final Settlement Agreement, December 10, 1986," briefing paper #7, included in *Animas-La Plata Water Rights Hearings* (H.R. 2642), and joint statement of the state of Colorado and the Ute Mountain and Southern Ute Tribes, December 3, 1987, *Animas-La Plata Hearings*, 430; Ute Mountain and Southern Ute Tribes, Animas-La Plata website, and its "Animas-La Plata Timeline"; Brooke, "Battle of the West's Last Big Dam"; L. Jones, "Animas-La Plata still flawed."

70. Colorado Ute Indian Final Water Rights Settlement Agreement (H.R. 2642), and An Act To Amend the Colorado Ute Indian Water Rights Settlement Act of 1988, 106th Cong, 1st Sess., October 20, 1999, H.R. 3112; Southwestern Conservation District, "Water Information Programs: Settlement Agreement."

71. L. Jones "Animas-La Plata Still Flawed"; *Animas-La-Plata Water Rights Hearings* (H.R. 2642), 26–32, 300–332, 351–63, 413–17.

72. Tom Wolf, "Water Boondoggle Wrapped in the Cause of Indian Rights," *Los Angeles Times*, April 26, 1998; National Wildlife Federation testimony, *Animas-LaPlata Water Rights Hearings* (H.R. 2642), 300–301; TCS, "Campaign to Stop Animas-La Plata, retrieved from www.taxpayer.net/TCS/States/co.html; Friends of the Earth (FOE), "Action Alert: Stop Jurassic Pork!: Cut the Animas-La Plata Irrigation Project" (posted online April 4, 1997), retrieved from www.foe.org/act.alpl.html; James Decker and the Sierra Club, *Animas-La Plata Hearings*, 285–94, 409.

73. Wolf, "Water Boondoggle"; *Animas-La Plata Hearings*, 288–300.

74. *Animas-La Plata Hearings*, 288–94, 300, 408–9. The hearing included testimony by the American River Association and the Sierra Club. See also Wolfe, "Water Boondoggle."

75. Wolf, "Water Boondoggle"; Sierra Club, "Petition to Congress regarding S. 2508" [against], posted online; *Deseret News*, March 14, 1996, May 17, 1997, February 2, 1998. Colorado pikeminnow, formerly Squawfish: *Ptychocheilus Lucius*.

76. American River Association, National Wildlife Federation, and the Sierra Club, in *Animas-LaPlata Hearing*, 288-92, 300-301, and 408-9; Wolf, "Water Boondoggle." See also Sierra Club, petition to Congress (posted online); L. Jones, "Animas-La Plata Still Flawed."

77. Sierra Club, "Petition to Congress"; Gail Brinkly, "A-LP Gets Federal A-OK," *High Country News*, August 27, 2001; L. Jones, "Animas-La Plata Still Flawed"; TCS, "Campaign to Stop Animas-La Plata"; FOE, "Action Alert: Stop Jurassic Pork!"; Citizens Against Waste (CAW) (Farmington, NM), lobbying letter re: H.R. 3112, posted online July 2000 at macinstruct.com/alpcentral/cawlobby.htm posted online July 2000.

78. CAW, lobbying letter re: H.R. 3112 (posted online); L. Jones, "Animas-La Plata Still Flawed"; James Decker, *Animas-La Plata Hearings*, 285–86; Sierra Club, petition to Congress, 2000 (online); Colorado Ute Settlement Act Amendments of 2000, S. 2508, May 4, 2000.

79. L. Jones, "Animas-La Plata Still Flawed," and quoting Frost; Southern Ute Grassroots Organization, "SUGO Legacy"; Brooke, "Battle of the West's Last Big Dam"; Ute Mountain and Southern Ute Tribes, "Animas-La Plata Timeline," at www.animaslp.com.

80. L. Jones, "Animas-La Plata Still Flawed"; Young, *Ute Indians of Colorado*, 194; Knight-Frank, "Excerpts of Testimony" (before the Senate), June 24, 1998, at www.animaslp.com/others.htm.

81. Ute Mountain and Southern Ute Tribes, "Animas-La Plata Timeline," at www.animaslp.com; DOI, "Notice of Intent to Prepare a Draft Supplemental Environmental Statement to the 1996 Final Supplement to the Final Environmental Statement for the Animas-La Plata Project," *Federal Register* 64, no. 1 (January 4, 1999); Southern Ute and Ute Mountain Ute, Animas-La Plata website, www.animaslp.com; Brooke, "Battle of the West's Last Big Dam"; L. Jones, "Animas-La Plata Still Flawed"; Young, *Ute Indians of Colorado*, 203–4.

82. Ute Mountain and Southern Ute Tribes, "Animas-La Plata Timeline"; FOE, "Action Alert! Stop Jurassic Pork."

83. DOI, "Notice of Intent to Prepare a Draft Supplemental Environmental Statement."

84. Ute Mountain and Southern Ute Tribes, "Animas-La Plata Timeline"; Brooke, "Battle of the West's Last Big Dam."

85. DOI, "Notice of Intent to Prepare a Draft Supplemental Environmental Statement"; Ute Mountain and Southern Ute Tribes, "Reconciliation Plan," Animas-La Plata Web site; Brooke, "Battle of the West's Last Big Dam."

86. DOI, "Notice of Intent to Prepare a Draft Supplemental Environmental Statement"; Ute Mountain and Southern Ute Tribes, Animas-La Plata website, including "Animas-La Plata Timeline"; Southwestern Conservation District, "Water Information Programs"; "Agency Probes Water Project's Cost Overruns," *Cortez Journal*, September 25, 2003. The term A-LP Lite was a reference to the low-calorie beer Coors-Lite, which was brewed in Colorado.

87. Russell Feingold, press release, March 13, 1997, and Tom Petri, press release, July 24, 1997, posted online, retrieved 2009 from www.senate.gov/~feingold/31rel.htm and www.house.gov/petri/press/alpmedia.htm. See also FOE, "Action Alert," 1998; TCS, "Campaign to Stop Animas-La Plata."

88. *Denver Post*, June 28, 1998; U.S. Senate, *A Bill to Amend the Colorado Ute Indian Water Rights Settlement Act*, 105 Cong., S. 1771, introduced March 17, 1998; Brooke "Battle of the West's Last Big Dam," and quoting SCALP, or "Stop Campbell's Animas La Plata."

89. Knight-Frank and Clement Frost, testimonies before the Senate regarding S. 1771, and posted on the Ute Mountain and Southern Ute Tribes, Animas-La Plata website.

90. DOI, "Notice of Intent to Prepare a Draft Supplemental Environmental Statement"; *Pueblo Chieftain*, June 19, 1998. See also Grand Junction's *Daily Sentinel*, January 24, 1999 ("little recourse"); and *Denver Post*, August 16, 1998, February 1, 1999; Bill Owens, gubernatorial candidate, statement posted on Ute Mountain and Southern Ute Tribes, Animas-La Plata Web site.

91. Jeanne W. Englert, "Let's Use Sense in Satisfying Tribes' Water Rights," *Rocky Mountain News*, February 20 1998; Englert to Ken Salazar [Colorado attorney general], August 13, 1999, posted at www.macinstruct.com/alpcentral/salazarpia.html; Richard G. Hamilton, testimony before the U.S. Senate Committee on Indian Affairs regarding S. 1771, and "Southern Ute Water Rights and the Date of Reservation under the Winters Doctrine," September 30, 1987, both posted online September 1997, updated June 15, 1998 at www.macinstruct.com/alpcentral/ute.html. See also *Winters v. U.S.* (1908); John Shurts, *Indian Reserved Water Rights: The* Winters *Doctrine in Its Social and Legal Context, 1880s–1930s* (Norman: University of Oklahoma Press, 2000); Getches, "The Unsettling of the West."

92. Hamilton, "Southern Ute Water Rights," and testimony before Congress regarding S. 1771; Englert, "Let's Use Sense"; Englert to Salazar, August 13, 1999. Hamilton quotes Judge Brennan for the Supreme Court who argued that "We find no creation of a reservation for the Southern Utes in the Act of 1880, nor can we find any words of cession in the Act of 1895."

93. Hamilton, "Southern Ute Water Rights," and testimony before Congress; Englert, "Let's Use Sense"; Englert to Salazar, August 13, 1999; Wolf, "Water Boondoggle." See also *U.S. v. Southern Utes or Band of Indians*, 402 U.S. 159, April 26, 1971, and quoted by Hamilton. While this Supreme Court action appeared to extinguish all future land claims and "demands of whatsoever nature in and to the land and property," Congress did not agree.

94. An Act to Amend the Colorado Ute Indian Water Rights Settlement Act of 1988, H.R. 3112, October 20, 1999; U.S. Senate, An Act To Amend the Colorado Ute Indian Water Rights Settlement Act of 1988, S. 2508, May 4, 2000; BOR, "Ridges Basin Dam Contract Awarded," press release posted online December 12, 2003; Ute Mountain Ute "Weeminuche Authority" at http://weeminuche.com; "Agency Probes," *Cortez Journal*, September 25, 2003.

95. "Agency Probes," *Cortez Journal*, September 25, 2003.

96. Details in McPherson, *As If the Land Owned Us*, 271–82; 342–45, 351–53.

97. McPherson, *As If the Land Owned Us*, 280–82; 342–45, 351–53; Cortez *Journal*, June 8, 2015, May 3, 2016, March 6, May 5, 13, 2017.

98. *Wall Street Journal*, June 13, 2003; *Durango Herald*, December 6, 2000; Thompson, "The Ute Paradox." For Jurrius, see Native American Resource Partners, "Our Team: John Jurrius, CEO," at http://narpllc.com, and Chapter 17 herein.

99. *The Wall Street Journal*, June 13, 2003; Thompson, "The Ute Paradox."

100. *The Wall Street Journal*, June 13, 2003; Southern Ute Tribe, "Tribal Economic/Business: Growth Fund Business Areas" posted online at Southern Ute Tribe webpage, and Southern Ute Growth

Fund at http://www.sugf.com. In 2005 the tribe's website had links detailing all current business ventures, including descriptions and pictures.

101. U.S. 2000 and 2010 Census, "Profiles of Selected Economic Characteristics," Colorado, Southern Ute and Ute Mountain Ute data sets; Colorado Fiscal Policy Institute, "Fact Sheet: Colorado Income October 2009," online; U.S. Census, "Fact Finder: Southern Utes CDP, Income," 2010–2014, online; "Ute Mountain Ute Colorado," city-data.com. Cf. Thompson, "The Ute Paradox."

102. "Business Empire Transforms Life For Colorado Ute Tribe," *Wall Street Journal*, June 13, 2003; *Denver Post*, June 8, 2001; *Durango Herald*, December 3, 2001, December 28, 2003; *Deseret News*, September, 24, 2006. See also "Fitch Rates Southern Ute Indian Tribe's Adjustable Rate GOs 'AAA'/ F1+; Outlook Stable," *Business Wire*, January 11, 2007; and Thompson, "The Ute Paradox." The tribe's value was estimated over $14 billion in 2013.

103. *Wall Street Journal*, June 13, 2003; Thompson, "The Ute Paradox."

104. Thompson, "The Ute Paradox"; *Durango Herald*, December 6, 2000; *Wall Street Journal*, June 13, 2003, quoting Annabelle Eagle, Ms. Vigil, and Sage Remington.

105. James A. Clifton, quoted in Young, *Ute Indians of Colorado*, 263.

106. Ibid.

107. Cross, "Tribes as Rich Nations," 956.

108. Diabetes statistics in Young, *Ute Indians of Colorado*, 262–63. Regarding diabetes among American Indians, see, e.g., National Diabetes Information Clearinghouse (NDIC), "Diabetes in American Indians and Alaska Natives," National Institute of Diabetes and Digestive and Kidney Diseases, National Institutes of Health, online report retrieved May 29, 2004, from http://www2.niddk.nih. gov/; Noah T. Boaz, "Diabetes Mellitus and the 'Thrifty Genotype,'" ch. 9 in *Evolving Health: the Origins of Illness and How the Modern World is Making Us Sick* (New York: Wiley, 2002). Regarding lifestyle changes, see Desmond E. Williams, et al., "The Effect of Indian or Anglo Dietary Preference on the Incidence of Diabetes in Pima Indians," *Diabetes Care* 24 (May 2001): 811–16; Eric Ravussin, et al., "Effects of a Traditional Lifestyle on Obesity in Pima Indians," *Diabetes Care* 17 (September 1994), 1067–72; J. V. Neel, "Diabetes Mellitus: A 'Thrifty' Genotype Rendered Detrimental by 'Progress'?" *American Journal of Human Genetics* 14 (1962): 352–53; Manu V. Chakravarthy and Frank W. Booth, "Eating, Exercise, and the 'Thrifty' Genotypes: Connecting the Dots toward an Evolutionary Understanding of Modern Chronic Disease," *Journal of Applied Physiology* 96, no. 10 (2004).

109. Young, *Ute Indians of Colorado*, 261–62; *Salt Lake Tribune*, October 10, 2000; Julie C. Abril, "Results from the Southern Ute Indian Community Safety Survey," prepared for the Department of Justice (DOJ), December 2005.

110. Warren Angus Ferris, *Life in the Rocky Mountains, 1830–1835*, edited and annotated by Leroy R. Hafen (Denver: Old West Publishing, 1983), 362–63.

111. Young, *Ute Indians of Colorado*, 264–65.

112. Justice William Rehnquist on unfairness of trying non-Indians in Indian courts, in *Oliphant v. Suquamish Tribe*, 435 U.S. 191 (1978). Statistics in Suzanne Gamboa, "Native American Women Seek Protections from Abuse," *Associated Press*, and *RezNet News: Reporting from Native America*, April 14, 2012. See also Felicia Fonesca, "American Indian Tribes New Authority over Non-Indians," *Huffington Post*, March 7, 2013; DOJ, "Office on Violence Against Women: Tribal Communities," at http://www.ovw.usdoj.gov/tribal.html; cf. Mathew L. M. Fletcher, "Addressing the Epidemic of Domestic Violence in Indian Country," legal brief prepared by the American Constitution society for Law and Policy, at www.acslaw.org/files/Fletcher%20Issue%20Brief.pdf; Violence against Women Reauthorization Act of 2013, S. 47 (P.L. 113-4), 113th Cong., 1st sess., signed March 7, 2013.

113. See, e.g., "New Violence against Women Act includes Historic Protections for Native American," *Democracy Now*, March 8, 2013 (online); Gamboa, "Native Women Seek Protections."

114. See, e.g., Young, *Ute Indians of Colorado*, 260–61.

115. Ralph Cloud, quoted in ibid., 269. L. Cesspooch (interview with author, March 19, 1999) said much the same about Uintah-Ouray youth.

116. Young, *Ute Indians of Colorado*, 269–70; Southern Ute Tribe, *Ute Dictionary and Ute Reference Grammar*, esp. "Foreword," and "Preface," i–iv; McPherson, *As If the Land Owned Us*, 361; *Southern Ute Drum* (online), April 20, 2013 (Language software), and June 2016 (New dictionary announced).

117. Young, *Ute Indians of Colorado*, 270; *Deseret News*, May 27, January 7, 1998; Carol Berry, *Indian Country Today*, January 17, 2013.

118. Young, *Ute Indians of Colorado*, 272–75, and quoting Terry Knight, 272; and see Chapter 13 herein.

119. Young, *Ute Indians of Colorado*, 214, 265, 273; L. Cesspooch, interview, March 19, 1999; Darrell Gardiner, conversations, March 18, July 1999, July 2000.

120. Young, *Ute Indians of* Colorado, 273–74; Eddie Box, interview with Robert R. Jones, 1978 (in author's possession). On Ute peyotism, see Omer C. Stewart, "Friend to the Ute: Omer C. Stewart Crusades for Indian Religious Freedom," *Colorado Heritage* (1982); Stewart, *Ute Peyotism: A Study of a Cultural Complex*, University of Colorado Studies, Series in Anthropology (Boulder: University of Colorado Press, 1948).

121. Young, *Ute Indians of Colorado*, 275–79. For in-depth discussion, see Jorgensen, *Sun Dance Religion*, 178–340; E. Box, interview with R. R. Jones, August 1978; D. Gardiner, personal communication, summers 1978–1981 and March 1999; L. Cesspooch, interview, March 18–19, 1999. My comments are also based on personal observation at Sundances and on Sundance grounds on all three reservations, 1979–1981, 1999, 2000. See also Lynda Grove D'Wolf, "Sun Dance Workshop Teaches Women Traditional Roles," *Ute Drum*, July 15, 2010.

122. Young, *Ute Indians of Colorado*, 279–90, including 1998 interviews with conservative councilmember and elder, Arthur Cuthair; *Wall Street Journal*, June 13, 2003, quoting Everett Burch, brother of Leonard Burch; Gonzales, "American Indians: Their Contemporary Reality," 52; Alexandra Harmon, "Gambling Money," in *Rich Indians: Native People and the Problem of Wealth in American History* (Chapel Hill: University of North Carolina Press, 2010), 349–79.

123. See Delaney, *Ute Mountain Ute*, 100–101; McPherson, *As If the Land Owned Us*, 346–51; "Demographics" on Ute Mountain Ute tribal website, retrieved 2006.

CHAPTER 19

1. On the "Eye-juggler" tale, see J. Alden Mason, "Myths of the Uintah Utes," *Journal of American Folk-Lore* 23 (1910): 314–16; and comments in Joseph G. Jorgensen, "Functions of Ute Folklore" (master's thesis, University of Utah, 1960). Cf. Robert H. Lowie, "Shoshonean Tales—Southern Ute," *Journal of American Folk-Lore* 37 (January–June 1924): 1–157, 26–27; Anne M. (Cooke) Smith, "Analysis of Basin Mythology" (PhD diss., Yale University, 1940), 2:5–6, 27–28, 37–38, 72–75, 81–83); and A. Smith, *Ute Tales* (Salt Lake City: University of Utah Press, 1992).

2. *Conscience collective*, the psychological undercurrent of cultural moral unanimity. See Emile Durkheim, *Elementary Forms of the Religious Life* (1912).

3. On character roles, see, e.g., Jorgensen, "Functions of Ute Folklore"; and Smith, "Analysis of Basin Mythology."

4. For more on criticism of tribal communalism being socialism, see, e.g., Graham D. Taylor, *The New Deal and American Indian Tribalism: The Administration of the Indian Reorganization Act, 1934–45* (Lincoln: University of Nebraska Press, 1980), x–xii, 139–50. Commentary on familial cooperation is in Katherine M. B. Osburn, *Southern Ute Women: Autonomy and Assimilation on the Reservation, 1887–1934* (Albuquerque: University of New Mexico Press, 1998), 117; and Frances Leon [Swadesh] Quintana, *Ordeal of Change: The Southern Utes and their Neighbors* (Walnut Creek: AltaMira Press, 2004), 108.

5. Max Weber, *Protestant Ethic and the Spirit of Capitalism*, 1905, English edition (New York: Charles Scribner's Sons, 1958). Cf. Johan Huizinga, *Homo Ludens: A Study of the Play Element in Culture* (Boston: The Beacon Press, 1950); Richard H. Grathoff, *The Structure of Social Inconsistencies: A Contribution to a Unified Theory of Play, Game, and Social Action* (The Hague: Martinus Nijhoff, 1970).

6. Jorgensen, *Sun Dance Religion*, 115–16; cf. Osburn, *Southern Ute Women*, 117.

7. On cynicism, see Omer C. Stewart, "Southern Ute Adjustment to Modern Living," in *Acculturation in the Americas* (Chicago: University of Chicago Press, 1952); Uintah-Ouray Utes revealed similar attitudes to the author in personal conversations (1978, 1979); and based on personal observation. Terry Knight is quoted in Richard K. Young, *The Ute Indians of Colorado in the Twentieth Century* (Norman: University of Oklahoma Press, 1997), 260. Square versus round houses (Indian wickiups, tipis, hogans) noted in *Black Elk Speaks* (1932; Lincoln: University of Nebraska, 1972), 194–96.

8. Personal communications with author, Uintah-Ouray Reservation, summer 1980; fall Bear Dance and powwow scheduled in the fall, announced in Cortez *Journal,* September 3, 2017. See also Marvin K. Opler, "The Integration of the Sun Dance in Ute Religion," *American Anthropologist* 43 (1941): 552 and fn.; cf. Angela A. Gonzales, "American Indians: Their Contemporary Reality and Future Trajectory," in *Challenges for Rural America in the Twenty-First Century* (University Park: University of Pennsylvania Press, 2003), 52.

9. *Wall Street Journal,* June 13, 2003; cf. Arrell Morgan Gibson, *The American Indian: Prehistory to the Present* (Norman: University of Oklahoma Press, 1980), 535–37. Examples are in Young, *Ute Indians of Colorado,* 181–92, 236–38, 260; Stewart, "Southern Ute Adjustment." Inculcated dependency in Richard White, *Roots of Dependency: Subsistence, Environment, and Social Change among the Choctaws, Pawnees, and Navajos* (Lincoln: University of Nebraska Press, 1983). Not everyone agrees with the so-called "dependency theory."

10. Anne M. (Cooke) Smith, *Ethnography of the Northern Utes,* Papers in Anthropology, no. 17 (Albuquerque: Museum of New Mexico Press, 1974), 19–24, and quoting Goss, 21; cf. Opler, "The Southern Ute," 126.

11. Denver, Chivers, and Hendricks to Inouye, March 3, 1992, and Resolutions. Posted on Affiliated Ute Citizens website, accessed March 2012, at http://www.undeclaredutes.net. Details in Chapter 15, herein.

12. On the Sundance community, see Jorgensen, *Sun Dance Religion,* esp. 280; Smith, *Ethnography of the Northern Utes,* 27. I experienced being part of the Sundance community when we tore open a gas tank on the rough road to the isolated Sundance grounds in the mountains above Towaoc. Ute Mountain members of the Sundance community, originally suspicious of strangers, assisted us (at no charge) by towing and welding the tank and providing some gas, after they discovered my husband was a Sundancer on the Uintah-Ouray reservation. Regarding Shoshone ancestry of the Reeds, see Henry Harris, Jr., interview, July 19, 1967, Doris Duke Oral History, 7–12; and Oran F. Curry, interview, July 20, 1967, Doris Duke Oral History Collection, box 3, no. 48, 19–21; and Colleen Gardiner and her sister Mrs. Reed (terminated mixed-bloods), personal communication to author, March 2009, 2011.

13. For various court battles, see, e.g., *Timpanogos Tribe, Snake Band of Shoshone Indians of Utah Territory v. Kevin Conway et al.* (April 15, 2002); *Ute Distribution Corporation v. Norton et al.* (July 25, 2002); *Felter et al. v. Kempthorne et al.,* No. 06-5092 (January 2007); and *Felter et al. v. Salazar et al.,* No. 10-5069 (March 2010). See also C. Gardiner and Mrs. Reed personal communication with author, March 2009, 2011; Larry Cesspooch, Northern Ute Public Relations Officer, personal interview, March 18–19, 1999.

14. Gregory E. Smoak, "Snakes and Diggers," in *Ghost Dances and Identity: Prophetic Religion and American Indian Ethnogenesis in the Nineteenth Century* (Berkeley: University of California, 2006), 15–47; David B. Madsen, "Mesa Verde and Sleeping Ute Mountain: The Geographical and Chronological Dimensions of the Numic Expansion," in *Across the West: Human Population Movement and the Expansion of the Numa* (Salt Lake City: University of Utah Press, 1994), 24–31; Mark Q. Sutton and David Rhode, "Background to the Numic Problem," in *Across the West,* 6–15;

15. C. Gardiner and Mrs. Reed, personal communication to author, 2009. See also numerous court cases, including *Timpanogos Tribe v. Conway* (2002), and still defiant claims in "Mixed Blood Group Prosecuted for Wire Fraud," *Ute Bulletin,* November 3, 2017.

16. On the development of tribal and ethnic identities, see, e.g., Smoak, *Ghost Dances and Identity,* 26–29; and Alexandra Harmon, *Indians in the Making: Ethnic Relations and Indian Identities around Puget Sound* (Los Angeles: University of California Press, 1998), esp. 9–10. Cf. Nancy Shoemaker, "How Indians Got to be Red," *American Historical Review* 102 (June 1997): 625–44. Peter Silver, *Our Savage Neighbors: How Indian War Transformed Early America* (New York: W. W. Norton, 2008); and general theories in Fredrik Barth, *Ethnic Groups and Boundaries: The Social Organization of Culture Difference,* edited by Fredrik Barth (1969; Long Grove, IL: Waveland Press, 1998).

17. Commentaries are in Smoak, *Ghost Dances and Identity,* 26–29; and Harman, *Indians in the Making,* esp. 9–10.

18. Barth, "Introduction," in *Ethnic Groups and Boundaries,* 11–15; Smith, *Ethnography of the Northern Utes,* 19–24; Opler, "Southern Ute," 126; Harmon, *Indians in the Making.*

19. Cf. Joane Nagel, *American Indian Ethnic Renewal: Red Power and the Resurgence of Identity and Culture* (New York: Oxford University Press, 1996), 205, and citing Anthony Cohen, *The Symbolic Construction of Community* (1985); Frances Densmore, *The Belief of the Indian in a Connection Between Song and the Supernatural*, Bureau of American Ethnology, Anthropology Papers 37 (Washington, D.C.: Smithsonian Institution, 1953), 217–23.

20. Opler, "Integration of the Sun Dance," 570; Joseph G. Jorgensen, "The Ethnohistory and Acculturation of the Northern Ute" (Ph.D. diss., Indiana University, Bloomington, 1964), 416; Clyde Ellis, *A Dancing People: Powwow Culture of the Southern Plains* (Lawrence: University of Kansas Press).

21. A. P. Medina, as remembered by his grandson, R. R. Jones, 1979.

Bibliography

PRIMARY AND ARCHIVAL SOURCES

Abel, Anne H., ed. *Official Correspondence of James S. Calhoun.* Washington: GPO, 1915.

Allred, R. N. "Journal of R. N. Allred." MS 8795, Church History Library, The Church of Jesus Christ of Latter-day Saints, Salt Lake City, Utah.

Anderson, William Marshall. *The Rocky Mountain Journals of William Marshall Anderson: The West in 1834.* Edited by Dale L. Morgan and Eleanor Towles Harris. San Marino, CA: Huntington Library, 1967.

Archuleta, Phillipe Santiago. "Testimony in Case of Libel." *United States v. Pedro León, et al.,* #1533. Utah State Archives.

Barker, Malcolm E., ed. *San Francisco Memoirs, 1835–1851.* San Francisco: Landborn Publications, 1994.

Bean, George W. "Autobiography." Holographic copy in the Church History Library, The Church of Jesus Christ of Latter-day Saints, Salt Lake City, Utah.

Beckwith, E. G. *Reports of Exploration for a Route for the Pacific Railroad by Capt. W. Gunnison,* Reports of Explorations and Surveys. Sen. Exec. Doc. 78, 33/2. Ser. 759:34–77.

Beckwourth, James P. *The Life and Adventures of James P. Beckwourth, As Told to Thomas D. Bonner.* Introduction and notes by Delmont R. Oswald. 1856. Reprint, Lincoln: University of Nebraska Press, 1972.

Blair, Seth M. "Reminiscences and Journals, 1851–1868." MS (microfilm). Church History Library, The Church of Jesus Christ of Latter-day Saints, Salt Lake City, Utah.

Bleak, James G., "Annals of the Southern Utah Mission." TS. Harold B. Lee Library, Special Collections, Brigham Young University, Provo, UT, 1928. Also online via University of Utah Marriott Library.

Booth, J. E. "A History of the Fourth Provo Ward, 1775–1858." Tms. Provo, UT: Harold B. Lee Library, Brigham Young University, 1941.

Brewerton, George Douglas. *Overland with Kit Carson: A Narrative of the Old Spanish Trail in '48.* 1930. Reprint, Lincoln: University of Nebraska Press, 1993. Originally published 1853, *Harper's New Monthly Magazine.*

Brown, Thomas D. *Journal of the Southern Indian Mission: Diary of Thomas D. Brown.* Edited by Juanita Brooks. Logan: Utah State University Press, 1972. Original journal in LDS Church History Library.

Carvalho, Solomon Nuñes. *Incidents of Travel and Adventure in the Far West with Colonel Fremont's Last Expedition.* New York: Derby and Jackson, 1856 and 1860.

Chavez, Angelico, trans., and Ted. J Warner, ed. *The Domínguez-Escalante Journal: Their Expedition through Colorado, Utah, Arizona, and New Mexico in 1776.* Provo, UT: Brigham Young University Press, 1976. Reprint, Salt Lake City: University of Utah Press, 1995.

Clayton, William. *William Clayton's Journal.* Salt Lake City: n.p., 1921.

"Col. Snow on the War Path." July 22, 1865, Brigham Young Collection (roll 92, book 58, folio 6). Church History Library, The Church of Jesus Christ of Latter-day Saints, Salt Lake City, UT.

Conard, Howard L. *"Uncle Dick" Wootton: Pioneer Frontiersman of the Rocky Mountain. Region.* Chicago: W. E. Dibble, 1890. Reprint, 1950.

Curry, Oran F. Interview. Doris Duke Oral History Collections. Marriot Library Special Collections, University of Utah, Salt Lake, 1967.

DeSmet, P. J. *Letters and Sketches: A Narrative of a Year's Residence among the Indian Tribes of the Rocky Mountains*. Philadelphia, 1843. In *Early Western Travels*, edited by Reuben Gold Thwaites. Vol. 27. Cleveland: Arthur H. Clark, 1906.

Doolittle, James. "The Doolittle Report," *Condition of the Indian Tribes: Report of the Joint Special Committee*. Washington: GPO, 1867.

Egan, Howard. *Pioneering the West 1846 to 1878: Major Howard Egan's Diary*. Richmond, UT: Howard R. Egan Estate, 1917.

Eldredge, Alma. "Diary, 1841–1925." MS 5125. Church History Library, The Church of Jesus Christ of Latter-day Saints, Salt Lake City, Utah.

Escalante, Silvestre Vélez de, and Francisco Atanasio Domínguez. *The Domínquez-Escalante Journal: Their Expedition through Colorado, Utah, Arizona, and New Mexico in 1776*. With notes. Trans. by Fray Angelico Chavez and edited by Ted J. Warner. Provo, UT: Brigham Young University Press, 1976. Reprint, Salt Lake City: University of Utah Press, 1995.

Ferris, Warren Angus. *Life in the Rocky Mountains, 1830–1835*. Rev. ed. Edited and annotated by Leroy R. Hafen and biography by Paul C. Phillips. Denver: Old West Publishing, 1983.

———. *Life in the Rocky Mountains, 1830 to 1835*. Edited by Paul C. Phillips. Denver: Old West Publishing, 1940.

Frémont, John Charles. *Report of the Exploring Expedition to the Rocky Mountains* [1844]. Ann Arbor, MI: University Microfilms, 1966.

Gottfredson, Peter. *Indian Depredations in Utah*. 2nd ed. 1919. Reprint, Salt Lake City: Shelton Publishing Co., 1969.

Gregg, Josiah. *Commerce of the Prairies*. 2 vols. New York: 1844.

Gunnison, John W. *The Mormons, or, Latter-day Saints, in the Valley of the Great Salt Lake*. Philadelphia: J. P. Lippincott, 1856.

Hackett, Charles W., ed. *Historical Documents Relating to New Mexico, Nueva Vizcaya, and Approaches Thereto, to 1773*. 3 vols. Collected by A. F. Bandelier and F. R. Bandelier. English translations, annotated by Hackett. Washington, D.C.: Carnegie Institution of Washington, 1937.

Hamblin, Jacob. *Jacob Hamblin: A Narrative of His Personal Experience as a Frontiersman, Missionary to the Indians and Explorer*. 2nd ed. Transcribed by James A. Little. Salt Lake City: *Deseret News* and *Juvenile Instructor*, 1881. Reprint, 1909, 1983, 1995 in New York and Provo, UT.

———. "Journals and Letters of Jacob Hamblin." 1969 typescript copy with original orthography. Harold B. Lee Library, Special Collections, Brigham Young University, Provo, Utah. Original six journals in Church History Library, The Church of Jesus Christ of Latter-day Saints, Salt Lake City, Utah.

Hamilton, W. T. *My Sixty Years on the Plains: Trapping, Trading, and Indian Fighting*. Norman: University of Oklahoma, 1905. Reprint, 1960.

Harris, Henry, Jr. Interview. 1967. Duke Oral Indian History Collection, Box 3 #46. Marriott Library Special Collections, University of Utah, Salt Lake City.

Hartman, Alonzo. "Memories and Experiences with the Utes in Colorado." MS, n.d. Reproduced in John B. Lloyd, "The Uncompahgre Utes," Master's thesis, Western State College of Colorado, Gunnison, 1939, 5–15.

Head, Lafayette. "Statement of Mr. Head of Abiquiú in Regard of the Buying and Selling of Payutahs—April 30, 1852." Doc. 2150, Rich Collection of Papers Pertaining to New Mexico. Huntington Library, San Marino, CA.

Heap, Gwinn Harris. *Central Route to the Pacific*. Edited and annotated by LeRoy R. Hafen and Ann W. Hafen. Glendale, CA: Arthur H. Clark, Co., 1957. Originally published in Philadelphia, 1854.

Heywood, Martha Spence. Journal of Martha Spence Heywood. n.d. Utah State Historical Society, Salt Lake City, Utah.

Huntington, Dimick B. *Vocabulary of the Utah and Shoshone or Snake Dialects*. Salt Lake City: Salt Lake City Herald Office, 1872.

Huntington, Oliver B. Diary. Harold B. Lee Library, n.d. Brigham Young University, Provo, Utah.

Hurt, Garland. "Indians of Utah." Appendix O. In J. H. Simpson, comp. *Report of Explorations across the Great Basin*.

Ingersoll, Ernest. *Knocking Around the Rockies*. New York: Harper & Bros., 1883.

Inman, "Colonel" Henry. *The Old Santa Fe Trail: The Story of a Great Highway*. Topeka: Crane and Co., 1916. Originally published 1897. Online as a Project Gutenberg EBook (2009) at http://www.gutenberg.org/files/7984/7984-h/7984-h.htm.

"Interview with Kit Carson." *New York World*, November 1866.

Jefferson, Thomas, *Notes on the State of Virginia, 1743–1826*. Edited by William Peden. Chapel Hill: University of North Carolina, 1955. Reprint, 1995.

Jocknick, Sidney. *Early Days on the Western Slope of Colorado, 1870–1883, inclusive*. Glorietta, NM: Rio Grande Press, 1913.

Johnson, Miles E. "Miles Egar Johnson: The Life Review of a Mormon." Typescript, edited by Rolla Virgil Johnson 1930–1933, revised 1970. MS 1187, Church History Library, The Church of Jesus Christ of Latter-day Saints, Salt Lake City, Utah.

Jones, Daniel W. *Forty Years among the Indians*. Los Angeles: Westernlore Press, [1890]. Reprint, 1960.

Journal History of the Church, 1830–1972. Church History Library, The Church of Jesus Christ of Latter-day Saints, Salt Lake City, Utah.

Kane, Elizabeth W. *Twelve Mormon Homes: Visited in Succession on a Journey through Utah to Arizona*. Salt Lake City: University of Utah Library, 1974.

Little, James Amasa. "Biography of Lorenzo Dow Young." *Utah Historical Quarterly* 14 (1946): 25–132.

Lyman, Platte D. Journal. L. Tom Perry Special Collections, Harold B. Lee Library, Brigham Young University, Provo, Utah.

Manly, William Lewis. *Death Valley in '49*. Ann Arbor, MI: University Microfilms, Inc., 1966. First published 1896.

Meeker, Josephine. *The Ute Massacre: Brave Miss Meeker's Captivity, Her Own Account of It*. Philadelphia: Old Franklin Publishing, 1879.

Miller, Thomas R. "Cause of the Ute Outbreak: An Unvarnished Tale." *Deseret News*, January 12, 1880.

Morgan, Dale. *The West of William Ashley: The International Struggle for the Fur Trade. Recorded in the Diaries and Letters of William Ashley and his Contemporaries, 1822–1838*. Denver: Old West Publishing, 1964.

Mowry, Sylvester (Lt.). Report given under command of Lt. Col. Steptoe, investigating Gunnison Massacre, July 23, 1855. Typescript of letter. Utah Writers Project. Utah State Historical Society, Salt Lake City, Utah.

New Mexico. Spanish, Mexican, and Territorial Archives of New Mexico. Microfilm. Santa Fe: State Historical Archives.

New Mexico Indian Superintendency. Microfilm. Record Group 75, T21. National Archives and Records Administration, Washington, D.C.

Office of Indian Affairs. *Annual Report of the Commissioner of Indian Affairs*. Washington, D.C.: GPO, 1855–1936.

Office of Indian Affairs. *Letters Received, Utah Superintendency, 1849–1880* [microfilm], Record Group 75, M-234, rolls 897–898. National Archives and Records Administration, Washington, D.C.

Olmsted, Virginia L., trans. and comp. *Spanish and Mexican Colonial Censuses of New Mexico: 1790, 1823, 1845*. Albuquerque: New Mexico Genealogical Society, 1975.

Pace, William B. "William B. Pace Collection." MS 10411, Church History Library, The Church of Jesus Christ of Latter-day Saints, Salt Lake City, Utah.

Pattie, James Ohio. "Pattie's Personal Narrative, 1824–1830." In *Early Western Travels, 1748–1846*. Edited by Reuben Gold Thwaites. Cleveland, OH: Arthur H. Clark, 1905.

Peacock, George. "The Original Diary of Judge George Peacock." MS 2251, Church History Library, The Church of Jesus Christ of Latter-day Saints, Salt Lake City, Utah.

Piercy, Frederick Hawkins. *Route from Liverpool to Great Salt Lake Valley*. Edited by Fawn M. Brodie. Cambridge: Belknap Press of Harvard University Press, 1962. First published 1854 in Liverpool, England.

Potts, Daniel. Letters. In Jerry Bagley "Appendixes," *Daniel Trotter Potts: First Known Man in Yellowstone Park*. Rigby, ID: Old Faithful Eye-Witness Publishing, 2000. Now available online, at http://user.xmission.com/~drudy/mtman/html/potts.

Powell, John Wesley. *Anthropology of the Numa: John Wesley Powell's Manuscripts on the Numic Peoples of Western North America, 1868–1880*. Edited by Don D. Fowler and Catherine S. Fowler. Washington, D.C.: Smithsonian Institution Press, 1971.

———. "The Life and Culture of the Ute—Methods of Marrying." 1873. MS 830-Ute, Anthropology Archives. Museum of Natural History, Smithsonian Institution, Washington, D.C.

———. "Religion of the Numas." 1873. MS 830-Ute, Anthropology Archives. Smithsonian Institution, Washington, D.C.

———. "Report on the Indians of the Numa Stock." In *Anthropology of the Numa.*

———. "Uintah Ute Relationship Terms in Powell's Hand." N.d. MS 831-a, Ute. Anthropology Archives. Smithsonian Institution, Washington, D.C.

Powell, John Wesley, and G. W. Ingalls. "Report of J. W. Powell and G. W. Ingalls." In *Report of the Secretary of the Interior, 1873* (409–417). U.S. Department of the Interior, Washington, D.C, 1873.

Records of United States Army Continental Command, 1871–1945, Record Group 394. National Archives and Records Administration, Washington, D.C.

Rees, Florence. "Miscellaneous Papers." Utah State Historical Society, Salt Lake City, Utah.

Report of the Secretary of the Interior. Washington, D.C.: GPO, 1860–1875.

Russell, Osborne. *Osborne Russell's Journal of a Trapper.* Lincoln: University of Nebraska Press, 1955/1975.

———. *Osborne Russell's Journal of a Trapper.* Portland: Oregon Historical Society, 1955. Reprint, 1965.

Ruxton, George Frederick. *Life in the Far West.* Edited by LeRoy R. Hafen. Norman: University of Oklahoma, 1849. Reprint, 1951.

———. *Ruxton of the Rockies.* Edited by LeRoy Hafen. Norman: University of Oklahoma Press, 1950.

———. *Wild Life in the Rocky Mountains.* New York: The MacMillan Company, copyright 1916. First published in London, 1847. Also online: http://user.xmission.com/ ~drudy/mtman/html/ruxton.html.

Sage, Rufus B. *Rocky Mountain Life; Startling Scenes and Perilous Adventures in the Far West.* Chicago: Donohue, Henneberry & Co., 1857.

Seeley, Orange Sr. "History of Orange Seeley, Sr., Told by Himself." MS 9942, Church History Library, The Church of Jesus Christ of Latter-day Saints, Salt Lake City, Utah.

Simpson, J. H. *Report of Explorations Across the Great Basin, etc.* Washington, D.C., 1876.

Smith, Anne M. (Cooke). "Analysis of Basin Mythology." [White River, Uintah, and Uncompahgre Ute folktales collected 1936–37.] In Vol. 2. Ph.D. dissertation, Yale University, 1940. Also in 1940, MS 4828-Ute, Anthropology Archives. Smithsonian Institution, Washington, D.C.

Smith, George A. "G. A. Smith Collection." Church History Library, The Church of Jesus Christ of Latter-day Saints, Salt Lake City, Utah.

———. "Journal of George Albert Smith (1817–1875). Principal Residence during this period (1850–1851) Parowan, Utah." Typescript. Special Collections, Harold B. Lee Library, Brigham Young University, Provo, UT.

Smith, Jedediah S. *The Southwest Expedition of Jedediah S. Smith: His Personal Account of the Journey to California, 1826–1827.* Edited by George R. Brooks. Glendale, CA: Arthur H. Clark, 1977.

Smith, Joseph. *History of the Church of Jesus Christ of Latter-day Saints.* 2nd ed., rev. 7 vols. Salt Lake City: Deseret Book, 1978.

Snow, William J. "Some Source Documents on Utah Indian Slavery." *Utah Historical Quarterly* 2 (July 1929): 76–90.

Southern Ute Tribe. *Constitution of the Southern Ute Indian Tribe of the Southern Ute Indian Reservation, Colorado.* University of Oklahoma Law Center website at http://thorpe.ou.edu/constitution/utecons.html.

Stansbury, Howard, *Exploration and Survey of the Valley of the Great Salt Lake of Utah.* Philadelphia: Lippincott, Grambo, 1852.

Stout, Hosea. Diary. 8 vols., TS. Provo, UT: Harold B. Lee Library, Brigham Young University, n.d.

———. *On the Mormon Frontier: The Diary of Hosea Stout: 1844–1861.* Edited by Juanita Brooks. Salt Lake City: University of Utah Press, 1964.

Sutter, John. A. "The Discovery of Gold in California." Originally published in *Hutchings California Magazine*, 1857. Retrieved from *The Virtual Museum of San Francisco* website.

Talbot, Theodore. *The Journals of Theodore Talbot, 1843 and 1849–52.* Edited by Charles H. Carey. Portland, OR: Metropolitan Press, 1931.

Thomas, A. B., trans. and ed. *Alonso de Posada Report, 1686: A Description of the Area of the Present Southern United States in the Late Seventeenth Century.* Vol. 4 in The Spanish Borderlands Series. Pensacola: The Perdido Bay Press, 1982.

Twitchell, Ralph E., comp. *Spanish Archives of New Mexico*. 2 vols. Cedar Rapids, MI: The Torch Press, 1914. Also available online at http://archive.org/stream/ spanisharchives001twituoft/spanishar-chives001twituoft_djvu.txt.

Uintah-Ouray Ute Tribe. *Constitution and By-laws of the Ute Indian Tribe of the Uintah and Ouray Reservation, Utah*. Approved January 19, 1937. Uintah-Ouray Tribal Offices and Tribal Museum Archives, Ft. Duchesne, Utah.

Utah Superintendency of Indian Affairs. Letters to the Office of Indian Affairs, 1849–80. Record Group 75, M-234, R 897-198. Bureau of Indian Affairs, Washington, D.C.

Utah Territorial Military Correspondence, 1849–1863. Microfilm ST-27. Utah State Historical Society, Salt Lake City.

Utah Territory. "Acts in Relation to Service." Ch. 24, in *Acts, Resolutions, and Memorials, Passed at the Several Sessions of the Legislative Assembly of the Territory of Utah*. Passed January 31, 1852; approved March 7, 1852. Salt Lake City, 1855.

——. First Judicial Court of Utah. "Information" in the case of *United States v. Pedro León et al.* February 10, 1852. Published in *Deseret News Weekly*, March 6, 1852.

——. "Minutes" of the First Judicial Court of Utah, 1851–52 (microfiche). Utah State Archives, Salt Lake City.

——. *United States v. Pedro León et al.* Doc. 1533 (microfiche). Utah State Archives, Salt Lake City.

Wells, Daniel H. "Daniel H. Wells' Narrative." *Utah Historical Quarterly* 6 (October 1933): 124–32.

White, E. E. *Experiences of a Special Indian Agent*. Norman: University of Oklahoma Press, 1893. Reprint, 1965.

Young, Brigham. Brigham Young Collection. Church History Library, Church of Jesus Christ of Latter-day Saints, Salt Lake City, Utah.

——. *Discourses of Brigham Young*. Edited by John A. Widtsoe. Salt Lake City, 1941. Reprint, 1978.

——. "Legislative Address," January 5, 1852. Published in *Deseret News Weekly*, January 10, 1852.

——. "Manuscript History." N.d. Church History Library, Church of Jesus Christ of Latter-day Saints, Salt Lake City, Utah.

——. Testimony given in First District Judicial Court, January 15, 1852, *United States v. Pedro León et al.* Doc. 1533, pp. 11–13 (microfiche). In *Minutes of the First Judicial Court*, Utah State Archives, Salt Lake City.

Young, Brigham, et al. *Journal of Discourses*. 26 vols. 1854–1886. Reprint, London: Latter-day Saints' Book Depot, 1966.

Young, Clara Decker. "A Woman's Experience with the Pioneer Band." *Utah Historical Quarterly* 14 (1946): 173–76.

Young, John R. *Memoirs of John R. Young, Utah Pioneer*. Salt Lake City: Deseret News, 1920.

Young, Lorenzo Dow. "Diary of Lorenzo Dow Young." *Utah Historical Quarterly* 14 (1946): 133–70. Written mostly by his wife, Harriet Page Wheeler Decker Young, 1846–1847.

Young, Susa Gates. "The Courtship of Kanosh: A Pioneer Love Story." *The Improvement Era* 9 (1906): 21–38.

Yount, George C. *George C. Yount and His Chronicles of the West*. Edited by Charles L. Camp. Denver: Old West Publishing, 1966.

GOVERNMENT SOURCES

Legislative and Government Agency Sources

Brookings Institute (Institute for Government Research). *The Problem of Indian Administration: Summary of Findings and Recommendations* ("Meriam Report"). Washington, D.C.: The Institute, 1928.

Kappler, Charles J., comp. and ed. *Indian Affairs: Laws and Treaties*. 5 vols. Washington, D.C.: GPO, 1902–1938.

Leupp, Frances E. *The Latest Phase of the Southern Ute Question: A Report*. Philadelphia: Indian Rights Association, 1895.

Nixon, Richard. "Message on Indian Affairs" (July 8, 1970). Public Papers of the Presidents of the United States, and in the Senate Committee on Indian Affairs Briefing Booklet, Presidential Policy Papers. Washington, D.C.

Roosevelt, Theodore. "Proclamation establishing the Uintah Forest Reserve in the State of Utah." In Charles J. Kappler, *Indian Affairs: Laws and Treaties*, Vol. 3, 602–3.

———. "Proclamation withdrawing certain Indian lands for a reservoir site [Strawberry]." In Charles J. Kappler, *Indian Affairs: Laws and Treaties*, Vol. 3, 610–11.

United States. Office of Indian Affairs. *Annual Report of the Commissioner of Indian Affairs [ARCIA]*. Washington, D.C.: GPO, 1856–1905.

U.S. Bureau of the Census. 1850, 1860, and 1870. Utah Territory. Family History Library microfilm 805314. Harold B. Lee Library, Brigham Young University, Provo, Utah.

———. 1850 and 1870. Rio Arriba County, New Mexico Territory. Family History Library microfilm 16603, and 552393. Harold B. Lee Library, Brigham Young University, Provo, Utah.

———. 1870. Conejos County, Colorado Territory. Family History Library microfilm 545595. Harold B. Lee Library, Brigham Young University, Provo, Utah.

U.S. Bureau of Reclamation. *Annual Report, 1910*. Vol. 36. Washington, D.C.: GPO, 1910.

U.S. Congress. James Buchanan. *Message from the President of the United States*, 35th Cong., 1st Sess., 1857. Ex. Doc. 2, 25.

U.S. Congress, House. *Changing the Boundary of the Uncompahgre Reservation*. 51st Cong., 1st and 2nd sess., 1890. H. Rept. 3305 and 3395.

———. Committee on Interior and Insular Affairs. *Animas-La Plata Water Rights Settlement: Hearings on H.R. 2642*. 100th Cong., 1st sess., September 16, 1987.

———. *Grant of Lands for Use of Certain Indians*. 58th Cong., 1st sess., 1903. H. Doc. 33.

———. *Investigation of the Bureau of Indian Affairs*. Committee on Interior and Insular Affairs. 82d Cong., 2d sess., 1953. H. Rept. 2503.

———. *Report of the Ute Commission*. Washington, D.C.: GPO, 1881.

———. *Surveys and Examinations of Uintah Indian Reservation*. [Rept. prepared by Cyrus Babb.] 57th Cong., 1st sess., 1902. H. Doc. 671.

———. *Ute Indians, A Special Report to the Congress*. Washington, D.C., 1880.

———. *White River Ute Commission Investigation*. Ute Commission. 46th Congress, 2d Sess., 1880. H. Ex. Doc. 83, 84, and H. Misc. Doc. 38.

U.S. Congress, Senate. *Colorado Ute Water Settlement Act Amendments of 2000*. 106th Cong., 2nd Sess. May 4, 2000. S. 2508.

———. Committee on Labor and Public Welfare, Special Subcommittee on Indian Education. *Indian Education: A National Tragedy—A National Challenge*. 91st Cong., 1st Sess, 1969. S. Rept. 91–501.

———. *Leasing of Indian Lands*. 57th Cong., 1st sess., 1902. S. Doc. 212.

———. *Report of the Secretary of War* [John B. Floyd], 35th Cong., 1st Sess., 1858. Ex. Doc. 11, 7.

U.S. Department of the Interior. *Report of the Secretary of the Interior*. Washington, D.C.: 1860–1875.

U.S. Department of War. *War of the Rebellion: A Compilation of the Official Records of the Union and Confederate Armies*. Series 1, Vols. 50 and 52, Part II. Washington, D.C., 1897.

Utah Territory. "Acts in Relation to Service." Chap. 24 in *Acts, Resolutions, and Memorials, Passed at the Several Sessions of the Legislative Assembly of the Territory of Utah*. Salt Lake City, 1855. [Passed January 31, 1852; approved March 7, 1852.]

ACTS AND RESOLUTIONS

An Act to Amend the Colorado Ute Indian Water Rights Settlement Act of 1988. 106th Cong, 1st Sess. October 20, 1999. H.R. 3112.

An Act to Amend the Colorado Ute Indian Water Rights Settlement Act of 1988. S. 2508, May 4, 2000.

An Act for the Appointment of a Commission to Make Allotments . . . upon the Uintah Indian Reservation, 55th Cong., 2nd Sess. June 4, 1898.

An Act to Disapprove [a] Treaty . . . with the Southern Ute Indians to be removed to the Territory of Utah . . . [and] providing for settling them down in severalty, etc. (Hunter Bill). 53rd Cong., 3rd sess. February 20, 1895.

An Act Granting the Utah Midland Railway Company the Right of Way, etc. 49th Cong., 2nd sess., March 3, 1887.

An Act to Promote Development of Indian Arts and Crafts, P.L. 101–644 (104 Stat. 4662)

American Indian Religious Freedom Act. U.S. Code. Title 42, Chap. 21, Sec 1996 (1978).

American Indian Religious Freedom Act Amendments of 1994. U.S. Code. Title 42, Chap. 21, Sec 1996a (P.L. 103–344).

Central Utah Project Completion Act, "Ute Indian Rights Settlement." 102nd Cong. (P.L. 102–575) (October 30, 1992).

Colorado Ute Indian Water Rights Settlement Act of 1988. 100th Cong., 2nd sess. (P.L. 100–585) (November 3, 1988).

Colorado Ute Water Settlement Act Amendments of 2000. 106th Cong., 2nd Sess. May 4, 2000. S. 2508.

Dawes Severalty (General Allotment) Act. 49th Cong., 2nd Sess., February 8, 1887.

Indian Child Welfare Act. U.S. Code 25, Chap. 21 (1978).

Indian Civil Rights Act, U.S. Code 25, ¶¶ 1301–1303 (1968).

Indian Education Act, U.S. Code 25, Chap 27 (P.L. 93–380 [1974], P.L. 100–129 [1988], P.L. 103–382 [1994], and P.L. 107–10 [2001]).

Indian Gaming Regulatory Act, U.S. Code 25, sec. 2701 (P.L. 100–497) (1988).

Indian Health Care Act. U.S. Code 25, Chap. 18 (1976).

Indian Homestead Act. 43rd Cong., 2nd Sess., March 3, 1875.

Indian Mineral Development Act (1982), U.S. Code 25, Sec. 2101–2108.

Indian Mineral Leasing Act (1938), U.S. Code. 25, Sec 396a–396g.

Indian Religious Freedom Act, Amended, 103rd Cong., 2nd Sess. (1994), P.L. 103–344.

Marriage. Utah Code. Title 30, Chap 1, Sec. 6 and 7, as amended 2004.

Mineral Leasing Act for Allotted Land (1909) 25 U.S.C. 396 25 CFR.

Native American Graves Protection and Repatriation Act, U.S. Code 25, Chap. 32 (1990).

Omnibus Tribal Leasing Act of (1969), 25 U.S.C. 396, 396a–396d.

Religious Freedom Restoration Act, 103 Cong., 1st Sess., 1993. U.S. Code 42, Chap. 21B, Sec. 2000bb (1993).

Self-Determination and Education Assistance Act, U.S. Code 25, Chap. 14, Stat. 2203 (P.L. 93–638) (1975).

JUDICIAL SOURCES

"Adoption of Halloway," Utah Supreme Court, 732 P.2d 962 (1986).

California v. Cabazon Band of Mission Indians, 480 U.S. 202 (1987).

Cherokee Tobacco, The, 78 U.S. 616 (1870).

City of Boerne v. Flores, 521 U.S. 507 (1997).

Confederated Bands of Ute Indians v. United States. U.S. Court of Claims. Nos. 45585, 46640, 47564, 47566 (March 17, 1950).

Confederated Bands of Ute Indians v. U.S., No. 30360 (May 23, 1910).

Employment Division, Oregon Dept. of Human Res. v. Smith et al., 494 U.S. 872 (1990)

Hagen v. Utah, U.S. 510–399 (1994).

Lone Wolf v. Hitchcock, 187 U.S. 553 (1903).

Merrion v. Jicarilla Apache Tribe, 455 U.S. 130 (1982).

Mississippi Choctaw Indian Band v. Holyfield, 490 U.S. 30 (1989).

Santa Clara Pueblo v. Martinez, 436 U.S. 49 (1978).

Solem v. Bartlett, 465 U.S. 463, 467 (1984).

Timpanogos Tribe v. Conway, No. 01-4056, 10th Circuit Court of Appeals (April 2002).

United States v. Pedro Leon et al., Doc. 1533 (microfiche). Utah State Archives, Salt Lake City.

United States v. Southern Utes or Band of Indians, 402 U.S. 159 (1971).

Ute Distribution Corporation v. Norton, No. 01-4020, 10th Circuit Court of Appeals (July 25, 2002).

Ute Distribution Corporation v. Ute Indian Tribe, D.C. No. 95-CV-37-W (1998).

Ute Indian Tribe v. State of Utah, 773 F. 2d 1087 (CA 10) (1985).

Ward vs. Race Horse, 163 U.S. 504 (1896).

Winters v. United States, 207 U.S. 564 (1908).

BOOKS

Aberle, David F., and Omer C. Stewart. *Navaho and Ute Peyotism: A Chronological and Distributional Study*. Series in Anthropology no. 6. Boulder: University of Colorado Press, 1957.

Albers, Patricia, and Beatrice Medicine. *The Hidden Half: Studies of Plains Indian Women*. New York: University Press of America, 1983.

Albers, Patricia, and Jennifer Lowry. *Cultural Resource and Properties of the Northern Ute Tribe: A Technical Report on Sites under Possible Impact by the Uinta Basin Replacement Project*. Salt Lake City: American West Center, 1995.

Alexander, Thomas G. *Utah: The Right Place*. Utah Statehood Centennial Project, Updated and rev. ed. Salt Lake City: Gibbs Smith, 2003.

Arrington, Leonard J., and Davis Bitton. *Saints Without Halos*. Salt Lake City: Signature Books, 1981.

Bagley, Jerry. *Daniel Trotter Potts: First Known Man in Yellowstone Park*. Rigby, ID: Old Faithful Eye-Witness Publishing, 2000.

Bailey, L. R. *Indian Slave Trade in the Southwest*. Los Angeles: Westernlore Press, 1966.

Bailey, Paul. *Walkara: Hawk of the Mountains*. Los Angeles: Westernlore Press, 1954.

Bancroft, Hubert Howe. *History of Arizona and New Mexico: 1530–1888*. San Francisco: History Company, 1889.

———. *History of Nevada, Colorado, and Wyoming, 1540–1880*. San Francisco: The History Company, 1890.

———. *History of Utah*. San Francisco: The History Company, 1890.

Bannon, John Francis. *The Spanish Borderlands Frontier: 1513–1821*. Histories of the American Frontier Series. Albuquerque: University of New Mexico Press, 1974.

Barber, Ruth K. *Indian Labor in the Spanish Colonies*. Albuquerque: University of New Mexico Press, 1932.

Barney, Garold. *Mormons, Indians, and the Ghost Dance Religion of 1890*. Lanham, MD: University Press of America, 1986.

Barth, Fredrik. "Introduction." *Ethnic Groups and Boundaries: The Social Organization of Culture Difference*. 1969; Long Grove, IL: Waveland Press, 1998.

Becker, Cynthia S., and P. David Smith. *Chipeta: Queen of the Utes*. Montrose, CO: Western Reflections, 2003.

Berkhofer, Robert F. *Salvation and the Savage: An Analysis of Protestant Missions, and American Indian Response, 1787–1862*. Lexington: University of Kentucky Press, 1965.

———. *The White Man's Indian*. New York: Alfred A. Knopf, 1978.

Bernstein, Alison R. *American Indians and World War II: Toward a New Era in Indian Affairs*. Norman: University of Oklahoma Press, 1991.

Billington, Allen, and Martin Ridge. *Westward Expansion: A History of the American Frontier*, 5th ed. New York: Macmillan Publishing, 1982.

Blackhawk, Ned. *Violence over the Land: Indians and Empires in the Early American West*. Cambridge, MA: Harvard University Press, 2006.

Boessenecker, John. *Gold Dust & Gunsmoke: Tales of Gold Rush Outlaws, Gunfighters, Lawmen, and Vigilantes*. New York: Wiley & Sons, 1999.

Bolton, Herbert E. *Coronado, Knight of Pueblo and Plain*. Albuquerque: University of New Mexico Press, 1949. Reprint, 1991.

———. *Pageant in the Wilderness: The Story of the Escalante Expedition to the Interior Basin, 1776*. Salt Lake City: Utah State Historical Society, 1950.

———. *Spanish Exploration in the Southwest, 1542–1700*. New York, 1916.

Boyd, David. *History of Greeley and the Union Colony of Colorado*. Greeley, CO, 1890.

Brooks, James F. *Captives & Cousins: Slavery, Kinship, and Community in the Southwest Borderlands*. Chapel Hill: University of North Carolina Press, 2002.

Brooks, Juanita. *The Mountain Meadows Massacre*. Stanford, CA: Stanford University Press, 1962.

———. *On the Ragged Edge: The Life and Times of Dudley Leavitt*. Salt Lake City: Utah State Historical Society, 1978.

Brooks, Juanita, ed. *On the Mormon Frontier: The Diary of Hosea Stout: 1844–1861*. 2 vols. Salt Lake City: University of Utah Press, 1964.

Brown, Dee. *Bury My Heart at Wounded Knee*. New York: Bantam Books, 1972.

Brugge, David M. *Navajos in the Catholic Church Records of New Mexico, 1694–1875*. Research Report no. 1. Window Rock, AZ: Navajo Tribe Parks and Recreation Department, 1968.

Campbell, Eugene E. *Establishing Zion: The Mormon Church in the American West, 1847–69*. Salt Lake City: Signature Books, 1988.

Campbell, Eugene E., and Fred R. Gowans. *Fort Supply: Brigham Young's Green River Experiment*. Provo, UT: Brigham Young University Press, 1976.

Carins, Mary Lyons. *The Pioneers*. Denver: World Press, 1946.

Carter, Harvey L., ed. *"Dear Old Kit": The Historical Christopher Carson*. Norman: University of Oklahoma, 1968.

Carter, Kate B., comp. *Heart Throbs of the West*. 12 vols. Salt Lake City: Daughters of the Utah Pioneers, 1939–1950.

———. *Our Pioneer Heritage*. 20 vols. Salt Lake City: Daughters of Utah Pioneers, 1958–1977.

Carter, William B. *Indian Alliances and the Spanish in the Southwest, 750–1750*. Norman: University of Oklahoma Press, 2009.

Champagne, Duane. *Social Change and Cultural Continuity among Native Nations*. Chicago: University of Chicago Press, 2006.

Christensen, Scott R. *Sagwitch: Shoshone Chieftain, Mormon Elder, 1822–1887*. Logan: Utah State University Press, 1999.

Church of Jesus Christ of Latter-day Saints. *The Book of Mormon*. Orig. printed 1829. Salt Lake City: The Church of Jesus Christ of Latter-day Saints, 1989.

Clemmer, Richard O., L. Daniel Myers, and Mary E. Rudden, eds. *Julian Steward and the Great Basin: The Making of an Anthropologist*. Salt Lake City: University of Utah Press, 1999.

Clifton, James A., ed. *Being and Becoming Indian: Biographical Studies of North American Frontiers*. Prospect Heights, IL: Waveland Press, 1989.

———. *The Invented Indian: Cultural Fictions and Government Policies*. New Brunswick, NJ: Transaction Publishers, 1990.

Conard, Howard Louis. *"Uncle Dick" Wootton: The Pioneer Frontiersman of the Rocky Mountain Region*. Edited by Milo Milton Quife, 1890. Reprint, Chicago: R. R. Donnelley and Sons, 1957.

Correll, J. Lee. *Through White Men's Eyes: A Contribution to Navajo History*. 2 vols. Window Rock, Arizona: Navajo Heritage Center, 1969.

Creer, Leland H. *Utah and the Nation*. Seattle: University of Washington Press, 1929.

Crosby, Alfred W., Jr. *The Columbian Exchange: Biological and Cultural Consequences of 1492*. Westport, CT: Greenwood, 1972.

Cuch, Forrest S., ed. *A History of Utah's American Indians*. Salt Lake City: Utah State Division of Indian Affairs/Utah State Division of History, 2000.

Culmsee, Carlton, *Utah's Black Hawk War: Lore and Reminiscences of Participants*. Logan: Utah State University, 1973.

Cutter, Donald, and Iris Engstrand. *Quest for Empire: Spanish Settlement in the Southwest*. Golden, CO: Fulcrum Press, 1996.

Daughters of Utah Pioneers, Sanpete County Company. *These—Our Fathers: A Centennial History of Sanpete County 1849 to 1947*. Springville, UT: Art City Publishing, 1947.

d'Azevedo, Warren L., Wilbur A. Davis, Don D. Fowler, and Wayne Suttles, eds. *The Current Status of Anthropological Research in the Great Basin: 1964*. Desert Research Institute, Technical Report Series S-H, Social Sciences and Humanities Publications, no. 1, 1966.

Delaney, Robert. *The Southern Ute People*. Phoenix: Indian Tribal Series, 1974.

———. *The Ute Mountain Utes*. Albuquerque: University of New Mexico Press, 1989.

Deloria, Philip Joseph. *Indians in Unexpected Places*. Lawrence: University Press of Kansas, 2006.

———. *Playing Indian*. New Haven, CT: Yale University Press, 1998.

Denison, Brandi. *Ute Land Religion in the American West, 1879–2009*. Lincoln: University of Nebraska Press and American Philosophical Society, 2017.

Densmore, Frances. *Northern Ute Music*. Bureau of American Ethnology, Bulletin, no. 75. Washington, D.C.: Smithsonian Institution, 1922.

Denver, Norma, and June Lyman, comp. *Ute People: An Historical Study*. Edited by Floyd A. O'Neil and John D. Sylvester. Salt Lake City: University of Utah, 1970.

Dixon, Madoline Cloward. *These Were the Utes: Their Lifestyles, Wars and Legends.* Provo, UT: Press Publishing Co., 1983.

Dunlay, Thomas. *Kit Carson and the Indians.* Lincoln: University of Nebraska, 2000.

Durkheim, Emile. *The Elementary Forms of the Religious Life.* Trans. by Joseph W. Swain. New York: Free Press, 1915.

Emmitt, Robert. *The Last War Trail: The Utes and the Settlement of Colorado.* Norman: University of Oklahoma Press, 1954.

Espinosa, J. Manuel. *Crusaders of the Rio Grande.* Chicago: Institute of Jesuit History, 1942.

Farmer, Jared. *On Zion's Mount: Mormons, Indians, and the American Landscape.* Cambridge: Harvard University Pres, 2008.

Farnham, T. J. *Life, Adventures, and Travels in California.* New York, 1849.

———. *Travels in the Great Western Prairies.* In *Early Western Travels.* Edited by Reuben Gold Thwaites. Vol. 28. Cleveland: Arthur H. Clark, 1906.

Fixico, Donald. *Termination and Relocation: Federal Indian Policy, 1945–1960.* Albuquerque: University of New Mexico Press, 1986.

Fowler, Don D., and Catherine S. Fowler, eds. *Anthropology of the Numa: John Wesley Powell's Manuscripts on the Numic Peoples of Western North America, 1868–1880.* Washington, D.C.: Smithsonian Institution Press, 1971.

Gallay, Alan. *The Indian Slave Trade: The Rise of the English Empire in the American South, 1670–1717.* New Haven, CT: Yale University Press, 2002.

Gallay, Alan, ed. *Indian Slavery in Colonial America.* Lincoln: University of Nebraska Press, 2009.

Garroutte, Eva Marie. *Real Indians: Identity and the Survival of Native America.* Berkeley: University of California Pres, 2003.

Gibson, Arrell Morgan. *The American Indian: Prehistory to the Present.* Norman: University of Oklahoma Press, 1980.

Goetzmann, William H. *Exploration and Empire: The Explorer and the Scientist in the Winning of the American West.* New York: Alfred Knopf, 1967.

Gowans, Fred R. *Fort Bridger: Island in the Wilderness.* Provo, UT: Brigham Young University Press, 1975.

———. *Rocky Mountain Rendezvous: A History of the Fur Trade Rendezvous, 1825–1840.* Salt Lake City: Gibbs-Smith, 1985.

Guild, Thelma S. and Harvey L. Carter. *Kit Carson.* Lincoln: University of Nebraska, 1984.

Gutiérrez, Ramón A. *When Jesus Came the Corn Mothers Went Away.* Stanford, CA: Stanford University Press, 1991.

Hafen, LeRoy R., ed. *The Mountain Men and The Fur Trade of the Far West: Biographical Sketches of the Participants by Scholars of the Subject and with Introduction by the Editor.* 10 vols. Glendale, CA: Arthur H. Clark Co., 1965–1972.

Hafen, LeRoy R., and Ann W. Hafen. *Colorado: A Story of the State and its People.* Denver: Old West Publishing, 1952.

———. *Old Spanish Trail: Santa Fe to Los Angeles.* Glendale, CA: Arthur H. Clark Co., 1954.

Hall, Frank. *History of the State of Colorado.* Vols. 2 and 4. Chicago: Blakely Printing Co., 1895.

Hämäläinen, Pekka. *Comanche Empire.* New Haven: Yale University Press, 2008.

Hammond, George P. *Don Juan de Oñate and the Founding of New Mexico.* Santa Fe: El Palacio Press, 1927.

Hammond, George P., and Agapito Rey. *Don Juan de Oñate, Colonizer of New Mexico, 1595–1628.* Albuquerque: University of New Mexico, 1953.

———. *The Rediscovery of New Mexico, 1580–1594: The Explorations of Chamuscado, Espejo, Castaño de Sosa, Morlete, and Leyva de Bonila and Humaña.* Albuquerque: University of New Mexico, 1966.

Harmon, Alexandra. *Indians in the Making: Ethnic Relations and Indian Identities around Puget Sound.* Los Angeles: University of California Press, 1998.

———. *Rich Indians: Native People and the Problem of Wealth in American History.* Chapel Hill: University of North Carolina Press, 2010.

Harrington, Anne, ed. *The Placebo Effect: An Interdisciplinary Exploration.* Cambridge, MA: Harvard University Press, 1997.

Harris, Dean. *The Catholic Church in Utah, 1776–1909.* Salt Lake City: Utah State Historical Society Library, 1909.

Hine, Robert V. and John M. Faragher. *The American West: A New Interpretive History*. New Haven, CT: Yale University Press, 2000.

Hittman, Michael. *Wovoka and the Ghost Dance*. Expanded edition. Edited by Don Lynch. Lincoln: University of Nebraska Press, 1990.

Hoebel, E. Adamson. *Anthropology: The Study of Man*. New York: McGraw-Hill, 1958.

Holt, Ronald L. *Beneath These Red Cliffs: An Ethnohistory of the Utah Paiutes*. Albuquerque: University of New Mexico Press, 1992.

Hunter, Milton R. *Utah in Her Western Setting*. Salt Lake City: Deseret News Press, 1943.

Jackson, William H. *Time Exposure: The Autobiography of William Henry Jackson*. Orig. published in 1940. Reprint, Tucson, AZ: Patrice Press, 1994.

Janetski, Joel C. *The Ute of Utah Lake*. Anthropological Papers no. 116. Salt Lake City: University of Utah Press, 1991.

Jefferson, James, Robert W. Delaney, and Gregory C. Thompson. *The Southern Utes: A Tribal History*. Edited by Floyd A. O'Neil. Ignacio, CO: Southern Ute Tribe, 1972.

Jennings, Francis. *The Invasion of America: Indians, Colonialism, and the Cant of Conquest*. Chapel Hill, NC: University of North Carolina Press, 1975.

Jocknick, Sidney. *Early Days on the Western Slope of Colorado, 1870–1883, inclusive*. Glorietta, NM: Rio Grande Press, 1913.

Jones, John A. *The Sun Dance of the Northern Ute*. Bureau of American Ethnology, Bulletin no. 157. Washington, D.C.: Smithsonian Institution, 1955. Anthropology Paper 47:203–64.

Jones, Sondra. *The Trial of Pedro León Luján: The Attack against Indian Slavers and Mexican Traders*. Salt Lake City: University of Utah Press, 1999.

Jorgensen, Joseph G. *The Sun Dance Religion: Power for the Powerless*. Chicago: University of Chicago Press, 1972.

Kehoe, Alice Beck. *The Ghost Dance: Ethnohistory & Revitalization*. 2nd ed. Milwaukee: University of Wisconsin, 2006.

Kelly, Isabel T. *Southern Paiute Ethnography*. University of Utah Anthropological Papers, no. 69. Salt Lake City: University of Utah Press, 1964.

Kidder, Alfred V. *Southwestern Archaeology*. Reprint ed. New Haven, CT: Yale University Press, 1962.

Kilpatrick, Jacquelyn. *Celluloid Indians: Native Americans and Film*. Lincoln: University of Nebraska Press, 1990.

Knack, Martha C. *Boundaries Between: The Southern Paiutes, 1775–1995*. Lincoln: University of Nebraska Press, 2004.

Kroeber, A. L. *Anthropology: Culture Patterns and Processes*. New York: Harcourt, Brace, 1948.

———. *Anthropology: Race, Culture, Psychology, Prehistory*. New York: Harcourt, Brace, 1923. Reprint, 1948.

LaBarre, Weston. *The Ghost Dance*. Garden City, NY: Doubleday, 1970.

———. *The Peyote Cult*. 4th ed., enl. New York: Schocken Books, 1975.

Lang, Gottfried Otto. *A Study in Culture Contact and Culture Change: The Whiterock Utes in Transition*. Anthropological Papers (Department of Anthropology), no. 15. Salt Lake City: University of Utah Press, 1953.

Lecompte, Janet. *Pueblo, Hardscrabble, Greenhorn: The Upper Arkansas, 1832–1856*. Norman: University of Oklahoma Press, 1978.

Lepore, Jill. *The Name of War: King Philip's War and the Origins of American Identity*. New York: Vintage Books, 1999.

Lewis, David Rich. *Neither Wolf nor Dog: American Indians, Environment, and Agrarian Change*. New York: Oxford University Press, 1994.

Look, Al. *Utes' Last Stand*. Denver: Golden Bell Press, 1972.

Lowie, Robert H. *Dances and Societies of the Plains Shoshone*. American Museum of Natural History Anthropological Papers, 11 (1915): 823–35.

———. *Notes on Shoshonean Ethnography*. American Museum of Natural History Anthropological Papers, 20 (1924): 185–314.

———. *The Sun Dance of the Shoshone, Ute and Hidatsa*. American Museum of Natural History Anthropological Papers, 16 (1919): 387–431.

Lyman, Albert R. *Indians and Outlaws: Settling of the San Juan Frontier*. Salt Lake City: Bookcraft, 1962.

——. *The Outlaw of Navaho Mountain*. Salt Lake City: Deseret Book, 1963.

Madsen, Brigham. *A Biography of Patrick Edward Connor*. Salt Lake City: University of Utah Press, 1990.

——. *Glory Hunter: Encounter with the Northwestern Shoshoni at Bear River in 1863: Battle or Massacre?* Dello G. Dayton Memorial Lecture, May 11, 1983. Ogden, UT: Weber State College Press, 1984.

——. *The Shoshoni Frontier and the Bear River Massacre*. Salt Lake City: University of Utah Press, 1985.

Madsen, David B., and David Rhode, eds. *Across the West: Human Population Movement and the Expansion of the Numa*. Salt Lake City: University of Utah Press, 1994.

Madsen, David B., and James F. O'Connell, ed. *Man and Environment in the Great Basin*. SAA Papers no. 2. Washington, D.C.: Society for American Archaeology, 1982.

Manly, William Lewis. *Death Valley in '49*. Orig. publication in 1896. Reprint, Ann Arbor: University Microfilms, Inc., 1966.

Manti, Utah. Centennial Committee. *Song of a Century, 1849–1949*. Provo, UT: Community Press, 1949. 2nd ed. 1978.

Martin, Curtis. *Ephemeral Bounty: Wickiups, Trade Goods, and the Final Years of the Autonomous Ute*. Salt Lake City: University of Utah Press, 2016.

May, Dean L. *Utah: A People's History*. Salt Lake City: University of Utah Press, 1987.

McPherson, Robert. S. *As If the Land Owned Us: An Ethnohistory of the White Mesa Utes*. Salt Lake City: University of Utah Press, 2011.

——. *A History of San Juan County: In the Palm of Time*. Salt Lake City: Utah Historical Society and San Juan Commissioner, 1995.

——. *The Northern Navajo Frontier, 1860–1900: Expansion through Adversity*. Logan: Utah State University Press, 2001.

——. *Staff Ride Handbook for the Battle of Bear River, 29 January 1863*. Riverton, UT: Utah National Guard, 2000.

Meeker, Nathan C. *The Adventures of Captain Armstrong*. New York, 1856.

Metcalf, R. Warren. *Termination's Legacy: The Discarded Indians of Utah*. Lincoln: University of Nebraska Press, 2002.

Moffitt, John Clifton. *The Story of Provo, Utah*. Provo, UT: Press Publishing, 1975.

Mooney, James. *The Ghost-dance Religion and the Sioux Outbreak of 1890*. Abridged and edited by Anthony Wallace. Chicago: University of Chicago Press, 1965. Originally published, 1896.

——. *The Ghost-dance Religion and the Sioux Outbreak of 1890*. 14th Annual Report of the Bureau of Ethnology, Part 2. 1896. Reprint, Lincoln, University of Nebraska Press, 1991.

Moorman, Donald R., with Gene A. Sessions. *Camp Floyd and the Mormons*. Salt Lake City: University of Utah Press, 1992.

Morgan, Dale L. *Jedediah Smith and the Opening of the West*. Orig. published in 1953. Lincoln: University of Nebraska Press, 1967.

Morgan, Edmund. *American Slavery, American Freedom*. New York: Norton and Company, 1975.

Nagel, Joane. *American Indian Ethnic Renewal: Red Power and the Resurgence of Identity and Culture*. 1996. New York: Oxford University Press, 1997.

Neff, Andrew Love. *History of Utah, 1847 to 1869*. Edited and annotated by Leland H. Creer. Salt Lake City: Deseret News Press, 1940.

Nielsen, Parker M. *The Dispossessed: Cultural Genocide of the Mixed-Blood Utes*. Norman: University of Oklahoma Press, 1998.

O'Neil, Floyd A., and Kathryn L. MacKay. *A History of the Uintah-Ouray Ute Lands*. American West Center Occasional Papers. Salt Lake City: University of Utah Press, n.d.

O'Brien, Sharon. *American Indian Tribal Governments*. Norman: University of Oklahoma Press, 1989.

Ortiz, Alfonso. *The Tewa World: Space, Time, Being, and Becoming in a Pueblo Indian Society*. Chicago: University of Chicago Press, 1969.

Osburn, Katherine M. B. *Southern Ute Women: Autonomy and Assimilation on the Reservation, 1887–1934*. Albuquerque: University of New Mexico Press, 1998.

Parkhill, Forbes. *The Last of the Indian Wars: The Final, Heroic Fight of the American Indian for Independence*. New York: Collier Books, 1961.

Peterson, Charles S. *Look to the Mountains: Southeastern Utah and the La Sal National Forest*. Provo, UT: Brigham Young University Press, 1975.

Peterson, John Alton. *Utah's Black Hawk War*. Salt Lake City: University of Utah Press, 1998.

Philp, Kenneth R. *Termination Revisited: American Indians on the Trail to Self-Determination, 1933–1953*. Lincoln: University of Nebraska Press, 1999.

———., ed. *Indian Self-Rule: First Hand Accounts of Indian-White Relations from Roosevelt to Reagan*. Salt Lake City: Howe Brothers, 1986.

Poll, Richard D., ed. *Utah's History*. Provo, UT: Brigham Young University Press, 1978.

Powell, A. Kent, ed. *Utah History Encyclopedia*. Salt Lake City: University of Utah Press, 1994. Also available online at http://www.uen.org/utah_history_encyclopedia.

Prucha, Francis Paul. *Indian Policy in the United States: Historical Essays*. Lincoln: University of Nebraska Press, 1981.

Quintana, Frances Leon [Swadesh]. *Ordeal of Change: The Southern Utes and their Neighbors*. Walnut Creek: AltaMira Press, 2004.

Reeve, W. Paul. *Making Space on the Western Frontier: Mormons, Miners, and Southern Paiutes*. Urbana: University of Illinois Press, 2006.

Roberts, B. H. *A Comprehensive History of The Church of Jesus Christ of Latter-day Saints: Century One*. 6 vols. 1930. Reprint, Provo, UT: The Church of Jesus Christ of Latter-day Saints, 1965.

Robinson, Lila W., and James Armagost, *Comanche Dictionary and Grammar*. Arlington: University of Texas, 1990.

Rockwell, Wilson. *The Utes: A Forgotten People*. Denver: Sage Books, 1956.

Sánchez, Joseph P. *Explorers, Traders, and Slavers: Forging the Old Spanish Trail, 1678–1850*. Salt Lake City: University of Utah Press, 1997.

Sapir, Edward. *Selected Writings of Edward Sapir in Language, Culture and Personality*. Edited by David G. Mandelbaum. Berkeley: University of California Press, 1949.

Schneider, David. *American Kinship: A Cultural Account*. Chicago: University of Chicago Press, 1968.

Shimkin, Demitri B. *The Wind River Shoshone Sun Dance*. Bureau of American Ethnology, Bulletin no. 151. Anthropology Paper 41:397–484. Washington, D.C.: Smithsonian Institution, 1953.

Shurts, John. *Indian Reserved Water Rights: The* Winters *Doctrine in Its Social and Legal Context, 1880s–1930s*. Norman: University of Oklahoma Press, 2000.

Sigler, William F., and Robert Rush Miller. *Fishes of Utah*. Salt Lake City: Utah State Dept. of Fish and Game, 1963.

Silver, Peter. *Our Savage Neighbors: How Indian War Transformed Early America*. New York: W. W. Norton, 2008.

Simmons, Marc. *The Last Conquistador: Juan de Oñate and the Settling of the Southwest*. Norman: University of Oklahoma Press, 1991.

Simmons, Virginia McConnell. *The Ute Indians of Utah, Colorado, and New Mexico*. Boulder: University of Colorado Press, 2000.

Smith, Anne M. (Cooke). *Ethnography of the Northern Utes*. Papers in Anthropology, no. 17. Albuquerque: Museum of New Mexico Press, 1974.

———. *Ute Tales*. Salt Lake City: University of Utah Press, 1992.

Smith, P. David. *Ouray, Chief of the Utes*. Ouray, CO: Wayfinder Press, 1986.

Smoak, Gregory E. *Ghost Dances and Identity: Prophetic Religion and American Indian Ethnogenesis in the Nineteenth Century*. Berkeley University of California, 2006.

Sonne, Conway B. *The World of Wakara*. San Antonio, TX: Naylor, 1962.

Southern Ute Tribe. *Ute Dictionary and Ute Reference Grammar*. 2 vols. Preliminary editions. Ignacio, CO: Ute Press, 1979.

Spicer, Edward H. *Cycles of Conquest: The Impact of Spain, Mexico, and the United States on the Indians of the Southwest, 1533–1960*. 6th ed. 1962. Tucson: University of Arizona Press, 1976.

———. *Perspectives in American Indian Culture Change*. Chicago: University of Chicago Press, 1961.

Sprague, Marshall. *Massacre: The Tragedy at White River*. Boston: Little, Brown & Co., 1957.

Stanley, F. [Stanley F. L. Crocchiola]. *The Abiquiú, New Mexico Story*. [Pamphlet]. Also bound in Crocchiola's *New Mexico Stories*, vol. 1, n.p., n.d.

Steward, Julian H. *Basin-Plateau Aboriginal Sociopolitical Groups. Bureau of American Ethnology, Bulletin* 120. United States: GPO, 1938. Reprint, Salt Lake City: University of Utah Press, 1997.

———. *Theory of Culture Change*. Urbana: University of Illinois Press, 1955.

———. *Ute Indians*. 3 vols. New York & London: Garland Publishing, 1974.

535

Stewart, Omer C. *Culture Element Distributions: XVIII, Ute—Southern Paiute*. Anthropological Records 6 (1942): 4:231–354.

———. *Peyote Religion: A History*. Norman: University of Oklahoma Press, 1987.

———. *Ute Peyotism: A Study of a Cultural Complex*. University of Colorado Studies, Series in Anthropology, no. 1. Boulder: University of Colorado Press, 1948.

Stewart, Omer C., and David F. Aberle. *Navaho and Ute Peyotism: A Chronological and Distributional Study*. University of Colorado Series in Anthropology, no. 6. Boulder: University of Colorado, 1957.

Sturm, Circe. *Becoming Indian: The Struggle over Cherokee Identity in the Twenty-first Century*. Santa Fe: School for Advanced Research Press, 2010.

———. *Blood Politics: Race, Culture, and Identity in the Cherokee Nation of Oklahoma*. Berkeley: University of California Press, 2002.

Sturtevant, William C., ed. *Handbook of North American Indians*. Washington, D.C.: Smithsonian Institution, 1978.

Swadesh [Quintana], Frances Leon. *Los Primeros Pobladores*. Notre Dame, IN: University of Notre Dame Press, 1974.

———. *Ordeal of Change: The Southern Utes and their Neighbors*. Walnut Creek: AltaMira Press, 2004. [See also, Quintana, Frances Leon].

Swanton, John R. *Indian Tribes of North America*. Washington, D.C.: Smithsonian Institution Press, 1952. Reprint, 1974.

Taylor, Graham D. *The New Deal and American Indian Tribalism: The Administration of the Indian Reorganization Act, 1934–45*. Lincoln: University of Nebraska Press, 1980.

Thomas, Alfred B. *After Coronado: Spanish Exploration Northeast of New Mexico, 1696–1727*. Norman: University of Oklahoma, 1935.

———. *Forgotten Frontiers: A Study of the Spanish Indian Policy of Don Juan Bautista de Anza, Governor of New Mexico, 1777–1787*. Norman: University of Oklahoma Press, 1932.

———. *Teodoro de Croix and the Northern Frontier of New Spain, 1776–1783*. Norman: University of Oklahoma Press, 1941. Reprint, 1968.

Thomas, David Hurst. *Skull Wars: Kennewick Man, Archaeology, and the Battle for Native American Identity*. New York: Basic Books, 2000.

Townsend, Kenneth W. *World War II and the American Indian*. Albuquerque: University of New Mexico Press, 2000.

Trafazer, Cliford. E., ed. *American Indian Identity: Today's Changing Perspectives*. CA: Sierra Oaks Publishing, 1986.

Trenholm, Virginia Cole, and Maurine Carley. *The Shoshones: Sentinels of the Rockies*. Norman: University of Oklahoma Press, 1964.

Tullidge, Edward W. *Tullidge's Histories*. 2 vols. Salt Lake City: Press of the Juvenile Instructor, 1889.

Twitchell, Ralph E., comp. *Spanish Archives of New Mexico*. 2 vols. Cedar Rapids, MI: The Torch Press, 1914. Also available online.

Tyler, Lyman S. *A History of Indian Policy*. Washington, D.C.: United States Department of Interior, Bureau of Indian Affairs, 1973.

Uintah-Ouray Ute Tribe. *Stories of Our Ancestors: A Collection of Northern-Ute Indian Tales*. Salt Lake City: Uintah-Ouray Ute Tribe, through University of Utah Printing Services, 1974.

———. *The Ute System of Government* [pamphlet]. Fort Duchesne: Uintah-Ouray Tribe, 1977.

———. *Weenoocheeyoo Peesaduehnee Yak:anup: Stories of Our Ancestors*. Salt Lake City: Uintah-Ouray Ute Tribe, through University of Utah Printing Services, 1974.

Ute Mountain Ute Tribe. *Ute Mountain Utes: A History Text*. Salt Lake City: University of Utah Printing Services, 1985.

Utley, Robert M. *Frontiersmen in Blue: The United States Army and the Indians, 1848–1865*. Lincoln: University of Nebraska Press, 1967.

———. *The Indian Frontier of the American West 1846–1890*. Histories of the American Frontier Series. Albuquerque: University of New Mexico, 1984.

Van Kirk, Sylvia. *Many Tender Ties: Women in Fur-trade Societies, 1670–1870*. Norman: University of Oklahoma Press, 1983.

Wallace, Ernest, and E. Adamson Hoebel. *The Comanches: Lords of the South Plains*. Norman: University of Oklahoma Press, 1952.

Weber, David J. *The Mexican Frontier, 1821–1846: The American Southwest under Mexico.* Albuquerque: University of New Mexico Press, 1982.

———. *The Spanish Frontier in North America.* New Haven and London: Yale University Press, 1992.

———. *Taos Trappers: The Fur Trade in the Far Southwest, 1540–1846.* Norman: University of Oklahoma, 1971.

Weber, Max. *The Protestant Ethic and the Spirit of Capitalism.* Trans. Talcott Parsons. New York: Charles Scribner's Sons, 1958.

West, Elliott. *The Contested Plains: Indians, Goldseekers, and the Rush to Colorado.* Lawrence: University Press of Kansas, 1998.

White, E. E. *Experiences of a Special Indian Agent.* 1893. Reprint, Norman: University of Oklahoma Press, 1965.

White, Richard, *Middle Ground: Indians, Empires, and Republics in the Great Lakes Region, 1650–1815.* Cambridge: University of Cambridge Press, 1991.

Whitney, Orson F. *History of Utah.* Vols. 1 and 2. Salt Lake City: George Q. Cannon and Sons, 1892–1904.

Wilkinson, Ernest L. *In the Court of Claims of the United States; in the Nos. 45585, 46640, 47564, 47566, Confederated Bands of Ute Indians, plaintiffs, v. United States, defendant.* United States: Court of Claims, 1950.

Wilkinson, Charles. *Blood Struggle: The Rise of Modern Indian Nations.* New York: W. W. Norton, 2005.

Wishart, David J. *The Fur Trade of the American West, 1807–1840.* Lincoln: University of Nebraska, 1979.

Wormington, H. M. *Prehistoric Indians of the Southwest.* Denver: Denver Museum of Natural History, 1947.

Writers Program, Work Projects Administration. *Provo: Pioneer Mormon City.* Portland, OR: Binsfords and Mort, 1942.

Young, Richard K. *The Ute Indians of Colorado in the Twentieth Century.* Norman: University of Oklahoma Press, 1997.

THESES AND DISSERTATIONS

Colton, Ray E. "A Historical Study of the Explorations of Utah Valley and the Story of Fort Utah." Master's thesis, Brigham Young University, 1946.

Combs, D. Gene. "Enslavement of Indians in the San Luis Valley of Colorado." Master's thesis, Adams State College, 1970.

Farnsworth, Melvin Taylor. "Ute Child Care—Part I: Ute Indian Opinion on Child Care at Uintah and Ouray Reservation, 1964." Master's thesis, University of Utah, 1964.

Goss, James A. "Ute Lexical and Phonological Patterns." Ph.D. diss., University of Chicago, 1972.

Horvath, Steven M., Jr. "The Social and Political Organization of the Genízaro of Plaza de Nuestra Señora de los Dolores de Belén, New Mexico, 1740–1812." Ph.D. diss., Brown University, 1979.

Jones, Robert R. "Some Effects of Modernization on the Ute Indian Religion." Master's thesis, University of Chicago, 1980. Also archived in the Marriott Library's Special Collections, University of Utah, Salt Lake City, UT.

Jones, Sondra. "Pedro León: Indian Slavery, Mexican Traders, and the Mormon Judiciary." Master's thesis, Brigham Young University, 1995.

Jorgensen, Joseph G. "The Ethnohistory and Acculturation of the Northern Ute." Ph.D. diss., Indiana University, 1964.

———. "Functions of Ute Folklore." Master's thesis, University of Utah, 1960.

Kitchen, Richard D. "Mormon-Indian Relations in Deseret: Intermarriage and Indenture, 1847 to 1877." Ph.D. diss., Arizona State University, 2002.

Leiby, Austin Nelson. "Borderland Pathfinders: The 1765 Diaries of Juan Maria Antonio de Rivera." Ph.D. diss., Northern Arizona University, 1985.

Lloyd, John B. "The Uncompahgre Utes: A Contribution of Data to the History of the Uncompahgre Ute." Master's thesis, Western State College of Colorado, 1932.

O'Neil, Floyd A. "A History of the Ute Indians until 1890." Ph.D. diss., University of Utah, 1973.

Peterson, John Alton. "Mormons, Indians, and Gentiles and Utah's Black Hawk War." Ph.D. diss., Arizona State University, 1993.

Smith, Anne M. (Cooke). "An Analysis of Basin Mythology." 2 vols. Ph.D. diss., Yale University, 1940.

Swadesh [Quintana], Frances Leon. "Hispanic Americans and the Ute Frontier from the Chama Valley to the San Juan Basin." Ph.D. diss., University of Colorado, Boulder, 1966.

———. "The Southern Utes and Their Neighbors, 1877–1926." Master's thesis, University of Colorado, Boulder, 1962

Tyler, Lyman S. "Before Escalante." Ph.D. diss., University of Utah, 1951.

Walker, Gary Lee. "A History of Fort Duchesne, Including Fort Thornburgh: The Military Presence in Frontier Uinta Basin." Ph.D. diss., Brigham Young University, 1992.

ARTICLES, CHAPTERS, AND CONFERENCE PAPERS

A.B.C. "Reminiscences of the Early Days of Manti." *Utah Historical Quarterly* 6 (October 1933): 117–23.

Alley, John R. "Prelude to Dispossession: The Fur Trade's Significance for the Northern Utes and Southern Paiutes." *Utah Historical Quarterly* 50 (Spring 1982): 104–24.

Alter, Cecil J. "Father Escalante and the Utah Indians." *Utah Historical Quarterly* 1 and 2 (July 1928–April 1929).

"America in Ferment: The Tumultuous 1960s—The Native American Power Movement." *Digital History: Online American History Textbook.* University of Houston, accessed March 16, 2004, http://www.digitalhistory.uh.edu.

Anderson, Robert T. "Blurring the Boundaries on Tribal and State Jurisdiction." *Washington State Bar News* [online], accessed November 2002, http://www.wsba.org/media/publications/barnews/archives/2002/nov-02-blurring.htm.

"Arthur V. Watkins & the Law of Unintended Consequences: Attorney, U.S. Senator, Historian." Brigham Young High School Alumni website, Class of 1906, accessed December 2, 2016, http://www.byhigh.org/Alumni_U_to_Z/Watkins/ArthurV.html.

Austin, Thomas E., and Robert S. McPherson. "Murder, Mayhem, and Mormons: The Evolution of Law Enforcement on the San Juan Frontier, 1880–1900." *Utah Historical Quarterly* 55 (Winter 1987): 36–49.

Baca, Luis, and Facundo Baca. "Hispanic Pioneer: Don Felipe Baca Brings His Family North to Trinidad." *Colorado Heritage* (1982): 27–35.

Bagley, Gerald C. "Daniel T. Potts." In Hafen, *Mountain Men and the Fur Trade*, 2:249–62.

Barker, Joanne. "Indian™ U.S.A." *Wicazo Sa Review* 18 (Spring, 2003): 25–79.

Beaulieu, David L. "Curly Hair and Big Feet: Physical Anthropology and the Implementation of Land Allotment on the White Earth Chippewa Reservation." *American Indian Quarterly* 18 (Autumn 1984): 281–314.

Bearnson, Margaret. "Moab." In Powell, *Utah History Encyclopedia* (online).

Beeton, Beverly. "Teach Them to Till the Soil: An Experiment with Indian Farms 1850–1862." *American Indian Quarterly* 3 (1977–78): 299–320.

Beinart, Peter. "Lost Tribes: Anthropologists Feud over Indian Identity." *Lingua Franca: The Review of Academic Life* (May/June 1999): 32–41.

Bird, Michael Yellow. "What We Want to be Called: Indigenous Peoples' Perspectives on Racial and Ethnic Identity Labels." *American Indian Quarterly* 23 (Spring 1999): 1–21.

Blackman, Craig H. "The Story of the Ute and the Grand Junction Indian School. In *Whispering Wind* (Cengage Learning, 2008). Available through The Free Library, online.

Boaz, Noel T. "Diabetes Mellitus and the 'Thrifty Genotype.'" Chap. 9 in *Evolving Health: The Origins of Illness and How the Modern World is Making Us Sick*. New York: Wiley, 2002.

Bolton, Herbert E. "Narrative of Antonio Espejo, 1582." In *Spanish Exploration in the Southwest, 1542–1700*. New York: 1916.

Box, Eddie, Sr. (Aka Nuche or Red Ute). "Sun Dance." Southern Ute Drum, reprinted on Southern Ute Tribe website: "Culture" (2016).

Brinkly, Gail. "A-LP Gets Federal A-OK." *High Country News* (online), August 27, 2001.

Brockman, Jason. Biographical sketch prefacing "The Governor Frederick W. Pitkin Collection." Colorado State Archives website, retrieved 2004.

Brooke, James, "Battle of What May Be the West's Last Big Dam," *New York Times* (online), September 20, 1997.

Brooks, James F. "'This Evil Extends Especially…to the Feminine Sex': Negotiating Captivity in the New Mexico Borderlands." *Feminist Studies* 22 (Summer 1996): 279–309.

———. "We Betray Our Own Nation." In *Indian Slavery in Colonial America*, 353–90.

Brooks, Juanita. "Indian Relations on the Mormon Frontier." *Utah Historical Quarterly* 12 (1944): 1–48.

———. "Indian Sketches from the Journals of T. D. Brown and Jacob Hamblin." *Utah Historical Quarterly* 29 (1961): 247–360.

Brown, Jennifer S. H. "Métis, Halfbreeds, and Other Real People: Challenging Cultures and Categories." *The History Teacher* 27 (November 1993): 19–26.

Byers, William N. "History of the Ute Nation." *Rocky Mountain News*, April 16, 1880.

Calloway, Donald, Joel Janetski, and Omer C. Stewart. "Ute." In *Handbook of the North American Indians*. Vol. 11, *Great Basin*. Warren L. D'Azevedo, volume editor. Washington, D.C.: Smithsonian Institution, 1986.

Camp, Charles L. "Pegleg Smith." In *George C. Yount and His Chronicles of the West*, edited by Charles L. Camp. Denver: Old West Publishing, 1966.

Cannon, Brian Q. "Adopted or Indentured, 1850–1870: Native Children in Mormon Households." In *Nearly Everything Imaginable: The Everyday Life of Utah's Mormon Pioneers*, edited by Ronald W. Walker and Doris R. Dant. Provo, UT: Brigham Young University Press, 1998.

Cannon, Brian Q., and Richard D. Kitchen. "Indenture and Adoption of Native American Children by Mormons on the Utah Frontier, 1850–1870." In *Common Frontiers: Proceedings of the 1996 Conference and Annual Meeting*. North Bloomfield, OH, 1997.

Carter, D. Robert. "Fish and the Famine of 1855–1856," *Journal of Mormon History* 27, no. 2 (2001): 92–124.

Carter, Harvey L. "Ewing Young." In Hafen, *Mountain Men and the Fur Trade* 2:379–401.

Carter, Kate B., ed. "Black Hawk Indian War." In *Our Pioneer Heritage*, 169–256. Vol. 9. Salt Lake City: Daughters of Utah Pioneers, 1966.

Castile, George Pierre. "The Commodification of Indian Identity." *American Anthropologist, New Series* 98 (December 1996): 743–49

Chakravarthy, M. V. C., and Frank W. Booth, "Eating, Exercise, and 'Thrifty' Genotypes: Connecting the Dots toward an Evolutionary Understanding of Modern Chronic Diseases." *Journal of Applied Physiology* 96 (2004): 3–10.

Chamberlin, Ralph V. "Some Plant Names of the Ute Indians." *American Anthropologist* (1909): 27–40.

Cheetham, Francis T. "The Early Settlements of Southern Colorado." *The Colorado Magazine* 5 (February 1928): 1–8.

Christy, Howard A. "Open Hand and Mailed Fist: Mormon-Indian Relations in Utah, 1847–52." *Utah Historical Quarterly* 46 (1978): 216–35.

———. Review of John Peterson's *Utah's Black Hawk War*. *Journal of Mormon History* 26 (Spring 2000): 282–89.

———. "The Walker War: Defense and Conciliation as Strategy." *Utah Historical Quarterly* 47 (1979): 395–420.

Churchill, Ward. "Radicals and Radicalism, 1900 to Present." *Encyclopedia of Native American Indians*. Edited by Fred Hoxie. NY: Houghton-Mifflin, 1996.

Clifton, James A. "Alternate Identities and Cultural Frontiers." In *Being and Becoming Indian: Biographical Studies of North American Frontiers*, edited by James A. Clifton. Chicago: Dorsey Press, 1989.

Coates, Lawrence G. "Brigham Young and Mormon Indian Policies: The Formative Period, 1836–1851." *BYU Studies* 18 (Spring 1978): 428–52.

———. "The Mormons and the Ghost Dance." *Dialogue: Journal of Mormon Thought* 18 (Winter 1985): 89–111.

"Commercial Elk Farming," Mountain Velvet, Ltd. (CO), accessed 1999 and 2005, http://www.elkusa.com/Elk_Farming.htm.

Correll, J. Lee. "Navajo Frontiers in Utah and Troublous Times in Monument Valley." *Utah Historical Quarterly* 39 (Spring 1971): 145–61.

Crampton, C. Gregory. "Utah's Spanish Trail." *Utah Historical Quarterly* 47 (Fall 1979): 361–83.

Creer, Leland Hargrave. "Spanish-American Slave Trade in the Great Basin, 1800–1853." *New Mexico Historical Review* 24 (July 1949): 171–83.

Cross, Raymond. "Tribes as Rich Nations." *Oregon Law Review* 79 (Winter 2000): 893–968.

539

"Clyde Warrior." In *Encyclopedia of Native American Indians* (online). NY: Houghton-Mifflin, accessed March 2004, http://college.hmco.com/history/readerscomp/naind/html/na_042100_warriorclyde. htm.

Dawson, Thomas F. "Major Thompson, Chief Ouray and the Utes: An Interview, May 23, 1921." *The Colorado Magazine* 7 (May 1930): 113–22.

Densmore, Frances. "The Belief of the Indian in a Connection Between Song and the Supernatural." Bureau of American Ethnology. Washington, D.C.: Smithsonian Institution, 1953. Anthropology Papers 37:217–23.

———. "Songs Used in the Treatment of the Sick." *Northern Ute Music.* Bulletin 75, Bureau of American Ethnology, 1922, and online, http://drumhop.com/music.php?page=96.

Defa, Dennis R. "The Goshute Indians of Utah." In Cuch, *Utah's American Indians*, 73–122.

DeHoyos, Genevieve. "Indian Student Placement Services." In *Encyclopedia of Mormonism*, edited by Daniel H. Ludlow. 2:679–80. New York: Macmillan, 1992.

d'Errico, Peter. "Sovereignty: A Brief History in the Context of U.S. 'Indian Law.'" Prepared for inclusion in *The Encyclopedia of Minorities in American Politics*, edited by Jeffery Schultz. Phoenix, AZ: Onyx Press, 2000. Posted online by the University of Massachusetts Legal Studies Department, Amherst, accessed June 2005, http://www.umass.edu/legal/derrico/sovereignty.html.

Duncan, Clifford. "The Northern Utes of Utah." In Cuch, *Utah's American Indians*, 167–224.

Englert, Jeanne W., "Let's Use Sense in Satisfying Tribes' Water Rights," *Rocky Mountain News* (online), February 20, 1998.

Espinosa, J. Manuel. "Governor Vargas in Colorado." *New Mexico Historical Review* 11 (April 1936): 179–87.

Foster, Robert L. "The Duchesne Strip: Part I, The Whiskey Tent Treaty." *True West* (August 1988): 26–29.

———. "The Duchesne Strip: Part II, A Lawless Land." *True West.* (September 1988): 52–56.

Fowler, Don D. "Great Basin Social Organization." In d'Azevedo et al., *Current Status of Anthropological Research in the Great Basin*, 37–73.

Friends of the Earth (FOE), "Action Alert: Stop Jurassic Pork!—Cut the Animas-La Plata Irrigation Project." Posted April 4, 1997, accessed June 14, 1999, www.foe.org/act.alpl.html.

Gallay, Alan. "Introduction." In *Indian Slavery in Colonial America*, 1–19.

Garroutte, Eva Marie. "The Racial Formation of American Indians: Negotiating Legitimate Identities within Tribal and Federal Law." *American Indian Quarterly* 25 (Spring 2001): 224–39.

Getches, David H. "The Unsettling of the West: How Indians Got the Best Water Rights." Review of John Shurts, *Indian Reserved Water Rights: The Winters Doctrine in Its Social and Legal Context, 1880s–1930s* (2000), in *Michigan Law Review* 99 (May 2001), 1473–99.

Gibbs, Josiah F. "Black Hawk's Last Raid—1866." *Utah Historical Quarterly* 4 (1931): 4:99–108.

———. "Gunnison Massacre—1853—Millard County, Utah—Indian Mareer's Version of the Tragedy—1894." *Utah Historical Quarterly* 1 (1928): 68–75.

———. "Moshoquop, the Avenger, as Loyal Friend." *Utah Historical Quarterly* 1 (1929): 6–7.

Gonzales, Angela A. "American Indians: Their Contemporary Reality and Future Trajectory." In *Challenges for Rural America in the Twenty-First Century*. University Park: University of Pennsylvania Press, 2003.

———. "Gaming and Displacement: Winners and Losers in American Indian Casino Development." *International Social Science Journal* 55 (March 2003): 123–33.

Goss, James A. "A Basin-Plateau Shoshonean Ecological Model." In *Great Basin Cultural Ecology: A Symposium*, 123–28.

———. "Culture-Historical Inference from Utaztekan Linguistic Evidence." In *Utaztekan Prehistory*, edited by Earl H. Swanson, Jr. Occasional Papers of the Idaho State University Museum, no. 22. Pocatello: Idaho State University, 1968.

———. "Linguistic Tools for the Great Basin Prehistorian." In *Models and Great Basin Prehistory (a symposium)*, edited by Don D. Fowler. Desert Research Institute Publications in the Social Sciences, no. 12, 1972.

———. "The Yamparica—Shoshones, Comanches, or Utes—or does It Matter?" In Clemmer, Myers, and Rudden, *Julian Steward and the Great Basin*, 74–84.

Gruenwald, Kim M. "American Indians and the Public School System: A Case Study of the Northern Utes." *Utah Historical Quarterly* 64 (Summer 1996): 246–63.

Hackett, C. W., and C. C. Shelby. "Revolt of the Pueblo Indians of New Mexico and Otermin's Attempted Reconquest, 1680–1682." *Coronado Cuarto Centennial Publications* (1912).

Hafen, LeRoy R. "A Brief History of the Fur Trade of the Far West." In Hafen, *Mountain Men and the Fur Trade*, 1:17–176.

———. "Elijah Barney Ward." In Hafen, *Mountain Men and the Fur Trade*, 7:343–51.

———. "Etienne Provost." In Hafen, *Mountain Men and the Fur Trade*, 6:371–85.

———. "The Fort Pueblo Massacre and the Punitive Expedition Against the Utes." *Colorado Magazine* 4 (March 1927): 49–58.

———. "Mountain Men before the Mormons." *Utah Historical Quarterly* 26 (1958): 307–28.

———. "Mountain Men of Utah." *Desert Magazine* 27 (1964): 4:13–14.

Hagen, William T. "Full Blood, Mixed Blood, Generic, and Ersatz: The Problem of Indian Identity." *Arizona and the West* 27 (Winter 1985): 309–26.

Harmon, Alexandra. "Tribal Enrollment Councils: Lessons on Law and Indian Identity." *Western Historical Quarterly* 32 (Summer 2001): 175–200.

———. "When is an Indian not an Indian? The 'Friends of the Indian' and the Problems of Indian Identity." *Journal of Ethnic Studies* 18 (Summer 1990): 95–123.

Hallowell, A. Irving. "Bear Ceremonialism in the Northern Hemisphere." *American Anthropologist* 28 (January 1926): 2–175.

Harvey, Mark W. T. "Misguided Reformer: Nathan Meeker Among the Ute." *Colorado Heritage* (1982): 36–44.

Herzog, George. "Plains Ghost Dance and Great Basin Music." *American Anthropologist* 37 (1935): 403–19.

Hill, Joseph J. "The Old Spanish Trail: A Study of the Spanish and Mexican Trade and Exploration Northwest from New Mexico to the Great Basin and California." *Hispanic American Historical Review* 4 (1921): 444–73.

———. "Spanish and Mexican Exploration and Trade Northwest From New Mexico Into the Great Basin, 1765–1853." *Utah Historical Quarterly* 3 (1930): 1:3–23.

Hoebel, E. Adamson. "The Sun Dance of the Hekandika Shoshone." *American Anthropologist* 37 (1935): 570–81.

Holladay, April. "Mormon Crickets March 50,000 strong." *USA Today,* July 23, 2004, accessed 2012, http://www.usatoday.com/tech/columnist/aprilholladay/2004-07-23-wonderquest_x.htm.

Holm, Tom. "Forgotten Warriors: American Indian Service Men in Vietnam." *Vietnam Generation* 1, no. 2 (1989): 56–68.

Humpherys, Alfred Glen. "Thomas L. (Peg-Leg) Smith." In Hafen, *Mountain Men and the Fur Trade*, 2:311–30.

Hurst, C. T. "A Ute Shelter." *Southwestern Lore* 5 (1939): 57–64.

"Indian Water Wars." *Newsweek,* June 13, 1983, 80–82.

Ismert, Cornelius M. "James Bridger." In Hafen, *Mountain Men and the Fur Trade*, 6:85–104.

Jackson, Steve. "Sage Remington." *Westword* (online), January 29, 1998, accessed 2016, www.westword.com/news/sage-remingtton-5058266.

Janes, Patricia L., and Collison, Jim. "Community Leader Perceptions of the Social and Economic Impacts of Indian Gaming." *UNLV Gaming Research & Review Journal* 8 (2004): 13–30.

Jennings, Jesse D. "Early Man in Utah." *Utah Historical Quarterly* 28 (January 1960): 4–5.

Jones, Lisa. "Animas-La Plata Still Flawed." *High Country News* (online), December 17, 1990, accessed 1999, www.hcn.org.

Jones, Sondra. "Redeeming the Indian: The Enslavement of Indian Children in Utah and New Mexico." *Utah Historical Quarterly* 67 (Summer 1999): 220–41.

———. "Saints or Sinners? The Evolving Perceptions of Mormon-Indian Relations in Utah Historiography." *Utah Historical Quarterly* 72 (Winter 2004): 19–46.

———. "Slave, Apprentice, Indian Chief: The Role of Indian Slavery in the Evolution of Ute and Paiute Cultures." Paper presented at the Western History Association Conference, September 2001.

———. "The Trial of Don Pedro León: Politics, Prejudice, and Pragmatism." *Utah Historical Quarterly* 65 (Spring 1997): 165–86.

"June Sucker." Utah Reclamation Mitigation and Conservation Commission (Salt Lake City), accessed March 21, 2012, http://www.mitigationcommission.gov/native/native_sucker.html

Kehoe, Alice B. "Primal Gaia: Primitivists and Plastic Medicine Men." In Clifton, *The Invented Indian*, 193–209.

———. "Where were Wovoka and Wuzzie George?" In Clemmer, Myers, and Rudden, *Julian Steward and the Great Basin*, 164–69.

Kelly, Isabel T., and Catherine S. Fowler. "Southern Paiute." In Sturtevant, *Handbook of North American Indians*. Vol. 11.

Kelly, Lawrence C. "The Indian Reorganization Act: The Dream and the Reality." *Pacific Historical Review* 44 (August 1975): 291–312.

Kimball, Spencer W. "The Evil of Intolerance." *LDS Conference Report* (April 1954): 103–8.

———. "The Expanding Indian Program," *Ensign*, October 6, 1956.

———. "Who is My Neighbor?" *LDS Conference Report* (1949): 103–13.

Kroeber, A. L. "Culture Process," and "Culture Change." Chap. 9 and 10. In *Anthropology: Race, Language, Culture, Psychology, Prehistory*, 344–444. Orig. published 1923. New York: Harcourt, Brace, 1948.

———. "Ute Tales." *Journal of American Folk-Lore* 14 (1901): 252–85.

"Lafayette Head." Colorado Lieutenant Governors Since 1877 with profiles. Colorado Archives, accessed 2012, http://www.colorado.gov/dpa/doit/archives/offic/ltgov.html#Head.

Lamb, Sidney M. "Linguistic Prehistory in the Great Basin." *International Journal of American Linguistics* 24 (April 1958): 95–100.

Larson, Gustive O. "Opening the Colorado Plateau." Chap. 20 in Poll, et al., *Utah's History*.

———. "Walkara, Ute Chief." In Hafen, *Mountain Men and the Fur Trade*, 2:339–50.

———. "Walkara's Half Century." *Western Humanities Review* 6 (Summer 1952): 235–59.

LaShell, Beth. "'Old' Fort Lewis College Web Site." Posted 2000, accessed December 2000, http://oldfort.fortlewis.edu.

Linton, Ralph. "The Comanche Sun Dance." *American Anthropologist* 35 (1935): 420–28.

———. "Nativistic Movements." *American Anthropologist* 45 (1943): 230–40.

Little, James Amasa. "Biography of Lorenzo Dow Young." *Utah Historical Quarterly* 14 (1946): 25–132.

Lowie, Robert H. "Shoshonean Tales: I—Southern Ute." *Journal of American Folk-Lore* 37 (January–June 1924): 1–157.

Lupo, Karen D. "The Historical Occurrence and Demise of Bison in Northern Utah." *Utah Historical Quarterly* 64 (Spring 1996): 168–80.

Lyman, Albert R. "A Relic of Gadianton: Old Posey as I Knew Him." *Improvement Era* 26 (July 1923): 793.

Lythgoe, Dennis L. "Negro Slavery in Utah." *Utah Historical Quarterly* 39 (Winter 1971): 40–54.

MacKay, Kathryn L. "The Strawberry Valley Reclamation Project and the Opening of the Uintah Indian Reservation." *Utah Historical Quarterly* 50 (Winter 1982): 68–89.

Madsen, David B. "Get It While the Gettin's Good: A Variable Model of Great Basin Subsistence and Settlement Based on Data from the Eastern Great Basin." In Madsen and O'Connell, *Man and Environment in the Great Basin*, 207–26.

Madsen, David B., and Brigham D. Madsen. "Mesa Verde and Sleeping Ute Mountain: The Geographical and Chronological Dimensions of the Numic Expansion." In Madsen and Rhode, *Across the West: Human Population Movement*, 24–31.

———. "One Man's Meat Is Another Man's Poison: A Revisionist View of the Seagull 'Miracle.'" *Nevada Historical Society Quarterly* 30 (Fall 1987): 165–81.

Madsen, David B., and David B. Rhode. "Introduction." In Madsen and Rhode, *Across the West: Human Population Movement*.

Malouf, Carling. "Ethnohistory in the Great Basin." In d'Azevedo, et al., *Anthropological Research in the Great Basin*, 1:1–38.

Malouf, Carling, and Arline Malouf. "The Effects of Spanish Slavery on the Indians of the Intermountain West." *Southwestern Journal of Anthropology* 1 (Spring 1945): 378–91.

Marshall, Joseph M., III. "Wounded Knee Takeover, 1973." *Encyclopedia of North American Indians*. NY: Houghton-Mifflin, accessed 2004, http://college.hmco.com/history/readerscomp/naind/html/na_043800_woundedkneet.htm.

Mason, J. Alden. "Myths of the Uintah Utes." *Journal of American Folk-Lore* 23 (1910): 299–363.

McCullough, Marie. "Adoption Anguish." March 4, 2003. Philadelphia, *The News-Sentinel* (online).

McDermott, R. "Ethics, Epidemiology and the Thrifty Gene: Biological Determinism as a Health Hazard." *Social Science and Medicine* 47, no. 9 (November 1999): 1189–95.

McNitt, Frank. "Foreword." In James Hervey Simpson, *Navaho Expedition: Journal of a Military Reconnaissance from Santa Fe…in 1849 by Lieutenant James. H. Simpson*, edited and annotated by Frank McNitt. Norman: University of Oklahoma, 1964.

McPherson, Robert. S. "Blanding." In Powell, *Utah History Encyclopedia* (online).

———. "Monticello." In Powell, *Utah History Encyclopedia* (online).

———. "Navajos, Mormons, and Henry L. Mitchell: Cauldron of Conflict on the San Juan." *Utah Historical Quarterly* 55 (Winter 1987): 50–65.

———. "Paiute Posey and the Last White Uprising." *Utah Historical Quarterly* 53 (Summer 1985): 248–67.

———. "Setting the Stage: Native America Revisited." In Cuch, *Utah's American Indians*, 3–24.

McPherson, Robert S., and Mary Jane Yazzie. "The White Mesa Utes." In Cuch, *Utah's American Indians*, 225–64.

Metcalf, R. Warren. "Lambs of Sacrifice: Termination, the Mixed-Blood Utes, and the Problem of Indian Identity." *Utah Historical Quarterly* 64 (Fall 1996): 322–43.

———. "A Precarious Balance: The Northern Utes and the Black Hawk War." *Utah Historical Quarterly* (Winter 1989): 24–35.

Meyer, Melissa "American Indian Blood Quantum Requirements: Blood is Thicker than Family." In *Over the Edge: Remapping the American West*, edited by Valerie Matsumoto and Blake Almendinger. Berkeley: University of California Press, 1999, 231–44.

Miller, Matthew. "Off the Reservation." *Forbes* 175 (June 2005): 152–53.

Morgan, Dale, and Eleanor Towles. "Étienne Provost." In *The Rocky Mountain Journals of William Marshall Anderson: The West in 1834*, edited by Dale L. Morgan and Eleanor Towles Harris. San Marino, CA: Huntington Library, 1967.

Murphy, Lawrence R. "Cantonment Burgwin, New Mexico 1852–1860." *Arizona and the West* 15 (Spring 1973).

Murray, Patty. "Murray Stands Up For Native American Veterans in Health Care Battle." Press Release, April 12, 2004, accessed November 13, 2006, http://murray.senate.gov/news.cfm?id=220410.

Nankivell, John H. "Colorado's Last Indian War." *The Colorado Magazine* 10 (1933): 222–34.

National Diabetes Information Clearinghouse. "Diabetes in American Indians and Alaska Natives." National Institute of Diabetes and Digestive and Kidney Diseases, *National Institutes of Health*, accessed May 29, 2004, http://diabetes.niddk.nih.gov/dm/pubs/americanindian/.

"National Indian Youth Council—History." Background summary for "Inventory of National Indian Youth Council Records." University of New Mexico, General Library, Center for Southwest Research, accessed March 2004, *http://elibrary.unm.edu/oanm/ NmU/nmu1%23mss703bc/ nmu1%23mss703bc_m4.html.*

Neel, J. V. "Diabetes Mellitus: A 'Thrifty' Genotype Rendered Detrimental by 'Progress'?" *American Journal of Human Genetics* 14 (1962): 352–53.

Nichols, Jeffrey D. "Ute Trek to South Dakota in 1906 Ended in Disappointment." Utah State Historical Society *History to Go* website, posted June 1995, accessed 1997, http://historytogo.utah.gov.

Nixon, Richard. "Special Message to the Congress on Indian Affairs." *Senate Committee on Indian Affairs Briefing Booklet: The Enduring Validity of Indian Self-Determination.* July 8, 1970. Presidential Policy Papers, online at senate.gov, accessed 1998, http://www.presidency.ucsb.edu/ws/?pid=2573.

Nykiel, Ronald A. "A Special Look at Indian Gaming: An Assessment of the Many Contributions of Native American Gaming—Connecticut Then and Now." *UNLV Gaming Research & Review Journal* 8 (2004): 51–56.

Oliva, Leo E. "Fort Union and the Frontier Army in the Southwest." Southwest Cultural Resources Center, National Park Service. Santa Fe: New Mexico, 1993.

Olsen, Ken. "Spiritual Pathways." *American Legion*, April 1, 2008.

Omi, Michael, and Howard Winant. "Racial Formations." In *Race Critical Theories: Text and Context*, edited by Philomena Essed and David Theo Goldberg, 123–45. Hoboken, NJ: Wiley-Blackwell, 2001.

O'Neil, Floyd A. "The Anguished Odyssey: The Flight of the Utes, 1906–1908." *Utah Historical Quarterly* 36 (1968): 315–37.

———. "The Reluctant Suzerainty." *Utah Historical Quarterly* 39 (1971): 130–44.

O'Neil, Floyd A., and Stanford J. Layton. "Of Pride and Politics: Brigham Young as Indian Superintendent." *Utah Historical Quarterly* 46 (1978): 236–50.

543

Opler, Marvin K. "The Character and History of the Southern Ute Peyote Rite." *American Anthropologist* 42 (1940): 463–78.

———. "Dream Analysis in Ute Indian Therapy." In *Culture and Mental Health*, edited by Marvin K. Opler. New York: Macmillan Co., 1959.

———. "The Integration of the Sun Dance in Ute Religion." *American Anthropologist* 43 (1941): 550–72.

———. "The Southern Ute of Colorado." In *Acculturation in Seven American Indian Tribes*, edited by Ralph Linton. New York: Harper & Son, 1940.

Oswald, Delmont R. "James Pierson Beckwourth." In Hafen, *Mountain Men and the Fur Trade*, 6:37–60.

Palmer, William R. "Indian Names in Utah Geography." *Utah Historical Quarterly* 1 (1928): 5–25.

———. "Pahute Indian Homelands." *Utah Historical Quarterly* 6 (1933): 88–102.

Parry, Mae. "The Northwestern Shoshone." In Cuch, *Utah's American Indians*, 25–72.

Patterson, M. R. (comp.). "T. T. Thornburgh." Arlington National Cemetery. Posted 28 June 2003, accessed 2010, www.arlingtoncemetery.net/ttthornburgh.htm.

"Peg-Leg Smith Liars Contest." Borrego Springs Chamber of Commerce, accessed 2012, http://www.borregospringschamber.com/ pegleg_liars-contest.html.

Peters, Mike. "The Obituary of Nathan Meeker: Written as it Would Appear Today." *Greeley Tribune* (online), July 2, 2001, accessed 2016, http://www.greeleytrib.com/article.php?Sid=2446.

Peterson, John A. "Lamanites in Rebellion: Another Look at the Origins of Utah's Black Hawk Indian War." Unpublished paper presented at Mormon History Conference, 1990.

Quinn, Frederick. "To Elevate the Red Man': The Episcopal Church's Native American Policy in Utah." *Utah Historical Quarterly* 73 (Winter 2005): 44–63.

Rapczynski, Joan. "Native American Culture in Crisis" (online). Yale University: Yale-New Haven Teacher's Institute, accessed March 2004, http://www.yale.edu/ynhti/curriculum/units/2001/4/01.04.09.x.html.

Ravussin E., and C. Bogardus. "Energy Expenditure in the Obese: Is There a Thrifty Gene?" *Infusiontherapie* 17 (April 1990): 108–12.

Reagan, Albert B. "The Bear Dance of the Ouray Utes." *Wisconsin Archaeologist* 9 (1931): 148–50.

Reagan, Albert, and Wallace Stark. "Chipeta, Queen of the Utes." *Utah Historical Quarterly* (April 1933): 791–97.

Redd, J. M. "The Last American Indian War." *Deseret News*, January 1, 1979.

Reed, Verner Z. "The Ute Bear Dance." *American Anthropologist* 9 (July 1896): 237–44.

Reeve, W. Paul. "'As Ugly as Evil' and 'as Wicked as Hell': Gadianton Robbers and the Legend Process among the Mormons." *Journal of Mormon History* 27 (Fall 2001): 125–49.

Rich, Christopher B., Jr. "The True Policy for Utah: Servitude, Slavery, and 'An Act in Relation to Service.'" *Utah Historical Quarterly* 80 (Winter 2012): 54–74.

Ronaasen, Sheree, Richard O. Clemmer, and Mary Elizabeth Rudden. "Rethinking Cultural Ecology, Multilinear Evolution, and Expert Witnesses: Julian Steward and The Indian Claims Commission Proceedings." In Clemmer, Myers, and Rudden, *Julian Steward and the Great Basin*, 170–202.

Russell, James. "Conditions and Customs of Present-day Utes In Colorado." *Colorado Magazine* 6 (1929): 104–12.

Salmon, Rusty, and Robert S. McPherson. "Cowboys, Indians, and Conflict: The Pinhook Draw Fight, 1881." *Utah Historical Quarterly* 69 (Winter 2001): 4–28.

Sapir, Edward. "Texts of the Kaibab Paiutes and Uintah Utes." *Proceedings of the American Academy of Arts and Sciences* 65 (1930): 297–535.

Scholes, Frances V. "Church and State in New Mexico." *New Mexico Historical Review* 11 (1936): 9–76, 145–78, 283–94, 297–99, 300–349.

Schroeder, Albert H. "A Brief History of the Southern Utes." *Southwestern Lore* 30 (1965): 53–78.

———. "The Cultural Position of Hurst's Tabeguache Caves and Pueblo Sites." *Southwestern Lore* 29 (1964): 4.

Schroeder, Albert H., and Omer C. Stewart. "Indian Servitude in the Southwest." Unpublished typescript. Santa Fe: Museum of New Mexico, n.d.

Searcy, Helen M. "Otto Mears and the Utes." In *Pioneers of the San Juan*. Vol. 1. Colorado Springs: Out West Printing & Stationery Co., 1942.

Shimkin, Demitri B. "Uto-Aztecan System of Kinship Terminology." *American Anthropologist* 43 (1941): 231–32.

Shoemaker, Nancy. "How Indians Got to be Red." *The American Historical Review* 102 (June 1997): 625–44.

Sierra Club. "Petition to Congress regarding S. 2508," posted online, accessed March 1999 (site discontinued).

Simmons, Virginia. "When Opportunity Knocked on Saguache's Door." *Colorado Central Magazine* 75 (May 2000): 20– (online), accessed March 1999, http://cozine.com/2000-may/when-opportunity-knocked-on-saguaches-door/.

Smedley, Audrey. "'Race' and the Construction of Human Identity." *American Anthropologist* 100 (September 1998): 690–702.

Smith, Duane A. "A Last Rush to Eden: The Settlement of Colorado's Ute Strip." *Our Public Lands* 30 (Spring 1980): 18–22.

Snow, William J. "Utah Indians and Spanish Slave Trade." *Utah Historical Quarterly* 2 (July 1929): 67–75.

Southern Ute Grassroots Organization. "SUGO Ute Legacy," an alternative to the tribes' A-LP Reconciliation Plan, accessed 14 June 1998, http://www.angelfire.com/al/alpcentral/sugo.html.

Southwestern Conservation District. "Water Information Programs: Colorado Ute Water Rights Settlement Agreement" (condensed), accessed June 25, 2004, www.waterinfo.org/indian.htm.

Sperry, T. J., and Harry C. Meyers. "A History of Fort Union." Kansas University Heritage Project, accessed February 6, 2006, http://www.kansasheritage.org/research/sft/ft-union.htm.

Steorts, Jason Lee. "Tribal Loyalties: The BIA—A Washington Disgrace." *National Review* (August 8, 2005): 39–41.

Steward, Julian H. "Introduction," and "The Great Basin Shoshonean Indians: An Example of a Family Level of Sociocultural Integration." In Steward, *Theory of Culture Change*, 3–8, and 101–21.

——. "A Uintah Ute Bear Dance, March, 1931." *American Anthropologist* 34 (1932): 263–73.

Stewart, Omer C. "The Basin." In *The Native Americans*, edited by Robert F. Spencer, Jesse D. Jennings, et al., 273–82 New York: Harper & Row, 1965.

——. "Friend to the Ute: Omer C. Stewart Crusades for Indian Religious Freedom." *Colorado Heritage* 2, no. 1 (1982): 45–52.

——. "Southern Ute Adjustment to Modern Living." In *Acculturation in the Americas*, edited by Sol Tax. Vol. 2. Proceedings of the 29th International Congress of Americanists. Chicago: University of Chicago Press, 1952.

——. "Tribal Distributions and Boundaries in the Great Basin." In d'Azevedo, et al., *Anthropological Research in the Great Basin*.

——. "Ute Indians: Before and after White Contact." *Utah Historical Quarterly* 34 (Winter 1966): 38–61.

Strong, Pauline Turner and Barrik Van Winkle. "'Indian Blood': Reflections on the Reckoning and Refiguring of Native North American Identity." *Cultural Anthropology*, Resisting Identities 11 (November 1996): 547–76.

Sturm, Circe. "Blood Politics, Racial Classification, and Cherokee National Identity." *American Indian Quarterly* 22 (Winter/Spring 1998): 230–57.

Sutton, Mark Q., and David Rhode. "Background to the Numic Problem." In Clemmer, Myers, and Rudden, *Across the West: Human Population Movement*, 6–15.

TallBear, Kimberly. "DNA, Blood, and Racializing the Tribe." *Wicazo Sa Review* 18 (Spring 2003): 81–107.

Taxpayers for Common Sense (TCS). "Animas-La Plata Irrigation Project," accessed March 19, 1999, *www.taxpayer.net*.

——. "Campaign to Stop Animas-La Plata," accessed April 1999, www.taxpayer.net/TCS/States/co.html.

Taylor, Walter W. "Archaeology and Language in Western North America." *American Antiquity* 27 (1961): 71–81.

Telonidis, Taki. "In Sweat Lodge, Vets Find Healing." National Public Radio, accessed May 28, 2012, npr.org.

Tessendorf, K. C. "Red Death on the Missouri." *American West* 14 (January/February, 1977).

Thompson, Gregory C. "The Unwanted Indians: The Southern Utes in Southeastern Utah." *Utah Historical Quarterly* 49 (Spring 1981): 189–203.

Tom, Gary and Ronald Holt. "The Paiute Tribe of Utah." In Cuch, *Utah's American Indians*, 123–66.

Tomlinson, Kenneth Y. "Scalping At Crow Creek." *Reader's Digest* (October 1979): 199–200.

Tullidge, Edward W. "History of Provo." *Tullidge's Quarterly Magazine* 3, no. 3 (July 1884): 240–41.

Tyler, Lyman S. "The Indians in Utah Territory." Chap. 19 in Poll, *Utah's History*.

——. "The Spaniard and the Ute." *Utah Historical Quarterly* 22, 4 (1954): 354.

———. "Ute Indians Along Civil War Communication Lines." *Utah Historical Quarterly* 46 (Summer 1978): 251–61.

U.S. Bureau of Reclamation. "Ridges Basin Dam Contract Awarded." Press release, December 12, 2003, accessed June 25, 2004, www.usbr.gov/uc/news/rdam_contract.html

U.S. Department of Education. "History of Indian Education: Legislative History," accessed at http://www.ed.gov/about/offices/list/ods/oie/history.html.

U.S. Department of the Interior. "Notice of Intent to Prepare a Draft Supplemental Environmental Statement to the 1996 Final Supplement to the Final Environmental Statement for the Animas-La Plata Project." *Federal Register* (online) 64, no. 1 (January 4, 1999), accessed July 2004.

U.S. Department of Justice. "Policy on Indian Sovereignty and Government-to-Government Relations with Indian Tribes," discussion, accessed June 2005, http://www.usdoj.gov/otj/sovtrb.htm; also http://www.ojp.usdoj.gov/americannative/ pubs/intro.htm.

Utah State Division of Indian Affairs. "Utah Tribes Today: Ute," accessed 2010, http://indian.utah.gov/utah_tribes_today/ute.html

Ute Tribe, "Veterans Day in the United States," *News from Ute Country: Ute Bulletin,* Vol. 52, no. 3 (November 3, 2017). Article lists all Northern Ute veterans.

Van Hoak, Stephen P. "And Who Shall Have the Children? The Indian Slave Trade in the Southern Great Basin, 1800–1865." *Nevada Historical Society Quarterly* 41 (Spring 1998): 3–25.

———. "The Other Buffalo: Native Americans, Fur Trappers, and the Western Bison, 1600–1860. *Utah Historical Quarterly* 72 (Winter 2004): 4–18.

———. "Waccara's Utes: Native American Equestrian Adaptations in the Eastern Great Basin, 1776–1876." *Utah Historical Quarterly* 67 (Fall 1999): 309–30.

Walker, Ronald W. "Native Women on the Utah Frontier." *Brigham Young University Studies* 32, no. 4 (1993): 87–124.

———. "President Young Writes Jefferson Davis about the Gunnison Massacre Affair." *Brigham Young University Studies* 35, no. 1 (1995): 146–70.

———. "Toward a Reconstruction of Mormon and Indian Relations, 1847–1877." *Brigham Young University Studies* 29, no. 4 (1989): 23–42.

Walker, Ronald W., and Jesse, Dean C. "Chief Walker and Brigham Young." *Brigham Young University Studies* 32 (1993): 125–35.

Wallace, Anthony F. C. "Revitalization Movements." *American Anthropologist* 58 (1956): 254–81.

Wallace, William S. "Antoine Robidoux." In Hafen, *Mountain Men and the Fur Trade,* 4:261–73.

Warner, Ted. J. "Peter Skene Ogden." In Hafen, *Mountain Men and the Fur Trade,* 3:213–238.

Washburn, Wilcomb E. "A Fifty-year Perspective on the Indian Reorganization Act." *American Anthropologist* 36 (June 1984): 279–89.

Watts, Sheldon. "Smallpox in the New World and the Old: From Holocaust to Eradication, 1518–1977." Chap. 3 in Watts, *Epidemics and History: Disease, Power, and Imperialism.* New Haven: Yale University Press, 1997.

Wiegel, C. W. "The Re-burial of Chief Ouray." *Colorado Magazine* 5 (1928): 165–73.

"William Henry Ashley." *Biographical Directory of the United States Congress.* Online at http://bioguide.congress.gov/ scripts/biodisplay.pl?index=A000315.

"William N. Byers." *Denver Characters*, at http://www.denvergov.org/AboutDenver/history_char_byers.asp

Winant, Howard. "Race and Race Theory," *Annual Review of Sociology* 26 (2000): 169–85.

Winkler, Albert. "The Circleville Massacre: A Brutal Incident in Utah's Black Hawk War." *Utah Historical Quarterly* 55 (Winter 1987): 4–21.

———. "Massacre at Thistle Valley." *Frontier Times* (April–May 1978): 12–13, 40–43.

Wilson, Iris Higbee. "William Wolfskill." In Hafen, *Mountain Men and the Fur Trade,* 2:351–62.

Wolf, Tom. "Water Boondoggle Wrapped in the Cause of Indian Rights." *Los Angeles Times* (online), April 26, 1998.

Wright, Coulsen, and Geneva Wright. "Indian-White Relations In the Uintah-Basin." *Utah Humanities Review* 2 (1945): 319–46.

Zeilo, Judy. "Tribes Bet on Gaining." *State Legislatures* 31 (March 2005): 26–28.

UNPUBLISHED COLLECTIONS

Monaghan, J. *Moffat County Interviews, Book I, 1933–34*. Pamphlet 356, Doc. 1–73. Denver: State Historical Society of Colorado, 1934.

Stewart, Omer C. "Data on the Identification and Group Leadership of Ute Indian Chiefs" ["Ute Chiefs List"]. Unpublished working papers prepared for Dockets 44–45, U.S. Indian Claims Commission, 1952. Omer C. Stewart Collection, 2nd Accession, box 1, Norlin Library Archives; also in Stewart Papers, Marriot Library Special Collections.

———. "The Eastern Ute" and "The Western Utes." Unpublished essays written in preparation for "Utes," in *Handbook of North American Indians*, vol. 11. Omer C. Stewart Collection, 2nd Accession, box 5, Norlin Library Archives; also in Stewart Papers, Marriot Library Special Collections.

———. Omer C. Stewart Collection. Norlin Library Archives, University of Colorado, Boulder.

———. Omer Call Stewart Papers, 1925–1992. Marriot Library Special Collections, University of Utah.

Wilkinson, Ernest L. "Ute Claims." Wilkinson Collection, Special Collections, Harold B. Lee Library, Brigham Young University, Provo, Utah.

VIDEO SOURCES

San Pete County Heritage Council, Manti-LaSal National Forest, and KBYU, producers. *Utah's Black Hawk War: Cultures in Conflict*. Moderated by John A. Peterson. Broadcast April 19, 1998.

"William Gilpin." *New Perspectives on the West*. In "The West Film Project." Public Broadcasting Services, 2001.

WEB SOURCES

Affiliated Ute Citizens website: http://affiliatedutecitizens.org/ and associated links (discontinued). See "The Terminated Mixed-Blood Uinta's [*sic*] of the Tribe" (formerly "The Mixed-Blood Uintas"), accessed 2018, at http://www.undeclaredutes.net/.

"Animas-La Plata Timeline," accessed March 9, 1999 from www.angelfire.com.

Citizens Against Waste [CAW] Lobbying letters, regarding H.R. 3112. Posted July 2000, accessed March 14, 2003, macinstruct.com/alpcentral/cawlobby.html.

Colorado Elk Breeders Association CEBA, accessed 1999, http://wapiti.net.

Colorado Fiscal Policy Institute. "Fact Sheet: Colorado Income October 2009," accessed 2009, http://www.cclponline.org/uploads/files/Colorado_Income_Fact_Sheet_FINAL10-14.pdf.

"Colorado Marriage Laws: Common Law Marriage." Larimer County Virtual Courthouse, website.

Colorado State Archives. Online biographies of influential figures in Colorado history. Available at http://www.colorado.gov/dpa/doit/archives/.

Englert, Jeanne, to Ken Salazar (Colorado attorney general), August 13, 1999, accessed 1999, www.macinstruct.com/alpcentral/salazarpia.html.

Feingold, Russel, press release, March 13, 1997, accessed 2003, www.senate.gov/~feingold/31rel.htm.

Hamilton, Richard G. Testimony before the U.S. Senate Committee on Indian Affairs regarding S. 1771, and "Ute Water Rights and the Date of Reservation under the Winters Doctrine," September 30, 1987, updated June 1998, accessed November 8, 2003, www.macinstruct.com/alpcentral/ute.html.

"Marriage codes." City and County recorder. At Denver.gov website.

National Indian Gaming Association Web site. Available at http://indiangaming.org.

Native American Resources Partners, LLC Website. Accessed 2010, http://narpllc.com.

Northern Ute Tribe, tribal website. Originally northernute.com (site discontinued). Now www.utetribe.com, last accessed December 2017.

Petri, Tom, press release, July 24, 1997, accessed 1998, www.house.gov/petri/press/alpmedia.htm.

Political Graveyard. Database of U.S. politicians and historic cemeteries. Available at http://politicalgraveyard.com/.

Southern Ute Tribe, tribal website, accessed most recently June 2018, www.southernute-nsn.gov.

U.S. Bureau of Land Management (Vernal Office). "Production and Revenue Statistics," updated December 3, 2002, accessed June 22, 2004 from BLM (Vernal Office) website. See https://www.blm.gov/office/vernal-field-office.

U.S. Census Bureau. 2000 Census. "Quickfacts" (online), Colorado. Southern Ute and Ute Mountain Ute data sets, accessed 2008, http://quickfacts.census.gov/qfdm and http://factfinder.census.gov.

U.S. Department of Commerce, Economic Development Administration. "Colorado: Ute Mountain Reservation." Online fact sheet, accessed 2004.

U.S. Department of Veterans Affairs. Diversity Awards Program, 2005, accessed November 13, 2006, http://www1.va.gov/ Diversity/page.cfm?pg=21.

U.S. Department of Veterans Affairs, "Chaplain Service Guidelines Concerning Native American Indian/Alaskan Native Traditional Practitioners." Online.

Utah Division of Indian Affairs, "Ute Tribe," accessed 2004, http://dced.utah.gov/indian_affairs/utah_tribes_today/ute.html.

Utah State Census 2000 Census Files. Compiled by the University of Utah Bureau of Economic and Business Research. Uintah and Duchesne Counties, accessed 2005, http://www.new.business.utah.edu/display.php?&pageId=1753

Utah State Data Center. Governor's Office of Planning and Budget. "Utah Data Guide," Fall 2002, accessed January 2005, http://governor.utah.gov/dea/DataGuide/02udg10.PDF.

Ute Mountain and Southern Ute Tribes. Animas-La Plata, accessed 1999–2005, www.animaslp.com (discontinued).

Ute Mountain Ute. Tribal website, accessed variously 1999–2018, originally www.utemountainute.com (discontinued); now www.utemountainutetribe.com.

Index

Note: page numbers printed in *italics* refer to figures, illustrations, or tables.